Y0-BPW-831

DAVE ELLIS

From Master Student to Master Employee

FOURTH EDITION

Doug Toft
Contributing Editor

Lorraine Fedrizzi
Instructor/Counselor,
Niagara County
Community College

Images: Oliver Cleve/Getty Images

 WADSWORTH
CENGAGE Learning·

Australia · Brazil · Japan · Korea · Mexico · Singapore · Spain · United Kingdom · United States

From Master Student to Master Employee, Fourth Edition
Ellis

Executive Editor: Shani Fisher

Development Editors: Marita Sermolins, Catherine Black

Assistant Editor: Joanna Hassel

Editorial Assistant: Erin Nixon

Media Editor: Amy Gibbons

Content Project Manager: Jill Quinn

Senior Art Director: Pam Galbreath

Manufacturing Planner: Sandee Milewski

Rights Acquisition Specialist: Shalice Shah-Caldwell

Production Service: MPS Limited

Text and Cover Designer: Riezebos Holzbaur/ Andrei Pasternak

Cover Image: © Oliver Cleve/Photographer's Choice/Corbis

Compositor: MPS Limited

> For product information and technology assistance, contact us at
> **Cengage Learning Customer & Sales Support, 1-800-354-9706**
>
> For permission to use material from this text or product,
> submit all requests online at **www.cengage.com/permissions**
> Further permissions questions can be emailed to
> **permissionrequest@cengage.com**

Library of Congress Control Number: 2012943889

Student Edition:

ISBN-13: 978-1-4354-6222-9

ISBN-10: 1-4354-6222-X

Annotated Instructor's Edition:

ISBN-13: 978-1-133-94168-2

ISBN-10: 1-133-94168-0

Wadsworth
20 Channel Center Street
Boston, MA 02210
USA

Cengage Learning is a leading provider of customized learning solutions with office locations around the globe, including Singapore, the United Kingdom, Australia, Mexico, Brazil and Japan. Locate your local office at **international.cengage.com/region**

Cengage Learning products are represented in Canada by Nelson Education, Ltd.

For your course and learning solutions, visit **www.cengage.com**

Purchase any of our products at your local college store or at our preferred online store **www.cengagebrain.com**

Instructors: Please visit **login.cengage.com** and log in to access instructor-specific resources.

Printed in the United States of America
1 2 3 4 5 6 7 16 15 14 13 12

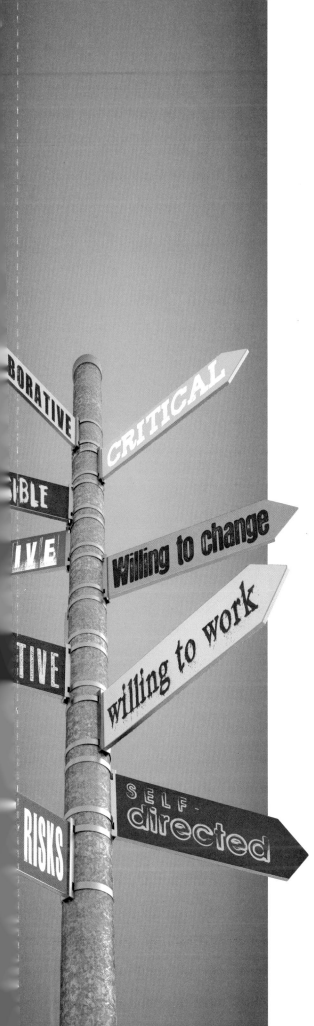

Images: Oliver Cleve/Getty Images

Brief Contents

Contents

CHAPTER 2 First Steps 49

CHAPTER 3 Time & Money 73

CHAPTER 4 Memory **113**

CHAPTER 5 Reading **133**

CHAPTER 6 Notes **159**

CHAPTER 7 Tests **185**

CHAPTER 8 Creative & Critical Thinking   **207**

CHAPTER 9 Communicating   **235**

CHAPTER 10 Collaborating **263**

CHAPTER 11 Health   **291**

CHAPTER 12 Career Management **319**

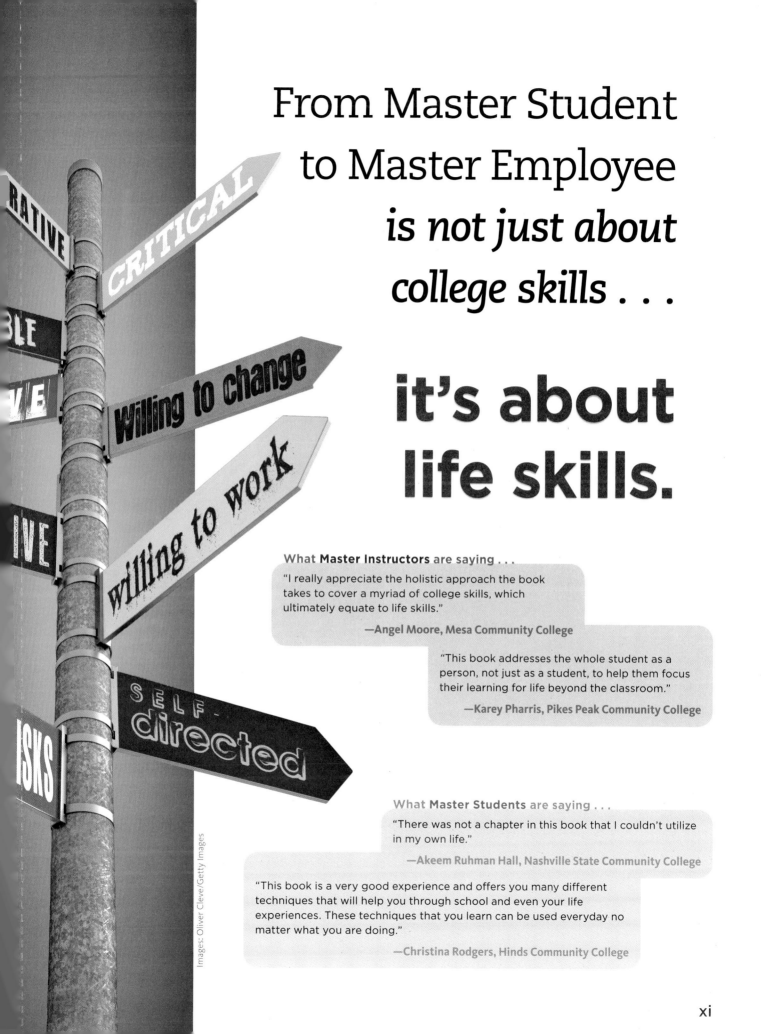

From Master Student to Master Employee *is not just about college skills . . .*

it's about life skills.

What **Master Instructors** are saying . . .

"I really appreciate the holistic approach the book takes to cover a myriad of college skills, which ultimately equate to life skills."

—Angel Moore, Mesa Community College

"This book addresses the whole student as a person, not just as a student, to help them focus their learning for life beyond the classroom."

—Karey Pharris, Pikes Peak Community College

What **Master Students** are saying . . .

"There was not a chapter in this book that I couldn't utilize in my own life."

—Akeem Ruhman Hall, Nashville State Community College

"This book is a very good experience and offers you many different techniques that will help you through school and even your life experiences. These techniques that you learn can be used everyday no matter what you are doing."

—Christina Rodgers, Hinds Community College

Images: Oliver Cleve/Getty Images

Behaviors *that* Point Students *In The* Right Direction

The master student qualities are the guiding force behind *From Master Student to Master Employee*. These are not just behaviors that every *student* should strive for, but that every *person* should strive for. The "Master student qualities" article that outlines these 30 qualities is now the first article students encounter in the Introduction. Students are reminded of these qualities throughout the book as they relate to study strategies and to life skills.

See pages 3-5

The Power Process articles—short, unique motivational articles designed to emphasize academic success in terms of life skills and behaviors—now appear at the beginning of each chapter to motivate students and illustrate how simple behaviors can lead to great changes and successes in academics, work, and life.

What Master Instructors are saying . . .

"The Power Processes are my favorite feature in *Becoming a Master Student*. They can be applied to all life situations. They're great for 'teachable moments' during the semester as well. I've heard students tell their classmates to 'Be here now' when they were engaged in side conversations or to apply 'I create it all' when they made excuses for not completing a homework assignment."

—Debbie Warfield, Seminole Community College

"The Power Processes are my favorite feature. They are applicable and very timely. They give students an opportunity to consciously explore problem situations. By presenting typical scenarios, my students are able to relate and begin to think outside the box."

—Dawn Shaffer, Central Piedmont Community College

What Master Students are saying . . .

"You will change profoundly and, even if you never apply any of the suggestions this book gives you, gain understanding about yourself that may just restore your confidence in tackling college."

— Jonathan Steinke, Mesa Community College

Critical Thinking *Skills that* *Produce* Master Students

NEW! `Critical Thinking Exercises` throughout the book have been developed to step students through Bloom's six levels of critical thought. Beginning with the earlier levels of remembering, understanding, and applying, students progress through the chapter exercises and are given more responsibility and exposure to the higher levels of analyzing, evaluating, and creating, an essential skill for master students. Chapter 8: Creative & Critical Thinking, now also presents the six different levels of higher thought with **Bloom's Taxonomy.**

What Master Instructors are saying . . .

"Becoming a Master Student promotes critical thinking in our students by having them use/consider the skills not only in the classroom setting but in other aspects of their life."

—**Terry Lee Rafter Carles, Valencia Community College**

"I really like how each activity addresses a level of Bloom's and gives good examples. I like how you built each exercise in conjunction to a level. I love, love, love the last few exercises that link to words used in essay questions. My students tend to answer all essay questions in the same way no matter what 'indicator' word is used. The fact that there are several exercises using the 'indicator' words in different scenarios is great!"

—**Krista Clay-Lieffring, Neosho County Community College**

Get the Skills Employers Value Most

This edition focuses on the Five Cs – character, creative thinking, critical thinking, communicating, and collaborating – the top five qualities employers seek in their employees. These skills are emphasized in Chapter 9: Communicating and three new chapters:

- Chapter 1: Character sets the stage for success in school and beyond by showing students how to define their values and align them with their actions. It focuses on forming positive and productive attitudes and changing poor habits to reach goals.

- Chapter 8: Creative & Critical Thinking now introduces students to the six different levels of higher thought with Bloom's Taxonomy and has a greater focus on how to bring creativity to the workplace.

- Chapter 10: Collaborating focuses on teamwork strategies useful both in college and in the workplace, as well as how to work effectively with a manager and how to manage a project efficiently.

What Master Instructors are saying . . .

"*Becoming a Master Student* is a tremendous asset and the basis for all things related to College and Career Planning."

—Rajone Lyman, Houston Community College—NE

NEW! Five Cs for Your Career. At the end of each chapter, this feature shows specific ways in which students can develop five crucial qualities that employers seek: character, creative thinking, critical thinking, communication, and collaboration skills. Students are asked to practice and develop these critical skills now, so that they may make a seamless transition from success in school to success on the job.

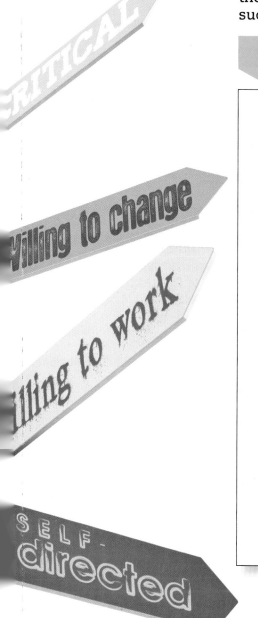

Now, make a personal commitment to developing the five Cs. Take another look at the Discovery Wheel in this chapter—especially the sections labeled Character, Creative and Critical Thinking, Communicating, and Collaborating. Take a snapshot of your current skills in these areas after reading and doing this chapter.

DISCOVERY

My scores on the "Five C" sections of the Discovery Wheel were:	As of today, I would give myself the following scores in these areas:	At the end of this course, I would like my scores in these areas to be:
Character _____	Character _____	Character _____
Creative & Critical Thinking _____	Creative & Critical Thinking _____	Creative & Critical Thinking _____
Communicating _____	Communicating _____	Communicating _____
Collaborating _____		

Next, skim this chapter and loo[k]...
rating in at least one of the five C...
by seeing, hearing and moving: Th...
collaborating with people who fav...

I discovered that my preferred t...

In light of the five Cs, I can use t...

INTENTION
To use this technique, I intend to...

NEXT ACTION
The specific action I will take is...

FIVE Cs
FOR YOUR CAREER

CHARACTER • CRITICAL THINKING • CREATIVE THINKING • COLLABORATION • COMMUNICATION

In the workplace, performance reviews often end with a personal development plan that includes specific ways to improve an employee's performance. After reading and using this book, you can think of these plans in a new way: They are opportunities to take a First Step about how you're doing at work.

Link your personal development plan to your character strengths. Standard advice from many self-development experts is to focus your plan on identifying and changing your greatest personal weaknesses. Think critically about this advice for three reasons:

- Tackling your weaknesses can feel threatening and lead to procrastination.
- A major weakness may be hard to change before your next performance review.
- Eliminating weaknesses might affect your life outside work and have little or no impact on your career.

Of course, it's fine to take a First Step about things you'd like to change. Another option is to focus your plan on listing and developing your strengths. This is a chance to think about character in a way that creates new possibilities for your future.

Think creatively and critically about your plan. Think about any of your recent accomplishments at work. Describe them in writing, including specific details about what you did and the results of your actions.

Next, set a goal to build on one of these accomplishments. This calls for creative thinking. Say that you made a suggestion to change the workflow in your department, and this change allowed your team to finish a project well before the scheduled due date. Consider setting a goal to make this a permanent change in your department's procedures. You could also set a goal to find other time-saving procedures.

You can always set a goal that targets one of your weaknesses. Just stay positive. Instead of focusing on a current behavior that you want to stop, for example, describe a new behavior that you want to start. Change "I will stop taking unclear notes at meetings" to "I will review my meeting notes to clarify the major agreements we made and next actions to take."

In any case, focus your development plan on goals that you can actually achieve in the near future, leading to clear benefits at work. Translate your goal into concrete behaviors. Ask yourself:

What exactly will I do differently based on my goal? Answering such questions involves critical thinking.

You can monitor your progress toward any goal, no matter how ambitious. To monitor listening skills, for example, you could count the number of times each day that you interrupt other people.

Remember that the point of monitoring your behavior is not to become a cold-blooded measurement machine. Rather, the idea is to make a change that really makes a difference over the long term. Behaviors that we measure carefully and consistently are likely to change.

As you monitor your behavior, remember the essence of a First Step: suspend all self-judgment. Just record the facts. If you deviate from your plan, just look for the next chance to practice your new behavior.

Use your knowledge of learning styles to communicate and collaborate with your boss. You probably feel more comfortable with a person when you feel that you have something in common. That feeling is called rapport. Whenever you establish rapport with someone in the workplace, you enter into a collaborative relationship.

When meeting with your boss for a performance review, for example, look for clues to that person's learning style. Then see if you can establish rapport by matching his or her style in a small, significant way.

For example, mirror your boss's word choice. She might like to process information visually. Clues to this preference are words such as, "I'll believe that when I see it" and "Give me an overview of your proposal." If she has a preference for verbal learning, she might say, "Let's talk through this" or "I'm hearing good things about you." And if she has kinesthetic preferences, she might signal those by referring to physical sensations ("I feel good about that idea") or action ("Walk me through your presentation before you give it").

Kinesthetic preferences are also expressed in posture, facial expressions, and other forms on nonverbal communication. Notice whether your boss is sitting with arms and legs crossed or open. If you can mirror that posture in a natural way, then do so.

As you look for ways to establish rapport, be subtle. The goal is not to manipulate. It's to communicate effectively and find common ground for collaboration.

CRITICAL

Willing to change

Willing to work

SELF-directed

What **Master Students** are saying . . .

"I have become a better student/person/employee and am way more reliable. My productivity each day is a max."

—Lauren Plagens, South Plains College

Self-Assessments *Get Students* Focusing *on* Metacognition

The Discovery Wheel. The most widely recognized feature of *From Master Student to Master Employee,* the Discovery Wheel gets students thinking about the kind of student they are and the kind of student that they want to become. Assigned at the outset of the course, this exercise helps students assess their current strengths and weaknesses in different areas of student success. Students are reminded of this when they complete the Discovery Wheel again, at the end of the textbook, to measure their growth.

What **Master Instructors** are saying . . .

"The Discovery Wheel is brilliant because it allows the students to quickly identify where they may be weak and directs them to the chapter that can assist them."

—Chris Douse, Indiana University–Purdue University Fort Wayne

"The Discovery Wheel is what starts and ends this course for us. It has become so integrated into the curriculum that we now use it as the implementation device for our Core Competency for the course—Personal Growth and Responsibility. It's easily assessed and it describes and prescribes areas for the students to develop."

—Laura Bazan, Central Piedmont Community College

Critical Thinking Exercises Only action makes this book work. Student critical thinking exercises found throughout the chapters encourage active learning and help develop critical thinking.

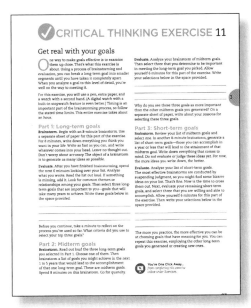

CRITICAL THINKING EXERCISE 11

Get real with your goals

One way to make goals effective is to examine them up close. That's what this exercise is about. Using a process of brainstorming and evaluation, you can break a long-term goal into smaller segments until you have taken it completely apart. When you analyze a goal to this level of detail, you're well on the way to meeting it.

For this exercise, you will use a pen, extra paper, and a watch with a second hand. (A digital watch with a built-in stopwatch feature is even better.) Timing is an important part of the brainstorming process, so follow the stated time limits. This entire exercise takes about an hour.

Part 1: Long-term goals

Brainstorm. Begin with an 8-minute brainstorm. Use a separate sheet of paper for this part of the exercise. For 8 minutes, write down everything you think you want in your life. Write as fast as you can, and write whatever comes into your head. Leave no thought out. Don't worry about accuracy. The object of a brainstorm is to generate as many ideas as possible.

Evaluate. After you have finished brainstorming, spend the next 6 minutes looking over your list. Analyze what you wrote. Read the list out loud. If something is missing, add it. Look for common themes or relationships among your goals. Then select three long-term goals that are important to you—goals that will take many years to achieve. Write these goals below in the space provided.

Before you continue, take a minute to reflect on the process you've used so far. What criteria did you use to select your top three goals?

Part 2: Midterm goals

Brainstorm. Read out loud the three long-term goals you selected in Part 1. Choose one of them. Then brainstorm a list of goals you might achieve in the next 1 to 5 years that would lead to the accomplishment of that one long-term goal. These are midterm goals. Spend 8 minutes on this brainstorm. Go for quantity.

Evaluate. Analyze your brainstorm of midterm goals. Then select three that you determine to be important in meeting the long-term goal you picked. Allow yourself 6 minutes for this part of the exercise. Write your selections below in the space provided.

Why do you see these three goals as more important than the other midterm goals you generated? On a separate sheet of paper, write about your reasons for selecting these three goals.

Part 3: Short-term goals

Brainstorm. Review your list of midterm goals and select one. In another 8-minute brainstorm, generate a list of short-term goals—those you can accomplish in a year or less that will lead to the attainment of that midterm goal. Write down everything that comes to mind. Do not evaluate or judge these ideas yet. For now, the more ideas you write down, the better.

Evaluate. Analyze your list of short-term goals. The most effective brainstorms are conducted by suspending judgment, so you might find some bizarre ideas on your list. That's fine. Now is the time to cross them out. Next, evaluate your remaining short-term goals, and select three that you are willing and able to accomplish. Allow yourself 6 minutes for this part of the exercise. Then write your selections below in the space provided.

The more you practice, the more effective you can be at choosing goals that have more meaning for you. You can repeat this exercise, employing the other long-term goals you generated or creating new ones.

You're One Click Away . . .
from completing this exercise online under Exercises.

a textbook and a workbook.

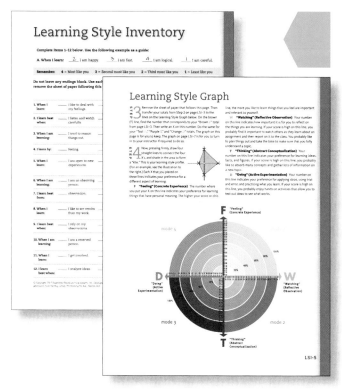

The Learning Style Inventory (LSI). People are fascinated by why they do what they do—and students are no exception. Students can take the Kolb Learning Style Inventory (LSI) in Chapter 1 to increase their self-awareness as learners. The LSI, which is printed on carbonless paper for easy scoring and is also available online, helps students make sense of what they're experiencing in college. Following the LSI, students get clear explanations of what their test results mean about how they learn.

The Discovery and Intention Journal Entry system. These journal prompts ask students to explain the whys, whats, and hows of applying the chapter skills to themselves in writing, and offer instructors a more specific and measurable form of journal writing than any other text. Students have an opportunity to reflect on their discoveries while setting a plan for action by writing their intentions.

What Master Instructors are saying . . .

"*Becoming a Master Student* gives students the knowledge necessary in the different areas that will help them be successful in college and in life, as well as the opportunity to reflect on where they are now and where they want to be. The intention statements encourage them to take the next step."

—Dana Dildine, Eastern New Mexico University–Ruidoso Branch

"Many students have reported in their evaluations the importance of the journal system, allowing them to reflect on what they have learned and then make a commitment to take action."

—Debbie Warfield, Seminole Community College

What Master Students are saying . . .

"Read this book and have it handy. It's a great resource to go to when you need a pick-me-up of where to start again."

—Lauren Plagens, South Plains College

Inspire *Your* Master Students *To* Learn

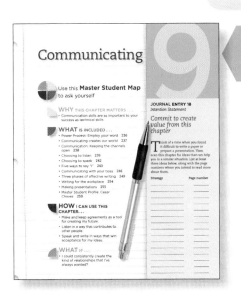

Master Student MAP. The Master Student MAP (an acronym for Metacognitive Application Process), located on the opening page of each chapter, provides an organizational framework that introduces each chapter and acts as a common theme throughout the text to guide students in monitoring thinking and learning. The map helps students understand why the chapter matters, what is included in the chapter, how they can use the chapter, and what to think about as they read. What makes this model so effective is that by utilizing the strengths of each learning style, students are empowered by their own metacognition.

Master Student Profiles. Master Student Profiles in every chapter are brief articles about a real person who encompasses master student qualities. Master Students include Al Gore, Nilofer Merchant, Randy Pausch, Lisa Price, and more!

ACKNOWLEDGMENTS

ADVISORY BOARD

Kinaya J. Ade' Medix College, GA

Mike Bohn Westwood College, TX

Justina Boyd Colorado University

Judy Brandon Clovis Community College, NM

Carl Bridges Career Education Corporation, IL

Julie Brown Corinthian Colleges, Inc., CA

Jodi Caldwell Georgia Southern University

Marla Cartwright Kaplan University

Jennifer Combs Fullerton College, CA

Audra Cooke Rock Valley College, IL

David Cooper Northwest Business College, IL

Katharine Davis Mississippi Delta Community College

Sylvia Edwards-Borens Texas State Technical College, Waco, TX

Steven Epstein SUNY—Suffolk Community College, NY

Mary Etter Davenport University, MI

Lorraine Fedrizzi Niagara County Community College

Marie Feuer Mt. Sierra College, CA

Mominka Fileva Davenport University, MI

Carol Forrey Kaplan University

Richard Gargan Florida Metropolitan University, Orlando, FL

Mark Gayden Westwood College, CA

James George Westwood College, Chicago Loop, IL

Vicki Gidney International Business College, TX

Dr. Andrea Goldstein South University, GA

Paul Gore University of Utah

Anne Gupton Mott Community College, MI

Dorothy Herndon National College of Business and Technology, VA

Jodi Hicks Davenport University

Pat Hunnicutt ITT-Technical Institutes, Little Rock, AR

Evelyn Hyde Brown Mackie College-Salina, KS

Jane Jepson Cypress College, CA

Martha Johnson Texas A&M University

James Jones Southwest Florida College, FL

Jill Jurgens Old Dominion University, VA

Linda Kester Erie Institute of Technology, PA

Pamela King Southwest Florida College, FL

Nicole E. Klues Missouri College

Patsy Krech University of Memphis, TN

Stephen Lewis Westwood College, O'Hare Campus, IL

Susan Loffredo Northeastern University, MA

Blake Mackesy Wilkes University, PA

Carole Mackewich Clark College, WA

Dean Mancina Golden West College, CA

Forrest Marston Sanford Brown Institute, Tampa, FL

Eldon L. McMurray Utah Valley State College

Amanda Millard Westwood College, Chicago Loop, IL

Jeneane Moore Anthem College Online

Katrina Neckuty-Fodness Globe University/ Minnesota School of Business, MN

Linda Nelson Davenport University, IN

Diane Noraas Baker College, MI

Sharon Occipinti Florida Metropolitan University, Tampa, FL

Keri O'Malley ECPI Technical College at Greensboro, NC

Rebecca Owens Colorado Technical University, CO

Nancy Porretto Katherine Gibbs Schools, Melville, NY

Margaret Puckett North Central State College, OH

Tracey Robinson DeVry University–South FL

Tara Ross Virginia College Online, AL

Diane Savoca St. Louis Community College, MO

Kathlene Scholljegeredes Bethel College, MN

Deidre Sepp Marist College, NY

Jocelyn Shaw Westwood College, South Bay, CA

Valerie Smolek Westwood College, Torrance, IL

Jake Sneva University at Buffalo, NY

David Southwell Westwood College, O'Hare Campus, IL

Zachary Stahmer Anthem Education Group

Jeffrey Swanberg Rockford Business College, IL

Pat Twaddle Moberly Area Community College, MO

Dr. Pamela D. Walker Northwestern College, IL

Debra Watson Mississippi Gulf Coast Community College

Diane Williams PIMA Medical Institute, AZ

Jean Wisuri American Education Centers, KY

Eric S. Wormsley PIMA Community College

STUDENT ADVISORY BOARD

Wylonda Bernstein East-West University

Valerie Cordes Alpena Community College

William Couch University of Maryland College Park

Jesse Decker Ocean County College

Theresa Francis Southwestern Illinois College

Alecia Jackson Phillips Community College of the University of Arizona

Kanisha Jackson Ohio University

Bradford Johnson Tallahassee Community College

Steven Kelley Drexel University

Joyce King Broward College

Kevin Kunz, Jr. Mesa Community College

Sally LaFleure Alpena Community College

Jose Ledesma II San Diego Mesa College

Jess Maggi Le Moyne College

Ashley Molton Central Texas College

Lindsay M. Ordone Delgado Community College

Christian Penaherrera University at Buffalo

Melody Reese Kent State University

Christopher Sampson University of Houston-Downtown

Jason Shah University of New Orleans

Lisa Shelley University of Texas at Arlington

Vanessa Silva Pace University

Ivory D. Wiggins Mesa College

Jamila Williams SUNY— University at Buffalo

Katherine Wood Washington and Lee University

Annotated Instructor's Edition Table of Contents

PART 1: RESOURCES AVAILABLE WITH *FROM MASTER STUDENT TO MASTER EMPLOYEE*

PART 2: TEACHING WITH *FROM MASTER STUDENT TO MASTER EMPLOYEE*

> **Chapter Annotations**
> **Please note:** Chapter annotations can be found on an insert that appears before the beginning of each of the main text chapters, starting with the Introduction.

Logging into *FROM MASTER STUDENT TO MASTER EMPLOYEE* digital resources

INSTRUCTOR ACCESS

To access instructor digital resources, such as the Instructor Companion Site or Instructor access for the College Success CourseMate for *From Master Student to Master Employee* follow these steps:

1. Visit **login.cengage.com**.

2. If you have not previously created a faculty account, choose the "Create a new Faculty Account" and follow the prompts.

3. If you have created a faculty account previously, log in with your email address or user name and password.

4. Search for *From Master Student to Master Employee* to add the available additional digital resources to your bookshelf.

   You will always need to return to **http://login.cengagebrain.com** and enter your email address and password to sign in to access these resources. Use this space to write down your email address or user name and password below:

   E-mail Address:_____

   Password:_____

STUDENT ACCESS

Note: the log in process for students is different from the way instructors access the resources.

To help your students navigate the log in process for the additional course materials, including the College Success CourseMate for *From Master Student to Master Employee*, have them follow these steps:

1. To register a product using your access code, go to **http://login.cengagebrain.com**.

2. Register as a new user or log in as an existing user if you already have an account with Cengage Learning or CengageBrain.com

3. Follow the online prompts.

   For future access, make sure students keep a record of their e-mail address, password, and course code. To access CourseMate, students will always need to return to **http://login.cengagebrain.com** and enter their email address and password to sign in.

Note: The access code is your password. Students will use the access code only once when they first register their product. They will then be prompted to create a password to use each time they return to the site.

PROBLEMS WITH ACCESS CODES? CONTACT CENGAGE LEARNING TECHNICAL SUPPORT:

www.cengage.com/support
Featuring 24/7 Live Chat!

Phone 1.800.354.9706

Monday—Thursday	8:30 A.M. to 9:00 P.M. EST
Friday	8:30 A.M. to 6:00 P.M. EST

ENRICH YOUR COURSE WITH **MEDIA ASSETS** FROM THE COLLEGE SUCCESS COURSEMATE

Interested in a simple way to complement *From Master Student to Master Employee* and your course content with study and practice materials? Cengage Learning's College Success CourseMate brings course concepts to life with interactive learning, study, and exam preparation tools that support the printed book. Watch student comprehension soar as your class works with the printed textbook. College Success CourseMate goes beyond *From Master Student to Master Employee* to deliver what you need!

 You're One Click Away... Look for the The One Click Away . . . icon! This directs students to the College Success CourseMate to the many available media resources, like reading more about a particular concept, doing an exercise electronically, or viewing a video related to the chapter's topic.

CHAPTER LEVEL RESOURCES

Master Students in Action Videos. Available for every chapter, students will hear first-hand from other students where their challenges are and their strategies for success. The Master Students in Action videos give your students a firsthand view of how the strategies in *From Master Student to Master Employee* have helped their peers overcome obstacles. In special segments, Dave Ellis offers students his best strategies for mastering each chapter's content.

Ruben C.
to being a student.

Video Skillbuilders. This online tool combines video clips featuring discussions with students, instructors, and experts, with articles and activities designed to give students a fully engaging learning experience. Available topics include:

Power Process Media. See how the Power Process articles from the textbook can come to life and apply to different learning styles. Watch the video, read, or listen to an audio version of the Power process article and then answer the accompanying questions. A PowerPoint presentation that summarizes the Power Process article's main points is also included.

Master Student Profiles. So students can learn more about each chapter's featured Master Student Profile, additional biographical information and Web links are available for students to do further research on how these individuals cultivated master student qualities.

Learning Styles Application. These activities have students apply the different Learning Styles Modes for each chapter topic.

Cultural Differences. These brief articles touch on aspects of diversity in our rapidly changing world.

Additional Resources. Concept Maps, Experiment with Strategies, Reflection Questions, and Interactive Quizzes all serve to help students study and apply chapter concepts to their own individual success.

BOOK LEVEL RESOURCES

Discovery Wheel. The Discovery Wheel has 12 spokes that represent the 12 themes (and chapters) in the book. The self-awareness that students gain through using this interactive tool provides them with a foundation for honestly assessing their experiences for the rest of their lives. Simply rate your responses to the questions and the wheel does the rest! Discover your key strengths and weaknesses in the 12 areas of success!

Learning Style Inventory. Students can complete the same Learning Style Inventory—a 12 question survey used to develop a personal profile of your current learning style—that appears in *From Master Student to Master Employee* (pages LSI-1–LSI-8) in an electronic environment. This digitized experience of the Kolb Learning Style Inventory tabulates students' scores and plots their results on the Learning Style Graph automatically. Students can then print or email their results.

Master Student Hall of Fame. Archive of biographies of Master Students featured in previous editions of the textbook.

Toolboxes. Specialized collections of articles geared for various student populations are available:

- Adult Learner Toolbox
- Community College Toolbox
- Student Athlete Toolbox
- Student Veteran Toolbox

Interactive eBook. With the interactive eBook, students can take notes, highlight, and search *From Master Student to Master Employee* with ease.

CL Assessment and Portfolio Builder. The CL Assessment and Portfolio Builder is a personal development tool that engages students in *self-assessment*, *critical thinking*, and *goal-setting* activities to prepare them for college and the workplace. Students build a portfolio by responding to questions about their skills, attitudes, values, and behaviors in four key life areas: *Personal, Interpersonal, Career,* and *Community.* The *Accomplishments Report* summarizes the results of their responses and asks students to provide supporting evidence for responses in which they rate themselves as highly proficient. This provides great practice for honing critical thinking skills as well as for creating a résumé or preparing for interviews. Students can view and update their portfolios throughout the semester, and they can print a hard copy to bring to class or use as a reference during an interview.

New! Access to Career Transitions, from Gale®, part of Cengage Learning, a world leader in e-research and educational publishing for libraries, schools and businesses. Career Transitions is the only complete, self-paced application that walks job-seekers through the entire process from assessing strengths and interests, to exploring new opportunities, to ultimately improving the chances of landing a job. Through CourseMate, your students have exclusive access to:

- **Prepare** – build, save, retrieve and update personal career information with a career toolkit
- **Assess** – explore current skills, occupational knowledge and interests and match them with fulfilling career paths
- **Explore** – investigate thousands of career paths, industries, locations and companies
- **Improve** – find educational opportunities and take classes to increase hiring chances
- **Apply** – search job listings from around the country that meet user criteria

Career Resource Center. The Career Resource Center offers tips, exercises, articles, and ideas to help students succeed on their journey from college to career.

- *The Bridge from College to Career* lets students practice new skills acquired in college that can be applied as they enter the job market.
- *Finding the Perfect Job* helps students fine-tune their résumé writing and interviewing skills.
- *Skills for Your Future* provides strategies for problem solving and decision making to help students learn to work with others and communicate on the job.

Plagiarism Prevention Zone. For strategies on how to avoid plagiarism when writing, direct students to the Plagiarism Prevention Zone where they can access various tutorials and opportunities to practice writing ethically.

Engagement Tracker. With CourseMate, you can use the Engagement Tracker to assess student preparation and engagement in your course. Use the tracking tools to see progress for the class as a whole or for individual students. Identify students at risk early in the course. Uncover which concepts are most difficult for your class. Monitor time on task with the resources you assign. Keep your students engaged. ■

INSTRUCTOR COMPANION SITE
is a ONE-STOP INSTRUCTOR'S RESOURCE

The Instructor Companion Site provides a one-stop teacher's resource to support your teaching of your course. Access to instructional materials, provided in electronic format, allows you to easily customize and then print, e-mail, or post materials to a Web site or course-management system. The Instructor Companion Site includes:

Online Course Manual. The online *Course Manual* serves as an invaluable reference for those developing and teaching a College Success course with *From Master Student to Master Employee*. The *Course Manual* provides advice on general teaching issues such as preparing for classes, classroom management, grading, and communicating with students of various backgrounds, as well as specific strategies on getting the most out of various features in *From Master Student to Master Employee* such as the Discovery Wheel and Learning Styles Inventory. Do a *Course Manual* reconnaissance to find ideas that you can use in your course right now.

Best Practices. The Best Practices facilitate an instructor community of sharing ideas, exercises, and practices. These additional ideas have been submitted by instructors to share tools they have developed for use with college students. Is your course feeling stale? Or perhaps you are new to teaching with *From Master Student to Master Employee* and want some tried and true ideas to use in your course? These Best Practices were collected as a way to simulate a free exchange of ideas among instructors. Find ideas for icebreakers, lectures ideas, classroom activities, and handouts.

PowerPoint Library. This master library of PowerPoint presentations makes it easy to find the right PowerPoint for you! In the library you will find PowerPoint slides for every chapter as well as every Power Process article covered in the book. All PowerPoint slides are downloadable and customizable to fit your needs.

- **Chapter PowerPoints:** Available for each chapter, these PowerPoints highlight the chapter's main points. Visually engaging and interactive, download these PowerPoints and customize them as you wish for your course.

- **Power Process PowerPoints:** Using the same concept as the Chapter PowerPoints these presentations cover the main points of the Power Process articles.

- **Walk Through Getting Started with the Instructor Companion Site:** This presentation will outline the contents of the Instructor Companion Site and act as a quick reference guide for you to locate the resource you want to access.

- **Walk Through Getting Started with CourseMate:** An outline of the available resources on the CourseMate, this walk through can also function as a quick reference guide for students.

Master Teachers in Action videos. The Master Teachers in Action videos provide you with an inside look at how *From Master Student to Master Employee* is used by professors, including information on their favorite parts, and how specific articles and activities from the text prepare students for achieving success. Hear from Dave Ellis himself and other instructors about what works for them when teaching the Learning Style Assessment and the Discovery Wheel.

Sample Syllabi. Sample syllabi instructors have generously shared for your inspiration.

Test Banks. These customizable, text-specific content quizzes are a great way to test student's knowledge and understanding of the text. Provided in ExamView, BlackBoard, WebCT, as well as Word you will have no problem accessing the multiple choice, true/false, completion, and short answer questions. ■

Master instructor resources to help you
REACH *your students and* TEACH *your course*

*F*rom Master Student to Master Employee is accompanied by various resources available to you through Cengage Learning to help make teaching your course easier. Take advantage of these valuable tools to assist you in designing your course. Remember to call your Cengage Learning sales representative or TeamUp consultant if you have any questions about acquiring materials or integrating them into your course, or if you have a suggestion you would like to see implemented in the future. Other instructor resources available via the Instructor Companion Site are described on page AIE-xxiv.

Powerlecture CD (ISBN 9781133941996). This Powerlecture CD-ROM contains the *From Master Student to Master Employee* test bank in the ExamView test-generating software, enhanced instructor PowerPoints, and a PDF of the Course Manual.

Discovery Wheel (ISBN 9781111840815). A standalone version of the Discovery Wheel is available so students can respond and hand in their results to you directly. Or consider using this Discovery Wheel as a handout to use in trainings or workshops with students and faculty.

Power-Up! Power Process DVD (ISBN 9780618949762). Show your students how to put the *power* into Power Processes with the *Power-Up!* DVD that contains 8- to 9-minute segments on each of the thirteen Power Processes in *From Master Student to Master Employee*. These video segments will enhance your lecture by bringing to life the concepts and metaphors in the text while speaking to the auditory and visual learners in your class. This closed-captioned Power Process DVD is free to adopters. These videos are also found on the College Success CourseMate for *From Master Student to Master Employee*.

College Success Planner. Package *From Master Student to Master Employee* with this twelve month, week-at-a-glance academic planner. The College Success Planner assists students in making the best use of their time both on and off campus, and includes additional reading about key learning strategies and life skills for success in college. Ask your Cengage Learning sales representative for more details.

WebTutor. The WebTutor on Blackboard offers a number of instructor resources to complement the main text including discussion questions and gradebook content. For students, Power Process media, Video Skillbuilders, and additional resources will enhance their understanding of the text's main points.

Noel-Levitz College Student Inventory. The Retention Management System™ College Student Inventory (CSI from Noel-Levitz) is an early-alert, early-intervention program that identifies students with tendencies that contribute to dropping out of school. Cengage Learning offers you three assessment options that evaluate students on nineteen different scales: Form A (194 items), Form B (100 items), or an online etoken (that provides access to either Form A, B, or C; 74 items). For more in-depth information, contact your Cengage Learning sales representative.

The Myers-Briggs Type Indicator® (MBTI®) Instrument. MBTI is the most widely used personality inventory in history—and it is also available for packaging with *From Master Student to Master Employee*. The standard Form M self-scorable instrument contains ninety-three items that determine preferences on four scales: Extraversion-Introversion, Sensing-Intuition, Thinking-Feeling, and Judging-Perceiving. For more in-depth information, contact your Cengage Learning sales representative. ■

Could your students use an
EXTRA $1,000?

*C*engage learning college success is proud to present three students each year with a $1,000 scholarship for tuition reimbursement. Students at postsecondary schools in the United States and Canada that offer a student success course are welcome to participate in this scholarship. To be considered, students must write an essay that answers the question "How do you define success?"

Here's one way to get your students to participate. Host a schoolwide competition for students enrolled in a first-year student success or study skills course. Consider having students participate by including the competition in your syllabus as a goal-setting or writing assignment. In your local contest, ask all of your students to write an essay on the topic "How do you define success?" The essay should not exceed 750 words.

Materials to advertise the scholarship competition are available on the Instructor Companion Site. Download flyers for posting on bulletin boards around campus, or for posting to online bulletin boards on your course Web site or in your course management system.

Students can send in their individual essays by filling out an entry form available on the College Success CourseMate for *From Master Student to Master Employee*. Multiple students from the same school may enter their essays. Entries are due each year on December 15. The winners are announced the following spring. Invite your students to read the winning essays of previous entrants, also available on the CourseMate.

Use the
College Success Factors Index
to measure and promote your
students' success!

How much of a difference does your college success course make in your students' academic success? The College Success Factors Index (CSFI) is an online survey that will give you the answers you're looking for. In use by colleges and universities for over twenty years, the CSFI contains 100 self-scoring statements designed to determine the readiness of college students to successfully complete their early years in higher education. At the start of the course, it helps you assess incoming students and tailor your course topics to meet their needs. As a post-test, it allows you and your students to measure their progress. The CSFI tool is accessed online, so students can take the assessment in a lab, their home, or anywhere there's a computer.

Many factors indicate potential academic success in universities and colleges throughout the country. Most notably, grade point average in high school and aptitude scores, such as SAT or ACT scores, are used to predict success in college. However, additional factors which are often unmeasured have a very important place in the retention of students and their continuing success in higher education. For example, how a student uses his or her time or approaches the tasks assigned may be more critical to success than aptitude and previous academic records.

Moreover, factors such as involvement in activities at the college and family interest may in fact be greater success indices than previously known. The former allows the student involvement with college activities, interaction with faculty and the development of peer relationships. The latter relates to a family that encourages success in college by providing encouragement, flexibility in the family calendar and the sharing of family resources.

With this in mind, the College Success Factors Index has been developed to help measure many of the undiscovered fundamentals and factors that are critical to academic success:

Responsibility/Control: If we do not take control over the responsibilities we assume in college, less success is possible.

Competition: The need to compete is part of our culture and thus an aspect of college and career success. For successful students, competition becomes internalized-they compete with themselves.

Task Planning: A strong task orientation and a desire to complete a task in a planned step-by-step manner are very important to college success.

Expectations: Successful students have goals that are related to assignments, areas of study, and future careers.

Family Involvement: Family encouragement and/or participation in planning and decision making are factors in a student's success.

College Involvement: Being involved in college activities, relating to faculty and developing strong peer relationships are important factors in retention.

Time Management: How people maximize their time and prioritize class assignments affects their productivity and success.

Wellness: People need ways to handle their problems. Stress, anger, sleeplessness, alcohol/drug use, inadequate diet and lack of exercise are deterrents to college success.

Precision: To approach one's education by being exact, careful with details and specific with assignments is a measure of success.

Persistence: To face a task with diligence, self-encouragement and a sense of personal urgency even when some tasks take extra effort and are repetitious is a mark of academic success.

The CSFI is coupled with Early Alert functionality. Early Alert allows students and professional staff to identify areas that need improvement the first day of school, thereby increasing the possibility for retention. Through Early Alert, staff may offer interventions that keep students in college.

For more information, visit our web site at **www.cengage.com/success/csfi2**. ∎

TeamUP College Survival:
Committed to
STUDENT SUCCESS

Cengage's teamup college survival group is dedicated to providing educators with proven instructional strategies and tools that lead to student success. For the past 24 years, our team of consultants has provided guidance and training for the design and implementation of student success and first-year courses.

The College Survival consulting team is available to assist with any stage of student success program development, including:

- Developing student retention strategies
- Implementing student success courses
- Training faculty members
- Helping faculty engage students as active learners
- Transforming the learning environment
- Presenting conferences and workshops

OUR TEAM

Our team of consultants has extensive experience in teaching and administering the first-year course and in facilitating training at national education conferences throughout the year. We provide full-time support to help educators establish and maintain effective student success programs.

WEB SITE

Visit our Web site at **www.cengage.com/teamup** for additional resources and more information about College Survival:

- Get the latest industry information
- Get updates on the latest technology available through Cengage Learning texts
- Get connected to our support services

CONFERENCES/WORKSHOPS

College Survival conferences and workshops offer highly interactive and informative sessions designed to equip you with ideas and activities that you can apply immediately in your classroom. All educators involved in enhancing instruction and improving students' motivation and performance are encouraged to attend.

- **About our national conferences.** Our two- to three-day conferences provide informative, interactive sessions on a wide range of topics, such as adult learners, learning styles, student retention, motivation, technology, and much more. Presenters include nationally known authors, student success instructors, and College Survival consultants who offer invaluable instructional strategies based on their experience teaching the first-year course. This forum for learning and sharing with colleagues will furnish you with activities and ideas to implement immediately in your course.

- **About our on-campus workshops.** Led by College Survival consultants, our on-campus workshops are customized to the needs of instructors on a particular campus. These workshops will equip you with ideas and activities to enliven the teaching and learning experience. The cost of a workshop is $1500 a day plus expenses, or free for schools ordering a minimum of $30,000 a year in College Success texts. Ask your Cengage Learning Representative to help you set up a training at your institution.

  - **Who should attend?** If you are an educator, new or experienced, who is dedicated to promoting student success in career schools, community colleges, or four-year colleges and universities, these events are for you! Those who will benefit from these workshops include:

  - Academic and student affairs administrators
  - Student success and freshman seminar coordinators
  - Faculty members (full-time and adjunct instructors)
  - Retention/enrollment management directors
  - Counselors and orientation directors

How can your Cengage Learning Consultant help? Your Cengage Learning Consultant can help you with ideas for introducing a topic, creating community in the classroom, designing your syllabus, and figuring out what to do in class tomorrow. All you have to do is contact them. Check the TeamUP website to find your consultant: **www.cengage.com/teamup** ■

TEAMup

Message From Master Instructor, LORRAINE FEDRIZZI

I am blessed to have worked at a community college as a counselor in Student Development teaching success courses for over 20 years. The course I presently teach (College & Career Skills) has evolved as a combination of Career Planning and College Success courses. I love that it hits home for most students connecting college material to the bigger picture of life and work skills. After reviewing a mountain of textbooks, I found *From Master Student to Master Employee* is a book that students can really relate to. Students have shared with me that they continued to use the book as a resource well after the course was over!

As you experiment with the many online and text tools available to you, cultivate a personal relationship with the author, David Ellis. Beyond the textbook and videos where you can experience actual lectures presented by David, seize the opportunity to go to a success workshop (especially if you see that David is a speaker). When I am working on class agenda, I often ask myself how David would present this material. His energy, joy, compassion, and creativity will help you adapt material to meet the needs of your particular class.

My goal is for students to learn to be their own master of skills and attitudes that will allow them to take things up a notch, to act and think in new and different ways that make life better. They are their own general managers. Early in the semester we talk about mediocrity, doing only what needs to be done to get by. We explore alternatives to go beyond surviving to thriving. We look at what is present in their tool boxes and explore what needs to be done to move it up a level, to do it better. Discovery/intention statements are perfect to help students develop a seemingly unconscious awareness of how things are and what adjustments can be done to make things even better. This system actually helps students identify potential problems and solutions before they play out, like taking too many courses! They become proactive managers of their own lives.

I started teaching years ago with a big agenda and I was on a quest to cover it all. I have finally learned to be a student centered teacher and look to the class for clues of what to do next. And sometimes that means abandoning the agenda and going with the flow. Some of the lessons I now incorporate:

Help students relax. Students learn best when they are relaxed. Devote time to do an icebreaker or tell a joke. Play a great song. Get students in the mood to listen and learn.

Help students feel that they matter. Remember something interesting or positive about each one as you learn their names. I have students fill out a biography questionnaire the first class that gives background information on career, academic, and personal life. Create avenues for students to have conversations with you in the classroom, on line, or through dialogue on their homework. Give students extra points for stopping in your office to introduce themselves. Throughout the class remember to say things like, "nice job, great work, absolutely, thank you for coming today, etc" while making eye contact with individuals who need it the most.

Monitor student outcomes. They may have lofty ideas of how easy something is or how much time they need to study. When results say otherwise, the handwriting is on the wall that a change in behavior is needed. Ask students to write about what they think their advisor or teacher knows about them based on their classroom behaviors, tests, homework, transcript and/or high school records. Do they think that advisor/teacher would hire them?

Help students feel they belong in the group. Foster group interaction. Begin with dyads. Move into triads. I find triads work best for keeping all three students engaged and I only need to move one student (based on criteria like who travelled the farthest) to mix up the groups. And, eventually, call on students to share information with the entire class, not only those that raise their hands. Assign projects students can work on as a team.

Make connections. Information is not learned in isolation! Students often do not understand why they must take general education courses. As time goes on, they find the material in science is connected to psychology! And they begin to find endless connections as they move through daily life (newspaper, tv, internet, conversations, etc). Actively use the "Five Cs for Your Career" at the end of each chapter to help students find the connection between the classroom and the work place.

Some things are not optional. Students truly seeking to learn and grow will be willing to listen to new ideas and try out new strategies on their mission to do things better. As they make choices, point out and reinforce that being on time for class, doing **all** the homework, attending **all** classes, taking notes, reviewing new class/book notes within 24 hours, etc, are necessary behaviors for college and career success.

And, above all, remember that you are a facilitator. There is something to be learned from every student in the class. Use your ingenuity to promote a learning, sharing atmosphere and let the magic begin. If we offer students help with skills, boost their self worth, and help them find and set meaningful goals, they are well on their way to becoming a master. The joy you put into this course is the joy you will get out of it. Make it fun. ■

using THE ANNOTATED INSTRUCTOR'S EDITION

master instructor
BEST PRACTICE

"Inevitably I end up having a class where what I've been doing just isn't working or, I'm just looking to try something different. I always find exciting ideas to take into class by reviewing the Annotated Instructor pages."

—Terry Carles,
Valencia Community College

GET FAMILIAR WITH THE ANNOTATED INSTRUCTOR'S EDITION

The Annotated Instructor's Edition of *From Master Student to Master Employee,* Fourth Edition, will help guide you as you use this textbook. Whether you are a first-time user of *From Master Student to Master Employee,* or a long-time fan, there is something here for you. In this Annotated Edition, strategies to aid your teaching are available at the front of the main text, and content-specific ideas appear prior to each chapter. All of these pages have a separate numbering system (AIE Chapter One, AIE Chapter Two, and so on) so that the textbook pages are numbered the same as the student edition of the text. This allows you to stay on the same page as your students when assigning readings and exercises.

DO A TEXTBOOK RECONNAISSANCE

Flip through the pages of this textbook right now to get the big picture of the fourth edition. Look for fresh ideas you can use to support your course objectives. The table of contents of this book outlines what's new and revised in this edition for each chapter. Explore new features, such as the new Five Cs for Your Career that help students see how the skills learned in each chapter can be applied in getting and keeping a job. Consider creating a textbook, e-book, or web site scavenger hunt for students to have them participate in the textbook reconnaissance, too. Locate exercises, articles, or activities, and ask students to work in groups, seeing who can successfully locate the resources. Possibly offer prizes or incentives.

GET TO KNOW YOUR TEAMUP COLLEGE SURVIVAL CONSULTANT

For more than 20 years, TeamUP College Survival has provided consultation and training for the design and implementation of student success and first-year courses. All members of the team of consultants have extensive experience in teaching and administering the first-year course and in facilitating training sessions and conferences. Get to know your consultant today by calling 1-800-856-5727. Or visit the team online at **www.cengage .com/teamup**. Be sure to ask a consultant how you can attend a conference or workshop—for free!

LISTEN TO YOUR PEERS

Throughout the Annotated Instructor's Edition, you will find tips from Master Instructor, Lorraine Fedrizzi of Niagara County Community College, as well as various Best Practices from Master Instructors across the country. As you dig into the following chapters, think about what you would say if you could add your voice to theirs. Send an e-mail to csweb.CollegeSurvival@cengage .com to share your comments. In addition, take what you have learned back to your campus. Consider hosting workshops on your campus, inviting instructors to share their best practices and success stories.

USE THE TRANSITION GUIDE TO FIND YOUR WAY

If you have used previous editions of *From Master Student to Master Employee,* you may need some help finding your favorite articles and exercises. The transition guide on the Instructor Companion Site will help you navigate the changes made to the fourteenth edition. This transition guide is also available on page AIE-xxxi.

MAKE THIS BOOK YOUR OWN

The length of student success courses varies, so there may be more content here than you can share during your course. If some sections of the book don't apply to your course at all, skip them. Take notes in the book signaling articles and exercises you plan to cover and how. Write down ideas for lesson plans, activities, quiz questions, guest speakers, and homework assignments. Change the exercises in the book to fit your needs. Create a new technique by combining several others. Create a technique out of thin air! Consider creating a document where you record the date, what you plan to cover in class that day, including homework to be assigned, upcoming test dates, and class announcements. You can add entries all semester, and then easily monitor your progress throughout the semester, noting what worked well, what didn't, and why. You can easily refer to this next semester, decreasing planning time and allowing you to document new ideas and assignments. In addition, when students ask about homework missed, you have a handy record. End your course by suggesting that students explore any unread sections of the book.

MODEL THE CONCEPTS

Action makes this book work. Completing the exercises along with your students will enable you to stay involved and speak from experience when you discuss each chapter in class. The exercises and articles will help you write, touch, feel, move, see, search, ponder, speak, listen, recall, choose, commit, and create. In this way you join your students on their road to success. Remember to explain your own personal journey of successes and challenges. You are a significant mentor and role model for your students and it is important to remind them that you have not always been the successful, self-actualized person they see before them today!

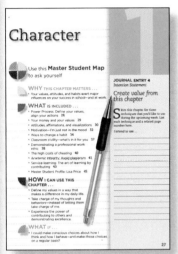

INTEGRATE LEARNING STYLES INTO YOUR TEACHING WITH THE MASTER STUDENT MAP

On the opening page of each chapter, the Master Student Map (**M**etacognitive **A**pplication **P**rocess) guides students toward maximum learning by asking the four basic questions—*Why? What? How?* and *What if?*—that correlate to the Learning Style Inventory as explained in Chapter 2. By becoming aware of their preferred learning style and by using the Master Student Map, students will be better able to understand and practice new styles. Read more about the Master Student Map and how it works on page AIE-xliv. For additional reinforcement, use the Master Student Map in class as a structure for reviewing the previous chapter and previewing the upcoming one.

USE THE MATERIALS BEFORE EACH CHAPTER TO HELP YOU CREATE LESSON PLANS

There are four instructor pages before each chapter. These sections provide content-related ideas for guest speakers, lectures, activities, homework assignments, and previews/reviews to help bring the classroom alive for your students. The organization of these pages is based on the seven-part lesson plan structure described on page AIE-xxxvi. Flip to one of the chapters and review the instructor pages now. Try to include a variety of activities that appeal to many learning styles, including short lectures, group work, hands-on activities, and textbook activities.

LINK TO THE WEB

Throughout this book, "You're One Click Away" icons remind students that additional resources are available on the College

Success CourseMate for *From Master Student to Master Employee*: There they'll find articles, videos, online exercises, and links to other useful Web sites. Part of the support for you when using this textbook is an Instructor Companion Site that contains best practices, lesson plan and lecture ideas, PowerPoints, activities, handouts, videos, test questions, and more. These tools were submitted by faculty around the country who wanted to share effective strategies they have used in their classrooms. Register now at login.cengage.com so that you can explore additional resources to use with your students. See page AIE-xxii for detailed instructions of how to access the available additional digital resources.

POWER PROCESSES

The Power Processes are a long-standing popular feature of *From Master Student to Master Employee*. To help motivate students at the start of each chapter, the Power Process now opens each chapter in the fourth edition. These articles describe approaches to student success that are more philosophical in nature than most of the tools in the text and serve to empower students at the onset of the chapter. Review the pre-chapter instructor resources in the book or on the Instructor Companion Site for strategies to help your students make full value of these special tools.

HELP STUDENTS TAKE THIS BOOK TO WORK

Though the focus of this textbook is success in college, students can apply nearly all of the techniques in this book to any career. Students with less experience in the workplace, however, may not see how these tools apply at work. Five Cs for Your Career at the end of each chapter suggests key strategies that will help students make a seamless transition from success in school to success at finding and applying for a job to success on the job. Skim one of them now.

MASTER STUDENT PROFILES

From Master Student to Master Employee has always included a brief article about a real person who encompasses master student qualities. In each new edition of the textbook, several of the stories are replaced with new ones. Read the article "Master student qualities" on page 3 and then check out the table of contents to discover the 12 people on the roster of master students for the fourth edition! ∎

A GUIDE FOR INSTRUCTORS *who have used* PREVIOUS EDITIONS OF THIS BOOK

The foundations and themes for student success in *From Master Student to Master Employee* have been used by millions of students. Since the first edition, students and instructors have helped shape this book by providing strategies, insights, and suggestions. As a result of its continuous evaluation and refinement, students are inspired and motivated by this book to adopt, develop, and commit to using the skills needed for success in college and throughout life. These ideas are now a part of the fourth edition.

Every word in every article has been evaluated for its helpfulness to students. Statistics have been updated, recent research has been included, and articles have been shortened or lengthened as necessary to maximize clarity of concepts and strategies. Here are some of the major changes you will see in this edition.

KEY UPDATES

- All chapters now begin on the right-hand page.
- The **Power Process** articles are now the first articles in each chapter to motivate students and help turn their negative attitudes around earlier in the chapter.
- A new chapter-ending feature called the **Five Cs for Your Career** presents specific ways in which students can develop five crucial qualities that employers seek: character, creative thinking, critical thinking, communication, and collaboration skills. Students are asked to practice and develop these critical skills now, so that they may make a seamless transition from success in school to success on the job.
- To allow for more coverage of the Five Cs, the Time and Money chapters from the previous edition have been combined into one chapter (Chapter 3). To focus on the five Cs, these topics have their own chapters: Chapter 1 (Character), Chapter 8 (Creative & Critical Thinking), Chapter 9 (Communicating), and Chapter 10 (Collaborating).

CHAPTER-BY-CHAPTER UPDATES

Introduction: Managing Change

- **Revised article** "Master student qualities" (pages 3–5) (previously "The master student" in Chapter 1) to emphasize the life skills associated with being a master student, encouraging students to mark which master student behaviors they possess and which they'd like to cultivate.
- **New Critical Thinking Exercise** "The master student in you" (page 6) gives students an opportunity to evaluate an experience in which they have exhibited master student qualities, as well as brainstorm new master student qualities to be added to the list.
- **Revised article** "Discovery and Intention Statement guidelines" (page 12) to be more succinct and functional for students, with checkboxes to use as they respond to journal entries.
- **Revised Journal Entry 1** "Declare what you want" (page 6), for students to put their Discovery and Intention Statement to use immediately after learning about the process, by responding to a prompt about the "Power Process: Discover what you want."
- **Revised article** "Making the transition to higher education" (pages 13–14) to address technology as a means for setting up students for academic and career success.
- **Expanded articles** "Jumpstart your education with transferrable skills" (pages 23–25) and "60 transferrable skills" (pages 24–25) to include the five Cs for your career—character, creative thinking, critical thinking, communication, and collaboration.
- **New Journal Entry** "Recognize the five Cs in yourself" (page 26) helps students create a detailed picture of the five Cs in themselves.
- **Moved articles** "Making the transition to higher education" (pages 13–14), "Enroll your instructor in your success" (pages 20–21), "Jumpstart your education with transferrable skills" (pages 23–25), and "60 transferrable skills" (pages 24–25) to introduce students to these essential key elements to success earlier.

Chapter 1: Character

- **New chapter** on the theme of character sets the stage for success in school and beyond by showing students how to define their values and align them with their actions. It focuses on forming positive and productive attitudes and changing poor habits to reach goals.
- **New article** "Your money and your values" (page 29) reveals how one's spending habits reflect the values that person possesses, and gives strategies for how to better align behaviors with beliefs.
- **Revised article** "Motivation—I'm just not in the mood" (pages 32–33) offers suggestions to practice maintaining motivation.
- **New Critical Thinking Exercise** "Change a habit" (page 36) takes students through the process of identifying a habit and changing that behavior.
- **New article** "Demonstrating a professional work ethic" (pages 38–39) helps make the connection from civility in the classroom to a professional environment.
- **New article** "Service learning: The art of learning by contributing" (pages 43–44) connects critical thinking to problems affecting our communities and how students can give back meaningfully.

Chapter 2: First Steps

- **Revised article** "First Step: Truth is a key to mastery" (page 51) emphasizes the characteristics of First Steps—universality, challenge, rewards, empowerment, and specificity.
- **Key revisions to the Learning Styles Inventory (pages LSI-1 through LSI-8)** include the following:
  - Clearer directions on how to take the LSI
  - New articles "Interpreting your Learning Style Graph" (page LSI-6) and "Developing all four modes" (page LSI-7) thoroughly explain to students how their LSI scores and graph relate to four different modes, and give students clearer explanations of what the test results mean and how they can apply that new knowledge about themselves to their academic coursework and success.
- **New** Master Student Profile: Fabian Pfortmüller (page 69)

Chapter 3: Time & Money

- **New** combined chapter on both time and money (Chapter 10 in the third edition) to allow for more coverage of the five Cs.
- **Revised article** "You've got the time—and the money" (page 75) to reflect the combined content of time and money.
- **Revised** directions for the exercise "The Time Monitor" (pages 76–80) that more clearly and accurately guide students on how they should track their time spent.
- **Revised** section in the article "Setting and achieving goals" (pages 81–82) about writing down goals, moving goals into actionable items, remembering how to keep benefits of goals at the forefront, and rewarding yourself for met goals.
- **New article** "Make choices about multitasking" (page 96) highlights how productivity goes down as more tasks are done simultaneously. This article provides realistic strategies on how to attempt to focus on one task at a time in today's world.
- **New articles** "Earn more money" (page 102) and "Spend less money" (page 103) offer strategies for increasing income as a way to build wealth and how to succeed in controlling expenses over the long term.
- **Revised article** "Managing money during tough times" (pages 104–105) accounts for the economic landscape today's students are faced with and provides additional strategies for how to manage finances and keeping one's education a priority.

Chapter 4: Memory

- **New** information in "20 memory techniques" (pages 118–122) about ways to organize and order lists—by category, alphabetically, chronologically, and spatially—and ways to use PowerPoint to create interactive flashcards as a study tool.
- **New sidebar** "You mind, online" (page 123) highlights ways students can use technology applications like social bookmarking, online notebooks, and personal information managers to organize topics and items they encounter electronically.
- **New article** "Your brain—its care and feeding" (pages 126–127) explains how students can maximize their brain's unique capacities to learn, study, and remember more efficiently.

Chapter 5: Reading

- **Revised** "Phase 2: While you read" of "How Muscle Reading works" (page 138) to more accurately describe how students should be focusing during their reading and flagging answers to questions they ask during Phase 1.
- **New article** "Getting past roadblocks to reading" (pages 143–144) gives students strategies for how to schedule time for reading, make choices about what to read, and avoid interruptions.
- **Revised article** "Word power—expanding your vocabulary" (page 147) focuses on the ways students can make use of print and online dictionaries.
- **Revised article** "Mastering the English language" (pages 148–149) explains to both ESL students and native speakers the importance of and strategies for using standard English.
- **New article** "Developing information literacy" (pages 150–153) guides students through the research process, how to use available research resources, and the steps they should take to evaluate and use researched information.
- **New article** "Muscle reading at work" (page 154) details how the techniques of Muscle Reading can help students read large amounts of material and extract what's needed in the workplace.
- **New** Master Student Profile: Michael Hyatt (page 155)

Chapter 6: Notes

- **New article** "Turn PowerPoints into powerful notes" (page 173) gives students suggestions for how to take effective notes when instructors use PowerPoint presentations as part of their lecture.
- **Revised** exercise "Taking notes under pressure" (page 174) to account for how today's students access videos.
- **Revised** section in the article "Taking notes while reading" (pages 175–177) includes more specific information about how to take research notes.
- **Revised article** "Taking effective notes for online coursework" (pages 179–180) provides more strategies for how to take notes on course materials and how to manage time when reading in an online environment.

Chapter 7: Tests

- **Revised article** "Let go of test anxiety" (pages 196–197) offers numerous methods for managing anxiety.

Chapter 8: Creative & Critical Thinking

- **Expanded** chapter includes the theme of creative thinking in addition to critical thinking, to emphasize these two essential skills for academic and career success.
- **Revised article and changed title** of "Thinking—a survival skill" to "Thinking: Moving from 'aha!' to follow through" (pages 209–210) to emphasize creative and critical thinking as part of the five Cs skills essential for academic and career success.
- **Revised article** "Ways to create ideas" (pages 211–212) adds suggestions for how to promote critical thinking in groups.
- **New article** "Creative thinking at work" (page 214) explains how creative thinking is essential in the workplace and the ways in which it needs to be carefully cultivated and sustained daily.

- **Expanded article** "Becoming a critical thinker" (pages 215–218) now includes higher levels of understanding as explained by Bloom's Taxonomy.
- **Expanded article** "Thinking critically about information on the Internet" (page 222) includes a section on how to distinguish between information and ideas, helping students to evaluate Internet content.
- **Revised article** "Asking questions—learning through inquiry" (pages 225–226) uncovers how asking questions can make on a better critical thinker in academic, personal, and professional life.
- **Expanded article** "Four ways to solve problems" (pages 228–229) expands on the skills of creative and critical thinking when looking to solve problems in the workplace.

Chapter 9: Communicating

- **Revised article** "Communication—keeping the channels open" (page 238) to emphasize that technology has transformed communicating and collaborating in both the educational and work settings.
- **Expanded article** "Choosing to listen" (pages 239–241) offers more techniques to improve listening skills.
- **New article** "Communicating with your boss" (pages 246–247) explains that this is a skill that can be mastered through preparation, practice, and taking time to see the world from one's boss's point of view.
- **New article** "Writing for the workplace" (page 254) provides strategies for writing success in the workplace.
- **New article** "Making presentations" (pages 255–258) outlines how to create and deliver a successful presentation to keep your audience interested and listening for the duration of a speech.

Chapter 10: Collaborating

- **New** chapter on the theme of collaboration, which is one of the five skills needed for academic and career success.
- **Expanded article** "Cooperative learning: Studying in groups" (page 265) connects studying to collaboration that is expected of employees in the workplace and offers technology suggestions for group work.
- **New article** "Four simple 'people skills'" (page 267) suggests ways in which students can practice their "people skills," which are vital in the workplace—and life.
- **New articles** "Getting to 'done'—the practical art of project planning" (page 268) and "The all-purpose project planner" (pages 269–270) outline how students should prepare for a leadership role in projects both in school and in the workplace. This includes forms to aid organizing projects.
- **New article** "Collaborate in effective teams" (pages 271–272) gives new suggestions for how to work successfully in teams and how this all applies to the workplace.
- **New Journal Entry** (page 272) asks students to reflect on their experience with collaboration.

- **New article** "Make the most of meetings" (page 273) provides tips about what to do before, during, and after meetings to ensure a meeting remains valuable to its participants.
- **Revised** article "Developing emotional intelligence (page 277) now lists and defines the traits that make up one's EQ.
- **New article** "Asking for help" (page 283) explains that asking for helps is not a sign of weakness and provides numerous strategies for how to ask for help in critical situations.
- **New** Master Student Profile: Nilofer Merchant (page 287)

Chapter 11: Health

- **Revised article** "Choose emotional health" (pages 297–299) replaces the previous "Choose mental health," to focus on one's complete emotional health, and identifies that emotional pain is not a sickness.
- **Revised article** "Developing a strong self-image" (pages 300–301) replaces the previous "Developing self-efficacy," to speak to students in terms they understand regarding self-image.

Chapter 12: Career Management

- **New** title for Chapter 12 (formerly entitled "Working") has been combined with the previous edition's chapter on "Careers" and revised to ensure a better flow of relevant content.
- **New article** "Tap the hidden job market" (pages 322–325) focuses on how networking is a powerful tool when job searching.
- **New article** "Build an irresistible résumé" (pages 327–329) puts the task of writing a résumé in the perspective of students beginning their college careers by giving strategies for how students can begin building experience and showcasing master student qualities for jobs desire in the future.
- **New sidebar** "Fine tune your cover letter" (page 329) gives quick suggestions to keep in mind when writing an eye-catching cover letter.
- **New article** "Use job interviews to 'hire' an employer" (pages 330–332) covers networking strategies entering students can use now, as well as what to do before, during, and after an interview.
- **Revised article** "Learning on the job" (pages 336–338) uncovers the benefits of coaching, mentoring, training, workshops, internships, and informal learning.
- **New article** "Creating value from any job" (page 340) focuses on managing expectations and how students can benefit from any job by using it as a steppingstone to the next job they want.
- **New article** "Create your career plan" (pages 343–345) provides an example of a personal development plan and gives students the opportunity to create their own.
- **New sidebar** "Don't plan your career" (page 345) gives advices and suggestions for staying true to one's values and skills while maintaining flexibility about one's career path in the midst of a changing work world.
- **Revised Critical Thinking Exercise** "Discovery Wheel—coming full circle" (pages 347–350) to accommodate new chapter structure and content. ■

Master Instructor
BEST PRACTICES

Throughout the Annotated Instructor's Edition, you will find Master Instructor Best Practices to inspire instructors to try new activities for *From Master Student to Master Employee* that have been successful for other instructors across the country. Whether it's to make a new course your own or to help keep the course fresh for yourself, this sampling of Best Practices reveal innovative ways to get your students involved and invested in becoming a master student and a master employee! For more Best Practices, visit the Best Practices library on the Instructor Companion Site.

EXPLORE FROM MASTER STUDENT TO MASTER EMPLOYEE WITH CHAPTER PAIRINGS (COURSE ORGANIZATION)

Exploring all of the chapters in sixteen weeks presents quite a challenge. Since all of the chapters offer valuable information for college and for life, I decided to pair the chapters. Emphasis is placed on the academic chapters, but these issues are linked with life-skill chapters. Students and I are pleased with this organization for all of the aspects for success are explored in six units. The pairings are as follows:

> Unit I—Introduction/Chapter 1 and Chapter 2—Managing Change, Character, and First Steps.
>
> Unit II—Chapter 3—Time & Money
>
> Unit III—Chapter 4 and Chapter 11—Success Is Mental and Physical
>
> Unit IV—Chapter 5 and Chapter 8—Reading and Creative & Critical Thinking
>
> Unit V—Chapter 6 and Chapter 9—Notes and Communicating
>
> Unit VI—Chapter 7, Chapter 10, and Chapter 12—Tests, Collaborating, and Career Management.

—Paula Wimbish,
Hinds Community College

LEARNING (AND REMEMBERING) VOCABULARY (ACCOMPANIES CHAPTERS 4 AND 5)

I believe that every moment/activity can be a learning moment, and try to incorporate several activities into each assignment. With this assignment students are not only learning and improving vocabulary and reading skills, but also exposing themselves to successful memory improving strategies as employed by other students.

A list of terms I create (mine has 325 terms) are distributed to the students. The students are required for homework to learn some, all, or part of the list. If the class meets once a week, I usually assign about 50 terms. They are told there will be a quiz where I will test them on 10 of the terms at the next class meeting. They are also told that they will have to report (orally and in writing!) on the strategy that they employed to learn the terms.

At the next class meeting I first have the students hand in their write-ups and then report on how they learned the terms. I then tell the class that the quiz has been postponed till the next class meeting. I urge them to try memory strategies suggested by their fellow students. By doing the quiz (usually consisting of only 10 of the fifty terms that have been assigned) a week later the students have an opportunity to try out memory strategies presented in class by their peers.

—Frank Baker,
Golden West College

BEST LISTENER (ACCOMPANIES CHAPTER 9)

This activity is used as part of a unit on communication, and prior to introducing the concept of Active Listening. First, I ask the students to think about the person in their life who they consider to be their "best listener."

Specifically, I ask them to think about the person they go the most often when they feel the need to talk about a problem or situation. Once they have that person in mind, I ask them to make a list of at least five behavioral characteristics that make this person a good listener. I try to avoid giving them examples, but will ask questions to get them thinking, like, what does this person do while they are listening to you or what specific words would you use to describe their actions and responses? I then divide them into groups of 3–4 and have them share their lists. The group then has to come up with their top five behavioral characteristics of a good listener and present them to the class. When we have debriefed all of the lists, I conclude by summarizing the responses and pointing out similarities among the lists.

At this point, I begin a brief presentation on the concept and characteristics of Active Listening (such as empathy, paraphrasing, probing (asking questions), reflection, summary, verbal prompts, silence). I conclude by pointing how many of the behaviors from their lists are considered to be a part of Active Listening. I follow this up with a quick discussion on open ended and closed ended questions. To illustrate the difference, we play a quick game of 20 questions. I think of an object and, in the first round, they can only ask questions that can be answered with a yes or a no (closed ended questions). I give them 3 or four minutes to ask questions, after which I tell them the object if they haven't guessed it. In the next round, they can ask any question. It usually doesn't take very long for them to guess the second item. Usually within the first 3 questions, someone asks, "What is it?" I conclude by discussing the role of appropriate questions in Active Listening and good communication in general.

—Maggie Seymour,
South Plains College

THE HEALTH MONITOR CHAPTER (ACCOMPANIES CHAPTER 11)

Mimicking the Time Monitor exercise from Chapter 3, students record all food and drink for 5-7 days. At the end of the assigned period of time, students analyze their eating and drinking habits and make a plan for possible changes. After monitoring their intake of food and drink for a period of them, students then write a 1-2 page essay which answers these questions:

- What have you learned about your diet/nutrition from keeping track of everything you consumed for 5 days? What surprised you? What did you notice that you did not notice before?
- What things can you add to or delete from your diet to make your nutrition healthier?
- What can you promise to change about your diet now that you have completed this exercise?

—Laura Bazan,
Central Piedmont Community College

PORTFOLIO ASSIGNMENT (CUMULATIVE PROJECT)

I have found this assignment to be one of the most rewarding, both for me as an instructor and for my students. Students apply and reflect upon the content and their experiences of From Master Student to Master Employee and the course. Students' Master Student Portfolios must begin with a two page reflective overview that describes the portfolio theme, the items chosen for the portfolio and their significance. The portfolio must include application examples, such as a copy of a page from a planner to demonstrate time management skills, a page (or pages) of notes taken for this or another class using either (or both) the Cornell or mind-map note-taking styles. The information that included in the portfolio should demonstrate how students have applied Master Student techniques and must also address how those techniques worked for them. Have students also discuss techniques they tried but didn't work, and explain why. Students should also answer these questions: In what areas has this class helped you to improve the most? What areas do you think you still need to work on? How do you plan to apply techniques from this class to continue to improve in those areas? This serves as their final exam and they must present their portfolio and a brief summary of the contents of their accompanying paper.

—Jane Speer,
Alpena Community College

CREATING ENGAGING CLASSES

USING THE SEVEN-PART COURSE MODEL IN YOUR CLASSROOM

Using the following lesson planning model as a framework can provide more opportunities to engage students as active participants and partners in their learning process. The objective is to use varying modes of instruction to facilitate a course that accesses and maximizes each student's method of learning. Try using this seven-part course model as a weekly guideline when developing your lesson plans:

Lectures	**20 percent**
Exercises	**20 percent**
Sharing	**20 percent**
Guest speakers	**20 percent**
Evaluation	
Preview/review	**20 percent**
Assignment	

It will not always be possible to include all parts each week and that's OK. Ideally, over the entire term, the recommendation is to spend 20 percent of class time for lectures; 20 percent for exercises; 20 percent for conversations and sharing; 20 percent for guest speakers; and the remaining 20 percent for previewing/reviewing, quizzes and evaluations, and giving assignments. A complete overview of this course model is available on the Instructor Companion Site. The revised Annotated Instructor's Edition models this structure for every chapter. Flip to the four pages before one of the chapters to see this model put into action.

Using this seven-part course model can be challenging at first and may seem like more work than lecturing. Although the initial investment to create or redesign your lesson plans may be significant, using this method to design lesson plans, class time is spent with students. Students enjoy the variety and class goes by much more quickly.

Here is a sample lesson plan for an 80 minute college success course.

CHAPTER 4: MEMORY

Collect homework (:05)
Preview the class agenda (:05)
Guest speaker or Master Students in Action video from CourseMate (:10)
Lecture—mnemonic devices (:20)
Activity—loci system and peg system (:20)
Class discussion—examples of memory techniques that worked for you in the past (:15)
Assignment—read/do pages 133–141 (Chapter 5) (:05)

COLLECT HOMEWORK

Try to collect homework at the beginning of each class. If homework is late, don't necessarily count it for full credit (unless following an absence). Once you have moved into another chapter, do not accept late work. This is in keeping with the workplace where late work is typically frowned upon or unacceptable. Additional suggestions regarding collecting and grading homework assignments are available on the Instructor Companion Site.

PREVIEW

Preview the Masters Student Map at the beginning of each chapter to give students an idea of the components to be found in each chapter. Survey the chapter, asking students to consider questions before covering the materials, including:

- What has been your experience with this topic?

- Have you experienced success or failure?

- Is this an area you would like to work on? If so, jot down personal ideas as you see strategies which you feel would be helpful.

- Consider putting a first-step toward these goals on your to-do list.

GUEST SPEAKER

Invite guest speakers from various departments on campus. In addition, the Masters Students in Action brings the best of all possible guest speakers, Dave Ellis, into the classroom. Search YouTube for relevant videos; many schools (perhaps even your own) have already uploaded clips with representatives from several departments on campuses, including the career employment center and the library. This allows instructors who teach online, are at an off-campus site, or can't schedule a speaker for a given time to still have access to critical members of the teaching community. Consider filming any guest speakers you may have come into your classroom and share that video with other instructors teaching the course at your institution. One of the important factors for student retention has been identified as campus involvement. Often this is difficult for online students, evening students, or off-campus site students to feel that connectedness to the institution. By seeing the faces and hearing the voices of members of your school community, students can build this connection beyond the walls of the school.

LECTURE

Each class period consider completing a mini lecture, utilizing your own notes and PowerPoints . PowerPoints for *From Master Student to Master Employee* are also available at the Instructor Companion Site that you can tailor to your course. Consider posting your PowerPoints online for students to preview before your lecture or access after the lecture to review. Make use of videos as part of your lecture to keep students engaged, like the Master Students in Action videos that feature Dave Ellis so that students to have an up-close encounter with the author.

ACTIVITY

Try to alternate types of activities you use in every class to provide variety and keep the class exciting for both yourself and the students. This also helps to incorporate different learning styles, appealing to individual student strengths. The Instructor Companion Site has many Best Practice activities tied to *From Master Student to Master Employee* content provided by advisors, consultants, and instructors. Skim them, pick a few that fit your teaching style and time constraints, and try them with your class.

SHARING

Consider including recurring group work in your classroom to emulate workforce structure. Throughout the semester, you can create "teachable moments" if group members are absent. For example, each group member must learn how to communicate effectively and to function as a whole just as they would on the job. Stress the fact that when projects are due, they may find other students in their group are absent. On the day when a group project is due, if only one or two students in a group attend, students may not have the materials needed because a vital group member is absent. Each group member is responsible for the material. Give them a personal example from the workplace where there's unprofessional outcome and remind students that in a time when the economy suffers and jobs are at a premium, they should attempt to secure themselves as an invaluable part of the work community, a member who is able, in spite of unforeseen circumstances, to "save the day."

EVALUATION

Encourage students to complete the interactive quizzes found in the *From Master Student to Master Employee* CourseMate. While tests are important, synthesis and application are more critical in this class; tell your students this. You can also use a portfolio approach, emphasizing product-based learning, with some ideas to include such as the CSFI 2.0, the Discovery Wheel, a college or academic plan, a résumé, and a PowerPoint presentation on the student's anticipated major and/or career.

ASSIGNMENTS

Emphasize to students that assignments are not intended as busy work. Assignments are intended for self-analysis and personal and professional growth. Consider consistently assigning certain portions, such as the Journal Entries. Certain CourseMate components might be especially helpful, like the Master Students in Action videos and Video Skillbuilders. Let other assignments evolve as you see needs or interests expressed in individual classes. ∎

gaining *support*

Student success courses and first-year seminar programs help students learn to be more effective in school, thereby improving their academic performance and increasing their level of commitment.

Gaining approval and support from administrators is important to the success of your course and requires preparation and communication. This backing is necessary to sustain the course long enough to establish both its effectiveness and its value. These suggestions can help you establish that base of support:

Write a statement of purpose for your course. One possibility is "The purpose of our student success course is to improve students' academic performance and increase their level of commitment to our college."

Refer to your statement of purpose often. When negotiating any aspect of your course, be sure to avoid compromises that would sabotage its purpose from either the institution's or the students' perspective. For example, it would be a mistake to settle for too few course contact hours.

Seek grassroots support. The more people who have a vested interest in your proposal, the more likely it is to be accepted. Ask for assistance from the top of the administrative hierarchy. Draw a political road map encompassing crucial factors for gaining support and identifying key individuals. Include those who have behind-the-scenes influence. Enlist the support of colleagues who trust you. Spend time with key individuals who may not support your concept but are key curriculum decision makers.

Become a retention expert on your campus. Familiarize yourself with all the data, research, and institutional studies related to student performance and retention at your school. Explore options your institution might use to improve student performance and reduce attrition.

SETTING UP
your syllabus

Both the students and the purpose and focus of the course will be different at each school. *From Master Student to Master Employee* is designed to give students and instructors a variety of topics and ideas. By using this Annotated Instructor's Edition and the Instructor Companion Site, you can select material that is most appropriate both for your students and for your course purpose.

There are dozens of approaches to creating your student success course's syllabus. It may be as brief as one page, providing only the most essential information for students, or it may be several pages long, with detailed assignments, due dates, and other information about the course. Here are some ideas to consider:

Choose what to include. In addition to the course name, class time and room, instructor name, office hours, and instructor contact information, here are some common elements that may be included in your syllabus:

- Required and optional textbook information

- Other materials you will require students to have. (This could include course codes for the Course Mate.) You should provide students with any needed online components, and suggest a consistent place for them to record their user name and passwords. This will save time and frustration.

- Class support Web site URL

- Assignments, with or without instructions and due dates

- Important dates, including midterm, final, last day to withdraw from classes

- Official course outline

- Agendas for each class meeting

- Learning outcomes

- Grading method

- Additional recommended readings and/or resources

- Class rules, including your policy for attendance, tardiness, late work, and plagiarism

If you're creating a syllabus for your course for the first time, a more general syllabus may be a better choice. As you progress through the course material, you may discover that some topics take more or less time than you anticipated. You will find that this varies from class to class, or semester to semester.

Organize and sequence the course topics. The official course outline of record and the total student contact hours for your course will provide you with parameters for organizing the material you will cover during the term. Based on the length of your course, decide how much time you will spend on each topic/chapter. Consider the order in which you will present the topics. Although the text chapters are organized in a logical sequence, once you complete the Introduction, each chapter has independent content, so you can teach the chapters in whatever order you prefer. Some teachers let the students prioritize the chapters by voting on each of the chapter topic names. Continue to get feedback from students. You may choose to vary the content and the delivery pace depending on student input. It is much better to successfully cover two topics than to hurriedly cover three. You can often "make up" the time by altering future assignments.

Identify key dates. After you have organized and sequenced the course topics/chapters, identify key dates for you and your students. Decide when the midterm will be given, when major projects will be due, and which guest speakers you want to invite and when during the term you want them to come. As you will read in chapter 3, it is important to prepare for the unexpected. Be flexible in your timeframe when possible. For example, an invited guest speaker may find he is unavailable at the last minute.

Choose a grading method. Decide how you will weight quizzes, tests, homework, and other assignments. How many quizzes will you give? Will students be allowed to drop their lowest quiz score? Will there be an option for extra credit? Develop an objective system for grading that is applied consistently to each student.

Choose class rules. Class rules include written clarification of the boundaries you set for behavior in the classroom, instructions on the way assignments should be presented for grading, and parameters for how your students should interact with each other and with you. For example, if you are more easily contacted by course e-mail than by phone, you might want to explain this to students. Topics you may want to address include:

- Attendance

- Assignments turned in with no name

- Late assignments

- Make-up test and quiz policy

- Word-processed (versus handwritten) assignments

- Side conversations

- Cell phone and laptop computer use in class

- Academic honesty

- Formatting requirements for electronically transmitted assignments (.pdf, .doc, etc.) It is helpful to be thorough in your instructions. The more detail you can give, the more likely students will be successful. For example, you can't assume students will understand how to upload a document or to log onto their course. Although this is especially true in online classes, it is also true of on-ground classes. You might consider including a document with screen shots of what students will see as they log in to the course. Or, you might consider including a tutorial for preparing, saving, or submitting documents.

- Logging-in frequency for online courses

Evaluate and refine. Each semester, make notes about what works and what doesn't work in your syllabus so that you can modify it for the next term. Consider asking your students at the end of the term to provide feedback as to how the syllabus could have been more helpful to them. Create your own evaluation form for your students. No later than midterm, ask questions to guide your instruction. These could include: Which methods in this course have been successful for you? Which methods have not been successful? What elements would you like to see used more in class (including such elements as group work, journals, lecture, and hands-on activities)? What ideas can you suggest for making this class more effective for you? For more sample syllabi, log on to the Instructor Companion Site and visit the Sample Syllabi Library there. ■

NCCC		Lorraine	Fedrizzi
GES 120		Mailbox:	A131
		Email:	Use Angel

WELCOME TO COLLEGE & CAREER PLANNING SKILLS

I. **CREDIT HOURS:** 3 (free elective)

II. **COURSE MATERIALS:** *From Master Student to Master Employee* (fourth edition) by Dave Ellis.

III. **PREREQUISITES:** None.

IV. **COURSE DESCRIPTION:** Concentration will be on strategies to create effective work habits and responsible decision-making that transfer from college to the workplace. This course offers a toolbox of strategies and skills practiced by successful, happy, and productive people. Learn to study smarter, build self-esteem, set goals, take responsibility, manage change, communicate effectively, manage time, solve problems, and take control of your school, work, and personal life.

V. **COURSE OBJECTIVES: At the end of this course, students will:**
- participate effectively within the college system.
- identify behaviors which influence academic, personal, and career success.
- identify a practical plan for choosing a major and a career that matches values, interests and abilities.
- use important academic skills including time management, textbook reading, note-taking, test-taking, memory strategies, listening, and creative and critical thinking.
- set educational and career objectives in view of tentative or definite career choices.
- Identify and solve problems using a systematic problem solving process.
- demonstrate a capability for self-direction.

Students may choose one of two grading options:
- S/U (Satisfactory/Unsatisfactory); student must file S/U card no later than deadline; a minimum of 630 points is required to earn an S grade.
- Standard Letter Grades:

Points	Grade Earned
900–1000	A
870–899	B+
800–869	B
770–799	C+
700–769	C
670–699	D+
600–669	D
000–599	F

SELLING THIS CLASS TO STUDENTS *on day 1*

If your student success course is required; you are likely to have a number of student resisters in your class. In colleges and universities where taking such a course is an option, some students enroll because they think it looks like an "easy A" in the catalog. In either case, you, as the course instructor, can positively influence students on the first day of class so that they'll be more likely to stay and discover for themselves the value of this course. Here are seven suggestions to help build interest and commitment on Day 1:

1. Student testimonial letters. At the end of each semester, ask students to write a letter of advice to a future student in your course. Encourage them to include the information they would have liked to have known on the first day of class. Consider making this assignment part of the final or another assignment for which credit is granted. Distribute copies of these letters to your students during the first class meeting. Since these letters consist of opinions and not always facts, it may be useful to have the students exchange letters or share key information in the letters in groups or with the class as a whole. Students believe the content in these letters from unknown peers, and many will be inspired by what they read. Faculty Advisor Dean Mancina puts these letters in envelopes before handing them out—the sealed envelopes add to the impact!

2. Student guest speakers. This idea can be used as an alternative or in conjunction with the testimonial letters above. At the end of the semester, invite students to return as guest speakers on the first day of your class the following semester. Get their e-mail address and/or phone number so that you can send them a reminder a week or two before the next term begins. Having two or three students tell their peers how valuable the course is raises the commitment level of students who are still "shopping" for classes during the first week of the term. Consider video recording these speakers. Many now have phones which have direct upload into YouTube. Or you may choose to save these interviews, allowing you to show these in your course's online platform. In addition, this allows you to save the most powerful speakers' thoughts for future semesters. Powerful student feedback builds buy-in from current students.

3. Show your enthusiasm. If you've taught this course before, you know the profound impact it can have on your students. Share that in a dramatic and enthusiastic way. Let your students know how much impact this course can have on their lives. Share some stories of the success your prior students have achieved, but don't mention names to protect your students' privacy.

4. Ask, "What do you want?" During the first class, ask students to write down three skills that would be so beneficial that if they could learn them, staying in this course would be "worth it." Brainstorm several such skills first to prompt their thinking. Use two-part paper. Have the students pass a copy forward. Read their responses aloud, anonymously, and announce whether each skill is part of the content of this course. This activity helps personalize the course and demonstrates that the content includes material that students want to learn. It also helps to clarify what this class is *not* about; as it's doubtful your course will cover everything the students want.

5. Talk about the text. *From Master Student to Master Employee* is one of the most used college textbooks on any subject in North America. This is a proven product that works. Hold the book up and turn to key pages such as the Discovery Wheel. Tell the students this is a book they will not want to burn or sell at the end of the semester, but will keep as a reference tool for the rest of their college years. . . and beyond! You can suggest that students consider the topics in terms of their families or other important individuals in their lives. For example, when discussing learning styles, encourage students to give the assessments to their significant others. This will help explain some of the frustrations in their personal interactions. For example, a boss who is a holistic thinker may cause frustration for a linear thinker. This student buy-in affects their personal lives, sometimes even resulting in family members or friends registering for the course in future semesters.

6. Group discussion and anonymous questions. Divide students into groups of four and ask them to brainstorm questions about this course that they don't know the answers to. Have the students submit their questions anonymously on 3 × 5 cards or in an online discussion board. Read the questions aloud and answer them. Addressing concerns students may not wish to state openly can help quell anxiety and fears that could result in students dropping the course.

7. Tell the truth. Be honest about both the "good news" and the "bad news." "This course is *not* an easy A! But it's also about more than you thought it was when you enrolled." ■

....

master instructor BEST PRACTICE

❝ *On the first day, I share this thought with my students: This course can change your life. But you need to be open to taking an honest look at yourself.* ❞

—Annette McCreedy,
Nashville State Community College

....

CLASSROOM
Management Strategies

Students can achieve maximum success in an environment that fosters creativity, critical thinking, focus, and commitment. Developing your classroom management skills can help you create that environment. There are as many approaches to effective classroom management as there are instructors. To be effective, a strategy has to fit your style. For example, if you like a structured, linear environment, set up your class to fit that style. Consider expanding your comfort zone, however, as you model flexibility. Brainstorm a list of answers to the following question: What is the optimum teaching environment for you and your students? The answers to this question may provide you with guidance in formulating strategies that will provide an environment conducive to learning. Consider asking tenured colleagues what works and what doesn't work for them. They know the culture of the students attending your institution.

After you decide what you want, make sure that you clearly communicate to your students how you conduct your class. Have a conversation with your students about this topic during the first week of class. Follow up with key aspects about your class in writing to enhance clarity. This information might be part of your syllabus or a separate handout.

Finally, implement consistently. Public institutions must be able to defend that students are not being discriminated against. No instructor wants to be accused of treating students with favoritism at any institution, public or private.

CLASS RULES TO CONSIDER
(You may want to include these rules in your class syllabus.)

- *Respect—for peers, for the instructor, and for guest speakers.* What are the minimum standards you want to set?

- *Side conversations.* Some side conversations in class are related to the class topic being discussed, but others may be unrelated to the topic. Seating students in groups promotes more active learning, but may also facilitate more side conversations. Side conversations may distract you from your lecture. Further, when two students engage in a side conversation, not only do they miss what's actually happening in class, but the students around them may be distracted as well. You can minimize this problem if you periodically change how you group students for class work. For example, if you are forming four groups, ask students to number off and form groups, thereby breaking up friends sitting together. For the next group assignment, start counting off from the opposite direction, again altering group structure.

- *Absences.* What is your policy regarding missed class meetings? How will students get the assignments, handouts, information, and class experiences they missed? Flexibility here is helpful for students, but if you're teaching many courses or are a part-time instructor, providing copies of all of your previous handouts and class summaries and taking the time to go over missed classes with students may not be realistic.

- *Arriving late to class.* Some instructors and students are distracted when students arrive late to class. How can late-arriving students minimize the disruption they cause? Will you still accept their homework? Does this count against students' grades? Will a set number of tardies count as an absence?

- *Cell phones/laptops/other technologies.* Many students have come to believe that they need to stay in touch with their family and friends even during class. If you don't want students constantly stepping out of the classroom to answer their phones, checking their e-mail, surfing the Web, or texting instead of being engaged in what's happening in class, you'll need to set parameters for the use of such devices. You should determine if you will allow students to use technology to take notes in class. It is difficult to monitor activity, especially if students have internet access. Temptations can be strong to surf social sites during class.

- *Turning in assignments late.* Will you accept assignments after they are due? If so, what are the limits to that policy, if any? Set limits early in the term. Put policies in the syllabus, and be consistent.

- *Makeups for missed quizzes and tests.* Can your students arrange to make up a quiz or test they miss? Consider giving quizzes at the beginning of class. This is especially effective if you do not allow make-up quizzes. You will deter tardiness by this strategy.

- *Accommodations.* Students should go through your campus' proper channels for obtaining accommodations. These should not be granted after the fact. In other words, after receiving a poor grade, a student may say he should have had special accommodations due to learning or physical challenges. These arrangements should be made early in the semester.

- *Cheating.* What is your policy regarding cheating?

- *Progressive discipline.* How will you handle violations of your class rules?

Some instructors provide a written list of class rules and review them during class. Other instructors create such a list with the students at the beginning of the course. Such documents can even take the form of a class contract that the instructor and students must sign.

As for discipline, first find out your college's policies and procedures regarding student discipline for cheating and disruptive classroom behavior. Your dean or another administrator may be responsible for student discipline and can give you guidance and direction that is consistent with the institution's policies. Decide ahead of time what your progressive discipline plan will be if a student violates or refuses to follow your rules. Your behavior in that situation will set an example and inform other students of the consequences of not following your rules. Depending on the specific infraction, you might start by approaching the student individually and reminding him of the rule he has broken. If he repeats the violation, you might call him out in front of the class, remind him that you have already talked to him about this, and say that the next time you will tell him to leave the class. Then follow through with his removal if he violates the rule a third time. Make sure you know your school's policy, including calling campus security for unmanageable or threatening conduct. ∎

See the example of Annette McCreedy's class rules below.

COURSE POLICIES & CLASS RULES

1. Attendance at each class meeting is required. Be in class on time. While I understand that there may be days when you may be unable to attend, there are no "excused" absences. In other words, an absence will be recorded. You are allowed 4 hours of absence before your grade is penalized. If you miss class, it is your responsibility to get make-up assignments and to stay current with class progress. If you are not certain how many absences you have accumulated, you can see me or e-mail me.

2. Be on time for class. Tardiness is disruptive, and you will miss vital information. Two tardies will count as one absence, Tardiness exceeding 15 minutes will be counted as an absence.

3. Side Conversations are not permitted. This includes texting!

4. Turn cell phones to Off or Silent and keep them out of sight during class.

5. Laptop computers may be used in class, but must focus at all times on course content.

6. Read and follow the Academic Integrity Policy in your syllabus. Ignorance of this policy is dangerous!

7. You are responsible for understanding and following the course syllabus and any other materials presented in this class. If you do not understand something, ask me BEFORE a due date arrives.

8. You must purchase a 3-ring binder for your text, handouts, notes, and other materials.

9. My course requires online access. Do not use an email address shared with others. Email attachments must be sent in WORD, rtf, or PDF format. No other formats will be accepted.

10. If you drop this course at any time during the semester, it is your responsibility to officially process the withdrawal paperwork. Note that failure to officially withdraw will result in a failure for non-attendance (FA). This will negatively impact your GPA.

11. My class and Website are hate-free zones. **Inappropriate, disrespectful, or disruptive behavior will not be tolerated.**

12. Achievement of Student Learning Outcomes is based on the premise that you attend all class meetings, participate actively, and complete all outside of class activities. Generally, students should expect to spend an average of 2 hours outside of class for every hour spent in class in most transferable college courses, including this one.

13. Students with disabilities who believe they may need accommodations should contact the Disabilities Coordinator as soon as possible. Any accommodations must be recommended by this office. You must fill out the correct paperwork and bring me a copy of the approved accommodations. All accommodations must be designated before due dates. In other words, it is not acceptable to complain about a grade after the fact, stating that you should have received accommodations. All disabilities and accommodations remain confidential.

TIPS FOR TEACHING
student success online

Many of the strategies in the the Instructor's Edition and on the Instructor Resources Web site can be adapted for use in your online student success course. For example, have students read a controversial article. Then at the Discussion Board, each student posts in the Subject Line— Strongly Agree, Agree, Disagree, or Strongly Disagree, with justification for their position in the body of the post. Further require that students respond to at least two other student posts in this thread.

One of the most important roles of the online instructor is to ensure a high degree of interactivity and participation by managing the discussion forum. In a classroom, the instructor builds motivation in front of the students by her on-stage demeanor. Online that role is portrayed in the projects, instructions, and guidance the instructor gives, which together promote a dynamic, interactive environment for online students. For example, when assigning text exercises such as the Discovery Wheel, instead of having students turn in the reflective responses to the exercise, have them post a Discovery and/or Intention Statement to the Discussion Board and respond to at least two classmates' posts. If you use the eBook with your online students, assign students to complete the pre-chapter assessment that appears as a link icon at the beginning of each chapter and post an intention statement about the results on the Discussion Board.

Here are some suggestions to help you manage your online Discussion Board:

- Stagger due dates for postings and replies each week to keep the conversation moving.

- Require discussion participation and make it part of the student's grade in the course.

- Provide post expectations to receive full credit. Include a rubric with specific expectations for Discussion postings. Students often try to piggy-back off of other students' postings, or they may only write a few words, trying to submit the bare minimum. Your rubric could include categories such as relevance, originality, and coherence. Then give the qualities necessary for certain points or grades on the discussion, including what makes up superior, average, and poor submissions.

- Teach students to create succinct, accurate titles for the subject line of their posts.

- Don't let students use abbreviated writing; teach netiquette. Search online for netiquette standards for other schools.

Consider the following examples of online activities:

1. Article Response. For example, after students read the article, "Ways to fool yourself: Common mistakes in logic" (page 219),

instruct them to pick one common mistake in logic and post a personal example to the Discussion Board. The second part of the assignment includes responding to classmates' posts.

2. Weekly Journal. The weekly journal is an avenue for students and the instructor to relate one-to-one. Solicit feedback from your students. Ask them how they are doing in class. Often an online class may be more difficult or time-consuming than they anticipated. In the journals, students often share frustrations with other classes, work, or not having enough time with family and friends. Direct them to a specific article in the textbook that may help, or quote something from the book in your reply.

3. Internet Search. Consider having students do some research on a topic. For example, use the "Building relationships across cultures" article (page 278). This activity is specifically for use with the eBook. After students have read the article, have them click on the *Activity* icon in their ebook. Instruct the students to read the activity article "The face of diversity, remembering cultural differences." Then ask each student to complete an Internet search on the phrase "cultural generalization" from the article. Finally, ask students to post their discovery statements about cultural generalization to the Discussion Board, backing up their discoveries with links to the Web sites they researched. As noted above, each student should also respond to two of these posts to keep the discussion moving. ■

Master Student Map

One of the most useful features in *From Master Student to Master Employee* is the Master Student Map (**M**etacognitive **A**pplication **P**rocess) located on the opening page of each chapter. The Master Student Map is a reasoning model based on the Learning Style Inventory. Even the most inexperienced students can quickly begin to apply this simple, systematic process to monitor their thinking and learning. What makes this model so effective is that by utilizing the strengths of each learning style, students can implement the monitoring aspect of metacognition as soon as they achieve awareness.

Each category of the Master Student Map begins with a basic question designed to engage student interest and lead to the important ideas presented in the chapter. A closer look at the design and formatting of each question in the Master Student Map will reveal the logic behind this innovative approach to introducing chapter topics.

WHY THIS CHAPTER MATTERS . . .

The role of this question is to encourage personal interest and a need to know in the learner. Initiating the Master Student Map with this type of question leads Mode 1 learners toward a deeper metacognitive understanding of their thinking, allowing them to call on principles within their prior knowledge that help structure the ideas in the chapter.

WHAT IS INCLUDED . . .

This question is followed by a list of specific, thought-provoking article titles from the chapter. This helps Mode 2 learners probe and analyze the factual and conceptual ideas presented in the chapter and become more aware of what will be expected of them.

HOW YOU CAN USE THIS CHAPTER . . .

Mode 3 students will experience the impact of acclaimed features of *From Master Student to Master Employee*, such as the Discovery and Intention Journal Entry system, Power Processes, and Master Student Profiles, which uplift and inspire students to make personal commitments and set goals to accomplish. In this stage, have students go through the list of articles and mark the ones they predict they will know something about. They may also identify topics that they suspect will be challenging to them. The articles they do not mark indicate topics they are least familiar with. Being aware of knowledge gaps will give students a better idea of what they need to study for tests.

AS YOU READ, ASK YOURSELF WHAT IF . . .

Taking advantage of the action-oriented strength of Mode 4 learners, *what if?* questions lead to more lateral thinking and thus better-quality decisions. Specific skills do not necessarily transfer from one mental schema to another. Asking provocative *what if?* questions trigger the students' imagination to transfer skills and create new schema for developing skills in their other classes. Students are intrigued by inquiry rather than pat answers. *What if?* questions stimulate discussion and further the transfer of skills in situations outside the classroom as well. Students are also practicing critical thinking. You can make this connection for the students since they may not even be aware that they are already practicing critical thinking skills.

Based on the latest theories of brain-active learning, the Master Student Map feature helps students activate relevant memories with regard to the subject matter in the chapter. Since all learning depends on prior knowledge, beginning each chapter with this reasoning model helps students in several ways. First, distractions can be reduced or eliminated because the model allows students to study the most interesting or important topics first, helping create student buy-in. Next, it helps increase the speed of students' learning by organizing the ideas in the beginning pages. Finally, it links all of the ideas in the entire textbook to the learning style of each student in a simple but powerful way.

Another important benefit of the Master Student Map is that it provides the instructor with a clear outline of what is going to be investigated in each chapter and a framework for guiding the discussion. In a pilot study using this model, instructors at Utah Valley University found these questions to be very helpful as teaching tools primarily because the questions gave them a place to begin instruction and a final destination.

The four basic questions not only help instructors better understand what the students need to know but also serve as a catalyst for both pre- and post-assessment in the students' minds. Instructors who were more adept at viewing the curriculum in a holistic fashion were able to use this feature of overarching guiding questions to help them convey to students the big picture of the chapter in an efficient and meaningful way. Those instructors who were more linear in their thinking leaned toward the *what?* category of guiding questions and allowed their students to discover how the other questions fit in during the course of the discussion. This flexibility instilled confidence in the instructors to teach the magazine format of *From Master Student to Master Employee* in their own preferred style and enabled them to be more comfortable with the teaching process. Consequently, students reported high satisfaction with both the course instructor and the material. Just as you encourage your students to increase their flexibility, you might want to increase your comfort with both linear and holistic preference. This could be a valuable discussion topic in meetings or workshops. This sharing will help you understand and acknowledge your students' styles as well. ■

Administering and interpreting the
LEARNING STYLE INVENTORY

The learning style inventory (LSI) is an important tool to help your students discover their preferred mode of learning. Some instructors have found their students feel overwhelmed when they are left on their own to take the LSI, score it, and interpret the results. Consider the following suggestions.

Begin by introducing the LSI to your students. The article "Learning Styles: Discovering How You Learn" page 57) will help you set the stage. It highlights the step-by-step directions for completing the LSI, which begins on page LSI-1. Review the directions with your students. If you are assigning the LSI as homework, consider walking students through the scoring process in class first. Or ask them to hold off scoring the inventory until they're in class with you. As you explain the process to students in class, ask them to help those sitting around them. This builds classroom connections. Guide them in using the interpretive material—help your students connect it with their own experience. Doing so will pay big dividends. Not only will your students begin to understand why they make the choices they do, but they'll be better partners in the learning process.

Be sure to review the cycle of learning with your students. The examples will be easily identifiable to your students and will encourage them to put the information they have discovered about themselves into practice right away. Begin your discussion by asking students about their preferred way to learn historical information or new technology. Ask students, "Did you ever have a difficult or unpleasant subject in school? But at one point you had a teacher who explained it in a way that connected for you—you understood the material and found yourself enjoying the process? This is an indication that the teacher appealed to your preferred learning style." Once you have your students in the proper mindset to think about their learning style, they will be better prepared to read the Master Student Map at the beginning of each chapter and will understand the value of completing the Learning Styles Application on the CourseMate.

Beginning on page 59, the article "Using Your Learning Style Profile to Succeed" will have your students participating in a Mode 4 activity. In the Five Cs for Your Career feature at the end of Chapter 2, your students will be invited to think specifically about learning styles and their application in the workplace.

Students can use their understanding of learning styles to make choices that support their academic progress. Ask them to apply *what? why? how?* and *what if?* questions to the LSI:

- "**Why** should I involve myself in this learning situation?"
  Self-awareness control is the ability to consciously monitor and intentionally control thinking and establish purposeful reasons for action. Asking the question *why?* helps students regulate their thinking by establishing purposeful reasons for their actions.

- "**What** will I need to do to understand the concept?"
  Critical analysis is the ability to identify key ideas, gather necessary information, and recognize the importance of essential ideas. Asking *what?* questions helps students recognize the knowledge level of essential ideas by their order of importance.

- "**How** is this learning meaningful to me?"
  Reasoned synthesis is the ability to combine essential ideas to create meaningful applications of knowledge. Asking *how?* questions helps students utilize essential ideas and create meaningful applications of their knowledge

- "**What if** I apply this strategy to my other courses or to my life?"
  Creative transfer application is the ability to adapt applications for different concepts and choose the most effective strategies for specific situations. Asking *what if?* questions helps students imagine alternative applications and choose the most effective strategy for the situation.

Integrating knowledge of learning styles into the curriculum can help instructors design a course that promotes success for all students. As you choose your teaching methods to address various preferences at different points in the course, you meet different students' needs. Students in your classes typically represent all four modes of learning, so some students will sometimes find a good fit with what you are doing, while at other times they'll need to stretch beyond their preferences. Acknowledging different learning styles allows instructors to shift their energy from lecturing to facilitating. Rather than just focusing on the transfer of knowledge, you can use feedback about your students' learning to inform your teaching. You may also find yourself challenged in new and exciting ways. Students come to realize that their interactions shape what happens in the classroom, and they become active participants in constructing their learning experience. Working together, instructors and students create an environment that promotes success.

More suggestions for creating lesson plans that support all four modes of learning are available at the Instructor Companion Site. In addition, video clips from the *Learning Style Inventory* video—an overview of the LSI and its application—are available at the Instructor Companion Site. ■

TEACHING LEARNING STYLES *in your classroom*

From *Master Student to Master Employee* includes three approaches to learning styles: the Learning Style Inventory, multiple intelligences, and the VAK (**v**isual, **a**uditory, and **k**inesthetic) system. That's a lot of information to absorb. It is important to recognize that each approach presents a valid option and is not the final word on learning styles. Encourage your students to look for ideas from any of these methods that they can put to immediate use. When they write Intention Statements, have your students keep these questions in mind: How can I use this idea to *be* more successful in school? What will I *do* differently as a result of reading about learning styles? If I develop new learning styles, what skill will I *have* that I don't have now?

The Learning Style Inventory (LSI). People are often fascinated by why they do what they do—and students are no exception.

Using learning styles to improve
LEARNING AND PROBLEM-SOLVING SKILLS

Students can improve their ability to learn and solve problems in three ways:

1. Develop learning and work relationships with people whose learning strengths and weaknesses are different from theirs. This is a valuable skill in the workplace as well.

2. Improve the fit between their learning style strengths and the kinds of learning and problem-solving experiences they face.

3. Practice and develop learning skills in their areas of weakness.

First strategy: Develop supportive relationships. This is the easiest way to improve learning skills. It is important for students to recognize their own learning style strengths and build on them. At the same time, it is important to understand and value other people's different learning styles. Also, students should not assume that they have to solve problems alone. Learning power is increased by working with others. Although students might be drawn to people who have similar learning skills, they'll learn more and experience the learning cycle more fully with friends and coworkers who have different learning skills. Try grouping students with the same learning styles and asking them to determine what does and does not work for them in a classroom setting. Share group responses aloud. For other exercises, try groups that combine students with different learning styles, encouraging them to discuss these differences and how they shape their decisions and behavior.

How? If someone has an abstract learning style, such as Mode 3, he can learn to communicate ideas more effectively by associating with those who are more concrete and people oriented, such as learners who prefer Mode 1. A person with a more reflective style can benefit from observing the risk taking and experimentation of people who are more active, such as learners who prefer Mode 4.

Second strategy: Improve the match or fit between students' learning styles and their tasks. This is a more difficult way to achieve better learning performance and life satisfaction.

How? There are a number of ways to do this. For some people, this might mean a change of career to a field where they feel more comfortable with the values and skills required of them. Most people, however, can improve the match between their learning style and their tasks by reorganizing their priorities and activities. They can concentrate on those tasks and activities that lie in their areas of learning strength and rely on other people's help in areas of learning weakness.

Third strategy: Become a flexible learner. Students can do this by strengthening their weakest learning skills. This strategy is the most challenging but also the most rewarding. By becoming flexible, students will be able to cope with problems of all kinds, and they will be more adaptable in changing situations. Because this strategy is more difficult, it requires more time and tolerance for mistakes and failures. Developing this skill can build confidence. Model this for your students. Discuss a time when you had to adjust to someone or some situation. Explain your thought process, and discuss the outcome.

How? First, students should develop a long-term plan. Look for improvements and payoffs over months and years, rather than right now. Next, look for safe opportunities to practice new skills. Students should find situations that can test new skills and will not punish them for failure. Lastly, students should reward themselves! Becoming a flexible learner is hard work. Ask students to take a few minutes to brainstorm immediate opportunities to work on this skill. Then pair students to discuss findings. Finally, discuss answers with the whole class. This process creates student bonds and encourages critical thinking.

Applying the learning styles for
critical thinking

Have students use the following scale to rate their confidence in their ability to utilize the four questions *Why? What? How?* and *What if?* to effectively accomplish the tasks listed below.

0 Never confident   1 Rarely confident

2 Occasionally confident   3 Sometimes confident

4 Often confident   5 Almost always confident

_____ 1. You are a learner, and your biology professor only shows you how to do an experiment. Rate your confidence in your ability to answer any questions (*Why? What?* and/or *What if?*) you still have.

_____ 2. After your professor repeats the instructions for an assignment, they are still not clear to you. How confident are you that you can gain the clarity you need to successfully complete the assignment by asking yourself the four questions?

_____ 3. As you plan your schedule for the next semester, you find there are a number of English classes to choose from. How confident are you in your ability to discover which class would be best for you to take?

_____ 4. You are preparing for a test, but you have little, if any, prior background knowledge about the subject.

_____ 5. You have a problem, and you are trying to understand all the factors that have contributed to the problem so that you can solve it.

_____ 6. You are reviewing your class notes for a test, and you do not remember why a certain entry was so important for you to remember.

_____ 7. You need to choose your career and declare a major, but you are not sure what steps to take first.

_____ 8. Your car breaks down, and you are the one responsible for fixing it.

_____ 9. You are planning a party, and you have been elected to be in charge of buying the food and arranging for the entertainment.

_____ 10. You are sending out invitations to an important event, and you discover that you have more friends and family on your list than you have designated funds for food and other expenses.

Others may actually avoid introspection (low intrapersonal intelligence according to Gardner's multiple intelligences theory) or may fear the results. Students may ask if their scores are "bad." It is important to point out to students that there are no right or wrong answers or learning styles. Taking the Learning Style Inventory (LSI) in Chapter 2 gives students a chance to increase their self-awareness as learners. The LSI helps students make sense of what they're experiencing in college. You should also complete the inventory to increase your understanding of the course content and to model the course concepts.

Developed by Dr. David Kolb at Case Western Reserve University in Cleveland, Ohio, the LSI measures a learner's preferences for *perceiving* information (taking it in) and *processing* information (making sense of what she takes in). When these preferences are plotted on two continuums, four unique modes of learning are formed. Students find that although every individual is capable of employing all four modes, each person has a preferred way of learning.

The Master Student Map on the first page of each chapter highlights these four modes to help students become more effective learners through an understanding of their own learning style preferences as related to the concepts found in each chapter. More important, the Master Student Map can help increase students' effectiveness by encouraging them to use those modes that they have previously underutilized.

Detailed information about administering and helping your students interpret the Learning Style Inventory appears on the next page. Support materials are also available at the Instructor Companion Site.

Multiple intelligences. Howard Gardner of Harvard University believes that no single measure of intelligence can tell us how smart we are. Instead, Gardner identifies many types of intelligence, described in *From Master Student to Master Employee* on page 63. By applying Gardner's concepts, students can explore additional methods for achieving success in school, work, and relationships. *From Master Student to Master Employee* is designed to help students develop these different intelligences. Charts accompany the definitions of Gardner's multiple intelligences in the text, highlighting the characteristics of each intelligence, the learning strategies that are preferred by people with this type of intelligence, and the careers that might interest them. Have your students apply this information to their core courses. For example, a student with musical/rhythmic intelligence could write songs using lyrics based on class notes and could experiment with various kinds of background music while studying. When students begin to acknowledge and trust all of their intelligences (realizing there are no right or wrong styles or intelligences), they can understand and appreciate themselves more.

The VAK system. The VAK system is a simple and powerful technique that focuses on perception through three sense channels: seeing, or *visual* learning; hearing, or *auditory* learning; and movement, or *kinesthetic* learning. Invite your students to discover their VAK preferences by taking the informal inventory included in the text.

Strategies in the text highlight ways students can build on their current learning preferences and develop new options by utilizing their other sense channels. It is important that you teach students to take in information efficiently through their preferred learning style, but it is equally important that you teach them to study and learn information efficiently through a variety of other learning styles. Understanding these concepts is helpful in dealing effectively in personal and workplace relationships, understanding that others also operate through their own styles and strengths. As their instructor, you can set an example by using a mix of strategies to teach them ways to learn the largest amount of material in the least amount of time. Additional ideas for implementing variety in your teaching strategies can be found at the Instructor Companion Site. ■

the **discovery** wheel

The Discovery Wheel is an opportunity for students to think about the kind of student they are and the kind of student that they want to become. Its twelve sections correspond to the twelve chapters in the text. This exercise is assigned at the outset of the course to help students assess their current strengths and weaknesses in different areas of student success. Students answer a series of questions and then plot their scores on their Discovery Wheel—a graphic illustration of their skill levels. This is especially helpful for visual learners. This exercise is also available for students to complete on the College Success CourseMate for *From Master Student to Master Employee* Web site.

At the end of Chapter 12 is an identical Discovery Wheel. By repeating the exercise at the completion of the course, students can trace their progress in acquiring skills and techniques that can ensure their success in school and later in life.

The purpose of this exercise is to give students the opportunity to change their behavior. Completing the Discovery Wheel a second time allows students to see what behaviors they have changed on their journey to becoming a master student and master employee.

Having your students complete the Journal Entry that follows the second Discovery Wheel provides them with another opportunity to state how they intend to change. Encourage them to reconsider tools that they did not think they could use the first time they encountered them in the text.

Note: Student scores may be lower on the second Discovery Wheel. That's OK. Lower scores might result from increased self-awareness and honesty, valuable assets in themselves.

Embracing diversity

Research indicates that although successful students benefit from having a relationship with a caring and competent adult, they are most likely to excel if they receive positive support from a peer group. The information below will help you foster that sense of belonging and assist students of all backgrounds in sharing with each other their discoveries and insights about higher education.

Research also shows that when students interact with diverse student groups, they experience many benefits including improved cultural understanding and tolerance, decreased cultural prejudice and discrimination, stronger connection to the campus community, preparation for challenges of global society, and development of creativity and critical thinking skills.

These benefits can be realized only if students extend themselves beyond both real and imagined barriers that exist.

One of the major goals of diversity awareness is to understand how each person fits into the lives and worlds of others. For some of your students, college may be their first experience with someone different from themselves. As you prepare for your course, keep in mind that some kinds of diversity can be less obvious, though just as profound, as others. To the student from rural America, a classmate from New York or Chicago might seem nearly as strange as one from Finland or Zimbabwe, and vice versa.

International students will have additional adjustment issues beyond those of the other students in your class. Keep in mind that some statements, activities, or attitudes that seem perfectly natural in our society may seem curious or even offensive to students from other countries. Familiarize yourself with cultural differences and issues that could frustrate these students.

Finding common ground can be an important learning experience in the classroom. . Routinely pairing students from different backgrounds and circumstances when assigning group projects and activities can provide students with the opportunity to encounter ideas, attitudes, and experiences different from their own. Throughout the semester, schedule a variety of activities involving students in individual, partner, small-group, and whole-class settings that exercise and accentuate the similarities among your students, and also celebrate the wealth of their differences.

CLASSROOM STRATEGIES

Help ensure success. You can individualize your instruction and structure your course so that students experience success. Total success in school is achieved by taking a series of small, successful steps. Set high but realistic expectations. If your course is too easy, students will lose interest. If it is too difficult, students may become discouraged. By continually evaluating students, monitoring their progress, and getting feedback from them, you can plan your classes in ways that help ensure student success. You are a valuable role model and mentor for your students as you go through this process.

Provide opportunities to talk. Invite students to speak about their perspectives. Suggest that students talk to others to share their concerns, celebrations, compliments, and complaints. Use small-group discussions and exercises. If you teach online or have a supplemental Web site for your class, use the Discussion Board for this purpose. Promote the idea of visiting with counselors and forming peer support groups. Try to find out what your students' options are, avoiding a generic "Get involved." Be as specific as possible. The suggestions for conversations and sharing at the Instructor Companion Site include many ideas for stimulating discussions.

Acknowledge and appreciate cultural differences. We can learn from each other and from exploring values that are different from our own. When we exchange ideas, we can expand our perceptions and examine our values. Use conversations, publications, and special events to recognize and celebrate diversity. Consider using YouTube, Public Radio, or other podcasts to provide viewpoints on global events.

Communicate the advantages of being bicultural. Learning new ways of speaking and behaving does not mean denying or letting go of our traditional languages or customs. Adding alternatives does not eliminate anything. Expanding our options increases our ability to operate effectively in a variety of situations and improves our chances of success.

Discuss how the school environment is similar to, and different from, students' home environments. Then discuss ways to make effective transitions back and forth from one to the other. Explore how the expectations of one environment can be assets or liabilities in another. Recognize that a strength in one culture might be a disadvantage in another. Tennis rackets are great on a tennis court, but they don't work very well in a golf game. How can a student adapt so that she is successful in both environments?

Recognize different beliefs regarding time, competitiveness, and respect for authority. In some cultures, punctuality is a plus. In others, time is not measured in hours, minutes, and seconds; instead, it is measured by the movement of the sun, the changing of the seasons, and an intuitive sense of community readiness. In some cultures, competitiveness is a common incentive toward achievement. In others, it is considered antisocial and insulting. Eye contact during conversations is considered respectful in some cultures and disrespectful in others.

You can acknowledge a wide range of beliefs and, at the same time, communicate the expectations of your institution. An advantage to being bicultural is the ability to adopt behaviors that promote success in a specific environment.

Encourage exposure to different backgrounds. Encourage students to break out of old patterns and habits by associating with people from different backgrounds as well as with those whose backgrounds are similar to their own. They could choose new lab partners, form groups with people they don't know for in-class exercises, sit in new areas in the student union, or attend events that are likely to draw crowds different from those with whom they are comfortable. Invite your class to brainstorm ways to gain exposure to people with different backgrounds. Research a variety of cultural events at your campus or in your community.

When students attend these events, uses these experiences as a springboard for class discussion.

Survey student needs. Evaluate frequently. When you become aware that a student is struggling in a certain area, make an appointment with that student to formulate an action plan.

Individualize feedback. Students appreciate getting specific feedback about their individual performance. Students may initially share cultural concerns or issues in their writing rather than speaking up in class or even individually to you. Write sensitive, relevant comments on papers you return. If possible, always try to include at least one encouraging comment on student assignments. Some students have a strong reaction to red ink, so consider using a more neutral color when correcting papers. Send messages and comments to students through the school e-mail. Thank a student who has actively participated as he leaves the classroom.

Set clear expectations. Communicate expectations clearly. State them several times in several different ways. Use examples to illustrate both what is acceptable and what isn't. Invite students to ask questions in class or to contact you during your office hours or via e-mail if they have any questions or concerns.

Be a mediator. You can facilitate communication between students and administrators. Pass students' complaints and compliments on to the people who are most directly involved. Ask for responses from those people and report back to the students. Follow up on all communications until the matter is resolved. Students often drop through the cracks without follow-up. Modeling advocacy can help create self-advocacy in students.

Include other cultural experiences. Use speakers, textbooks, classroom materials, activities, and media presentations that incorporate diverse cultural experiences. Ask students, colleagues, administrators, and community members for recommendations.

Use a critical thinking approach. Ask students to decide what they think about relevant issues and, more importantly, why they think it. Then ask them to seek other views and gather evidence to support the various viewpoints. Discuss which view or views are the most reasonable. When discussing issues, you can apply the strategies outlined in the articles on critical thinking in the text to recognize any errors in thinking.

Encourage proaction. When students face uncomfortable and difficult situations, they sometimes choose avoidance. Help students consider the long-term costs of giving up. Help them see the benefits of a positive, healthy, and proactive approach. Rather than giving up, students can garner support and find or create forums to discuss and resolve their issues. Sometimes, thoughtful grouping of students in class can create a critical connection. For example, a young mother or a defiant young man can be effectively grouped with a more mature student who can provide wisdom and guidance, and model critical thinking skills.

Allow personal expression. Invite students to translate material into their own words. Ask them how certain techniques, or variations of those techniques, might be applied in their own culture. For example, a gay, lesbian, or transgender student may want to "come out" to the class while sharing in groups or with the whole class. Be ready to provide leadership and support if students respond in an insensitive or inappropriate manner.

Acknowledge student expertise. Ask students to communicate course content from their unique cultural perspective. Experiencing a concept from a different cultural perspective reinforces it. Give an assignment requiring students to combine a student success strategy with some cultural event, personality, tradition, or value. For example, they could create original music and lyrics or describe the role that a particular success strategy may have played in how a cultural hero changed history.

Use guest speakers. Invite guest speakers to your class who represent successful role models. Ask them to share struggles they have experienced and successes they have achieved. Be sure to include time for a question-and-answer period. For off-site, online, or evening classes, record these speakers for class use.

PERSONAL STRATEGIES

Avoid generalizations. All generalizations are suspect—even this one. Avoid tendencies to lump together all people of one race or culture. Consider speaking up when you hear generalizations being made.

Examine your own prejudices. If you have painful memories that contribute to your prejudices, judgments, and generalizations, examine them. Tell the truth about the costs and benefits of holding on to them. Look at how your history encouraged you to be prejudiced in certain ways. Talk about your prejudices and formulate a plan to heal and grow.

Examine your assumptions about students. Where do you think your students go during their vacations? How would you expect them to spend extra money? What type of music do they enjoy? Who are their heroes? Which holidays do they celebrate? Consider how often your assumptions direct your teaching and your conversations with students. How would your teaching and your conversations be different if you assumed nothing about your students? Get to know them as individuals, and allow them to see a personal side of you as well.

Find a translator. Taking a First Step by admitting that you are unfamiliar or uncomfortable with students from other cultures helps bridge the gap. Ask around to find someone who can act as a translator. In this sense, a translator is someone from the students' ethnic or cultural background who has successfully adapted to the mainstream environment. Ask students if they are willing to have this person present when you discuss various issues.

Increase your sensitivity to society's exclusions and inclusions. When you become aware of what to look for, you can see many examples of how one cultural or ethnic group excludes or includes others. Watch advertising and television shows. Examine the policies and notice the membership demographics of schools, businesses, neighborhoods, religious institutions, and athletic clubs. Look for subtle or hidden messages of exclusion and inclusion as well as blatant, formal structures. Expand your personal comfort zone, just as you request of your students.

Give specific feedback. Feedback promotes student success. When feedback is given with a sincere desire to promote success, it is likely to be appreciated. ■

MANAGING CHANGE

Instructor Tools & Tips

"Change and growth take place when a person has risked himself and dares to become involved with experimenting with his own life." —Herbert Otto

Each chapter in the *Annotated Instructor Edition* is preceded by pages with suggestions for instructors. These suggestions are organized using the seven-part course model on page AIE xxxvi. You can quickly find ideas to use in your classroom for preview, guest speakers, lectures, class activities, sharing, homework, and evaluation.

PREVIEW

The introductory chapter, Managing Change, is an important gateway to *From Master Student to Master Employee* because it sets the stage for entering the culture of higher education and connecting to new surroundings. It also explains how students should write the important Discovery and Intention Journal Entries throughout the book. Encourage your students to read "Managing Change" the first week of class.

GUEST SPEAKER

Two or three students from your class in the previous term can make great guest speakers for the first week of class. Students respond well to hearing from their peers. You might provide some guidance about the types of experiences the speakers should share. Ask them to briefly discuss why they enrolled in this course and the three most useful tools they learned in the class. Then invite students to ask the guests questions about the course. Consider taping the presentation in case no former students are available to speak. As many courses may be taught online or on off-campus sites, these students miss out in activities in daytime classes on the main campus. You might want to videotape guest speakers to allow these students the ability to feel a connection to the campus. Today, cell phones or other electronic devices can easily videotape and upload to YouTube. This option will also provide closed captioning, which can help your campus be more ADA compliant. Captioning also facilitates second language students, as often the understanding of the written word can come before understanding of spoken English.

Consider inviting the elected president of student government or an officer from another student organization to speak to your students. Prompt the president to discuss why he or she became involved in student activities and what he or she has gotten out of the experience. Did the president gain unexpected benefits from being involved?

master instructor
BEST PRACTICE

During the first class, I ask my students to preview the text, paying particular attention to the Table of Contents. I then give students my course syllabus, which lists a suggested schedule of topics for the semester. The students' first assignment is to look at the Table of Contents and rearrange the schedule of topics in a way that fits their needs. (Another way to do this is to use students' completed Discovery Wheels—see Chapter 2.) During the second class meeting, we list the topics on a flip chart and vote on the order of the chapters. Then we rearrange the syllabus according to the preferences of the students. This method helps me design the course to meet students' immediate needs. Since the course is mandatory, some of the students have negative feelings when they come to class. Allowing them input on the order of the topics sparks interest and gives them ownership of the course.

–Dr. Jennifer Hurd, TeamUP Consultant

LECTURE

Master Student Map (page 1) Teach students how to use the Master Student Map right from the start of *From Master Student to Master Employee*. If you have ever had trouble convincing your students to read the Introduction, this simply formatted framework helps them grasp the value of this book right away. Use the Master Student Map (Map is an acronym for **M**etacognitive **A**pplication **P**rocess) as a jumping-off point for sparking classroom discussion. Teach your students how they can use this model to preview chapter content in this textbook. Take the Map a step further and show your students how creating a similar schema for textbooks in other courses can help activate background knowledge and provide a "hook" to get them ready for the material within any chapter. Start now by asking the following questions that you can write on your whiteboard, post to your discussion board in an online course, or create a PowerPoint presentation with them.

Why? *Why* is it important to read the Introduction?

What? *What* kind of information does an Introduction provide for the reader? *What* information does the Introduction to *From Master Student to Master Employee* provide?

How? Rate your level of effectiveness with the information presented in the Introduction now. (*How* much do you already know about the topics presented? *How* will this book help you become a better student?) Ask yourself, "*How* can I get more value from my textbook by reading the Introduction?"

What if? *What if* you skipped the Introduction? Ask yourself, "*What if* I could use this Introduction right now to become a better student? And then, "*What if* I could use this material right now in my other classes?"

Discovery and Intention Statements (pages 11–12) The Discovery and Intention Journal Entry system allows students to begin the reflective critical thinking process they will need to grasp the concepts and develop the skills studied in this student success course and to transfer those skills to their other classes. This simple yet powerful system is one of the foundations of the textbook. As students read the book, they are often asked to write Discovery Statements about what they are learning and Intention Statements about what they plan to do, based on the new information they are assimilating.

In addition to assigning the many Discovery and Intention Statements in the book, ask students to write statements in class after activities such as guest speakers, videos, or lectures.

Here is one formula for writing Discovery Statements:

"When I [what you experienced], I discovered that [specifically what you became aware of]."

A formula for Intention Statements:

"I intend to [specifically what action you plan to take] by [time frame or date]. My reward will be [the tangible reward you'll give yourself if you complete your intended goal]."

Sharing these aloud can also help students model the thought process for each other.

Organize for success Encourage your students to identify a student in each class who seems responsible and dependable. Have them exchange e-mail addresses and phone numbers and record them. Suggest to students that if they know they won't be

in class, they should contact this student ahead of time to ask her to pick up extra copies of handouts and request to copy her notes. Take this opportunity to invite your students to visit you during office hours. Provide your e-mail address, phone number, and office location. You might choose to share your office schedule with your students. If you are an adjunct, you might want to provide a sample schedule. Students often are confused about how to read a door schedule. Although we are accustomed to terms such as *office* and *open hours*, this may be confusing to new students.

Barriers to Success Students often have good intentions but fall short of completing them. There are three obstacles that may get in the way of change: not knowing what they really want, lacking skills to succeed, and for some students (unconsciously or consciously) not believing they deserve to succeed. Ask students which one of these barriers is most likely to interfere with their progress, and discuss some options to overcome those barriers. Reaffirm that this book addresses all of these issues, starting with the first Power Process: Discover what you want. The process of Discovery/ Intention statements is a great tool to help students monitor their outcomes and make immediate adjustments for improvement. Chapter 1 addresses character; Chapter 11 addresses a strong self-image; and Chapters 5, 6, and 7 address academic skills. Students will find help to overcome barriers in every chapter of this book.

EXERCISES/ACTIVITIES

1. **Power Process: Discover what you want (page 2)**
   Begin using the idea presented by the Master Student Map to think critically about the Power Process in the Introduction. Explain the purpose of each Power Process to your students: The Power Process will change the way they think, or change their consciousness, because it is their consciousness that determines their behavior. Ask students to consider and discuss in groups: (1) *Why* this Power Process might matter to them (or to their children, family, coworkers, and the like), (2) *What* this Power Process means with regard to the transition to college, (3) *How* they will make this transition work for them, and (4) *What* they risk by not making this transition now.

2. **Master student qualities (pages 3–5)** After students read this article outside class, reinforce the concept of mastery with the following team-building activity in class. Randomly assign students to groups of four, and ask each group to select five of the most important master student qualities for the classroom and also to select five of the most important qualities in the workplace. The group members must agree on the five qualities they pick and be able to justify their decision to choose them. Ask students to examine the qualities on both lists. Do the lists overlap? What does this tell them? Have each group report to the whole class on their choices.

3. **Commitment exercise (page 6)** After students have read the Introduction and completed this exercise, at the following class meeting ask them to open their books to this exercise so that they can review what they wrote. This simple exercise,

which takes less than 5 minutes to complete, helps students confirm their commitment to this course and, indirectly, to their entire college experience. To reinforce this exercise and remind students of it throughout the semester, have them write in large letters on a sheet of paper the words of the level of commitment they chose and then sign their name at the bottom. Have them put this paper at the very front of their three-ring binder for this course so that every time they open their binder, they'll be reminded of their commitment to this textbook—and to their student success.

4. **Making the transition to higher education (pages 13–15)** Have your students choose partners and review the list of expectations in this article. Ask them to predict the two transition areas in the list from the article that would cause students the most trouble and to discuss why. Then they should discuss some possible solutions for students who might be facing these problems. To help students connect to the article on a personal level, ask them which of the items listed in the article present a challenge for them. Collecting these from students allows you to recognize issues early on. It also allows you to keep challenges in mind when grouping students. For example, a struggling, exhausted young mother can benefit from a group assignment with a mature, more experienced parent. This can create life-changing bonds.

5. **First day activity** On the first day of class, ask your students, "What do you want?" Ask if anyone in the class knows or has received recommendations about the class from a former student. Ask, "What did these students recommend about this class?" Later this semester, consider recording students' life-changing experiences to show to next semester's students in these critical early weeks of the term. Give them 10 minutes to write a list of 10 skills they might learn in this class that would be useful for them in college and in their lives. Challenge them to think about things that are worth working hard for. Then have the students form groups of four to share what they wrote. Have them complete this list on two-part paper so that they can keep their list and you can have a copy. This will help you get to know your students right away.

CONVERSATION/SHARING

This book is worthless—if you just read it (pages 7–8) This article helps you "sell" this course to resistant students, whether your course is required or not. Consider going over the seven pitches on the first day of class, even though the students haven't read this article yet.

If you share with your class an experience that you had as a student in college, your students may feel that you are more of a partner with them in their educational explorations. Students particularly enjoy hearing stories of the mistakes you made while in college!

60 Transferable skills (pages 24–25) Students can be encouraged to think about and work with the concept of transferable skills by considering how different skills are learned and practiced in different in-class and out-of-class collegiate experiences. Have

students pick 10 skills from the list and identify how they are currently learning to develop these skills in both classroom-based and out of class contexts.

HOMEWORK

Critical Thinking Exercise 1 (page 1) Even though many students won't have purchased the textbook on the first day of class, hold up your copy of the book and show them the Textbook Reconnaissance exercise on page 1. When you assign textbook reading each week, tell students that they must read the articles *and* do all of the chapter exercises, practicing Critical Thinking Exercises and Discovery/Intention Journal Entries within the assigned pages. The thinking/writing assignments in the book help students personalize what they are reading. To encourage students to buy the textbook early in the term, you might want to assign homework early, pointing out that in college courses, grading begins early, placing students at a disadvantage if they do not come prepared. For example, you might want to count the Discovery Wheel as an early grade, especially given the fact that this should be completed as early as possible if it is to be a true gauge of accomplishment when the Discovery Wheel is given again at the close of the term.

Journal Entry 3 Discovery/Intention Statement (page 26) The five Cs is a recurring theme at the end of each chapter and each "C" (Character, Creative and Critical Thinking, Communicating, and Collaborating) is addressed in corresponding chapters. This journal exercise helps students create a detailed picture of the five Cs in themselves that will then be related to their continued exploration at the end of each chapter.

EVALUATION

Frequent quizzes ensure that students focus attention during class and keep up with the text reading assignments. Quizzes also provide students with opportunities for written reflection regarding new discoveries and intentions. In addition, evaluations help you identify topics and concepts that students have not yet mastered. Questions may be based on the textbook reading assignment, guest speakers, class activities, and/or the lecture. Possible answers are provided for the end-of-chapter quizzes in the Annotated Instructor's Edition.

At your request, Cengage Learning will provide packages of three-part NCR quiz paper to facilitate quick quizzes in class. First make up your quiz question(s). These may be multiple-choice, true/false, short-answer, or essay questions. Students answer the quiz question(s) on the white (top) sheet, simultaneously making two copies on the yellow and pink paper. When the quiz time is up, direct students to tear off the white copy and pass it forward. They can no longer change their answers because you have the original white sheet. Then direct them to look up the correct answers in their book and grade their own quiz. Finally, have them pass the yellow copy forward for your review so you can record their scores. Students keep the pink copy.

Additional Digital Resources for the Introduction

What can you ASSIGN FROM THE COURSEMATE *for From Master Student to Master Employee?*

- **Master Students in Action Videos.** Available for every chapter, students will hear firsthand from other students about their challenges and their strategies for success. The Master Students in Action videos give your students a firsthand view of how the strategies in *From Master Student to Master Employee* have helped their peers overcome obstacles. In special segments, Dave Ellis offers students his best strategies for mastering each chapter's content.

- **Interactive eBook.** For students who are more likely to read onscreen than in print, assign the ebook chapter as an option where students can take notes, highlight, and search, and are directly connected to all the additional digital resources available for the chapter. Challenge your students with a virtual scavenger hunt to help them learn to maneuver the ebook and locate features and exercises you assign.

- **Sample Quiz and Interactive Quiz.** To see if your students have read and understood the reading you've assigned from the Introduction, assign the Sample Quiz for practice and the Interactive Quiz for a grade. Note that quizzes are available for every chapter.

CourseMate *To access CourseMate, your students need to visit* www.cengagebrain .com. *At the CengageBrain.com home page, students search for the ISBN of* From Master Student to Master Employee *(from the back cover of the book), using the search box at the top of the page. This takes them to the product page where these resources can be found.*

Did you know that THESE RESOURCES (and many more) ARE AVAILABLE on the INSTRUCTOR COMPANION SITE?

- **Need some general advice about using *From Master Student to Master Employee* in your course?** The online *Course Manual* serves as an invaluable reference for those developing and teaching a College Success course with *From Master Student to Master Employee*. The *Course Manual* provides advice on general teaching issues such as preparing for classes, classroom management, grading, and communicating with students of various backgrounds, as well as specific strategies on getting the most out of various features in *From Master Student to Master Employee* such as the Discovery Wheel and Learning Styles Inventory. Download the *Course Manual* now and do a reconnaissance to find ideas that you can use in your course.

- **Looking for test banks?** Customizable, text-specific content quizzes are a great way to test student's knowledge and understanding of the text and are available for every chapter. Because they are provided in ExamView, BlackBoard, and WebCT as well as Word, you will have no problem accessing the multiple choice, true/false, completion, and short-answer questions.

- **Check out the new PowerPoint Library!** This master library of PowerPoint presentations makes it easy to find the right PowerPoint for you! In the library, you will find PowerPoint slides for every chapter as well as every Power Process article covered in the book. All PowerPoint slides are downloadable and customizable to fit your needs.

  - **Walk through Getting Started with Instructor Companion Site.** This presentation outlines the contents of the Instructor Companion Site and acts as a quick reference guide for you to locate the resource you want to access.

  - **Walk through Getting Started with CourseMate.** This outlines and defines the resources on the CourseMate and can also be used as a quick reference guide for students.

  - **Chapter PowerPoints.** For each chapter, there is a set of PowerPoints that highlights the main points. Use these PowerPoints in your lecture.

  - **Power Process PowerPoints.** Using the same concept as the Chapter PowerPoints, these presentations cover the main points of the Power Process articles at the end of each chapter.

Please visit login.cengage.com *to log in and access the Instructor Companion Site.*

Managing Change

Use this **Master Student Map** to ask yourself

WHY THE INTRODUCTION MATTERS . . .

- You can ease your transition to higher education and set up a lifelong pattern of success by starting with some key strategies.

WHAT IS INCLUDED . . .

HOW I CAN USE THIS INTRODUCTION . . .

- Connect with the natural learner within me.
- Discover a way to interact with books that multiplies their value.
- Use a journal to translate personal discoveries into powerful new behaviors.

WHAT IF . . .

- I could use the ideas in this book to more consistently get what I want in my life?

✔ CRITICAL THINKING EXERCISE 1

Textbook reconnaissance

Start becoming a master employee this moment by doing a 15-minute "textbook reconnaissance." First, read this book's Table of Contents. Do it in 3 minutes or less. Next, look at every page in the book. Move quickly. Scan headlines. Look at pictures. Notice forms, charts, and diagrams.

Look especially for ideas you can use. When you find one, write the page number and a short description of the idea here. You also can use sticky notes to flag pages that look useful. (If you're reading *From Master Student to Master Employee* as an ebook, you can flag pages electronically.)

_____

_____

_____

_____

_____

_____

_____

_____

_____

© Ruslan Ivantsov/Shutterstock.com

POWER process

Discover what you want

Imagine a person who walks up to a counter at the airport to buy a plane ticket for his next vacation. "Just give me a ticket," he says to the reservation agent. "Anywhere will do."

The agent stares back at him in disbelief. "I'm sorry, sir," she replies. "I'll need some more details. Just minor things—such as the name of your destination city and your arrival and departure dates."

"Oh, I'm not fussy," says the would-be vacationer. "I just want to get away. You choose for me."

Compare this person to another traveler who walks up to the counter and says, "I'd like a ticket to Ixtapa, Mexico, departing on Saturday, March 23, and returning Sunday, April 7. Please give me a window seat, first class, with vegetarian meals."

Now, ask yourself which traveler is more likely to end up with a vacation that he'll enjoy.

The same principle applies in any area of life. Knowing where we want to go increases the probability that we will arrive at our destination. Discovering what we want makes it more likely that we'll attain it.

Okay, so the example about the traveler with no destination is far-fetched. Before you dismiss it, though, do an informal experiment: Ask three other students what they want to get out of their education. Be prepared for hemming and hawing, vague generalities, and maybe even a helping of pie in the sky à la mode.

This is amazing, considering the stakes involved. Students routinely invest years of their lives and thousands of dollars, with only a hazy idea of their destination in life.

Now suppose that you asked someone what she wanted from her education and you got this answer: "I plan to get a degree in journalism with double minors in earth science and Portuguese so that I can work as a reporter covering the environment in Brazil." The details of a person's vision offer clues to their skills and sense of purpose.

Another clue is the presence of "stretch goals"—those that are big *and* achievable. A 40-year-old might spend years talking about his desire to be a professional athlete some day. Chances are, that's no longer achievable. However, setting a goal to lose 10 pounds by playing basketball at the gym 3 days a week is another matter. That's a stretch—a challenge. It's also doable.

Discovering what you want helps you succeed in higher education. Many students quit school simply because they are unsure about what they want from it. With well-defined goals in mind, you can look for connections between what you want and what you study. The more connections, the more likely you'll stay in school—and get what you want in every area of life.[1]

You're One Click Away...
from accessing Power Process media online and finding out more about "Discovering what you want."

Master student
qualities

This book is about something that cannot be taught. It's about becoming a master student and master employee.

Mastery means attaining a level of skill that goes beyond technique. For a master, work is effortless; struggle evaporates. The master carpenter is so familiar with her tools that they are part of her. To a master chef, utensils are old friends. Because these masters don't have to think about the details of the process, they bring more of themselves to their work.

Mastery can lead to flashy results: an incredible painting, for example, or a gem of a short story. In basketball, mastery might result in an unbelievable shot at the buzzer. For a musician, it might be the performance of a lifetime, the moment when everything comes together. You could describe the experience as "flow" or being "in the zone."

Often, the result of mastery is a sense of profound satisfaction, well-being, and timelessness. Distractions fade. Time stops. Work becomes play. After hours of patient practice, after setting clear goals and getting precise feedback, the master has learned to be fully in control.

At the same time, he lets go of control. Results happen without effort, struggle, or worry. Work seems self-propelled. The master is in control by being out of control. He lets go and allows the creative process to take over. That's why after a spectacular performance by an athlete or performer, observers often say, "He played full out—and made it look like he wasn't even trying."

Likewise, the master student is one who makes learning look easy. She works hard without seeming to make any effort. She's relaxed *and* alert, disciplined *and* spontaneous, focused *and* fun-loving.

You might say that those statements don't make sense. Actually, mastery does *not* make sense. It cannot be captured with words. It defies analysis. Mastery cannot be taught. It can only be learned and experienced.

By design, you are a learning machine. As an infant, you learned to walk. As a toddler, you learned to talk. By the time you reached age five, you'd mastered many skills needed to thrive in the world. And you learned all these things without formal instruction, without lectures, without books, without conscious effort, and without fear.

Shortly after we start school, however, something happens to us. Somehow we start forgetting about the master student inside us. Even under the best teachers, we experience the discomfort that sometimes accompanies learning. We start avoiding situations that might lead to embarrassment. We turn away from experiences that could lead to mistakes. We accumulate a growing list of ideas to defend, a catalog of familiar experiences that discourages us from learning anything new. Slowly, we restrict our possibilities and potentials.

However, the story doesn't end there. You can open a new chapter in your life, starting today. You can rediscover the natural learner within you. Each chapter of this book is about a step you can take on this path.

Master students share certain qualities. These are attitudes and core values. Though they imply various strategies for learning, they ultimately go beyond what you do. Master student qualities are ways of *being* exceptional.

Following is a list of master student qualities. Remember that the list is not complete. It merely points in a direction.

As you read the following list, look to yourself. Put a check mark next to each quality that you've already demonstrated. Put another mark, say an exclamation point, next to each quality you want to actively work on possessing. This is not a test. It is simply a chance to celebrate what you've accomplished so far—and start thinking about what's possible for your future.

☐ **Inquisitive.** The master student is curious about everything. By posing questions, she can generate interest in the most mundane, humdrum situations. When she is bored during a biology lecture, she thinks to herself, "I always get bored when I listen to this instructor. Why is that? Maybe it's because he reminds me of my boring Uncle Ralph, who always tells those endless fishing stories. He even looks like Uncle Ralph. Amazing! Boredom is certainly interesting." Then she asks herself, "What can I do to get value out of this lecture, even though it seems boring?" And she finds an answer.

☐ **Able to focus attention.** Watch a two-year-old at play. Pay attention to his eyes. The wide-eyed look reveals an energy and a capacity for amazement that keep his attention absolutely focused in the here and now. The master student's focused attention has a childlike quality. The world, to a child, is always new. Because the master student can focus attention, to him the world is always new too.

☐ **Willing to change.** The unknown does not frighten the master student. In fact, she welcomes it—even the unknown in herself. We all have pictures of who we think we are, and these pictures can be useful. But they also can prevent learning and growth. The master student is open to changes in her environment and in herself.

☐ **Able to organize and sort.** The master student can take a large body of information and sift through it to discover relationships. He can play with information, organizing data by size, color, function, timeliness, and hundreds of other categories. He has the guts to set big goals—and the precision to plan carefully so that those goals can be achieved.

☐ **Competent.** Mastery of skills is important to the master student. When she learns mathematical formulas, she studies them until they become second nature. She practices until she knows them cold, then puts in a few extra minutes. She also is able to apply what she learns to new and different situations.

☐ **Joyful.** More often than not, the master student is seen with a smile on his face—sometimes a smile at nothing in particular other than amazement at the world and his experience of it.

☐ **Able to suspend judgment.** The master student has opinions and positions, and she is able to let go of them when appropriate. She realizes she is more than her thoughts. She can quiet her internal dialogue and listen to an opposing viewpoint. She doesn't let judgment get in the way of learning. Rather than approaching discussions with a "Prove it to me and then I'll believe it" attitude, she asks herself, "What if this is true?" and explores possibilities.

☐ **Energetic.** Notice the student with a spring in his step, the one who is enthusiastic and involved in class. When he reads, he often sits on the very edge of his chair, and he plays with the same intensity. He is determined and persistent. He is a master student.

☐ **Well.** Health is important to the master student, though not necessarily in the sense of being free of illness. Rather, she values her body and treats it with respect. She tends to her emotional and spiritual health as well as her physical health.

☐ **Self-aware.** The master student is willing to evaluate himself and his behavior. He regularly tells the truth about his strengths and those aspects that could be improved.

☐ **Responsible.** There is a difference between responsibility and blame, and the master student knows it well. She is willing to take responsibility for everything in her life—even for events that most people would blame on others.

For example, if a master student takes a required class that most students consider boring, she chooses to take responsibility for her interest level. She looks for ways to link the class to one of her goals. She sees the class as an opportunity to experiment with new study techniques that will enhance her performance in any course. She remembers that by choosing her thoughts and behaviors, she can create interesting classes, enjoyable relationships, fulfilling work experiences, or just about anything else she wants.

☐ **Willing to take risks.** The master student often takes on projects with no guarantee of success. He participates in class dialogues at the risk of looking foolish. He tackles difficult subjects in term papers. He welcomes the risk of a challenging course.

☐ **Willing to participate.** Don't look for the master student on the sidelines. She's in the game. She is a team player who can be counted on. She is engaged at school, at work, and with friends and family. She is willing to make a commitment and to follow through on it.

☐ **A generalist.** The master student is interested in everything around him. In the classroom, he is fully present.

Outside the classroom, he actively seeks out ways to deepen his learning—through study groups, campus events, student organizations, and team-based projects,. Through such experiences, he develops a broad base of knowledge in many fields that can apply to his specialties.

☐ **Willing to accept paradox.** The word *paradox* comes from two Greek words, *para* ("beyond") and *doxen* ("opinion"). A paradox is something that is beyond opinion or, more accurately, something that might seem contradictory or absurd yet might actually have meaning.

For example, the master student can be committed to managing money and reaching her financial goals. At the same time, she can be totally detached from money, knowing that her real worth is independent of how much money she has. The master student recognizes the limitations of the mind and is at home with paradox. She can accept that ambiguity.

☐ **Courageous.** The master student admits his fear and fully experiences it. For example, he will approach a tough exam as an opportunity to explore feelings of anxiety and tension related to the pressure to perform. He does not deny fear; he embraces it. If he doesn't understand something or if he makes a mistake, he admits it. When he faces a challenge and bumps into his limits, he asks for help. And, he's just as willing to give help as to receive it.

☐ **Self-directed.** Rewards or punishments provided by others do not motivate the master student. Her desire to learn comes from within, and her goals come from herself. She competes like a star athlete—not to defeat other people but to push herself to the next level of excellence.

☐ **Spontaneous.** The master student is truly in the here and now. He is able to respond to the moment in fresh, surprising, and unplanned ways.

☐ **Relaxed about grades.** Grades make the master student neither depressed nor euphoric. She recognizes that sometimes grades are important. At the same time, grades are not the only reason she studies. She does not measure her worth as a human being by the grades she receives.

☐ **Intuitive.** The master student has an inner sense that cannot be explained by logic alone. He trusts his "gut instincts" as well as his mind.

☐ **Able to communicate.** Human beings are sending messages every second that they're awake. These messages are verbal and nonverbal, intellectual and emotional, clear and confused. The master student communicates at all these levels by transforming the raw material of words and gestures into a chorus of shared meaning. And when conflict occurs between people, the master student sees it as a chance to create a new level of understanding.

☐ **Able to collaborate.** The master student knows that when people passionately share a goal, they can accomplish more by acting as a group than acting alone. When team members polarize around two competing points of view, the master student seizes the power of the "third force"—a new option that includes the best elements of everyone's ideas.

☐ **Able to think creatively.** Where others see dull details and trivia, the master student sees opportunities to create. She can gather pieces of knowledge from a wide range of subjects and put them together in new ways. The master student is creative in every aspect of her life.

☐ **Able to think critically.** Not all ideas are created equal. The master student has the rare ability to remain open-minded and skeptical at the same time. She can analyze, evaluate, and apply ideas with a keen eye for logic, evidence, and usefulness.

☐ **Willing to be uncomfortable.** The master student does not place comfort first. When discomfort is necessary to reach a goal, he is willing to experience it. He can endure personal hardships and can look at unpleasant things with detachment.

☐ **Optimistic.** The master student sees setbacks as temporary and isolated, knowing that he can choose his response to any circumstance.

☐ **Willing to laugh.** The master student might laugh at any moment, and his sense of humor includes the ability to laugh at himself. While going to school is a big investment, with high stakes, you don't have to enroll in the deferred-fun program. A master student celebrates learning, and one of the best ways of doing that is to laugh now and then.

☐ **Hungry.** Human beings begin life with a natural appetite for knowledge. In some people it soon gets dulled. The master student has tapped that hunger, and it gives her a desire to learn for the sake of learning.

☐ **Willing to work.** Once inspired, the master student is willing to follow through with sweat. He knows that genius and creativity are the result of persistence and work. When in high gear, the master student works with the intensity of a child at play.

☐ **Caring.** A master student cares about knowledge and has a passion for ideas. She also cares about people and appreciates learning from others. She collaborates on projects and thrives on teams. She flourishes in a community that values win-win outcomes, cooperation, and love. ■

✔ CRITICAL THINKING EXERCISE 2

The master student in you

The purpose of this exercise is to demonstrate to yourself that you truly are a master student. Start by remembering a time in your life when you learned something well or demonstrated mastery. This experience does not have to relate to school. It might be a time when you aced a test, played a flawless soccer game, created a work of art that won recognition, or burst forth with a blazing guitar solo. It might be a time when you spoke from your heart in a way that moved someone else. Or it might be a time when you listened deeply to another person who was in pain, comforted him, and connected with him at a level beyond words.

Describe the details of such an experience in your life. Include the place, time, and people involved. Describe what happened and how you felt about it.

_____

_____

_____

_____

_____

_____

Now, review the article "Master student qualities" and take a look at the master student qualities that you checked off. These are the qualities that apply to you. Give a brief example of how you demonstrated at least one of those qualities.

_____

_____

_____

_____

_____

Now think of other qualities of a master student—characteristics that were not mentioned in the article. List those qualities here, along with a one-sentence description of each.

_____

_____

_____

_____

_____

JOURNAL ENTRY 1
Discovery Statement

Declare what you want

Review the "Power Process: Discover what you want" on page 2. Then, writing on separate paper, brainstorm possible ways to complete the following sentence. When you're done, choose the ending that feels best to you and write it below.

I discovered that what I want most from my education is . . .

_____

_____

_____

_____

_____

_____

This book is worthless—
if you just read it

iStockphoto.com/Franck-Boston

The first edition of this book began with the sentence *This book is worthless.* Many students thought beginning this way was a trick to get their attention. It wasn't. Others thought it was reverse psychology. It wasn't that either. Still others thought it meant that the book was worthless if they didn't read it. It meant more than that.

This book is worthless *even if you read it*—if reading it is all you do. What was true of that first edition is true of this one as well. Until you take action and use the ideas in it, *From Master Student to Master Employee* really is worthless.

The purpose of this book is to help you make a successful transition to higher education by setting up a pattern of success that will last the rest of your life. You probably won't take action and use the ideas in this book until you are convinced that you have something to gain. That's the reason for this introduction—to persuade you to use this book actively.

Before you stiffen up and resist this sales pitch, remember that you have already bought the book. Now you can get something for your money by committing yourself to take action—in other words, by committing yourself to From Master Student to Master Employee. Here's what's in it for you.

Pitch #1: You can save money now and make more money later. Start with money. Your college education is one of the most expensive things you will ever buy. You might find yourself paying $100 an hour to sit in class. (See Critical Thinking Exercise 13: "Education by the hour," on page 106, to come up with a specific figure that applies to your own education.)

As a master student, you control the value you get out of your education, and that value can be considerable. The joy of learning aside, higher levels of education relate to higher lifetime income and more consistent employment.[2] It pays to be a master student.

Pitch #2: You can rediscover the natural learner in you. Joy is important too. As you become a master student, you will learn to gain knowledge in the most effective way possible—by discovering the joyful, natural learner within you.

Children are great natural students. They quickly master complex skills, such as language, and they have fun doing it. For young children, learning is a high-energy process involving experimentation, discovery, and sometimes broken dishes. Then comes school. For some students, drill and drudgery replace discovery and dish breaking. Learning can become a drag. You can use this book to reverse that process and rediscover what you knew as a child—that laughter and learning go hand in hand.

Sometimes—and especially in college—learning does take effort. As you become a master student, you will learn many ways to get the most out of that effort.

Pitch #3: You can choose from hundreds of techniques. *From Master Student to Master Employee* is packed with hundreds of practical, nuts-and-bolts techniques. And you can begin using them immediately. For example, during the "Textbook reconnaissance," on page 1, you might find three powerful learning techniques in one exercise. Even if you doze in lectures, drift off during tests, or dawdle on term papers, you'll find ideas in this book that you can use to become a more effective student.

Not all of these ideas will work for you. That's why there are so many of them in *From Master Student to Master Employee*. You should experiment with the techniques. As you discover what works, you will develop a unique style of learning that you can use for the rest of your life.

Pitch #4: You get the best suggestions from thousands of students. The concepts and techniques in this book are here not just because learning theorists, educators, and psychologists say they work, but because tens of thousands of students from all kinds of backgrounds have tried them and agree that they work. These are students who dreaded giving speeches, couldn't read their own notes, and fell behind in their course work. Then they figured out how to solve those problems. Now you can use their ideas.

Pitch #5: You can learn about yourself. The process of self-discovery is an important theme in *From Master Student to Master Employee*. Throughout the book, you can use Journal Entries for everything from organizing your desk to choosing long-term goals. Studying for an organic chemistry quiz is a lot easier with a clean desk and a clear idea of the course's importance to you.

Pitch #6: You can use a proven product. The previous editions of this book have proved successful for hundreds of thousands of students. Student feedback has been positive. In particular, students with successful histories have praised the techniques in this book.

Pitch #7: You can learn the secret of student success. If this sales pitch still hasn't persuaded you to use this book actively, maybe it's time to reveal the secret of student success.

(Provide your own drum roll here.)

The secret is . . . there are no secrets. The ultimate formula is to give up formulas, keep experimenting, and find strategies that actually help you meet your goals.

The strategies that successful students use are well-known. You have hundreds of them at your fingertips right now, in this book. Use them. Modify them. Invent new ones. You're the authority on what works for you.

However, what makes any technique work is commitment—and action. Without them, the pages of *From Master Student to Master Employee* are just 2.1 pounds of expensive mulch.

Add your participation to the mulch, and these pages become priceless. ■

Master Employees
IN ACTION

I had a lot of difficulties in interviews, especially when an interviewer would ask me to describe myself. Looking back now, I realize that I was lucky I wasn't hired for any of those positions. It forced me to stop and be more critical about the type of person I was, and the type of job that would truly suit me. When I finally found a job opening that *interested me, I discovered that I didn't have any problem in the interview.*

—*Matt Carle,*
Graphic Designer

© iStockphoto.com/kryczka

You're One Click Away...
from watching a video about
Master Students in Action online.

✔ CRITICAL THINKING EXERCISE 3

Commitment

This book is worthless unless you actively participate in its activities and exercises. One powerful way to begin taking action is to make a commitment. Conversely, if you don't make a commitment, then sustained action is unlikely. The result is a worthless book. Therefore, in the interest of saving your valuable time and energy, this exercise gives you a chance to declare your level of involvement up front. From the options below, choose the sentence that best reflects your commitment to using this book. Write the number of the sentence in the space provided at the end of the list.

1. "Well, I'm reading this book right now, aren't I?"
2. "I will skim the book and read the interesting parts."
3. "I will read the book, think about it, and do the exercises that look interesting."
4. "I will read the book, do some exercises, and complete some of the Journal Entries."
5. "I will read the book, do some exercises and Journal Entries, and use some of the techniques."
6. "I will read the book, do most of the exercises and Journal Entries, and use some of the techniques."
7. "I will study this book, do most of the exercises and Journal Entries, and use some of the techniques."
8. "I will study this book, do most of the exercises and Journal Entries, and experiment with many of the techniques in order to discover what works best for me."
9. "I promise myself that I will create value from this course by studying this book, doing all the exercises and Journal Entries, and experimenting with most of the techniques."
10. "I will use this book as if the quality of my education depended on it—doing all the exercises and Journal Entries, experimenting with most of the techniques, inventing techniques of my own, and planning to reread this book in the future."

Write the sentence number that best describes your commitment level and today's date here:

Commitment level _____ Date _____

If you selected commitment level 1 or 2, you probably won't create a lot of value in this class, and you might consider passing this book on to a friend. If your commitment level is 9 or 10, you are on your way to terrific success in school. If your level is somewhere in between, experiment with the techniques and learning strategies in this book. If you find that they work, consider returning to this exercise and raising your level of commitment.

Get the most out of this book

Get used to a new look and tone. This book looks different from traditional textbooks. *From Master Student to Master Employee* presents major ideas in magazine-style articles. There are lots of lists, blurbs, one-liners, pictures, charts, graphs, illustrations, and even a joke or two.

Rip 'em out. The pages of *From Master Student to Master Employee* are perforated because some of the information here is too important to leave in the book. For example, Journal Entry 2 asks you to list some important things you want to get out of your education. To keep yourself focused on these goals, you could rip out that page and post it on your bathroom mirror—or some other place where you'll see it several times each day.

You can rip out pages and reinsert them later by sticking them into the spine of the book. A piece of tape will hold them in place.

Skip around. Feel free to use this book in several different ways. Read it straight through. Or pick it up, turn to any page, and find an idea you can use right now. For example, if you want to learn how to set and achieve goals, skip directly to the article on this topic in Chapter 3.

You might find that this book presents similar ideas in several places. This repetition is intentional. Repetition reinforces key points. Also, a technique that works in one area of your life might work in others as well.

If it works, use it. If it doesn't, lose it. If there are sections of this book that don't apply to you at all, skip them—unless, of course, they are assigned. In that case, see if you can gain value from those sections anyway. When you commit to get value from this book, even an idea that seems irrelevant or ineffective at first can turn out to be a powerful tool in the future.

Listen to your peers. Throughout this book you will find features titled Master Employees in Action. These are short quotations from people in the workforce who are using the ideas presented in this text. As you dig into the following chapters, think about what you would say if you could add your voice to theirs.

Own this book. Determine what you want to get out of school, and create a record of how you intend to get it by completing the Journal Entries throughout this book. Every time your pen touches a page, you move closer to mastery.

Do the exercises. Action makes this book work. To get the most out of this book, do most of the critical thinking exercises. (It's never too late to go back and do the ones you skipped.) Exercises invite you to write, touch, feel, move, see, search, ponder, speak, listen, recall, choose, commit, and create. You might even sing and dance. Learning often works best when it involves action.

⊘ CRITICAL THINKING EXERCISE 19

Take your thinking to another level

Recall an idea or suggestion from the chapter that you'd like to explore in more detail. Summarize it, and include the page number where it appears.

You've just done some thinking at Level 1: **Remembering**—Now, take your thinking about this idea or suggestion to one of the higher levels:

Level 2: Understanding—Explain this idea in your own words and give examples from your own experience.

Level 3: Applying—Use the idea to produce a desired result.

Level 4: Analyzing—Divide this idea into parts or steps.

Level 5: Evaluating—Rate the truth, usefulness or quality of the idea—and give reasons for your rating.

Level 6: Creating—Invent something new based on the idea.

Demonstrate your higher-level thinking by writing a brief paragraph in the space below. If you want to show your thinking in another way, then check with your instructor. In either case, clearly state your intended level of thinking (For example, "To apply this idea, I would . . . ")

Learn about learning styles. Check out the Learning Styles Inventory and related articles in Chapter 2. This material can help you discover your preferred learning styles and allow you to explore new styles. Then, throughout the rest of this book, you'll find suggestions for applying your knowledge of learning styles. The modes of learning can be accessed by asking four basic questions: *Why? What? How?* and *What if?*

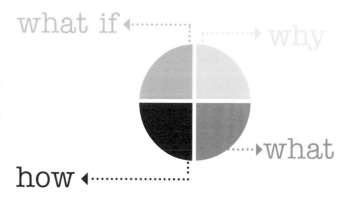

what if ← ┈┈┈ ┈┈┈ → why

how ← ┈┈┈ ┈┈┈ → what

Master Employees **IN ACTION**

❝ *The budgeting work that I do in the office has made me a better money manager in my own life. It has taught me that money is just a way to ascribe value, and not a value in and of itself. I've been better able to evaluate the things I care about and the things I can do without.* ❞

–Bill White, Construction Manager

▶ You're One Click Away...
from a video about Master
Students in Action

Navigate through learning experiences with the Master Student Map. You can orient yourself for maximum learning every time you open this book by asking those same four questions: *Why? What? How?* and *What if?* That's the idea behind the Master Student Map included on the first page of each chapter, which includes sample answers to those questions. Remember that you can use the four-part structure of this map to effectively learn anything.

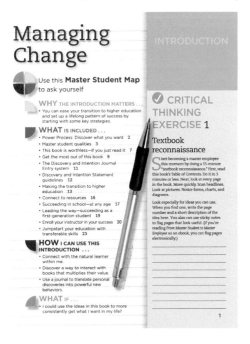

Experience the power of the Power Processes. A *Power Process* is a suggestion to shift your perspective or try on a new behavior. Look for this feature on the second page of each chapter. Users of *From Master Student to Master Employee* often refer to these articles as their favorite part of the book. Approach them with a sense of play and possibility. Start with an open mind, experiment with the ideas, and see what works.

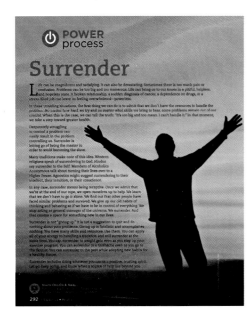

Link to the Web. Throughout this book, you'll notice reminders to visit the College Success CourseMate for *From Master Student to Master Employee*. There you'll discover ways to take your involvement with this book to a deeper level. For example, access the Web site to do an online version of the Discovery Wheel exercise. Also look for videos, additional exercises, articles, PowerPoint slides, practice tests, and forms.

You're One Click Away...

To get access, visit CengageBrain.com

© Cengagelearning 2013

Read the sidebars. Look for sidebars—short bursts of words placed between longer articles—throughout this book. These short pieces might offer insights that transform your experience of higher education.

Focus on developing the "five Cs." One of the major goals of this book is to assist you in gaining skills that are valued in the workplace. In particular, you can benefit from developing the "five Cs"—character, creative thinking, critical thinking, communicating, and collaborating. For more details, see "Jumpstart your education with transferable skills" on page 23 and the Five Cs for Your Career articles near the end of each chapter. Use this material to make a seamless transition from success in school to success on the job. ■

Rewrite IN
this book

Some books should be preserved in pristine condition. This book isn't one of them.

Something happens when you interact with your book by writing in it. *From Master Student to Master Employee* is about learning, and learning results when you are active. When you make notes in the margin, you can hear yourself talking with the author. When you doodle and underline, you see the author's ideas taking shape. You can even argue with the author and come up with your own theories and explanations. In all of these ways, you can become a coauthor of this book. Rewrite it to make it yours.

While you're at it, you can create symbols or codes that will help you when reviewing the text later on. You might insert a "Q" where you have questions or put exclamation points or stars next to important ideas. You could also circle words to look up in a dictionary.

Remember, if any idea in this book doesn't work for you, you can rewrite it. Change the exercises to fit your needs. Create a new technique by combining several others. Create a technique out of thin air!

Find something you agree or disagree with on

CHARACTER • CRITICAL THINKING • CREATIVE THINKING • COLLABORATION • COMMUNICATION

See character as a career asset. At the end of every workday, character boils down to two ideas that are weaved throughout this book: Define your values and align your actions. Another word for acting in alignment with your values is *integrity*, and it is a personal quality that your employers, clients, or customers will come to value.

When people know that they can count on you to make commitments and follow through, they'll be more willing to work with you over the long term. Integrity is more than an abstract word. It's also a practical strategy for surviving layoffs and increasing job security.

Think creatively about mistakes. Recall a mistake you made at work and then write about it. In a Discovery Statement, describe what you did to create a result you didn't want ("I discovered that I tend to underestimate the number of hours projects take"). Then write an Intention Statement describing something you can do differently in the future ("I intend to keep track of my actual hours on each project so that I can give more accurate estimates"). Doing these two things will help you mine valuable lessons and graduate from the school of hard knocks—with honors.

Thinking critically about your successes. You can also use journal entries to think critically about things that go well in your work life. Throughout your career, keep track of the positive outcomes you produce at work, including financial successes. Summarize these results in a sentence or two and add them to your résumé as well. Whenever you deliver a project on time and on budget, write Discovery Statements about how you created that result. Follow up with Intention Statements about ways to be even more effective on your next project.

Stay in communication about trends that will affect your career. Keep up to date with breaking changes in the job market

leaders and major players in your industry on social networks such as Twitter, Facebook, and LinkedIn.

Periodicals. Read the business sections of the *New York Times* and the *Wall Street Journal*, for example. Most newspapers also have online editions, as do magazines such as *Wired* and *Business Week*.

Professional associations. People in similar jobs like to band together and give each other heads up on emerging trends—one reason for professional associations. These range from the American Medical Association to the Society of Actuaries. There's bound to be one for people in your field. Ask colleagues and search the Internet. *Note:* Many associations maintain Web sites and publish newsletters or trade magazines.

Conferences and conventions. Many professional associations sponsor annual meetings. Here's where you can meet people face to face and use your networking skills. Print and online publications are powerful sources of news, but sometimes nothing beats plain old schmoozing. Ask people at work what professional organizations they have joined.

Use the Power Processes to become a rock-star collaborator. They're full of ideas for producing results *and* building relationships.

Take the "Power Process: I create it all," for example. Before blaming a snafu on a coworker, look for any ways that you might have contributed to the problem. Even if you did *not* contribute to the problem, look for ways that you can contribute to the solution. Write Intention Statements to clarify what you will think, say, and do in the future to create a more positive work environment. In the workplace, problem solvers are valued.

By the way, one of the ideas behind "I create it all" is to create a gap between stimulus and response. See if you can fill this gap

The **Discovery and Intention Journal Entry system**

Using the Discovery and Intention Journal Entry system is a little like flying a plane. Airplanes are seldom exactly on course. Human and automatic pilots are always checking an airplane's positions and making corrections. The resulting flight path looks like a zigzag. The plane is almost always flying in the wrong direction, but because of constant observation and course correction, it arrives at the right destination.

As a student, you can use a similar approach. Journal Entries throughout this book are labeled as Discovery Statements, Intention Statements, or Discovery/Intention Statements. Each Journal Entry contains a short set of suggestions that involve writing.

Hello Author I Agree :)

Through Discovery Statements, you gain **awareness** of "where you are." These statements are a record of what you are learning about yourself as a student—both your strengths and your weaknesses. **Discovery Statements can also be declarations of your goals, descriptions of your attitudes, statements of your feelings, transcripts of your thoughts, and chronicles of your behavior.**

Sometimes Discovery Statements chronicle an "aha!" moment—a flash of insight that results when you connect a new idea with your prior experiences, preferred styles of learning, or both. Perhaps a solution to a long-standing problem suddenly occurs to you. Or a life-changing insight wells up from the deepest recesses of your mind. Don't let such moments disappear. Capture them in Discovery Statements.

Intention Statements can be used to alter your course. These statements are about your **commitment** to take action based on increased awareness. An intention arises out of your choice to direct your energy toward a specific task and to aim at a particular goal. The processes of discovery and intention reinforce each other.

Even simple changes in behavior can produce results. If you feel like procrastinating, then tackle just one small, specific task related to your intention. Find something you can complete in 5 minutes or less, and do it *now*. For example, access just one Web site related to the topic of your next assigned paper. Spend just 3 minutes previewing a reading assignment. Taking "baby steps" like these can move you into action with grace and ease.

The purpose of this system is not to get you pumped up and excited to go out there and try harder. In fact, Discovery and Intention Statements are intended to help you work smarter rather than harder.

The process of discovery, intention, and action creates a dynamic and efficient cycle. First, you write Discovery Statements about where you are now. Next, you write Intention Statements about where you want to be and the specific steps you will take to get there. Finally, you follow up with action—the sooner, the better.

Then you start the cycle again. Write Discovery Statements about whether or how you act on your Intention Statements—and what you learn in the process. Follow up with more Intention Statements about what you will do differently in the future. Then move into action and describe what happens next.

This process never ends. Each time you repeat the cycle, you get new results. It's all about getting what you want and becoming more effective in everything you do. This is the path of mastery—a path that you can travel for the rest of your life.

Sometimes a Discovery or Intention Statement will be long and detailed. Usually, it will be short—maybe just a line or two. With practice, the cycle will become automatic.

Don't panic when you fail to complete an intended task. Straying off course is normal. Simply make the necessary corrections. Consider the first word in the title of this book—*becoming*. This word implies that mastery is not an end state or final goal. Rather, mastery is a process that never ends.

Miraculous progress might not come immediately. Do not be concerned. Stay with the cycle. Give it time. Use Discovery Statements to get a clear view of your world. Then use Intention Statements to direct your actions. Whenever you notice progress, record it.

The following statement might strike you as improbable, but it is true: It can take the same amount of energy to get what you *don't* want in school as it takes to get what you *do* want. Sometimes getting what you don't want takes even more effort. An airplane burns the same amount of fuel flying away from its destination as it does flying toward it. It pays to stay on course.

You can use the Discovery and Intention Journal Entry system to stay on your own course and get what you want out of school. Start with the Journal Entries included in the text. Then go beyond them. Write Discovery and Intention Statements of your own at any time, for any purpose. Create new strategies whenever you need them, based on your current situation.

Once you get the hang of it, you might discover you can fly. ■

Discovery and Intention Statement Guidelines

Writing Journal Entries helps you to develop self-awareness, self-direction, and other master student qualities. Use the following guidelines as a checklist. Consider removing this page from the book and posting it in a prominent place where you'll typically be writing your responses to the Journal Entries.

DISCOVERY STATEMENTS

☐ **Record the specifics about your thoughts, feelings, and behavior.** Notice your thoughts, observe your actions, and record them accurately. Get the facts.

Thoughts include inner voices. We talk to ourselves constantly in our heads. When internal chatter gets in your way, write down what you are telling yourself. If this seems difficult at first, just start writing. The act of writing can trigger a flood of thoughts.

Also notice how you feel when you function well. Use Discovery Statements to pinpoint exactly where and when you learn most effectively.

☐ **Use discomfort as a signal.** When you approach a daunting task, such as a difficult math problem, notice your physical sensations. Feeling uncomfortable, bored, or tired might be a signal that you're about to do valuable work. Stick with it. Write about it. Tell yourself you can handle the discomfort just a little bit longer. You will be rewarded with a new insight.

☐ **Suspend judgment.** When you are discovering yourself, be gentle. Suspend self-judgment. If you continually judge your behaviors as "bad" or "stupid" or "galactically imbecilic," sooner or later your mind will revolt. Rather than put up with the abuse, it will quit making discoveries. For your own benefit, be kind to yourself.

☐ **Tell the truth.** Suspending judgment helps you tell the truth about yourself. "The truth will set you free" is a saying that endures for a reason. The closer you get to the truth, the more powerful your Discovery Statements. If you notice that you are avoiding the truth, don't blame yourself. Just tell the truth about it.

INTENTION STATEMENTS

☐ **Make intentions positive.** The purpose of writing Intention Statements is to focus on what you want rather than what you don't want. Instead of writing "I will not to fall asleep while studying chemistry," write, "I intend to stay awake when studying chemistry." Also avoid the word *try*. Trying is not doing. When we hedge our bets with *try*, we can always tell ourselves, "Well, I *tried* to stay awake." We end up fooling ourselves into thinking we succeeded.

☐ **Make intentions observable.** Rather than writing "I intend to work harder on my history assignments," write, "I intend to review my class notes, and I intend to make summary sheets of my reading." Then, when you review your progress, you can determine more precisely whether you have accomplished what you intended.

☐ **Make intentions small and achievable.** Give yourself opportunities to succeed by setting goals you can meet. Break large goals into small, specific tasks that can be accomplished quickly. If you want to get an A in biology, ask yourself, "What can I do today?" You might choose to study biology for an extra hour. Make that your intention.

☐ **Set time lines.** For example, if you are assigned a paper to write, break the assignment into small tasks and set a precise due date for each one: "I intend to select a topic for my paper by 9 A.M. Wednesday."

Time lines are especially useful when your intention is to experiment with a technique suggested in this book. The sooner you act on a new idea, the better. Consider practicing a new behavior within four hours after you first learn about it.

☐ **Anticipate self-sabotage.** Be aware of what you might do, consciously or unconsciously, to undermine your best intentions. If you intend to study differential equations at 9 p.m., notice when you sit down to watch a two-hour movie that starts at 8 p.m. Also be careful of intentions that depend on others. If you write that you intend for your study group to complete an assignment by Monday, then your success depends on the other students in the group.

☐ **Include rewards.** When you meet your goal on time, reward yourself. Rewards that are an integral part of a goal are powerful. For example, your reward for earning a degree might be the career you've always dreamed of. External rewards, such as a movie or an afternoon in the park, are also valuable. These rewards work best when you're willing to withhold them. If you plan to take a nap on Sunday afternoon whether or not you've finished your chemistry assignment, the nap is not an effective reward.

☐ **Move from intention to action.** IIntention Statements are of little use until you act on them. If you want new results in your life, then take action. Life responds to what you *do*. ■

You share one thing in common with other students at your vocational school, college, or university: Entering higher education represents a major change in your life. You've joined a new culture with its own set of rules, both spoken and unspoken.

MAKING THE TRANSITION TO higher education

Whether you've just graduated from high school or have been out of the classroom for decades, you'll discover many differences between secondary and post-secondary education. The sooner you understand such differences, the sooner you can deal with them. Some examples of what you might face include the following:

- **New academic standards.** Once you enter higher education, you'll probably find yourself working harder in school than ever before. Instructors will often present more material at a faster pace. There probably will be fewer tests in higher education than in high school, and the grading might be tougher. Compared to high school, you'll have more to read, more to write, more problems to solve, and more to remember.

- **A new level of independence.** College instructors typically give less guidance about how or when to study. You may not get reminders about when assignments are due or when quizzes and tests will take place. You probably won't get study sheets before a test. Overall, you might receive less consistent feedback about how well you are doing in each of your courses. Don't let this tempt you into putting off work until the last minute. You will still be held accountable for all course work. And anything that's said in class or included in assigned readings might appear on an exam.

- **Differences in teaching styles.** Instructors at colleges, universities, and vocational schools are often steeped in their subject matter. Many did not take courses on how to teach and might not be as interesting as some of your high school teachers. And some professors might seem more focused on research than on teaching.

- **A larger playing field.** The institution you've just joined might seem immense, impersonal, and even frightening. The sheer size of the campus, the variety of courses offered, the large number of departments—all of these opportunities can add up to a confusing array of options.

- **More students and more diversity.** The school you're attending right now might enroll hundreds or thousands more students than your high school. And the range of diversity among these students might surprise you.

In summary, you are now responsible for structuring your time and creating new relationships. Perhaps more than ever before, you'll find that your life is your own creation. You are free to set different goals, explore alternative ways of thinking, change habits, and expand your circle of friends. All this can add up to a new identity—a new way of being in the world.

At first, this world of choices might seem overwhelming or even frightening. You might feel that you're just going through the motions of being a student or playing a role that you've never rehearsed.

That feeling is understandable. Use it to your advantage. Consider that you *are* assuming a new role in life—that of being a student in higher education. And just as actors enter the minds of the characters that they portray, you can take on the character of a master student.

When you're willing to take responsibility for the quality of your education, you can create the future of your dreams. Keep the following strategies in mind.

Decrease the unknowns. To reduce surprise, anticipate changes. Before classes begin, get a map of the school property and walk through your first day's schedule, perhaps with a classmate or friend. Visit your instructors in their offices and introduce yourself. Anything you can do to get familiar with the new routine will help. In addition, consider buying your textbooks before class begins. Scan them to get a preview of your courses.

Admit your feelings—whatever they are. School can be an intimidating experience for new students. People of diverse cultures, adult learners, commuters, and people with disabilities may feel excluded. Anyone can feel anxious, isolated, homesick, or worried.

Those emotions are common among new students, and there's nothing wrong with them. Simply admitting the truth about how you feel—to yourself and to someone else—can help you cope. And you can almost always do something constructive in the present moment, no matter how you feel.

If your feelings about this transition make it hard for you to carry out the activities of daily life—going to class, working, studying, and relating to people—then get professional help. Start with a counselor at the student health service on your campus. The mere act of seeking help can make a difference.

Allow time for transition. You don't have to master the transition to higher education right away. Give it some time. Also, plan your academic schedule with your needs for transition in mind. Balance time-intensive courses with others that don't make as many demands.

Find resources. A supercharger increases the air supply to an internal combustion engine. The resulting difference in power can be dramatic. You can make just as powerful a difference in your education if you supercharge it by using all of the resources available to students. In this case, your "air supply" includes people, campus clubs and organizations, and school and community services.

Of all resources, people are the most important. You can isolate yourself, study hard, and get a good education. However,

doing this is not the most powerful use of your tuition money. When you establish relationships with teachers, staff members, fellow students, and employers, you can get a *great* education. Build a network of people who will personally support your success in school.

Meet with your academic advisor. One person in particular —your academic advisor—can help you access resources and make the transition to higher education. Meet with this person regularly. Advisors generally know about course requirements, options for declaring majors, and the resources available at your school. Peer advisors might also be available.

When you work with an advisor, remember that you're a paying customer and have a right to be satisfied with the service you get. Don't be afraid to change advisors when that seems appropriate.

Learn the language of higher education. Terms such as *grade point average (GPA), prerequisite, accreditation, matriculation, tenure,* and *syllabus* might be new to you. Ease your transition to higher education by checking your school catalog or school Web site for definitions of definitions of these words and others that you don't understand. Also ask your academic advisor for clarification.

Show up for class. In higher education, teachers generally don't take attendance. Yet you'll find that attending class is essential to your success. The amount that you pay in tuition and fees makes a powerful argument for going to classes regularly and getting your money's worth. In large part, the material that you're tested on comes from events that take place in class.

Showing up for class occurs on two levels. The most visible level is being physically present in the classroom. Even more important, though, is showing up mentally. This kind of attendance includes taking detailed notes, asking questions, and contributing to class discussions.

Research on college freshmen indicates a link between regular class attendance and academic success.[3] Succeeding in school can help you get almost anything you want, including the career, income, and relationships you desire. Attending class is an investment in yourself.

Manage out-of-class time. For students in higher education, time management takes on a new meaning. What you do *outside* class matters as much—or even more than—what you do in class. Instructors give you the raw materials for understanding a subject while a class meets. You then take those materials, combine them, and *teach yourself* outside of class.

To allow for this process, schedule two hours of study time for each hour that you spend in class. Also, get a calendar that covers the entire academic year. With the syllabus for each of your courses in hand, note key events for the entire term—dates for tests, papers, and other projects. Getting a big picture of your course load makes it easier to get assignments done on time and prevents all-night study sessions.

Experiment with new ways to study. You can cope with increased workloads and higher academic expectations by putting all of your study habits on the table and evaluating them. Don't assume that the learning strategies you used in the past—in high school or the workplace—will automatically transfer to your new role in higher education. Keep the habits that serve you, drop those that hold you back, and adopt new ones to promote your success. On every page of this book, you'll find helpful suggestions.

Take the initiative in meeting new people. Introduce yourself to classmates and instructors. Just before or after class is a good time. Realize that most of the people in this new world of higher education are waiting to be welcomed. You can help them and help yourself at the same time.

Make peace with new technology. Turn back the clock just one decade. Google was just getting started. There was no Facebook, no Twitter, no iPad, and no iPhone.

Today, you can get a job in some companies as director of social media. Tablets and smartphones are as popular in the workplace as in higher education. And when people ask you to research the topic on the Internet, they tell you to "just Google it."

If you don't feel comfortable with the latest technology, welcome to the club. Many people who are going back to school will admit the same thing. Students in higher education are asked to engage with technology at a level that has no precedent in our history.

To make the transition to this world, remember two things. First, it's OK to admit the truth whenever you're outside of your comfort zone. Second, it's also OK to get help. Go to your academic advisor and ask about "help desks," technology workshops, classes, and other campus resources for getting up to speed with technology. One way to overcome fear of change is to get hands-on experience with digital tools as soon as possible.

Become a self-regulated learner. Reflect on your transition to higher education. Think about what's working well, what you'd like to change, and ways to make those changes. Psychologists use the term *self-regulation* to describe this kind of thinking.[4] Self-regulated learners set goals, monitor their progress toward those goals, and change their behavior based on the results they get.

From Master Student to Master Employee promotes self-regulation through the ongoing cycle of discovery, intention, and action. Write Discovery Statements to monitor your behavior and evaluate the results you're currently creating in any area of your life. Write about your level of commitment to school, your satisfaction with your classes and grades, your social life, and your family's support for your education.

Based on your discoveries, write Intention Statements about your goals for this term, this year, next year, and the rest of your college career. Describe exactly what you will do to create new

Rewrite IN
this book

Some books should be preserved in pristine condition. This book isn't one of them.

Something happens when you interact with your book by writing in it. *From Master Student to Master Employee* is about learning, and learning results when you are active. When you make notes in the margin, you can hear yourself talking with the author. When you doodle and underline, you see the author's ideas taking shape. You can even argue with the author and come up with your own theories and explanations. In all of these ways, you can become a coauthor of this book. Rewrite it to make it yours.

While you're at it, you can create symbols or codes that will help you when reviewing the text later on. You might insert a "Q" where you have questions or put exclamation points or stars next to important ideas. You could also circle words to look up in a dictionary.

Remember, if any idea in this book doesn't work for you, you can rewrite it. Change the exercises to fit your needs. Create a new technique by combining several others. Create a technique out of thin air!

Find something you agree or disagree with on this page, and write a short note in the margin about it. Or draw a diagram. Better yet, do both. Let creativity be your guide. Have fun.

Begin rewriting now.

results in each of these time frames. Then follow through with action. In this way, you take charge of your transition to higher education—starting now. ■

You're One Click Away...
from finding more strategies for mastering the art of transition online.

Connect to
RESOURCES

EDHAR/Shutterstock.com

As a student in higher education, you can access a world of student services and community resources. Any of them can help you succeed in school. Many of them are free.

Name a problem that you're facing right now or that you anticipate facing in the future: finding money to pay for classes, resolving conflicts with a teacher, lining up a job after graduation. Chances are that a school or community resource can help you. The ability to access resources is a skill that will serve you long after you stop being a student. In addition, taking advantage of services and getting involved with organizations can lead you to new experiences that expand your learning styles.

Resources often go unused. Following are examples of what you can find. Check your school and city Web sites for more options. Remember that you can connect with many of them online as well as in person.

Academic advisors/counselors can help you select courses, choose a major, plan your career, and adjust in general to the culture of higher education.

Arts organizations connect you to local museums, concert venues, clubs, and stadiums.

Athletic centers often open weight rooms, swimming pools, indoor tracks, basketball courts, and racquetball and tennis courts to all students.

Child care is sometimes made available to students at a reasonable cost through the early childhood education department on campus or community agencies.

Churches, synagogues, mosques, and temples have members who are happy to welcome fellow worshippers who are away from home.

Computer labs on campus are places where students can go to work on projects and access the Internet. Computer access is often available off-campus as well. Check public libraries for this service. Some students get permission to use computers at their workplace after hours.

Consumer credit counseling can help even if you've really blown your budget. And it's usually free. Do your research, and choose a reputable and not-for-profit consumer credit counselor.

Counseling centers in the community can assist you with a problem when you can't get help at school. Look for career-planning services, rehabilitation offices, outreach programs for veterans, and mental health clinics.

The **financial aid office** assists students with loans, scholarships, work-study, and grants.

Governments (city, county, state, and federal) often have programs for students. Check the government listings in your local telephone directory.

Hotlines offer a way to get emergency care, personal counseling, and other kinds of help via a phone call. Do an Internet search on *phone hotlines* in your area that assist with the specific kind of help you're looking for, and check your school catalog for more resources.

Job placement offices can help you find part-time employment while you are in school and a full-time job after you graduate.

Legal aid services provide free or inexpensive assistance to low-income people.

Libraries are a treasure on campus and in any community. They employ people who are happy to help you locate information.

Newspapers published on campus and in the local community list events and services that are free or inexpensive.

The **school catalog** lists course descriptions, and tuition fees, requirements for graduation, and information on everything from the school's history to its grading practices.

School security agencies can tell you what's safe and what's not. They can also provide information about parking, bicycle regulations, and traffic rules.

Special needs and disability services assist college students who have learning disabilities or other disabilities.

Student health clinics often provide free or inexpensive counseling and other medical treatment.

Student organizations present opportunities for extracurricular activities. Explore student government, fraternities, sororities, service clubs, religious groups, sports clubs, and political groups. Find women's centers; multicultural student centers; and organizations for international students, disabled students with disabilities, and gay, lesbian, bisexual, and transgender (GLBT) students.

Support groups exist for people with almost any problem, from drug addiction to cancer. You can find people with problems who meet every week to share suggestions, information, and concerns about problems they share.

Tutoring is usually free and is available through academic departments or counseling centers and is often free or low cost. ■

Succeeding in school—
at any age

David Buffington/Getty Images

David Buffington/Getty Images

Being an adult learner puts you on a strong footing. With a rich store of life experiences, you can ask meaningful questions and make connections between course work and daily life. Any abilities that you've developed to work on teams, manage projects, meet deadlines, and solve problems are assets. Many instructors will especially enjoy working with you.

Following are some suggestions for adult learners who want to ease their transition to higher education. If you're a younger student, commuting student, or community college student, look for useful ideas here as well.

Acknowledge your concerns. Adult learners might express any of the following fears:

- *I'll be the oldest person in all my classes.*
- *I've been out of the classroom too long.*
- *I'm concerned about my math, reading, and writing skills.*
- *I'm worried about making tuition payments.*
- *How will I ever make the time to study, on top of everything else I'm doing?*
- *I won't be able to keep up with all the new technology.*

Those concerns are understandable. Now consider some facts:

- College classrooms are more diverse than ever before. According to the U.S. Census Bureau, 37 percent of students in the nation's colleges are age 25 and older. The majority of these older students attend school part-time.[5]
- Adult learners can take advantage of evening classes, weekend classes, summer classes, distance learning, and online courses. Also look for classes in off-campus locations, closer to where you work or live.
- Colleges offer financial aid for students of all ages, including scholarships, grants, and low-interest loans.

- You can meet other students and make new friends by taking part in orientation programs. Look for programs that are targeted to adult learners.

- You are now enrolled in a course that can help boost your skills at math, reading, writing, note taking, time management, and other key skills.

Ease into it. If you're new to higher education, consider easing into it. You can choose to attend school part-time before making a full-time commitment. If you've taken college-level classes in the past, find out if any of those credits will transfer into your current program.

Plan ahead. By planning a week or month at a time, you get a bigger picture of your multiple roles as a student, an employee, and a family member. With that awareness, you can make conscious adjustments in the number of hours you devote to each domain of activity in your life. For example:

- If your responsibilities at work or home will be heavy in the near future, then register for fewer classes next term.

- Choose recreational activities carefully, focusing on those that relax you and recharge you the most.

- Don't load your schedule with classes that require unusually heavy amounts of reading or writing.

For related suggestions, see Chapter 3: Time & Money.

Delegate tasks. If you have children, delegate some of the household chores to them. Or start a meal co-op in your neighborhood. Cook dinner for yourself and someone else one night each week. In return, ask that person to furnish you with a meal on another night. A similar strategy can apply to child care and other household tasks.

Get to know other returning students. Introduce yourself to other adult learners. Being in the same classroom gives you an immediate bond. You can exchange work, home, or cell phone numbers and build a network of mutual support. Some students adopt a buddy system, pairing up with another student in each class to complete assignments and prepare for tests.

In addition, learn about student services and organizations. Many schools have a learning assistance center with workshops geared to adult learners. Sign up and attend. Meet people on campus. Personal connections are key to your success.

Find common ground with traditional students. Traditional and nontraditional students have many things in common. They seek to gain knowledge and skills for their chosen careers. They desire financial stability and personal fulfillment. And, like their older peers, many younger students are concerned about whether they have the skills to succeed in higher education.

Consider pooling resources with younger students. Share notes, edit one another's papers, and form study groups. Look for ways to build on one another's strengths. If you want help with using a computer for assignments, you might ask a younger student for help. In group projects and case studies, you can expand the discussion by sharing insights from your experiences.

Enlist your employer's support. Let your employer in on your educational plans. Point out how the skills you gain in the classroom will help you meet work objectives. Offer informal seminars at work to share what you're learning in school. You might find that your company reimburses its employees for some tuition costs or even grants time off to attend classes.

Get extra mileage out of your current tasks. Look for ways to relate your schoolwork to your job. For example, when you're assigned a research paper, choose a topic that relates to your current job tasks. Some schools even offer academic credit for work and life experience.

Review your subjects before you start classes. Say that you've registered for trigonometry and you haven't taken a math class since high school. Consider brushing up on the subject before classes begin. Also, talk with future instructors about ways to prepare for their classes.

"Publish" your schedule. After you plan your study and class sessions for the week, write up your schedule and post it in a place where others who live with you will see it. If you use an online calendar, print out copies to put in your school binder or on your refrigerator door, bathroom mirror, or kitchen cupboard.

Enroll family and friends in your success. School can cut into your social life. Prepare friends and family members by discussing this issue ahead of time. See Chapter 9: Communicating for ways to prevent and resolve conflict.

You can also involve your spouse, partner, children, or close friends in your schooling. Offer to give them a tour of the campus, introduce them to your instructors and classmates, and encourage them to attend social events at school with you. Share ideas from this book, and from your other courses.

Take this process a step further, and ask the key people in your life for help. Share your reason for getting a degree, and talk about what your whole family has to gain from this change in your life. Ask them to think of ways that they can support your success in school and to commit to those actions. Make your own education a joint mission that benefits everyone. ■

You're One Click Away...
from finding more strategies for adult learners online.

Leading the way—
succeeding as a
first-generation student

American history confirms that people who are the first in their family to enter higher education can succeed. Examples range from the former slaves who enrolled in the country's first African-American colleges to the ex-soldiers who used the GI Bill to win advanced degrees. From their collective experience, you can take some life-changing lessons.

REMEMBER YOUR STRENGTHS

The fact that you're reading this book right now is a sign of your accomplishments. You applied to school. You got admitted. You've already taken a huge step to success: You showed up.

Celebrate every one of your successes in higher education, no matter how small they seem. Every assignment you complete, every paper you turn in, and every quiz question you answer is a measurable and meaningful step to getting a degree.

Discover more of your strengths by taking any fact that others might see as a barrier and looking for the hidden advantage. Did you grow up in a family that struggled to make ends meet financially? Then you know about living on a limited budget. Did you work to help support your family while you were in high school? Then you know about managing your time to balance major commitments. Did you grow up in a neighborhood with people of many races, religions, and levels of income? Then you already have an advantage when it comes to thriving with diversity.

Put your strengths in writing. Write Discovery Statements about specific personal, academic, and financial challenges you faced in the past. Describe how you coped with them. Then follow up with Intention Statements about ways to meet the challenges of higher education.

Also keep showing up. Going to every class, lab session, and study group meeting is a way to squeeze the most value from your tuition bills.

EXPECT CHANGE—AND DISCOMFORT

Entering higher education means walking into a new culture. At times you might feel that all the ground rules have changed, and you have no idea how to fit in. This is normal.

When you walked into your first class this semester, you carried your personal hopes for the future along with the expectations of your parents, siblings, and other relatives. Those people might assume that you'll return home and be the same person you were last year.

The reality is that you will change while you're in school. Your beliefs, your friends, and your career goals may all shift. You might feel critical of people back home and think that some of their ideas are limited. And in turn, they might criticize you.

First-generation students sometimes talk about standing between two worlds. They know that they're changing. At the same time, they are uncertain about what the future holds.

This, too, is normal. Education is all about change. It can be exciting, frustrating, and frightening—all at once. Making mistakes and moving through disappointments is part of the process.

ASK FOR SUPPORT

You don't have to go it alone. Your tuition buys access to many services. These are sources of academic and personal support. You'll find examples listed in "Connect to Resources" on page 16. Ask your school about any programs geared specifically to first-generation students.

The key point is to *ask for help right away*. Do this as soon as you feel stuck in class or experience conflict in a relationship.

Also keep a list of every person who stands behind you— relatives, friends, instructors, advisors, mentors, tutors, and counselors. Remind yourself that you are surrounded by people who want you to succeed. Furthermore, thank each of them for their help.

PAY IT FORWARD

You are an inspiration to your family, friends, and fellow students. Several people you know might apply to school on the strength of your example. Talk to these people about what you've learned. Your presence in their lives is a contribution. ■

Enroll your instructor
in your SUCCESS

Faced with an instructor you don't like, you have two basic choices. One is to label the instructor a "dud." When you make this choice, you endure class and complain to other students. This choice gives your instructor sole responsibility for the quality of your education and the value of your tuition payments.

There is another option. Don't give away your power. Instead, take responsibility for your education.

The word *enroll* in this headline is a play on words. Usually we think of students as the people who enroll in school. Turn this idea on its head. See whether you can enlist instructors as partners in getting what you want from higher education.

Research the instructor. When deciding what classes to take, you can look for formal and informal sources of information about instructors. One source is the school catalog. Alumni magazines or newsletters or the school newspaper might run articles on teachers. At some schools, students post informal evaluations of instructors on Web sites. Also talk to students who have taken courses from the instructor you're researching.

Or introduce yourself to the instructor. Set up a visit during office hours, and ask about the course. This conversation can help you get the flavor of a class and the instructor's teaching style. Other clues to an instructor's style include the *types* of material he presents (ranging from theory or fact) and the *ways* that the material is presented (ranging from lectures to discussion and other in-class activity).

Show interest in class. Students give teachers moment-by-moment feedback in class. That feedback comes through posture, eye contact, responses to questions, and participation in class discussions. If you find a class boring, recreate the instructor through a massive display of interest. Ask lots of questions. Sit up straight, make eye contact, take detailed notes. Your enthusiasm might enliven your instructor. If not, you are still creating a more enjoyable class for yourself.

Release judgments. Maybe your instructor reminds you of someone you don't like—your annoying Aunt Edna or a rude store clerk. Your attitudes are in your own head and beyond the instructor's control. Likewise, an instructor's beliefs about politics, religion, or feminism are not related to teaching ability. Being aware of such things can help you let go of negative judgments.

Instructors are a lot like you. They have opinions about politics, sports, and music. They worry about their health, finances, and career path. They're sometimes in a good mood and sometimes sad or angry. What distinguishes them is a lifelong passion for the subject that they teach.

© Ron Chapple/Getty Images

Get to know the instructor. Meet with your instructor during office hours. Teachers who seem boring in class can be fascinating in person. Prepare to notice your pictures and let them go. An instructor that someone told you to avoid might become one of your favorite teachers. You might hear conflicting reports about teachers from other students. The same instructor could be described by two different students as a riveting speaker and as completely lacking in charisma. Decide for yourself what descriptions are accurate.

Students who do well in higher education often get to know at least one instructor outside of class. In some cases, these instructors become mentors and informal advisors.

Open up to diversity. Sometimes students can create their instructors by letting go of pictures about different races and ethnic groups. According to one picture, a Hispanic person cannot teach English literature. According to other pictures, a white teacher cannot have anything valid to say about African music, and a teacher in a wheelchair cannot command the attention of a hundred people in a lecture hall. All of those pictures can clash with reality. Releasing them can open up new opportunities for understanding and appreciation.

Separate liking from learning. You don't have to like an instructor to learn from her. See whether you can focus on content instead of form. *Form* is the way something is organized or presented. If you are irritated at the sound of an instructor's voice, you're focusing on form. When you put aside your concern about her voice and turn your attention to the points she's making, you're focusing on *content*.

Seek alternatives. You might feel more comfortable with another teacher's style or method of organizing course materials. Consider changing teachers, asking another teacher for help outside class, or attending an additional section taught by a different instructor.

If you cannot change instructors, then take charge of your learning. Actively use the suggestions in this article. You can also learn from other students, courses, tutors, study groups, books, and DVDs. Be a master student, no matter who teaches your classes. Your education is your own creation.

Avoid excuses. Instructors know them all. Most teachers can see a snow job coming before the first flake hits the ground. Accept responsibility for your own mistakes, and avoid thinking that you can fool the teacher.

Submit professional work. Prepare papers and projects as if you were submitting them to an employer. Imagine that your work will determine whether you get a promotion and raise. Instructors often grade hundreds of papers during a term. Your neat, orderly, well-organized paper can stand out and lift a teacher's spirits.

Accept criticism. Learn from your teachers' comments about your work. It is a teacher's job to give feedback. Don't take it personally.

Use course evaluations. In many classes, you'll have an opportunity to evaluate the instructor. Respond honestly. Write about the aspects of the class that did not work well for you. Offer specific ideas for improvement. Also note what *did* work well.

Communicate effectively by phone and e-mail. Ask your instructors how they prefer to be contacted. If they take phone calls, leave a voice mail message that includes your first and last name, course name, section, and phone number.

If your instructor encourages contact via e-mail, then craft your messages with care. Start by including your name, course title, and section number in the subject line. Keep the body of your message brief and get to the point immediately.

Remember that the recipient of online communication is a human being whose culture, language, and humor may have different points of reference from your own. Write clearly, and keep the tone positive. Do not type in FULL CAPS, which is equivalent to shouting.

If there's a problem to solve, focus on solutions rather than blame. For example, avoid: "Why do you grade so unfairly?" Instead, write, "I'd like to understand your criteria for grading our assignments so that I can raise my scores."

Also proofread your message carefully and fix any errors. Write with full words and complete sentences. Avoid the abbreviations that you might use in a text message.

Finally, remember that instructors are busy people with personal lives. Don't expect them to be online at the same time as you.

Take further steps, if appropriate. Sometimes severe conflict develops between students and instructors. In such cases, you might decide to file a complaint or ask for help from an administrator.

Be prepared to document your case in writing. Describe specific actions that created problems. Stick to the facts—events that other class members can verify. Your school has grievance procedures to use in these cases. Use them. You are a consumer of education and have a right to fair treatment. ■

You're One Click Away...
from discovering more ways to create positive relationships with instructors online.

Meeting with
YOUR INSTRUCTOR

Meeting with an instructor outside class can save hours of study time and help boost your grade. Instead of trying to resolve a conflict with an instructor in the few minutes before or after class, schedule a time during office hours. During this meeting, state your concerns in a respectful way. Then focus on finding solutions. To get the most from these meetings, consider doing the following:

- Schedule a meeting time during the instructor's office hours. These are often listed in the course syllabus and on the instructor's office door.

- If you need to cancel or reschedule an appointment, let your instructor know well in advance.

- During the meeting, relax. This activity is not graded.

- Come prepared with a list of questions and any materials you'll need. During the meeting, take notes on the instructor's suggestions.

- Show the instructor your class notes to see whether you're capturing essential material.

- Get feedback on outlines that you've created for papers.

- Go over items you missed on exams.

- Get overall feedback on your progress.

- Ask about ways to prepare for upcoming exams.

- If the course is in a subject area that interests you, ask about the possibilities of declaring a major in that area and the possible careers associated with that major.

- Avoid questions that might offend your instructor—for example, "I missed class on Monday. Did we do anything important?"

- Ask whether your instructor is willing to answer occasional short questions via e-mail or a phone call.

- When the meeting is over, thank your instructor for making time for you.

- Remember that meeting during office hours is something that you do in addition to attending class regularly.

Choosing your purpose

Success is a choice—your choice. To *get* what you want, it helps to *know* what you want. That is the purpose of this two-part Journal Entry. You can begin choosing success by completing this Journal Entry right now. If you choose to do it later, then plan a date, time, and place and then block out the time on your calendar.

Date: _____ Time: _____ Place: _____

Part 1

Select a time and place when you know you will not be disturbed for at least 20 minutes. (The library is a good place to do this exercise.) Relax for two or three minutes, clearing your mind. Next, complete the following sentences—and then keep writing. When you run out of things to write, stick with it just a bit longer. Be willing to experience a little discomfort. Keep writing. What you discover might be well worth the extra effort.

What I want from my education is . . . _____

_____

When I complete my education, I want to be able to . . . _____

_____

I also want . . . _____

_____

_____

_____

Part 2

After completing Part 1, take a short break. Reward yourself by doing something that you enjoy. Then come back to this Journal Entry.

Now, review the list you just created of things that you want from your education. See whether you can summarize them in one sentence. Start this sentence with "My purpose for being in school is. . . ." Allow yourself to write many drafts of this mission statement, and review it periodically as you continue your education. With each draft, see whether you can capture the essence of what you want from higher education and from your life. State it in a vivid way—in a short sentence that you can easily memorize, one that sparks your enthusiasm and makes you want to get up in the morning.

You might find it difficult to express your purpose statement in one sentence. If so, write a paragraph or more. Then look for the sentence that seems most charged with energy for you. Following are some sample purpose statements:

- My purpose for being in school is to gain skills that I can use to contribute to others.
- My purpose for being in school is to live an abundant life that is filled with happiness, health, love, and wealth.
- My purpose for being in school is to enjoy myself by making lasting friendships and following the lead of my interests.

Write at least one draft of your purpose statement here:

_____

_____

_____

_____

Jumpstart your education with
transferable skills

One dictionary defines *skill* as "the ability to do something well, usually gained by training or experience." Some skills—such as the ability to repair fiber-optic cables or do brain surgery—are acquired through formal schooling, on-the-job training, or both. These abilities are called *work-content skills*. People with such skills have mastered a specialized body of knowledge needed to do a specific kind of work.

However, there is another category of skills that we develop through experiences both inside and outside the classroom. These are *transferable skills*. Transferable skills are abilities that help people thrive in any job—no matter what work-content skills they have. You are developing these skills right now, even before you take your next job.

Perhaps you've heard someone described this way: "She's really smart and knows what she's doing, but she's got lousy people skills." People skills—such as *listening* and *negotiating*—are prime examples of transferable skills. Transferable skills are key to building the career you want over the long-term.

SUCCEED IN MANY SITUATIONS

Transferable skills are often invisible to us. The problem begins when we assume that a given skill can be used in only one context, such as working at a particular job. Thinking in this way places an artificial limit on our possibilities.

As an alternative, think about the things you routinely do to succeed in school. Analyze your activities to isolate specific skills. Then brainstorm a list of jobs where you could use the same skills.

Consider the task of writing a research paper. This calls for the following skills:

- *Planning*, including setting goals for completing your outline, first draft, second draft, and final draft.
- *Managing time* to meet your writing goals.
- *Interviewing* people who know a lot about the topic of your paper.
- *Researching* using the Internet and campus library to discover key facts and ideas to include in your paper.
- *Writing* to present those facts and ideas in an original way.
- *Editing* your drafts for clarity and correctness.

Now consider the kinds of jobs that draw on these skills.

For example, you could transfer your skill at writing papers to a possible career in journalism, technical writing, or advertising copywriting.

You could use your editing skills to work in the field of publishing as a magazine or book editor.

Interviewing and research skills could help you enter the field of market research. And the abilities to plan, manage time, and meet deadlines will help you succeed in all the jobs mentioned so far.

Use the same kind of analysis to think about transferring skills from one job to another. Say that you work part-time as an administrative assistant at a computer dealer that sells a variety of hardware and software. You take phone calls from potential customers, help current customers solve problems using their computers, and attend meetings where your coworkers plan ways to market new products. You are developing skills at *selling*, *serving customers*, and *working on teams*. These skills could help you land a job as a sales representative for a computer manufacturer or software developer.

The basic idea is to take a cue from the word *transferable*. Almost any skill you use to succeed in one situation can *transfer* to success in another situation.

The concept of transferable skills creates a powerful link between higher education and the work world. Skills are the core elements of any job. While taking any course, list the specific skills you are developing and how you can transfer them to the work world. Almost everything you do in school can be applied to your career—if you consistently pursue this line of thought.

Getting past the "I-don't-have-any-skills" syndrome means that you can approach job hunting with more confidence. As you uncover these hidden assets, your list of qualifications will grow as if by magic. You won't be padding your résumé. You'll simply be using action words to tell the full truth about what you can do.

Identifying your transferable skills takes a little time. And the payoffs are numerous. A complete and accurate list of transferable skills can help you land jobs that involve more responsibility, more variety, more freedom to structure your time, and more money. Careers can be made—or broken—by the skills that allow you to define your job, manage your workload, and get along with people.

Transferable skills help you thrive in the midst of constant change. Technology will continue to develop. Ongoing discoveries in many fields could render current knowledge obsolete. Jobs that exist today may disappear in a few years, only to be replaced by entirely new ones.

In the economy of the twenty-first century, you might not be able to count on job security. What you *can* count on is "skills security"—abilities that you can carry from one career to another or acquire as needed. Even though he only completed eight years of formal schooling,[6] Henry Ford said, "The only real security that a person can have in this world is a reserve of knowledge, experience, and ability. Without these qualities, money is practically useless."[7]

ASK FOUR QUESTIONS

To experiment further with this concept of transferable skills, ask and answer four questions derived from the Master Student Map.

Why identify my transferable skills? Identifying your transferable skills takes a little time. And the payoffs are numerous. A complete and accurate list of transferable skills can help you land jobs that involve more responsibility, more variety, more freedom to structure your time, and more money. Careers can be made—or broken—by the skills that allow you to define your job, manage your workload, and get along with people.

What are my transferable skills? Discover your transferable skills by reflecting on key experiences. Recall a time when you performed at the peak of your ability, overcame obstacles, won an award, gained a high grade, or met a significant goal. List the skills you used to create those successes.

For a more complete picture of your transferable skills, describe the object of your action. Say that one of the skills on your list is *organizing*. This could refer to organizing ideas, organizing people, or organizing objects in a room. Specify the kind of organizing that you like to do.

How do I perform these skills? You can bring your transferable skills into even sharper focus by adding adverbs—words that describe *how* you take action. You might say that you edit *accurately* or learn *quickly*.

In summary, you can use a three-column chart to list your transferable skills. For example:

Verb	Object	Adverb
Organizing	Records	Effectively
Serving	Customers	Courteously
Coordinating	Special events	Efficiently

Add a specific example of each transferable skill to your skills list, and you're well on the way to an engaging résumé and a winning job interview.

What if I could expand my transferable skills? In addition to thinking about the skills you already have, consider the skills you'd like to acquire. Describe them in detail. List experiences that can help you develop them. Let your list of transferable skills grow and develop as you do.

FOCUS ON THE FIVE Cs

Throughout much of the nineteenth and twentieth centuries, people with basic skills in reading, writing, and arithmetic—the "three R's"—could expect to find entry-level jobs. The economy of the twenty-first century changes that. According to the *AMA 2010 Critical Skills Survey*, conducted by the American Management Association, employers are now looking for people with a specific set of transferable skills—the "four Cs." These include:

- **Creative thinking**—creating ideas for new products and services, presenting those ideas to others, and working with teams to refine and implement them. People who think creatively see failures as opportunities to learn and look for results over the long-term.

- **Critical thinking**—stating questions precisely, examining a variety of possible answers, testing the logical accuracy of and evidence for each answer, and using the results to make effective decisions and solve problems.

- **Communication**—creating and sharing meaning through speaking, listening, writing, and reading. Skilled communicators stay aware of their purpose—to inform, instruct, or persuade—and choose ways to meet that purpose with a variety of audiences.

- **Collaboration**—working effectively with diverse teams to set shared goals and to meet them. Skilled collaborators respect their peers, stay open to new ideas, manage conflict, and bring projects to completion.

Most of the employers included in the AMA Survey said that they evaluate current employees based on the four Cs. In addition, skills in thinking, communication, and collaboration are key factors in deciding who gets hired when a job opening occurs.

This edition of *From Master Student to Master Employee* adds a fifth and equally important "C" that employers seek:

- **Character**—demonstrating a positive attitude, commitment, flexibility, willingness to learn, and trustworthiness.

Character takes skills, such as the four Cs, and embeds them in a larger context. While skills are about what you can *do*, character is about who you *are*. When employers talk about a *professional work ethic*, they're referring to character. Many of the master student qualities related to character as well.

You can use the articles, exercises, and journal entries in this book to develop a variety of transferable skills. Chapters 1, 8, 9, and 10 in particular deal with the five Cs. Also look for *Five Cs for Your Career* at the end of every chapter for ways to develop these crucial qualities now—and take them with you into the workplace. ▪

 You're One Click Away...
from learning more about transferable skills online.

60 transferable skills

There are literally hundreds of transferable skills. Start with the following list, which is organized by the chapter topics in this book. To learn more transferable skills, check out O*Net OnLine, a Web site from the federal government at online.onetcenter.org. There you'll find tools for discovering your skills and matching them to specific occupations. Additional information on careers and job hunting is available through CareerOneStop at www.careeronestop.org.

Self-management

1. Assessing your current knowledge and skills.

2. Seeking out opportunities to acquire new knowledge and skills.

3. Choosing and applying learning strategies.

4. Showing flexibility by adopting new attitudes and behaviors.

5. Persisting in order to meet goals.

For more information about self-management skills, see Chapter 1 of this book.

Self-discovery

6. Assessing your current knowledge and skills.

7. Seeking out opportunities to acquire new knowledge and skills.

8. Choosing and applying learning strategies.

9. Showing flexibility by adopting new attitudes and behaviors.

10. Changing habits.

For more information about self-discovery skills, see Chapter 2.

Time and money management

11. Scheduling due dates for project outcomes.

12. Scheduling time for goal-related tasks.

13. Monitoring income and expenses.

14. Raising funds.

15. Preparing budgets.

For more information about time and money skills, see Chapter 3.

Memory

16. Focusing attention to learn new information and ideas.

17. Selecting key information and ideas to remember.

18. Associating new information and ideas with prior knowledge.

19. Discovering meaningful ways to organize new information and ideas.

20. Encoding new information and ideas in ways that appeal to the senses.

For more information about memory skills, see Chapter 4.

Reading

21. Reading for key ideas and major themes.

22. Reading for detail.

23. Reading to synthesize ideas and information from several sources.

24. Reading to discover strategies for solving problems or meeting goals.

25. Reading to understand and follow instructions.

For more information about reading skills, see Chapter 5.

Note taking

26. Taking notes on material presented verbally, in print, or online.

27. Creating pictures, graphs, and other visuals to summarize and clarify information.

28. Organizing information and ideas in digital and paper-based forms.

29. Researching by finding information online or in the library.

30. Gathering data through field research or working with primary sources.

For more information about note-taking skills, see Chapter 6.

Test taking and related skills

31. Assessing personal performance at school or at work.

32. Using test results and other assessments to improve performance.

33. Working cooperatively in study groups and project teams.

34. Managing stress.

35. Using mathematics to do basic computations and solve problems.

For more information about test-taking skills, see Chapter 7.

Creative and critical thinking

36. Thinking to create new ideas, products, or services.

37. Thinking to evaluate ideas, products, or services.

38. Evaluating material presented verbally, in print, or online.

39. Making decisions.

40. Solving problems.

For more information about thinking skills, see Chapter 8.

Communication

41. Listening fully (without judgment or distraction).

42. Interpreting and responding to nonverbal messages.

43. Writing.

44. Editing.

45. Speaking to diverse audiences.

For more information about communication skills, see Chapter 9.

Collaboration

46. Leading and participating in project teams.

47. Assigning and delegating tasks.

48. Giving people feedback about the quality of their performance.

49. Preventing and resolving conflict.

50. Managing multiple projects at the same time.

For more information about collaboration skills, see Chapter 10.

Health

51. Changing habits that affect health.

52. Making health-related decisions based on sound information.

53. Maintaining reserves of energy and alertness for the tasks of daily life.

54. Managing stress and negative emotions in constructive ways.

55. Monitoring habits that affect health.

For more information about health-related skills, see Chapter 11.

Career management

56. Finding employment based on self-knowledge and accurate information about the work world.

57. Finding and learning from a mentor.

58. Taking the initiative with tasks and going beyond the minimum requirements of a job.

59. Updating skills continuously.

60. Working well with people from a variety of backgrounds.

For more information about career management skills, see Chapter 12.

JOURNAL ENTRY 3 *Discovery/Intention Statement*

Recognize the "five Cs" in yourself

Before you begin this Journal Entry, gather at least a hundred 3 × 5 cards and a pen or pencil. Or, start a new file in a word processing program or any software that allows you to create lists. Allow about one hour to do the suggested thinking and writing.

STEP 1 **List recent activities** Recall your activities during the past week or month. Write down as many of these activities as you can. (If you're using 3 × 5 cards, list each item on a separate card.) Include work-related activities, school activities, and hobbies. Spend 10 minutes on this step.

STEP 2 **List rewards and recognitions** Next, list any rewards you've received, or other recognition of your achievements, during the past year. Examples include scholarship awards, athletic awards, or recognitions for volunteer work. Allow 10 minutes for this step as well.

STEP 3 **List work-content skills** Now review the two lists you just created. Then take another 10 minutes to list any specialized areas of knowledge needed to do those activities, win those awards, and receive those recognitions.

These areas of knowledge indicate your *work-content skills*. For example, tutoring a French class requires a working knowledge of that language.

List all of your skills that fall into this category, labeling each one as "work-content."

STEP 4 **List transferable skills** Go over your list of activities one more time. Spend 10 minutes looking for examples of *transferable skills*— those that can be applied to a variety of situations. For instance, giving a speech or working as a salesperson in a computer store requires the ability to persuade people. Tuning a car means that you can attend to details and troubleshoot.

List all your skills that fall into this category, labeling each one as "transferable." Give special attention to the four Cs—skills that relate to creative thinking, critical thinking, communication, and collaboration.

STEP 5 **Describe your character** Your activities, rewards, and recognitions also reveal a deeper dimension of how you show up in the world— your character. Ask yourself: What are the qualities of a master student that I've demonstrated so far in my life? Create another list with your answers to this question.

STEP 6 **Review and plan** You now have a detailed picture of the five Cs in yourself. Review all the lists you created in the previous steps. See if you can add any new items that occur to you.

Save your lists in a place where you can easily find them again. Plan to update all of them at least once each year. Your lists will come in handy for writing your résumé, preparing for job interviews, and doing other career-planning tasks.

CHAPTER 1 CHARACTER

"You either change things or you don't; Excuses rob you of power and induce apathy." —Agnes Whistling Elk

· "We must all suffer from one of two pains: the pain of discipline or the pain of regret. The difference is discipline weighs ounces, while regret weighs tons." —Jim Rohn

PREVIEW

Values, attitudes, and habits exert major influences on success in school, relationships, and the work place. Life works to the extent that we align our behaviors with our values. The alternative is an endless stream of bad choices. Students begin to understand that their college experiences are opportunities to grow in character and integrity. This chapter reinforces self-awareness and change for the better.

GUEST SPEAKER

Consider inviting the administrator responsible for student discipline. In addition to explaining the office's broader role at the college, prompt the administrator to talk about the college's policies regarding cheating. When students cheat and get caught, they don't talk about it, so students have a misperception that no one's getting caught. The administrator's firsthand discussion of the topic may hit home with students who have considered cheating or have cheated in the past. Learn about your school's policy regarding academic integrity, and consider putting this in your course syllabus.

Play a video or audio of a renowned motivational speaker for students. One idea is to play part of Wayne Dyer's *Choosing Your Own Greatness*, talking about motivated and unmotivated employees and comparing them to eagles and ducks. This will spark discussion in class of the characteristics of motivated people and why we want to be like them.

If a speaker isn't available, consider using the Master Student Profile articles as guest speakers. Each chapter of this text includes a profile of a person who embodies several qualities of a master student. Invite your students to look for timeless qualities in the people they read about. Ask students to think of a person in their lives who embodies the qualities of a master student. Share these stories aloud.

LECTURE

Power Process: Define your values, align your actions (page 28) Students are often not very clear on what values are and why they are important to them. There are three criteria that must be met for identifying values:

They must be chosen freely. A child may practice habits of cleanliness because of fear or reward; it does not become a value until it is chosen regardless of parental influence.) They must be prized and cherished. (True values are publicly affirmed; is it obvious to others that this is really important to you: race, citizenship, religion, beliefs, or opinions)? And, they must be acted upon. (A divorced man who promises he will always support his children and then does so is living his values; a person against racism will stand up for someone being treated unfairly.) If all three criteria are not present when examining

master instructor
BEST PRACTICE

"I do this exercise to help students identify their top qualities, accomplishments, and talents, and discover which ones are really, really important to them. I ask them to complete this statement 10 times with their responses: "I respect me for …"

Then I ask them based on these statements to generate words that describe them based on these statements (competitive kind, honest, intelligent, religious, forgiving, generous, etc). From these words, they select the top three considered the most important and evaluate them using the three criteria of a value (chosen freely, prized and cherished, and acted upon). I also ask them to list five things they dislike in others and identify what values they represent."

—Lorraine Fedrizzi, Niagara County Community College

goals, purposes, attitudes, interests, feelings, beliefs, convictions, and also worries, problems or obstacles, it is not truly a value but a value in progress. Three global values that are really, really important to people of all cultures are health, family, and work or school. The most important of these values is health; you are not much good for your family or your employer if you do not make the commitment to take care of yourself. This is the value that tends to get neglected the most. Ask students to skim Chapter 11 and identify ways they can create the habit of taking care of their health now. Life flows when our behaviors are in line with our values and when we learn to take care of our own well-being.

Motivation—I'm just not in the mood (pages 32–33) Students often look to the teacher for motivation. Ask students, "Who is responsible for your learning?" The start of this course is a good time to help students learn and practice the art of self-motivation. Present the five Ms of Motivation to students:

- **Motive:** If motive is missing, there is nothing to work for. Give yourself motive; create desire to learn or so something meaningful. Where intention goes, energy flows.
- **Manage:** Overwhelmed or bored states result in lack of motivation. Turn up or turn down the pressure.
- **Mirror:** See your reflection in others and self. Seek honest feedback from friends and family. Use this to set goals.
- **Model:** Hang around the masters. Find someone you consider successful and spend time with that person. Take workshops. Meet similar people. Find a mentor.
- **Move:** Change your body/change your mind. You do not need to feel like it to get moving. Motivation can follow action. Fake it until you make it! Ask students to pay attention to what goes on in their heads and hearts that prevents them from participating fully in life. Motivation and success are inner concepts. You do not get them from other people or gaining fame, possessions, or riches. You bring them with you wherever you go.

EXERCISES/ACTIVITIES

1. **Attitudes, affirmations, and visualizations (page 30)** Self-awareness is the key to self-regulation and eventually self-mastery. This article encourages students to begin positive self-talk early in the course. Affirmations are employed to help students sustain a positive self-image and develop attitudes that lead to success. To help students grasp the power of visualization, try the classroom exercise "Creating Their Place." Begin this exercise by providing students with names for this place such as power place, caring place, peaceful place, or happy place. Students select the name that feels best to them. This allows all students, introverts and extroverts, to be positive about their choice. Instruct students to close their eyes and create this place in their mind. Follow a script (which is available on the

master instructor
BEST PRACTICE

"I cover classroom civility in my classes. I have found that we can't assume that students know what is expected of them in terms of what are appropriate college classroom behaviors. For many, they are the first in their family to attend college. There is a misconception among students that because they pay for classes, any behavior is acceptable in the classroom. (The customer is always right!) Many of the students are also under a great deal of stress right now due to the state of the economy. This also influences their behaviors. During the first week of class, we have a discussion on classroom civility, and I have them sign the student agreement."

–Debbie Warfield, Seminole Community College

master instructor
BEST PRACTICE

"Kick off the class by helping students develop the habit of using and carrying their calendars with them. Assign students to bring a student calendar to the next class. I give them large paper clips they can clip in their calendars and easily open up to the current day. I routinely have them post important college dates on their monthly calendars (like last day to drop courses without penalty, holidays, major tests, college fairs, etc). At the end of each class, they are directed to write down the assignment in their weekly calendars. The first couple of classes, I tell students that they must have calendars and books with them to be marked present."

–Lorraine Fedrizzi, Niagara County Community College

Instructor Web site) to help them discover the effectiveness of guided visualization. Once they have created this "mind place" in class two or three times, it can help reduce stress and test anxiety, and it can serve as a strategic memory tool.

2. **Ways to change a habit (pages 34–35)** Challenge your students in class to brainstorm habits they would like to start, stop, or change. Then ask them to pick a habit that they would like to commit to change successfully over the course of the term. Using the two-part notepaper from TeamUP, have them write down their habit and separate the paper. Tell the students to put one part in a self-addressed envelope and to keep the copy for themselves as a reference and reminder of their habit change plan. Collect the self-addressed envelopes and mail them to the students in four months (after the course is over) as an incentive for them to keep working on their habit change.

CONVERSATION/SHARING

The article on Motivation (pages 32–33) provides students with tools that enable them to take responsibility for their own motivation in college. Motivation is often high at the beginning of the semester but may drop as the term progresses. Have students form groups of four and share which of the tools each student intends to use to keep motivation high for the entire term. Make a note to revisit this list at mid-semester to reconnect with this motivation. Ask each group to print out a summary for the whole class.

HOMEWORK

Critical Thinking Exercise 4, page 31, Reprogram your attitude Have students read the article, Attitudes, Affirmations, and Visualizations, and complete Critical Thinking Exercise 4. Ask students to report on their progress of practicing their affirmations and visualizations over time in later classes. Discuss how this process worked or did not work for them, and if there is something they could do differently to make a positive change.

EVALUATION

Quiz Ideas for Chapter 1

Ask students to:

- Give an example of a value they hold, and explain why it is considered a value.
- Choose one power process from any chapter, and relate it to how it would be valued by an employer.
- List characteristics of a professional work ethic.
- Explain two approaches to thinking about motivation.
- Give an example of classroom civility.

Frequent quizzes ensure that students focus attention during class and keep up with the text reading assignments. Quizzes also provide students with opportunities for written reflection regarding new discoveries and intentions. In addition, evaluations help you identify topics and concepts that students have not yet mastered. Questions may be based on the textbook reading assignment, guest speakers, class activities, and/or the lecture. Possible answers are provided for the end-of-chapter quizzes in the Annotated Instructor's Edition.

....

master instructor
BEST PRACTICE

❝*One of the assignments in my class is a group presentation on a Power Process. Early in the term, students pick a Power Process to work on. Small groups are formed with students interested in the same one. At mid-term time, presentations are given. It is one of the highlights of the term.*❞

–Joe Rine, Minneapolis Community and Technical College

....

Additional Digital Resources for Chapter 1

What can you **ASSIGN FROM THE COURSEMATE** *for From Master Student to Master Employee?*

• **Master Students in Action Videos.** Available for every chapter, students will hear firsthand from other students about their challenges and their strategies for success. The Master Students in Action videos give your students a firsthand view of how the strategies in *From Master Student to Master Employee* have helped their peers overcome obstacles. In special segments, Dave Ellis offers students his best strategies for mastering each chapter's content.

• **Interactive eBook.** For students who are more likely to read onscreen than in print, assign the ebook chapter as an option where students can take notes, highlight, and search, and are directly connected to all the additional digital resources available for the chapter. Challenge your students with a virtual scavenger hunt to help them learn to maneuver the ebook and locate features and exercises you assign.

• **Power Process Media.** See how the Power Process articles from the textbook can come to life and apply to different learning styles. Watch the video, read, or listen to an audio version of the Power Process article, and then answer the accompanying questions. A PowerPoint presentation that summarizes the Power Process article's main points is also included.

CourseMate *To access CourseMate, your students need to visit www.cengagebrain.com. At the CengageBrain.com home page, students search for the ISBN of From Master Student to Master Employee (from the back cover of the book), using the search box at the top of the page. This takes them to the product page where these resources can be found.*

Did you know that **THESE RESOURCES** (and many more) **ARE AVAILABLE** on the **INSTRUCTOR COMPANION SITE**?

• **Need some general advice about using** *From Master Student to Master Employee* **in your course?** The online *Course Manual* serves as an invaluable reference for those developing and teaching a College Success course with *From Master Student to Master Employee*. The *Course Manual* provides advice on general teaching issues such as preparing for classes, classroom management, grading, and communicating with students of various backgrounds, as well as specific strategies on getting the most out of various features in *From Master Student to Master Employee* such as the Discovery Wheel and Learning Styles Inventory. Download the *Course Manual* now and do a reconnaissance to find ideas that you can use in your course.

• **Looking for test banks?** Customizable, text-specific content quizzes are a great way to test students' knowledge and understanding of the text and are available for every chapter. Because they are provided in ExamView, BlackBoard, WebCT, as well as Word, you will have no problem accessing the multiple choice, true/false, completion, and short-answer questions.

• **Check out the new PowerPoint Library!** This master library of PowerPoint presentations makes it easy to find the right PowerPoint for you! In the library, you will find PowerPoint slides for every chapter as well as every Power Process article covered in the book. All PowerPoint slides are downloadable and customizable to fit your needs.

- **Walk through Getting Started with Instructor Companion Site.** This presentation outlines the contents of the Instructor Companion Site and acts as a quick reference guide for you to locate the resource you want to access.

- **Walk through Getting Started with CourseMate.** This outlines and defines the resources on the CourseMate and can also be used as a quick reference guide for students.

- **Chapter PowerPoints.** For each chapter, there is a set of PowerPoints that highlights the main points. Use these PowerPoints in your lecture.

- **Power Process PowerPoints.** Using the same concept as the Chapter PowerPoints, these presentations cover the main points of the Power Process articles at the end of each chapter.

Please visit login.cengage.com *to log in and access the Instructor Companion Site.*

Character

Use this **Master Student Map** to ask yourself

WHY THIS CHAPTER MATTERS . . .

- Your values, attitudes, and habits exert major influences on your success in school—and at work.

WHAT IS INCLUDED . . .

HOW I CAN USE THIS CHAPTER . . .

- Define my values in a way that makes a difference in my daily life.
- Take charge of my thoughts and behaviors—instead of letting them take charge of me.
- Experience the power of contributing to others and demonstrating excellence.

WHAT IF . . .

- I could make conscious choices about how I think and how I behave—and make those choices on a regular basis?

© Ruslan Ivantsov/Shutterstock.com

JOURNAL ENTRY 4
Intention Statement

Create value from this chapter

Skim this chapter for three techniques that you'd like to use during the upcoming week. List each technique and a related page number here.

I intend to use ...

_____

_____

_____

_____

_____

_____

_____

_____

_____

_____

_____

_____

_____

_____

⏻ **POWER** process Define your values, align your actions

Some people are guided by values that they automatically adopt from others or by values that remain largely unconscious. Other people focus on short-term gain and forget about how their behavior violates their values over the long term.

All these people could be missing the opportunity to live a life that's truly of their own choosing. This book offers you a way to escape that fate by discovering what you want and how you intend to get it. In short, this book is about defining your values and aligning your actions.

The Master Student qualities explained in this book are based on a specific set of values:

- Focused attention
- Self-responsibility
- Integrity
- Risk taking
- Contributing

You'll find these values and related ones directly stated in the Power Processes throughout the text. For instance, "Discover what you want" is about the importance of living a purpose-based life. "Ideas are tools" points to the benefits of being willing to experiment with new ideas. "Be here now" expresses the value of focused attention. "Love your problems (and experience your barriers)" is about seeing difficulties as opportunities to develop new skills. "Notice your pictures and let them go" is about adopting an attitude of open-mindedness. "I create it all" is about taking responsibility for our beliefs and behaviors.

"Detach" reminds us that our core identity and value as a person does not depend on our possessions, our circumstances, or even our accomplishments. "Employ your word" expresses the value of making and keeping agreements. "Choose your conversations and your community" reminds us of the power of language, and that we can reshape our lives by taking charge of our thoughts. "Risk being a fool" is about courage—the willingness to take risks for the sake of learning something new. "Surrender" points to the value of human community and the power of asking for help. "Be it" is specifically about the power of attitudes—the idea that change proceeds from the inside out as we learn to see ourselves in new ways.

In addition, most of the skills you read about in these pages have their source in values. The Time Monitor/Time Plan process in Chapter 3, for example, calls for focused attention. Even the simple act of sharing your notes with a student who missed a class is an example of contributing.

Gaining a liberal education is all about adopting and acting on values. As you begin to define your values, consider the people who have gone before you. In creeds, scriptures, philosophies, myths, and sacred stories, the human race has left a vast and varied record of values. Be willing to look everywhere. The creed of your local church or temple might eloquently describe some of your values. So might the mission statement of your school, company, or club. Another way to define your values is to describe the qualities of people you admire.

To experience the full power of this process, translate your values into behavior. Although defining your values is powerful, it doesn't guarantee any results. To achieve your goals, take actions that align with your values.

ryby/Shutterstock.com

Your money
and your values

Want a clue to your values? Look at the way you handle money. The amount you spend on fast food shows how much you value convenience. The amount you spend on clothes shows how much you value appearance. And the amount you spend on tuition shows how much you value education. You might not think about values when you pull out a credit card or put cash on the counter. Even so, your values are at work.

Think of any value as having two aspects. One is invisible—a belief about what matters most in life. You can define this belief by naming something you want and asking, "*Why* do I want that?" Keep asking until you reach a point where the question no longer makes sense. At that point, you'll bump into one of your values.

Suppose that you want to start dating. Why do you want that? Perhaps you want to find someone who will really listen to you and also share his deepest feelings. Why do you want *that*? Perhaps because you want to love and be loved. If someone asks why you want *that*, you might say, "I want that because . . . well, I just want it." At that point, the *why?* question no longer applies. To you, love is an end in itself. You desire love simply for its own sake. Love is one of your values.

The second aspect of any value is a behavior. If you value love, you will take action to meet new people. You'll develop close friendships. You'll look for a spouse or life partner and build a long-term relationship. These behaviors are visible signs that you value love.

We experience peace of mind when our behaviors align with our values. However, this is not always the case. If you ever suspect that there's a conflict between your values and your behavior, then look at your money life for clues.

For example, someone says that he values health. After monitoring his expenses, he discovers that he spent $200 last month on fast food. He's discovered a clear source of conflict. He can resolve that conflict by redefining his values or changing his behavior. We sometimes work to buy more things that we have no time to enjoy . . . because we work so much. This can be a vicious cycle.

Sometimes we live values that are not our own. Values creep into our lives due to peer pressure or advertising. Movies, TV, and magazines pump us full of images about the value of owning more *stuff*—bigger houses, bigger cars, better clothes. All that stuff costs a lot of money. The process of acquiring it can drive us into debt—and into jobs that pay well but deny our values.

Money gives us plenty of opportunities for critical thinking. For example, think about the wisdom of choosing to spend money on the latest video game or digital gadget rather than a textbook or other resource needed for your education. Games and gadgets can deliver many hours of entertainment before they break down. Compare that to the value of doing well in a course, graduating with better grades, and acquiring skills that increase your earning power for the rest of your career.

One way to align your behaviors with your beliefs is to ask one question whenever you spend money: *Is this expense consistent with my values?* Over time, this question can lead to daily changes in your behavior that make a big difference in your peace of mind.

Keeping track of your income and expenses allows you to make choices about money with your eyes open. It's all about handling money on purpose and living with integrity. With the financial facts at hand, you can spend and earn money in ways that demonstrate your values. ■

Master Employees
IN ACTION

" *The budgeting work that I do in the office has made me a better money manager in my own life. It has taught me that money is just a way to ascribe value, and not a value in and of itself.*

I've been better able to evaluate the things I care about and the things I can do without. "

—Bill White, Construction Manager

You're One Click Away...
from a video about Master Students in Action.

© iStockphoto.com/Csaba Peterdi

ATTITUDES, AFFIRMATIONS, and VISUALIZATIONS

"**I** have a bad attitude." Some of us say this as if we were talking about having the flu. An attitude is certainly as strong as the flu, but it isn't something we have to live with forever anymore than the flu is.

Attitudes are judgments—enduring, deeply rooted views about what we like and what we dislike. Attitudes are also powerful. They mold behavior. If your attitude is that you're not interesting at a party, then your behavior will probably match your attitude. If your attitude is that you are fun at a party, then your behavior is more likely to be playful.

Visible measures of success—such as top grades and résumés filled with accomplishments—start with invisible assets called attitudes. Some attitudes will help you benefit from all the money and time you invest in higher education, for example: "Every course is worthwhile." "I learn something from any instructor." "The most important factors in the quality of my education are my own choices."

Other attitudes will render your investment worthless, for instance: "This required class is a total waste of time." "You can't learn anything from some instructors." "Success depends on luck more than anything else." "I've never been good at school."

Changing attitudes starts with detecting them. One clue to the presence of a negative attitude is sadness, anger, or fear. Our attitudes and emotions are closely connected. If you feel a negative emotion, then there's probably a negative attitude hiding behind it. Chances are also good that those attitudes lean heavily on words such as *must, should,* and *have to*: "Other people must always behave the way I want them to." "Things should always turn out well." "I have to be in control at all times."

One way to change such attitudes is to change your language. Practice dropping *must, should,* and *have to*. Also stop behaving on the basis of those thoughts. Over time and with repeated practice, your attitudes will change.

You can also change your attitudes through regular practice with affirmations and visualizations.

Affirm it.

An affirmation is a statement describing what you want. The most effective affirmations are personal, positive, and written in the present tense.

To use affirmations, first determine what you want, then describe yourself as if you already have it. To get what you want from your education, you could write, "I, Malika Jones, am a master student. I take full responsibility for my education. I learn with joy, and I use my experiences in each course to create the life that I want."

If you decide that you want a wonderful job, you might write, "I, Peter Webster, have a wonderful job. I respect and love my colleagues, and they feel the same way about me. I look forward to going to work each day."

Effective affirmations include detail. Use brand names, people's names, and your own name. Involve all of your senses—sight, sound, smell, taste, touch. Take a positive approach. Instead of saying, "I am not fat," say, "I am slender."

Once you have written an affirmation, repeat it. Practice saying it out loud several times a day. Do this at a regular time, such as just before you go to sleep or just after you wake up. Sit in a chair in a relaxed position. Take a few deep and relaxing breaths, and then repeat your affirmation with emotion. It's also effective to look in a mirror while saying the affirmation. Keep looking and repeating until you are saying your affirmation with conviction.

Visualize it.

You can improve your golf swing, tennis serve, or batting average while lying in bed. You can become a better driver, speaker, or cook while sitting silently in a chair. In line at the grocery store, you can improve your ability to type or to take tests. This is all possible through visualization—the technique of seeing yourself being successful.

Here's one way to begin. Choose what you want to improve. Then describe in writing what it would look like, sound like, and feel like to have that improvement in your life. If you are learning to play the piano, write down briefly what you would see, hear, and feel if you were playing skillfully. If you want to improve your relationships with your children, write down what you would see, hear, and feel if you were communicating with them successfully.

Once you have a sketch of what it would be like to be successful, practice it in your imagination. Then wait for the results to unfold in your life. Whenever you toss the basketball, it swishes through the net. Every time you invite someone out on a date, the person says "yes." Each test the teacher hands back to you is graded an "A." Practice at least once a day. Then wait for the results to unfold in your life.

You can also use visualizations to replay errors. When you make a mistake, replay it in your imagination. After a bad golf shot, stop and imagine yourself making that same shot again, this time very successfully. If you just had a discussion with your roommate that turned into a fight, replay it successfully.

Visualizations and affirmations can alter your attitudes and behaviors. Reinforce them by writing them down and posting them in prominent places, such as your refrigerator and bathroom mirror. Also surround yourself with positive people—those who support and demonstrate your values and goals.

Be clear about what you want, and then practice it. ■

Attitude REPLACEMENTS

You can use affirmations to replace a negative attitude with a positive one. There are no limitations, other than your imagination and your willingness to practice. Modify these sample affirmations to suit your individual hopes and dreams, and then practice them.

I, _____, have abundant energy and vitality throughout the day.

I, _____, exercise regularly.

I, _____, work effectively with many different kinds of people.

I, _____, eat wisely.

I, _____, plan my days and use time wisely.

I, _____, have a powerful memory.

I, _____, take tests calmly and confidently.

I, _____, fall asleep quickly and sleep soundly.

I, _____, have relationships that are mutually satisfying.

I, _____, contribute to other people through my job.

I, _____, know ways to play and have fun.

I, _____, focus my attention easily.

I, _____, like myself.

I, _____, have an income that far exceeds my expenses.

I, _____, live my life in positive ways for the highest good of all people.

For more ideas, review "Master student qualities," on page 3. You can turn any of those qualities into an affirmation.

You're One Click Away...
from finding an online version of these affirmations.

✓ CRITICAL THINKING EXERCISE 4

Reprogram your attitude

Step 1
Pick something in your life that you would like to change. It can be related to anything—relationships, work, money, or personal skills. Write a brief description here of what you choose to change.

_____

_____

Step 2
Add more details about the change you described in Step 1. Write down how you would like the change to come about. Be outlandish. Imagine that you are about to ask your fairy godmother for a wish she will grant. Be detailed in your description of your wish.

_____

_____

Step 3
Use affirmations and visualizations to start on the path to creating exactly what you wrote about in Step 2. Write at least two affirmations that describe your dream wish.

Also, briefly outline a visualization that you can use to picture your wish. Be specific, detailed, and positive.

_____

_____

_____

Step 4
Put your new attitudes to work. Set up a schedule to practice them. Let the first time you practice be right now. Then set up at least five other times and places.

I intend to relax and practice my affirmations and visualizations for at least 5 minutes on the following dates and at the time(s) and location(s) given.

Date	Time	Location
1.		
2.		
3.		
4.		
5.		

You're One Click Away...
from completing this exercise online under Exercises.

MOTIVATION—
I'm just not in the mood

In large part, this chapter is about your motivation to succeed in school. And there are at least two ways to think about motivation. One is to use the terms *self-discipline*, *willpower*, and *motivation* to describe something in ourselves that's missing. We use these words to explain another person's success—or our own shortcomings: "Of course she got an 'A.' She has self-discipline." "If I had more willpower, I'd lose weight." It seems that certain people are born with lots of motivation, whereas others miss out on it.

A second approach to thinking about motivation is to stop assuming that motivation is mysterious, determined at birth, or hard to come by. Perhaps there's nothing missing in you. What we call motivation could be something that you already possess—the ability to do a task even when you don't feel like it. This is a habit that you can develop with practice. The following suggestions offer ways to do that.

Promise It. Motivation can come simply from being clear about your goals and acting on them. Say that you want to start a study group. You can commit yourself to inviting people and setting a time and place to meet. Promise your classmates that you'll do this, and ask them to hold you accountable. Self-discipline, willpower, motivation—none of these mysterious characteristics has to get in your way. Just make a promise and keep your word.

Focus on one change at a time. On January 1, you might feel tempted to start a grand program of self-improvement by listing a dozen New Year's resolutions. To increase your odds of success, resist this temptation. Reduce your list to just one intention for now. Focus on achieving this new goal or changing this habit. When this resolution is accomplished, then choose a new one and bring it to completion.

Using this one-at-a-time method, you can move a large list of intentions with success. In contrast, tackling too many challenges at the same time makes them harder to remember. Sometimes the failure to follow through on an intention results from a lack of clarity rather than a lack of willpower.

Start small and build on early success. It's a cliché to say that the journey of a thousand miles begins with one step. And some clichés persist because they're so useful. Making the smallest change in behavior—and doing it on a consistent basis—can lead to surprising results. Flossing your teeth might take just one minute each day. Do it every day, however, and you might be able to reduce your dental bill by hundreds of dollars over your lifetime.

Success at changing any behavior is often a matter of finding balance—the sweet spot between "too easy" and "too hard." If you're currently inactive and want to run a marathon, for example, then don't start by setting an intention to run a mile every day. Instead, plan to walk 10 blocks. Over the coming weeks, gradually increase that amount. Then start jogging one out of every three blocks. Slow and steady, as they say, wins the race.

Befriend your discomfort. Sometimes keeping your word means doing a task you'd rather put off. The mere thought of doing laundry or proofreading a term paper can lead to discomfort. In the face of such discomfort, you can procrastinate. Or you can use this barrier as a means to getting the job done.

Begin by investigating the discomfort. Notice the thoughts running through your head, and speak them out loud: "I'd rather walk on a bed of coals than do this." "This is the last thing I want to do right now."

Also observe what's happening with your body. For example, are you breathing faster or slower than usual? Are your shoulders tight? Do you feel any tension in your stomach?

Once you're in contact with your mind and body, stay with the discomfort a few minutes longer. Don't judge it as good or bad. Accepting the thoughts and body sensations robs them of power. They might still be there, but in time they can stop being a barrier for you.

Also remember that discomfort with many new tasks tends to be short-lived and can disappear within a few minutes. You might find that the hardest part of following through with an intention is simply getting started.

With this in mind, direct most of your attention and energy to the initial step. If your intention is to exercise, for example, then focus on packing your workout clothes in a bag and getting to the gym. By the time you reach the gym your initial resistance to exercising might be a dim memory.

The word *motivation* is derived from the Latin word for "move." This is useful to remember. Don't wait until you feel like moving into action. Just move. Now. Then notice what happens to your mood.

Discomfort can be a gift—an opportunity to do valuable work on yourself. On the other side of discomfort lies mastery.

Change your mind—and your body. You can also get past discomfort by planting new thoughts in your mind or changing your physical stance. For example, instead of slumping in a chair, sit up straight or stand up. You can also get physically active by taking a short walk. Notice what happens to your discomfort.

Work with your thoughts, also. Replace "I can't stand this" with "I'll feel great when this is done" or "Doing this will help me get something I want."

Another option is to become aware of your internal debate about whether to follow through with a task. Remember that your mind is brilliant. It can manufacture a long list of reasons to procrastinate almost any task. Some of the reasons will sound— well, *reasonable*. Simply notice them, then let them go. Thank your mind for being so creative. And then remind yourself that you don't have to believe everything you think.

Sweeten the task. Sometimes it's just one aspect of a task that holds you back. You can stop procrastinating merely by changing that aspect. If distaste for your physical environment keeps you from studying, you can change that environment. Reading about social psychology might seem like a yawner when you're alone in a dark corner of the house. Moving to a cheery, well-lit library can sweeten the task.

When you're done with an important task, reward yourself for a job well done. The simplest rewards—such as a walk, a hot bath, or a favorite snack—can be the most effective.

Talk about how bad it is. One way to get past negative attitudes is to take them to an extreme. When faced with an unpleasant task, launch into a no-holds-barred gripe session. Pull out all the stops: "There's no way I can start my income taxes now. This is terrible beyond words—an absolute disaster. This is a catastrophe of global proportions!" Griping taken this far can restore perspective. It shows how self-talk can turn inconveniences into crises.

Turn up the pressure. Sometimes motivation is a luxury. Pretend that the due date for your project has been moved up one month, one week, or one day. Raising the stress level slightly can spur you into action. Then the issue of motivation seems beside the point, and meeting the due date moves to the forefront.

Turn down the pressure. The mere thought of starting a huge task can induce anxiety. To get past this feeling, turn down the pressure by taking "baby steps." Divide a large project into small tasks. In 30 minutes or less, you could preview a book, create a rough outline for a paper, or solve two or three math problems. Careful planning can help you discover many such steps to make a big job doable.

Create an environment that supports your intention. You can often reduce the need for "willpower" simply by changing the people and things that surround you. Even rearranging the objects in a room—or using different objects—can help. For example, if your intention is to drink more water, then keep a bottle of water at your desk and in your car, making sure it's within easy reach.

It's easy to confuse a lack of motivation with a lack of follow-through. Design an environment that removes the obstacles to acting on your intention. Make the task easier to do than *not* do. Then you can move from intention to action with a minimum of friction.

Ask for support. Other people can become your allies in overcoming procrastination. For example, form a support group and declare what you intend to accomplish before each meeting. Then ask members to hold you accountable. If you want to begin exercising regularly, ask another person to walk with you three times weekly.

Adopt a model. One strategy for succeeding at any task is to hang around the masters. Find someone you consider successful, and spend time with her. Observe this person and use her as a model for your own behavior. You can "try on" this person's actions and attitudes. Look for tools that feel right for you. This person can become a mentor for you.

Compare the payoffs to the costs. All behaviors have payoffs and costs. Even unwanted behaviors, such as cramming for exams or neglecting exercise, have payoffs. Cramming might give you more time that's free of commitments. Neglecting exercise can give you more time to sleep.

Skipping a reading assignment can give you time to go to the movies. However, you might be unprepared for class and have twice as much to read the following week.

Maybe there is another way to get the payoff (going to the movies) without paying the cost (skipping the reading assignment). With some thoughtful weekly planning, you might choose to give up a few hours of television and end up with enough time to read the assignment *and* go to the movies.

Comparing the costs and benefits of any behavior can fuel our motivation. We can choose new behaviors because they align with what we want most.

Do it later. At times, it's effective to save a task for later. For example, writing a résumé can wait until you've taken the time to analyze your job skills and map out your career goals. Putting it off does not show a lack of motivation—it shows planning.

When you do choose to do a task later, turn this decision into a promise. Estimate how long the task will take, and schedule a specific date and time for it on your calendar.

Heed the message. Sometimes lack of motivation carries a message that's worth heeding. An example is the student who majors in accounting but seizes every chance to be with children. His chronic reluctance to read accounting textbooks might not be a problem. Instead, it might reveal his desire to major in elementary education. His original career choice might have come from the belief that "real men don't teach kindergarten." In such cases, an apparent lack of motivation signals a deeper wisdom trying to get through. ▪

Jason Stitt/Shutterstock.com

Ways to *change a habit*

Consider a new way to think about the word *habit*. Imagine for a moment that many of our most troublesome problems and even our most basic traits are just habits.

The expanding waistline that your friend is blaming on her spouse's cooking—maybe that's just a habit called overeating.

The fit of rage that a student blames on a teacher—maybe that's just the student's habit of closing the door to new ideas.

Procrastination, stress, and money shortages might just be names that we give to collections of habits—scores of simple, small, repeated behaviors that combine to create a huge result. The same goes for health, wealth, love, and many of the other things that we want from life.

One way of thinking about success or failure is to focus on habits. Behaviors such as failing to complete reading assignments or skipping class might be habits leading to outcomes that "could not" be avoided, including dropping out of school. In the same way, behaviors such as completing assignments and attending class might lead to the outcome of getting an "A."

When you confront a behavior that undermines your goals or creates a circumstance that you don't want, consider a new attitude: That behavior is just a habit. And it can be changed.

Thinking about ourselves as creatures of habit actually gives us power. Then we are not faced with the monumental task of changing our very nature. Rather, we can take on the doable job of changing our habits. One change in behavior that seems insignificant at first can have effects that ripple throughout your life.

After interviewing hundreds of people, psychologists James Prochaska, John Norcross, and Carlo DiClemente identified stages that people typically go through when adopting a new behavior.[1] These stages take people from *contemplating* a change and making a clear *determination* to change, to taking *action* and *maintaining* the new behavior. Following are ways to help yourself move successfully through each stage as you attempt to change a habit.

TELL THE TRUTH

Telling the truth about any habit—from chewing our fingernails to cheating on tests—frees us. Without taking this step, our efforts to change might be as ineffective as rearranging the deck chairs on the *Titanic*. Telling the truth allows us to see what's actually sinking the ship.

When we admit what's really going on in our lives, our defenses are down. We're open to accepting help from others. The support we need to change a habit has an opportunity to make an impact.

CHOOSE AND COMMIT TO A NEW BEHAVIOR

It often helps to choose a new habit to replace an old one. First, make a commitment to practice the new habit. Tell key people in your life about your decision to change. Set up a plan for when and how. Answer questions such as these: When will I apply the new habit? Where will I be? Who will be with me? What will I be seeing, hearing, touching, saying, or doing? Exactly how will I think, speak, or act differently?

For example, consider the student who always snacks when he studies. Each time he sits down to read, he positions a bag of potato chips within easy reach. For him, opening a book is a cue to start chewing. Snacking is especially easy, given the place he chooses to study: the kitchen. He decides to change this habit by studying at a desk in his bedroom instead of at the kitchen table. And every time he feels the urge to bite into a potato chip, he drinks from a glass of water instead.

Richard Malott, a psychologist who specializes in helping people overcome procrastination, lists three key steps in committing to a new behavior.[2] First, *specify* your goal in numerical terms whenever possible. For example, commit to reading 30 pages per day, Monday through Friday. Second, *observe* your behavior and record the results—in this case, the number of pages that you actually read every day. Finally, set up a small *consequence* for failing to keep your commitment. For instance, pay a friend one quarter for each day that you read less than 30 pages.

AFFIRM YOUR INTENTION

You can pave the way for a new behavior by clearing a mental path for it. Before you apply the new behavior, rehearse it in your mind. Mentally picture what actions you will take and in what order.

Say that you plan to improve your handwriting when taking notes. Imagine yourself in class with a blank notebook poised before you. See yourself taking up a finely crafted pen. Notice how comfortable it feels in your hand. See yourself writing clearly and legibly. You can even picture how you will make individual letters: the *e*'s, *i*'s, and *r*'s. Then, when class is over, see yourself reviewing your notes and taking pleasure in how easy they are to read.

START WITH A SMALL CHANGE

You can sometimes rearrange a whole pattern of behaviors by changing one small habit. If you have a habit of always being late for classes, then be on time for one class. As soon as you change the old pattern by getting ready and going on time to one class, you might find yourself arriving at all of your classes on time. You might even start arriving everywhere else on time too.

The joy of this process is watching one small change of habit ripple through your whole life.

GET FEEDBACK AND SUPPORT

Getting feedback and support is a crucial step in adopting a new behavior. It is also a point at which many plans for change break down. It's easy to practice your new behavior with great enthusiasm for a few days. After the initial rush of excitement, though, things can get a little tougher. You begin to find excuses for slipping back into old habits: "One more cigarette won't hurt." "I can get back to my paper tomorrow." "It's been a tough day. I deserve to skip the rest of my classes."

One way to get feedback is to bring other people into the picture. Ask others to remind you that you are changing your habit if they see you backsliding. If you want to stop an old behavior, such as cramming for tests, then tell everyone about your goal. When you want to start a new behavior, though, consider telling only a few people—those who truly support your efforts.

Starting new habits might call for the more focused, long-lasting support that close friends or family members can give. Support from others can be as simple as a quick phone call: "Hi. Have you started that outline for your research paper yet?" Or it can be as formal as a support group that meets once a week to review everyone's goals and action plans.

One effective source of feedback is yourself. You know yourself better than anyone else does and can design a system to monitor your behavior. Create your own charts to track your behavior, or write about your progress in your journal. Figure out a way to monitor your progress.

Jerry Seinfeld told one aspiring comedian that "the way to be a better comic was to create better jokes, and the way to create better jokes was to write every day."[3] Seinfeld also revealed his own system for creating a writing habit: He bought a big wall calendar that displayed the whole year on one page. On each day that he wrote jokes, Seinfeld marked a big red "X" on the appropriate day on the wall calendar. He knew that he'd established a new habit when he looked at the calendar and saw an unbroken chain of "X's." You can use the same strategy to take a series of small steps that add up to a big change.

PRACTICE, PRACTICE, PRACTICE— WITHOUT SELF-JUDGMENT

Psychologists such as B. F. Skinner define learning as a stable change in behavior that comes as a result of practice.[4] This widely accepted idea is key to changing habits. Act on your intention over and over again. If you fail or forget, let go of any self-judgment. Just keep practicing the new habit. Allow whatever time it takes to make a change.

Accept the feelings of discomfort that might come with a new habit. Keep practicing the new behavior, even if it feels unnatural. Trust the process. Grow into the new behavior. However, if this new habit doesn't work, simply note what happened (without guilt or blame), select a new behavior, and begin this cycle of steps over again.

Making mistakes as you practice doesn't mean that you've failed. Even when you don't get the results you want from a new behavior, you learn something valuable in the process. Once you understand ways to change one habit, you understand ways to change almost any habit. ∎

 You're One Click Away...
from finding more strategies for changing a habit online.

✔ CRITICAL THINKING EXERCISE 5

Change a habit

In his book *The Power of Habit*, Charles Duhigg explains that any habit has three elements. These include the following:

- *Routine.* This is a behavior that we repeat, usually without thinking. Examples are taking a second helping at dinner, biting fingernails, or automatically hitting the "snooze" button when the alarm goes off in the morning.

- *Cue.* Also known as a trigger, this is an event that occurs right before we perform the routine. It might be an internal event, such as change in mood. Or it could be an external event, such as seeing an advertisement that triggers food cravings.

- *Reward.* This is the "payoff" for the routine—usually a feeling a pleasure or a reduction in stress.

Taken together, the above elements form a habit loop: You perceive a *cue* and then perform a *routine* in order to get a *reward*.

For this exercise, you will choose a habit loop in your own life and use the following four steps to change it. (Duhigg arrived at these steps after reviewing hundreds of published studies.) Once you master this process, you'll be able to change a variety of habits—and enjoy new results in your life. To increase your odds of success, focus on just one habit for now. Also start with a small change in behavior.

Step 1: Identify the routine

In the space below, describe the habit that you want to change. Refer to a specific behavior that anyone could observe—preferably a physical, visible action that you perform every day.

_____

_____

_____

_____

_____

Step 2: Identify the cue

Next, think about what takes place immediately before you perform the routine. For instance, drinking a cup of coffee (cue) might trigger the urge to eat a chocolate chip cookie (routine). Use the following space to describe the cue for the behavior you listed in Step 1.

_____

_____

_____

_____

Step 3: Identify the reward

Now for the "goodie." Reflect on the reward you get from your routine. Do you gain a distraction from discomfort? A pleasant sensation in your body? A chance to socialize with friends or coworkers? Write about your reward below.

_____

_____

_____

_____

_____

Step 4: Choose a new routine

Once you've collected the data from Steps 1 to 3, you're prepared to actually change your habit. This means creating a specific intention—choosing a different *routine* that you can perform in response to the *cue*. The challenge is to choose a behavior that offers a *reward* with as few disadvantages as possible. Instead of eating a whole chocolate chip cookie, for example, you could break off just one small section and eat it slowly, with full attention. This would allow you to experience a familiar pleasure with a fraction of the calories.

Describe your new routine here.

_____

_____

_____

_____

Act on your intention every day for the next week and keep track of the results. If you don't succeed at changing the habit, just tell the truth about it. Then experiment with different routines until you discover one that works.

CLASSROOM CIVILITY—
what's in it for you

This topic might seem like common sense, yet some students forget that simple behaviors create a sense of safety, mutual respect, and community.

Consider an example: A student arrives 15 minutes late to a lecture and lets the door slam behind her. She pulls a fast-food burger out of a crackling paper bag. Then her cell phone rings at full volume—and she answers it. Behaviors like these send a message to everyone in the room: "I'm ignoring you."

Without civility, you lose. Even a small problem with classroom civility can create a barrier for everyone. Learning gets interrupted. Trust breaks down. Your tuition dollars go down the drain. You deserve to enter classrooms that are free of discipline problems and bullies. Many schools have formal policies about classroom civility. Find out what policies apply to you. The consequences for violating them can be serious and may include dismissal or legal action.

With civility, you win. When you treat instructors with respect, you're more likely to be treated that way in return. A respectful relationship with an instructor could turn into a favorable reference letter, a mentorship, a job referral, or a friendship that lasts for years after you graduate. Politeness pays.

Classroom civility does not mean that you have to be passive or insincere. You can present your opinions with passion and even disagree with an instructor in a way that leaves everyone enriched rather than threatened.

Lack of civility boils down to a group of habits. Like any other habits, these can be changed. The following suggestions reflect common sense, and they make an uncommon difference.

Attend classes regularly and on time. If you know that you're going to miss a class or be late, let your instructor know. Take the initiative to ask your instructor or another student about what you missed.

If you arrive late, do not disrupt class. Close the door quietly and take a seat. When you know that you will have to leave class early, tell your instructor before class begins, and sit near an exit. If you leave class to use the restroom or handle an emergency, do so quietly.

During class, participate fully. Take notes and join in discussions. Turn off your cell phone or any other electronic device that you don't need for class. Remember that sleeping, texting, or doing work for another class is a waste of your time and money. Instructors notice distracting activities and take them as a sign of your lack of interest and commitment. So do employers.

Before packing up your notebooks and other materials, wait until class has been dismissed. Instructors often give assignments or make a key point at the end of a class period. Be there when it happens.

Communicate respect. When you speak in class, begin by addressing your instructor as *Ms., Mrs., Mr., Dr., Professor,* or whatever the teacher prefers.

Discussions gain value when everyone gets a chance to speak. Show respect for others by not monopolizing class discussions. Refrain from side conversations and profanity. When presenting viewpoints that conflict with those of classmates or your instructor, combine the passion for your opinion with respect for the opinions of others. Similarly, if you disagree with a class requirement or grade you received, then talk to your instructor about it after class in a respectful way. In a private setting, your ideas will get more attention.

Respect gets communicated in small details. Don't make distracting noises. Cover your mouth if you yawn or cough. Avoid wearing inappropriate clothing. And even if you meet your future spouse in class, refrain from public displays of affection.

Embrace diversity. Master students—and teachers—come in endless variety. They are old and young, male and female. They come from every culture, race, and ethnic group. Part of civility is staying open to the value that other people have to offer. For more ideas, see Chapter 10.

See civility as a contribution. Every class you enter has the potential to become a community of people who talk openly, listen fully, share laughter, and arrive at life-changing insights. These are master student qualities. Every time you demonstrate them, you make a contribution to your community. ■

Demonstrating a professional WORK ETHIC

Through their behavior at work, some people give the impression that they are merely warming chairs and taking up office space. They perform just up to minimum requirements without much energy, enthusiasm, or commitment. Their verbal and nonverbal behavior often conveys a single message: *I'd really rather be somewhere else.*

This is not a strategy for success. Being a "warm body" at work will not cut it. Even being "generally competent" in your field or "better than average" may not be enough for you to get hired—or to survive a round of layoffs.

If you want to prosper in your next job and open up new career options for the future, then demonstrate a *professional work ethic.* You'll see those three words in many job descriptions, and they're not just filler. Employers value people who are willing to stand out from the crowd and consistently demonstrate excellence.

People with a professional work ethic use their job as a venue for constant learning and contribution. They function as team players, and they're also willing to take the lead. They contribute ideas, and they're also willing to change their mind. They learn new tasks quickly and push through obstacles until projects are completed. In short, these people care about what they do.

Demonstrating a professional work ethic means more than showing up for work on time and dressing smartly. Those are important, and there's much more. Consider the following qualities that turn Master Students into Master Employees.

DEMONSTRATE COMPETENCE

The basis of a work ethic is a set of skills that are appropriate for your job. Gaining those skills is one of the major reasons you're in school right now.

Getting a degree or a certificate will do a lot to help you get hired, and that's just a starting point. Many professions have a core of knowledge and best practices that's constantly changing. Some of the things that you learn in school might be outdated on the first day of your next job. Demonstrating a professional work ethic calls for a commitment to lifelong learning so that you can stay up to date with new developments in your field.

In addition, competence means aligning your daily activities with your organization's core mission. Lift your eyes to the horizon and look beyond the lines of your job description. Ask how your work enables the organization to generate more revenue, improve efficiency, or reach new clients or customers. If you can show

> Demonstrating a professional work ethic means more than showing up for work on time and dressing smartly.

that you're helping to meet those goals, you'll be perceived as professional—and valuable.

DEMONSTRATE INITIATIVE

When people spot a problem at work, there are two distinct ways for them to respond. The unprofessional response is to ignore the problem or complain about it. The professional response is to try to help solve the problem while still attending to their regular job tasks.

Demonstrating initiative means thinking carefully before making statements such as these:

- *I'm not going to do that—it's not in my job description.*
- *This problem has been around for years, and it's here to stay.*
- *I'll wait until I get a promotion; then I'll think about getting involved.*

Remember that you don't need a new job title in order to become a leader. When you spot a problem in your workplace, describe it an objective way—without judgment or blame. Stick to the facts about what's working and what's not working. Then offer a possible solution. Better yet, offer several solutions.

Also keep in mind that becoming a leader does not always involve telling people what to do. Instead, leadership is about going to meetings and asking questions such as these:

- What's our desired outcome?
- What our next action on this project?
- Who's doing it?
- What's the due date?
- How can I help?

You'll know you've succeeded at demonstrating initiative when coworkers start coming to you for answers—or when they refuse to start a meeting until you're present.

DEMONSTRATE HUMILITY

During the course of your career, you'll meet people who value prestige above all else. These people tend to be fussy about their job title and position on the company's organization chart. They typically consider certain tasks to be "beneath" them. If they think that their achievements are ignored, they take offense and look for ways to get revenge.

In contrast, people with a professional work ethic see what needs to be done and pitch in. Instead of worrying about status or recognition, they join a team and look for ways to contribute.

Humility has other meanings as well. These include:

- *Assuming the posture of a learner.* A professional doesn't pretend to know all the answers or speak the final words on any topic. She asks other people for their suggestions. She respects points of view that differ from her own. And she refuses to criticize an idea until she's taken the time to fully understand it.

- *Admitting mistakes.* A professional is open to coaching. He routinely asks for feedback, and he receives it without becoming defensive. If he makes an error, he quickly admits it and apologizes. He also looks for ways to make amends.

- *Giving others credit.* When a project goes well, unprofessional people try to take credit. In contrast, professional people look for ways to *give* credit. They make a habit of expressing appreciation for coworkers.

Humility is a word that's often misunderstood. It does not mean downplaying your strengths or being the first to take blame. The true mark of a humble person is treating everyone in a workplace—from the janitor to the chief executive officer—as a fellow member of the human race.

"Whenever I hire an executive, I always like to take him or her to dinner," says Michael Hyatt, chairman of Thomas Nelson Publishers. "I am always interested to see how he treats the hostess, the waiters, and even the busboys. Is he curt? Is he demanding or brusque? Does he treat them with dignity? Is he appreciative? Does he even notice them?"[5] If the answer to such questions is no, then the problem is a lack of humility.

DEMONSTRATE ETIQUETTE

Etiquette refers to common courtesy, such as greeting people when they enter a room, saying *please* when making a request, and saying thank you when the request is granted. In the workplace, etiquette takes on additional meanings—for example, opening an e-mail with a personal greeting for the recipient and closing it with *Sincerely* or *Thanks*, followed by your name.

Also remember *netiquette*, the online equivalent of etiquette. This is a set of guidelines for using computers, cell phones, or any

> The true mark of a humble person is treating everyone in a workplace—from the janitor to the chief executive officer—as a fellow member of the human race.

other form of technology to communicate. To promote a cordial online community, abide by the following guidelines:

- *Respect others' time.* Send concise messages. Adopt the habit of getting to your point, sticking to it, and getting to the end. Also use the "reply to all" feature sparingly—only when everyone on the recipient list will truly benefit from receiving your reply.

- *Fine-tune the mechanics.* Proofread your message for spelling and grammar—just as you would a printed message. Give your readers the gift of clarity and precision. Use electronic communications as a chance to hone your writing skills.

- *Avoid messages* in ALL UPPERCASE LETTERS. This is the online equivalent of shouting.

The people who receive your digital communication miss out on voice inflection and nonverbal cues that are present in face-to-face communication. Without these cues, words can be easily misinterpreted. Reread your message before sending it and ask: *Would I say this to the person's face?*

DEMONSTRATE SOUND JUDGMENT

While they're at work, some people forget that they can be friendly without sharing all the details of their personal life. Comments such as *I really got wasted last Saturday night* or *Thank God it's Friday* could come back to them at a future performance review.

Being professional means monitoring the quality of your conversations to ensure that they build the reputation you want. Make a commitment to stop dwelling on faults of coworkers or complaining about the state of the economy. Instead, talk about what you're learning, how you intend to develop new skills, and what you value in life. The act of changing your speaking can shift your attitude. And in most work environments, attitude counts as much as competence. ■

The HIGH COSTS of cheating

Cheating on tests can be a tempting strategy. It offers the chance to get a good grade without having to study.

Instead of studying, you could spend more time watching TV, partying, sleeping, or doing anything that seems like more fun. Another benefit is that you could avoid the risk of doing poorly on a test—which could happen even if you *do* study.

Remember that cheating carries costs. Here are some consequences to consider.

You risk failing the course or getting expelled from college. The consequences for cheating are serious. Cheating can result in failing the assignment, failing the entire course, getting suspended, or getting expelled from college entirely. Documentation of cheating may also prevent you from being accepted to other colleges.

You learn less. Although you might think that some courses offer little or no value, you can create value from any course. If you look deeply enough, you can discover some idea or acquire some skill to prepare you for future courses or a career after graduation.

You lose time and money. Getting an education costs a lot of money. It also calls for years of sustained effort. Cheating sabotages your purchase. You pay full tuition and invest your energy without getting full value for it. You shortchange yourself and possibly your future coworkers, customers, and clients. Think about it: You probably don't want a surgeon who cheated in medical school to operate on you.

Fear of getting caught promotes stress. When you're fully aware of your emotions about cheating, you might discover intense stress. Even if you're not fully aware of your emotions, you're likely to feel some level of discomfort about getting caught.

Violating your values promotes stress. Even if you don't get caught cheating, you can feel stress about violating your own ethical standards. Stress can compromise your physical health and overall quality of life.

Cheating on tests can make it easier to violate your integrity again. Human beings become comfortable with behaviors that they repeat. Cheating is no exception.

Think about the first time you drove a car. You might have felt excited—even a little frightened. Now driving is probably second nature, and you don't give it much thought. Repeated experience with driving creates familiarity, which lessens the intense feelings you had during your first time at the wheel.

You can experience the same process with almost any behavior. Cheating once will make it easier to cheat again. And if you become comfortable with compromising your integrity in one area of life, you might find it easier to compromise in other areas.

Cheating lowers your self-concept. Whether or not you are fully aware of it, cheating sends the message that you are not smart enough or responsible enough to make it on your own. You deny yourself the celebration and satisfaction of authentic success.

An alternative to cheating is to become a master student. Ways to do this are described on every page of this book. ■

Perils of high-tech CHEATING

Digital technology offers many blessings, but it also expands the options for cheating during a test. For example, one student loaded class notes onto a smartphone and tried to read them. Another student dictated his class notes into files stored on his iPod and tried to listen to them. At one school, students used cell phones to take photos of test questions. They sent the photos to classmates outside the testing room, who responded by text-messaging the answers.[6]

All of these students were caught. Schools are becoming sophisticated about detecting high-tech cheating. Some install cameras in exam rooms. Others use software that monitors the programs running on students' computers during tests. And some schools simply ban all digital devices during tests.

The bottom line: If you cheat on a test, you are more likely than ever before to get caught.

There's no need to learn the hard way—through painful consequences—about the high costs of high-tech cheating. Using the suggestions in this chapter can help you succeed on tests *and* preserve your academic integrity.

ACADEMIC INTEGRITY:
Avoid plagiarism

Using another person's words, images, or other original creations without giving proper credit is called *plagiarism*. Plagiarism amounts to taking someone else's work and presenting it as your own—the equivalent of cheating on a test.

Higher education consists of a community of scholars who trust one another to speak and write with integrity. Plagiarism undermines this trust. The consequences of plagiarism can range from a failing grade to expulsion from school.

Plagiarism can be unintentional. Some students don't understand the research process. Sometimes they leave writing until the last minute and don't take the time to organize their sources of information. Also, some people are raised in cultures where identity is based on group membership rather than individual achievement. These students may find it hard to understand how an individual can own creative work. Remember, however, that even accidental plagiarism can lead to a lowered grade and other penalties.

To avoid plagiarism, ask an instructor where you can find your school's written policy on this issue. Read this document carefully, and ask questions about *anything* you don't understand.

> Higher education consists of a community of scholars who trust one another to speak and write with integrity. Plagiarism undermines this trust. The consequences of plagiarism can range from a failing grade to expulsion from school.

The basic guideline for preventing plagiarism is to cite a source for any fact or idea that is new to you. These include words and images created by another person. The overall goal is to clearly distinguish your own work from the work of others. A secondary goal is to give enough information about your sources so that they are easy to find. There are several ways to ensure that you meet both of these goals consistently.

Know the perils of "paper mills." A big part of the problem is misuse of the Internet. Anyone with a computer can access thousands of Web pages on a given topic. Images and text from those sources are easily copied and pasted into another document. Technology makes it easy to forget that some information is free for the taking—and some is privately owned.

Plagiarism is now a growth industry. A quick Web search will uncover hundreds of online business that sell term papers, essays, and book reports. These businesses are often called "paper mills." Some of them offer to customize their products for an additional fee. Even so, these services are based on plagiarism.

Students who use these services might answer, "When I buy a paper online, it's not plagiarism. I paid for those words, so now they're mine." But in fact, those words were still created by someone else. Plagiarism is more than merely copying words from another source: It's turning in thoughts and work that you did not produce.

Also remember that plagiarism includes turning in a paper—or portions of a paper—that you have already written for another class. If you want to draw on prior research, talk to your instructor first.

Identify direct quotes. If you use a direct quote from another writer or speaker, put that person's words in quotation marks. If you do research online, you might find yourself copying sentences or paragraphs from a Web page and pasting them directly into your notes. *This is the same as taking direct quotes from your source.* To avoid plagiarism, identify such passages in an obvious way. Besides enclosing them in quotation marks, you could format them in a different font or color to help you remember that these are quotes from other sources. Just remember to reverse the formatting before turning in your paper.

Paraphrase carefully. Instead of using a direct quote, you might choose to paraphrase an author's words. Paraphrasing means restating the original passage in your own words, usually making it shorter and simpler. Students who copy a passage word for word and then just rearrange or delete a few phrases are running a serious risk of plagiarism. Consider this paragraph:

> *Higher education also offers you the chance to learn how to learn. In fact, that's the subject of this book. Employers value the person who is a "quick study" when it comes to learning a new job. That makes your ability to learn a marketable skill.*

Following is an improper paraphrase of that passage:

> *With higher education comes the chance to learn how to learn. Employers value the person who is a "quick study" when it comes to learning a new job. Your ability to learn is a marketable skill.*

A better paraphrase of the same passage would be this one:

> *The author notes that when we learn how to learn, we gain a skill that is valued by employers.*

Remember to cite a source for paraphrases, just as you do for direct quotes.

When you use the same sequence of ideas as one of your sources—even if you have not paraphrased or directly quoted—cite that source.

Summarize carefully. For some of your notes, you may simply want to summarize your source in a few sentences or paragraphs. To do this effectively:

- Read your source several times for understanding.
- Put your source away; then write a summary in your own words.
- In your summary, include only the author's major points.
- Check your summary against your source for accuracy.

Identify distinctive terms and phrases. Some ideas are closely identified with their individual creators. Students who present such ideas without mentioning the individual are plagiarizing. This is true even if they do not copy words, sentence structure, or overall organization of ideas.

For example, the phrase "seven habits of highly effective people" is closely linked to Stephen Covey, author of several books based on this idea. A student might write a paper titled "Habits of Effective People," using words, sentences, and a list of habits that differ completely from Covey's. However, the originality of this student's thinking could still be called into question. This student would be wise to directly mention Covey in the paper and acknowledge Covey's idea that effectiveness and habits are closely linked.

Note details about each source. Identify the source of any material that you quote, paraphrase, or summarize. For books, details about each source include the author, title, publisher, publication date, location of publisher, and page number. For articles from print sources, record the article title and the name of the magazine or journal as well. If you found the article in an academic or technical journal, also record the volume and number of the publication. A librarian can help identify these details.

If your source is a Web page, record as many identifying details as you can find—author, title, sponsoring organization, URL, publication date, and revision date. In addition, list the date that you accessed the page.

Cite your sources as endnotes or footnotes to your paper. Ask your instructor for examples of the format to use.

Submit only your own work. Turning in materials that have been written or revised by someone else puts your education at risk.

Allow time to digest your research. If you view research as a task that you can squeeze into a few hours, then you may end up more confused than enlightened. Instead, allow for time to reread and reflect on the facts you gather. This creates conditions for genuine understanding and original thinking.

In particular, take the time to do these things:

- Read over all your notes without feeling immediate pressure to write.
- Summarize major points of view on your topic, noting points of agreement and disagreement.
- Look for connections in your material—ideas, facts, and examples that occur in several sources.
- Note direct answers to your main and supporting research.
- Revise your thesis statement, based on discoveries from your research.
- Put all your notes away and write informally about what you want to say about your topic.
- Look for connections between your research and your life— ideas that you can verify based on personal experience. ■

You're One Click Away...
from finding examples online of the suggestions in this article.

SERVICE-LEARNING:
The art of learning by
CONTRIBUTING

As part of a service-learning project for a sociology course, students volunteer at a community center for older adults. For another service-learning project, history students interview people in veterans' hospitals about their war experiences. These students plan to share their interview results with a psychiatrist on the hospital staff.

Meanwhile, business students provide free tax-preparation help at a center for low-income people. Students in graphic arts classes create free promotional materials for charities. Other students staff a food cooperative and a community credit union.

These examples of actual projects from the National Service-Learning Clearinghouse demonstrate the working premise of service-learning: Volunteer work and other forms of contributing can become a vehicle for higher education.

Fill yourself up and give it back. In the spirit of the Power Process included earlier in this chapter, think of service-learning as a way to "find a bigger problem." This suggestion is based on one of the core values behind this book—making a positive contribution to the lives of other people.

From Master Student to Master Employee is about filling yourself up, taking care of yourself, being selfish, and meeting your needs. The techniques and suggestions in these pages focus on ways to get what you want out of school, work, and the rest of your life.

One of the results of all this successful selfishness is the capacity to contribute. This means giving back to your community in ways that enhance the lives of other people.

People who are satisfied with life can share that satisfaction with others. It is hard to contribute to another person's joy until you experience joy yourself. The same is true for love. When people are filled with love, they can more easily contribute love to others. Contributing is what's left to do when your needs are met. It completes the circle of giving and receiving.

Elements of service-learning. Service-learning generally includes three elements: meaningful community service, a formal academic curriculum, and time for students to reflect on what they learn from service. That reflection can include speeches, journal writing, and research papers.

> People who are satisfied with life can share that satisfaction with others. It is hard to contribute to another person's joy until you experience joy yourself. Contributing is what's left to do when your needs are met. It completes the circle of giving and receiving.

Service-learning creates a win–win scenario. For one thing, students gain the satisfaction of contributing. They also gain experiences that can guide their career choices and help them develop job skills.

At the same time, service-learning adds to the community a resource with a handsome return on investment. For example, participants in the Learn and Serve America program (administered by the Corporation for National and Community Service) provided community services valued at four times the program cost.[7]

Find service-learning courses. Many schools offer service-learning programs. Look in the index of your school catalog under "service-learning," and search your school's Web site using those key words. There might be a service-learning office on your campus.

Also turn to national organizations that keep track of service-learning opportunities. One is the Corporation for National and Community Service, a federal government agency (www.nationalservice.gov, 202-606-5000). You can also contact the National Service-Learning Clearinghouse (www.servicelearning.org, 866-245-7378). These resources can lead you to others, including service-learning programs in your state.

GETTING THE MOST FROM SERVICE-LEARNING

When you design a service-learning project, consider the following suggestions.

Follow your interests. Think of the persistent problems in the world—illiteracy, hunger, obesity, addictions, unemployment, poverty, and more. Which of them generate the strongest feelings in you? Which of them link to your possible career plans and choice of major? The place where passion intersects with planning often creates a useful opportunity for service-learning.

Choose partners carefully. Work with a community organization that has experience with students. Make sure that the organization has liability insurance to cover volunteers.

Learn about the organization. Once you connect with community organization, learn everything you can about it. Find its mission statement and explore its history. Find out what makes this organization unique. If the organization partners with others in the community, learn about those other organizations as well.

Handle logistics. Integrating service-learning into your schedule can call for detailed planning. If your volunteer work takes place off campus, arrange for transportation and allow for travel time.

Include ways to evaluate your project. From your Intention Statements, create action goals and outcome goals. *Action goals* state what you plan to do and how many people you intend to serve; for instance, "We plan to provide 100 hours of literacy tutoring to 10 people in the community." *Outcome goals* describe the actual impact that your project will have: "At the end of our project, 60 percent of the people we tutor will be able to write a résumé and fill out a job application." Build numbers into your goals whenever possible. That makes it easier to evaluate the success of your project.

Build long-term impact into your project. One potential pitfall of service-learning is that the programs are often short-lived. After students pack up and return to campus, programs can die. To avoid this outcome, make sure that other students or community members are willing to step in and take over for you when the semester ends.

Build transferable skills. Review the list of 60 transferable skills on page 24. Use this list as a way to stimulate your thinking. List the specific skills that you're developing through service-learning. Keep this list. It will come in handy when you write a résumé and fill out job applications. And before you plan to do another service-learning project, think about the skills you'd like to develop from that experience.

Make use of mistakes. If your project fails to meet its goals, then turn this result into an opportunity to learn. State—in writing—the obstacles you encountered and possible ways to overcome them. The solutions you offer will be worth gold to the people who follow in your footsteps. Sharing the lessons learned from mistakes is an act of service in itself.

Connect service-learning to critical thinking. Remember that a *service* activity does not necessarily become a *service* attitude. Students can engage in service-learning merely to meet academic requirements and add a line to their résumé. Or students can engage in service-learning as a way to make long-term changes in their beliefs and behavior.

The idea behind service-learning is that community action is a strategy for academic achievement. This is what distinguishes service-learning from other forms of volunteer activity. A service-learning course combines work in the community with activities in the classroom. Contributing to others becomes a powerful and effective way to learn.

Turn to a tool you've used throughout this book—the Discovery and Intention Journal Entry system. Write Discovery Statements about what you gain from service-learning and how you feel about what you're doing. Follow up with Intention Statements about what you'll do differently for your next service-learning experience.

To think critically and creatively about your service-learning project, also ask questions such as these:

- What service did you perform?

- What roles did your service project include, and who filled those roles?

- What knowledge and skills did you bring to this project?

- After being involved in this project, what new knowledge and skills do you want to gain?

- What did you learn from this experience that can make another service-learning project more successful?

- Will this service-learning project affect your choice of a major? If so, how?

- Will this service-learning project affect your career plans? If so, how?

Service-learning provides an opportunity to combine theory and practice, reflection and action, "book learning" and "real-world" experience. Education takes place as we reflect on our experiences and turn them into new insights and intentions. Use service-learning as a way to take your thinking skills to a whole new level. ■

You're One Click Away...
from finding more strategies online for effective service-learning.

masterstudentprofile

Lisa Price

(1962–) Author of Success Never Smelled So Sweet: How I Followed My Nose and Found My Passion

Today I am a successful businesswoman. But when I was twenty-eight years old, I filed for personal bankruptcy. I had spent a number of years chasing dreams, living over my head and hoping that I would be able to pay for it later. Well . . . I did pay—just not the way I had hoped. I reached a point where my credit-card balances were sky high. And I would later learn that with penalties and interest, I was also about $33,000 in debt to the Internal Revenue Service. I wasn't even thirty and I had already screwed up my life. . . .

. . . Over the next ten years, I focused on turning my life around—and did. . . . In my early thirties, I had taken one hundred dollars and created a business out of my love of good scents and lifelong hobby of creating fragrances. I started selling perfumes at flea markets as a way of supplementing my income, always reinvesting the profit back into my business. As it turns out, people liked my products and my venture began to blossom. My hobby-turned-business grew slowly, without bank loans or credit cards—my finances were too bad to qualify for either. . . . In time, my company, Carol's Daughter: Beauty by Nature, transformed itself into a successful boutique in the Fort Greene neighborhood of Brooklyn and online business. . . .

. . . How did I get myself into such a tough situation—and, more importantly, how did I dig myself out? Like many people I overextended myself by trying to keep up with others. . . . But when we're open to it, life's difficulties can teach us lessons . . . . I stopped trying to keep up with the Joneses and began to pay attention to myself—my inner Self. I learned to listen to the internal voice that spoke to me without fail, each and every day, whether or not I paid attention.

. . . As this was happening I learned to trust my gifts and talents. In my case I literally followed my nose

out of my difficulties and into a life I could never have imagined.

. . . As I run my company, teach classes, and speak to people, many tell me they long to do work that they love. Most tell me that financial fear keeps them stuck where they are. Not too long ago I felt trapped in a dead-end job like the seekers I describe. I want more women and men to experience the feeling of exhilaration and sense of satisfaction that living your passion brings.

LISA PRICE ... is willing to take risks.

YOU ... can take risks with more confidence when you define your values and align them with your actions.

Source: Excerpt from *Success Never Smelled So Sweet* by Lisa Price and Hillary Beard, pp. vii–x, © 2004 by Lisa Price and Hilary Beard. Reprinted by permission of Ballantine Books, a division of Random house, Inc. and William Morris Endeavor Entertainment, LLC on behalf of the Author. Any third party use of this material, outside of this publication, is prohibited. Interested parties must apply directly to Random House, Inc. for permission.

You're One Click Away...
from learning more about Lisa Price online at the Master Student Profiles. You can also visit the Master Student Hall of Fame to learn about other master students.

©iStockphoto.com/Mustang_79

FIVE Cs
FOR YOUR CAREER

CHARACTER • CRITICAL THINKING • CREATIVE THINKING • COLLABORATION • COMMUNICATION

One theory of education separates life into two distinct domains: work and school. One domain is the "real" world. The other is the place where you attend classes to prepare for the real world.

Consider another point of view: Success in higher education promotes success in the workplace. Starting now, read this book with a mental filter in place. Ask yourself:

- How can I use the content of this course to meet my career goals?

- How can I apply a technique from this book to my current job—or the next job I want to get?

- What ideas from this class would be worthwhile to share with my coworkers?

The answers to such questions can help you thrive in any job—and get the most value from every dollar that you spend on tuition.

Following are examples of ways to put suggestions from this chapter to work for you in the areas of:

- Character
- Communicating
- Creative thinking
- Collaborating
- Critical thinking

Look for an exercise like this one at the end of each chapter in this book. Use them to keep exploring these five crucial connections between work and school.

Develop character by seeing work as a way to align with your values. Review the "Power Process: Define your values, align your actions." Then think about your planned career. With what values does it align? How will your work contribute to the human community? How can you increase the value that your work creates? Put your answers to these questions in writing.

Consider that every job is grounded in certain values. People who work in health care are grounded in the value of promoting wellness and freedom from disease. Teachers are grounded in the value of promoting learning. Sales people are grounded in creating value for people by delivering products and services that solve problems for customers and clients.

It's been said that "profit comes from the creation of value." The same idea applies to any job.

Use the Discovery and Intention Journal Entry system to promote creative and critical thinking at work. Write Discovery Statements to note your current job skills, as well as areas for improvement. Also use Discovery Statements to describe what you want from your current job, and from your career over the long term. For encouragement to do this kind of creative thinking, review the "Power Process: Discover what you want" on page 2.

Follow up with Intention Statements that detail specifically what you want to be doing one year, five years, and ten years or more from today. Write additional Intention Statements about specific actions you can take to meet those career goals.

Any time that you take a general statement (such as a goal you want to meet) and translate it into more specific terms (such as specific actions you will take to meet that goal), you are engaging in critical thinking.

Develop communication skills by demonstrating civility in the workplace. Much of civility is communicated on a nonverbal level—not through specific words, but through your posture, gestures, and tone of voice. Civil behavior sends these unmistakable and valuable messages to your coworkers:

- *I regard you as equal in worth to me.*

- *It is worthwhile for me to grant you my full attention.*

- *I am going to work with you as a willing collaborator.*

Gain collaboration skills by developing a professional work ethic now. Most projects in the workplace get done by teams of people who collaborate. And people are more willing to collaborate with you when they know that you can be trusted to add value to a group, take on tasks, and complete them on time.

This characteristic—trustworthiness—is something that you can develop while you're in school. For example, a student who knows how to show up for class on time is ready to show up for work on time. A student who knows how to focus attention during a lecture is ready to focus attention during a training session at work. And a student who's worked cooperatively in a study group brings skills to the table when joining a project team at work.

Now, make a personal commitment to developing the five Cs. The first exercise in this book asked you to do a "reconnaissance" of its contents. Now it's time to take similar action with the five Cs in mind.

Start becoming a master employee this moment by reviewing this book's Table of Contents and scanning every page in the book. Focus especially on this chapter and Chapters 8 through 10, which explore the five Cs in detail.

As you do your reconnaissance, look for ways to complete the following sentences:

CHARACTER
An article with useful ideas for developing character is (include the title and page number) . . .

_____

One specific suggestion from this article that I want to know more about is . . .

_____

_____

CREATIVE THINKING
An article with useful ideas for creative thinking is (include the title and page number) . . .

_____

One specific suggestion from this article that I want to know more about is . . .

_____

_____

CRITICAL THINKING
An article with useful ideas for critical thinking is . . .

_____

One specific suggestion from this article that I want to know more about is . . .

_____

_____

COMMUNICATION
An article with useful ideas for communicating effectively is . . .

_____

One specific suggestion from this article that I want to know more about is . . .

_____

_____

COLLABORATION
An article with useful ideas for collaborating on a project with other people is . . .

_____

One specific suggestion from this article that I want to know more about is . . .

_____

_____

CHAPTER **1** QUIZ

Name _____

Date _____

1. This chapter explains two approaches to thinking about motivation. Summarize those approaches in one sentence each.
   One approach is to use the terms *self-discipline*, *willpower*, and *motivation* to describe something in ourselves that's missing. A second approach is thinking about motivation as something you already possess; stop assuming that motivation is mysterious, determined at birth, or hard to come by. (*Motivation—I'm just not in the mood*, page 32)

2. Define *plagiarism*, and list a strategy for preventing it.
   Plagiarism amounts to taking someone else's work and presenting it as your own—the equivalent of cheating on a test. Strategies to prevent (any one of the following): Know the perils of "paper mills." Identify direct quotes. Paraphrase carefully. Summarize carefully. Identify distinctive terms and phrases. Note details about each source. Cite your sources as endnotes or footnotes to your paper. Submit only your own work. Allow time to digest your research. (*Academic integrity: Avoid plagiarism*, page 41)

3. To use affirmations effectively, first determine what you want and then describe yourself as having it in the future. True or false? Explain your answer.
   False. Describe yourself as if you already have it. The most effective affirmations are personal, positive, and written in the present tense. (*Attitudes, affirmations, and visualizations*, page 30)

4. Define the term *classroom civility*, and give an example of it.
   Classroom civility refers to being respectful of others when you choose your behaviors. (Examples will vary.) If you must leave the class early, be sure to tell your instructor before class begins, sit near the exit, and leave quietly. (*Classroom civility—what's in it for you?* page 37)

5. According to the text, a professional work ethic includes
   (a) competence. **(b)** initiative. **(c)** humility. **(d)** sound judgment. **(e)** all of the above.
   (e) all of the above. (*Demonstrating a professional work ethic*, page 38)

6. List three costs of cheating.
   Any three of the following: You risk failing the course or getting expelled from college. You learn less. You lose time and money. Fear of getting caught promotes stress. Violating your values promotes stress. Cheating on tests can make it easier to violate your integrity again. Cheating lowers your self-concept. (*The high costs of cheating*, page 40)

7. According to the text, the simple act of defining your values will guarantee new results in your life. True or false? Explain your answer.
   False. Although defining your values is powerful, it doesn't guarantee any results. To achieve your goals, take actions that align with your values. (*Power Process: Define your values, align your actions*, page 28)

8. The recommended strategies for changing a habit do not include
   (a) telling the truth.
   (b) choosing and committing to a new behavior.
   (c) affirming your intention.
   (d) starting with a large change.
   (e) getting feedback and support.
   (d) starting with a large change. (*Ways to change a habit*, page 34)

9. According to the text, one sure-fire way to increase motivation is to try making many changes in your life all at once. True or false? Explain your answer.
   False. Focus on one change at a time. Tackling too many challenges at the same time makes them harder to follow through. (*Motivation—I'm just not in the mood*, page 32)

10. Define the word *etiquette*, and give an example of it.
    Etiquette refers to common courtesy, such as greeting people when you enter a room, saying please when making a request, saying thank you when the request is granted, opening an e-mail with a personal greeting for the recipient, and closing an e-mail with *Sincerely* or *Thank you* followed by your name.. (Examples will vary.) (*Demonstrating a professional work etiquette*, page 38)

CHAPTER 2

FIRST STEPS

Instructor Tools & Tips

"Once we have identified our special talents, it doesn't matter whether or not we find immediate success in them; what does matter is that we take a step each day towards our intended goal! " —Josh Hinds

"In oneself lies the whole world, and if you know how to look and learn, then the door is there, and the key is in your hand. Nobody on earth can give you either that key or the door to open, except yourself." —J. Krishnamurti

PREVIEW

Many students taking a student success course start out the semester with a high level of enthusiasm and energy, and that's good because there's a lot of meaty and important foundation material in the Introduction and in Chapter 1. If students learn the important concepts presented here, they are well on the way to achieving their educational goals. Remind your students that this chapter is about First Steps—and this includes exercises in self-discovery learning styles, and making transitions. Use the Master Student Map on the chapter opener page to inspire your students, stimulate class discussion, and preview the chapter topics.

GUEST SPEAKER

Consider inviting a faculty member from a popular course or two to talk about learning strategies used by their most successful students. Courses such as writing, math, psychology, and biology give students insight into what it takes to become a flexible learner.

LECTURE

Learning Style Inventory (pages LSI-1 through LSI-8)
Being aware of learning styles is an important strategy for success because it helps students understand differences in the ways people like to perceive and process new information. Your students will learn about their own preferred style of learning and how this tool can help them observe and ascertain the preferred teaching styles of their professors. Encourage students to share the instruments in this vital chapter with their significant others—friends and family. This helps create a support network for course principles, and also helps students understand that some issues may be a result of differences in learning styles and strengths. You may even find this buy-in leads to family members and friends enrolling in the course once they see the power of the principles in action.

The Learning Style Inventory (LSI) is a unifying theme woven throughout *From Master Student to Master Employee*. Activities are crafted to engage students not only in the strengths of their own learning preference but in the strengths of other styles as well. The Master Student Map at the beginning of each chapter can help students internalize the strategies taught in each chapter. Study skills do not transfer from a student success class to other courses accidentally. Explain that some individuals are not necessarily strong in the area of intrapersonal intelligence (Gardner's multiple intelligences) and may not be accustomed to thinking about their thinking (metacognition). But this is something that can be taught to a large extent. Even unaccustomed students can be made aware of the importance of understanding their own strengths and learning styles. It takes a talented and prepared instructor to help students build other schema and develop the confidence that is necessary to transfer new strategies to different learning settings. Teaching this might seem intimidating for first-time instructors. Remember, when you teach with *From Master Student to Master Employee*, you are not alone. Network with experienced college success teachers on your own campus. This saves time and can help you avoid frustration. Your support materials include a talented team of TeamUP consultants. Call (1-800-528-8323) or visit www.cengage.com/teamup today!

Additional resources to help guide you in administering the LSI and applying the Master Student Map and Learning Styles Application are on the Instructor Web site. A video for instructors is also available online.

Claim your multiple intelligences (page 63) Howard Gardner's theory of several types of intelligence complements this chapter's discussion of different learning styles: Both recognize that there are alternative ways for people to learn and assimilate knowledge. This article provides students with concepts for exploring additional methods to achieve success in school, work, and relationships. A chart on pages presents an overview of the characteristics of each type of intelligence, suggests possible learning strategies for each, and links the different types with possible careers. Have your students further explore these career choices as they consider different majors or areas of focused study.

EXERCISES/ACTIVITIES

1. **Power Process: Ideas are tools (page 50)** Each Power Process can be illustrated by a simple yet meaningful object lesson. For example, to illustrate this Power Process, bring a drinking straw, a spoon, a hammer, and a piece of chalk or whiteboard marker to class. Ask for volunteers to help write an assignment on the board. Hand out the various "ideas/tools" for them to use to write on the board. In seconds, all of the students will realize the power of this process. Although each of these ideas is an excellent tool for the job it was designed to do, only the student with the right tool is successful at the current task.

2. **Learning by seeing, hearing, and moving: The VAK system (pages 66–68)** Learning by seeing (visual learning), hearing (auditory learning), and moving (kinesthetic learning) allows students to perceive information through their senses. Engage your students by asking them to take the informal inventory and to continue to take First Steps of self-discovery. Have your students submit Discovery Statements to highlight the new strategies they have discovered and Intention Statements to describe the new options for learning that they intend to implement. Ask students to remember a time in their education when a teacher finally presented course material in a way that "connected" for them. Perhaps it was a science teacher who presented a concept in a hands-on manner that finally made sense. Suggest that students reflect on what learning style this successful teaching strategy used.

3. **The Discovery Wheel (pages 53–56)** The Discovery Wheel is a critical tool in this course. After students complete the Discovery Wheel in the book or online, ask them to consider their three lowest areas identified by the Discovery Wheel. Discuss these results in class. Did these test results surprise students? Do they agree with their results? Suggest that students notice their lowest areas. There are many resources available in the book and on the College Success CourseMate Web site that you may not assign. Encourage students to go on a reconnaissance mission through the book and the CourseMate Web site, focusing on their three lowest areas of the Discovery Wheel. Ask them to locate at least one exercise in the textbook or online, or one video online, they feel may be especially useful as they address these lowest areas. Share responses in class.

4. **Celebrate strengths** Assign students to create a visual representation of their strengths and multiple intelligences. This can be in the form of a collage, concept map, or other visual elements. Ask students to focus on the highest areas on the Discovery Wheel and on their multiple intelligences and learning styles. This is an interesting exercise for students who are not visual learners! Emphasize that students do not need to be good at drawing or art to complete a visual representation. Remind them that they all enjoyed cutting, coloring, and creating as children. Invite them to relax and have fun with this exercise. Share student creations in class.

CONVERSATION/SHARING

Refer students to the article First Step: Truth is a key to mastery on page 51. Assure students that even though this journey may feel intimidating at first, first steps are indeed challenging—and rewarding! As students complete the inventories in this chapter, remind them there are no right or wrong answers, but using these inventories as opportunities to take charge makes this an exciting process. Remind students that the work will be hard but rewarding if they are willing to invest the time and energy in the process. Ask students if they have heard about this course from former students. Share these stories aloud.

master instructor
BEST PRACTICE

" *I make this concrete comparison, which usually gets students' attention: If during this course, you put forth the effort and attention that most of us do when purchasing a cell phone, you will be surprised at your progress in this course. How sad it is that we will often research and do the legwork required to buy a phone, but we will not make improvements in the quality of our own lives and futures! This course is a gift that you can give yourselves and your families—a new and more aware you!* "

–Annette McCreedy, Nashville State Community College

HOMEWORK

The Discovery Wheel (pages 53–56) is an opportunity for students to take a First Step in telling the truth about the kind of student they are and the kind of student they want to become. This is not a test, but an opportunity for change. Students complete the Discovery Wheel in Chapter 2 and then again in Chapter 12. This enables them to measure their progress. Results from the Discovery Wheel exercises can be used in your course in a variety of ways. Consider the following suggestions:

- Ask students to list their intentions or commitments for improving particular skills during the term. At the end of the term, they can assess their progress in those areas by using the Discovery Wheel in Chapter 12.

- As an alternative to the textbook version of the Discovery Wheel, have your students fill out the online interactive Discovery Wheel found on the CourseMate Web site. Note that this online version does not include number ratings, so the results will be formatted differently from the results of the Discovery Wheel in the text.

- Create an assignment requiring students to contact people on campus or in the community who can assist them in enhancing particular skills. For example, the reading center or learning center can provide specific strategies for improving comprehension, word attack skills, and concentration.

- Allow the Discovery Wheel exercises to help shape course content. You can use the results to plan future lessons or to determine what students want to learn or accomplish during the course as a result of their self-assessments. You might create assignments for each component of the Discovery Wheel, asking students to complete the assignments for their three lowest areas of the Discovery Wheel. This allows students to focus on their own self-identified weak areas, without feeling like they are involved in "busywork." Suggest the following analogy: The components of your Discovery Wheel are like the components of a functioning automobile. Although the car can function even though the tires are somewhat worn, it can perform optimally when all components receive attention. Likewise, by addressing their lowest areas of the Discovery Wheel, they can improve their performance and increase their chances of college success.

- Ask students to form small groups and coach each other. Coaching could include how to capitalize on and share talents and how to strengthen areas for growth. If you choose to do this activity, let students know your reasons for forming small groups. For many, self-assessment is personal, and sharing the results might seem risky. Ask students to take their best suggestions and implement them.

- Create a resource network. List the titles from each section of the Discovery Wheel (Self-Discovery, Time & Money, Memory, and so on) on a piece of paper. Ask students to add their names to a sign-up sheet if they are willing to assist others in enhancing their skills in a particular area. Then distribute the lists to the class or post them on your course Web site.

EVALUATION

Quiz Ideas for Chapter 2

Ask students to:

- Describe the role of truth in the mastery of student success.

- Describe their discoveries from completing the Discovery Wheel.

- Describe their preferred Learning Style and the characteristics of students who like to learn using this style.

- List some challenges in college for someone with their particular Learning Style. Ask students to explain and give examples.

- Name and give examples of two multiple intelligences.

- Describe the ways in which they are smart (their talents and gifts), and relate these to the appropriate multiple intelligences.

master instructor
BEST PRACTICE

"To save class time for instruction and discussion, I tell my students that I am going to select only one 10-point question for the quiz. It will be one of the questions in the book quiz. I present the question and ask students to respond using the three-part quiz forms (available through your sales rep). When they are through answering the question, I remind students to write their name on the quiz before tearing off the white sheet and handing it in. Then they compare answers with the person next to them to seek insights from each other. If they did not have the answer, I tell them that if they return the pink sheet with the answers to all 10 questions, I will give them 7 out of 10 points."

—Eldon McMurray, Utah Valley State College

Additional Digital Resources for Chapter 2

What can you ASSIGN FROM THE COURSEMATE for From Master Student to Master Employee?

- **Discovery Wheel.** The Discovery Wheel has 12 spokes that represent the 12 themes (and chapters) in the book. The self-awareness that students gain through using this interactive tool provides them with a foundation for honestly assessing their experiences for the rest of their lives. Students simply rate their responses to the questions, and the wheel does the rest! The online Discovery Wheel is particularly useful in an online class where paper versions can't be turned in or reviewed.

- **Video Skillbuilders.** These interactive online tools combine video clips featuring discussions with students, instructors, and experts, with articles and activities designed to give students a fully engaging learning experience. Either view and experience these together in class, or have students view them as a homework assignment and respond to the viewing questions and reflective exercise. These modules are good matches for Chapter 2:

  - Motivation and Goal Setting: Staying Motivated and Making a Contribution
  - Motivation and Goal Setting: Staying Motivated as an Adult Learner
  - Learning Styles: The VAK
  - Learning Styles: The Kolb Learning Style Inventory

  Note that Video Skillbuilders are available for every chapter.

- **Learning Style Inventory.** Students can take the full Learning Style Inventory online and have their results immediately plotted on the Learning Styles Graph. Descriptions of what each style and mode means are provided, as well a video about how one's Learning Style Profile can impact group work. Students are able to print and e-mail their results, so consider having students take the inventory and print out or e-mail their results to you.

CourseMate *To access CourseMate, your students need to visit* www.cengagebrain .com. *At the CengageBrain.com home page, students search for the ISBN of* Becoming a Master Student *(from the back cover of the book), using the search box at the top of the page. This takes them to the product page where these resources can be found.*

Did you know that THESE RESOURCES (and many more) ARE AVAILABLE on the INSTRUCTOR COMPANION SITE?

- **Need guidance on how to teach with the Discovery Wheel and Learning Style Inventory?** The **Master Teachers in Action videos** provide you with an inside look at how *From Master Student to Master Employee* is used by professors, including information on their favorite parts, and how specific articles and activities from the text prepare students for achieving success. Hear from Dave Ellis himself and other instructors about what works for them when teaching the Discovery Wheel and the Learning Style Inventory.

- **Looking for fresh, innovative ways to teach Chapter 2 topics?** Browse through the Best Practices library to see what other Master Instructors have been successfully doing with their students.

master instructor
BEST PRACTICE

Your Multiple Intelligence, Dissected. *Have students take the free multiple intelligence inventory at http://www.ldpride.net/learningstyles.MI.htm. This exercise helps students identify their particular type of intelligence and shows them characteristics, possible learning strategies, and careers unique to them. Because this inventory is located on a site for individuals with disabilities, we talk about why it would be important for people with disabilities to understand how they learn the best. We discuss what it will do for them in their work environment as well as everyday life. We have many thought provoking conversations about this topic just by accessing the site!*

–Krista Clay-Lieffring, Neosho County Community College

Please visit login.cengage.com *to log in and access the Instructor Companion Site.*

First Steps

Use this **Master Student Map** to ask yourself

WHY THIS CHAPTER MATTERS . . .

- Success starts with telling the truth about what is working—and what isn't—in our lives right now.

WHAT IS INCLUDED . . .

HOW I CAN USE THIS CHAPTER. . .

- Experience the power of telling the truth about my current skills.
- Discover my preferred learning styles.
- Choose learning strategies that promote my success.

WHAT IF . . .

- I could start to create new outcomes in my life by accepting the way I am right now?

© Ruslan Ivantsov/Shutterstock.com

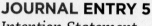

JOURNAL ENTRY 5
Intention Statement

Create value from this chapter

S kim this chapter for three techniques that you'd like to use in school or in your personal life during the upcoming week. List each technique and a related page number here.

I intend to use . . .

_____

_____

_____

_____

_____

_____

_____

_____

_____

_____

_____

_____

_____

_____

_____

_____

POWER process

Ideas are tools

There are many ideas in this book. When you first encounter them, don't believe any of them. Instead, think of the ideas as tools.

For example, you use a hammer for a purpose—to drive a nail. You don't try to figure out whether the hammer is "right." You just use it. If it works, you use it again. If it doesn't work, you get a different hammer.

People have plenty of room in their lives for different kinds of hammers, but they tend to limit their openness to different kinds of ideas. A new idea, at some level, is a threat to their very being—unlike a new hammer, which is simply a new hammer.

Most of us have a built-in desire to be right. Our ideas, we often think, represent ourselves.

Some ideas are worth dying for. But please note: This book does not contain any of those ideas. The ideas on these pages are strictly "hammers."

Imagine someone defending a hammer. Picture this person holding up a hammer and declaring, "I hold this hammer to be self-evident. Give me this hammer or give me death. Those other hammers are flawed. There are only two kinds of people in this world: people who believe in this hammer and people who don't."

That ridiculous picture makes a point. This book is not a manifesto. It's a toolbox, and tools are meant to be used.

If you read about a tool in this book that doesn't sound "right" or one that sounds a little goofy, remember that the ideas here are for using, not necessarily for believing. Suspend your judgment. Test the idea for yourself. If it works, use it. If it doesn't, don't use it.

Any tool—whether it's a hammer, a computer program, or a study technique based on your knowledge of learning styles—is designed to do a specific job. A master mechanic carries a variety of tools, because no single tool works for all jobs. If you throw a tool away because it doesn't work in one situation, you won't be able to pull it out later when it's just what you need. So if an idea doesn't work for you and you are satisfied that you gave it a fair chance, don't throw it away. File it away instead. The idea might come in handy soon.

And remember, this book is not about figuring out the "right" way. Even the "ideas are tools" approach is not "right."

It's a hammer . . . (or maybe a saw).

You're One Click Away...
from accessing the Power Process Media online and finding out more about how "ideas are tools."

First Step: Truth is a *key to mastery*

The First Step technique is simple: Tell the truth about who you are and what you want. The First Step is one of the most valuable tools in this book. It magnifies the power of all the other techniques. It is a key to becoming a master student—and employee.

To succeed in school, tell the truth about what kind of student you are and what kind of student you want to become. Success starts with telling the truth about what *is* working—and what is *not* working—in our lives right now. When we acknowledge our strengths, we gain an accurate picture of what we can accomplish. When we admit that we have a problem, we are free to find a solution. Ignoring the truth, on the other hand, can lead to problems that stick around for decades.

FIRST STEPS ARE UNIVERSAL

An article about telling the truth might sound like pie-in-the-sky moralizing. However, there is nothing pie-in-the-sky or moralizing about a First Step. It is a practical, down-to-earth principle to use whenever we want to change our behavior.

When you see a doctor, the First Step is to tell the truth about your current symptoms. That way you can get an accurate diagnosis and effective treatment plan. This principle is universal. It works for just about any problem in any area of life.

First Steps are used by millions of people who want to turn their lives around. No technique in this book has been field-tested more often or more successfully—or under tougher circumstances.

For example, members of Alcoholics Anonymous start by telling the truth about their drinking. Their First Step is to admit that they are powerless over alcohol. That's when their lives start to change.

People dealing with a variety of other challenges—including troubled relationships with food, drugs, sex, and work—also start by telling the truth. They use First Steps to change their behavior, and they do it for a reason: First Steps work.

FIRST STEPS ARE CHALLENGING— AND REWARDING

Let's be truthful: It's not easy to tell the truth about ourselves. It's not fun to admit our weaknesses. We might end up admitting that we don't complete term papers on time or that coming up with the money to pay for tuition is a constant challenge.

There is another way to think about self-evaluations. If we could see them as opportunities to solve problems and take charge of our lives, we might welcome them.

It may seem natural to judge our own shortcomings and feel bad about them. Some people believe that such feelings are necessary to correct their errors. Others think that a healthy dose of shame can prevent the moral decay of our society.

Think again. Consider the opposite idea: We can gain skill without feeling rotten about the past. We can change the way things *are* without having to criticize the way things *have been*. We can learn to see shame or blame as excess baggage and set them aside.

If the whole idea of telling the truth about yourself puts a knot in your stomach, that's good. Notice the knot. It is your friend. It is a reminder that First Steps call for courage and compassion. These are qualities of a master student.

FIRST STEPS FREE US TO CHANGE

Master students get the most value from a First Step by turning their perceived shortcomings into goals. "I don't exercise enough" turns into "I will walk briskly for 30 minutes at least three times per week."

Another quality of master students is that they refuse to let their First Steps turn into excuses. These students avoid using the phrase "I can't" and its endless variations.

The key is to state First Steps in a way that allows for new possibilities in the future. Use language in a way that reinforces your freedom to change. For example, "I can't succeed in math" is better stated like this: "During math courses, I tend to get confused early in the term and find it hard to ask questions. I could be more assertive in asking for help right away."

Telling the truth about what we don't want gives us more clarity about what we *do* want. By taking a First Step, we can free up all the energy that it takes to deny our problems and avoid change. We can redirect that energy and use it to take actions that align with our values.

FIRST STEPS INCLUDE STRENGTHS

For some of us, it's even harder to recognize our strengths than to recognize our weaknesses. Maybe we don't want to brag. Maybe we're attached to a poor self-image.

The reasons don't matter. The point is that using the First Step technique means telling the truth about our positive qualities, too.

Remember that weaknesses are often strengths taken to an extreme. The student who carefully revises her writing can make significant improvements in a term paper. If she revises too much and hands in the paper late, though, her grade might suffer. Any success strategy carried too far can backfire.

FIRST STEPS ARE SPECIFIC

Whether written or verbal, the ways that we express our First Steps are more powerful when they are specific. For example, if you want to improve your note-taking skills, you might write, "I am an awful note taker"; but it would be more effective to write, "I can't read 80 percent of the notes I took in Introduction to Psychology last week, and I have no idea what was important in that class."

The exercises and Journal Entries in this chapter are all about getting specific. They can help you tap resources you never knew you had. For example, do the Discovery Wheel to get a big-picture view of your personal effectiveness. And use the Learning Styles Inventory, along with the articles about multiple intelligences and the VAK system, to tell the truth about how you perceive and process information.

As you use these elements of this book you might feel surprised at what you discover. You might even disagree with the results of an exercise. That's fine. Just tell the truth about it. Use your disagreement as a tool for further discussion and self-discovery. ■

✓ CRITICAL THINKING EXERCISE 6

Taking the First Step

The purpose of this exercise is to give you a chance to discover and acknowledge your own strengths, as well as areas for improvement. For many students, this exercise is the most difficult one in the book. To make the exercise worthwhile, do it with courage.

Some people suggest that looking at areas for improvement means focusing on personal weaknesses. They view it as a negative approach that runs counter to positive thinking. Well, perhaps. Positive thinking is a great technique. So is telling the truth, especially when we see the whole picture—the negative aspects as well as the positive ones.

If you admit that you can't add or subtract and that's the truth, then you have taken a strong, positive First Step toward learning basic math. On the other hand, if you say that you are a terrible math student and that's not the truth, then you are programming yourself to accept unnecessary failure.

The point is to tell the truth. This exercise is similar to the Discovery Statements that appear throughout the chapters. The difference is that, in this case, for reasons of confidentiality, you won't write down your discoveries in the book.

You are likely to disclose some things about yourself that you wouldn't want others to read. You might even write down some truths that could get you into trouble. Do this exercise on separate sheets of paper; then hide or destroy them. Protect your privacy. To make this exercise work, follow these suggestions.

Be specific. It is not effective to write, "I can improve my communication skills." Of course you can. Instead, write down precisely what you can *do* to improve your communication skills—for example, "I can spend more time really listening while the other person is talking, instead of thinking about what I'm going to say next."

Be self-aware. Look beyond the classroom. What goes on outside school often has the greatest impact on your ability to be an effective student. Consider your strengths and weaknesses that you may think have nothing to do with school.

Be courageous. This exercise calls for an important master student quality—courage. It is a waste of time if this exercise is done half-heartedly. Be willing to take risks. You might open a door that reveals a part of yourself that you didn't want to admit was there. The power of this technique is that once you know what is there, you can do something about it.

Part 1

Time yourself, and for 10 minutes write as fast as you can, completing each of the following sentences at least 10 times with anything that comes to mind. If you get stuck, don't stop. Just write something—even if it seems crazy.

I never succeed when I . . .

I'm not very good at . . .

Something I'd like to change about myself is . . .

Part 2

When you have completed the first part of the exercise, review what you have written, crossing off things that don't make any sense. The sentences that remain suggest possible goals for becoming a master student.

Part 3

Here's the tough part. Time yourself, and for 10 minutes write as fast as you can, completing the following sentences with anything that comes to mind. As in Part 1, complete each sentence at least 10 times. Just keep writing, even if it sounds silly.

I always succeed when I . . .

I am very good at . . .

Something I like about myself is . . .

Part 4

Review what you have written, and circle the things that you can fully celebrate. This list is a good thing to keep for those times when you question your own value and worth.

You're One Click Away...
from completing this exercise online under Exercises.

✔ CRITICAL THINKING EXERCISE 7

THE DISCOVERY WHEEL

The Discovery Wheel is another opportunity to tell the truth about the kind of student you are and the kind of student you want to become. Like many other students, you might find the Discovery Wheel to be the most valuable exercise in the book.

This is not a test. There are no trick questions, and the answers will have meaning only for yourself.

Here are two suggestions to make this exercise more effective. First, think of it as the beginning of an opportunity to change. There is another Discovery Wheel at the end of this book. You will have a chance to measure your progress there, so be honest about where you are now. Second, lighten up. A little laughter can make self-evaluations a lot more effective.

Here's how the Discovery Wheel works. By the end of this exercise, you will have filled in a circle similar to the one on this page. The Discovery Wheel circle is a picture of how you see yourself as a student. The closer the shading comes to the outer edge of the circle, the higher the evaluation of a specific skill. In the example below, the student has rated her reading skills low and her note-taking skills high.

The terms *high* and *low* are not meant to reflect judgment. The Discovery Wheel is not a permanent picture of who you are. It is a picture of how you view your strengths and weaknesses as a student today. To begin this exercise, read the statements beginning on the next page and award yourself points for each one, using the point system described below. Then add up your point total for each section, and shade the Discovery Wheel on page 56 to the appropriate level.

5 points: This statement is always or almost always true of me.

4 points: This statement is often true of me.

3 points: This statement is true of me about half the time.

2 points: This statement is seldom true of me.

1 point: This statement is never or almost never true of me.

© Cengage Learning

1. _____ I live by a set of values that translates into daily actions.
2. _____ I am willing to accept challenges even when I'm not sure how to meet them.
3. _____ I take responsibility for the quality of my education—and my life.
4. _____ I am gaining skills to support my success in school and in the workplace.
5. _____ I monitor my attitudes and change them when appropriate.
6. _____ I monitor my habits and change them when appropriate.
7. _____ I take effective action even when I don't feel "motivated."
8. _____ I demonstrate a professional work ethic.

_____ Total score (1) Character

1. _____ I enjoy learning.
2. _____ I understand and apply the concept of multiple intelligences.
3. _____ I connect my courses to my purpose for being in school.
4. _____ I make a habit of assessing my personal strengths and areas for improvement.
5. _____ I am satisfied with how I am progressing toward achieving my goals.
6. _____ I use my knowledge of learning styles to support my success in school.
7. _____ I am willing to consider any idea that can help me succeed in school—even if I initially disagree with that idea.
8. _____ I regularly remind myself of the benefits I intend to get from my education.

_____ Total score (2) Self-discovery

1. _____ I set long-term goals and periodically review them.
2. _____ I set short-term goals to support my long-term goals.
3. _____ I write a plan for each day and each week.
4. _____ I assign priorities to what I choose to do each day.
5. _____ I can access a variety of resources to finance my education.
6. _____ I take on debts carefully and repay them on time.
7. _____ I have long-range financial goals and a plan to meet them.
8. _____ I pay off the balance on credit card accounts each month.

_____ Total score (3) Time & Money

1. _____ I am confident of my ability to remember.
2. _____ I can remember people's names.
3. _____ At the end of a lecture, I can summarize what was presented.
4. _____ I apply techniques that enhance my memory skills.
5. _____ I can recall information when I'm under pressure.
6. _____ I remember important information clearly and easily.
7. _____ I can jog my memory when I have difficulty recalling.
8. _____ I can relate new information to what I've already learned.

_____ Total score (4) Memory

1. _____ I preview and review reading assignments.
2. _____ When reading, I ask myself questions about the material.
3. _____ I underline or highlight important passages when reading.
4. _____ When I read textbooks, I am alert and awake.
5. _____ I relate what I read to my life.
6. _____ I select a reading strategy to fit the type of material I'm reading.
7. _____ I take effective notes when I read.
8. _____ When I don't understand what I'm reading, I note my questions and find answers.

_____ Total score (5) Reading

1. _____ When I am in class, I focus my attention.
2. _____ I take notes in class.
3. _____ I am aware of various methods for taking notes and choose those that work best for me.
4. _____ I distinguish important material and note key phrases in a lecture.
5. _____ I copy down material that the instructor writes on the board or overhead display.
6. _____ I can put important concepts into my own words.
7. _____ My notes are valuable for review.
8. _____ I review class notes within 24 hours.

_____ Total score (6) Notes

1. _____ I use techniques to manage stress related to exams.
2. _____ I manage my time during exams and am able to complete them.
3. _____ I am able to predict test questions.
4. _____ I adapt my test-taking strategy to the kind of test I'm taking.
5. _____ I understand what essay questions ask and can answer them completely and accurately.
6. _____ I start reviewing for tests at the beginning of the term.
7. _____ I continue reviewing for tests throughout the term.
8. _____ My sense of personal worth is independent of my test scores.

_____ **Total score (7) Tests**

1. _____ I have flashes of insight and think of solutions to problems at unusual times.
2. _____ I use brainstorming to generate solutions to a variety of problems.
3. _____ When I get stuck on a creative project, I use specific methods to get unstuck.
4. _____ I apply the results of my thinking to make effective decisions and solve problems.
5. _____ I am willing to consider different points of view and alternative solutions.
6. _____ I can detect common errors in logic.
7. _____ I construct viewpoints by drawing on information and ideas from many sources.
8. _____ As I share my viewpoints with others, I am open to their feedback.

_____ **Total score (8) Creative & Critical Thinking**

1. _____ I am honest with others about who I am, what I feel, and what I want.
2. _____ Other people tell me that I am a good listener.
3. _____ I can communicate anger, sadness, and fear without blaming others.
4. _____ I can make friends and create valuable relationships in a new setting.
5. _____ I am open to being with people I don't especially like in order to learn from them.
6. _____ I can effectively plan and research a large writing assignment.
7. _____ I create first drafts without criticizing my writing, then edit later for clarity, accuracy, and coherence.
8. _____ I know ways to prepare and deliver effective presentations.

_____ **Total score (9) Communicating**

1. _____ I build rewarding relationships with people from diverse backgrounds.
2. _____ I work cooperatively with others to meet shared goals.
3. _____ I add value to study groups and to teams in the workplace.
4. _____ I can plan a project with multiple steps and deliver quality results on time.
5. _____ I am willing to assume a leadership role when that's appropriate.
6. _____ I can resolve conflict with family members, friends, and coworkers.
7. _____ I ask for help when a problem is too big for me to handle alone.
8. _____ I respond effectively to my emotions and stay aware of how other people feel.

_____ **Total score (10) Collaborating**

1. _____ I have enough energy to study and work—and still enjoy other areas of my life.
2. _____ If the situation calls for it, I have enough reserve energy to put in a long day.
3. _____ The way I eat supports my long-term health.
4. _____ The way I eat is independent of my feelings of self-worth.
5. _____ I exercise regularly to maintain a healthful weight.
6. _____ My emotional health supports my ability to learn.
7. _____ I notice changes in my physical condition and respond effectively.
8. _____ I am in control of any alcohol or other drugs I put into my body.

_____ **Total score (11) Health**

1. _____ I see learning as a lifelong process.
2. _____ I relate school to what I plan to do for the rest of my life.
3. _____ I have a written career plan and update it regularly.
4. _____ I am building positive relationships with people who support my career plan.
5. _____ I use effective strategies to find a job.
6. _____ I find ways to create value from any job.
7. _____ I use mentoring, internships, on-the-job training, and other strategies to learn at work.
8. _____ I stay up to date on new developments in my career field.

_____ **Total score (12) Career Management**

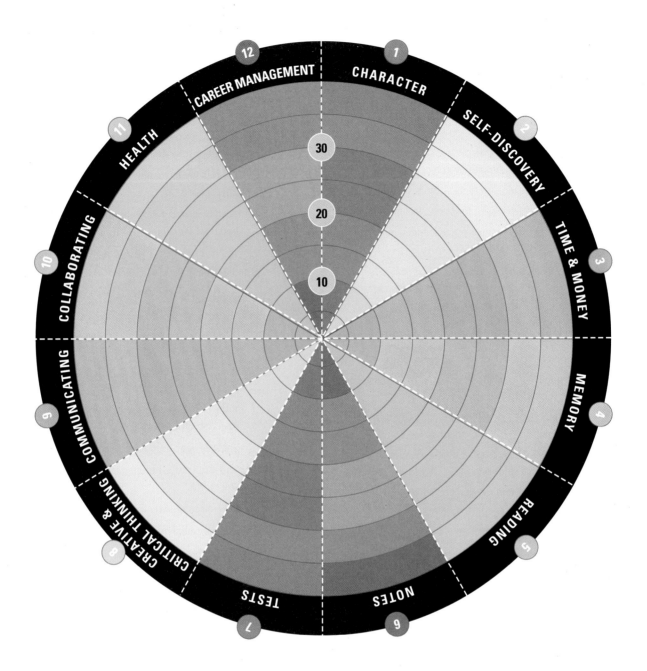

FILLING IN YOUR DISCOVERY WHEEL

Using the total score from each category, shade in each section of the Discovery Wheel. Use different colors, if you want. For example, you could use green to denote areas you want to work on. ■

You're One Click Away...
from having your Discovery Wheel scores calculated automatically for you online.

LEARNING STYLES
Discovering how you learn

Right now, you are investing substantial amounts of time, money, and energy in your education. What you get in return for this investment depends on how well you understand the process of learning and use it to your advantage.

If you don't understand learning, you might feel bored or confused in class. After getting a low grade, you might have no idea how to respond. Over time, frustration can mount to the point where you question the value of being in school.

Some students answer that question by dropping out of school. These students lose a chance to create the life they want, and society loses the contributions of educated workers.

You can prevent that outcome. Gain strategies for going beyond boredom and confusion. Discover new options for achieving goals, solving problems, listening more fully, speaking more persuasively, and resolving conflicts between people. Start by understanding the different ways that people create meaning from their experience and change their behavior. In other words, learn about *how* we learn.

WE LEARN BY PERCEIVING AND PROCESSING

When we learn well, says psychologist David Kolb, two things happen.[1] First, we *perceive*. That is, we notice events and "take in" new experiences.

Second, we *process*. We "deal with" experiences in a way that helps us make sense of them.

Some people especially prefer to perceive through *feeling* (also called *concrete experience*). They like to absorb information through their five senses. They learn by getting directly involved in new experiences. When solving problems, they rely on intuition as much as intellect. These people typically function well in unstructured classes that allow them to take initiative.

Some people prefer to process by *watching* (also called *reflective observation*). They prefer to stand back, watch what is going on, and think about it. They consider several points of view as they attempt to make sense of things and generate many ideas about how something happens. They value patience, good judgment, and a thorough approach to learning.

Other people like to perceive by *thinking* (also called *abstract conceptualization*). They take in information best when they can think about it as a subject separate from themselves. They analyze, intellectualize, and create theories. Often these people take a scientific approach to problem solving and excel in traditional classrooms.

Other people like to process by *doing* (also called *active experimentation*). They prefer to jump in and start doing things immediately. These people do not mind taking risks as they attempt to make sense of things; this helps them learn. They are results oriented and look for practical ways to apply what they have learned.

PERCEIVING AND PROCESSING—AN EXAMPLE

Suppose that you get a new cell phone. It has more features than any phone you've used before. You have many options for learning how to use it. For example:

- Just get your hands on the phone right away, press some buttons, and see whether you can dial a number or send a text message.
- Recall experiences you've had with phones in the past and what you've learned by watching other people use their cell phones.
- Read the instruction manual and view help screens on the phone before you try to make a call.
- Ask a friend who owns the same type of phone to coach you as you experiment with making calls and sending messages.

These actions illustrate the different approaches to learning:

- Getting your hands on the phone right away and seeing whether you can make it work is an example of learning through *feeling* (or *concrete experience*).
- Recalling what you've experienced in the past is an example of learning through *watching* (or *reflective observation*).
- Reading the manual and help screens before you use the phone is an example of learning through *thinking* (or *abstract conceptualization*).
- Asking a friend to coach you through a "hands-on" activity with the phone is an example of learning through *doing* (or *active experimentation*).

In summary, your learning style is the unique way that you blend feeling, thinking, watching, and doing. You tend to use this approach in learning anything—from cell phones to English composition to calculus. Reading the next few pages and doing the recommended activities will help you explore your learning style in more detail. ▪

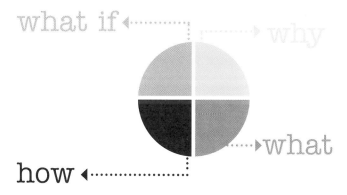

Journal Entry 6
Discovery Statement

Prepare for the Learning Style Inventory (LSI)

As a "warm-up" for the Learning Style Inventory that follows, think about times when you felt successful at learning. Underline or highlight any of the following statements that describe those situations.

- I was in a structured setting, with a lot of directions about what to do.
- I was free to learn at my own pace and in my own way.
- I learned as part of a small group.
- I learned mainly by working alone in a quiet place.
- I learned in a place where there was a lot of activity going on.
- I formed pictures in my mind.
- I learned by *doing* something—moving around, touching something, or trying out a process for myself.
- I learned by talking to myself or explaining ideas to other people.
- I got the "big picture" before I tried to understand the details.
- I listened to a lecture and then thought about it after class.
- I read a book or article and then thought about it afterward.
- I used a variety of media—such as videos, films, audio recordings, or computers—to assist my learning.
- I was considering where to attend school and had to actually set foot on each campus before choosing.
- I was shopping for a car and paid more attention to how I felt about test-driving each one than to the sticker prices or mileage estimates.
- I was thinking about going to a movie and carefully read the reviews before choosing one.

Reviewing this list, do you see any patterns in the way you prefer to learn? If so, briefly describe them.

Directions for completing the Learning Style Inventory

To help you become more aware of learning styles, a psychologist named David Kolb developed the Learning Style Inventory (LSI). This inventory is included on the next page. Responding to the items in the LSI can help you discover a lot about the ways you learn. Following the LSI are suggestions for using your results to promote your success.

The LSI is not a test. There are no right or wrong answers. Your goal is simply to develop a profile of your current learning style. So, take the LSI quickly. You might find it useful to recall a recent time when you learned something new at school, home, or work. However, do not agonize over your responses.

Note that the LSI consists of 12 sentences, each with four different endings. You will read each sentence, and then write a "4" next to the ending that best describes the way you currently learn. Then you will continue ranking the other endings with a "3," "2," or "1," representing the ending that least describes you. This is a forced-choice inventory, so you must rank each ending. Do not leave any endings blank. Use each number only once for each question.

Following are more specific directions:

1. Before you write on page LSI–1, remove the sheet of paper following page LSI–2.
2. Read the instructions at the top of page LSI–1. When you understand example A, you are ready to begin.
3. While writing on page LSI–1, *press firmly* so that your answers will show up on page LSI–3.

Learning Style Inventory

Complete items 1–12 below. Use the following example as a guide:

A. When I learn: _2_ I am happy.   _3_ I am fast.   _4_ I am logical.   _1_ I am careful.

Remember: **4** = Most like you   **3** = Second most like you   **2** = Third most like you   **1** = Least like you

Do not leave any endings blank. Use each number only once for each question. Before completing the items, remove the sheet of paper following this page. While writing, press firmly.

1. When I learn:	_____ I like to deal with my feelings.	_____ I like to think about ideas.	_____ I like to be doing things.	_____ I like to watch and listen.
2. I learn best when:	_____ I listen and watch carefully.	_____ I rely on logical thinking.	_____ I trust my hunches and feelings.	_____ I work hard to get things done.
3. When I am learning:	_____ I tend to reason things out.	_____ I am responsible about things.	_____ I am quiet and reserved.	_____ I have strong feelings and reactions.
4. I learn by:	_____ feeling.	_____ doing.	_____ watching.	_____ thinking.
5. When I learn:	_____ I am open to new experiences.	_____ I look at all sides of issues.	_____ I like to analyze things, break them down into their parts.	_____ I like to try things out.
6. When I am learning:	_____ I am an observing person.	_____ I am an active person.	_____ I am an intuitive person.	_____ I am a logical person.
7. I learn best from:	_____ observation.	_____ personal relationships.	_____ rational theories.	_____ a chance to try out and practice.
8. When I learn:	_____ I like to see results from my work.	_____ I like ideas and theories.	_____ I take my time before acting.	_____ I feel personally involved in things.
9. I learn best when:	_____ I rely on my observations.	_____ I rely on my feelings.	_____ I can try things out for myself.	_____ I rely on my ideas.
10. When I am learning:	_____ I am a reserved person.	_____ I am an accepting person.	_____ I am a responsible person.	_____ I am a rational person.
11. When I learn:	_____ I get involved.	_____ I likc to observe.	_____ I evaluate things.	_____ I like to be active.
12. I learn best when:	_____ I analyze ideas.	_____ I am receptive and open-minded.	_____ I am careful.	_____ I am practical.

Taking the next steps

Now that you've finished taking the Learning Style Inventory, you probably have some questions about what it means. You're about to discover some answers! In the following pages, you will find instructions for:

- *Scoring your inventory (page LSI–3)*
- *Plotting your scores on to a Learning Style Graph that literally gives a "big picture" of your learning style (page LSI–5)*
- *Interpreting your Learning Style Graph by seeing how it relates to four distinct modes, or styles, of learning (page LSI–6)*
- *Developing all four modes of learning (page LSI–7)*
- *Balancing your learning preferences (page LSI–8)*

Take your time to absorb all this material. Be willing to read through it several times and ask questions.

Your efforts will be rewarded. In addition to discovering more details about *how* you learn, you'll gain a set of strategies for applying this knowledge to your courses. With these strategies, you can use your knowledge of learning styles to actively promote your success in school.

Above all, aim to recover your natural gift for learning—the defining quality of a master student. Rediscover a world where the boundaries between learning and fun, between work and play, all disappear. While immersing yourself in new experiences, blend the sophistication of an adult with the wonder of a child. This path is one that you can travel for the rest of your life.

Remove this sheet before completing the Learning Style Inventory.

This page is inserted to ensure that the other writing you do in this book doesn't show through on page LSI–3.

Remove this sheet before completing the Learning Style Inventory.

This page is inserted to ensure that the other writing you do in this book doesn't show through on page LSI–3.

Scoring your Inventory

Now that you have taken the Learning Style Inventory, it's time to fill out the Learning Style Graph (page LSI-5) and interpret your results. To do this, follow these steps.

STEP 1 First, add up all of the numbers you gave to the items marked with brown F letters. Then write down that total in the box to the right, next to **"Brown F."**

Next, add up all of the numbers for **"Teal W," "Purple T,"** and **"Orange D,"** and also write down those totals in the box to the right.

STEP 2 Add the four totals to arrive at a GRAND TOTAL, and write down that figure in the box to the right. (**Note:** The grand total should equal 120. If you have a different amount, go back and re-add the colored letters; it was probably just an addition error.) Now remove this page and continue with Step 3 on page LSI-5.

Brown **F** total _____

Teal **W** total _____

Purple **T** total _____

Orange **D** total _____

GRAND TOTAL _____

F	T	D	W
W	T	F	D
T	D	W	F
F	D	W	T
F	W	T	D
W	D	F	T
W	F	T	D
D	T	W	F
W	F	D	T
W	F	D	T
F	W	T	D
T	F	W	D

Remove this page after you have completed
Steps 1 and 2 on page LSI-3.
Then continue with Step 3 on page LSI-5.

Learning Style Graph

STEP 3 Remove the sheet of paper that follows this page. Then transfer your totals from Step 2 on page LSI–3 to the lines on the Learning Style Graph below. On the brown (F) line, find the number that corresponds to your "Brown F" total from page LSI–3. Then write an X on this number. Do the same for your "Teal W," "Purple T," and "Orange D" totals. The graph on this page is for you to keep. The graph on page LSI–7 is for you to turn in to your instructor if required to do so.

STEP 4 Now, pressing firmly, draw four straight lines to connect the four X's, and shade in the area to form a "kite." This is your learning style profile. (For an example, see the illustration to the right.) Each X that you placed on these lines indicates your preference for a different aspect of learning:

F "Feeling" (Concrete Experience) The number where you put your X on this line indicates your preference for learning things that have personal meaning. The higher your score on this line, the more you like to learn things that you feel are important and relevant to yourself.

W "Watching" (Reflective Observation) Your number on this line indicates how important it is for you to reflect on the things you are learning. If your score is high on this line, you probably find it important to watch others as they learn about an assignment and then report on it to the class. You probably like to plan things out and take the time to make sure that you fully understand a topic.

T "Thinking" (Abstract Conceptualization) Your number on this line indicates your preference for learning ideas, facts, and figures. If your score is high on this line, you probably like to absorb many concepts and gather lots of information on a new topic.

D "Doing" (Active Experimentation) Your number on this line indicates your preference for applying ideas, using trial and error, and practicing what you learn. If your score is high on this line, you probably enjoy hands-on activities that allow you to test out ideas to see what works.

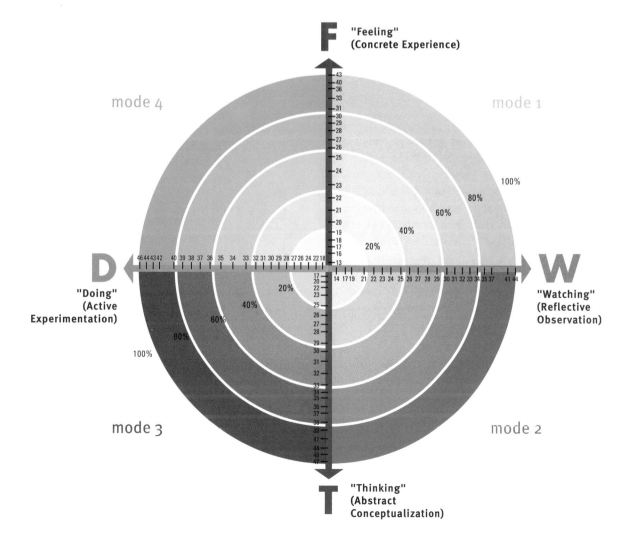

Interpreting your Learning Style Graph

When you examine your completed Learning Style Graph on page LSI–5, you will notice that your learning style profile (the "kite" that you drew) might be located primarily in one part of the graph. This will give you an idea of your preferred **mode** of learning—the kind of behaviors that feel most comfortable and familiar to you when you are learning something.

Using the descriptions below and the sample graphs, identify your preferred learning mode.

 Mode 1 blends feeling and watching. If the majority of your learning style profile is in the upper right-hand corner of the Learning Style Graph, you probably prefer Mode 1 learning. You seek a purpose for new information and a personal connection with the content. You want to know why a course matters and how it challenges or fits in with what they already know. You embrace new ideas that relate directly to their current interests and goals.

 Mode 2 blends watching and thinking. If your learning style profile is mostly in the lower right-hand corner of the Learning Style Graph, you probably prefer Mode 2 learning. You are interested in knowing what ideas or techniques are important. You seek a theory to explain events and are interested in what experts have to say. You enjoy learning lots of facts and then arranging these facts in a logical and concise manner. You break a subject down into its key elements or steps and master each one in a systematic way.

 Mode 3 blends thinking and doing. If most of your learning style profile is in the lower left-hand corner of the Learning Style Graph, you probably prefer Mode 3 learning. You hunger for an opportunity to try out what you're studying. You get involved with new knowledge by testing it out. You investigate how ideas and techniques work, and you put into practice what you learn. You thrive when you have well-defined tasks, guided practice, and frequent feedback.

 Mode 4 blends doing and feeling. If most of your learning style profile is in the upper left-hand corner of the Learning Style Graph, you probably prefer Mode 4 learning. You get excited about going beyond classroom assignments. You like to take what you have practiced and find other uses for it. You seek ways to apply this newly gained skill or information at your workplace or in your personal relationships.

It might be easier for you to remember the modes if you summarize each one as a single question:

- Mode 1 means asking, *Why* learn this?
- Mode 2 means asking, *What* is this about?
- Mode 3 means asking, *How* does this work?
- Mode 4 means asking, *What if* I tried this in a different setting?

 Combinations. Some learning style profiles combine all four modes. The profile to the left reflects a learner who is focused primarily on gathering information—*lots* of information! People with this profile tend to ask for additional facts from an instructor, or they want to know where they can go to discover more about a subject.

 The profile to the left applies to learners who focus more on understanding what they learn and less on gathering lots of information. People with this profile prefer smaller chunks of data with plenty of time to process it. Long lectures can be difficult for these learners.

 The profile to the left indicates a learner whose preferences are fairly well balanced. People with this profile can be highly adaptable and tend to excel no matter what the instructor does in the classroom. ■

Remove this sheet before completing the Learning Style Graph.

This page is inserted to ensure that the other writing you do in this book does not show through on page LSI–7.

Remove this sheet before completing the Learning Style Graph.

This page is inserted to ensure that the other writing you do in this book does not show through on page LSI–7.

Developing all four modes of learning

Each mode of learning represents a unique blend of feeling, watching, thinking, and doing. No matter which of these you've tended to prefer, you can develop the ability to use all four modes:

- **To develop Mode 1,** ask questions that help you understand *why* it is important for you to learn about a specific topic. You might also want to form a study group.
- **To develop Mode 2,** ask questions that help you understand *what* the main points and key facts are. Also, learn a new subject in stages. For example, divide a large reading assignment into sections and then read each section carefully before moving on to the next one.
- **To develop Mode 3,** ask questions about *how* a theory relates to daily life. Also allow time to practice what you learn. You can do experiments, conduct interviews, create presentations, find a relevant work or internship experience, or even write a song that summarizes key concepts. Learn through hands-on practice.
- **To develop Mode 4,** ask *what-if* questions about ways to use what you have just learned in several different situations. Also, seek opportunities to demonstrate your understanding. You could coach a classmate about what you have learned, present findings from your research, explain how your project works, or perform your song.

Developing all four modes offers many potential benefits. For example, you can excel in many types of courses and find more opportunities to learn outside the classroom. You can expand your options for declaring a major and choosing a career. You can also work more effectively with people who learn differently from you.

In addition, you'll be able to learn from instructors no matter how they teach. Let go of statements such as "My teachers don't get me" and "The instructor doesn't teach to my learning style." Replace those excuses with attitudes such as "I am responsible for what I learn" and "I will master this subject by using several modes of learning."

The graph on this page is here for you to turn in to your instructor if required to do so.

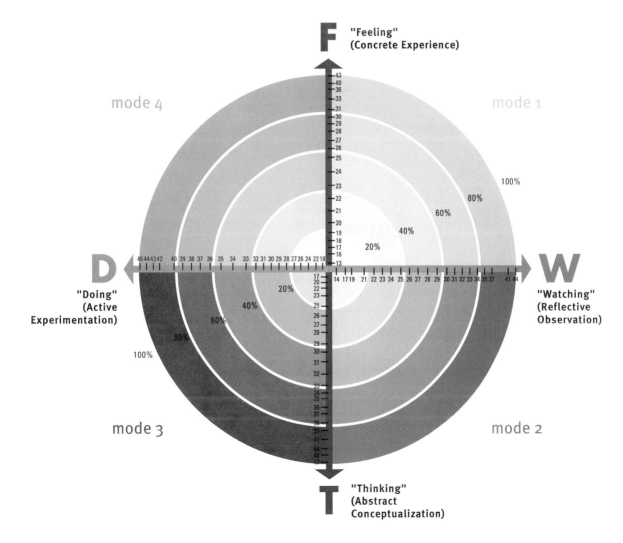

Balancing your preferences

The chart below identifies some of the natural talents people have, as well as challenges for people who have a strong preference for any one mode of learning. For example, if most of your "kite" is in Mode 2 of the Learning Style Graph, then look at the lower right-hand corner of the following chart to see whether it gives an accurate description of you.

After reviewing the description of your preferred learning mode, read all of the sections that start with the words "People with other preferred modes." These sections explain what actions you can take to become a more balanced learner.

Feeling

mode 4

Strengths:
• Getting things done
• Leadership
• Risk taking

Too much of this mode can lead to:
• Trivial improvements
• Meaningless activity

Too little of this mode can lead to:
• Work not completed on time
• Impractical plans
• Lack of motivation to achieve goals

People with other preferred modes can develop Mode 4 by:
• Making a commitment to objectives
• Seeking new opportunities
• Influencing and leading others
• Being personally involved
• Dealing with people

mode 1

Strengths:
• Imaginative ability
• Understanding people
• Recognizing problems
• Brainstorming

Too much of this mode can lead to:
• Feeling paralyzed by alternatives
• Inability to make decisions

Too little of this mode can lead to:
• Lack of ideas
• Not recognizing problems and opportunities

People with other preferred modes can develop Mode 1 by:
• Being aware of other people's feelings
• Being sensitive to values
• Listening with an open mind
• Gathering information
• Imagining the implications of ambiguous situations

Doing ← | → **Watching**

mode 3

Strengths:
• Problem solving
• Decision making
• Deductive reasoning
• Defining problems

Too much of this mode can lead to:
• Solving the wrong problem
• Hasty decision making

Too little of this mode can lead to:
• Lack of focus
• Reluctance to consider alternatives
• Scattered thoughts

People with other preferred modes can develop Mode 3 by:
• Creating new ways of thinking and doing
• Experimenting with fresh ideas
• Choosing the best solution
• Setting goals
• Making decisions

mode 2

Strengths:
• Planning
• Creating models
• Defining problems
• Developing theories

Too much of this mode can lead to:
• Vague ideals ("castles in the air")
• Lack of practical application

Too little of this mode can lead to:
• Inability to learn from mistakes
• No sound basis for work
• No systematic approach

People with other preferred modes can develop Mode 2 by:
• Organizing information
• Building conceptual models
• Testing theories and ideas
• Designing experiments
• Analyzing quantitative data

Thinking

Using your
LEARNING STYLE PROFILE
to succeed

DEVELOP ALL FOUR MODES OF LEARNING

Each mode of learning highlighted in the Learning Style Inventory represents a unique blend of concrete experience ("feeling"), reflective observation ("watching"), abstract conceptualization ("thinking"), and active experimentation ("doing"). You can explore new learning styles simply by adopting new habits related to each of these activities. Consider the following suggestions as places to start. Also remember that any idea about learning styles will make a difference in your life only when it leads to changes in your behavior.

- Conduct an informational interview with someone in your chosen career or "shadow" that person for a day on the job.

- Look for a part-time job, internship, or volunteer experience that complements what you do in class.

- Deepen your understanding of another culture and extend your foreign language skills by studying abroad.

To become more reflective:

- Keep a personal journal, and write about connections among your courses.

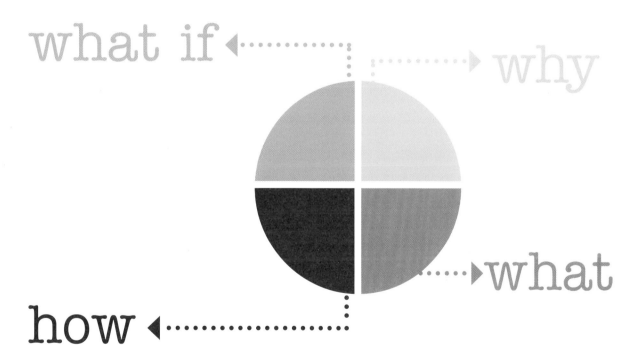

To gain concrete experiences:

- See a live demonstration or performance related to your course content.

- Engage your emotions by reading a novel or seeing a video related to your course.

- Interview an expert in the subject you're learning or a master practitioner of a skill you want to gain.

- Conduct role-plays, exercises, or games based on your courses.

- Form a study group to discuss and debate topics related to your courses.

- Set up a Web site, blog, e-mail listserv, or online chat room related to your major.

- Create analogies to make sense of concepts; for instance, see whether you can find similarities between career planning and putting together a puzzle.

- Visit your course instructor during office hours to ask questions.

- During social events with friends and relatives, briefly explain what your courses are about.

To develop abstract thinking:

- Take notes on your reading in outline form; consider using word-processing software with an outlining feature.
- Supplement assigned texts with other books, magazine and newspaper articles, and related Web sites.
- Attend lectures given by your current instructors and others who teach the same subjects.
- Take ideas presented in text or lectures and translate them into visual form—tables, charts, diagrams, and maps (see Chapter 6: Notes).
- Create visuals and use computer software to recreate them with more complex graphics and animation.

To become more active:

- Conduct laboratory experiments or field observations.
- Go to settings where theories are being applied or tested.
- Make predictions based on theories you learn, and then see whether events in your daily life confirm your predictions.
- Try out a new behavior described in a lecture or reading, and observe its consequences in your life.

LOOK FOR EXAMPLES OF THE MODES IN ACTION

To understand the modes of learning, notice when they occur in your daily life. You are a natural learner, and this means that the modes are often at work. You use them when you solve problems, make choices, and experiment with new ideas.

Suppose that your family asks about your career plans. You've just enrolled for your first semester of classes, and you think it's too early to think about careers. Yet you choose to brainstorm some career options anyway. If nothing else, it might be fun, and you'll have some answers for when people ask you what you're going to do after college. This is an example of Mode 1. You asked, "Why learn about career planning?" and came up with an answer.

During the next meeting of your psychology class, your instructor mentions the career planning center on campus. You visit the center's Web site and discover its list of services. While you're online, you also register for one of the center's workshops because you want more information about writing a career plan. This illustrates Mode 2: You asked, "What career planning options are available?" and discovered several answers.

In this workshop, you learn about the role that internships and extracurricular activities play in career planning. All of these are ways to test an early career choice and discover

whether it appeals to you. You enjoy being with children, so you choose to volunteer at a campus-based child care center. You want to discover how this service learning experience might help you choose a career. This is Mode 3: You asked, "How can I use what I learned in the workshop?" This led you to working with children.

Your experience at the center leads to a work-study assignment there. On the basis of this new experience, you choose to declare a major in early childhood education. This is an example of Mode 4: You asked, "What if this assignment points to a new direction for my future?" The answer led to a new commitment.

USE THE MODES WHILE CHOOSING COURSES

Remember your learning style profile when you're thinking about which classes to take and how to study for each class. Look for a fit between your preferred mode of learning and your course work.

If you prefer Mode 1, for example, then look for courses that sound interesting and seem worthwhile to you. If you prefer Mode 2, then consider classes that center on lectures, reading, and discussion. If you prefer Mode 3, then choose courses that include demonstrations, lab sessions, role-playing, and others ways to take action. And if you prefer Mode 4, then look for courses that could apply to many situations in your life—at work, at home, and in your relationships.

You won't always be able to match your courses to your learning styles. View those situations as opportunities to practice becoming a flexible learner. By developing your skills in all four modes, you can excel in many types of courses.

USE THE MODES TO EXPLORE YOUR MAJOR

If you enjoy learning in Mode 1, you probably value creativity and human relationships. When choosing a major, consider the arts, English, psychology, or political science.

If Mode 2 is your preference, then you enjoy gathering information and building theories. A major related to math or science might be ideal for you.

If Mode 3 is your favorite, then you like to diagnose problems, arrive at solutions, and use technology. A major related to health care, engineering, or economics is a logical choice for you.

And if your preference is Mode 4, you probably enjoy taking the initiative, implementing decisions, teaching, managing projects, and moving quickly from planning into action. Consider a major in business or education.

As you prepare to declare a major, remain flexible. Use your knowledge of learning styles to open up possibilities rather than restrict them. Remember that regardless of your mode, you can excel at any job or major; it just may mean developing new skills in other modes.

USE THE MODES OF LEARNING TO EXPLORE YOUR CAREER

Knowing about learning styles becomes especially useful when planning your career.

People who excel at Mode 1 are often skilled at tuning in to the feelings of clients and coworkers. These people can listen with an open mind, tolerate confusion, be sensitive to people's feelings, open up to problems that are difficult to define, and brainstorm a variety of solutions. If you like Mode 1, you may be drawn to a career in counseling, social services, the ministry, or another field that centers on human relationships. You might also enjoy a career in the performing arts.

People who prefer Mode 2 like to do research and work with ideas. They are skilled at gathering data, interpreting information, and summarizing—arriving at the big picture. They may excel at careers that center on science, math, technical communications, or planning. Mode 2 learners may also work as college teachers, lawyers, technical writers, or journalists.

People who like Mode 3 are drawn to solving problems, making decisions, and checking on progress toward goals. Careers in medicine, engineering, information technology, or another applied science are often ideal for them.

People who enjoy Mode 4 like to influence and lead others. These people are often described as "doers" and "risk takers." They like to take action and complete projects. Mode 4 learners often excel at managing, negotiating, selling, training, and teaching. They might also work for a government agency.

Keep in mind that there is no strict match between certain learning styles and certain careers. Learning is essential to success in all careers. Also, any career can attract people with a variety of learning styles. For instance, the health care field is large enough to include people who prefer Mode 3 and become family physicians—*and* people who prefer Mode 2 and become medical researchers.

> # Keep in mind that there is no strict match between certain learning styles and certain careers. Learning is essential to success in all careers.

EXPECT TO ENCOUNTER DIFFERENT STYLES

As higher education and the workplace become more diverse and technology creates a global marketplace, you'll meet people who differ from you in profound ways. Your fellow students and coworkers will behave in ways that express a variety of preferences for perceiving information, processing ideas, and acting on what they learn. Consider these examples:

- A roommate who's continually moving while studying—reciting facts out loud, pacing, and gesturing—probably prefers concrete experience and learning by taking action.

- A coworker who talks continually on the phone about a project may prefer to learn by listening, talking, and forging key relationships.

- A supervisor who excels at abstract conceptualization may want to see detailed project plans and budgets submitted in writing well before a project swings into high gear.

- A study group member who always takes the initiative, manages the discussion, delegates any work involved, and follows up with everyone probably prefers active experimentation.

Differences in learning style can be a stumbling block—or an opportunity. When differences intersect, there is the potential for conflict as well as for creativity. Succeeding with peers often means seeing the classroom and workplace as a laboratory for learning from experience. Resolving conflict and learning from mistakes are all part of the learning cycle.

LOOK FOR SPECIFIC CLUES TO ANOTHER PERSON'S STYLE

You can learn a lot about other people's styles of learning simply by observing them during the work day. Look for clues such as these:

Approaches to a task that requires learning. Some people process new information and ideas by sitting quietly and reading or writing. When learning to use a piece of equipment, such as a new computer, they'll read the instruction manual first. Others will skip the manual, unpack all the boxes, and start setting up equipment. And others might ask a more experienced colleague to guide them in person, step by step.

Word choice. Some people like to process information visually. You might hear them say, "I'll look into that" or "Give me the big picture first." Others like to solve problems verbally: "Let's talk through this problem" or "I hear you!" In contrast, some people focus on body sensations ("This product feels great") or action ("Let's run with this idea and see what happens").

Body language. Notice how often coworkers or classmates make eye contact with you and how close they sit or stand next to you. Observe their gestures, as well as the volume and tone of their voice.

Content preferences. Notice what subjects coworkers or classmates openly discuss and which topics that they avoid. Some people talk freely about their feelings, their families, and even their personal finances. Others choose to remain silent on such topics and stick to work-related matters.

Process preferences. Look for patterns in the way that your coworkers and classmates meet goals. When attending meetings, for example, some of them might stick closely to the agenda and keep an eye on the clock. Other people might prefer to go with the flow, even if it means working an extra hour or scrapping the agenda.

ACCOMMODATE DIFFERING STYLES

Once you've discovered differences in styles, look for ways to accommodate them. As you collaborate on projects with other students or coworkers, keep the following suggestions in mind:

Remember that some people want to reflect on the big picture first. When introducing a project plan, you might say, "This process has four major steps." Before explaining the plan in detail, talk about the purpose of the project and the benefits of completing each step.

Allow time for active experimentation and concrete experience. Offer people a chance to try out a new product or process for themselves—to literally get the feel of it.

Allow for abstract conceptualization. When leading a study group or conducting a training session, provide handouts that include plenty of visuals and step-by-step instructions. Visual learners and people who like to think abstractly will appreciate it. Also schedule periods for questions and answers.

When planning a project, encourage people to answer key questions. Remember the four essential questions that guide learning. Answering *Why?* means defining the purpose and desired outcomes of the project. Answering *What?* means assigning major tasks, setting due dates for each task, and generating commitment to action. Answering *How?* means carrying out assigned tasks and meeting regularly to discuss things that are working well and ways to improve the project. And answering *What if?* means discussing what the team has learned from the project and ways to apply that learning to the whole class or larger organization.

When working on teams, look for ways that members can complement one another's strengths. If you're skilled at planning, find someone who excels at doing. Also seek people who can reflect on and interpret the team's experience. Pooling different styles allows you to draw on everyone's strengths.

RESOLVE CONFLICT WITH RESPECT FOR STYLES

When people's styles clash in educational or work settings, you have several options. One is to throw up your hands and resign yourself to personality conflicts. Another option is to recognize differences, accept them, and respect them as complementary ways to meet common goals. Taking that perspective allows you to act constructively. You might do one of the following:

Resolve conflict within yourself. You might have mental pictures of classrooms and workplaces as places where people are all supposed to have the same style. Notice if you have those pictures and gently let them go. If you *expect* to find differences in styles, you can more easily respect those differences.

Introduce a conversation about learning styles. Attend a workshop on learning styles. Then bring such training directly to your classroom or office.

Let people take on tasks that fit their learning styles. People gravitate toward the kinds of tasks they've succeeded at in the past, and that's fine. Remember, though, that learning styles are both stable and dynamic. People can also broaden their styles by tackling new tasks to reinforce different modes of learning.

Rephrase complaints as requests. "This class is a waste of my time" can be recast as "Please tell me what I'll gain if I participate actively in class." "The instructor talks too fast" can become "What strategies can I use for taking notes when the instructor covers the material rapidly?"

ACCEPT CHANGE—AND OCCASIONAL DISCOMFORT

Seek out chances to develop new modes of learning. If your instructor asks you to form a group to complete an assignment, avoid joining a group where everyone shares your learning style. Work on project teams with people who learn differently than you. Get together with people who both complement and challenge you.

Also look for situations where you can safely practice new skills. If you enjoy reading, for example, look for ways to express what you learn by speaking, such as leading a study group on a textbook chapter.

Discomfort is a natural part of the learning process. Allow yourself to notice any struggle with a task or lack of interest in completing it. Remember that such feelings are temporary and that you are balancing your learning preferences. By choosing to move through discomfort, you consciously expand your ability to learn in new ways. ■

Claim your multiple INTELLIGENCES

People often think that being smart means the same thing as having a high IQ, and that having a high IQ automatically leads to success. However, psychologists are finding that IQ scores do not always foretell which students will do well in academic settings—or after they graduate.[2]

Howard Gardner of Harvard University believes that no single measure of intelligence can tell us how smart we are. Instead, Gardner defines intelligence in a flexible way as "the ability to solve problems, or to create products, that are valued within one or more cultural settings." He also identifies several types of intelligence, as described here.[3]

People using **verbal/linguistic intelligence** are adept at language skills and learn best by speaking, writing, reading, and listening. They are likely to enjoy activities such as telling stories and doing crossword puzzles.

People who use **mathematical/logical intelligence** are good with numbers, logic, problem solving, patterns, relationships, and categories. They are generally precise and methodical, and are likely to enjoy science.

When people learn visually and by organizing things spatially, they display **visual/spatial intelligence**. They think in images and pictures, and understand best by seeing the subject. They enjoy charts, graphs, maps, mazes, tables, illustrations, art, models, puzzles, and costumes.

People using **bodily/kinesthetic intelligence** prefer physical activity. They enjoy activities such as building things, woodworking, dancing, skiing, sewing, and crafts. They generally are coordinated and athletic, and they would rather participate in games than just watch.

Individuals using **musical/rhythmic intelligence** enjoy musical expression through songs, rhythms, and musical instruments. They are responsive to various kinds of sounds; remember melodies easily; and might enjoy drumming, humming, and whistling.

People using **intrapersonal intelligence** are exceptionally aware of their own feelings and values. They are generally reserved, self-motivated, and intuitive.

Outgoing people show evidence of **interpersonal intelligence.** They do well with cooperative learning and are sensitive to the feelings, intentions, and motivations of others. They often make good leaders.

People using **naturalist intelligence** love the outdoors and recognize details in plants, animals, rocks, clouds, and other natural formations. These people excel in observing fine distinctions among similar items.

Each of us has all of these intelligences to some degree. And each of us can learn to enhance them. Experiment with learning in ways that draw on a variety of intelligences—including those that might be less familiar. When we acknowledge all of our intelligences, we can constantly explore new ways of being smart. ■

istockphoto.com/pavlen

2

✓ CRITICAL THINKING EXERCISE 8

Develop your multiple intelligences

Gardner's theory of multiple intelligences complements the discussion of different learning styles in this chapter. The main point is that there are many ways to gain knowledge and acquire new behaviors. You can use Gardner's concepts to explore a range of options for achieving success in school, work, and relationships.

The chart on the next page summarizes the content of "Claim your multiple intelligences" and suggests ways to apply the main ideas. Instead of merely

glancing through this chart, get active. Place a check mark next to any of the "Possible characteristics" that describe you. Also check off the "Possible learning strategies" that you intend to use. Finally, underline or highlight any of the "Possible careers" that spark your interest.

Remember that the chart is *not* an exhaustive list or a formal inventory. Take what you find merely as points of departure. You can invent strategies of your own to cultivate different intelligences.

Type of intelligence	Possible characteristics	Possible learning strategies	Possible careers
Verbal/linguistic	❏ You enjoy writing letters, stories, and papers. ❏ You prefer to write directions rather than draw maps. ❏ You take excellent notes from textbooks and lectures. ❏ You enjoy reading, telling stories, and listening to them.	❏ Highlight, underline, and write notes in your textbooks. ❏ Recite new ideas in your own words. ❏ Rewrite and edit your class notes. ❏ Talk to other people often about what you're studying.	Librarian, lawyer, editor, journalist, English teacher, radio or television announcer
Mathematical/logical	❏ You enjoy solving puzzles. ❏ You prefer math or science class over English class. ❏ You want to know how and why things work. ❏ You make careful, step-by-step plans.	❏ Analyze tasks so you can order them in a sequence of steps. ❏ Group concepts into categories, and look for underlying patterns. ❏ Convert text into tables, charts, and graphs. ❏ Look for ways to quantify ideas—to express them in numerical terms.	Accountant, auditor, tax preparer, mathematician, computer programmer, actuary, economist, math or science teacher
Visual/spatial	❏ You draw pictures to give an example or clarify an explanation. ❏ You understand maps and illustrations more readily than text. ❏ You assemble things from illustrated instructions. ❏ You especially enjoy books that have a lot of illustrations.	❏ When taking notes, create concept maps, mind maps, and other visuals (see Chapter 6: Notes). ❏ Code your notes by using different colors to highlight main topics, major points, and key details. ❏ When your attention wanders, focus it by sketching or drawing. ❏ Before you try a new task, visualize yourself doing it well.	Architect, commercial artist, fine artist, graphic designer, photographer, interior decorator, engineer, cartographer
Bodily/kinesthetic	❏ You enjoy physical exercise. ❏ You tend not to sit still for long periods of time. ❏ You enjoy working with your hands. ❏ You use a lot of gestures when talking.	❏ Be active in ways that support concentration; for example, pace as you recite, read while standing up, and create flash cards. ❏ Carry materials with you, and practice studying in several different locations. ❏ Create hands-on activities related to key concepts; for example, create a game based on course content. ❏ Notice the sensations involved with learning something well.	Physical education teacher, athlete, athletic coach, physical therapist, chiropractor, massage therapist, yoga teacher, dancer, choreographer, actor

Type of intelligence	Possible characteristics	Possible learning strategies	Possible careers
Musical/rhythmic	❏ You often sing in the car or shower. ❏ You easily tap your foot to the beat of a song. ❏ You play a musical instrument. ❏ You feel most engaged and productive when music is playing.	❏ During a study break, play music or dance to restore energy. ❏ Put on background music that enhances your concentration while studying. ❏ Relate key concepts to songs you know. ❏ Write your own songs based on course content.	Professional musician, music teacher, music therapist, choral director, musical instrument sales representative, musical instrument maker, piano tuner
Intrapersonal	❏ You enjoy writing in a journal and being alone with your thoughts. ❏ You think a lot about what you want in the future. ❏ You prefer to work on individual projects over group projects. ❏ You take time to think things through before talking or taking action.	❏ Connect course content to your personal values and goals. ❏ Study a topic alone before attending a study group. ❏ Connect readings and lectures to a strong feeling or significant past experience. ❏ Keep a journal that relates your course work to events in your daily life.	Minister, priest, rabbi, professor of philosophy or religion, counseling psychologist, creator of a home-based or small business
Interpersonal	❏ You enjoy group work over working alone. ❏ You have plenty of friends and regularly spend time with them. ❏ You prefer talking and listening over reading or writing. ❏ You thrive in positions of leadership.	❏ Form and conduct study groups early in the term. ❏ Create flash cards, and use them to quiz study partners. ❏ Volunteer to give a speech or lead group presentations on course topics. ❏ Teach the topic you're studying to someone else.	Manager, school administrator, salesperson, teacher, counseling psychologist, arbitrator, police officer, nurse, travel agent, public relations specialist, creator of a midsize to large business
Naturalist	❏ As a child, you enjoyed collecting insects, leaves, or other natural objects. ❏ You enjoy being outdoors. ❏ You find that important insights occur during times you spend in nature. ❏ You read books and magazines on nature-related topics.	❏ During study breaks, take walks outside. ❏ Post pictures of outdoor scenes where you study, and play recordings of outdoor sounds while you read. ❏ Invite classmates to discuss course work while taking a hike or going on a camping trip. ❏ Focus on careers that hold the potential for working outdoors.	Environmental activist, park ranger, recreation supervisor, historian, museum curator, biologist, criminologist, mechanic, woodworker, construction worker, construction contractor or estimator

2

LEARNING BY SEEING, HEARING, AND MOVING: the VAK system

Another way to approach the topic of learning styles is to use a system that focuses on just three ways of perceiving through your senses:

• Seeing, or visual learning

• Hearing, or auditory learning

• Movement, or kinesthetic learning

To recall this system, remember the letters VAK, which stand for **visual**, **auditory**, and **kinesthetic**. The theory is that each of us prefers to learn through one of these senses. And we can enrich our learning with activities that draw on the other channels.

To reflect on your VAK preferences, answer the following questions. Each question has three possible answers. Circle the answer that best describes how you would respond in the stated situation. This is not a formal inventory—just a way to prompt some self-discovery.

When you have problems spelling a word, you prefer to:

1. Look it up in the dictionary.

2. Say the word out loud several times before you write it down.

3. Write out the word with several different spellings and then choose one.

You enjoy courses the most when you get to:

1. View slides, overhead displays, videos, and readings with plenty of charts, tables, and illustrations.

2. Ask questions, engage in small-group discussions, and listen to guest speakers.

3. Take field trips, participate in lab sessions, or apply the course content while working as a volunteer or intern.

When giving someone directions on how to drive to a destination, you prefer to:

1. Pull out a piece of paper and sketch a map.

2. Give verbal instructions.

3. Say, "I'm driving to a place near there, so just follow me."

When planning an extended vacation to a new destination, you prefer to:

1. Read colorful, illustrated brochures or articles about that place.

2. Talk directly to someone who's been there.

3. Spend a day or two at that destination on a work-related trip before taking a vacation there.

You've made a commitment to learn to play the guitar. The first thing you do is:

1. Go to a library or music store and find an instruction book with plenty of diagrams and chord charts.

2. Pull out your favorite CDs, listen closely to the guitar solos, and see if you can play along with them.

3. Buy or borrow a guitar, pluck the strings, and ask someone to show you how to play a few chords.

You've saved up enough money to lease a car. When choosing from among several new models, the most important factor in your decision is:

1. The car's appearance.

2. The information you get by talking to people who own the cars you're considering.

3. The overall impression you get by taking each car on a test drive.

You've just bought a new computer system. When setting up the system, the first thing you do is:

1. Skim through the printed instructions that come with the equipment.

2. Call someone with a similar system and ask her for directions.

3. Assemble the components as best as you can, see if everything works, and consult the instructions only as a last resort.

You get a scholarship to study abroad next semester, which starts in just three months. You will travel to a country where French is the most widely spoken language. To learn as much French as you can before you depart, you:

1. Buy a video-based language course that's recorded on a DVD or downloaded from the Internet.

2. Set up tutoring sessions with a friend who's fluent in French.

3. Sign up for a short immersion course in an environment in which you speak only French, starting with the first class.

Now take a few minutes to reflect on the meaning of your responses. All of the answers numbered "1" are examples of visual learning. The "2's" refer to auditory learning, and the "3's" illustrate kinesthetic learning. Finding a consistent pattern in your answers indicates that you prefer learning through one sense channel more than the others. Or you might find that your preferences are fairly balanced.

Listed here are suggestions for learning through each sense channel. Experiment with these examples, and create more techniques of your own. Use the suggestions to build on your current preferences and develop new options for learning.

TO ENHANCE VISUAL LEARNING:

- Preview reading assignments by looking for elements that are highlighted visually—bold headlines, charts, graphs, illustrations, and photographs.

- When taking notes in class, leave plenty of room to add your own charts, diagrams, tables, and other visuals later.

- Whenever an instructor writes information on a blackboard or overhead display, copy it exactly in your notes.

- Transfer your handwritten notes to your computer. Use word-processing software that allows you to format your notes in lists, add headings in different fonts, and create visuals in color.

- Before you begin an exam, quickly sketch a diagram on scratch paper. Use this diagram to summarize the key formulas or facts you want to remember.

- During tests, see if you can visualize pages from your handwritten notes or images from your computer-based notes.

TO ENHANCE AUDITORY LEARNING:

- Reinforce memory of your notes and readings by talking about them. When studying, stop often to recite key points and examples in your own words.

- After reciting several summaries of key points and examples, record your favorite version or write it out.

- Read difficult passages in your textbooks slowly and out loud.

- Join study groups, and create short presentations about course topics.
- Visit your instructors during office hours to ask questions.

TO ENHANCE KINESTHETIC LEARNING:

- Look for ways to translate course content into three-dimensional models that you can build. While studying biology, for example, create a model of a human cell, using different colors of clay.

- Supplement lectures with trips to museums, field observations, lab sessions, tutorials, and other hands-on activities.
- Recite key concepts from your courses while you walk or exercise.
- Intentionally set up situations in which you can learn by trial and error.
- Create a practice test, and write out the answers in the room where you will actually take the exam.

Master Employees
IN ACTION

You're One Click Away...
from a video about Master Students in Action.

"*The skills I learned in college are initiative and being proactive. Similar to making the effort to attend office hours to speak with a professor about a project, I have been proactive in reaching out to people within my division to learn more about their job responsibilities. Through doing so, I have been able to gain insights as to areas I may want to learn more about as well as further my knowledge about how our jobs are connected.*"

—*Kristen Oats*
Financial Analyst

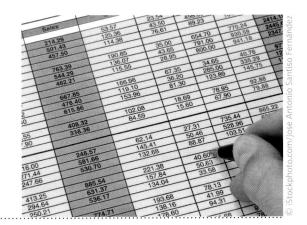

masterstudentprofile

Fabian Pfortmüller

(1983–) Cofounder of Holstee, a company that aims to "*create the greatest social impact while simultaneously creating the smallest environmental impact.*"

Most mission statements contain words like *value* and *service* but often fail to explain what the founders truly care about, much less inspire anyone else to care. Holstee's mission statement is an exception. The Brooklyn, New York–based company, which sells eco-friendly clothing and accessories, rose from obscurity last year after its statement, dubbed the Holstee Manifesto, went viral. The document has been viewed online more than 50 million times and translated into 12 languages. ...

Inc. reporter Issie Lapowsky recently spoke with [Holstee cofounder] Pfortmüller about the impact a strong mission statement can have on a company.

Q: How did you come up with your mission statement?

A: We wrote it a few months after we started Holstee, in 2009. We were talking about how every entrepreneur, including us, wants to build a lifestyle for himself. But even though you're your own boss, sometimes a start-up becomes something you can't control. You build your business, but at the end of the day, you might not even want to work there. So we wanted to define what success means to us in nonmonetary terms. We also knew that down the road, it would help to have a reminder of why we started Holstee. Dave and Mike quit their jobs in the middle of the recession to start the company. The manifesto was a reminder that we took all these risks for a reason, to live a lifestyle we loved.

Q: How did it get so big?

A: Two bloggers picked it up. That just kicked off a chain reaction. We saw it all over Tumblr and Twitter. People started making it their Facebook photo. We were so surprised at how people responded to it. I think society is just hungry for genuine values.

Q: Whose idea was it to turn the manifesto into merchandise?

A: Actually, customers started asking for it. At first, we were hesitant about putting it on a poster. It was really personal to us, and putting anything on a big poster or T-shirt can cheapen it. But we got so many requests that one of our freelancers convinced us to try it. We got amazing feedback. We sold about 11,000 posters last year. They accounted for roughly 50 percent of our revenue in November.

Q: How has the popularity of the posters influenced your brand?

A: Usually people make a product first, then build a brand around it. In our case, it happened the other way around. That has helped us build trust with customers. People see the manifesto and automatically understand what we stand for. Then again, we're not a manifesto company, whatever that would be. The success of the posters helped us bootstrap, but at the end of the day, we're about products with a unique story that are designed with a conscience.

Fabian Pfortmüller ... is willing to take risks.
YOU ... can take appropriate risks by defining what success means to you.

Read the Holstee Manifesto online at http://shop.holstee.com /pages/about.

You're One Click Away...
from learning more about Fabian Pfortmüller online at the Master Student Profiles. You can also visit the Master Student Hall of Fame to learn more about other master students.

FIVE Cs
FOR YOUR CAREER

CHARACTER • CRITICAL THINKING • CREATIVE THINKING • COLLABORATION • COMMUNICATION

In the workplace, performance reviews often end with a personal development plan that includes specific ways to improve an employee's performance. After reading and using this book, you can think of these plans in a new way: They are opportunities to take a First Step about how you're doing at work.

Link your personal development plan to your character strengths. Standard advice from many self-development experts is to focus your plan on identifying and changing your greatest personal weaknesses. Think critically about this advice for three reasons:

- Tackling your weaknesses can feel threatening and lead to procrastination.

- A major weakness may be hard to change before your next performance review.

- Eliminating weaknesses might affect your life outside work and have little or no impact on your career.

Of course, it's fine to take a First Step about things you'd like to change. Another option is to focus your plan on listing and developing your strengths. This is a chance to think about character in a way that creates new possibilities for your future.

Think creatively and critically about your plan. Think about any of your recent accomplishments at work. Describe them in writing, including specific details about what you did and the results of your actions.

Next, set a goal to build on one of these accomplishments. This calls for creative thinking. Say that you made a suggestion to change the workflow in your department, and this change allowed your team to finish a project well before the scheduled due date. Consider setting a goal to make this a permanent change in your department's procedures. You could also set a goal to find other time-saving procedures.

You can always set a goal that targets one of your weaknesses. Just stay positive. Instead of focusing on a current behavior that you want to stop, for example, describe a new behavior that you want to start. Change "I will stop taking unclear notes at meetings" to "I will review my meeting notes to clarify the major agreements we made and next actions to take."

In any case, focus your development plan on goals that you can actually achieve in the near future, leading to clear benefits at work. Translate your goal into concrete behaviors. Ask yourself:

What exactly will I do differently based on my goal? Answering such questions involves critical thinking.

You can monitor your progress toward any goal, no matter how ambitious. To monitor listening skills, for example, you could count the number of times each day that you interrupt other people.

Remember that the point of monitoring your behavior is not to become a cold-blooded measurement machine. Rather, the idea is to make a change that really makes a difference over the long term. Behaviors that we measure carefully and consistently are likely to change.

As you monitor your behavior, remember the essence of a First Step: suspend all self-judgment. Just record the facts. If you deviate from your plan, just look for the next chance to practice your new behavior.

Use your knowledge of learning styles to communicate and collaborate with your boss. You probably feel more comfortable with a person when you feel that you have something in common. That feeling is called rapport. Whenever you establish rapport with someone in the workplace, you enter into a collaborative relationship.

When meeting with your boss for a performance review, for example, look for clues to that person's learning style. Then see if you can establish rapport by matching his or her style in a small, significant way.

For example, mirror your boss's word choice. She might like to process information visually. Clues to this preference are words such as, "I'll believe that when I see it" and "Give me an overview of your proposal." If she has a preference for verbal learning, she might say, "Let's talk through this" or "I'm hearing good things about you." And if she has kinesthetic preferences, she might signal those by referring to physical sensations ("I feel good about that idea") or action ("Walk me through your presentation before you give it").

Kinesthetic preferences are also expressed in posture, facial expressions, and other forms on nonverbal communication. Notice whether your boss is sitting with arms and legs crossed or open. If you can mirror that posture in a natural way, then do so.

As you look for ways to establish rapport, be subtle. The goal is not to manipulate. It's to communicate effectively and find common ground for collaboration.

Now, make a personal commitment to developing the five Cs. Take another look at the Discovery Wheel in this chapter—especially the sections labeled Character, Creative and Critical Thinking, Communicating, and Collaborating. Take a snapshot of your current skills in these areas after reading and doing this chapter.

DISCOVERY

My scores on the "Five C" sections of the Discovery Wheel were:	As of today, I would give myself the following scores in these areas:	At the end of this course, I would like my scores in these areas to be:
Character _____	Character _____	Character _____
Creative & Critical Thinking _____	Creative & Critical Thinking _____	Creative & Critical Thinking _____
Communicating _____	Communicating _____	Communicating _____
Collaborating _____	Collaborating _____	Collaborating _____

Next, skim this chapter and look for a technique that you want to explore in depth. Choose one that would enhance your self-rating in at least one of the five Cs. For example, you could choose a technique for enhancing visual learning presented in "Learning by seeing, hearing and moving: The VAK system." Practicing this technique could help you become more skilled at communicating and collaborating with people who favor visual learning.

I discovered that my preferred technique is . . .

_____

_____

_____

_____

In light of the five Cs, I can use this technique to become more . . .

_____

_____

_____

_____

INTENTION
To use this technique, I intend to . . .

_____

_____

_____

_____

NEXT ACTION
The specific action I will take is . . .

_____

_____

_____

_____

Name _____

Date _____

1. The Power "Process: Ideas are tools" states that if you want to use an idea, you must believe in it. True or false? Explain your answer.

   False. If you read about a tool in this book that doesn't sound right, or one that sounds a little goofy, remember that the ideas here are for using, not necessarily for believing. Suspend your judgment. Test the idea for yourself. If it works, use it. If it doesn't, don't use it. *(Power Process: Ideas are tools,* page 50)

2. The First Step technique refers only to telling the truth about your areas for improvement. True or false? Explain your answer.

   False. Although the First Step is all about telling the truth, telling the truth about your areas for improvement is just one part. Taking the First Step involves telling the truth about what is working as well as what isn't, who you are, and what you want. (Answers may vary.) *(First Step: Truth is a key to mastery,* page 51)

3. The four modes of learning are associated with certain questions. Give the appropriate question for each mode.

   Mode 1: Why? Mode 2: What? Mode 3: How? Mode 4: What if? *(Learning styles: Discovering how you learn,* page 57)

4. List the types of intelligence defined by Howard Gardner.

   Verbal/linguistic intelligence, mathematical/logical intelligence, visual/spatial intelligence, bodily/kinesthetic intelligence, musical/rhythmic intelligence, intrapersonal intelligence, interpersonal intelligence, naturalist intelligence. *(Claim your multiple intelligences,* page 63)

5. Describe two learning strategies related to one type of intelligence that you listed.

   (Answers will vary.) Visual/spatial intelligence: charts, maps, graphs, mazes, puzzles. *(Claim your multiple intelligences,* page 63)

6. The word kinesthetic refers to

   (a) Moving   **(b)** Hearing   **(c)** Seeing   **(d)** Listening

   (a) Moving *(Learning by seeing, hearing, and moving: The VAK system,* page 66)

7. Give an example of turning a First Step into a goal.

   (Answers will vary.) A student who is aware of "not exercising enough" can set a goal, such as "I will walk briskly for 30 minutes at least three times per week." *(First Step: Truth is a key to mastery,* page 51)

8. According to the text, the process of change starts with making negative judgments about our personal shortcomings. True or false? Explain your answer.

   False. First Steps allow you to admit your shortcomings as a way to take charge of your life and create positive change. It is your opportunity to gain skill and change the way things are without having to criticize the way things have been. *(First Step: Truth is a key to mastery,* page 51)

9. List three strategies for gaining concrete experiences when you learn something.

   Any three of the following: See a live demonstration; read a novel; interview an expert; conduct role plays, exercises, or games; form a study group; set up a Web site; create analogies; visit your instructor; discuss course material with friends. *(Using your learning style profile to succeed,* page 59)

10. Clues to another person's learning style include

    (a) approaches to a task that requires learning.

    (b) word choice.

    (c) body language.

    (d) all of the above.

    (d) all of the above. *(Using your learning style profile to succeed,* page 59)

CHAPTER 3

TIME & MONEY

Instructor Tools & Tips

"Dost thou love life, then do not squander time, for that's the stuff life is made of." —Benjamin Franklin

"There are people who have money and people who are rich." —Coco Chanel

PREVIEW

Chapter 3 addresses one of the greatest challenges for students—managing their time and money. There is no lack of time and money in the universe. Even when times are tough, we see and hear stories of people who figure out how to make things work. These people are prepared for emergencies and make decisions about how they spend their time and money that keeps them thriving. It's really about how students respond to their changing environments. Time and money are vital resources that students can learn to manage effectively. Planning offers them the freedom to act in response to their intentions rather than to their moods. And planning vastly increases the odds of getting what they want out of life. And when we are thriving, we are in a good position to contribute to people less fortunate.

Whether they are traditional students attending college right out of high school or returning students attending college for the first time after an absence from formal education, your students each have only 168 hours per week to allocate to their many priorities. Time is an equal opportunity resource: All people, regardless of race, gender, creed, or national origin, have exactly the same number of hours per week. As you help your students choose how to allocate their 168 hours per week, set goals, and overcome procrastination, remind them that planning increases their options.

Money, or rather the lack of money, is the most common reason students give for withdrawing from college. This important issue has been covered in all editions of *From Master Student to Master Employee*, but with tuition increases on the rise in most states, the need for first-year college students to develop a mature financial literacy is crucial to their college survival. Understanding the economic aspects of completing a degree is more essential now than ever. New articles help students explore ways to manage money during tough times and relate their learning style to how they spend their money. This chapter also challenges students to think about what money means to them and how they can use money to achieve their goals without letting money use them. Spend time explaining the concept of credit scores to your students. For many, this is a new concept. Encourage students to share their success stories as well as financial challenges as you cover this topic.

GUEST SPEAKER

Consider inviting experts from your college or from off-campus who work in fields that emphasize planning, goal setting, or organization. A representative from the counseling department may provide some planning tips and also share information about advisement, scheduling, and personal counseling services. Invite the financial a director to talk about financial aid opportunities, deadlines, and forms students need to fill out. If you have a credit union on campus, invite the manager to talk about building a good credit record, saving money, and identity protection. You may discover that your students have more questions for these speakers than any of the others! Discussing time and money in class can raise student awareness and provide an opportunity to model critical thinking.

LECTURE

Suggested lecture topics for this chapter include the following: planning strategies for effective use of time and money, structure and freedom, organizing your space, committing to attend class, completing projects, budgeting, credit cards, and Power Process: Be here now. For specific lecture ideas and key lecture points on text articles, visit the lecture ideas area of the chapter-by-chapter instructor materials at the Online Instructor Resources Web site.

EXERCISES/ACTIVITIES

1. **Power Process: Be here now (page 74)** This Power Process teaches the skill of focusing attention—a skill essential for taking effective notes in class, maximizing comprehension when reading textbooks, and memorizing content. After students read the article and review it with them in class, have them stand up and find a partner for this brief "hand mirror" exercise. Facing their partner, students put their hands up, palms facing toward their

partner, without touching. In this position, students appear as a mirror image of their partner. Without speaking, for 1 minute, one student is in charge of moving her hands slowly in different directions—up, down, left, right, forward, backward. Her partner focuses his attention and mirrors the movement of her hands with his hands, even when they do not move symmetrically. After 1 minute, they reverse roles for another minute. Afterwards, discuss the paradox that it feels both easy and difficult to focus attention for just 60 seconds. It may be beneficial to bring a student forward and demonstrate the activity with him first.

2. **Why? What? How? and What if?** Consider writing these questions on the chalkboard or whiteboard. Post them to your online course discussion board. Tap into all the different learning styles of your students by asking these questions in class:

   Why? Why does From *Master Student to Master Employee* cover the topic of planning your time and money?

   What? What is planning? Read through the list of articles in this chapter, and pick three that look interesting. What about these three articles interests you?

   How? How would you rate your level of success with the ideas covered in this chapter? (How much do you already know about prioritizing your time, setting goals, avoiding procrastination, or managing money?)

   What if? What if you start to apply these strategies to your life right now? And what if you don't? Connect to the workplace: What if an employee can't meet deadlines or spends more than he or she makes?

3. **The ABC daily to-do list (pages 84–85)** Some students have had prior experience with to-do lists. Their testimonials in class can help convince students who have not yet tried to-do lists to experiment with them. Students can see different perspectives and gain new ideas. For example, a visual learner can gain motivation when another visual learner shares about a visually appealing technique—a unique to-do list pad, use of stickers, and colorful markers and pens. The ABC priority aspect is usually a new concept for all students. Learning this technique helps them make better decisions about *what* to do and *when* to do it. Practicing this skill in groups during class helps students get started with to-do lists.

4. **Stop procrastination now (pages 89–90)** Many students report that procrastination is their number one obstacle to success in school, work, and their personal lives. After they have read the antiprocrastination article and sidebar, divide them into groups of four, and ask them to list situations in which they often procrastinate. Then discuss as a group which of the antiprocrastination strategies might be most appropriate for each situation. Making this an active learning exercise puts the strategies in motion. Have the students create summary charts on poster paper and then present a brief report to the rest of the class.

5. **25 ways to get the most out of now (pages 91–95) and Spend less money (page 103)** After students have read these articles, divide them into groups of four, and ask them to discuss which of the 25 tools and which of the tips to spend less they have had success with in the past. Have each group list on poster paper the top five tools from each article that promote effective use of time and money. Then have group members place their initials next to at least four of the tools that they are willing to commit to for the next week. Save the posters for the next class, and ask students to report back to their groups to discuss which strategies worked and which did not.

6. **Critical Thinking Exercise 13: Education by the hour (page 106)** Consider having your students complete this exercise during class. When all the students have computed their actual direct and indirect costs of attending one class meeting, have them write the figure anonymously on a 3×5 card and put the cards on the chalk or whiteboard tray in order from lowest to highest. Then point out that the amount on the card is also the amount that students throw away each time they miss a class meeting during the term. I bring $100 in $1 bills and select a card with an amount that is close to $100 without going over it. I dramatically pull the hundred bills out of my pocket and count out the total on the 3×5 card, tossing the $1 bills onto a table one by one. Then I pick up the wad of cash and throw it into the classroom trash can as a graphic illustration of how money is lost every time a class meeting is skipped. Without fail, you'll likely hear students gasp! Of course, the money loss is just one aspect of missing class, but students will get the point. Ask them each to retrieve their card and put it where they will see it frequently and be reminded of the cost of missing classes.

   Preparation note: While students are doing their calculations and filling out their cards, sneak over to the trashcan and line it with another trash bag to protect the dollar bills you'll throw in it later! Don't worry about forgetting to retrieve your cash—the students' eyes won't leave the trashcan until you pull out the liner with the cash! (*Note:* I adapted this activity from a similar presentation by Dave Ellis when he was teaching me and other instructors how to illustrate the articles in *From Master Student to Master Employee*.)

7. **Take charge of your credit (pages 107–108)** Tell students to keep all credit card offers they receive in the mail. Have them bring the offers to class on a specific day. Divide the class into groups, and ask them to analyze the offers in terms of the promotional interest rate, regular interest rate, credit limits, annual fees, and penalties for late payments. Students who did not receive any offers can borrow some from students who receive several daily! Then ask the students if any of the offers in their group provides a better deal than the rate, limit, fees, and penalties on the credit card(s) they currently use. Most students won't know these facts about their current credit card(s). This is a good lead-in to a homework assignment to investigate their credit cards. Remind students to shred these offers when you finish this exercise.

CONVERSATION/SHARING

The ABC daily to-do list (pages 84–85) Many students have had prior experience with to-do lists. Their testimonials in class can help convince students who have not yet tried making to-do lists to experiment with them. The ABC priority aspect is usually a new concept for all students. Learning this technique helps them make better decisions about what to do and when to do It. Ask students to discuss how they can apply the ABC priority process to a list of monthly expenses to decide how to best spend their money. This is an opportunity to talk about "first things first"; spend time and money on the most important things first before you work on the less important ones.

HOMEWORK

Critical Thinking Exercise 9: The Time Monitor (pages 76–80) Assign the monitoring step of this exercise the week before you get to this chapter, because the exercise asks students to monitor their activities first so that they will have a detailed picture of how they spend their time. When students complete this exercise *before* they read the chapter, they are motivated to learn strategies to make the most of their 168 hours per week. It is not easy to keep track of oneself for 24 hours a day for a week, so talk about the importance of this exercise ahead of time. To show students that you know how challenging this exercise really is, share with them that you did it yourself.

Critical Thinking Exercise 10: Create a lifeline (page 82) Have students tape two sheets of paper side by side to allow for a long lifeline, drawn diagonally from the bottom left-hand corner to the upper right-hand corner. Have them spread the next 10 years across the left-hand page and then 50 years of highlights across the right-hand page. An alternative to doing this on paper is using the "Create a lifeline" online exercise on the Student Web site. Students who are skilled in computers may be able to create a powerful visual through Excel or PowerPoint, which could include images of what they imagine that goal to include.

Break it down, get it done: Using a long-term planner (page 86) The words *planning* and *time management* strike terror into many students' hearts. Yet this is the number one skill research tells us that students need. Tell students that they cannot control time, but they *can* control the way they respond to it. They cannot control the past, but they *can* learn from it, and they can have an impact on their future by planning the semester. As Spanish-born philosopher and poet George Santayana observed, "Those who do not learn from history are doomed to repeat it." And we only get one shot at life and time! The master monthly calendar is an opportunity for you to work with your students to plan an entire semester. Using the blank monthly calendar in the textbook (with additional sheets at the back of the text or available on the Student Web site), have students create their master plan based on the course syllabi from all of their classes. Have them transfer key dates for tests and papers, and tell them to plug in interim deadlines, such as "Write draft of English paper." Some students have success with developing master plans if, during this exercise, they also create a timeline for each of the bigger projects. An example of such a timeline is available on the Instructor Web site. Encourage students to personalize their schedules and planners, using visual elements such as design, color stickers, markers, and whatever it takes to make this a pleasant tool. If a planner feels cold and impersonal, students are not as likely to use and enjoy it.

Critical Thinking Exercise 12: The Money Monitor/Money Plan (pages 97–101) Tell your students that this is similar to the Time Monitor. The first step in managing their money is to see objectively how much money they have and how they spend it. As students examine the findings of this exercise, remind them that simple changes can make a big difference. Start by examining small possibilities: making coffee at home in the mornings, changing to energy-saving light bulbs, cutting down on their driving, or just slowing down to conserve fuel when driving. See if your local electric company provides hints for cutting down energy usage in the home. Ask students to make a note in their planners to examine their financial progress in a month or more.

Time/Money Management Article Ask students to search the Internet and bring in an interesting article on either time or money management, to share in the next class. Tell them to read their article, highlight important points, and be prepared to give a 2-minute summary. Information can be shared with the entire class or in groups of four.

EVALUATION

Quiz Ideas for Chapter 3

Ask students to:

- Write a Discovery statement regarding the Power Process: Be here now.
- Write a Discovery statement regarding time monitoring/planning and money monitoring/planning.
- Create an Intention statement regarding goal setting.
- Name antiprocrastination tools.
- Describe strategies for getting the most out of now.
- Describe ways to make more money and spend less money.
- Discuss one or more money management strategies that are especially useful during tough economic times.
- Ask students how they can take charge of their credit cards.

Additional Digital Resources for Chapter 3

What can you ASSIGN FROM THE COURSEMATE *for From Master Student to Master Employee?*

• **Master Students in Action Video.** Students hear firsthand from other students about their time management challenges and their strategies for success. The Master Students in Action videos give your students a firsthand view of how the strategies in *From Master Student to Master Employee* have helped their peers overcome obstacles. In special segments, Dave Ellis offers students his best strategies for mastering each chapter's content. Note that these videos are available for every chapter.

• **Power Process Media: Be here now.** To help students understand the importance of "be here now" as described in the Power Process for Chapter 3, have them watch a video about being here now, listen to an audio version, and then answer the accompanying questions. A PowerPoint presentation that summarizes the Power Process article's main points is also included. Or have students create group multimedia PowerPoint presentations based on their understanding of how to "be here now." Note that Power Process media are available for every chapter.

• **Learning Style Application.** To keep the information learned in Chapter 2 fresh, the Learning Style Applications, available under the Chapter Reflections tab, invite students to cycle through the four styles of learning and apply it to managing their time. In answering the four questions about freeing up for extra hours per week posted in this chapter's Learning Styles Application, students explore the different modes and apply their new knowledge. Note that Learning Style Applications are available for every chapter.

Download a list of all the resources available on the CourseMate for From Master Student to Master Employee *for Chapter 3 at the Instructor Companion Site.*

 CourseMate *To access CourseMate, your students need to visit* www.cengagebrain.com. *At the CengageBrain.com home page, students search for the ISBN of* From Master Student to Master Employee *(from the back cover of the book), using the search box at the top of the page. This takes them to the product page where these resources can be found.*

Did you know that THESE RESOURCES (and many more) ARE AVAILABLE on the INSTRUCTOR COMPANION SITE?

• **Do you have trouble managing your time?** Consider looking at the strategies for instructors who have little time to prepare, and get advice about how to develop and plan your course in the online *Course Manual*. You can also browse through the sample syllabi provided by other Master Instructors to get ideas for how you might want to reorganize your course for the future.

• **Need some energizing lecture ideas?** Browse through the lecture ideas provided for Chapter 3, including the following:

• **Committing Coming to Class.** Through a short case study of a student going to a movie, you can show the value of coming to class.

• **Complete It.** Explain to students how sorting and planning can help them become more organized.

Please visit login.cengage.com *to log in and access the Instructor Companion site.*

Time & Money

Use this **Master Student Map** to ask yourself

WHY THIS CHAPTER MATTERS . . .

- Procrastination, lack of planning, and money problems can undermine your success.

WHAT IS INCLUDED . . .

HOW I CAN USE THIS CHAPTER . . .

- Discover the details about how I currently manage time and money.
- Set time and money goals that make a difference in the quality of my life.
- Eliminate procrastination.

WHAT IF . . .

- I could meet my goals with time and money to spare?

JOURNAL ENTRY 7
Intention Statement

Create value from this chapter

Take a few minutes to skim this chapter. Find at least three techniques that you intend to use. List them below, along with their associated page numbers.

Strategy	Page number

© Ruslan Ivantsov/Shutterstock.com

POWER process

Be here now

Being right here, right now is such a simple idea. It seems obvious. Where else can you be but where you are? When else can you be there but when you are there?

The answer is that you can be somewhere else at any time—in your head. It's common for our thoughts to distract us from where we've chosen to be. When we let this happen, we lose the benefits of focusing our attention on what's important to us in the present moment.

To "be here now" means to do what you're doing when you're doing it. It means to be where you are when you're there. Students consistently report that focusing attention on the here and now is one of the most powerful tools in this book.

We all have a voice in our head that hardly ever shuts up. If you don't believe it, conduct this experiment: Close your eyes for 10 seconds, and pay attention to what is going on in your head. Please do this right now.

Notice something? Perhaps a voice in your head was saying, "Forget it. I'm in a hurry." Another might have said, "I wonder when 10 seconds is up?" Another could have been saying, "What little voice? I don't hear any little voice."

That's the voice.

This voice can take you anywhere at any time—especially when you are studying. When the voice takes you away, you might appear to be studying, but your brain is somewhere else.

All of us have experienced this voice, as well as the absence of it. When our inner voices are silent, time no longer seems to exist. We forget worries, aches, pains, reasons, excuses, and justifications. We fully experience the here and now. Life is magic.

Do not expect to be rid of the voice entirely. That is neither possible nor desirable. Inner voices serve a purpose. They enable us to analyze, predict, classify, and understand events out there in the "real" world. The trick is to consciously choose when to be with your inner voice and when to let it go.

Instead of trying to force a stray thought out of your head, simply notice it. Accept it. Tell yourself, "There's that thought again." Then gently return your attention to the task at hand. That thought, or another, will come back. Your mind will drift. Simply notice again where your thoughts take you, and gently bring yourself back to the here and now.

Also remember that planning supports this Power Process. Goals are tools that we create to guide our action in the present. Time management techniques—calendars, lists, and all the rest—have only one purpose. They reveal what's most important for you to focus on right *now*.

The idea behind this Power Process is simple. When you listen to a lecture, listen to a lecture. When you read this book, read this book. And when you choose to daydream, daydream. Do what you're doing when you're doing it. Be where you are when you're there.

Be here now . . . and now . . . and now.

You're One Click Away...
from accessing Power Process Media online and finding out more about how to "be here now."

You've got the time—
and the money

The words *time management* may call forth images of restriction and control. You might visualize a prune-faced Scrooge hunched over your shoulder, stopwatch in hand, telling you what to do every minute. Bad news.

Good news: You do have enough time for the things you want to do. All it takes is thinking about the possibilities and making conscious choices.

Time is an equal opportunity resource. All of us, regardless of gender, race, creed, or national origin, have exactly the same number of hours in a week. No matter how famous we are, no matter how rich or poor, we get 168 hours to spend each week—no more, no less.

Time is also an unusual commodity. It cannot be saved. You can't stockpile time like wood for the stove or food for the winter. It can't be seen, heard, touched, tasted, or smelled. You can't sense time directly. Even scientists and philosophers find it hard to describe. Because time is so elusive, it is easy to ignore. That doesn't bother time at all. Time is perfectly content to remain hidden until you are nearly out of it. And when you are out of it, you are out of it.

Time is a nonrenewable resource. If you're out of wood, you can chop some more. If you're out of money, you can earn a little extra. If you're out of love, there is still hope. If you're out of health, it can often be restored. But when you're out of time, that's it. When this minute is gone, it's gone.

Sometimes it seems that your friends control your time; your boss controls your time; your teachers or your parents or your kids or somebody else controls your time. Maybe that is not true, though.

Approach time as if you were in control. When you say you don't have enough time, you might really be saying that you are not spending the time you *do* have in the way that you want. This chapter is about ways to solve that problem.

The same idea applies to money. When you say you don't have enough money, the real issue might be that you are not spending the money you *do* have in the way that you want.

Most money problems result from spending more than is available. It's that simple, even though we often do everything we can to make the problem much more complicated. The solution also is simple: Don't spend more than you have. If you are spending more than you have, then increase your income, decrease your spending, or do both.

Again, you are in control of what you spend. This idea has never won a Nobel Prize in Economics, but you won't go broke applying it.

Everything written about time and money management can be reduced to three main ideas:

1. **Know exactly *what* you want.** State your wants as clear, specific goals. And put them in writing.

2. **Know *how* to get what you want.** Take action to meet your goals, including financial goals. Determine what you'll do *today* to get what you want in the future. Put those actions in writing as well.

3. **Take action to *get* what you want.** When our lives lack this quality, we spend most of our time responding to interruptions, last-minute projects, and emergencies. Life feels like a scramble to just survive. We're so busy achieving someone else's goals that we forget about getting what *we* want.

When schedules get tight, we often drop important activities such as exercising and fixing nutritious meals. We postpone them for that elusive day when we'll finally "have the time" or "have the money."

Don't wait for that time to come. *Make* the time. Use the suggestions and exercises in this chapter to empower yourself.

The most useful strategies for managing time and money are not new. They apply to people at *any* stage of their lives. These strategies are all based on the cycle of discovery, intention, and action that you're already practicing in this book. Throw in the ability to add and subtract, and you have everything you need to manage your time and your money. Spend these valuable resources in ways that align with your values. ■

CRITICAL THINKING EXERCISE 9

The Time Monitor

The purpose of this exercise is to transform time into a knowable and predictable resource. To do this, monitor your time in 15-minute intervals, 24 hours a day, for 7 days. Record how much time you spend sleeping, eating, studying, attending lectures, traveling to and from class, working, watching television, listening to music, taking care of the kids, running errands—everything.

If this sounds crazy, hang on for a minute. This exercise is not about keeping track of the rest of your life in 15-minute intervals. It is an opportunity to become conscious of how you spend your time—your life. Use the Time Monitor only for as long as it helps you do that.

When you know exactly how you spend your time, you can make choices with open eyes. You can plan to spend more time on the things that are most important to you and less time on the unimportant. Monitoring your time puts you in control of your life.

To do this exercise, complete the following steps:

1. **Look at Figure 3.2, a sample Time Monitor, on page 77.** On Monday, the student in this sample got up at 6:45 A.M., showered, and got dressed. He finished this activity and began breakfast at 7:15. He put this new activity in at the time he began, and drew a line just above it. He ate from 7:15 to 7:45. It took him 15 minutes to walk to class (7:45 to 8:00), and he attended classes from 8:00 to 11:00.

    You will list your activities in the same way. When you begin an activity, write it down next to the time you begin. Round off to the nearest 15 minutes. If, for example, you begin eating at 8:06, enter your starting time as 8:00.

2. **Fill out your Time Monitor.** Now it's your turn. Make copies of the blank Time Monitor (Figure 3.3 on page 78), or plan to do this exercise online. With your instructor, choose a day to begin monitoring your time. On that day, start filling out your Time Monitor. Keep it with you all day and use it for one full week. Take a few moments every couple of hours to record what you've done. Or, enter a note each time that you change activities.

3. **After you've monitored your time for one week, group your activities together into categories.** List them in the "Category" column in Figure 3.4 on page 80. This chart already includes the categories "sleep," "class," "study," and "meals." Think of other categories to add. "Grooming" might include showering, putting on makeup, brushing teeth, and getting dressed. "Travel" could include walking, driving, taking the bus, and riding your bike. Other categories might be "exercise," "entertainment," "work," "television," "domestic," and "children." Write in the categories that work for you.

4. **List your *estimated* hours for each category of activity.** Guess how many hours you *think* you spent on each category of activity. List these hours in the "Estimated" column in Figure 3.4.

5. **List your *actual* hours for each category of activity.** Now, add up the figures from your Time Monitor. List these hours in the "Actual" column in Figure 3.4. Make sure that the grand total of all categories is 168 hours.

6. **Reflect on the results of this exercise.** Compare the "Estimated" and "Actual" columns. Take a few minutes and let these numbers sink in. Notice your reactions. You might feel disappointed or even angry about where your time goes. Use those feelings as motivation to make different choices. Complete the following sentences:

    I was surprised at the amount of time I spent on . . .

    _____

    I want to spend more time on . . .

    _____

    I want to spend less time on . . .

    _____

7. **Repeat this exercise.** Do this exercise as many times as you want. The benefit is developing a constant awareness of your activities. With that awareness, you can make informed choices about how to spend the time of your life.

You're One Click Away...
from doing this exercise online under Exercises.

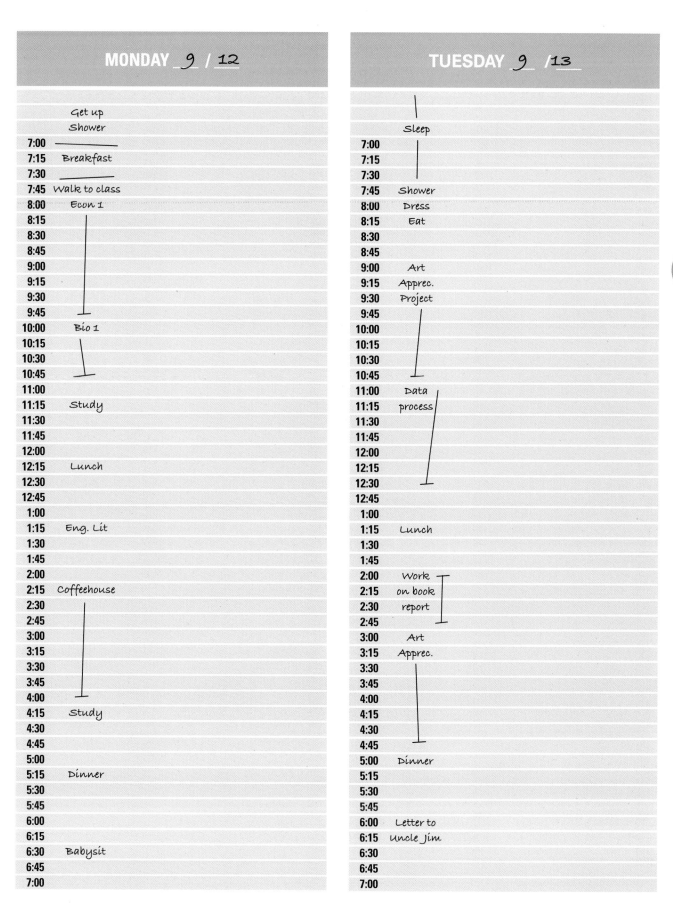

MONDAY _9_ / _12_		TUESDAY _9_ /_13_	
	Get up		
	Shower		Sleep
7:00	————	7:00	
7:15	Breakfast	7:15	
7:30	————	7:30	
7:45	Walk to class	7:45	Shower
8:00	Econ 1	8:00	Dress
8:15		8:15	Eat
8:30		8:30	
8:45		8:45	
9:00		9:00	Art
9:15		9:15	Apprec.
9:30		9:30	Project
9:45		9:45	
10:00	Bio 1	10:00	
10:15		10:15	
10:30		10:30	
10:45		10:45	
11:00		11:00	Data
11:15	Study	11:15	process
11:30		11:30	
11:45		11:45	
12:00		12:00	
12:15	Lunch	12:15	
12:30		12:30	
12:45		12:45	
1:00		1:00	
1:15	Eng. Lit	1:15	Lunch
1:30		1:30	
1:45		1:45	
2:00		2:00	Work
2:15	Coffeehouse	2:15	on book
2:30		2:30	report
2:45		2:45	
3:00		3:00	Art
3:15		3:15	Apprec.
3:30		3:30	
3:45		3:45	
4:00		4:00	
4:15	Study	4:15	
4:30		4:30	
4:45		4:45	
5:00		5:00	Dinner
5:15	Dinner	5:15	
5:30		5:30	
5:45		5:45	
6:00		6:00	Letter to
6:15		6:15	Uncle Jim
6:30	Babysit	6:30	
6:45		6:45	
7:00		7:00	

Figure 3.2 Sample Time Monitor

MONDAY ___ / ___ / ___ /	TUESDAY ___ / ___ / ___ /	WEDNESDAY ___ / ___ / ___ /	THURSDAY ___ / ___ / ___ /
7:00	7:00	7:00	7:00
7:15	7:15	7:15	7:15
7:30	7:30	7:30	7:30
7:45	7:45	7:45	7:45
8:00	8:00	8:00	8:00
8:15	8:15	8:15	8:15
8:30	8:30	8:30	8:30
8:45	8:45	8:45	8:45
9:00	9:00	9:00	9:00
9:15	9:15	9:15	9:15
9:30	9:30	9:30	9:30
9:45	9:45	9:45	9:45
10:00	10:00	10:00	10:00
10:15	10:15	10:15	10:15
10:30	10:30	10:30	10:30
10:45	10:45	10:45	10:45
11:00	11:00	11:00	11:00
11:15	11:15	11:15	11:15
11:30	11:30	11:30	11:30
11:45	11:45	11:45	11:45
12:00	12:00	12:00	12:00
12:15	12:15	12:15	12:15
12:30	12:30	12:30	12:30
12:45	12:45	12:45	12:45
1:00	1:00	1:00	1:00
1:15	1:15	1:15	1:15
1:30	1:30	1:30	1:30
1:45	1:45	1:45	1:45
2:00	2:00	2:00	2:00
2:15	2:15	2:15	2:15
2:30	2:30	2:30	2:30
2:45	2:45	2:45	2:45
3:00	3:00	3:00	3:00
3:15	3:15	3:15	3:15
3:30	3:30	3:30	3:30
3:45	3:45	3:45	3:45
4:00	4:00	4:00	4:00
4:15	4:15	4:15	4:15
4:30	4:30	4:30	4:30
4:45	4:45	4:45	4:45
5:00	5:00	5:00	5:00
5:15	5:15	5:15	5:15
5:30	5:30	5:30	5:30
5:45	5:45	5:45	5:45
6:00	6:00	6:00	6:00
6:15	6:15	6:15	6:15
6:30	6:30	6:30	6:30
6:45	6:45	6:45	6:45
7:00	7:00	7:00	7:00
7:15	7:15	7:15	7:15
7:30	7:30	7:30	7:30
7:45	7:45	7:45	7:45
8:00	8:00	8:00	8:00
8:15	8:15	8:15	8:15
8:30	8:30	8:30	8:30
8:45	8:45	8:45	8:45
9:00	9:00	9:00	9:00
9:15	9:15	9:15	9:15
9:30	9:30	9:30	9:30
9:45	9:45	9:45	9:45
10:00	10:00	10:00	10:00
10:15	10:15	10:15	10:15
10:30	10:30	10:30	10:30
10:45	10:45	10:45	10:45
11:00	11:00	11:00	11:00
11:15	11:15	11:15	11:15
11:30	11:30	11:30	11:30
11:45	11:45	11:45	11:45
12:00	12:00	12:00	12:00

Figure 3.3 Your Time Monitor

FRIDAY ___ / ___ / ___ /	SATURDAY ___ / ___ / ___ /	SUNDAY ___ / ___ / ___ /
7:00	7:00	7:00
7:15	7:15	7:15
7:30	7:30	7:30
7:45	7:45	7:45
8:00	8:00	8:00
8:15	8:15	8:15
8:30	8:30	8:30
8:45	8:45	8:45
9:00	9:00	9:00
9:15	9:15	9:15
9:30	9:30	9:30
9:45	9:45	9:45
10:00	10:00	10:00
10:15	10:15	10:15
10:30	10:30	10:30
10:45	10:45	10:45
11:00	11:00	11:00
11:15	11:15	11:15
11:30	11:30	11:30
11:45	11:45	11:45
12:00	12:00	12:00
12:15	12:15	12:15
12:30	12:30	12:30
12:45	12:45	12:45
1:00	1:00	1:00
1:15	1:15	1:15
1:30	1:30	1:30
1:45	1:45	1:45
2:00	2:00	2:00
2:15	2:15	2:15
2:30	2:30	2:30
2:45	2:45	2:45
3:00	3:00	3:00
3:15	3:15	3:15
3:30	3:30	3:30
3:45	3:45	3:45
4:00	4:00	4:00
4:15	4:15	4:15
4:30	4:30	4:30
4:45	4:45	4:45
5:00	5:00	5:00
5:15	5:15	5:15
5:30	5:30	5:30
5:45	5:45	5:45
6:00	6:00	6:00
6:15	6:15	6:15
6:30	6:30	6:30
6:45	6:45	6:45
7:00	7:00	7:00
7:15	7:15	7:15
7:30	7:30	7:30
7:45	7:45	7:45
8:00	8:00	8:00
8:15	8:15	8:15
8:30	8:30	8:30
8:45	8:45	8:45
9:00	9:00	9:00
9:15	9:15	9:15
9:30	9:30	9:30
9:45	9:45	9:45
10:00	10:00	10:00
10:15	10:15	10:15
10:30	10:30	10:30
10:45	10:45	10:45
11:00	11:00	11:00
11:15	11:15	11:15
11:30	11:30	11:30
11:45	11:45	11:45
12:00	12:00	12:00

3

WEEK OF ___ / ___ / ___ /		
Category	Estimated Hours	Actual Hours
Sleep		
Class		
Study		
Meals		

Figure 3.4 Your Estimated and Actual Hours

SETTING *and* ACHIEVING *goals*

Many people have no goals, or have only vague, idealized notions of what they want. These notions float among the clouds in their heads. They are wonderful, fuzzy, safe thoughts such as "I want to be a good person," "I want to be financially secure," or "I want to be happy."

Generalized outcomes have great potential as achievable goals. When we keep these goals in a nonspecific form, however, we may become confused about ways to actually achieve them.

Make your goal as real as a finely tuned engine. There is nothing vague or fuzzy about engines. You can see them, feel them, and hear them. You can take them apart and inspect the moving parts. Goals can be every bit as real and useful. If you really want to meet a goal, then take it apart. Inspect the moving parts—the physical actions that you will take to make the goal happen and fine-tune your life.

There are many useful methods for setting goals. You're about to learn one of them. This method is based on writing goals that relate to several time frames and areas of your life. Experiment, and modify as you see fit.

Write down your goals. Writing down your goals greatly increases your chances of meeting them. Writing exposes undefined terms, unrealistic time frames, and other symptoms of fuzzy thinking. If you've been completing Intention Statements as explained in the Introduction to this book, then you've already had experience writing goals. Both goals and Intention Statements address changes you want to make in your behavior, your values, your circumstances—or all of these.

To keep track of your goals, write each one on a separate 3 × 5 card, or type them all into a file on your computer. Update this file as your goals change, and back it up when you back up your other files. Consider storing this file on a flash drive so you can access it any time you are at a computer.

Write specific goals. State your goals in writing as observable actions or measurable results. Think in detail about how things will be different once your goals are attained. List the changes in what you'll see, feel, touch, taste, hear, be, do, or have.

Suppose that one of your goals is to become a better student by studying harder. You're headed in a powerful direction; now translate that goal into a concrete action, such as "I will study 2 hours for every hour I'm in class." Specific goals make clear what actions are needed or what results are expected.

Vague goal	Specific goal
Get a good education.	Graduate with B.S. degree in engineering, with honors, by 2012.
Get good grades.	Earn a 3.5 grade point average next semester.
Enhance my spiritual life.	Meditate for 15 minutes daily.
Improve my appearance.	Lose 6 pounds during the next 6 months
Get control of my money.	Transfer $100 to my savings account each month.

When stated specifically, a goal might look different to you. If you examine it closely, a goal you once thought you wanted might not be something you want after all. Or you might discover that you want to choose a new path to achieve a goal that you are sure you want.

Write goals in several time frames. To get a comprehensive vision of your future, write down the following:

- *Long-term goals.* Long-term goals represent major targets in your life. These goals can take 5 to 20 years to achieve. In some cases, they will take a lifetime. They can include goals in education, careers, personal relationships, travel, financial security—whatever is important to you. Consider the answers to the following questions as you create your long-term goals: What do you want to accomplish in your life? Do you want your life to make a statement? If so, what is that statement?

- *Midterm goals.* Midterm goals are objectives you can accomplish in 1 to 5 years. They include goals such as completing a course of education, paying off a car loan, or achieving a specific career level. These goals usually support your long-term goals.

- *Short-term goals.* Short-term goals are the ones you can accomplish in a year or less. These goals are specific achievements, such as completing a particular course, hiking the Appalachian Trail, or organizing a family reunion. A short-term financial goal would probably include a dollar amount. Whatever your short-term goals are, they require action now or in the near future.

Write goals in several areas of life. People who set goals in only one area of life—such as their career—may find that their personal growth becomes one-sided. They might experience success at work while neglecting their health or relationships with family members and friends.

To avoid this outcome, set goals in a variety of categories. Consider what you want to experience in these areas and add goals in other areas as they occur to you:

- Education
- Career
- Financial life
- Family life or relationships
- Social life
- Spiritual life
- Level of health

Reflect on your goals. Each week, take a few minutes to think about your goals. You can perform the following spot checks:

- *Check in with your feelings.* Think about how the process of setting your goals felt. Consider the satisfaction you'll gain in attaining your objectives. If you don't feel a significant emotional connection with a written goal, consider letting it go or filing it away to review later.
- *Check for alignment.* Look for connections among your goals. Do your short-term goals align with your midterm goals? Will your midterm goals help you achieve your long-term goals? Look for a fit between all of your goals and your purpose for taking part in higher education, as well as your overall purpose in life.
- *Check for obstacles.* All kinds of things can come between you and your goals, such as constraints on time and money. Anticipate obstacles, and start looking now for workable solutions.

Move into action immediately. To increase your odds of success, take immediate action. Decrease the gap between stating a goal and starting to achieve it. If you slip and forget about the goal, you can get back on track at any time by *doing* something about it. Here's a way to link goal setting to time management. Decide on a list of small, achievable steps you can take right away to accomplish each of your short-term goals. Write these small steps down on a daily to-do list. If you want to accomplish some of these steps by a certain date, enter them in a calendar that you consult daily. Then, over the coming weeks, review your to-do list and calendar. Take note of your progress and celebrate your successes.

One of the most effective actions you can take is to share your goals with people who will assist you to achieve them. Tap into the the power of a supportive community.

Reward yourself with care. When you meet your goal on time, reward yourself. Remember that there are two types of rewards. The first type includes rewards that follow naturally from achieving a goal. For example, your reward for earning a degree might be getting the job you've always wanted.

The second type of reward is something that you design. After turning in a paper, you might reward yourself with a nap or an afternoon in the park. A reward like this works best when you're willing to withhold it. If you plan to take a nap on Sunday afternoon, whether you've finished your chemistry assignment or not, then the nap is not an effective reward.

Another way to reward yourself after you achieve a goal is to just sit quietly and savor the feeling. One reason why success breeds success is that it feels good.

Get back to benefits. Achieving a long-term goal, such as graduating from school, poses a special challenge. You might go through periods when you lose enthusiasm. The payoff in the future seems so distant. And the work in the present seems so hard.

See whether you can close that gap in time. Take the future rewards of your goals and make them as vivid as possible in the present. Post visible reminders of the benefits you'll gain. If you want to graduate, then post photographs of people wearing caps and gowns at a ceremony. If you want to stop smoking, then post a list of the benefits that you'll gain from quitting.

Some presentations about goal setting make the whole process seem like a dry, dusty exercise in self-discipline. Don't believe it. In the end, setting and achieving goals is about having the most fun over the long run. It's about getting what you want in the future and enjoying every step along the way. ■

 CRITICAL THINKING EXERCISE 10

Create a lifeline

On a large sheet of paper, draw a horizontal line. This line will represent your lifetime. Now add key events in your life to this line, in chronological order. Examples are birth, first day at school, graduation from high school, and enrollment in higher education.

Now extend the lifeline into the future. Write down key events you would like to see occur 1 year, 5 years, and 10 or more years from now. Choose events that align with your core values. Work quickly in the spirit of a brainstorm, bearing in mind that this plan is not a final one.

Afterward, take a few minutes to review your lifeline. Select one key event for the future, and list any actions

you could take in the next month to bring yourself closer to that goal. Do the same with the other key events on your lifeline. You now have the rudiments of a comprehensive plan for your life.

Finally, extend your lifeline another 50 years beyond the year when you would reach age 100. Describe in detail what changes in the world you'd like to see as a result of the goals you attained in your lifetime.

You're One Click Away...
from doing this exercise online under Exercises.

✔CRITICAL THINKING EXERCISE 11

Get real with your goals

One way to make goals effective is to examine them up close. That's what this exercise is about. Using a process of brainstorming and evaluation, you can break a long-term goal into smaller segments until you have taken it completely apart. When you analyze a goal to this level of detail, you're well on the way to meeting it.

For this exercise, you will use a pen, extra paper, and a watch with a second hand. (A digital watch with a built-in stopwatch feature is even better.) Timing is an important part of the brainstorming process, so follow the stated time limits. This entire exercise takes about an hour.

Part 1: Long-term goals

Brainstorm. Begin with an 8-minute brainstorm. Use a separate sheet of paper for this part of the exercise. For 8 minutes, write down everything you think you want in your life. Write as fast as you can, and write whatever comes into your head. Leave no thought out. Don't worry about accuracy. The object of a brainstorm is to generate as many ideas as possible.

Evaluate. After you have finished brainstorming, spend the next 6 minutes looking over your list. Analyze what you wrote. Read the list out loud. If something is missing, add it. Look for common themes or relationships among your goals. Then select three long-term goals that are important to you—goals that will take many years to achieve. Write these goals below in the space provided.

_____

_____

_____

Before you continue, take a minute to reflect on the process you've used so far. What criteria did you use to select your top three goals?

Part 2: Midterm goals

Brainstorm. Read out loud the three long-term goals you selected in Part 1. Choose one of them. Then brainstorm a list of goals you might achieve in the next 1 to 5 years that would lead to the accomplishment of that one long-term goal. These are midterm goals. Spend 8 minutes on this brainstorm. Go for quantity.

Evaluate. Analyze your brainstorm of midterm goals. Then select three that you determine to be important in meeting the long-term goal you picked. Allow yourself 6 minutes for this part of the exercise. Write your selections below in the space provided.

_____

_____

_____

Why do you see these three goals as more important than the other midterm goals you generated? On a separate sheet of paper, write about your reasons for selecting these three goals.

Part 3: Short-term goals

Brainstorm. Review your list of midterm goals and select one. In another 8-minute brainstorm, generate a list of short-term goals—those you can accomplish in a year or less that will lead to the attainment of that midterm goal. Write down everything that comes to mind. Do not evaluate or judge these ideas yet. For now, the more ideas you write down, the better.

Evaluate. Analyze your list of short-term goals. The most effective brainstorms are conducted by suspending judgment, so you might find some bizarre ideas on your list. That's fine. Now is the time to cross them out. Next, evaluate your remaining short-term goals, and select three that you are willing and able to accomplish. Allow yourself 6 minutes for this part of the exercise. Then write your selections below in the space provided.

_____

_____

_____

The more you practice, the more effective you can be at choosing goals that have meaning for you. You can repeat this exercise, employing the other long-term goals you generated or creating new ones.

 You're One Click Away...
from completing this exercise online under Exercises.

One of the most effective ways to stay on track and actually get things done is to use a daily to-do list. Although the Time Monitor gives you a general picture of the week, your daily to-do list itemizes specific tasks you want to complete within the next 24 hours.

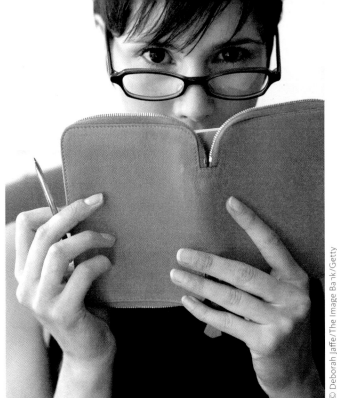

© Deborah Jaffe/The Image Bank/Getty

The ABC
daily to-do list

One advantage of keeping a daily to-do list is that you don't have to remember what to do next. It's on the list. A typical day in the life of a student is full of separate, often unrelated tasks—reading, attending lectures, reviewing notes, working at a job, writing papers, researching special projects, running errands. It's easy to forget an important task on a busy day. When that task is written down, you don't have to rely on your memory.

The following steps present one method for creating and using to-do lists. This method involves ranking each item on your list according to three levels of importance—A, B, or C. Experiment with these steps, modify them as you see fit, and invent new techniques that work for you.

STEP 1 BRAINSTORM TASKS

To get started, list all of the tasks you want to get done tomorrow. Each task will become an item on a to-do list. Don't worry about putting the entries in order or scheduling them yet. Just list everything you want to accomplish on a sheet of paper or planning calendar, or in a special notebook. You can also use 3 × 5 cards, writing one task on each card. Cards work well because you

can slip them into your pocket or rearrange them, and you never have to copy to-do items from one list to another.

STEP 2 ESTIMATE TIME

For each task you wrote down in Step 1, estimate how long it will take you to complete it. This can be tricky. If you allow too little time, you end up feeling rushed. If you allow too much time, you become less productive. For now, give it your best guess. If you are unsure, overestimate rather than underestimate how long it will take for each task. Overestimating has two benefits: (1) It avoids a schedule that is too tight, missed deadlines, and the resulting feelings of frustration and failure; and (2) it allows time for the unexpected things that come up every day—the spontaneous to-dos. Now pull out your calendar or Time Monitor. You've probably scheduled some hours for activities such as classes or work. This leaves the unscheduled hours for tackling your to-do lists.

Add up the time needed to complete all your to-do items. Also add up the number of unscheduled hours in your day. Then compare the two totals. The power of this step is that you can spot overload in advance. If you have 8 hours' worth of to-do items but only 4 unscheduled hours, that's a potential problem. To solve it, proceed to Step 3.

Step 1: Brainstorm tasks
Step 2: Estimate time
Step 3: Rate each task by priority
Step 4: Cross off tasks
Step 5: Evaluate
Bonus Step: Tinker

ALEXEY GRIGOREV/Shutterstock.com

STEP 3 RATE EACH TASK BY PRIORITY

To prevent overscheduling, decide which to-do items are the most important, given the time you have available. One suggestion for making this decision comes from the book *How to Get Control of Your Time and Your Life,* by Alan Lakein: Simply label each task A, B, or C.[1]

The A's on your list are those things that are the most critical. They include assignments that are coming due or jobs that need to be done immediately. Also included are activities that lead directly to your short-term goals.

The B's on your list are important, but less so than the A's. B's might someday become A's. For the present, these tasks are not as urgent as A's. They can be postponed, if necessary, for another day.

The C's do not require immediate attention. C priorities include activities such as "shop for a new blender" and "research genealogy on the Internet." C's are often small, easy jobs with no set time line. They too can be postponed.

Once you've labeled the items on your to-do list, schedule time for all of the A's. The B's and C's can be done randomly during the day when you are in between tasks and are not yet ready to start the next A. Even if you only get only one or two of your A's done, you'll still be moving toward your goals.

STEP 4 CROSS OFF TASKS

Keep your to-do list with you at all times. Cross off activities when you finish them, and add new ones when you think of them. If you're using 3 × 5 cards, you can toss away or recycle the cards with completed items. Crossing off tasks and releasing cards can be fun—a visible reward for your diligence. This step fosters a sense of accomplishment.

When using the ABC priority method, you might experience an ailment common to students: C fever. Symptoms include the uncontrollable urge to drop that A task and begin crossing C's off your to-do list. If your history paper is due tomorrow, you might feel compelled to vacuum the rug, call your third cousin in Tulsa, and make a trip to the store for shoelaces. The reason C fever

is so common is that A tasks are usually more difficult or time-consuming to achieve, with a higher risk of failure.

If you notice symptoms of C fever, ask yourself, "Does this job really need to be done now? Do I really need to alphabetize my DVD collection, or might I better use this time to study for tomorrow's data-processing exam?" Use your to-do list to keep yourself on task, working on your A's. But don't panic or berate yourself when you realize that in the last 6 hours, you have completed eleven C's and not a single A. Just calmly return to the A's.

STEP 5 EVALUATE

At the end of the day, evaluate your performance. Look for A priorities you didn't complete. Look for items that repeatedly turn up as B's or C's on your list and never seem to get done. Consider changing them to A's or dropping them altogether. Similarly, you might consider changing an A that didn't get done to a B or C priority.

Be willing to admit mistakes. You might at first rank some items as A's only to realize later that they are actually C's. And some of the C's that lurk at the bottom of your list day after day might really be A's. When you keep a daily to-do list, you can adjust these priorities *before* they become problems.

When you're done evaluating, start on tomorrow's to-do list. That way you can wake up and start getting things done right away.

BONUS STEP TINKER

When it comes to to-do lists, one size does not fit all. Feel free to experiment. Tweak the format of your list so that it works for you.

For example, the ABC system is not the only way to rank items on your to-do list. Some people prefer the 80-20 system. This method is based on the idea that 80 percent of the value of any to-do list comes from only 20 percent of the tasks on that list. So on a to-do list of 10 items, find the 2 that will contribute most to your life today. Complete those tasks without fail.

Another option is to rank items as "yes," "no," or "maybe." Do all of the tasks marked "yes." Delete those marked "no." And put all of the "maybes" on the shelf for later. You can come back to the "maybes" at a future point and rank them as "yes" or "no."

You might find that grouping items by categories such as "errands" and "calls" works best. Be creative.

In any case, use your to-do list in close connection with your calendar. On your calendar, note appointments, classes, and other events that take place on a specific date, a specific time, or both. Use your to-do list for items that you can complete between scheduled events. Keeping a separate to-do list means that you don't have to clutter up your calendar with all those reminders.

In addition, consider planning a whole week or even 2 weeks in advance. Planning in this way can make it easier to put activities in context and see how your daily goals relate to your long-term goals. Weekly planning can also free you from feeling that you have to polish off your whole to-do list in 1 day. Instead, you can spread tasks out over the whole week.

In any case, make starting your own to-do list an A priority. ■

You're One Click Away...
from finding more strategies online for daily planning.

BREAK IT DOWN, GET IT DONE
Using a long-term planner

With a long-term planner, you can eliminate a lot of unpleasant surprises. Long-term planning allows you to avoid scheduling conflicts—the kind that obligate you to be in two places at the same time 3 weeks from now. You can also anticipate busy periods, such as finals week, and start preparing for them now. Good-bye, all-night cram sessions. Hello, serenity.

Find a long-term planner, or make your own. Many office supply stores carry academic planners in paper form that cover an entire school year. Computer software for time management offers the same features. You can also be creative and make your own long-term planner. A big roll of newsprint pinned to a bulletin board or taped to a wall will do nicely. You can also search the Internet for a computer application or smartphone app that's designed for planning.

Enter scheduled dates that extend into the future. Use your long-term planner to list commitments that extend beyond the current month. Enter test dates, lab sessions, days that classes will be canceled, and other events that will take place over this term and next term.

Create a master assignment list. Find the syllabus for each course you're currently taking. Then, in your long-term planner, enter the due dates for all of the assignments in all of your courses. This step can be a powerful reality check.

The purpose of this technique is to not to make you feel overwhelmed with all the things you have to do. Rather, its aim is to help you take a First Step toward recognizing the demands on your time. Armed with the truth about how you use your time, you can make more accurate plans.

Include nonacademic events. In addition to tracking academic commitments, you can use your long-term planner to mark significant events in your life outside school. Include birthdays, doctors' appointments, concert dates, credit card payment due dates, and car maintenance schedules.

> Planning a day, a week, or a month ahead is a powerful practice. Using a long-term planner—one that displays an entire quarter, semester, or year at a glance—can yield even more benefits.

Use your long-term planner to divide and conquer. For some people, academic life is a series of last-minute crises punctuated by periods of exhaustion. You can avoid that fate. The trick is to break down big assignments and projects into smaller assignments and subprojects, each with their own due date.

When planning to write a paper, for instance, enter the final due date in your long-term planner. Then set individual due dates for each milestone in the writing process—creating an outline, completing your research, finishing a first draft, editing the draft, and preparing the final copy. By meeting these interim due dates, you make steady progress on the assignment throughout the term. That sure beats trying to crank out all those pages at the last minute. ■

 You're One Click Away...
from finding printable copies of this long-term planner online.

Week of	Monday	Tuesday	Wednesday	Thursday	Friday	Saturday	Sunday
9 / 5							
9 / 12		English quiz					
9 / 19			English paper due		Speech #1		
9 / 26	Chemistry test					Skiing at the lake	
10 / 3		English quiz			Speech #2		
10 / 10				Geography project due			
10 / 17				--- No classes ---			

LONG-TERM PLANNER ___ / ___ / ___ to ___ / ___ / ___

Week of	Monday	Tuesday	Wednesday	Thursday	Friday	Saturday	Sunday
___ / ___							
___ / ___							
___ / ___							
___ / ___							
___ / ___							
___ / ___							
___ / ___							
___ / ___							
___ / ___							
___ / ___							
___ / ___							
___ / ___							
___ / ___							
___ / ___							
___ / ___							
___ / ___							
___ / ___							
___ / ___							
___ / ___							
___ / ___							
___ / ___							
___ / ___							
___ / ___							
___ / ___							
___ / ___							
___ / ___							
___ / ___							
___ / ___							
___ / ___							
___ / ___							

3

Name _____

LONG-TERM PLANNER ___ / ___ / ___ to ___ / ___ / ___

Week of	Monday	Tuesday	Wednesday	Thursday	Friday	Saturday	Sunday
___ / ___							
___ / ___							
___ / ___							
___ / ___							
___ / ___							
___ / ___							
___ / ___							
___ / ___							
___ / ___							
___ / ___							
___ / ___							
___ / ___							
___ / ___							
___ / ___							
___ / ___							
___ / ___							
___ / ___							
___ / ___							
___ / ___							
___ / ___							
___ / ___							
___ / ___							
___ / ___							
___ / ___							
___ / ___							
___ / ___							
___ / ___							
___ / ___							
___ / ___							
___ / ___							
___ / ___							

STOP
Procrastination
Now

Consider a bold idea: The way to stop procrastinating is to stop procrastinating. Giving up procrastination is actually a simple choice. People just make it complicated.

Sound crazy? Well, test this idea for yourself.

Think of something that you've been putting off. Choose a small, specific task—one that you can complete in 5 minutes or less. Then do that task today.

Tomorrow, choose another task and do it. Repeat this strategy each day for 1 week. Notice what happens to your habit of procrastination.

If the above suggestion just doesn't work for you, then experiment with any strategy from the 7-day antiprocrastination plan on page 90.

DISCOVER THE COSTS. Find out whether procrastination keeps you from getting what you want. Clearly seeing the side effects of procrastination can help you kick the habit.

DISCOVER YOUR PROCRASTINATION STYLE. Psychologist Linda Sapadin identifies different styles of procrastination.[2] For example, *dreamers* have big goals that they seldom translate into specific plans. *Worriers* focus on the worst-case scenario and are likely to talk more about problems than about solutions. *Defiers* resist new tasks or promise to do them and then don't follow through. *Overdoers* create extra work for themselves by refusing to delegate tasks and neglecting to set priorities. And *perfectionists* put off tasks for fear of making a mistake.

Awareness of your procrastination style is a key to changing your behavior. If you exhibit the characteristics of an overdoer, for example, then say no to new projects. Also ask for help in completing your current projects.

To discover your procrastination style, observe your behavior. Avoid judgments. Just be a scientist: Record the facts. Write Discovery Statements about specific ways you procrastinate. Follow up with Intention Statements about what to do differently.

TRICK YOURSELF INTO GETTING STARTED. If you have a 50-page chapter to read, then grab the book and say to yourself, "I'm not really going to read this chapter right now. I'm just going to flip through the pages and scan the headings for 10 minutes." Tricks like these can get you started on a task you've been dreading.

LET FEELINGS FOLLOW ACTION. If you put off exercising until you feel energetic, you might wait for months. Instead, get moving now. Then watch your feelings change. After 5 minutes of brisk walking, you might be in the mood for a 20-minute run. This principle—action generates motivation—can apply to any task that you've put on the back burner.

CHOOSE TO WORK UNDER PRESSURE. Sometimes people thrive under pressure. As one writer puts it, "I don't do my *best* work under deadline. I do my *only* work under deadline." Used selectively, this strategy might also work for you.

Put yourself in control. If you choose to work with a due date staring you right in the face, then schedule a big block of time during the preceding week. Until then, enjoy!

THINK AHEAD. Use the long-term planner on page 87 to list due dates for assignments in all your courses. Using these tools, you can anticipate heavy demands on your time and take action to prevent last-minute crunches. Make *From Master Student to Master Employee* your home base—the first place to turn in taking control of your schedule.

CREATE GOALS THAT DRAW YOU FORWARD. A goal that grabs you by the heartstrings is an inspiration to act now. If you're procrastinating, then set some goals that excite you. Then you might wake up one day and discover that procrastination is part of your past. ■

You're One Click Away...
from finding more strategies online for ending procrastination.

THE 7-DAY
antiprocrastination plan

Listed here are seven strategies you can use to reduce or eliminate many sources of procrastination. The suggestions are tied to the days of the week to help you remember them. Use this list to remind yourself that each day of your life presents an opportunity to stop the cycle of procrastination.

MONDAY Make it Meaningful. What is important about the task you've been putting off? List all the benefits of completing that task. Look at it in relation to your short-, mid-, or long-term goals. Be specific about the rewards for getting it done, including how you will feel when the task is completed. To remember this strategy, keep in mind that it starts with the letter **M**, as in the word *Monday*.

TUESDAY Take it Apart. Break big jobs into a series of small ones you can do in 15 minutes or less. If a long reading assignment intimidates you, divide it into two- or three-page sections. Make a list of the sections, and cross them off as you complete them so you can see your progress. Even the biggest projects can be broken down into a series of small tasks. This strategy starts with the letter **T**, so mentally tie it to *Tuesday*.

WEDNESDAY Write an Intention Statement. If you can't get started on a term paper, you might write, "I intend to write a list of at least 10 possible topics by 9:00 p.m. I will reward myself with an hour of guilt-free recreational reading." Write your intention on a 3 × 5 card. Carry it with you or post it in your study area, where you can see it often. In your memory, file the first word in this strategy—*write*—with *Wednesday*.

THURSDAY Tell Everyone. Publicly announce your intention to get a task done. Tell a friend that you intend to learn 10 irregular French verbs by Saturday. Tell your spouse, roommate, parents, and children. Include anyone who will ask whether you've completed the assignment or who will suggest ways to get it done. Make the world your support group. Associate *tell* with *Thursday*.

FRIDAY Find a Reward. Construct rewards to yourself carefully. Be willing to withhold them if you do not complete the task. Don't pick a movie as a reward for studying biology if you plan to go to the movie anyway. And when you legitimately reap your reward, notice how it feels. Remember that *Friday* is a fine day to *find* a reward. (Of course, you can find a reward on any day of the week. Rhyming *Friday* with *fine* day is just a memory trick.)

SATURDAY Settle it Now. Do it now. The minute you notice yourself procrastinating, plunge into the task. Imagine yourself at a cold mountain lake, poised to dive. Gradual immersion would be slow torture. It's often less painful to leap. Then be sure to savor the feeling of having the task behind you. Link *settle* with *Saturday*.

SUNDAY Say No. When you keep pushing a task into a low-priority category, reexamine your purpose for doing that task at all. If you realize that you really don't intend to do something, quit telling yourself that you will. That's procrastinating. Just say no. Then you're not procrastinating. You don't have to carry around the baggage of an undone task. *Sunday*—the last day of this 7-day plan—is a great day to finally let go and just *say* no.

25 WAYS
TO GET THE MOST OF OUT OF
now

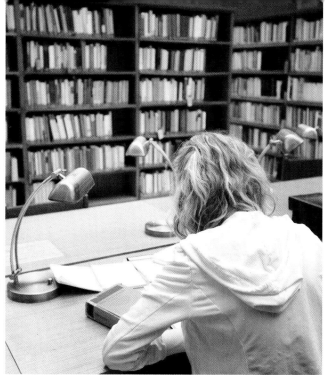

Ferenc Szelepcsenyi/Shutterstock.com

The following techniques are about getting the most from study time. They're listed in four categories:

• When to study

• Where to study

• Getting focused when you study

• Questions that keep you focused

Don't feel pressured to use all of the techniques or to tackle them in order. As you read, note the suggestions you think will be helpful. Pick one technique to use now. When it becomes a habit, come back to this article and select another one. Repeat this cycle, and enjoy the results as they unfold in your life.

WHEN TO STUDY

Study difficult (or boring) subjects first. If your chemistry problems put you to sleep, get to them first, while you are fresh. We tend to give top priority to what we enjoy studying, yet the courses that we find most difficult often require the most creative energy. Save your favorite subjects for later. If you find yourself avoiding a particular subject, get up an hour earlier to study it before breakfast. With that chore out of the way, the rest of the day can be a breeze.

Continually being late with course assignments indicates a trouble area. Further action is required. Clarify your intentions about the course by writing down your feelings in a journal, talking with an instructor, or asking for help from a friend or counselor. Consistently avoiding study tasks can also be a signal to reexamine your major or course program.

Be aware of your best time of day. Many people learn best in daylight hours. If this is true for you, schedule study time for your most difficult subjects or most difficult people before nightfall.

Unless you grew up on a farm, the idea of being conscious at 5:00 A.M. might seem ridiculous. Yet many successful businesspeople begin the day at 5:00 A.M. or earlier. Athletes and yoga practitioners use the early morning too. Some writers complete their best work before 9:00 A.M.

Others experience the same benefits by staying up late. They flourish after midnight. If you aren't convinced, then experiment. When you're in a time crunch, get up early or stay up late. You might even see a sunrise.

Use waiting time. Five minutes waiting for a subway, 20 minutes waiting for the dentist, 10 minutes in between classes—waiting time adds up fast. Have short study tasks ready to do during these periods, and keep your study materials handy. For example, carry 3 × 5 cards with facts, formulas, or definitions and pull them out anywhere. A mobile phone with an audio recording app can help you use commuting time to your advantage. Make a recording of yourself reading your notes. Play back the recording as you drive, or listen through headphones as you ride on the bus or subway.

Study 2 hours for every hour you're in class. Students in higher education are regularly advised to allow 2 hours of study time for every hour spent in class. If you are taking 15 credit hours, then plan to spend 30 hours a week studying. That adds up to 45 hours each week for school—more than a full-time job. The benefits of thinking in these terms will be apparent at exam time.

This guideline is just that—a guideline, not an absolute rule. Consider what's best for you. If you do the Time Monitor exercise in this chapter, note how many hours you actually spend studying for each hour of class. Then ask how your schedule is working. You might want to allow more study time for some subjects.

Keep in mind that the "2 hours for 1" rule doesn't distinguish between focused time and unfocused time. In one 4-hour block of study time, it's possible to use up 2 of those hours with phone calls, breaks, daydreaming, and doodling. With study time, quality counts as much as quantity.

Avoid marathon study sessions. With so many hours ahead of you, the temptation is to tell yourself, "Well, it's going to be a long day. No sense rushing into it. Better sharpen about a dozen of these pencils and change the light bulbs." Three 3-hour sessions are usually more productive than one 9-hour session.

If you must study in a large block of time, work on several subjects. Avoid studying similar topics one after the other.

Whenever you study, stop and rest for a few minutes every hour. Give your brain a chance to take a break. Simply moving to a new location might be enough to maintain your focus. When taking breaks fails to restore your energy, it's time to close the books and do something else for a while.

Monitor how much time you spend online. To get an accurate picture of your involvement in social networking and other online activities, use the Time Monitor process in this chapter. Then make conscious choices about how much time you want to spend on these activities. Staying connected is fine. Staying on constant alert for a new text, Twitter stream, or Facebook update distracts you from achieving your goals.

WHERE TO STUDY

Use a regular study area. Your body and your mind know where you are. Using the same place to study, day after day, helps train your responses. When you arrive at that particular place, you can focus your attention more quickly.

Study where you'll be alert. In bed, your body gets a signal. For most students, that signal is more likely to be "Time to sleep!" than "Time to study!" Just as you train your body to be alert at your desk, you also train it to slow down near your bed. For that reason, don't study where you sleep.

Easy chairs and sofas are also dangerous places to study. Learning requires energy. Give your body a message that energy is needed. Put yourself in a situation that supports this message. For example, some schools offer empty classrooms as places to study. If you want to avoid distractions, look for a room where friends are not likely to find you.

Use a library. Libraries are designed for learning. The lighting is perfect. The noise level is low. A wealth of material is available. Entering a library is a signal to focus the mind and get to work. Many students can get more done in a shorter time frame at the library than anywhere else. Experiment for yourself.

GETTING FOCUSED WHEN YOU STUDY

Pay attention to your attention. Breaks in concentration are often caused by internal interruptions. Your own thoughts jump in to divert you from your studies. When this happens, notice these thoughts and let them go. Perhaps the thought of getting something else done is distracting you. One option is to handle that other task now and study later. Or you can write yourself a note about it or schedule a specific time to do it.

Agree with living mates about study time. This agreement includes roommates, spouses, and children. Make the rules about study time clear, and be sure to follow them yourself. Explicit agreements—even written contracts—work well. One student always wears a colorful hat when he wants to study. When his wife and children see the hat, they respect his wish to be left alone.

Get off the phone. The phone is the ultimate interrupter. People who wouldn't think of distracting you in person might call or text you at the worst times because they can't see that you are studying. You don't have to be a victim of your cell phone. If a simple "I can't talk; I'm studying" doesn't work, use dead silence. It's a conversation killer. Or short-circuit the whole problem: Turn off your phone or silence it.

Learn to say no. Saying no is a time-saver and a valuable life skill for everyone. Some people feel it is rude to refuse a request. But you can say no effectively and courteously. Others want you to succeed as a student. When you tell them that you can't do what they ask because you are busy educating yourself, most people will understand.

Hang a "do not disturb" sign on your door. Many hotels will give you a free sign, for the advertising. Or you can create a sign yourself. They work. Using signs can relieve you of making a decision about cutting off each interruption—a time-saver in itself.

Get ready the night before. Completing a few simple tasks just before you go to bed can help you get in gear the next day. If you need to make some phone calls first thing in the morning, look up those numbers, write them on 3 × 5 cards, and set them near the phone. If you need to drive to a new location, make a note of the address and put it next to your car keys. If you plan to spend the next

SETTING LIMITS ON screen time

Access to the Internet and wireless communication offers easy ways to procrastinate. We call it "surfing," "texting," "IMing,"—and sometimes "researching" or "working." In his book *Crazy Busy: Overstretched, Overbooked, and About to Snap*, Edward Hallowell coined a word to describe these activities when they're done too often—*screensucking*.

Digital devices create value. With a computer you can stream music, watch videos, listen to podcasts, scan newspapers, read books, check e-mail, and send instant messages. With a smartphone you consume online content while staying available to key people when it counts. And any of these activities can become a constant source of distraction.

Discover how much time you spend online. People who update their Twitter stream or Facebook page every hour may be sending an unintended message—that they have no life offline.

To get an accurate picture of your involvement in social networking and other online activity, use the Time Monitor exercise included earlier in this chapter. Then make conscious choices about how much time you want to spend online and on the phone. Don't let social networking distract you from meeting personal and academic goals.

Go offline to send the message that other people matter. It's hard to pay attention to the person who is right in front of you when you're hammering out text messages or updating your Twitter stream. You can also tell when someone else is doing these things and only half-listening to you. How engaged in your conversation do you think that person is?

An alternative is to close up your devices and "be here now." When you're eating, stop answering the phone. Notice how the food tastes. When you're with a friend, close up your laptop. Hear every word he says. Rediscover where life actually takes place—in the present moment.

Developing emotional intelligence requires being with people and away from a computer or cell phone. People who break up with a partner through text messaging are not developing that intelligence. True friends know when to go offline and head across campus to resolve a conflict. They know when to go back home and support a family member in crisis. When it counts, your presence is your greatest present.

3

---

afternoon writing a paper, get your materials together: dictionary, notes, outline, paper, pencil, flash drive, laptop—whatever you need. Pack your lunch or put gas in the car. Organize the baby's diaper bag and your briefcase or backpack.

Call ahead. We often think of talking on the telephone as a prime time-waster. Used wisely, though, the telephone can actually help manage time. Before you go shopping, call the store to see whether it carries the items you're looking for. A few seconds on the phone or computer can save hours in wasted trips and wrong turns.

Avoid noise distractions. To promote concentration, avoid studying in front of the television, and turn off the radio. Many students insist that they study better with background noise, and it might be true. Some students report good results with carefully selected and controlled music. For many others, silence is the best form of music to study by.

At times noise levels might be out of your control. A neighbor or roommate might decide to find out how far she can turn up her music before the walls crumble. Meanwhile, your ability to concentrate on the principles of sociology goes down the drain. To avoid this scenario, schedule study sessions during periods when your living environment is usually quiet. If you live in a residence

hall, ask whether study rooms are available. Or go somewhere else where it's quiet, such as the library. Some students have even found refuge in quiet coffee shops, self-service laundries, and places of worship.

Manage interruptions. Notice how others misuse your time. Be aware of repeat offenders. Ask yourself whether there are certain friends or relatives who consistently interrupt your study time.

If avoiding the interrupter is impractical, send a clear message. Sometimes others don't realize that they are breaking your concentration. You can give them a gentle, yet firm, reminder: "What you're saying is important. Can we schedule a time to talk about it when I can give you my full attention?" If this strategy doesn't work, there are other ways to make your message more effective. For more ideas, see Chapter 9: Communicating.

See whether you can "firewall" yourself for selected study periods each week. Find a place where you can count on being alone and work without interruption.

Sometimes interruptions still happen, though. Create a system for dealing with them. One option is to take an index card and write a quick note about what you're doing the moment an interruption occurs. As soon as possible, return to the card and pick up the task where you left off.

QUESTIONS THAT
KEEP YOU FOCUSED

Ask: "What is one task I can accomplish toward achieving my goal?" This technique is helpful when you face a big, imposing job. Pick out one small accomplishment, preferably one you can complete in about 5 minutes; then do it. The satisfaction of getting one thing done can spur you on to get one more thing done. Meanwhile, the job gets smaller.

Ask: "Am I being too hard on myself?" If you are feeling frustrated with a reading assignment, your attention wanders repeatedly, or you've fallen behind on math problems that are due tomorrow, take a minute to listen to the messages you are giving yourself. Are you scolding yourself too harshly? Lighten up. Allow yourself to feel a little foolish, and then get on with the task at hand. Don't add to the problem by berating yourself.

Worrying about the future is another way people beat themselves up: "How will I ever get all this done?" "What if every paper I'm assigned turns out to be this hard?" "If I can't do the simple calculations now, how will I ever pass the final?" Instead of promoting learning, such questions fuel anxiety and waste valuable time.

Labeling and generalizing weaknesses are other ways people are hard on themselves. Being objective and specific in the messages you send yourself will help eliminate this form of self-punishment and will likely generate new possibilities. An alternative to saying "I'm terrible in algebra" is to say, "I don't understand factoring equations." This rewording suggests a plan to improve.

You might be able to lighten the load by discovering how your learning styles affect your behavior. For example, you may have a bias toward concrete experience rather than abstract thinking. If so, after setting a goal, you might want to move directly into action.

In large part, the ability to learn through concrete experience is a valuable trait. After all, action is necessary to achieve goals. At the same time, you might find it helpful to allow extra time to plan. Careful planning can help you avoid unnecessary activity. Instead of using a planner that shows a day at a time, experiment with a calendar that displays a week or month at a glance. The expanded format can help you look further into the future and stay on track as you set out to meet long-term goals.

Ask: "Is this a piano?" Carpenters who construct rough frames for buildings have a saying they use when they bend a nail or accidentally hack a chunk out of a two-by-four: "Well, this ain't no piano." It means that perfection is not necessary. Ask yourself whether what you are doing needs to be perfect. Perhaps you don't have to apply the same standards of grammar to lecture notes that you would apply to a term paper. If you can complete a job 95 percent perfectly in 2 hours and 100 percent perfectly in 4 hours, ask yourself whether the additional 5 percent improvement is worth doubling the amount of time you spend.

Sometimes, though, it *is* a piano. A tiny miscalculation can ruin an entire lab experiment. A misstep in solving a complex math problem can negate hours of work. Computers are notorious for turning little errors into nightmares. Accept lower standards only when appropriate.

A related suggestion is to weed out low-priority tasks. The to-do list for a large project can include dozens of items, not all of which are equally important. Some can be done later, while others can be skipped altogether, if time is short.

Apply this idea when you study. In a long reading assignment, look for pages you can skim or skip. When it's appropriate, read chapter summaries or article abstracts. As you review your notes, look for material that might not be covered on a test, and decide whether you want to study it.

Ask: "Would I pay myself for what I'm doing right now?" If you were employed as a student, would you be earning your wages? Ask yourself this question when you notice that you've taken your third snack break in 30 minutes. Then remember that you are, in fact, employed as a student. You are investing in your own productivity and are paying a big price for the privilege of being a student. Doing a mediocre job now might result in fewer opportunities in the future.

Ask: "Can I do just one more thing?" Ask yourself this question at the end of a long day. Almost always you will have enough energy to do just one more short task. The overall increase in your productivity might surprise you.

Ask: "Can I delegate this?" Instead of slogging through complicated tasks alone, you can draw on the talents and energy of other people. Busy executives know the value of delegating tasks to coworkers. Without delegation, many projects would flounder or die.

You can apply the same principle in your life. Instead of doing all the housework or cooking by yourself, for example, you can assign some of the tasks to family members or roommates. Rather than making a trip to the library to look up a simple fact, you can call and ask a library assistant to research it for you. Instead of driving across town to deliver a package, you can hire a delivery service to do so. All of these tactics can free up extra hours for studying.

It's not practical to delegate certain study tasks, such as writing term papers or completing reading assignments. However, you can still draw on the ideas of others in completing such tasks. For instance, form a writing group to edit and critique papers, brainstorm topics or titles, and develop lists of sources.

If you're absent from a class, find a classmate to summarize the lecture, discussion, and any upcoming assignments. Presidents depend on briefings. You can use the same technique.

Ask: "How did I just waste time?" Notice when time passes and you haven't accomplished what you had planned to do. Take a minute to review your actions and note the specific ways you wasted time. We tend to operate by habit, wasting time in the same ways over and over again. When you are aware of things you do that drain your time, you are more likely to catch yourself in the act next time. Observing one small quirk might save you hours. But keep this in mind: Asking you to notice how you waste time is not intended to make you feel guilty. The point is to increase your skill by getting specific information about how you use time.

Ask: "Could I find the time if I really wanted to?" The way people speak often rules out the option of finding more time. An alternative is to speak about time with more possibility.

The next time you're tempted to say, "I just don't have time," pause for a minute. Question the truth of this statement. Could you find 4 more hours this week for studying? Suppose that someone offered to pay you $10, 000 to find those 4 hours. Suppose too that you will get paid only if you don't lose sleep, call in sick for work, or sacrifice anything important to you. Could you find the time if vast sums of money were involved?

Remember that when it comes to school, vast sums of money *are* involved.

Ask: "Am I willing to promise it?" This time-management idea might be the most powerful of all: If you want to find time for a task, promise yourself—and others—that you'll get it done. Unleash one of the key qualities of master students and take responsibility for producing an outcome.

To make this technique work, do more than say that you'll try to keep a promise or that you'll give it your best shot. Take an oath, as you would in court. Give it your word.

One way to accomplish big things in life is to make big promises. There's little reward in promising what's safe or predictable. No athlete promises to place seventh in the Olympic games. Chances are that if you're not making big promises, you're not stretching yourself.

The point of making a promise is not to chain yourself to a rigid schedule or impossible expectations. You can promise to reach goals without unbearable stress. You can keep schedules flexible and carry out your plans with ease, joy, and satisfaction.

At times, though, you might go too far. Some promises may be truly beyond you, and you might break them. However, failing to keep a promise is just that—failing to keep a promise. A broken promise is not the end of the world.

Promises can work magic. When your word is on the line, it's possible to discover reserves of time and energy you didn't know existed. Promises can push you to exceed your expectations. ■

 You're One Click Away...
from discovering even more ways online to get the most out of now.

Master Employees
IN ACTION

 You're One Click Away...
from a video about Master Students in Action.

"*In my college classes I would get syllabi from professors that laid out the whole year. Assignments were never mentioned again and it was up to me to do them on time. At work, I have a whole series of tasks to complete on my own from week to week. And I now know how/when to do those things without being asked.*"

–Karlis Bryan,
Assistant Media Buyer

© Wendy White / Alamy

Make choices about
MULTITASKING

When we get busy, we get tempted to do several things at the same time. It seems like such a natural solution: Watch TV *and* read a textbook. Talk on the phone *and* outline a paper. Write an e-mail *and* listen to a lecture. These are examples of multitasking.

There's a problem with this strategy: Multitasking is much harder than it looks.

Despite the awe-inspiring complexity of the human brain, research reveals that we are basically wired to do one thing at a time.[3] One study found that people who interrupted work to check e-mail or surf the Internet took up to 25 minutes to get back to their original task.[4] In addition, people who use cell phones while driving have more accidents than anyone except drunk drivers.[5]

The solution is an old-fashioned one: Whenever possible, take life one task at a time. Develop a key quality of master students—focused attention. Start by reviewing and using the "Power Process: Be here now." Then add the following strategies to your toolbox.

UNPLUG FROM TECHNOLOGY

To reduce the temptation of multitasking, turn off distracting devices. Shut off your TV and cell phone. Disconnect from the Internet unless it's required for your planned task. Later, you can take a break to make calls, send texts, check e-mail, and browse the Web.

CAPTURE FAST-BREAKING IDEAS WITH MINIMAL INTERRUPTION

Your brain is an expert nagger. After you choose to focus on one task, it might issue urgent reminders about 10 more things you need to do. Keep 3 × 5 cards or paper and a pen handy to write down those reminders. You can take a break later and add them to your to-do list. Your mind can quiet down once it knows that a task has been captured in writing.

MONITOR THE MOMENT-TO-MOMENT SHIFTS IN YOUR ATTENTION

Whenever you're studying and notice that you're distracted by thoughts of doing something else, make a tally mark on a sheet of paper. Simply being aware of your tendency to multitask can help you reclaim your attention.

HANDLE INTERRUPTIONS WITH CARE

Some breaking events are so urgent that they call for your immediate attention. When this happens, note what you were doing when you were interrupted. For example, write down the number of the page you were reading, or the name of the computer file you were creating. When you return to the task, your notes can help you get up to speed again.

MULTITASK BY CONSCIOUS CHOICE

If multitasking seems inevitable, then do it with skill. Pair one activity that requires concentration with another activity that you can do almost automatically. For example, studying for your psychology exam while downloading music is a way to reduce the disadvantages of multitasking. Pretending to listen to your children while watching TV is not.

ALIGN YOUR ACTIVITIES WITH YOUR PASSIONS

Our attention naturally wanders when we find a task to be trivial, pointless, or irritating. At those times, switching attention to another activity becomes a way to reduce discomfort.

Handling routine tasks is a necessary part of daily life. But if you find that your attention frequently wanders throughout the day, ask yourself: Am I really doing what I want to do? Do my work and my classes connect to my interests?

If the answer is no, then the path beyond multitasking might call for a change in your academic and career plans. Determine what you want most in life. Then use the techniques in this chapter to set goals that inspire you. Whenever an activity aligns with your passion, the temptation to multitask loses power. ■

CRITICAL THINKING EXERCISE 12

The Money Monitor/Money Plan

Many of us find it easy to lose track of money. It likes to escape when no one is looking. And usually, no one is looking. That's why the simple act of noticing the details about money can be so useful—even if this is the only idea from the chapter that you ever apply.

Use this exercise as a chance to discover how money flows into and out of your life. The goal is to record all the money you receive and spend over the course of 1 month. This sounds like a big task, but it's simpler than you might think. Besides, there's a big payoff for this action. With increased awareness of income and expenses, you can make choices about money that will change your life. Here's how to begin.

STEP 1 Tear out the Money Monitor/Money Plan form on page 100. Make photocopies of this form to use each month. The form helps you do two things. One is to get a big picture of the money that flows in and out of your life. The other is to plan specific and immediate changes in how you earn and spend money.

STEP 2 Keep track of your income and expenses. Use your creativity to figure out how you want to carry out this step. The goal is to create a record of exactly how much you earn and spend each month. Use any method that works for you. And keep it simple. Following are some options:

- **Carry 3 × 5 cards in your pocket, purse, backpack, or briefcase.** Every time you buy something or get paid, record a few details on a card. List the date. Add a description of what you bought or what you got paid. Note whether the item is a source of income (money coming in) or an expense (money going out). Be sure to use a separate card for each item. This makes it easier to sort your cards into categories at the end of the month and fill out your Money Monitor/Money Plan.

- **Save all receipts and file them.** This method does not require you to carry any 3 × 5 cards. But it does require that you faithfully hang on to every receipt and record of payment. Every time you buy something, ask for a receipt. Then stick it in your wallet, purse, or pocket. When you get home, make notes about the purchase on the receipt. Then file the receipts in a folder labeled with the current month and year (for example, January 2011). Every time you get a paycheck during that month, save the stub and add it to the folder. If you do not get a receipt or record of payment, whip out a 3 × 5 card and create one of your own. Detailed receipts will help you later on when you file taxes, categorize expenses (such as food and entertainment), and check your purchases against credit card statements.

- **Use personal finance software.** Learn to use Quicken or a similar product that allows you to record income and expenses on your computer and to sort them into categories.

- **Use online banking services.** If you have a checking account that offers online services, take advantage of the records that the bank is already keeping for you. Every time you write a check, use a debit card, or make a deposit, the transaction will show up online. You can use a computer to log in to your account and view these transactions at any time. If you're unclear about how to use online banking, go in to your bank and ask for help.

- **Experiment with several of the above options.** Settle into one that feels most comfortable to you. Or create a method of your own. Anything will work, as long as you end each month with an *exact and accurate* record of your income and expenses.

STEP 3 On the last day of the month, fill out your Money Monitor/Money Plan. Pull out a blank Money Monitor/Money Plan. Label it with the current month and year. Fill out this form using the records of your income and expenses for the month.

Notice that the far left column of the Money Monitor/Money Plan includes categories of income and expenses. (You can use the blank rows for categories of income and expenses that are not already included.) Write your total for each category in the middle column.

For example, if you spent $300 at the grocery store this month, write that amount in the middle column next to *Groceries*. If you work a part-time job and received two paychecks for the month, write the total in the middle column next to *Employment*. See the sample Money Monitor/Money Plan on page 99 for more examples.

Remember to split expenses when necessary. For example, you might write one check each month to pay the balance due on your credit card. The purchases listed on your credit card bill might fall into several categories. Total up your expenses in each category, and list them separately.

Suppose that you used your credit card to buy music online, purchase a sweater, pay for three restaurant meals, and buy two tanks of gas for your car. Write the online music expense next to *Entertainment*. Write the amount you paid for the sweater next to *Clothes*. Write the total you spent at the restaurants next to *Eating Out*. Finally, write the total for your gas stops next to *Gas*.

Now look at the column on the far right of the Money Monitor/Money Plan. This column is where the magic happens. Review each category of income and expense. If you plan to reduce your spending in a certain category during the next month, write a minus sign (−) in the far right column. If you plan a spending increase

in any category next month, write a plus sign (+) in the far right column. If you think that a category of income or expense will remain the same next month, leave the column blank.

Look again at the sample Money Monitor/Money Plan on page 99. This student plans to reduce her spending for clothes, eating out, and entertainment (which for her includes movies and DVD rentals). She plans to increase the total she spends on groceries. She figures that even so, she'll save money by cooking more food at home and eating out less.

STEP 4 **After you've filled out your first Money Monitor/ Money Plan, take a moment to congratulate yourself.** You have actively collected and analyzed the data needed to take charge of your financial life. No matter how the numbers add up, you are now in conscious control of your money. Repeat this exercise every month. It will keep you on a steady path to financial freedom.

 You're One Click Away...
from doing this exercise online at your College Success CourseMate.

No budgeting required

Notice one more thing about the Money Monitor/Money Plan: It does not require you to create a budget. Budgets—like diets—often fail. Many people cringe at the mere mention of the word *budget*. To them it is associated with scarcity, drudgery, and guilt. The idea of creating a budget conjures up images of a penny-pinching Ebenezer Scrooge shaking a bony, wrinkled finger at them and screaming, "You spent too much, you loser!"

That's not the idea behind the Money Monitor/Money Plan. In fact, there is no budget worksheet for you to complete each month. And no one is pointing a finger at you. Instead of budgeting, you simply write a plus sign or a minus sign next to each expense or income category that you *freely choose* to increase or decrease next month. There's no extra paperwork, no shame, and no blame.

Sample Money Monitor/Money Plan

Income	This Month	Next Month
Employment	500	
Grants	100	
Interest from Savings		
Loans	300	
Scholarships	100	
Total Income	1000	

Expenses	This Month	Next Month
Books and Supplies		
Car Maintenance		
Car Payment		
Clothes		−
Deposits into Savings Account		
Eating Out	50	−
Entertainment	50	−
Gas	100	
Groceries	300	+
Insurance (Car, Life, Health, Home)		
Laundry	20	
Phone	55	
Rent/Mortgage Payment	400	
Tuition and Fees		
Utilities	50	
Total Expenses	1025	−

3

Money Monitor/Money Plan
Month_____ Year_____

Income	This Month	Next Month	Expenses	This Month	Next Month
Employment			Books and Supplies		
Grants			Car Maintenance		
Interest from Savings			Car Payment		
Loans			Clothes		
Scholarships			Deposits into Savings Account		
			Eating Out		
			Entertainment		
			Gas		
			Groceries		
			Insurance (Car, Life, Health, Home)		
			Laundry		
			Phone		
			Rent/Mortgage Payment		
			Tuition and Fees		
			Utilities		
Total Income			Total Expenses		

Money Monitor/Money Plan
Month_____ Year_____

Income	This Month	Next Month	Expenses	This Month	Next Month
Employment			Books and Supplies		
Grants			Car Maintenance		
Interest from Savings			Car Payment		
Loans			Clothes		
Scholarships			Deposits into Savings Account		
			Eating Out		
			Entertainment		
			Gas		
			Groceries		
			Insurance (Car, Life, Health, Home)		
			Laundry		
			Phone		
			Rent/Mortgage Payment		
			Tuition and Fees		
			Utilities		
Total Income			Total Expenses		

EARN MORE MONEY

For many people, finding a way to increase income is the most appealing way to fix a money problem. This approach is reasonable, but it has a potential problem: When their income increases, many people continue to spend more than they make. This means that money problems persist even at higher incomes. To avoid this problem, manage your expenses no matter how much money you make.

If you do succeed at controlling your expenses over the long term, then increasing your income is definitely a way to build wealth.

Focus on your education. Your most important assets are not your bank accounts, your car, or your house, but your skills. That's why your education is so important. Right now, you're developing knowledge, experience, and abilities that you can use to create income for the rest of your life.

Once you graduate and land a job in your chosen field, continue your education. Look for ways to gain additional skills or certifications that lead to higher earnings and more fulfilling work assignments.

Work while you're in school. If you work while you're in school, you earn more than money. You gain experience, establish references, interact with a variety of people, and make contact with people who might hire you in the future. Also, regular income in any amount can make a difference in your monthly cash flow.

Many students work full-time or part-time jobs. Work and school don't have to conflict, especially if you plan carefully and ask for your employer's support.

See if you can find a job related to your chosen career. Even an entry-level job in your field can provide valuable experience. Once you've been in such a job for a while, explore the possibilities for getting a promotion.

Treat people well. No matter where you work, you are meeting people. Build positive relationships. Do this with people at any level of an organization—from the CEO to the people who empty the trash. Treat them all as equals. Look for common ground and make friendly conversation. And if you ever feel someone at work has taken advantage of you, take steps to protect yourself while letting go of the desire to get revenge.

Treating people well offers two benefits. First, you create a more pleasant work environment. Second, someone that you treat with kindness today might be in a position to recommend you for a promotion or a higher-paying job in the future. Kindness pays off in many ways.

Use "downtime" to your advantage. Some jobs involve workloads that come in cycles. During certain times of the year—when a new product is launched, for example—people work longer

> If your employer offers training and development programs, take advantage of them. Use downtime to contribute to your employer and yourself.

hours. At other points in the year, they experience downtimes—days when they have much less to do.

If your work slows down, look for something useful to do. Instead of sharpening pencils or surfing the Internet, do a task that's important but not urgent. If your employer offers training and development programs, take advantage of them. Use downtime to contribute to your employer and yourself.

Do your best at every job. Once you get a job, make it your intention to excel as an employee. A positive work experience can pay off for years by leading to other jobs, recommendations, and contacts.

This means doing every task with full attention and care—even the "menial" jobs. Straightening up shelves or updating a mailing list are opportunities to shine as an employee.

Every job involves tasks that are less than glamorous. Think beyond what you're *doing* to who you're *being*. Any task allows you to align your actions with a commitment to quality and other core values.

Take the long view. To maximize your earning power, keep honing your job-hunting and career-planning skills. You can find a wealth of ideas on these topics in Chapter 12: Career Management.

Finally, keep things in perspective. If your current job is lucrative and rewarding, great. If not, remember that almost any job can support you in becoming a master student and a master employee. ■

You're One Click Away...
from discovering more ways online to increase your income.

SPEND LESS MONEY

Controlling your expenses is something you can do right away, and it's usually easier than increasing your income. Start with the following ideas.

Look at big-ticket items. When you look for places to cut expenses, start with the items that cost the most. Choices about where to live, for example, can save you thousands of dollars. Sometimes a place a little farther from campus, or a smaller house or apartment, will be much less expensive.

Use "Critical Thinking Exercise 12: The Money Monitor/Money Plan" on page 97 to discover the main drains on your finances. Then focus on one or two areas where you can reduce spending.

Do comparison shopping. Prices vary dramatically. Shop around, wait for off-season sales, and use coupons. Check out secondhand stores, thrift stores, and garage sales. Before plunking down the full retail price for a new item, consider whether you could buy it used.

Be aware of quality. The cheapest product is not always the least expensive over the long run. Sometimes, a slightly more expensive item is the best buy because it will last longer. Remember, there is no correlation between the value of something and the amount of money spent to advertise it.

Save money on eating and drinking. This single suggestion could significantly lower your expenses. Instead of hitting a restaurant or bar, head to the grocery store. Fresh fruits, fresh vegetables, and whole grains are not only better for you than processed food—they also cost less.

Cooking for yourself doesn't need to take much time. Do a little menu planning. Create a list of your five favorite home-cooked meals. Learn how to prepare them. Then keep ingredients for these meals always on hand. To reduce grocery bills, buy these ingredients in bulk.

Lower your phone bills. If you use a cell phone, pull out a copy of your latest bill. Review how many minutes you used last month. Perhaps you could get by with a less expensive phone, fewer minutes, fewer text messages, and a cheaper plan.

Go "green." To conserve energy and save money on utility bills, turn out the lights when you leave a room. Keep windows and doors closed in winter. In summer, keep windows open early in the day to invite lots of cool air into your living space. Then close up the apartment or house to keep it cool during the hotter hours of the day. Leave air-conditioning set at 72 degrees or above. In cool weather, dress warmly and keep the house at 68 degrees or less. In hot weather, take shorter, cooler showers.

Postpone purchases. If you plan to buy something, leave your credit card at home when you first go shopping. Look at all the possibilities. Then go home and make your decision when you don't feel pressured. When you are ready to buy, wait a week, even if the salesperson pressures you. What seems like a necessity today may not even cross your mind the day after tomorrow.

Use the envelope system. After reviewing your monthly income and expenses, put a certain amount of cash each week in an envelope labeled *Entertainment/Eating Out*. When the envelope is empty, stop spending money on these items for the rest of the week. If you use online banking, see if you can create separate accounts for various spending categories. Then deposit a fixed amount of money into each of those accounts. This is an electronic version of the envelope system.

Use the money you save to prepare for emergencies and reduce debt. If you apply strategies such as those listed here, you might see your savings account swell nicely. Congratulate yourself. Then choose what to do with the extra money. To protect yourself during tough times, create an emergency fund. Then reduce your debt by paying more than the minimum on credit card bills and loan payments (see "Take Charge of Your Credit" on page 107.) ■

> Remember, there is no correlation between the value of something and the amount of money spent to advertise it.

You're One Click Away...
from discovering more cost-cutting strategies online.

Managing money during tough times

A short-term crisis in the overall economy can reduce your income and increase your expenses. So can the decision to go back to school. The biggest factor in your long-term financial well-being, though, is your daily behavior. Habits that help you survive during tough times will also help you prosper after you graduate and when the economy rebounds. Taking informed action is a way to cut through financial confusion and move beyond fear.

Start by doing "Critical Thinking Exercise 12: Money Monitor/Money Plan" on page 97, if you have not yet completed it. This exercise will give you the details about what you're spending and earning right now. With that knowledge, you can choose your next strategy from among the following.

TAKE A FIRST STEP

If the economy tanks, we can benefit by telling the truth about it. We can also tell the truth about ourselves. It's one thing to condemn the dishonesty of mortgage bankers and hedge fund managers. It's another thing to have an unpaid balance on a credit card or wipe out a savings accounts and still believe that we are in charge of our money. The first step to changing such behaviors is simply to admit that they don't work.

SPEND LESS AND SAVE MORE

The less you spend, the more money you'll have on hand. Use that money to pay your monthly bills, pay off your credit cards,

and create an emergency fund to use in case you lose your job or a source of financial aid. See "Spend less money" on page 103 for ideas.

Author Suze Orman recommends three actions to show that you can reduce spending at any time: (1) Do not spend money for 1 day, (2) do not use your credit card for 1 week, and (3) do not eat out for 1 month. Success with any of these strategies can open up your mind to other possibilities for spending less and saving more.[6]

MAKE SURE THAT YOUR SAVINGS ARE PROTECTED

The Federal Deposit Insurance Corporation (FDIC) backs individual saving accounts. The National Credit Union Administration (NCUA) offers similar protection for credit union members. If your savings are protected by these programs, every penny you deposit is safe. Check your statements to find out, or go online to www.myfdicinsurance.gov.

PAY OFF YOUR CREDIT CARDS

If you have more than one credit card with an outstanding balance, then find out which one has the highest interest rate. Put as much money as you can toward paying off that balance while making the minimum payment on the other cards. Repeat this process until all unpaid balances are erased.

INVEST ONLY AFTER SAVING

The stock market is only for money that you can afford to lose. Before you speculate, first save enough money to live on for at least 6 months in case you're unemployed. Then consider what you'll need over the next 5 years to finish your schooling and handle other major expenses. Save for these expenses before taking any risks with your money.

DO STELLAR WORK AT YOUR CURRENT JOB

The threat of layoffs increases during a recession. However, companies will hesitate to shed their star employees. If you're working right now, then think about ways to become indispensable. Gain skills and experience that will make you more valuable to your employer.

No matter what job you have, be as productive as possible. Look for ways to boost sales, increase quality, or accomplish tasks in less time. Ask yourself every day how you can create extra value by solving a problem, reducing costs, improving service, or attracting new clients or customers.

THINK ABOUT YOUR NEXT JOB

Create a career plan that describes the next job you want, the skills that you'll develop to get it, and the next steps you'll take to gain those skills. Stay informed about the latest developments in your field. Find people who are already working in this area, and contact them for information interviews.

You might want to start an active job hunt now, even if you have a job. Find time to build your network, go to job-related conferences, and stay on top of current job openings in your field. For related ideas, see Chapter 12: Career Management.

RESEARCH UNEMPLOYMENT BENEFITS

Unemployment benefits have limits and may not replace your lost wages. However, they can cushion the blow of losing a job while you put other strategies in place. To learn about the benefits offered in your state, go online to www.servicelocator.org. Click "Unemployment Benefits." Then enter your state.

GET HEALTH INSURANCE

A sudden illness or lengthy hospital stay can drain your savings. Health insurance can pick up all or most of the costs instead. If possible, get health insurance through your school or employer. Another option is private health insurance. This can be cheaper than extending an employer's policy if you lose your job. To find coverage, go online to the Web site of the National Association of Health Underwriters (www.nahu.org) and www.ehealthinsurance.com.

GET HELP THAT YOU CAN TRUST

Avoid debt consolidators that offer schemes to wipe out your debt. What they don't tell you is that their fees are high, and that using them can lower your credit rating. Turn instead to the National Foundation for Credit Counseling (www.nfcc.org). Find a credit counselor that is accredited by this organization. Work with someone who is open about fees and willing to work with all your creditors. Don't pay any fees up front, before you actually get help.

PUT YOUR PLAN IN WRITING

List the specific ways that you will reduce spending and increase income. If you have a family, consider posting this list for everyone to see. The act of putting your plan in writing can help you feel in control of your money. Review your plan regularly to make sure that it's working and that everyone who's affected is on board.

COPE WITH STRESS IN POSITIVE WAYS

When times get tough, some people are tempted to reduce stress with unhealthy behaviors like smoking, drinking, and overeating. Find better ways to cope. Exercise, meditation, and a sound sleep can do wonders. For specific suggestions, see Chapter 11: Health.

Social support is one of the best stress busters. If you're unemployed or worried about money, connect with family members and friends often. Turn healthy habits such as exercising and preparing healthy meals into social affairs.

CHOOSE YOUR MONEY CONVERSATIONS

When the economy tanks, the news is filled with gloomy reports and dire predictions. Remember that reports are constantly competing for your attention. Sometimes they use gloom-and-doom headlines to boost their ratings.

Keep financial news in perspective. Recessions can be painful. And they eventually end. The mortgage credit crisis in recent years was due to speculation, not to a lack of innovation. Our economy will continue to reward people who create valuable new products and services.

To manage stress, limit how much attention you pay to fear-based articles and programs. You can do this even while staying informed about news. Avoid conversations that focus on problems. Instead, talk about ways to take charge of your money and open up job prospects. Even when the economy takes a nosedive, there is always at least one more thing you can do to manage stress and get on a firmer financial footing.

Talk about what gives your life meaning beyond spending money. Eating at home instead of going out can bring your family closer together and save you money weekly, monthly, and annually. Avoiding loud bars and making time for quiet conversation can deepen your friendships. Finding free sources of entertainment can lead you to unexpected sources of pleasure. Letting go of an expensive vacation can allow you to pay down your debts and find time for a fun hobby. Keeping your old car for another year might allow you to invest in extra skills training.

When tough times happen, use them as a chance to embrace the truth about your money life rather than resist it. Live from conscious choice rather than unconscious habit. Learning to live within your means is a skill that can bring financial peace of mind for the rest of your life. ■

You're One Click Away...
from finding more ways online to thrive during tough times.

Education is worth it—
and you can pay for it

Education is one of the few things you can buy that will last a lifetime. It can't rust, corrode, break down, or wear out. It can't be stolen, repossessed, or destroyed. Once you have a degree, no one can take it away. That makes your education a safer investment than real estate, gold, oil, diamonds, or stocks.

Higher levels of education are associated with the following:[7]

- Greater likelihood of being employed
- Greater likelihood of having health insurance
- Higher income
- Higher job satisfaction
- Higher tax revenues for governments, which fund libraries, schools, parks, and other public goods
- Lower dependence on income support services, such as food stamps
- Higher involvement in volunteer activities

In short, education is a good deal for you and for society. It's worth investing in it periodically to update your skills, reach your goals, and get more of what you want in life.

Millions of dollars are waiting for people who take part in higher education. The funds flow to students who know how to find them. There are many ways to pay for school. The kind of help you get depends on your financial need. In general, *financial need* equals the cost of your schooling minus what you can reasonably be expected to pay. A financial aid package includes three major types of assistance:

- Money you do not pay back (grants and scholarships)
- Money you *do* pay back (loans)
- Work-study programs

Many students who get financial aid receive a package that includes all of the above elements.

To find out more, visit your school's financial aid office on a regular basis. Also go online. Start with Student Aid on the Web at http://studentaid.ed.gov. ■

You're One Click Away...
from discovering more ways online to pay for school.

✓ CRITICAL THINKING EXERCISE 13

Education by the hour

Determine exactly what it costs you to go to school. Fill in the blanks, using totals for one term. **Note:** Include only the costs that relate directly to going to school. For example, under "Transportation," list only the amount that you pay for gas to drive back and forth to school—not the total amount you spend on gas in a term.

Tuition	$_____
Books	$_____
Fees	$_____
Transportation	$_____
Clothing	$_____
Food	$_____
Housing	$_____
Entertainment	$_____
Other expenses (such as insurance, medical costs, and child care)	$_____
Subtotal	$_____
Salary you could earn per term if you weren't in school	$_____
Total (A)	$_____

Now figure out how many classes you attend in one term. This is the number of your scheduled class periods per week multiplied by the number of weeks in your school term. Put that figure below:

Total (B) $_____

Divide the **Total (B)** into the
Total (A), and put that amount here: $_____

This is what it costs you to go to one class one time.

On a separate sheet of paper, describe your responses to discovering this figure. Also list anything you will do differently as a result of knowing the hourly cost of your education.

You're One Click Away...
from completing this exercise online under Exercises.

Take charge of *your credit*

A good credit rating will serve you for a lifetime. With this asset, you'll be able to borrow money any time you need it. A poor credit rating, however, can keep you from getting a car or a house in the future. You might also have to pay higher insurance rates, and you could even be turned down for a job.

To take charge of your credit, borrow money only when truly necessary. If you do borrow, make all of your payments, and make them on time. This is especially important for managing credit cards and student loans.

iStockphoto.com/Laurent davoust

3

USE CREDIT CARDS WITH CAUTION

A credit card is compact and convenient. That piece of plastic seems to promise peace of mind. Low on cash this month? Just whip out your credit card, slide it across the counter, and relax. Your worries are over—that is, until you get the bill.

Credit cards do offer potential benefits, of course. Having one means that you don't have to carry around a checkbook or large amounts of cash, and they're pretty handy in emergencies. Used unwisely, however, credit cards can create a debt that takes decades to repay. Use the following strategies to take control of your credit cards.

Pay off the balance each month. An unpaid credit card balance is a sure sign that you are spending more money than you have. To avoid this outcome, keep track of how much you spend with credit cards each month. Pay off the card balance each month, on time, and avoid finance or late charges.

If you do accumulate a large credit card balance, go to your bank and ask about ways to get a loan with a lower interest rate. Use this loan to pay off your credit cards. Then promise yourself never to accumulate credit card debt again.

Scrutinize credit card offers. Finding a card with a lower interest rate can make a dramatic difference. However, look carefully at credit card offers. Low rates might be temporary. After a few months, they could double or even triple. Also look for annual fees, late fees, and other charges buried in the fine print.

Be especially wary of credit card offers made to students. Remember that the companies who willingly dispense cards on campus are not there to offer an educational service. They are in business to make money by charging you interest.

Avoid cash advances. Due to their high interest rates and fees, credit cards are not a great source of spare cash. Even when you get a cash advance on a card from an ATM, it's still borrowed money. As an alternative, get a debit card tied to a checking account, and use that card when you need cash on the go.

Check statements against your records. File your credit card receipts each month. When you get the bill for each card, check it against your receipts for accuracy. Mistakes in billing are rare, but they can happen. In addition, checking your statement reveals the interest rate and fees that are being applied to your account.

Credit card companies can change the terms of your agreement with little or no warning. Check bills carefully for any changes in late fees, service charges, and credit limits. When you get letters about changes in your credit card policies, read them carefully. Cancel cards from companies that routinely raise fees.

Use just one credit card. To simplify your financial life and take charge of your credit, consider using only one card. Choose one with no annual fee and the lowest interest rate. Consider the bottom line, and be selective. If you do have more than one credit card, pay off the one with the highest interest rate first. Then consider canceling that card.

Get a copy of your credit report. A credit report is a record of your payment history and other credit-related items. You are entitled to get a free copy each year. Go to your bank and ask someone there how to do this. You can also request a copy of your credit report online at https://www.annualcreditreport.com. This site was created by three nationwide consumer credit–reporting companies—Equifax, Experian, and TransUnion. Check your report carefully for errors or accounts that you did not open. Do this now, before you're in financial trouble.

Protect your credit score. Whenever you apply for a loan, the first thing a lender will do is check your credit score. The higher your score, the more money you can borrow at lower interest rates. To protect your credit score:

- Pay all your bills on time.
- Hold on to credit cards that you've had for a while.
- Avoid applying for new credit cards.
- Pay off your credit card balance every month—especially for the cards that you've had the longest.
- If you can't pay off the entire balance, then pay as much as you can above the minimum monthly payment.
- Never charge more than your limit.
- Avoid using a credit card as a source of cash.
- Avoid any actions that could lead a credit card company to reduce your credit limit.

MANAGE STUDENT LOANS

A college degree is one of the best investments you can make. But you don't have to go broke to get that education. You can make that investment with the lowest debt possible.

Choose schools with costs in mind. If you decide to transfer to another school, you can save thousands of dollars the moment you sign your application for admission. In addition to choosing schools on the basis of reputation, consider how much they cost and the financial aid packages that they offer.

> A college degree is one of the best investments you can make. But you don't have to go broke to get that education. You can make that investment with the lowest debt possible.

Avoid debt when possible. The surest way to manage debt is to avoid it altogether. If you do take out loans, borrow only the amount that you cannot get from other sources—scholarships, grants, employment, gifts from relatives, and personal savings. Predict what your income will be when the first loan payments are due and whether you'll make enough money to manage continuing payments.

Also set a target date for graduation, and stick to it. The fewer years you go to school, the lower your debt.

Shop carefully for loans. Go the financial aid office and ask if you can get a Stafford loan. These are fixed-rate, low-interest loans from the federal government. If you qualify for a subsidized Stafford loan, the government pays the interest due while you're in school. Unsubsidized Stafford loans do not offer this benefit, but they are still one of the cheapest student loans you can get. Remember that *anyone* can apply for a Stafford loan.

If your parents are helping to pay for your education, they can apply for a PLUS loan. There is no income limit, and parents can borrow up to the total cost of their children's education. With these loans, your parents—not you—are the borrowers. A new option allows borrowers to defer repayment until after they graduate. For more information on the loans that are available to you, visit www.studentaid.ed.gov.

If at all possible, avoid loans from privately owned companies. These companies often charge higher interest rates and impose terms that are less favorable to students.

While you're shopping around, ask about options for repaying your loans. Lenders might allow you to extend the payments over a longer period, or adjust the amount of your monthly payment based on your income.

Some lenders will forgive part of a student loan if you agree to take a certain type of job for a few years—for example, teaching in a public school in a low-income neighborhood, or working as a nurse in a rural community.

Repay your loans. If you take out student loans, find out exactly when the first payment is due on each of them. Make all your payments, and make them on time.

Also ask your financial aid office about whether you can consolidate your loans. This means that you lump them all together and owe just one payment every month. Loan consolidation makes it easier to stay on top of your payments and protect your credit score. ■

You're One Click Away...
from finding more strategies online for credit mastery.

masterstudentprofile

Richard Anderson

(1955–) CEO of Delta Airlines

Q: What was the most important leadership lesson you learned?

A: I've learned to be patient and not lose my temper. And the reason that's important is everything you do is an example, and people look at everything you do and take a signal from everything you do. And when you lose your temper, it really squelches debate and sends the wrong signal about how you want your organization to run. . . .

Q: Are there other things that you've learned to do more of, or less?

A: You've got to be thankful to the people who get the work done, and you've got to be thankful to your customers. So, I find myself, more and more, writing hand-written notes to people. I must write a half a dozen a day.

Q. Looking back over your career, even to the early years, do you recall an insight that set you on a different trajectory?

A: Yes, and it was actually at my first job while I went to night law school at South Texas College of Law. And I had a good full-time job as the administrative assistant to the D.A. And what you understood was you really needed to be a problem-solver, not a problem-creator. You know, don't bring a Rubik's cube to the table, unless you have an idea on how you're going to try to get an answer. And always try to be a leader that comes up with the creative answers to the hard problems.

Q: And what about advice on your career?

A: If you just focus on getting your job done and being a good colleague and a team player in an organization, and not focused about being overly ambitious and wanting pay raises and promotions and the like, and just doing your job and being a part of a team, the rest of it all takes care of itself.

Q: Did somebody give you that advice, or was that something that you came to understand yourself?

A: My mother and father died from cancer when I was 20, and so I was working full time, and I was pretty fortunate to be around a lot of good people that had that kind of culture and approach to things. It was just by osmosis that I came to those kinds of conclusions. . . .

Q: And is there any change in the kind of qualities you're looking for [in job candidates] compared with 5, 10 years ago?

A: I think this communication point is getting more and more important. People really have to be able to handle the written and spoken word. And when I say written word, I don't mean PowerPoints. I don't think PowerPoints help people think as clearly as they should because you don't have to put a complete thought in place. You can just put a phrase with a bullet in front of it. And it doesn't have a subject, a verb and an object, so you aren't expressing complete thoughts. . . .

Q: What about time management?

A: Only touch paper once. No. 2, always have your homework done. No. 3, return your calls very promptly. No. 4, stick to your schedule. I keep my watch about 10 minutes ahead. It's important to run on time, particularly at an airline. And use your time wisely. And then, once a month, take the rest of the calendar year, or the next six months and re-review how you are using your time and reprioritize what you're doing.

© Mark Wilson/Getty Images

RICHARD ANDERSON ... is responsible.
YOU ... can see time and money as areas for practicing responsibility.

You're One Click Away...
from learning more about Richard Anderson online at the Master Student Profiles. You can also visit the Master Student Hall of Fame to learn about other master students.

FIVE Cs
FOR YOUR CAREER

CHARACTER • CRITICAL THINKING • CREATIVE THINKING • COLLABORATION • COMMUNICATION

Jobs involve managing time, money, or both. This chapter is rich with strategies that you can take to work. Consider the following examples.

See time and money management as elements of your character. When you're looking for work, be on time for job interviews. When you're employed, be punctual, and work with full energy until you leave. Also find ways to help your employer, customers, or clients to increase their revenue, decrease their expenses, or both. Behaviors such as these show people that you value their time and their money.

Think creatively to "show me the money." See if you can use *From Master Student to Master Employee* to create a financial gain that is many times more than the cost of the book. Scan the entire text and look for suggestions that could help you save money or increase income in significant ways. For example, use suggestions in "Tap the hidden job market" in Chapter 12 to find your next job more quickly—and start earning money sooner. Get a higher-paying job with strategies from the article "Use job interviews to 'hire' an employer" in Chapter 12. Use suggestions from this chapter to reduce your monthly expenses and fatten up your savings account.

Practice creative thinking by expanding this list. Focus on strategies that will work for you.

Think critically to create balance in your life. If you're used to planning one day or one week in advance, then try your hand at planning *two weeks ahead*. This allows enough time for you to spot potential "crunches" in your schedules at work and at home. If you discover that you're pressed for time, you can take action to prevent burnout. Following are the major steps in two-week planning.

List upcoming tasks. Write down all the significant tasks you want to complete in the next 14 days. List each task on a separate 3 × 5 card, or create your list with a computer.

Estimate the time you need for these tasks. Take the tasks you listed in the previous step and estimate the number of hours needed to complete each one. When in doubt, take your first estimate and double it. Add up all your estimates to get a total number of hours.

Sort tasks into categories and choose how much time you want to spend on each category. Common categories are work, school, and family. Figure out the number of hours you want to spend on each category. If you're employed full-time, for instance, you might want to limit yourself to 80 hours at work (40 hours per week for the next two weeks).

Assign task priorities. Rate each task based on your commitment to completing it. Tasks that you're absolutely committed to getting done in the next two weeks get an "A" priority. Tasks that you could get done but are less urgent or important get a "C" priority. *Note:* This is a twist on the ABC priority system recommended in this chapter. See if using just two levels of priority rather than three helps you to get a clearer sense of your commitments.

Schedule "A" priority tasks. Now take your calendar and block out an appropriate number of hours for "A" priority tasks. Schedule specific dates and times.

Add up the number of hours for all your "A" priority tasks. This step could be revealing. For example, you might discover that you need 100 hours to complete work tasks over the next two weeks—even though you only want to work 80 hours. If something like this happens, use the "three D's" to reduce your "A" priority tasks: Downgrade some of them to C-priority; delay some tasks to the following two-week period; delegate tasks to someone else.

Collaborate through effective delegating. The last bullet in the above list is key to success at work. Skilled collaborators are master delegators.

To delegate effectively, get permission from your coworkers to do so. Also think about their individual learning styles. Find common ground between the tasks that *you* want to delegate and the tasks that *they* want to complete.

When delegating tasks to members of a project team, set a clear due date for each task. Also keep a list of tasks that you've delegated, when they're due, and who's handling each task. Check this list at least once each week.

Communicate about time and money in more powerful ways. Comments about time and money often reinforce a view of the world that doesn't leave much room for learning and mastery. Consider statements such as *I've love to pursue that possibility, but there's never enough time* and *I always have more "month" left over at the end of my money.* These suggest that we are victims of forces beyond our control.

In response, you can open up conversations about time and money that create real possibilities for change. For example, talk about what you learned by doing the Time Monitor and Money Monitor exercises in this chapter. Also share any successes you experienced in freeing up more hours per week, increasing income, or reducing expenses. Your speaking can open up new options for other people and make a lasting contribution to their lives.

Now, make a personal commitment to developing the five Cs. Take another look at the Discovery Wheel in Chapter 2—especially the sections labeled Character, Creative and Critical Thinking, Communicating, and Collaborating. Take a snapshot of your current skills in these areas after reading and doing this chapter.

DISCOVERY

My scores on the "Five C" sections of the Discovery Wheel were:	As of today, I would give myself the following scores in these areas:	At the end of this course, I would like my scores in these areas to be:
Character _____	Character _____	Character _____
Creative & Critical Thinking _____	Creative & Critical Thinking _____	Creative & Critical Thinking _____
Communicating _____	Communicating _____	Communicating _____
Collaborating _____	Collaborating _____	Collaborating _____

Next, skim this chapter and look for a time or money management technique that you want to explore in depth. Choose one that would enhance your self-rating in at least one of the five Cs.

I discovered that my preferred technique is . . .

_____
_____
_____
_____

In light of the five Cs, I can use this technique to become more . . .

_____
_____
_____
_____

INTENTION
To use this technique, I intend to . . .

_____
_____
_____
_____

NEXT ACTION
The specific action I will take is . . .

_____
_____
_____
_____

1. The "Power Process: Be here now" rules out planning. True or false? Explain your answer.

    False. Remember that planning supports this Power Process. Goals are tools that we create to guide our action in the present. Time management techniques—calendars, lists, and all the rest—have only one purpose. They reveal what's most important for you to focus on right now.   (*Power Process: Be here now*, page 74)

2. According to the text, everything written about time and money management can be reduced to three main ideas. What are they?

    (1) Know exactly what you want. State your wants as clear, specific goals, and put them in writing. (2) Know how to get what you want. Take action to meet your goals, including financial goals. Determine what you'll do today to get what you want in the future. Put those actions in writing as well. (3) Take action to get what you want. When our lives lack this quality, we spend most of our time responding to interruptions, last-minute projects, and emergencies. Life feels like a scramble just to survive. We're so busy achieving someone else's goals that we forget about getting what we want.   (*You've got the time—and the money*, page 75)

3. Rewrite the statement "I want to study harder" so that it becomes a specific goal.

    (Answers will vary.) "I will study one more hour each night, Monday through Friday, for the next 30 days. After that, I will reflect and evaluate on the impact it has had on my performance in college."   (*Setting and achieving goals*, page 81)

4. Define *C fever* as it applies to the ABC priority method.

    (Answers will vary.) When using the ABC priority method, you might experience an ailment common to students: C fever. Symptoms include the uncontrollable urge to drop that "A" task and begin crossing "Cs off your to-do list. If your history paper is due tomorrow, you might feel compelled to vacuum the rug, call your third cousin in Tulsa, and make a trip to the store for shoelaces. The reason C fever is so common is that "A" tasks are usually more difficult or time-consuming to achieve, with a higher risk of failure.   (*The ABC daily to-do list*, page 84)

5. You can rank your to-do list items with the ABC system. Explain an alternative to this system.

    (Answers will vary.) Some people prefer the 80–20 system. This method is based on the idea that 80 percent of the value of any to-do list comes from only 20 percent of the tasks on that list. So on a to-do list of 10 items, find the 2 that will contribute most to your life today. Complete these tasks without fail.   (*The ABC daily to-do list*, page 84)

6. According to the text, overcoming procrastination is a complex process that can take months or even years. True or false? Explain your answer.

    False. The way to stop procrastinating is to stop procrastinating. Giving up procrastination is actually a simple choice.   (*Stop procrastination now*, page 89)

7. Describe a strategy for increasing your income.

    (Answers will vary.) Consider financial aid—by applying for financial aid, you can free yourself from having to work full-time or even part-time. Never assume you do not qualify for any type of financial aid.   (*Earn more money*, page 102)

8. List three ways to decrease your expenses.

    (Answers will vary.) List any three of the following: Look to big-ticket items. Look to small-ticket items. Ask for student discounts. Do comparison shopping. Be aware of quality. Save money on eating and drinking.   (*Spend less money*, page 103)

9. According to the text, the biggest factor in your long-term financial well-being is

    (a) the state of the overall economy.

    (b) the interest rates on your credit cards.

    (c) the federal deficit.

    (d) your daily behavior.

    (e) none of the above.

    (d) your daily behavior.   (*Managing money during tough times*, page 104)

10. What are three ways that you can avoid getting into financial trouble when you use credit cards?

    List any three of the following (answers will vary): Pay off the balance each month. Scrutinize credit card offers. Avoid cash advances. Check statements against your records. Use just one credit card. Get a copy of your credit report. Protect your credit score.   (*Take charge of your credit*, page 107)

4 MEMORY

CHAPTER

"The art of true memory is the art of attention." —Samuel Johnson

"Memory is the mother of imagination, reason and skill. . . . This is the companion, this is the tutor, the poet, the library with which you travel." —Mark Van Doren

PREVIEW

A primary objective of student success courses is to foster the fundamental skill of memorizing key information. Simplified, memory is a biological brain change. In one of the most remarkable discoveries about memory and the human brain, neuroscientists at Washington University in St. Louis, using functional MRI technology, point to literal changes in the brain's activity as different learning processes take place. Educational psychologists recently discovered that all long-term memories are set by emotional markers.[1]

New learning is accomplished when, within the brain's cognitive neural structure, the student's existing emotional markers match or connect the new information to be learned within the existing brain structure. Understanding the principles of brain-active learning presented in this chapter will help students learn more in less time. It is frustrating when we can't remember something we're certain that we know, especially in a high-stakes situation, such as during a test or at a job interview.

This chapter opens with new information about the brain—how it changes physically by growing more connections between neurons. Understanding that the limbic processor is the gateway to learning and to remembering what they learn can

---

[1] J. G. Ojemann, R. L. Buckner, E. Akbudak, A. Z. Snyder, J. M. Ollinger, et al., "Functional MRI Studies of Word-Stem Completion: Reliability across Laboratories and Comparison to Blood Flow Imaging with PET," *Human Brain Mapping* 6, no. 4 (1998): 203–215; and M. I. Posner and M. E. Raichle, "The Neuroimaging of Human Brain Function," *Proceedings of the National Academy of Sciences of the United States of America* 95, no. 3 (1998): 763–764.

help students become more confident that their brain really is "college material." How your students feel about what they are learning has become more important than ever. Help your students improve their memory by learning to "wire" those neural networks into place.

master instructor
BEST PRACTICE

"*I have always loved the 20 memory techniques . ... In my classes, I stress the importance of making all techniques your own. Needless to say, the custom-made memory system is right on target! Throughout the list of techniques, I especially like that each technique has a clear-cut example for the student. It also gives each student choices. "Be aware of attitudes" and "Give your 'secret brain' a chance" also fit right in with the information I'm already teaching my students. This also helps to show the reader what is significant.*"

–Maria Parnell, Brevard Community College, Florida

GUEST SPEAKER

Consider inviting a psychology or anatomy colleague as your guest speaker to talk to your students about how the brain works. Your current or former students can also be used as guest speakers. Most students are more receptive to hearing about these profiles from their peers. Having a student presentation also helps to break up the amount of time you spend as the instructor in front of the classroom. Ask former students to talk about *Why* Scott Heiferman is an example of a master student; *What* qualities Heiferman has that they would like to emulate; *How* they could obtain and practice these qualities; and *What if*, like Scott Heiferman, they fought to overcome barriers to success and found a way to give back to the community. Consider videotaping these students as they present the material. A well-stocked library of guest speakers can come in handy when experienced students are not readily available. This can become a valuable shared resource among other faculty on your campus teaching the course as well. Pool your resources to help make your jobs easier.

LECTURE

Consider lecturing about some of the 20 memory techniques you used when you were a student, clarifying how students can use these techniques to maximize their effectiveness in college classes. Provide personal examples of what did and what didn't work for you as a student. For example, you may recall a time when you crammed for an exam, memorizing material, only to forget everything in a week. Students relate to us more readily when they realize that learning is challenging for all of us at times. Another approach is to invite students to ask you for additional information about articles in this chapter.

master instructor
BEST PRACTICE

"Here's how I explained Q-Cards (page 124) to a student. This explanation could be expanded as a lecture for all students about this useful tool. I had a frustrated student tell me that, although she had studied and studied, she had failed her exam in biology. We reviewed her study methods: She had created flash cards by putting a question on one side and the answer on the other. Her review questions did not align well with the instructor's test questions, so she was unable to retrieve answers from her memory during the exam. Q-Cards have a question on both sides. Here's the trick: The question on each side of the card contains the answer to the question on the other side. This portable studying device helps students break information into manageable pieces and forces them to use a higher level of thinking. You can promote even further connection with materials by asking students to draw pictures to help them remember concepts. Reviewing these materials consistently before an exam will aid students' recall."

–Eldon Mcmurray, Utah State College

For additional lecture ideas, visit the Chapter 4, "Lecture Ideas" on the Instructor Web site.

EXERCISES/ACTIVITIES

1. **Power Process: Love your problems (and experience your barriers) (page 114)** One of many problem-solving tools in *From Master Student to Master Employee*, this Power Process helps students explore an alternative to avoiding problems that they encounter in college. By embracing a problem, you can diffuse its energy and find a solution. To illustrate this process with an in-class activity, bring a word puzzle or mind game to class. Students who hate these types of puzzles get frustrated. Competitive students become anxious because each wants to be the first to solve it. Allow time for your students to try to solve the problem by loving it. Tell them to relax; enjoy the process; notice their frustration level, competitiveness, and anxiety; and just love the problem. Many students are able to solve the puzzle, individually or in groups. The Instructor Web site has a sample puzzle that you can hand out to your students as part of this exercise. Ask the students who enjoy this process to share aloud why they find this process exciting

2. **The memory jungle (pages 116–117)** Students enjoy the book's analogy of the memory as a jungle. For the visual learner, it is helpful to use the interactive version on the *From Master Student to Master Employee* Web site to illustrate the concept in a step-by-step manner. You can project it onto a screen in class as a means for review, or you can have students visit the site outside class.

3. **Mnemonic devices (page 128)** Get your students involved in creating mnemonic devices in class, and they will discover how easy it is to apply these devices outside class. Divide students into groups. Ask each group to teach the class a simple concept (changing a tire, making bread, a simple yoga movement), using an original mnemonic device. Students can't use a mnemonic device they learned elsewhere. It must be a new device they created for this purpose. Ask students to share their devices with the class. To reinforce neural connections, groups should be encouraged to include visuals—drawn pictures, props, photos, and so forth.

4. **The loci system (page 128)** Humor can be an effective memory motivator. Memory techniques that include bizarre, humorous elements stick with us. Demonstrate in class how making up a funny story can help with memorizing word lists. Explain the concept of the loci system, pointing out that because you are all familiar with the classroom, it will serve as the "location" from which to model this technique. Normally, however, students would choose a location such as their living room or bedroom, which they can visualize easily. Start by asking for a show of hands from students who think they can name the first six presidents of the United States. Some students will raise their hands. Then ask how many students think they can remember the Presidents in order—that is, if asked for the fifth president, they recall the fifth president's name. Usually, only one or two students will raise their hands. Write this list on the board for reference:

1. George Washington
2. John Adams
3. Thomas Jefferson

4. James Madison
5. James Monroe
6. John Quincy Adams

Now, position six students around the classroom. Because location is a key element in the loci system, you can make special note of the placement of students. Then ask each student to make some distinct, unique movement and to state the president's name. For example, the first student standing near the door can wave and say, "I am George Washington." The second student, standing perhaps near the instructor's desk, can jump up and down, saying, "I am John Adams." Then farther to the left, a student standing at the board can shake his head and announce, "I am Thomas Jefferson." Continue with all six students (presidents). Ask these students to repeat this pattern several times. Point out that repetition and recitation help the memory process. Also, the students watching heard the student "presidents" speak (auditory) and watched their motions (visual). This linked the order of the presidents with the space order in the room—left to right, near to far. Linking funny gestures and voice patterns can contribute to the strength of the memory process.

Students usually find the process foolishly humorous, which helps them remember it. As you repeat the process, remind students to focus completely on the presidents' names ("Be here now"). Repeat the names, and ask students to join you and talk through the list in unison. The next step is to erase or cover up the words on the board and recite the list again in unison. Next, go up and down the rows, asking students to name the president that goes with a certain number. If a student can't recall the name, ask her to say the list aloud from the beginning. By the time the student gets to the name, she usually can recall it. This ordinarily takes a total of about 5 minutes. Next, say a number, and ask students to raise their hands if they know the president's name that goes with that number. Select one student to confirm the name. Continue until it is clear that everyone knows all the names and the number order associated with them.

Point out that if students can memorize 6 names in 5 minutes, in order, then they can also memorize important terms for tests fairly quickly if they focus their attention and create a system for memorization. This chapter contains many memorization tools. Most students initially think they can't memorize these names in order, so this exercise boosts confidence in their memory, too.

5. **Remembering names** This exercise can be used as an opportunity for building relationships. Start students off in groups of four. Have them use tools described in the article to help remember the names of the people in each small group. Then the groups combine to make groups of 8, then 16, then 32, and so on, until everyone in the class can say the first name of every classmate. Talk about how it feels when someone remembers your name, and conversely, how it feels when someone fails to remember your name. Ask students to share stories of times when they failed to remember an important name, and the consequences or embarrassment this may have caused them. Emphasize the importance of this skill in their personal lives and in the workplace as well.

CONVERSATION/SHARING

Divide students into small groups to discuss the topic of memorization in college. Students should share their frustration with memorization as well as a successful experience they've had remembering something important.

You can also facilitate a conversation using the Master Student Map. After your students begin to read about memory and learn to activate the connections between neurons, you will have empowered them to connect memory to their Learning Styles. So they see the connection, be sure to articulate this to your students.

Why?	Why do master students need to have confidence in their ability to remember what they study? Why do master students need these skills in the workplace? Ask students for examples in their own work experiences.
What?	What is memory? Read through the list of articles in this chapter and pick three that look interesting. What about these three articles interests you?
How?	How can knowing more about how your memory works improve your memory skills? How will this help you in college and in life?
What if?	What if you start to apply these memory techniques to your other classes? And what if you don't? What if employees are unable to demonstrate these skills in the workplace?

HOMEWORK

Use Q-Cards to reinforce memory (page 124) Ask students to create five Q-cards for one of their other courses and bring them to class to share with their classmates.

Critical Thinking Exercise 15: Remembering your car keys—or anything else (page 125) This exercise helps students practice Learning Styles Mode 3, "How can I use this?" Students are asked to apply the strategies they are learning to a specific, personal memorization situation. An alternative to this assignment would be to ask students to bring in a memorization task from one of their current classes for discussion and analysis in class in groups. As an optional assignment, ask students to research Temple Grandin. As a primarily visual learner diagnosed with autism, Grandin has used her unique visual memory to pave the way for human autistic intervention as well as thoughtful and humane handling of animals.

EVALUATION

Quiz Ideas for Chapter 4

Ask students to:
- Describe four memory techniques from the chapter that work for them and explain how they have used them.

- Describe the tool of setting a trap for your memory.

- Explain three ways to keep the brain fit for life.

- Explain what "love your problems" means.

- Discuss why Scott Heiferman is considered a master student.

Additional Digital Resources for Chapter 4

What can you **ASSIGN FROM THE COURSEMATE** for *From Master Student to Master Employee?*

• **Memory Strategies Video Skillbuilder.** This interactive online tool combines video clips featuring discussions with students, instructors, and experts, with articles and activities designed to give students a fully engaging learning experience. Students are given a quick memory test and then learn strategies for maximizing their memory. Note that Video Skillbuilders are available for every chapter.

• **The Memory Jungle.** This PowerPoint presentation explains to students the concept behind The memory jungle (page 116). Consider showing this in class or assigning students to create their own PowerPoint interpretation of The memory jungle.

• **Reflection Questions.** This diverse set of questions available at the Chapter Reflections tab can get students thinking about how memory strategies apply to the different learning style modes, how to remember something by making it personally meaningful, and other topics that allow students to experiment with strategies from the chapter.

CourseMate *To access CourseMate, your students need to visit* www.cengagebrain .com. *At the CengageBrain.com home page, students search for the ISBN of* From Master Student to Master Employee *(from the back cover of the book), using the search box at the top of the page. This takes them to the product page where these resources can be found.*

Did you know that **THESE RESOURCES** (and many more) **ARE AVAILABLE** on the **INSTRUCTOR COMPANION SITE**?

• **Looking for fresh, innovative ways to teach Chapter 4 topics?** Browse through the Best Practices library to see what other Master Instructors have been successfully doing with their students.

master instructor BEST PRACTICE

Name That Tune. *Divide students into five groups. Assign groups to one of the following techniques: songs and rhymes, peg system, loci, visuals, and acronyms. They are then required to teach the class about a subject of their choosing, using the group's assigned memory technique. Topics should be very simple, allowing the groups to teach topics in approximately 5 minutes per group. Examples might include changing a tire, performing a simple yoga move, or baking a cake. Groups should be encouraged to choose a topic quickly, and consensus may be difficult. This allows you to encourage effective group decision making. The groups must come up with a unique strategy for teaching the subject and present it to the class. Students may find this assignment more difficult than expected, as they are required to process and apply the memory techniques explained in the textbook, calling for higher levels of Bloom's Taxonomy. This assignment allows students to practice creating their own mnemonics, and this is a wonderful way to celebrate the diversity and interests of the students. Students usually find this assignment challenging but entertaining!*

–Annette Mccreedy, Nashville State Community College

• **Check out the PowerPoint Library for a PowerPoint specifically created for Chapter 4.** This master library of PowerPoint presentations makes it easy to find the right PowerPoint for you! If you're looking for a way to freshen up your lecture, the PowerPoint Library is a great place to start.

Please visit login.cengage.com *to log in and access the Instructor Companion Site.*

Memory

Use this **Master Student Map**
to ask yourself

WHY THIS CHAPTER MATTERS . . .

- Learning memory techniques can boost your skills at test taking, reading, note taking, and many other tasks.

WHAT IS INCLUDED . . .

HOW I CAN USE THIS CHAPTER . . .

- Focus my attention.
- Make conscious choices about what to remember.
- Recall facts and ideas with more ease.

WHAT IF . . .

- I could use my memory to its full potential?

© Ruslan Ivantsov/Shutterstock.com

JOURNAL ENTRY 8
Intention Statement

Create value from this chapter

Think of a time when you struggled to remember something that was important. Perhaps you were trying to remember someone's name or recall some key information for a test. Then scan this chapter and find at least three strategies that you will use to prevent this problem in the future.

Strategy	Page number

POWER process

Love your problems
(and experience your barriers)

We all have problems and barriers that block our progress or prevent us from moving into new areas. Often, the way we respond to our problems places limitations on what we can be, do, and have.

Problems often work like barriers. When we bump up against one of our problems, we usually turn away and start walking along a different path. And all of a sudden—bump!—we've struck another barrier. And we turn away again.

As we continue to bump into problems and turn away from them, our lives stay inside the same old boundaries. Inside these boundaries, we are unlikely to have new adventures. We are unlikely to keep learning.

If we respond to problems by loving them instead of resisting them, we can expand the boundaries in which we live our lives.

The word *love* might sound like an overstatement. In this Power Process, the word means to unconditionally accept the fact that your problems exist. The more we deny or resist a problem, the stronger it seems to become. When we accept the fact that we have a problem, we can find effective ways to deal with it.

Suppose one of your barriers is speaking in front of a group. You fear that you'll forget everything you planned to say.

One option for dealing with this barrier is denial. You could get up in front of a group and pretend that you're not afraid. You could tell yourself, "I'm not going to be scared," and then try to keep your knees from knocking.

A more effective approach is to love your fear. Go to the front of the room, look out into the audience, and say to yourself, "I am scared. I notice that my knees are shaking and my mouth feels dry, and I'm having a rush of thoughts about what might happen if I say the wrong thing. Yup, I'm scared, and I'm not going to fight it. I'm going to give this speech anyway."

The beauty of this Power Process is that you continue to take action—giving your speech, for example—no matter what you feel. You walk right up to the barrier and then *through* it. You might even find that if you totally accept and experience a barrier, such as fear, it shrinks or disappears. When you relax, you reclaim your natural abilities. You can recall memories, learn something new, and even laugh a little. Even if this does not happen right away, you can still open up to a new experience.

Loving a problem does not need *liking* it. Instead, loving a problem means admitting the truth about it. This helps us take effective action—which can free us of the problem once and for all.

 You're One Click Away...
from accessing Power Process Media online and finding out more ways to love your problems.

iStockphoto.com/Miroslav Ferkuniak

Take your memory
out of the closet

Once upon a time, people talked about human memory as if it were a closet. You stored individual memories there as you would old shirts and stray socks. Remembering something was a matter of rummaging through all that stuff. If you were lucky, you found what you wanted.

This view of memory creates some problems. For one thing, closets can get crowded. Things too easily disappear. Even with the biggest closet, you eventually run out of space. If you want to pack some new memories in there—well, too bad. There's no room.

Brain researchers shattered this image to bits. Memory is not a closet. It's not a place or a thing. Instead, memory is a *process*.

On a conscious level, memories appear as distinct and unconnected mental events: words, sensations, images. They can include details from the distant past—the smell of cookies baking in your grandmother's kitchen or the feel of sunlight warming your face through the window of your first-grade classroom.

On a biological level, each of those memories involves millions of brain cells, or neurons, firing chemical messages to one another. If you could observe these exchanges in real time, you'd see regions of cells all over the brain glowing with electrical charges at speeds that would put a computer to shame.

When a series of brain cells connects several times in a similar pattern, the result is a memory. Psychologist Donald Hebb explains it this way: "Neurons which fire together, wire together."[1] It means that memories are not really stored. Instead, remembering is a process in which you *encode* information as links between active neurons that fire together. You also *decode*, or reactivate, neurons that wired together in the past.

There are critical moments in this process. Say that you're enjoying a lecture in introduction to psychology. It really makes sense. In fact, it's so interesting that you choose to just sit and listen—without taking notes. Two days later, you're studying for a test and wish you'd made a different choice. You remember that the lecture was interesting, but you don't recall much else. In technical terms, your decision to skip note taking was an *encoding error*.

So, you decide to change your behavior and take extensive notes during the next psychology lecture. Your goal is to capture everything the instructor says. This too has mixed results—a case of writer's cramp and 10 pages of dense, confusing scribbles. Oops. Another encoding error.

Effective encoding is finding a middle ground between these two extremes. As you listen and read, you make

> # Memory is the probability that certain patterns of brain activity will occur again in the future. In effect, you recreate a memory each time you recall it. In more practical terms, a good memory is not something you *have*. It's something you *do*.

moment-to-moment choices about what you want to remember. You distinguish between key points, transitions, and minor details. You predict what material is likely to appear on a test. You also stay alert for ideas you can actively apply. These are things you capture in your notes.

Signs of memory mastery are making choices about *what* to remember and *how* to remember it. This in turn makes it easier for you to decode, or recall, the material at a crucial point in the future—such as during a test.

Whenever you efficiently encode and decode something new, your brain changes physically. You grow more connections between neurons. The more you learn, the greater the number of connections. For all practical purposes, there's no limit to how many memories your brain can process.

There's a lot you can do to wire those neural connections into place. That's where the memory techniques described in this chapter come into play. Use them to step out of your crowded mental closet into a world of infinite possibilities. ∎

The MEMORY JUNGLE

Think of your memory as a vast, overgrown jungle. This memory jungle is thick with wild plants, exotic shrubs, twisted trees, and creeping vines. It spreads over thousands of square miles—dense, tangled, forbidding.

Imagine that the jungle is encompassed on all sides by towering mountains. There is only one entrance to the jungle, a small meadow that is reached by a narrow pass through the mountains.

In the jungle there are animals, millions of them. The animals represent all of the information in your memory. Imagine that every thought, mental picture, or perception you ever had is represented by an animal in this jungle. Every single event ever perceived by any of your five senses—sight, touch, hearing, smell, or taste—is a thought animal that has also passed through the meadow and entered the jungle. Some of the thought animals, such as the color of your seventh-grade teacher's favorite sweater, are well hidden. Other thoughts, such as your cell phone number or the position of the reverse gear in your car, are easier to find.

The memory jungle has two rules: Each thought animal must pass through the meadow at the entrance to the jungle. And once an animal enters the jungle, it never leaves.

The meadow represents short-term memory. You use this kind of memory when you look up a telephone number and hold it in your memory long enough to make a call. Short-term memory appears to have a limited capacity (the meadow is small) and disappears fast (animals pass through the meadow quickly).

The jungle itself represents long-term memory. This kind of memory allows you to recall information from day to day, week to week, and year to year. Remember that thought animals never leave the long-term memory jungle. The following visualizations can help you recall useful concepts about memory.

VISUALIZATION #1: A WELL-WORN PATH

Imagine what happens as a thought—in this case, we'll call it an elephant—bounds across short-term memory and into the jungle. The elephant leaves a trail of broken twigs and hoof prints that you can follow.

Brain research suggests that thoughts can wear "paths" in the brain.[2] These paths consist of dendrites—string-like fibers that connect brain cells. The more these connections are activated, the easier it is to retrieve (recall) the thought. In other words, the more often the elephant retraces the path, the clearer the path becomes. The more often you recall information and the more often you put the same information into your memory, the easier it is to find.

Tippawan Kunkeaw/Shutterstock.com

When you buy a new car, for example, the first few times you try to find reverse, you have to think for a moment. After you have found reverse gear every day for a week, the path is worn into your memory. After a year, the path is so well-worn that when you dream about driving your car backward, you even dream the correct motion for putting the gear in reverse.

VISUALIZATION #2: A HERD OF THOUGHTS

The second picture you can use to your advantage in recalling concepts about memory is the picture of many animals gathering at a clearing—like thoughts gathering at a central location in memory. It is easier to retrieve thoughts that are grouped together, just as it is easier to find a herd of animals than it is to find a single elephant.

Pieces of information are easier to recall if you can associate them with similar information. For example, you can more readily remember a particular player's batting average if you can associate it with other baseball statistics.

VISUALIZATION #3: TURNING YOUR BACK

Imagine releasing the elephant into the jungle, turning your back, and counting to 10. When you turn around, the elephant is gone. This is exactly what happens to most of the information you receive.

Psychological research consistently shows that we start forgetting new material almost as soon as we learn it. The memory loss is steep, with most of it occurring within the first 24 hours.[3] This means that much of the material is not being encoded. It is wandering around, lost in the memory jungle.

The remedy is simple: Review quickly. Do not take your eyes off the thought animal as it crosses the short-term memory meadow. Look at it again (review it) soon after it enters the long-term memory jungle. Wear a path in your memory immediately.

VISUALIZATION #4: DIRECTING THE ANIMAL TRAFFIC

The fourth picture is one you are in. You are standing at the entrance to the short-term memory meadow, directing herds of thought animals as they file through the pass, across the meadow, and into your long-term memory. You are taking an active role in the learning process. You are paying attention. You are doing more than sitting on a rock and watching the animals file past into your brain. You have become part of the process, and in doing so, you have taken control of your memory. ■

You're One Click Away...
from finding guided visualizations based on the memory jungle online.

4

Master Employees **IN ACTION**

You're One Click Away...
from a video about Master Students in Action.

My field is constantly developing, and I have to memorize new code, programs, and even programming languages on a monthly basis. Whenever a new program is introduced into our office, I find that it's easiest if I take it home and play with it. By interacting with it creatively, I can transform it from something I need to memorize into a tool I can use.

—*Raul Olivo,
Software Engineer*

© iStockphoto.com/Alex Slobodkin

20 MEMORY *Techniques*

Experiment with these techniques to develop a flexible, custom-made memory system that fits your style of learning.

The 20 techniques discussed here are divided into four categories, each of which represents a general principle for improving memory:

Organize it. Organized information is easier to find.

Use your body. Learning is an active process; get all of your senses involved.

Use your brain. Work *with* your memory, not *against* it.

Recall it. Regularly retrieve and apply key information.

ORGANIZE IT

1 Be selective. There's a difference between gaining understanding and drowning in information. During your stay in higher education, you will be exposed to thousands of facts and ideas. No one expects you to memorize all of them. To a large degree, the art of memory is the art of selecting what to remember in the first place.

As you dig into your textbooks and notes, make choices about what is most important to learn. Imagine that you are going to create a test on the material, and consider the questions you would ask.

When reading, look for chapter previews, summaries, and review questions. Pay attention to anything printed in bold type. Also notice visual elements—tables, charts, graphs, and illustrations. They are all clues pointing to what's important. During lectures, notice what the instructor emphasizes. Anything that's presented visually—on the board, in overheads, or with slides—is probably key.

2 Make it meaningful. You remember things better if they have meaning for you. One way to create meaning is to learn from the general to the specific. Before you begin your next reading assignment, skim the passage to locate the main ideas. If you're ever lost, step back and look at the big picture. The details then might make more sense.

You can organize any list of items—even random items—in a meaningful way to make them easier to remember. Although there

are probably an infinite number of facts, there are only a finite number of ways to organize them.

One option is to organize any group of items by *category*. You can apply this suggestion to long to-do lists. For example, write each item on a separate index card. Then create a pile of cards for calls to make, errands to run, and household chores to complete. These will become your working categories.

The same concept applies to the content of your courses. In chemistry, a common example of organizing by category is the periodic table of chemical elements. When reading a novel for a literature course, you can organize your notes in categories such as theme, setting, and plot. Then take any of these categories and divide them into subcategories such as major events and minor events in the story. Use index cards to describe each event.

Another option is to organize by *chronological order*. Any time that you create a numbered list of ideas, events, or steps, you are organizing by chronological order. To remember the events that led up to the stock market crash of 1929, for instance, create a time line. List the key events on index cards. Then arrange the cards by the date of each event.

A third option is to organize by *spatial order*. In plain English, this means making a map. When studying for a history exam, for example, you can create a rough map of the major locations where events take place.

Fourth, there's an old standby for organizing lists—putting a list of items in *alphabetical* order. It's simple, and it works.

3 Create associations. The data already encoded in your neural networks are arranged according to a scheme that makes sense to you. When you introduce new data, you can remember them more effectively if you associate them with similar or related data.

Think about your favorite courses. They probably relate to subjects that you already know something about. If you have been interested in politics over the last few years, you'll find it easier to remember the facts in a modern history course. Even when you're tackling a new subject, you can build a mental store of basic background information—the raw material for creating associations. Preview reading assignments, and complete those readings before you attend lectures. Before taking upper-level courses, master the prerequisites.

USE YOUR BODY

4 Learn actively. Action is a great memory enhancer. Test this theory by studying your assignments with the same energy that you bring to the dance floor or the basketball court.

You can use simple, direct methods to infuse your learning with action. When you sit at your desk, sit up straight. Sit on the edge of your chair as if you were about to spring out of it and sprint across the room.

Also experiment with standing up when you study. It's harder to fall asleep in this position. Some people insist that their brains work better when they stand. Pace back and forth and gesture as you recite material out loud. Use your hands. Get your body moving.

Don't forget to move your mouth. During a lecture, ask questions. Read key passages from textbooks out loud. Use a louder voice for the main points.

Active learning also involves a variety of learning styles. In Chapter 2, the article "Learning styles: Discovering how you learn" explains four aspects of learning: feeling, watching, thinking, and doing. Many courses in higher education lean heavily toward thinking—lectures, papers, and reading. These courses might not offer chances to actively experiment with ideas or test them by "feeling."

Create those opportunities yourself. For example, your introductory psychology book probably offers some theories about how people remember information. Choose one of those theories, and test it on yourself. See whether you can discover a new memory technique.

Your sociology class might include a discussion about how groups of people resolve conflict. See whether you can apply any of those ideas to resolving conflict in your own life. The point behind each of these examples is the same: To remember an idea, go beyond thinking about it. Make it personal. *Do* something with it.

5 Relax. When you're relaxed, you absorb new information quickly and recall it with greater ease and accuracy. Students who can't recall information under the stress of a final exam can often recite the same facts later when they are relaxed.

Relaxing might seem to contradict the idea of active learning as explained in technique #4, but it doesn't. Being relaxed is not the same as being drowsy, zoned out, or asleep. Relaxation is a state of alertness, free of tension, during which your mind can play with new information, roll it around, create associations with it, and apply many of the other memory techniques. You can be active *and* relaxed. See "Critical Thinking Exercise 16: Relax," in Chapter 5, for some tips on how to relax.

6 Create pictures. Draw diagrams. Make cartoons. Use these images to connect facts and illustrate relationships. You can "see" and recall associations within and among abstract concepts more easily when you visualize both the concepts and the associations. The key is to use your imagination. Creating pictures reinforces visual and kinesthetic learning styles.

For example, Boyle's law states that at a constant temperature the volume of a confined ideal gas varies inversely with its pressure. Simply put, cutting the volume in half doubles the pressure. To remember this concept, you might picture someone "doubled over," using a bicycle pump. As she increases the pressure in the pump by decreasing the volume in the pump cylinder, she seems to be getting angrier. By the time she has doubled the pressure (and halved the volume), she is boiling ("Boyle-ing") mad.

Another reason to create pictures is that visual information is associated with a part of the brain that is different from the part that processes verbal information. When you create a picture of a concept, you are anchoring the information in a second part of your brain. Doing so increases your chances of recalling that information.

To visualize abstract relationships effectively, create an action-oriented image, such as the person using the pump. Make the picture vivid too. The person's face could be bright red. And involve all of your senses. Imagine how the cold metal of the pump would feel and how the person would grunt as she struggled with it.

You can also create pictures as you study by using *graphic organizers*. These preformatted charts prompt you to visualize relationships among facts and ideas.

One example is a *topic-point-details* chart. At the top of this chart, write the main topic of a lecture or reading assignment. In the left column, list the main points you want to remember. And in the right column, list key details related to each point. Figure 4.1 is the beginning of a chart based on this article.

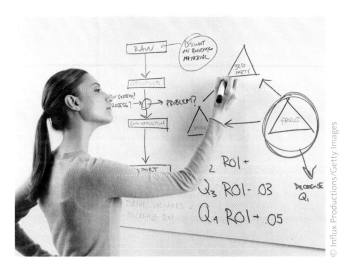

© Influx Productions/Getty Images

20 MEMORY TECHNIQUES

Point	Details
1. Be selective	Choose what not to remember. Look for clues to important material.
2. Make it meaningful	Organize by time, location, category, continuum, or alphabet.
3. Create associations	Link new facts with facts you already know.
4. Learn actively	Sit straight. Stand while studying. Recite while walking.
5. Relax	Release tension. Remain alert.

Figure 4.1 Topic-Point-Details Chart

STIMULATE THE ECONOMY WITH TAX CUTS?

Opinion	Support
Yes	Savings from tax cuts allow businesses to invest money in new equipment.
	Tax cuts encourage businesses to expand and hire new employees.
No	Years of tax cuts under the Bush administration failed to prevent the mortgage credit crisis.
	Tax cuts create budget deficits.
Maybe	Tax cuts might work in some economic conditions.
	Budget deficits might be only temporary.

Figure 4.2 Question-Opinion-Support Chart

You could use a similar chart to prompt critical thinking about an issue. Express that issue as a question, and write it at the top. In the left column, note the opinion about the issue. In the right column, list notable facts, expert opinions, reasons, and examples that support each opinion. Figure 4.2 is about tax cuts as a strategy for stimulating the economy.

Sometimes you'll want to remember the main actions in a story or historical event. Create a time line by drawing a straight line. Place points in order on that line to represent key events. Place earlier events toward the left end of the line and later events toward the right. Figure 4.3 shows the start of time line of events relating the U.S. war with Iraq.

When you want to compare or contrast two things, play with a Venn diagram. Represent each thing as a circle. Draw the circles so that they overlap. In the overlapping area, list characteristics that the two things share. In the outer parts of each circle, list the unique characteristics of each thing. Figure 4.4 compares the two types of journal entries included in this book—Discovery Statements and Intention Statements.

The graphic organizers described here are just a few of the many kinds available. To find more examples, do an Internet search. Have fun, and invent graphic organizers of your own.

7 Recite and repeat. When you repeat something out loud, you anchor the concept in two different senses. First, you get the physical sensation in your throat, tongue, and lips when voicing the concept. Second, you hear it. The combined result is synergistic, just as it is when you create pictures. That is, the effect of using two different senses is greater than the sum of their individual effects.

The "out loud" part is important. Reciting silently in your head can be useful—in the library, for example—but it is not as effective as making noise. Your mind can trick itself into thinking it knows something when it doesn't. Your ears are harder to fool.

The repetition part is important too. Repetition is a common memory device because it works. Repetition blazes a trail through the pathways of your brain, making the information easier to find. Repeat a concept out loud until you know it; then say it five more times.

Recitation works best when you recite concepts in your own words. For example, if you want to remember that the acceleration of a falling body due to gravity at sea level equals 32 feet per second per second, you might say, "Gravity makes an object accelerate 32 feet per second faster for each second that it's in the air at sea level." Putting a concept into your own words forces you to think about it.

Have some fun with this technique. Recite by writing a song about what you're learning. Sing it in the shower. Use any style you want. (Country, jazz, rock, or rap—when you sing out loud, learning's a snap!)

Or imitate someone. Imagine your textbook being read by Will Ferrell, Madonna, or Clint Eastwood. ("Go ahead, punk. Make my density equal mass over volume.")

8 Write it down. The technique of writing things down is obvious, yet easy to forget. Writing a note to yourself helps you remember an idea, even if you never look at the note again. Writing notes in the margins of your textbooks can help you remember what you read.

You can extend this technique by writing down an idea not just once, but many times. Let go of the old image of being forced to write "I will not throw paper wads" a hundred times on the chalkboard after school. When you choose to remember something, repetitive writing is a powerful tool.

Writing engages a different kind of memory than speaking. Writing prompts us to be more logical, coherent, and complete. Written reviews reveal gaps in knowledge that oral reviews miss, just as oral reviews reveal gaps that written reviews miss.

Another advantage of written reviews is that they more closely match the way you're asked to remember

3/19/03 U.S. invades Iraq	3/30/03 Rumsfeld announces location of WMD	4/9/03 Soldiers topple statue of Saddam	5/1/03 Bush declares mission accomplished	5/29/03 Bush: We found WMD

Figure 4.3 Time Line

Discovery Statements
- Describe specific thoughts
- Describe specific feelings
- Describe current and past behaviors

- Are a type of journal entry
- Are based on telling the truth
- Can be written at any time on any topic
- Can lead to action

Intention Statements
- Describe future behaviors
- Can include timelines
- Can include rewards

Figure 4.4 Venn Diagram

materials in school. During your academic career, you'll probably take far more written exams than oral exams. Writing can be an effective way to prepare for such tests.

Finally, writing is physical. Your arm, your hand, and your fingers join in. Remember, learning is an active process—you remember what you *do*.

USE YOUR BRAIN

9 Engage your emotions. One powerful way to enhance your memory is to make friends with your amygdala. This area of your brain lights up with extra neural activity each time you feel a strong emotion. When a topic excites love, laughter, or fear, the amygdala sends a flurry of chemical messages that say, in effect, *This information is important and useful. Don't forget it.*

You're more likely to remember course material when you relate it to a goal—whether academic, personal, or career—that you feel strongly about. This is one reason why it pays to be specific about what you want. The more goals you have and the more clearly they are defined, the more channels you create for incoming information.

You can use this strategy even when a subject seems boring at first. If you're not naturally interested in a topic, then create interest. Find a study partner in the class—if possible, someone you know and like—or form a study group. Also consider getting to know the instructor personally. When a course creates a bridge to human relationships, you engage the content in a more emotional way.

10 Overlearn. One way to fight mental fuzziness is to learn more than you need to know about a subject simply to pass a test. You can pick a subject apart, examine it, add to it, and go over it until it becomes second nature.

This technique is especially effective for problem solving. Do the assigned problems and then do more problems. Find another textbook and work similar problems. Then make up your own problems and solve them. When you pretest yourself in this way,

the potential rewards are speed, accuracy, and greater confidence at exam time. Being well prepared can help you prevent test anxiety.

11 Escape the short-term memory trap. Short-term memory is different from the kind of memory you'll need during exam week. For example, most of us can look at an unfamiliar seven-digit phone number once and remember it long enough to dial it. See whether you can recall that number the next day.

Short-term memory can fade after a few minutes, and it rarely lasts more than several hours. A short review within minutes or hours of a study session can move material from short-term memory into long-term memory. That quick mini-review can save you hours of study time when exams roll around.

12 Use your times of peak energy. Study your most difficult subjects during the times when your energy peaks. Some people can concentrate more effectively during daylight hours. The early morning hours can be especially productive, even for those who hate to get up with the sun. Observe the peaks and valleys in your energy flow during the day, and adjust study times accordingly. Perhaps you experience surges in memory power during the late afternoon or evening.

13 Distribute learning. As an alternative to marathon study sessions, experiment with several shorter sessions spaced out over time. You might find that you can get far more done in three 2-hour sessions than in one 6-hour session.

For example, when you are preparing for your American history exam, study for an hour or two and then wash the dishes. While you are washing the dishes, part of your mind will be reviewing what you studied. Return to American history for a while, then call a friend. Even when you are deep in conversation, part of your mind will be reviewing history.

You can get more done if you take regular breaks. You can even use the breaks as mini-rewards. After a productive study session, give yourself permission to log on and check your e-mail, listen to a song, or play 10 minutes of hide-and-seek with your kids.

Distributing your learning is a brain-friendly activity. You cannot absorb new information and ideas during all of your waking hours. If you overload your brain, it will find a way to shut down for a rest—whether you plan for it or not. By taking periodic breaks while studying, you allow information to sink in. During these breaks, your brain is taking the time to rewire itself by growing new connections between cells. Psychologists call this process *consolidation*.[4]

The idea of allowing time for consolidation does have an exception. When you are so engrossed in a textbook that you cannot put it down, when you are consumed by an idea for a term paper and cannot think of anything else—keep going. The master student within you has taken over. Enjoy the ride.

14 Be aware of attitudes. People who think history is boring tend to have trouble remembering dates and historical events. People who believe math is difficult often have a hard time recalling mathematical equations and formulas. All of us can forget information that contradicts our opinions.

If you think a subject is boring, remind yourself that everything is related to everything else. Look for connections that relate to your own interests.

For example, consider a person who is fanatical about cars. He can rebuild a motor in a weekend and has a good time doing so. From this apparently specialized interest, he can explore a wide realm of knowledge. He can relate the workings of an engine to principles of physics, math, and chemistry. Computerized parts in newer cars can lead him to the study of data processing. He can research how the automobile industry has changed our cities and helped create suburbs, a topic that relates to urban planning, sociology, business, economics, psychology, and history.

Being aware of your attitudes is not the same as fighting them or struggling to give them up. Just notice your attitudes and be willing to put them on hold. For more ideas, see the "Power Process: Notice your pictures and let them go" on page 134.

15 Elaborate. According to Harvard psychologist Daniel Schacter, all courses in memory improvement are based on a single technique—elaboration. *Elaboration* means consciously encoding new information. Repetition is one basic way to elaborate. However, current brain research indicates that other types of elaboration are more effective for long-term memory.[5]

One way to elaborate is to ask yourself questions about incoming information: "Does this remind me of something or someone I already know?" "Is this similar to a technique that I already use?" and "Where and when can I use this information?"

When you learned to recognize Italy on a world map, your teacher probably pointed out that the country is shaped like a boot. This is a simple form of elaboration.

The same idea applies to more complex material. When you meet someone new, for example, ask yourself, "Does she

remind me of someone else?" Or when reading this book, preview the material using the Master Student Map that opens each chapter.

16 Intend to remember. To instantly enhance your memory, form the simple intention to *learn it now* rather than later. The intention to remember can be more powerful than any single memory technique.

You can build on your intention with simple tricks. During a lecture, for example, pretend that you'll be quizzed on the key points at the end of the period. Imagine that you'll get a $5 reward for every correct answer.

Also pay attention to your attention. Each time your mind wanders during class, make a tick mark in the margins of your notes. The act of writing reengages your attention.

If your mind keeps returning to an urgent or incomplete task, then write an Intention Statement about how you will handle it. With your intention safely recorded, return to what's important in the present moment.

USE YOUR COMPUTER TO enhance memory

The outlining feature of a word-processing program offers a way to combine some of the memory techniques in this chapter. Outlining allows you to organize information in a meaningful way. Stating key points in your own words also helps you learn actively. To create outlined summaries of your textbooks and lecture notes:

- Divide a book chapter or set of handwritten notes into sections.

- Open up a new document in your word-processing program, and list the main points from each section.

- Shift to the outline view of your document, and turn each point into a level-one heading.

- Enter key facts and other details as normal text under the appropriate heading.

- When reviewing for a test, shift your document into outline view so that only the headings are displayed. Scan them as you would scan the headlines in a newspaper.

- In the outline view, see whether you can recall the details you included. Then open up the normal text underneath each headline to check the accuracy of your memory.

RECALL IT

17 **Remember something else.** When you are stuck and can't remember something that you're sure you know, remember something else that is related to it.

If you can't remember your great-aunt's name, remember your great-uncle's name. During an economics exam, if you can't remember anything about the aggregate demand curve, recall what you do know about the aggregate supply curve. If you cannot recall specific facts, remember the example that the instructor used during her lecture. Any piece of information is encoded in the same area of the brain as a similar piece of information. You can unblock your recall by stimulating that area of your memory.

A brainstorm is a good memory jog. If you are stumped when taking a test, start writing down lots of answers to related questions, and—pop!—the answer you need is likely to appear.

18 **Notice when you do remember.** Everyone has a different memory style. Some people are best at recalling information they've read. Others have an easier time remembering what they've heard, seen, or done.

To develop your memory, notice when you recall information easily, and ask yourself what memory techniques you're using naturally. Also notice when you find it difficult to recall information. Be a reporter. Get the facts and then adjust your learning techniques. And remember to congratulate yourself when you remember.

The memory strategies that work best for you might relate to the preferred learning style that you identified in Chapter 2. See whether you can combine those strategies with new ones that are based on a different learning style. This approach might increase your effectiveness in the same way that cross-training works for athletes.

19 **Use it before you lose it.** Even information encoded in long-term memory becomes difficult to recall when we don't use it regularly. The pathways to the information become faint with disuse. For example, you can probably remember your current phone number. What was your phone number 10 years ago?

This example points to a powerful memory technique. To remember something, access it a lot. Read it, write it, speak it, listen to it, apply it—find some way to make contact with the material regularly. Each time you do so, you widen the neural pathway to the material and make it easier to recall the next time.

One classic technique for this purpose is making flash cards. Write a sample test question on one side of a 3×5 card and the answer to that question on the other side of the card. Use these cards to quiz yourself. Or ask someone else to read the questions, listen to your answers, and compare them to the answers on the card.

You can also use PowerPoint or other presentation software to create flash cards. Add illustrations, color, and other visual effects—a simple and fun way to activate your visual intelligence. A related option is to go online. Do an Internet search with the words *flash, card,* and *online.* You'll find a list of sites that allow you to select from a library of printable flash cards—or create and print your own cards. You can get flash card apps for your smart phone too.

Another way to make contact with the material is to teach it. Teaching demands mastery. When you explain the function of the pancreas to a fellow student, you discover quickly whether you really understand it yourself. Study groups are especially effective because they put you on stage. The friendly pressure of knowing that you'll teach the group helps focus your attention.

20 **Adopt the attitude that you never forget.** You might not believe that an idea or a thought never leaves your memory. That's okay. In fact, it doesn't matter whether you agree with the idea or not. It can work for you anyway.

Test the concept. Instead of saying, "I don't remember," you can say, "It will come to me." The latter statement implies that the information you want is encoded in your brain and that you can retrieve it—just not right now. You might be surprised to find that the information obediently pops into mind. ■

Your mind,
online

Imagine how useful—and fun—it would be to download everything you've ever read or thought and then instantly locate what you know about a particular topic. Something like this is possible with digital tools. Web sites and computer applications give you a variety of ways to store text and images, organize, search them, and even share them. These applications fall into three major categories.

Social bookmarking. Some Web sites allow you to store, tag, share, and search links to specific pages. Examples are Delicious (www.delicious.com), Diigo (www.diigo.com), and Pinboard (pinboard.in).

Online notebooks. Evernote (www.evernote.com), Springpad (springpadit.com), Zoho Notebook (notebook.zoho.com), and similar Web sites allow you to "clip" images and text from various Web pages, categorize all this content, search it, and add your own notes.

Personal information managers. Examples of personal information managers include Evernote, Zotero, and Yojimbo. These applications share many features with online notebooks. However, some of them allow you to add "offline" content such as digital photos of business cards and receipts. You can search through all this content by using tags and key words.

 You're One Click Away...
from finding more memory strategies online.

Use Q-Cards to reinforce memory

One memory strategy you might find useful involves a special kind of flash card. It's called a *Question Card*, or *Q-Card* for short.

To create a standard flash card, you write a question on one side of a 3 × 5 card, and its answer on the other side. Q-Cards have a question on *both* sides. Here's the trick: The question on one side of the card contains the answer to the question on the other side.

The questions you write on Q-Cards can draw on both lower- and higher-order thinking skills. Writing these questions forces you to encode material in different ways. You activate more areas of your brain and burn the concepts even deeper into your memory.

For example, say that you want to remember the subject of the Eighteenth Amendment to the U.S. Constitution—the one that prohibited the sale of alcohol. On one side of a 3 × 5 card, write *Which amendment prohibited the sale of alcohol?* Turn the card over, and write *What did the Eighteenth Amendment do?*

To get the most from Q-Cards:

- Add a picture to each side of the card. Doing so helps you learn concepts faster and develop a more visual learning style.

- Read the questions and recite the answers out loud. Two keys to memory are repetition and novelty, so use a different voice whenever you read and recite. Whisper the first time you go through your cards, then shout or sing the next time. Doing this develops an auditory learning style.

- Carry Q-Cards with you, and pull them out during waiting times. To develop a kinesthetic learning style, handle your cards often.

- Create a Q-Card for each new and important concept within 24 hours after attending a class or completing an assignment. This is your *active stack* of cards. Keep answering the questions on these cards until you learn each new concept.

- Review all of the cards for a certain subject on one day each week. For example, on Monday, review all cards from biology; on Tuesday, review all cards from history. These cards make up your *review stacks*.

Get started with Q-Cards right now. Use the blanks below. One blank represents the front of the card; the other blank represents the back. Start by creating a Q-Card about remembering how to use Q-Cards!

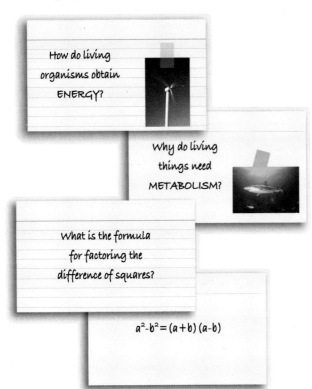

How do living organisms obtain ENERGY?

Why do living things need METABOLISM?

What is the formula for factoring the difference of squares?

$a^2 - b^2 = (a+b)(a-b)$

Windmill: Robert Harding/Getty Images; Reef shark: Stephen Frink/Getty Images

SET A TRAP FOR
your memory

When you want to remind yourself to do something, link this activity to another event you know will take place. The key is to "trap" your memory by picking events that are certain to occur.

Say that you're walking to class and suddenly remember that your accounting assignment is due tomorrow. If you wear a ring, then switch it to a finger on the opposite hand. Now you're "trapped." Every time you glance at your hand and notice that you switched the ring, you get a reminder that you were supposed to remember something else. If you empty your pockets every night, put an unusual item in your pocket in the morning to remind yourself to do something before you go to bed. For example, to remember to call your younger sister on her birthday, pick an object that reminds you of her—a photograph, perhaps—and put it in your pocket. When you empty your pocket that evening and find the photo, you're more likely to make the call.

Everyday rituals that you seldom neglect, such as feeding a pet or unlacing your shoes, provide opportunities for setting traps. For example, tie a triple knot in your shoelace as a reminder to set the alarm for your early morning study group meeting.

You can even use imaginary traps. To remember to pay your phone bill, visualize a big, burly bill collector knocking on your front door to talk to you about how much you owe. The next time your arrive at your front door, you'll be glad that you got there before he did. You still have time to make your payment!

Mobile devices work well for setting memory traps. To remind yourself to bring your textbook to class, for example, set an alarm on your cell phone to go off 10 minutes before you leave the house. Visualize yourself picking up the book when the alarm goes off.

Link two activities together, and make the association unusual. ■

©Istockphoto.com/Tatiana Popova

✓ CRITICAL THINKING EXERCISE 15

Remembering your car keys—or anything else

Pick something you frequently forget. Some people chronically lose their car keys or forget to pay their bills on time. Others let anniversaries and birthdays slip by.

Pick an item or a task you're prone to forget. Then design a strategy for remembering it. Use any of the techniques from this chapter, research others, or make up your own from scratch. Describe your technique and the results in the space provided.

In this exercise, as in most of the exercises in this book, a failure is also a success. Don't be concerned with whether your technique will work. Design it, and then find out whether it works. If it doesn't work for you this time, use another method.

4

_____

_____

_____

_____

_____

_____

_____

_____

_____

_____

_____

_____

_____

_____

YOUR BRAIN—
its care and feeding

When asked about brain-based learning, skeptics might say: "Well, obviously—how could learning be based anywhere other than the brain?"

That's a fair question. One answer is this: Although all learning involves the brain, some learning strategies use more of the brain's unique capacities.

BRAINS THRIVE ON MEANINGFUL PATTERNS

Your brain is a pattern-making machine. It excels at taking random bits of information and translating them into meaningful wholes. Build on this capacity with *elaborative rehearsal*. For example:

- *Use your journal.* Write Discovery and Intention Statements like the ones in this book. Journal Entries prompt you to

Your brain is a pattern-making machine. It excels at taking random bits of information and translating them into meaningful wholes. Build on this capacity with *elaborative rehearsal.*

elaborate on what you hear in class and read in your textbooks. You can create your own writing prompts. For example: "In class today, I discovered that . . . ." "In order to overcome my confusion about this topic, I intend to . . . ."

- *Send yourself a message.* Imagine that an absent classmate has asked you to send her an e-mail about what happened in class today. Write up a reply and send this e-mail to yourself. You'll actively process your recent learning—and create a summary that you can use to review for tests.

- *Play with ideas.* Copy your notes on to 3 × 5 cards, one fact or idea per card. Then see whether you can arrange them into new patterns—chronological order, order of importance, or main ideas and supporting details.

BRAINS THRIVE ON RICH SENSORY EXPERIENCE

Your brain's contact with the world comes through your five senses. So, anchor your learning in as many senses as possible. Beyond seeing and hearing, this can include touch, movement, smell, and taste:

- *Create images.* Draw mind map summaries of your readings and lecture notes. Include visual images. Put main ideas in larger letters and brighter colors.

- *Translate ideas in physical objects.* If one of your career goals is to work from a home office, for example, then create a model of your ideal workspace. Visit an art supplies store to find appropriate materials.

- *Immerse yourself in concrete experiences.* Say that you're in a music appreciation class and learning about jazz. Go to a local jazz club or concert to see and hear a live performance.

BRAINS THRIVE ON LONG-TERM CARE

Starting now, adopt habits to keep your brain lean and fit for life. Consider these research-based suggestions from the Alzheimer's Association.[6]

- *Stay mentally active.* If you sit at a desk most of the workday, take a hiking class or start a garden. If you seldom travel, start reading maps of new locations and plan a cross-country trip. Play challenging games and work crossword puzzles. Seek out museums, theaters, concerts, and other cultural

> Even after you graduate, consider learning another language or taking up a musical instrument. Learning gives your brain a workout, much like sit-ups condition your abs.

4

events. Even after you graduate, consider learning another language or taking up a musical instrument. Learning gives your brain a workout, much like sit-ups condition your abs.

- *Stay socially active.* Having a network of supportive friends can reduce stress levels. In turn, stress management helps to maintain connections between brain cells. Stay socially active by working, volunteering, and joining clubs.

- *Stay physically active.* Physical activity promotes blood flow to the brain. It also reduces the risk of diabetes, cardiovascular disease, and other diseases that can impair brain function. Exercise that includes mental activity—such as planning a jogging route and watching for traffic signals—offers added benefits.

- *Adopt a brain-healthy diet.* A diet rich in dark-skinned fruits and vegetables boosts your supply of antioxidants—natural chemicals that nourish your brain. Examples of these foods are raisins, blueberries, blackberries, strawberries, raspberries, kale, spinach, brussels sprouts, alfalfa sprouts, and broccoli. Avoid foods that are high in saturated fat and cholesterol, which may increase the risk of Alzheimer's disease.

- *Protect your heart.* In general, what's good for your heart is good for your brain. Protect both organs by eating well, exercising regularly, managing your weight, staying tobacco-free, and getting plenty of sleep. These habits reduce your risk of heart attack, stroke, and other cardiovascular conditions that interfere with blood flow to the brain. ■

MNEMONIC DEVICES

It's pronounced "ne-MON-ik." The word refers to tricks that can increase your ability to recall everything from grocery lists to speeches.

Some entertainers use mnemonic devices to perform "impossible" feats of memory, such as recalling the names of everyone in a large audience after hearing them just once. Using mnemonic devices, speakers can go for hours without looking at their notes. The possibilities for students are endless.

There is a catch, though. Mnemonic devices have three serious limitations:

- They don't always help you understand or digest material. Mnemonics rely only on rote memorization.

- The mnemonic device itself is sometimes complicated to learn and time-consuming to develop.

- Mnemonic devices can be forgotten.

In spite of their limitations, mnemonic devices can be powerful. There are five general categories: new words, creative sentences, rhymes and songs, the loci system, and the peg system.

Make up new words. Acronyms are words created from the initial letters of a series of words. Examples include NASA (**N**ational **A**eronautics and **S**pace **A**dministration) and laser (**l**ight **a**mplification by **s**timulated **e**mission of **r**adiation).

You can make up your own acronyms to recall a series of facts. A common mnemonic acronym is Roy G. Biv, which has helped millions of students remember the colors of the visible spectrum (**r**ed, **o**range, **y**ellow, **g**reen, **b**lue, **i**ndigo, and **v**iolet). IPMAT helps biology students remember the stages of cell division (**i**nterphase, **p**rophase, **m**etaphase, **a**naphase, and **t**elophase). OCEAN helps psychology students recall the five major personality factors: **o**pen-mindedness, **c**onscientiousness, **e**xtraversion, **a**greeableness, and **n**euroticism.

Use creative sentences. Acrostics are sentences that help you remember a series of letters that stand for something. For example, the first letters of the words in the sentence *Every good boy does fine* (E, G, B, D, and F) are the music notes of the lines of the treble clef staff.

Create rhymes and songs. Madison Avenue advertising executives spend billions of dollars a year on advertisements designed to burn their messages into your memory. The song "It's the Real Thing" was used to market Coca-Cola, despite the soda's artificial ingredients.

Rhymes have been used for centuries to teach basic facts. "*I* before *e*, except after *c*" has helped many a student on spelling tests.

Use the loci system. The word *loci* is the plural of *locus,* a synonym for *place* or *location.* Use the loci system to create visual associations with familiar locations. Unusual associations are the easiest to remember.

The loci system is an old one. Ancient Greek orators used it to remember long speeches, and politicians use it today. For example, if a politician's position were that road taxes must be raised to pay for school equipment, his loci visualizations before a speech might look like the following.

First, as he walks in the door of his house, he imagines a large *porpoise* jumping through a hoop. This reminds him to begin by telling the audience the *purpose* of his speech.

Next, he visualizes his living room floor covered with paving stones, forming a road leading into the kitchen. In the kitchen, he pictures dozens of schoolchildren sitting on the floor because they have no desks.

Now it's the day of the big speech. The politician is nervous. He's perspiring so much that his clothes stick to his body. He stands up to give his speech and his mind goes blank. Then he starts thinking to himself:

I can remember the rooms in my house. Let's see, I'm walking in the front door and—wow!—I see a porpoise. That reminds me to talk about the purpose of my speech. And then there's that road leading to the kitchen. Say, what are all those kids doing there on the floor? Oh, yeah, now I remember—they have no desks! We need to raise taxes on roads to pay for their desks and the other stuff they need in classrooms.

Use the peg system. The peg system is a technique that employs key words that are paired with numbers. Each word forms a "peg" on which you can "hang" mental associations. To use this system effectively, learn the following peg words and their associated numbers well:

bun goes with 1	*sticks* goes with 6
shoe goes with 2	*heaven* goes with 7
tree goes with 3	*gate* goes with 8
door goes with 4	*wine* goes with 9
hive goes with 5	*hen* goes with 10

You can use the peg system to remember the Bill of Rights (the first ten amendments to the U.S. Constitution). For example, amendment number *four* is about protection from unlawful search and seizure. Imagine people knocking at your *door* who are demanding to search your home. This amendment means that you do not have to open your door unless those people have a proper search warrant. ■

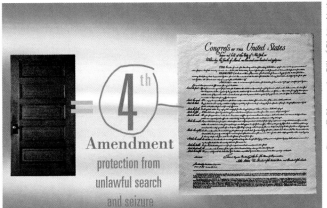

master**student**profile

Scott Heiferman

(1972—) Cofounder and CEO of Meetup, a Web site for organizing local groups

I grew up with four siblings who were 12 to 17 years older, so I was exposed early to the fields they were interested in and the diversity influenced me. When I was a preteen, I programmed an Apple II computer to manage the inventory for my parents' paint store.

I was 16 when my mother died, and I realized that life is short. It motivated me to take risks and have fun.

I studied engineering at the University of Iowa, but I wasn't good enough in math to focus solely on engineering, so I got a business degree. I wasn't much interested in the business classes, but I saw business as a means to bring innovation to a large number of people....

During senior year, I had two job offers, one in Silicon Valley and one at Sony in Montvale, N.J. When I looked at a map, Montvale seemed as if it was practically New York City, so I chose the job there. But Montvale isn't New York City and I lasted less than a year there.

I moved to Queens and in 1995 started an online ad agency called i-traffic, which was bought by Agency.com in 1999.

I was 27, with a staff of more than 100, when Agency.com bought the company, and I was totally over my head managing a large operation. I left the company in 2000. I was so sick of working with lawyers and accountants and investment bankers that I worked the counter at a McDonald's in Manhattan for a couple of weeks.

The attacks on Sept. 11 got me thinking and I came up with 30 ideas for my next project. I narrowed them to two.

One, which I developed with a co-founder, was a company called Fotolog, now a social network that is big in South America. The other was Meetup, a way for people to self-organize locally. I pulled a team together and we started Meetup.com in 2002.

A Meetup is about the simple idea of using the Internet to get people off the Internet. People feel a need to commiserate or get together and talk about what's important to them.

When we were designing the site, we were wrong about almost everything we thought people would want to use it for. I thought it would be a niche lifestyle venture, perhaps for fan clubs. I had no idea that people would form new types of P.T.A.'s, chambers of commerce or health support groups. And we weren't thinking that anyone would want to meet about politics, but there are thousands of these Meetups.

People have organized more than 200,000 monthly Meetups in more than 100 countries. There's nothing more powerful than a community coming together around a purpose. We spend increasingly more time in front of screens. We're more connected technologically, but we're less connected physically.

Meetup earns most of its revenue from the small monthly fee charged to organizers, 1 percent of our users. There are 60 of us in our Manhattan office, and we had our first profitable month in July.

Critics have predicted our death three times. If no one is predicting your company's death, then you're not taking enough risks in what you're doing.

In 2008, I married Emily Krasnor, a human-rights professional. In a few years, we hope to move to a developing country, perhaps in Africa. She'll continue her human-rights work while I will help expand Meetup's operations around the world.

As told to Patricia R. Olsen.

Scott J. Ferrell/Congressional Quarterly/Getty Images

Scott Heiferman ... is willing to change.

YOU ... can master change by remembering how you've handled transitions in the past.

Excerpt from Scott Heiferman, "The Pursuit of Community," *New York Times*, September 5, 2009, http://www.nytimes.com/2009/09/06/jobs/06boss.html?emc=eta1.

You're One Click Away...
from learning more about Scott Heiferman online at the Master Student Profiles. You can also visit the Master Student Hall of Fame to learn about other master students.

FIVE Cs
FOR YOUR CAREER

CHARACTER • CRITICAL THINKING • CREATIVE THINKING • COLLABORATION • COMMUNICATION

Use your memory skills to succeed in the workplace. Retain information from workshops, training sessions, and business books. Recall details about products and services. And look for connections between memory and the four Cs.

See memory skills as ways to develop character. At first glance, you might find it hard to connect the content of this chapter with the topic of character. If you persist with this line of thinking, you might make some unexpected connections. By their very nature, memory techniques call for focused attention, self-awareness, and self-direction. Every time you use a strategy from this chapter, you are developing these key qualities of a master student.

Use creative thinking to enhance your memory. Experiment with organizing facts and ideas into creative lists. For instance, you could recall many of the memory techniques presented in this chapter with the following list of "R's":

Relax. Notice and release tension. Reduce distractions in the external environment and within yourself.

Reduce. Distinguish between essential and inessential information. Focus your attention on a limited number of items that you want to remember.

Restructure. Organize the material you want to learn. Group items into logical categories and sequences.

Relate. Create meaningful associations and connect new material to a topic that interests you, or to personal experiences.

Recite. Summarize facts and ideas by speaking, writing, and creating visuals.

Rephrase. Go beyond rote learning by translating material into your own words.

Repeat. Over-learn the material. Recite up to the point that the material feels second nature.

Use critical thinking to enhance your memory. One simple but powerful means of elaboration is to ask questions about incoming information and ideas. Asking questions forces you to slow down, focus your attention, and think critically. All these mental activities are memory boosters.

For starters, use the "five W" questions:

• *Who* will ask me to remember this information?

• *What* are the main points and significant details?

• *Why* (or *how*) would it create value for me to remember this new information?

• *Where*—in what situations—would I be asked to remember this information?

• *When* is such a situation likely to occur?

Become a better communicator by remembering what you want to say. Before a job interview, for example, make a short list of things you want to mention. Start with key facts from the research you've done about your prospective employer—company history, products, and services. Also list key points from your skills analysis and résumé. (For more on these topics, see Chapter 12.) Use your favorite memory techniques to keep these lists in mind.

Become a better collaborator by remembering names. Starting your first day at a new job, you'll be asked to remember coworkers' names. You can do it. Impress your team by using any of the following techniques.

Comment on the name. This technique acts as a conversation starter while allowing you to recite and repeat the person's name: "I have a cousin named Theresa, so that will be easy to remember." "You're the second person named James that I've met today."

Ask for the spelling. This allows you to hear the name again. It also helps you distinguish between common names with different spellings: *Stephen* versus *Steven*; *Joanne* versus *Joann*. Once you get the spelling, visualize yourself writing it on a blank sheet of paper in big, bold letters.

Break the name down into simpler parts and then say them to yourself. Exaggerate the key sounds. For Tina, say *teeeeee-na*. For Jamal, say *ja-maaaaaaal*.

Take notes. Keep a pen and a few 3 × 5 cards in your purse or pocket. After meeting someone, jot the person's name on a card, along with a notable fact: "Sophie works in accounting." "Melissa started working here on the same day I did."

File names for future reference. Gather up all your handwritten notes about people you've met. Then key this information into a document that you can access with your computer or other digital device.

Look for visual cues. If name tags are required in your workplace, then you've got a handy tool for remembering names. Also look for name cards posted on office doors and workstations.

Be sensitive to cultural norms. In workplaces with a more formal tone, you might be wise to refer to people by their last name: Mr. Hassad or Ms. Washington. Notice how your experienced coworkers handle this situation.

Give yourself a break. Stop saying things such as "I'm bad at names." Instead, say: "I'm *getting better* with names." Notice whether this new way of speaking affects your ability to remember.

Now, make a personal commitment to developing the five Cs. Take another look at the Discovery Wheel in Chapter 2—especially the sections labeled Character, Creative and Critical Thinking, Communicating, and Collaborating. Take a snapshot of your current skills in these areas after reading and doing this chapter.

DISCOVERY

My scores on the "Five C" sections of the Discovery Wheel were:	As of today, I would give myself the following scores in these areas:	At the end of this course, I would like my scores in these areas to be:
Character _____	Character _____	Character _____
Creative & Critical Thinking _____	Creative & Critical Thinking _____	Creative & Critical Thinking _____
Communicating _____	Communicating _____	Communicating _____
Collaborating _____	Collaborating _____	Collaborating _____

Next, skim this chapter and look for a memory technique that you want to explore in depth. Choose one that would enhance your self-rating in at least one of the five Cs.

I discovered that my preferred technique is . . .

_____

_____

_____

_____

In light of the five Cs, I can use this technique to become more . . .

_____

_____

_____

_____

This technique can also enhance my character by helping me to develop master student qualities, including . . .

_____

_____

_____

_____

INTENTION
To use this technique, I intend to . . .

_____

_____

_____

_____

NEXT ACTION
The specific action I will take is . . .

_____

_____

_____

_____

Name _____

Date _____

1. Briefly define the word *love* as it is used in the "Power Process: Love your problems (and experience your barriers)."

   In the Power Process, the word love means to unconditionally accept the fact that your problems exist.   (*Power Process: Love your problems and experience your barriers*, page 114)

2. According to the latest research, memory is

   (a) A process rather than a thing.

   (b) A process of encoding and decoding.

   (c) Not something you *have* but something you *do*.

   (d) All of the above.

   (d) all of the above.   (*Take your memory out of the closet*, page 115)

3. In the article about the memory jungle, the meadow:

   (a) is a place that every animal (thought or perception) must pass through.

   (b) represents short-term memory.

   (c) represents the idea that one type of memory has a limited capacity.

   (d) all of the above.

   (d) all of the above.   (*The memory jungle*, page 116)

4. Give two examples of ways in which you can organize a long list of items.

   (Answers will vary.) One way of organizing a long list for memorization is by location. An example is a biology student memorizing the leg muscles from the foot up to the hip. She could organize the muscles by location by grouping the muscles in the foot, those in the calf, those in the knee, and so on. Another way of organizing a list is by continuum. An example is a student memorizing the types of business organization. He could organize them on a continuum, from the smallest and simplest type (a sole proprietorship) to the largest and most complex (a multinational corporation).   (*20 memory techniques*, page 118)

5. Memorization on a deep level can take place if you

   (a) repeat the idea.   **(b)** repeat the idea.   **(c)** repeat the idea.   **(d)** all of the above.

   (d) all of the above.   (*20 memory techniques*, page 118)

6. The article "20 memory techniques" is divided into four categories. What are those categories?

   (1) Organize it (organized information is easier to find). (2) Use your body (learning is an active process; get all of your senses involved). (3) Use your brain (work with your memory, not against it). (4) Recall it (regularly retrieve and apply key information).   (*20 memory techniques*, page 118)

7. Define the term *graphic organizer*, and give two examples.

   (Answers will vary.) *Graphic organizer* can be defined as preformatted charts used to prompt the student to visualize relationships among facts and ideas. Examples: topic-point-details chart, Venn diagram.   (*20 memory techniques*, page 118).

8. Define *acronym*, and give an example of one.

   (Answers will vary.) Acronyms are words created from the initial letters of a series of words. Examples include NASA (National Aeronautics and Space Administration) and laser (light amplification by stimulated emission of radiation).   (*Mnemonic devices*, page 128)

9. Mnemonic devices are the most efficient ways to memorize facts and ideas. True or false? Explain your answer.

   True. These memory tricks can help you learn information quickly. Therefore, they are efficient. However, they may not be effective for long-term memorization or for understanding.   (*Mnemonic devices*, page 128)

10. According to the text, the human brain thrives on elaborative rehearsal. Give an example of this process.

    Use your journal. Discovery intention statements prompt you to elaborate on what you have learned. For example, "In class today, I discovered that …" and In order to overcome this confusion, I intend to …" Other examples: Send yourself a message or play with ideas.   (*Your brain–its care and feeding*, page 126).

5 CHAPTER — READING

Instructor Tools & Tips

"Reading furnishes our mind only with materials of knowledge; it is thinking that makes what we read ours."
—John Locke

"There would seem to be almost no limit to what people can and will misunderstand when they are not doing their utmost to get at a writer's meaning." —Ezra Pound

PREVIEW

Chapter 5 is the first chapter in the text's academic development section, which includes Chapters 5 through 7. This section of the book employs a time-sensitive critical thinking approach to organize academic learning by considering strategies to employ before, during, and after learning. All three chapters (Chapter 5: Reading, Chapter 6: Notes, and Chapter 7: Tests) follow this approach. This structure makes Chapter 3: Time & Money even more relevant to student success.

Although much of this chapter appears to be simply a review of what students should have learned in elementary or high school, the reality is that many students do not learn the critical reading skills they need to survive and thrive in the academic rigors of college. College reading is more than just the ability to read the words. Critical reading is a complex thinking process and thus is unlike any other "subject" they study in school. The academic literacy training that students receive in this chapter will prove invaluable throughout their academic careers. It is not uncommon for students enrolled in certificate programs or in courses which do not require proficiency in reading college textbooks to face difficulty in comprehending their college materials. Even though students may resist this necessary skill, it can directly impact their success in their classes and in the workplace. You may want to point out to students the need to read and respond effectively in a career: interoffice communication (e-mails and memos), communication with clients and outside parties, and reading professional journals and other publications.

Our motivation, maturity, and life experiences all lead us to value the skills of reading comprehension and reading speed more than we might have as children. Most importantly, you can help your students accelerate their ability to learn new material by helping them activate any prior knowledge to engage with the reading they must do to succeed. Encourage your students to use the information they have learned about the brain in Chapter 4: Memory, to enhance their skill at reading. You may want to briefly review this material in class. Consider the Master Student Map at the beginning of the chapter as a stepping-stone.

GUEST SPEAKER

This is a good time to invite a librarian as your guest speaker to talk to students about how they can use the library to research topics for classes. See also a related assignment in the Homework section.

Although the following strategy may take a bit of advance planning and a mobile cart, you may want to gather books from several academic disciplines and take them into the classroom. You can spend time looking at the structure and organization of the textbooks. Ask students to survey the texts, looking for such things as chapter layout and organization, appendices, and details that may differ from other disciplines. These are concepts that may escape students' notice otherwise.

Another possibility is to invite instructors from a variety of disciplines to talk about reading strategies appropriate to their course content. Ask them to come prepared to answer the following questions for your students:

Why? Why is the reading material in your discipline area unique?

What? What strategies would work best for tackling the reading material in your discipline area? Suggest that your discipline expert bring a sample passage (as a handout) for students so that they can use this new strategy to read it.

How? How can students improve their reading comprehension in your discipline area using these strategies?

What if? What if the students are still having trouble with reading in this discipline? What resources do you suggest (on-campus labs, ancillary textbooks, Web sites, and the like)?

master instructor
BEST PRACTICE

"*The article 'Getting past road blocks to reading' is one of my favorites. I usually have many students in my online college survival course who are parents. Often, somewhere along the way, they will mention the problems they have with studying because of their kids. I immediately suggest that they read this article, and I have received some really positive feedback from the students who have not only read the article but have successfully used some of the techniques. Many of them have written back to me to thank me for alerting them to this article before it became part of an assigned chapter. Their children have also responded positively to the attention they receive while 'helping' Mom or Dad to study!*"

–*Diane Beecher, Lake Superior College, Minnesota*

LECTURE

Students may ask, "Why use Muscle Reading? I have been reading since first grade!" Muscle Reading is designed as a balanced literacy approach. It incorporates the three aspects of a metacognitive learning system. This means that it presents specific strategies for students to use before, during, and after reading.

Students may also grumble that this approach to reading requires "too much." Lecture on Muscle Reading by walking them through the nine steps for the next chapter, Chapter 6: Notes.

- Tell them to *preview* the chapter by turning the pages, looking at graphs, pictures, article titles, and anything else that stands out for them.

- Next, on a sheet of paper, students create an *outline* by listing the titles of the articles, double-spacing between the article titles. Instruct the students to turn each title into a *Question*.

- Then students *read* the chapter, highlighting or *underlining* the *answers* they discover to their outline list of questions.

- Students *recite*, *review*, and periodically *review again* their outline questions and highlighted answers in the book.

This lecture and demonstration helps your students see how the nine-step process can be efficiently streamlined while retaining its effectiveness. For more information, review the sidebar article Muscle reading—a leaner approach on page 140.

EXERCISES/ACTIVITIES

1. **Power Process: Notice your pictures and let them go (page 134)** Present this Power Process as a problem-solving technique. When students feel frustrated because reality does not match their expectations, Notice your pictures and let them go helps them let go of those expectations and experience what their reality *does* have to offer. In class, have students individually brainstorm "pictures" that interfere with their success in college. Examples include "I'm not smart enough to get a college degree" or "I'll never graduate—I can't stick with anything for four years." Then ask students to select one picture to "let go." Have them write their picture on a piece of paper and fold it up. Take an empty cardboard box into the classroom. Ask the entire class to tear their papers (negative pictures) into shreds and throw them into the box—literally letting them go Ask students to write briefly about a new, positive picture to replace the negative one they have let go. For some students, this will be a personal exercise, and they may not feel comfortable talking about it with others. Other students may be willing to share with the class their experience of letting their negative picture go.

2. **Muscle Reading (pages 135–141)** Divide your class into three groups: Before, During, and After. Have each group prepare a 10-minute presentation on the three steps within their given phase. Each group aims for a memorable lesson that provides examples of their strategies. In conclusion, the three groups come up with a sample test question to help determine how the rest of the class understood their presentation. Give feedback as a class. If students did not understand a presentation, ask them to try to articulate how it might have been made clearer for them. We all understand feedback best when comments are specific and we receive suggestions for future projects.

CONVERSATION/SHARING

Now that your students have practiced using the Master Student Map in previous chapters, see if they can generate their own questions before you present yours to the class.

Why? Why does *From Master Student to Master Employee* include a chapter on reading?

What? Read through the list of articles and select three that you believe will enhance your reading skills.

How? How can you be more successful in college with these additional strategies for successful reading? How can these skills be useful in the workplace?

What if? What if you apply these reading strategies to your coursework for other classes?

HOMEWORK

Developing information literacy (pages 150–153) You can tie library research to the workplace. After students have read this article and heard from a librarian (as a guest speaker), give them an assignment to go to the college library to (1) select a potential career to research and (2) narrow topics within the broad career topic. Ask the librarian to discuss library resources that would help in this career research. Librarians can suggest reference books within the library on your campus. Students often rely only on online sources because they are unfamiliar with books and other sources in the library facility. In addition, you can suggest student research the following site: http://online.onetcenter .org. This U.S. Department of Labor site provides attributes and characteristics about hundreds of occupations.

Developing critical thinking strategies throughout the semester will help your students master their college-level reading. Use this exercise to help students further develop their skills. This assignment works best as either an extra-credit assignment or as homework.

You can find additional career resources within the General Resources folder on the *From Master Student to Master Employee* Web site. You will find the Career Resource Center helpful as you connect this chapter to the workplace.

Practicing Critical Thinking One of the strategies suggested for understanding difficult reading material (When reading is tough, page 142) is to read another publication on the same subject. This is one example of critical thinking skills—explaining and assessing alternative views on an issue.

Apply this strategy now. Ask your students to find and read a newspaper or magazine article that's relevant to one of their current reading assignments. Have your students summarize and compare the viewpoints on the subject presented by both authors. Ask them to list the major questions addressed, along with the

answers that are offered, and have them highlight points of disagreement and agreement. Finally, have your students consider the methods that the authors use to reach their conclusions and the evidence they present. Have students determine if one author's viewpoint is more reasonable, given all of the suitable evidence, and then write a paragraph that supports their conclusion.

If you assign this for extra credit or homework, be sure to clarify for your students exactly which materials they should submit. Consider asking them to submit their articles or a bibliography page. If you are trying to encourage students to become familiar with technology, ask them to forward the materials to you in an e-mail attachment or post the materials to your online course management system. You might ask students to create a PowerPoint presentation based on this assignment, allowing you to introduce students to this important presentation tool. Students can find Microsoft tutorials online to help them get started. This provides a comfortable environment for guidance in new technology.

EVALUATION

Quiz Ideas for Chapter 5

Ask students to:

- Explain the nine steps of the Muscle Reading process.

- Describe tools to use when reading tough material.

- List techniques for reading faster.

Additional Digital Resources for Chapter 5

What can you **ASSIGN FROM THE COURSEMATE** *for From Master Student to Master Employee?*

- **Master Student Profile: Michael Hyatt.** Assign students to read about Michael's success as a leader in a major publishing company and ask them to recap the process Michael applies to his mentoring group that helps them retain what they have read.

- **Master Students in Action Video.** Students will hear firsthand from other students about their reading challenges and their strategies for success. The Master Students in Action videos give your students a firsthand view of how the strategies in *From Master Student to Master Employee* have helped their peers overcome obstacles. In special segments, Dave Ellis offers students his best strategies for muscle reading. Note that these videos are available for every chapter.

- **Learning Styles Application.** In answering the four questions about Muscle Reading posted in this chapter's Learning Styles Application available in the Chapter Reflections tab gives you the opportunity to see how well students are applying their Learning Style Profile to reading.

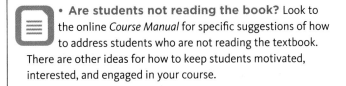

To access CourseMate, your students need to visit www.cengagebrain.com. *At the CengageBrain.com home page, students search for the ISBN of* From Master Student to Master Employee *(from the back cover of the book), using the search box at the top of the page. This takes them to the product page where these resources can be found.*

Did you know that **THESE RESOURCES** *(and many more)* **ARE AVAILABLE** *on the* **INSTRUCTOR COMPANION SITE***?*

- **Are students not reading the book?** Look to the online *Course Manual* for specific suggestions of how to address students who are not reading the textbook. There are other ideas for how to keep students motivated, interested, and engaged in your course.

- **Need some energizing lecture ideas?** Browse through the lecture ideas provided for Chapter 5, including the following:

  - **Children Underfoot.** Geared for students who are also parents, these share some success tips from other parents about how to get reading completed with children around.
  - **Reading Rates.** This explains to students the different categories of reading rates and how to decide which rate works for which type of reading situation.

Please visit login.cengage.com *to log in and access the Instructor Companion Site.*

Reading

Use this **Master Student Map**
to ask yourself

WHY THIS CHAPTER MATTERS . . .

- Higher education requires extensive reading of complex material.

WHAT IS INCLUDED . . .

HOW I CAN USE THIS CHAPTER. . .

- Analyze what effective readers do and experiment with new techniques.
- Increase my vocabulary and adjust my reading speed for different types of material.
- Comprehend difficult texts with more ease.

WHAT IF . . .

- I could finish my reading with time to spare and easily recall the key points?

© Ruslan Ivantsov/Shutterstock.com

JOURNAL ENTRY 9
Intention Statement

Declare what you want from this chapter

Recall a time when you encountered problems with reading, such as finding words you didn't understand or pausing to reread paragraphs more than once. Then list at least three specific reading skills you want to gain from this chapter.

I intend to . . .

POWER process

Notice your pictures and let them go

One of the brain's primary jobs is to manufacture images. We use mental pictures to make predictions about the world, and we base much of our behavior on those predictions.

Pictures can sometimes get in our way. Take the student who plans to attend a school he hasn't visited. He chose this school for its strong curriculum and good academic standing, but his brain didn't stop there. In his mind, the campus has historic buildings with ivy-covered walls and tree-lined avenues. The professors, he imagines, will be as articulate as Barack Obama and as entertaining as Conan O'Brien. The cafeteria will be a cozy nook serving everything from delicate quiche to strong coffee. He will gather there with fellow students for hours of stimulating, intellectual conversation. The library will have every book, while the computer lab will boast the newest technology.

The school turns out to be four gray buildings downtown, next to the bus station. The first class he attends is taught by an overweight, balding professor wearing a purple and orange bird-of-paradise tie. The cafeteria is a nondescript hall with machine-dispensed food, and the student's apartment is barely large enough to accommodate his roommate's tuba. This hypothetical student gets depressed. He begins to think about dropping out of school.

The problem with pictures is that they can prevent us from seeing what is really there. That is what happened to the student in this story. His pictures prevented him from noticing that his school is in the heart of a culturally vital city—close to theaters, museums, government offices, clubs, and all kinds of stores. The professor with the weird tie is not only an expert in his field but also a superior teacher. The school cafeteria is skimpy because it can't compete with the variety of inexpensive restaurants in the area.

Our pictures often lead to our being angry or disappointed. We set up expectations of events before they occur. Sometimes we don't even realize that we have these expectations. The next time you discover you are angry, disappointed, or frustrated, look to see which of your pictures aren't being fulfilled.

When you notice that pictures are getting in your way, in the gentlest manner possible let your pictures go. Let them drift away like wisps of smoke picked up by a gentle wind.

This Power Process can be a lifesaver when it comes to reading. Some students enter higher education with pictures about all the reading they'll be required to do before they graduate. They see themselves feeling bored, confused, and worried about keeping up with assignments. If you have such pictures, be willing to let them go. This chapter can help you recreate your whole experience of reading, which is crucial to your success.

Sometimes when we let go of old pictures, it's helpful to replace them with new, positive pictures. These new images can help you take a fresh perspective. Your new pictures might not feel as comfortable and genuine as your old ones. That's okay. Give it time. It's your head, and you're ultimately in charge of the pictures that live there.

© peterglanville

You're One Click Away...
from accessing Power Process Media online and finding out more about how to "notice your pictures and let them go."

> Picture yourself sitting at a desk, a book in your hands. Your eyes are open, and it looks as if you're reading. Suddenly your head jerks up. You blink. You realize your eyes have been scanning the page for 10 minutes, and you can't remember a single thing you have read.

MUSCLE READING

Or picture this: You've had a hard day. You were up at 6:00 A.M. to get the kids ready for school. A coworker called in sick, and you missed your lunch trying to do his job as well as your own. You picked up the kids, then had to shop for dinner. Dinner was late, of course, and the kids were grumpy.

Finally, you get to your books at 8:00 P.M. You begin a reading assignment on something called "the equity method of accounting for common stock investments." "I am preparing for the future," you tell yourself, as you plod through two paragraphs and begin the third. Suddenly, everything in the room looks different. Your head is resting on your elbow, which is resting on the equity method of accounting. The clock reads 11:00 P.M. Say good-bye to 3 hours.

Sometimes the only difference between a sleeping pill and a textbook is that the textbook doesn't have a warning on the label about operating heavy machinery.

Contrast this scenario with the image of an active reader, who exhibits the following behaviors:

- Stays alert, poses questions about what she reads, and searches for the answers.
- Recognizes levels of information within the text, separating the main points and general principles from supporting details.
- Quizzes herself about the material, makes written notes, and lists unanswered questions.
- Instantly spots key terms and takes the time to find the definitions of unfamiliar words.
- Thinks critically about the ideas in the text and looks for ways to apply them.

That sounds like a lot to do. Yet skilled readers routinely accomplish all these things and more—while enjoying the process.

Master students engage actively with reading material. They're willing to grapple with even the most challenging texts. They wrestle meaning from each page. They fill the margins with handwritten questions. They underline, highlight, annotate, and nearly rewrite some books to make them their own.

Master students also commit to change their lives based on what they read. Of every chapter, they ask, "What's the point? And what's the payoff? How can I use this to live my purpose and achieve my goals?" These students are just as likely to create to-do lists as to take notes on their reading. And when they're done with a useful book, master students share it with others for continuing conversation. Reading becomes a creative act and a tool for building community.

One way to experience this kind of success is to approach reading with a system in mind. An example is Muscle Reading. You can use Muscle Reading to avoid mental minivacations and reduce the number of unscheduled naps during study time, even after a hard day. Muscle Reading is a way to decrease difficulty and struggle by increasing energy and skill. Once you learn this system, you might actually spend less time on your reading and get more out of it.

Boosting your reading skills will promote your success in school. It can also boost your income. According to a report from the National Endowment for the Arts, proficient readers earn more than people with only basic reading skills. In addition, better readers are more likely to work as managers or other professionals.[1]

This is not to say that Muscle Reading will make your job or education a breeze. Muscle Reading might even look like more work at first. Effective textbook reading is an active, energy-consuming, sit-on-the-edge-of-your-seat business. That's why this strategy is called Muscle Reading. ∎

5

How Muscle Reading WORKS

Muscle Reading is a three-phase technique you can use to extract the ideas and information you want.

- Phase 1 includes steps to take *before* you read.
- Phase 2 includes steps to take *while* you read.
- Phase 3 includes steps to take *after* you read.

Each phase has specific steps.

PHASE ONE:
Before you read
Step 1: **Preview**
Step 2: **Outline**
Step 3: **Question**

PHASE TWO:
While you read
Step 4: **Focus**
Step 5: **Flag Answers**

PHASE THREE:
After you read
Step 6: **Recite**
Step 7: **Review**
Step 8: **Review again**

Brent Walker/Shutterstock.com

To jog your memory, write the first letters of the Muscle Reading acrostic in a margin or at the top of your notes. Then check off the steps you intend to follow.

To assist your recall of Muscle Reading strategies, memorize three short sentences:

Pry **O**ut **Q**uestions.

Focus and **F**lag **A**nswers.

Recite, **R**eview, and **R**eview again.

These three sentences correspond to the three phases of the Muscle Reading technique. Each sentence is an acrostic. The first letter of each word stands for one of the steps listed above.

Take a moment to invent images for each of those sentences.

For *Phase 1*, visualize or feel yourself prying out questions from a text. These questions are ones you want answered based on a brief survey of the assignment. Make a mental picture of yourself scanning the material, spotting a question, and reaching into the text to pry it out. Hear yourself saying, "I've got it. Here's my question."

Then for *Phase 2*, focus on finding answers to your questions. Feel free to underline, highlight, or mark up your text in other ways. Make the answers so obvious that they lift up from the page.

Finally, you enter *Phase 3*. Hear your voice reciting what you have learned. Listen to yourself making a speech or singing a song about the material as you review it.

To jog your memory, write the first letters of the Muscle Reading acrostic in a margin or at the top of your notes. Then check off the steps you intend to follow. Or write the Muscle Reading steps on 3 × 5 cards and then use them for bookmarks.

Muscle Reading might take a little time to learn. At first you might feel it's slowing you down. That's natural when you're gaining a new skill. Mastery comes with time and practice.

PHASE 1 Before you read

STEP 1 PREVIEW

Before you start reading, preview the entire assignment. You don't have to memorize what you preview to get value from this step. Previewing sets the stage for incoming information by warming up a space in your mental storage area.

If you are starting a new book, look over the table of contents and flip through the text page by page. If you're going to read one chapter, flip through the pages of that chapter. Even if your assignment is merely a few pages in a book, you can benefit from a brief preview of the table of contents.

Read all chapter headings and subheadings. Like the headlines in a newspaper, these are usually printed in large, bold type. Often headings are brief summaries in themselves.

Keep an eye out for summary statements. If the assignment is long or complex, read the summary first. Many textbooks have summaries in the introduction or at the end of each chapter.

When previewing, seek out familiar concepts, facts, or ideas. These items can help increase comprehension by linking new information to previously learned material. Take a few moments to reflect on what you already know about the subject—even if you think you know nothing. This technique prepares your brain to accept new information.

Look for ideas that spark your imagination or curiosity. Inspect drawings, diagrams, charts, tables, graphs, and photographs.

Imagine what kinds of questions will show up on a test. Previewing helps to clarify your purpose for reading. Ask yourself what you will do with this material and how it can relate to your long-term goals. Will you be reading just to get the main points? Key supporting details? Additional details? All of the above? Your answers will guide what you do with each step that follows.

Keep your preview short. If the entire reading assignment will take less than an hour, your preview might take 5 minutes. Previewing is also a way to get yourself started when an assignment looks too big to handle. It is an easy way to step into the material.

STEP 2 OUTLINE

With complex material, take time to understand the structure of what you are about to read. Outlining actively organizes your thoughts about the assignment and can help make complex information easier to understand.

If your textbook provides chapter outlines, spend some time studying them. When an outline is not provided, sketch a brief one in the margin of your book or at the beginning of your notes on a separate sheet of paper. Later, as you read and take notes, you can add to your outline.

Headings in the text can serve as major and minor entries in your outline. For example, the heading for this article is "Phase 1: Before you read," and the subheadings list the three steps in this phase. When you outline, feel free to rewrite headings so that they are more meaningful to you.

The amount of time you spend on this outlining step will vary. For some assignments, a 10-second mental outline is all you might need. For other assignments (fiction and poetry, for example), you can skip this step altogether.

STEP 3 QUESTION

Before you begin a careful reading, determine what you want from the assignment. Then write down a list of questions, including any questions that resulted from your preview of the materials.

Another useful technique is to turn chapter headings and subheadings into questions. For example, if a heading is "Transference and Suggestion," you can ask yourself, "What are *transference* and *suggestion*? How does *transference* relate to *suggestion*?" Make up a quiz as if you were teaching this subject to your classmates.

If there are no headings, look for key sentences and turn them into questions. These sentences usually show up at the beginnings or ends of paragraphs and sections.

Have fun with this technique. Make the questions playful or creative. You don't need to answer every question that you ask. The purpose of making up questions is to get your brain involved in the assignment. Take your unanswered questions to class, where they can be springboards for class discussion.

Demand your money's worth from your textbook. If you do not understand a concept, write specific questions about it. The more detailed your questions, the more powerful this technique becomes.

> Have fun with this technique. Make the questions playful or creative. You don't need to answer every question that you ask. The purpose of making up questions is to get your brain involved in the assignment. Take your unanswered questions to class, where they can be springboards for class discussion.

You're One Click Away...
from finding examples of Phase 1 strategies online.

PHASE 2 While you read

STEP 4 FOCUS

You have previewed the reading assignment, organized it in your mind or on paper, and formulated questions. Now you are ready to begin reading.

It's easy to fool yourself about reading. Just having an open book in your hand and moving your eyes across a page doesn't mean that you are reading effectively. Reading takes mental focus.

As you read, be conscious of where you are and what you are doing. Use the "Power Process: Be here now" in Chapter 3. When you notice your attention wandering, gently bring it back to the present moment. There are many ways to do this.

To begin, get in a position to stay focused. If you observe chief executive officers, you'll find that some of them wear out the front of their chair first. They're literally on the edge of their seat. Approach your reading assignment in the same way. Sit up. Keep your spine straight. Avoid reading in bed, except for fun.

Avoid marathon reading sessions. Schedule breaks and set a reasonable goal for the entire session. Then reward

FIVE SMART WAYS
to highlight text

Step 5 in Muscle Reading mentions a powerful tool: highlighting. It also presents a danger—the ever-present temptation to highlight too much text. Excessive highlighting leads to wasted time during reviews. Get the most out of all that money you pay for books and the time you spend reading. Highlight in an efficient way that leaves texts readable for years to come and provides you with an easy reviewing method.

Read carefully first. Read an entire chapter or section at least once before you begin highlighting. Don't be in a hurry to mark up your book. Get to know the text first. Make two or three passes through difficult sections before you highlight.

Make choices up front about what to highlight. Perhaps you can accomplish your purposes by highlighting only certain chapters or sections of a text. When you highlight, remember to look for passages that directly answer the questions you posed during Step 3 of Muscle Reading. Within these passages, highlight individual words, phrases, or sentences rather than whole paragraphs. The important thing is to choose an overall strategy before you put highlighter to paper.

Recite first. You might want to apply Step 6 of Muscle Reading before you highlight. Talking about what you read—to yourself or with other people—can help you grasp the essence of a text. Recite first; then go back and highlight. You'll probably highlight more selectively.

Underline, then highlight. Underline key passages lightly in pencil. Then close your text and come back to it later. Assess your underlining. Perhaps you can highlight less than you underlined and still capture the key points.

Use highlighting to monitor your comprehension. Critical thinking plays a role in underlining and highlighting. When highlighting, you're making moment by-moment decisions about what you want to remember from a text. You're also making inferences about what material might be included on a test. Take your critical thinking a step further by using highlighting to check your comprehension. Stop reading periodically and look back over the sentences you've highlighted. See whether you are making accurate distinctions between main points and supporting material. Highlighting too much—more than 10 percent of the text—can be a sign that you're not making this distinction and that you don't fully understand what you're reading. See the article "When Reading Is Tough" later in this chapter for suggestions that can help.

You're One Click Away...
from finding an example of smart highlighting online.

It's easy to fool yourself about reading. Just having an open book in your hand and moving your eyes across a page doesn't mean that you are reading effectively. Reading takes mental focus.

yourself with an enjoyable activity for 10 or 15 minutes every hour or two.

For difficult reading, set more limited goals. Read for a half hour and then take a break. Most students find that shorter periods of reading distributed throughout the day and week can be more effective than long sessions.

Visualize the material. Form mental pictures of the concepts as they are presented. If you read that a voucher system can help control cash disbursements, picture a voucher handing out dollar bills. Using visual imagery in this way can help deepen your understanding of the text while allowing information to be transferred into your long-term memory.

Read material out loud, especially if it is complicated. Some of us remember better and understand more quickly when we hear an idea.

Get a "feel" for the subject. For example, let's say you are reading about a microorganism—a paramecium—in your biology text. Imagine what it would feel like to run your finger around the long, cigar-shaped body of the organism. Imagine feeling the large fold of its gullet on one side and the tickle of the hairy little cilia as they wiggle in your hand.

In addition, predict how the author will answer your key questions. Then read to find out if your predictions were accurate.

STEP 5 FLAG ANSWERS

As you read, seek out the answers to your questions. You are a detective, watching for every clue. When you do find an answer, flag it so that it stands out on the page.

Deface your books. Have fun. Flag answers by highlighting, underlining, writing comments, filling in your outline, or marking up pages in any other way that helps you. Indulge yourself as you never could with your grade school books.

Marking up your books offers other benefits. When you read with a highlighter, pen, or pencil in your hand, you involve your kinesthetic senses of touch and motion. Being physical

with your books can help build strong neural pathways in your memory.

You can mark up a text in many ways. For example:

- Place an asterisk (*) or an exclamation point (!) in the margin next to an especially important sentence or term.
- Circle key terms and words to look up later in a dictionary.
- Write short definitions of key terms in the margin.
- Write a *Q* in the margin to highlight possible test questions, passages you don't understand, and questions to ask in class.
- Write personal comments in the margin—points of agreement or disagreement with the author.
- Write mini-indexes in the margin—that is, the numbers of other pages in the book where the same topic is discussed.
- Write summaries in your own words.
- Rewrite chapter titles, headings, and subheadings so that they're more meaningful to you.
- Draw diagrams, pictures, tables, or maps that translate text into visual terms.
- Number each step in a list or series of related points.
- In the margins, write notes about the relationships between elements in your reading. For instance, note connections between an idea and examples of that idea.
- If you infer an answer to a question or come up with another idea of your own, write that down as well.

Avoid marking up a text too soon. Wait until you complete a chapter or section to make sure you know the key points. Then mark up the text. Sometimes, flagging answers after you read each paragraph works best.

Also remember that the purpose of making marks in a text is to call out important concepts or information that you will review later. Flagging key information can save lots of time when you are studying for tests. With this in mind, highlight or underline sparingly—usually less than 10 percent of the text. If you mark up too much on a page, you defeat the purpose: to flag the most important material for review.

Finally, jot down new questions, and note when you don't find the answers you are looking for. Ask these questions in class, or see your instructor personally. Demand that your textbooks give you what you want—answers.

5

You're One Click Away...
from finding examples of Phase 2 strategies online.

PHASE 3 After you read

STEP 6 RECITE

Talk to yourself about what you've read. Or talk to someone else. When you finish a reading assignment, make a speech about it. When you recite, you practice an important aspect of metacognition—synthesis, or combining individual ideas and facts into a meaningful whole.

One way to get yourself to recite is to look at each underlined point. Note what you marked; then put the book down and start talking out loud. Explain as much as you can about that particular point.

To make this technique more effective, do it in front of a mirror. It might seem silly, but the benefits can be enormous. Reap them at exam time.

A related technique is to stop reading periodically and write a short, free-form summary of what you just read. In one study, this informal "retrieval practice" helped students recall information better than other study techniques.[2]

Classmates are even better than mirrors. Form a group and practice teaching one another what you have read. One of the best ways to learn anything is to teach it to someone else.

In addition, talk about your reading whenever you can. Tell friends and family members what you're learning from your textbooks.

Talking about your reading reinforces a valuable skill—the ability to summarize. To practice this skill, pick one chapter (or one section of one chapter) from any of your textbooks. State the main topic covered in this chapter. Then state the main points that the author makes about this topic.

For example, the main topic up to this point in this chapter is Muscle Reading. The main point about this topic is that Muscle Reading includes three phases—steps to take before you read, while you read, and after you read. For a more detailed summary, you could name each of the steps.

Note: This topic-point method does not work so well when you want to summarize short stories, novels, plays, and other works of fiction. Instead, focus on action. In most stories, the main character confronts a major problem and takes a series of actions to solve it. Describe that problem and talk about the character's key actions—the turning points in the story.

STEP 7 REVIEW

Plan to do your first complete review within 24 hours of reading the material. Sound the trumpets! This point is critical: A review within 24 hours moves information from your short-term memory to your long-term memory.

Review within 1 day. If you read it on Wednesday, review it on Thursday. During this review, look over your notes and clear up anything you don't understand. Recite some of the main points again.

This review can be short. You might spend as little as 15 minutes reviewing a difficult 2-hour reading assignment.

Muscle Reading—
a leaner approach

Keep in mind that Muscle Reading is an overall approach, not a rigid, step-by-step procedure. Here's a shorter variation that students have found helpful. Practice it with any chapter in this book:

- **Preview and question.** Flip through the pages, looking at anything that catches your eye—headings, subheadings, illustrations, photographs. Turn the title of each article into a question. For example, "How Muscle Reading works" can become "How does Muscle Reading work?" List your questions on a separate sheet of paper, or write each question on a 3 × 5 card.

- **Read to answer your questions.** Read each article. Then go back over the text and underline or highlight answers to the appropriate questions on your list.

- **Recite and review.** When you're done with the chapter, close the book. Recite by reading each question—and answering it—out loud. Review the chapter by looking up the answers to your questions. (It's easy—they're already highlighted.) Review again by quizzing yourself one more time with your list of questions.

Investing that time now can save you hours later when studying for exams.

STEP 8 REVIEW AGAIN

The final step in Muscle Reading is the weekly or monthly review. This step can be very short—perhaps only 4 or 5 minutes per assignment. Simply go over your notes. Read the highlighted parts of your text. Recite one or two of the more complicated points.

The purpose of these reviews is to keep the neural pathways to the information open and to make them more distinct. That way, the information can be easier to recall. You can accomplish these short reviews anytime, anywhere, if you are prepared.

Conduct a 5-minute review while you are waiting for a bus, for your socks to dry, or for the water to boil. Three-by-five cards are a handy review tool. Write ideas, formulas, concepts, and facts on cards, and carry them with you. These short review periods can be effortless and fun.

Sometimes longer review periods are appropriate. For example, if you found an assignment difficult, consider rereading it. Start over, as if you had never seen the material before. Sometimes a second reading will provide you with surprising insights.

Decades ago, psychologists identified the primacy-recency effect, which suggests that we most easily remember the first and last items in any presentation.[3] Previewing and reviewing your reading can put this theory to work for you. ∎

You're One Click Away...
from finding examples of Phase 3 strategies online.

JOURNAL ENTRY 10   *Discovery/Intention Statement*

Experimenting with Muscle Reading

After reading the steps included in Muscle Reading, reflect on your reading skills. Are you a more effective reader than you thought you were? Less effective? Record your observations below.

I discovered that I . . .

_____

_____

_____

_____

_____

_____

_____

_____

_____

_____

_____

_____

_____

Many students find that they only do the "read" step with their textbooks. You've just read about the advantages of eight additional steps you should perform. Depending on the text, reading assignment, your available time, and your commitment level to the material, you may discover through practice which additional steps work best for you. Right now, make a commitment to yourself to experiment with all or several of the additional Muscle Reading steps by completing the following Intention Statement.

I intend to use the following Muscle Reading steps for the next 2 weeks in my _____ class:

❏ Preview

❏ Outline

❏ Question

❏ Focus

❏ Flag answers

❏ Recite

❏ Review

❏ Review again

5

When reading is
TOUGH

© Graham Bell/Corbis

Sometimes ordinary reading methods are not enough. It's easy to get bogged down in a murky reading assignment. The solution starts with a First Step: When you are confused, tell the truth about it. Successful readers monitor their understanding of reading material. They do not see confusion as a mistake or a personal shortcoming. Instead, they take it as a cue to change reading strategies and process ideas at a deeper level.

Read it again. Somehow, students get the idea that reading means opening a book and dutifully slogging through the text—line by line, page by page—moving in a straight line from the first word until the last. Actually, this method can be an ineffective way to read much of the published material you'll encounter in college.

Feel free to shake up your routine. Make several passes through tough reading material. During a preview, for example, just scan the text to look for key words and highlighted material. Next, skim the entire chapter or article again, spending a little more time and taking in more than you did during your preview. Finally, read in more depth, proceeding word by word through some or all of the text. Difficult material—such as the technical writing in science texts—is often easier the second time around. Isolate difficult passages and read them again, slowly.

This suggestion comes with one caution. If you find yourself doing a lot of rereading, then consider a change in reading strategies. For example, you might benefit from reciting after each paragraph or section rather than after each chapter. For more ideas, review the steps of Muscle Reading and consider the following suggestions.

Look for essential words. If you are stuck on a paragraph, mentally cross out all of the adjectives and adverbs, and then read the sentences without them. Find the important words—usually verbs and nouns.

Hold a mini-review. Pause briefly to summarize—either verbally or in writing—what you've read so far. Stop at the end of a paragraph and recite, in your own words, what you have just read. Jot down some notes, or create a short outline or summary.

Read it out loud. Make noise. Read a passage out loud several times, each time using a different inflection and emphasizing a different part of the sentence. Be creative. Imagine that you are the author talking.

Talk to someone who can help. Admit when you are stuck. Then bring questions about reading assignments to classmates and members of your study group. Also make an appointment with your instructor. Most teachers welcome the opportunity to work individually with students. Be specific about your confusion. Point out the paragraph that you found toughest to understand.

Stand up. Changing positions periodically can combat fatigue. Experiment with standing as you read, especially if you get stuck on a tough passage and decide to read it out loud.

Skip around. Jump to the next section or to the end of a tough article or chapter. You might have lost the big picture. Simply seeing the next step, the next main point, or a summary might be all you need to put the details in context. Retrace the steps in a chain of ideas, and look for examples. Absorb facts and ideas in whatever order works for you—which may be different than the author's presentation.

Find a tutor. Many schools provide free tutoring services. If your school does not, other students who have completed the course can assist you.

Use another text. Find a similar text in the library. Sometimes a concept is easier to understand if it is expressed another way. Children's books—especially children's encyclopedias—can provide useful overviews of baffling subjects.

Note where you get stuck. When you feel stuck, stop reading for a moment and diagnose what's happening. At these stop points, mark your place in the margin of the page with a penciled *S* for *Stuck*. A pattern to your marks over several pages might indicate a question you want to answer before going further.

Stop reading. When none of the above suggestions work, do not despair. Admit your confusion and then take a break. Catch a movie, go for a walk, study another subject, or sleep on it. The concepts you've already absorbed might come together at a subconscious level as you move on to other activities. Allow some time for that process. When you return to the reading material, see it with fresh eyes. ■

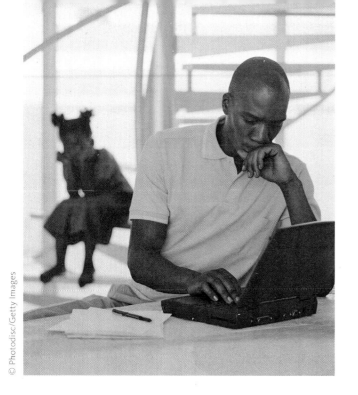

© Photodisc/Getty Images

Getting past ROADBLOCKS *to* READING

Even your favorite strategies for reading can fail when you're dealing with bigger issues. Those roadblocks to getting your reading done can come from three major sources:

- Finding enough time to keep up with your reading.
- Making choices about what to read once you find the time.
- Getting interrupted by other people while you're reading.

For solutions to each of these problems, read on.

SCHEDULING TIME FOR READING

Planning dispels panic (*I've got 300 pages to read before tomorrow morning!*) and helps you finish off your entire reading load for a term. Creating a reading plan is relatively simple if you use the following steps.

Step 1. Estimate the total number of pages that you'll read. To arrive at this figure, check the course syllabus for each class that you're taking. Look for lists of reading assignments. Based on what you find, estimate the total number of pages that you'll read for all your classes.

Step 2. Estimate how many pages you can read during 1 hour. Remember that your reading speed will be different for various materials. It depends on everything from the layout of the pages to the difficulty of the text. To give your estimate some credibility, base it on actual experience. During your first reading assignment in each course, keep track of how many pages you read per hour.

Step 3. Estimate your total number of reading hours. Divide the total number of pages from Step 1 by your pages-per-hour from Step 2. For example, look at this calculation:

600 (total pages for all courses this term) ÷ 10 (pages read per hour)
= 60 (total reading hours needed for the term)

The result is the total number of hours you'll need to complete your reading assignments this term. Remember to give yourself some "wiggle room." Allow extra hours for rereading and unplanned events. Consider taking your initial number of projected hours and doubling it. You can always back off from there to an estimate that seems more reasonable.

Step 4. Schedule reading time. Take the total number of hours from Step 3 and divide it by the number of weeks in your current term. That will give you the number of hours to schedule for reading each week.

60 (total reading hours needed for the term) ÷ 16 (weeks in the term)
= 3.75 (hours per week to schedule for reading)

Now, go to your calendar or long-term planner and reflect on it for a few minutes. Look for ways to block out those hours next week. For ideas, review Chapter 3.

Step 5. Refine your reading plan. Scheduling your reading takes time. The potential benefits are beyond calculation. With a plan, you can be more confident that you'll actually get your reading done. Even if your estimates are off, you'll still go beyond blind guessing or leaving the whole thing to chance. Your reading matters too much for that.

MAKING CHOICES ABOUT WHAT TO READ

Books about time management often mention the "80/20" principle. According to this principle, 80 percent of the value created by any group derives from only 20 percent of its members. If you have a to-do list of 10 items, for example, you'll get 80 percent of your desired results by doing only 2 items on the list.

The point is not to take these figures literally but to remember the underlying principle: *Focus on what creates the most value.* Look at your reading in light of the 80/20 principle. For instance:

- In a 10-paragraph article, you might find 80 percent of the crucial facts in the headline and first paragraph. (In fact, journalists are *taught* to write this way.)

- If you have a 50-page assignment, you may find that the most important facts and ideas in 10 pages of that total.

- If you're asked to read five books for a course, you may find that most exam questions come from just one of them.

A caution is in order here. The 80/20 principle is not a suggestion to complete only 20 percent of your reading assignments. That choice can undermine your education. To find the most important parts of anything you read, first get familiar with the whole. Only then can you make sound choices about where to focus.

Skilled readers constantly make choices about what to read and what *not* to read. They realize that some texts are more valuable for their purposes than others and that some passages within a single text are more crucial than the rest. When reading, they instantly ask, "What's most important here?"

The answer to this question varies from assignment to assignment, and even from page to page within a single assignment. Pose this question each time that you read, and look for clues to the answers. Pay special attention to the following:

- Any readings that your instructor refers to in class

- Readings that are emphasized in a class syllabus

- Readings that generate the most questions on quizzes and tests

- Parts of a text that directly answer the questions you generated while previewing

- Chapter previews and summaries (usually found at the beginning and end of a chapter or section)

DEALING WITH INTERRUPTIONS

Sometimes the people you live with and care about the most—a friend, roommate, spouse, or child—can become a temporary roadblock to reading. The following strategies can help you stay focused on your reading:

Attend to people first. When you first come home from school, keep your books out of sight. Spend some time with your roommates or family members before you settle in to study. Make small talk and ask them about their day. Give the important people in your life a short period of full, focused attention rather than a longer period of partial attention. Then explain that you have some work to do. Set some ground rules for the amount of time you need to focus on studying. You could be rewarded with extra minutes or hours of quiet time.

Plan for interruptions. It's possible that you'll be interrupted even if you set up guidelines for your study time in advance. If so, schedule the kind of studying that can be interrupted. For instance, you could write out or review flash cards with key terms and definitions. Save the tasks that require sustained attention for more quiet times.

Use "pockets" of time. See whether you can arrange a study time in a quiet place at school before you come home. If you arrive at school 15 minutes earlier and stay 15 minutes later, you can squeeze in an extra half hour of reading that day. Also look for opportunities to study on campus between classes.

When you can't read everything, read something. Even if you can't absorb an entire chapter while your roommates are blasting music, you can skim a chapter. Or you can just read the introduction and summary. When you can't get it *all* done, get *something* done.

Caution: If you always read this way, your education will be compromised. Supplement this strategy with others from this chapter so that you can get your most important reading done.

Read with children underfoot. It is possible to have both effective study time and quality time with your children. The following suggestions come mostly from students who are also parents. The specific strategies you use will depend on your schedule and the ages of your children.

- *Find a regular playmate for your child.* Some children can pair off with close friends and safely retreat to their rooms for hours of private play. You can check on them occasionally and still get lots of reading done.

- *Create a special space for your child.* Set aside one room or area of your home as a play space. Childproof this space. The goal is to create a place where children can roam freely and play with minimal supervision. Consider allowing your child in this area *only* when you study. Your homework time then becomes your child's reward. If you're cramped for space, just set aside some special toys for your child to play with during your study time.

- *Use television responsibly.* Whenever possible, select educational programs that keep your child's mind active and engaged. Also see whether your child can use headphones while watching television. That way, the house stays quiet while you study.

- *Schedule time to be with your children when you've finished studying.* Let your children in on the plan: "I'll be done reading at 7:30. That gives us a whole hour to play before you go to bed."

- *Ask other adults for help.* Getting help can be as simple as asking your spouse, partner, neighbor, or fellow student to take care of the children while you study. Offer to trade child care with a neighbor: You will take his kids and yours for 2 hours on Thursday night if he'll take them for 2 hours on Saturday morning.

- *Find community activities and services.* Ask whether your school provides a day care service. In some cases, these services are available to students at a reduced cost. ■

Reading faster

One way to read faster is to read faster. This idea might sound like double-talk, but it is a serious suggestion. The fact is, you can probably read faster—without any loss in comprehension—simply by making a conscious effort to do so. Your comprehension might even improve.

Experiment with the "just do it" method right now. Read the rest of this article as fast as you can. After you finish, come back and reread the same paragraphs at your usual rate. Note how much you remember from your first sprint through the text. You might be surprised to find out how well you comprehend material even at dramatically increased speeds. Build on that success by experimenting with the following guidelines.

Get your body ready. Gear up for reading faster. Get off the couch. Sit up straight at a desk or table, on the edge of your chair, with your feet flat on the floor. If you're feeling adventurous, read standing up.

Set a time limit. When you read, use a clock, cell phone, or a digital watch with a stopwatch feature to time yourself. You are not aiming to set speed records, so be realistic. For example, set a goal to read two or three sections of a chapter in an hour, using all of the Muscle Reading steps. If that works, set a goal of 50 minutes for reading the same number of sections. Test your limits. The idea is to give yourself a gentle push, increasing your reading speed without sacrificing comprehension.

Relax. It's not only possible to read fast when you're relaxed; it's easier. Relaxation promotes concentration. And remember, relaxation is not the same as sleep. You can be relaxed *and* alert at the same time.

Move your eyes faster. When we read, our eyes leap across the page in short bursts called *saccades* (pronounced "să-käds"). A saccade is also a sharp jerk on the reins of a horse—a violent pull to stop the animal quickly. Our eyes stop like that too, in pauses called *fixations*.

Although we experience the illusion of continuously scanning each line, our eyes actually take in groups of words, usually about three at a time. For more than 90 percent of reading time, our eyes are at a dead stop, in those fixations.

One way to decrease saccades is to follow your finger as you read. The faster your finger moves, the faster your eyes move. You can also use a pen, pencil, or 3 × 5 card as a guide.

Your eyes can move faster if they take in more words with each burst—for example, six instead of three. To practice taking in more words between fixations, find a newspaper with narrow columns. Then read down one column at a time, and fixate only once per line.

In addition to using the above techniques, simply make a conscious effort to fixate less. You might feel a little uncomfortable at first. That's normal. Just practice often, for short periods of time.

Notice and release ineffective habits. Our eyes make regressions; that is, they back up and reread words. You can reduce regressions by paying attention to them. Use a handy 3 × 5 card to cover words and lines that you have just read. You can then note how often you stop and move the card back to reread the text. Don't be discouraged if you stop often at first. Being aware of it helps you regress less frequently.

Also notice vocalizing. You are more likely to read faster if you don't read out loud or move your lips. You can also increase your speed if you don't subvocalize—that is, if you don't mentally "hear" the words as you read them. To stop doing it, just be aware of it.

Another habit to release is reading letter by letter. When we first learn to read, we do it one letter at a time. By now you have memorized many words by their shape, so you don't have to focus on the letters at all. Read this example: "Rasrhcers at Cbmrigae Uivnretisy funod taht eprxert raeedrs dno't eevn look at the lteters." You get the point. Skilled readers recognize many words and phrases in this way, taking them in at a single glance.

When you first attempt to release these habits, choose simpler reading material. That way, you can pay closer attention to your reading technique. Gradually work your way up to more complex material.

If you're pressed for time, skim. When you're in a hurry, experiment by skimming the assignment instead of reading the whole thing. Read the headings, subheadings, lists, charts, graphs, and summary paragraphs. Summaries are especially important. They are usually found at the beginning or end of a chapter or section.

This suggestion is not about reading faster, but reading smarter. In many cases, you can read for main points and let go of the rest. You might not need to process all the facts, examples, and quotations that are used to *support* those main points. Ask

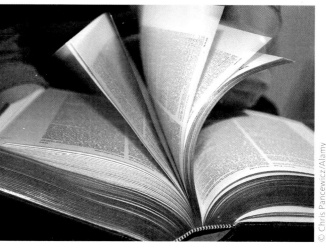

© Chris Pancewicz/Alamy

5

whether you can meet your purpose for reading by skimming or skipping that supporting material.

The essence of many nonfiction books can be summarized in just a few pages. That core message may be all you want from an author.

Stay flexible. Remember that speed isn't everything. Skillful readers vary their reading rate according to their purpose and the nature of the material. An advanced text in analytic geometry usually calls for a different reading rate than the Sunday comics.

You also can use different reading rates on the same material. For example, you might first sprint through an assignment for the key words and ideas, and then return to the difficult parts for a slower and more thorough reading.

Another option is to divide a large reading assignment into smaller sections and use different reading strategies for each one. You might choose to read the first and last sections in detail, for example, and skim the middle sections.

As a general guideline, slow down your reading pace for material that's technical and unfamiliar to you. Speed up for material that's familiar, staying alert for anything that seems new or significant.

Also remember that reading faster *without comprehension* can actually increase the amount of time that you study. Balance a desire for speed with the need for understanding what you read.

Explore more resources. You can find many books about speed-reading. Ask a librarian to help you find a few. Using them can be a lot of fun. For more possibilities, including courses and workshops, go to your favorite search engine on the Internet, and key in the word *speed-reading*.

In your research, you might discover people who offer to take you beyond speed-reading. According to some teachers, you can learn to flip through a book and "mentally photograph" each page—hundreds or even thousands of words at once. To prepare for this feat, you first do relaxation exercises to release tension while remaining alert. In this state, you can theoretically process vast quantities of information at a level other than with your conscious mind.

You might find these ideas controversial. Approach them in the spirit of the "Power Process: Ideas are tools." Also remember that you can use more conventional reading techniques at any time.

One word of caution: Courses and workshops in speed-reading range from free to expensive. Before you lay out any money, check the instructor's credentials and talk to people who've taken the course. Also find out whether the instructor offers free "sampler sessions" and whether you can cancel at some point in the course for a full refund.

Finally, remember the first rule of reading fast: Just do it! ▨

Master Employees
IN ACTION

❝College gave me the tools to understand the technical data involved in maps and scientific reports, but in my job, it isn't enough to simply understand the technical aspects. I also have to be able to translate this data into a format that a layperson can understand. This means that I have to be able to read my own writing from the perspective of someone who doesn't necessarily have my technical background.❞

© ailenn/Shutterstock

–Monica Edmonds, Hydrologist

You're One Click Away...
from a video about Master Students in Action.

✔ CRITICAL THINKING EXERCISE 16

Relax

 yestrain can be the result of continuous stress. Take a break from your reading and use this exercise to release tension.

1. Sit on a chair or lie down, and take a few moments to breathe deeply.

2. Close your eyes, place your palms over them, and visualize a perfect field of black.

3. Continue to be aware of the blackness for 2 or 3 minutes while you breathe deeply.

4. Now remove your hands from your eyes, and open your eyes slowly.

5. Relax for a minute more; then continue reading.

WORD POWER—expanding your VOCABULARY

Having a large vocabulary makes reading more enjoyable and increases the range of materials you can explore. In addition, building your vocabulary gives you more options for self-expression when speaking or writing. With a larger vocabulary, you can think more precisely by making finer distinctions between ideas. And you won't have to stop to search for words at crucial times—such as a job interview.

Strengthen your vocabulary by taking delight in words. Look up unfamiliar terms. Pay special attention to words that arouse your curiosity.

Before the age of the Internet, students used two kinds of printed dictionaries: the desk dictionary and the unabridged dictionary. A desk dictionary is an easy-to-handle abridged dictionary that you can use many times in the course of a day. You can keep this book within easy reach (maybe in your lap) so you can look up unfamiliar words while reading.

In contrast, an unabridged dictionary is large and not made for you to carry around. It provides more complete information about words and definitions not included in your desk dictionary, as well as synonyms, usage notes, and word histories. Look for unabridged dictionaries in libraries and bookstores.

You might prefer using one of several online dictionaries, such as Dictionary.com. Another common option is to search for definitions by using a search engine such as Google.com. If you do this, inspect the results carefully. They can vary in quality and be less useful than the definitions you'd find in a good dictionary or thesaurus.

Construct a word stack. When you come across an unfamiliar word, write it down on a 3 × 5 card. Below the word, copy the sentence in which it was used, along with the page number. You can look up each word immediately, or you can accumulate a stack of these cards and look up the words later. Write the definition of each word on the back of the 3 × 5 card, adding the diacritics—marks that tell you how to pronounce it.

To expand your vocabulary and learn the history behind the words, take your stack of cards to an unabridged dictionary. As you find related words in the dictionary, add them to your stack. These cards become a portable study aid that you can review in your spare moments.

Learn—even when your dictionary is across town. When you are listening to a lecture and hear an unusual word or when you are reading on the bus and encounter a word you don't know, you can still build your word stack. Pull out a 3 × 5 card and write down the word and its sentence. Later, you can look up the definition and write it on the back of the card.

Divide words into parts. Another suggestion for building your vocabulary is to divide an unfamiliar word into syllables and look for familiar parts. This strategy works well if you make it a point to learn common prefixes (beginning syllables) and suffixes (ending syllables). For example, the suffix *-tude* usually refers to a condition or state of being. Knowing this makes it easier to conclude that *habitude* refers to a usual way of doing something and that *similitude* means being similar or having a quality of resemblance.

Infer the meaning of words from their context. You can often deduce the meaning of an unfamiliar word simply by paying attention to its context—the surrounding words, phrases, sentences, paragraphs, or images. Later, you can confirm your deduction by consulting a dictionary.

Practice looking for context clues such as these:

- *Definitions.* A key word might be defined right in the text. Look for phrases such as *defined as* or *in other words.*

- *Examples.* Authors often provide examples to clarify a word meaning. If the word is not explicitly defined, then study the examples. They're often preceded by the phrases *for example, for instance,* or *such as.*

- *Lists.* When a word is listed in a series, pay attention to the other items in the series. They might define the unfamiliar word through association.

- *Comparisons.* You might find a new word surrounded by synonyms—words with a similar meaning. Look for synonyms after words such as *like* and *as.*

- *Contrasts.* A writer might juxtapose a word with its antonym. Look for phrases such as *on the contrary* and *on the other hand.* ∎

5

Mastering the English LANGUAGE

The complexity of English makes it a challenge for people who grew up with another language—and for native speakers of English as well. To get the most benefit from your education, analyze the ways that you speak and write English. Look for patterns that might block your success. Then take steps to increase your mastery.

LEARN TO USE STANDARD ENGLISH WHEN IT counts

Standard English (also called *standard written English*) is the form of the language used by educated speakers and writers. It is the form most likely to be understood by speakers and writers of English, no matter where they live.

Using non-standard English in the classroom or workplace might lead people to doubt your skills, your intentions, or your level of education. Non-standard English comes in many forms, including these:

- *Slang.* These informal expressions often create vivid images. When students talk about "acing" a test or "hanging loose" over spring break, for example, they're using slang.

- *Idioms.* These are colorful expressions with meanings that are not always obvious. For instance, a "fork in the road" does not refer to an eating utensil discarded on a street but rather to a place where a part of the road branches off. Even native speakers of English can find idioms hard to understand.

- *Dialects.* A sentence such as "I bought me a new phone" is common in certain areas of the United States. If you use such an expression in a paper or presentation, however, your audience might form a negative impression of you.

- *Jargon.* Some terms are used mainly by people who work in certain professions. If you talk about "hacking a site" or finding a "workaround," for example, then only students majoring in software engineering might understand you.

Any community of English speakers and writers can reshape the language for its own purposes. People who send text messages are doing that now. So are people who post on Twitter.com, a Web site that limits updates to 140 characters. Even your family, friends, and coworkers might develop expressions that no one else comprehends.

Learning when and how to use non-standard English is part of mastering the language. However, save non-standard expressions for informal conversations with friends. In that context, you can safely try out new words and ask for feedback about how you're using them. If you're not sure whether a particular expression is standard English, then talk to an instructor. And if someone points out that you're using nonstandard English, be willing to learn from that experience. You can do this even when the feedback is not given with skill or sensitivity.

BUILD CONFIDENCE

Students who grew up with a language other than English might fall under the category of English as a Second Language (ESL) student, or English Language Learner (ELL). Many ESL/ELL students feel insecure about using English in social settings, including the classroom. Choosing not to speak, however, can delay your mastery of English and isolate you from other students.

As an alternative, make it your intention to speak up in class. List several questions beforehand and plan to ask them. Also schedule a time to meet with your instructors during office hours to discuss any material that you find confusing. These strategies can help you build relationships while developing English skills.

In addition, start a conversation with at least one native speaker of English in each of your classes. For openers, ask about their favorite instructors or ideas for future courses to take.

English is a complex language. Whenever you extend your vocabulary and range of expression, the likelihood of making mistakes increases. The person who wants to master English yet seldom makes mistakes is probably being too careful. Do not look upon mistakes as a sign of weakness. Mistakes can be your best teachers—if you are willing to learn from them.

Remember that the terms *English as a Second Language* and *English Language Learner* describe a difference—not a deficiency. The fact that you've entered a new culture and are mastering another language gives you a broader perspective than people who speak only one language. And if you currently speak two or more languages, you've already demonstrated your ability to learn.

ANALYZE ERRORS IN USING ENGLISH

To learn from your errors, make a list of those that are most common for you. Next to the error, write a corrected version. For examples, see the chart below. Remember that native speakers of English also use this technique—for instance, by making lists of words they frequently misspell.

Errors	Corrections
Sun is bright.	The sun is bright.
He cheerful.	He is cheerful.
I enjoy to play chess.	I enjoy playing chess.
Good gifts received everyone.	Everyone received good gifts.
I knew what would present the teachers.	I knew what the teachers would present.
I like very much burritos.	I like burritos very much.
I want that you stay.	I want you to stay.
Is raining.	It is raining.
My mother, she lives in Iowa.	My mother lives in Iowa.
I gave the paper to she.	I gave the paper to her.
They felt safety in the car.	They felt safe in the car.
He has three car.	He has three cars.
I have helpfuls family members.	I have helpful family members.
She don't know nothing.	She knows nothing.

LEARN BY SPEAKING AND LISTENING

You probably started your English studies by using textbooks. Writing and reading in English are important. Both can help you add to your English vocabulary and master grammar. To gain greater fluency and improve your pronunciation, also make it your goal to *hear* and *speak* standard English.

For example, listen to radio talk shows hosted by educated speakers with a wide audience. Imitate the speaker's pronunciation by repeating phrases and sentences that you hear. During TV shows and personal conversations, notice the facial expressions and gestures that accompany certain English words and phrases.

If you speak English with an accent, do not be concerned. Many people speak clear, accented English. Work on your accent only if you can't be easily understood.

Take advantage of opportunities to read and hear English at the same time. For instance, turn on English subtitles when watching

a film on DVD. Also, check your library for books on tape or CD. Check out the printed book, and follow along as you listen.

USE COMPUTER RESOURCES

Some online dictionaries allow you to hear words pronounced. They include Answers.com (www.answers.com) and Merriam-Webster Online (www.m-w.com).

Other resources include online book sites with a read-aloud feature. An example is Project Gutenberg (www.gutenberg.org; search on *audio books*). Speaks for Itself (www.speaksforitself.com) is a free download that allows you to hear text from Web sites read aloud.

Also, check general Web sites for ESL students. A popular one is Dave's ESL Café (www.eslcafe.com), which will lead you to others.

GAIN SKILLS IN NOTE TAKING AND TESTING

When taking notes, remember that you don't have to capture everything that an instructor says. To a large extent, the art of note taking consists of choosing what *not* to record. Listen for key words, main points, and important examples. Remember that instructors will often repeat these things. You'll have more than one chance to pick up on the important material. When you're in doubt, ask for repetition or clarification. For additional suggestions, see Chapter 6: Notes.

Taking tests is a related challenge. You may find that certain kinds of test questions—such as multiple-choice items—are more common in the United States than in your native country. Chapter 7: Tests can help you master these and many other types of tests.

CREATE A COMMUNITY OF ENGLISH LEARNERS

Learning as part of a community can increase your mastery. For example, when completing a writing assignment in English, get together with other people who are learning the language. Read each other's papers and suggest revisions. Plan on revising your paper a number of times based on feedback from your peers.

You might feel awkward about sharing your writing with other people. Accept that feeling—and then remind yourself of everything you have to gain by learning from a group. In addition to learning English more quickly, you can raise your grades and make new friends.

Native speakers of English might be willing to assist your group. Ask your instructors to suggest someone. This person can benefit from the exchange of ideas and the chance to learn about other cultures.

CELEBRATE YOUR GAINS

Every time you analyze and correct an error in English, you make a small gain. Celebrate those gains. Taken together over time, they add up to major progress in mastering English as a second language. ■

Developing information literacy

© Masterfile

Information literacy is a set of skills to use whenever you want to answer questions or find information. For example, you might want to learn more about a product, a service, a vacation spot, or a potential job. You might want to follow up on something you heard on the radio or saw on TV. Or you might want to develop a topic for a paper or speech.

In any case, the fruit of curiosity is research. And research involves finding information, which means reading—sometimes *lots* of reading.

An important quality of master students is curiosity. To answer questions, these students find information from appropriate sources, evaluate the information, organize it, and use it to achieve a purpose. The ability to do this in a world where data is literally at your fingertips is called information literacy.

DISCOVER YOUR PURPOSE

One of the early steps in Muscle Reading involves asking questions. Research means asking questions as well.

Discover your *main question*. This is the thing that sparked your curiosity in the first place. Answering it is your purpose for doing research.

Your main question will raise a number of smaller, related questions. These are *supporting questions*. They also call for answers.

Suppose that your main question is: "During the mortgage credit crisis of 2007 to 2010, what led banks to lend money to people with poor credit histories?" Your list of supporting questions might include these:

• What banks were involved in the mortgage credit crisis?

• How do banks discover a person's credit history?

• What are the signs of a poor credit history?

Listing your main and supporting questions can save hours of time. If you ever feel overwhelmed or get sidetracked, pull out your list of questions. When the information you're finding answers one of those questions, then you're on track. If you're wading through material that's not answering your questions, then it's time to find another source of information or revise your questions.

CONSIDER PRIMARY AND SECONDARY SOURCES OF INFORMATION

Consider the variety of information sources that are available to you: billions of Web pages, books, magazines, newspapers, and audio and video recordings. You can reduce this vast range of materials to a few manageable categories. Start with the distinction between primary and secondary sources.

Primary sources. These can lead to information treasures. Primary sources are firsthand materials—personal journals, letters, speeches, government documents, scientific experiments, field observations, interviews with recognized experts, archeological digs, artifacts, and original works of art.

Primary sources can also include scholarly publications such as the *New England Journal of Medicine*, *Contemporary Literary Criticism*, and similar publications. One clue that you're dealing with primary source is the title. If it includes the word *journal*, then you're probably reading a primary source. Signs of scholarly articles include these:

• Names of authors with their credentials and academic affiliations

• A brief abstract (summary) of the article, along with a section on research methods (how the authors tested their ideas and reached their conclusions)

• Lengthy articles with detailed treatment of the main topic and definitions of key terms

- Conclusions based on an extensive review of relevant publications, survey research, data collected in a laboratory experiment, or a combination of these
- Extensive bibliographies and references to the work of other scholars in the form of footnotes (at the bottom of each page) or endnotes (at the end of the article)

If you pick up a magazine with pages of full-color advertisements and photos of celebrities, you're not reading a scholarly journal. Though some scholarly articles run just a few pages, many run to 10, 20, or even more. While that's a lot to read, you get more information to use for your assignment or to answer your questions.

Though many kinds of publications can be useful, scholarly journals and other primary sources are unmatched in depth and credibility. In addition, journal articles are often peer reviewed. This means that other experts in the field read and review the articles to make sure that they are accurate.

Secondary sources. These sources summarize, explain, and comment on primary sources:

- Popular magazines such as *Time* and *Newsweek*.
- Magazines—such as the *Atlantic Monthly* and *Scientific American*—with wide circulation and long articles.
- Nationally circulated newspapers such as the *Washington Post*, *New York Times*, and *Los Angeles Times*.
- General reference works such as the *Encyclopaedia Britannica* and the *Oxford Companion to English Literature*.

Secondary sources are useful places to start your research. Use them to get an overview of your topic. Depending on the assignment, these may be all you need for informal research.

GET TO KNOW YOUR LIBRARY

Remember that many published materials are available in print as well as online. For a full range of sources, head to your campus library.

Ask a librarian. One reason for a trip to the library is to find a reference librarian. Tell this person about the questions you want to answer, and ask for good sources of information.

Take a tour. Libraries—from the smallest one in your hometown to the Smithsonian in Washington, D.C.—consist of just three basic elements:

- *Catalogs*—online databases that list all of the library's accessible sources.
- *Collections*—materials, such as periodicals (magazines, journals and newspapers), books, pamphlets, audiovisual materials, and materials available from other libraries via interlibrary loan.
- *Computer resources*—Internet access; connections to campuswide computer networks; and databases stored on CD-ROMs, CDs, DVDs, or online. Online databases—which allow you to look at full-text articles from magazines, journals, and newspapers—are sometimes available from your personal computer or smartphone

with a password. Many libraries have access to special databases that are not available on the Internet. Also ask about ebooks that can be delivered straight to your computer.

Before you start your next research project, take some time to investigate all three elements of your school's library.

Dig in to the collection. When inspecting a library's collections, look for materials such as the following, making sure to ask about both print and online versions:

- *Encyclopedias.* Use leading print and online encyclopedias, such as *Encyclopaedia Britannica.* Specialized encyclopedias can cover many fields and include, for example, *Encyclopedia of Psychology, Encyclopedia of the Biological Sciences, Encyclopedia of Asian History, Violence in America* and *McGraw-Hill Encyclopedia of Science and Technology.*

- *Biographies.* Read accounts of people's lives in biographical works such as *Who's Who, Dictionary of American Biography, Contemporary Musicians,* and *Biography Index: A Cumulative Index to Biographical Material in Books and Magazines.*

- *Critical works.* Read what scholars have to say about works of art and literature in Oxford Companion volumes (such as *Oxford Companion to Art, Masterplots, Poetry Criticism, Novels for Students,* and *Oxford Companion to African American Literature*).

- *Statistics and government documents.* Among the many useful sources are *Statistical Abstract of the United States, Handbook of Labor Statistics, Occupational Outlook Handbook,* and U.S. Census Bureau publications.

- *Almanacs, atlases, and gazetteers.* For population statistics and boundary changes, see the *World Almanac and Book of Facts, Atlas of Crime,* the *New York Times Almanac,* or the *CIA World Factbook.*

- *Dictionaries.* Consult the *American Heritage Dictionary of the English Language, Oxford English Dictionary,* and other specialized dictionaries such as the *Penguin Dictionary of Literary Terms and Literary Theory, The New Grove Dictionary of Music and Musicians,* and the *Dictionary of the Social Sciences.*

- *Indexes and databases.* Databases contain publication information and an abstract, or sometimes the full text, of an article available for downloading or printing from your computer. Your library houses print and CD-ROM databases and subscribes to some online databases; others are accessible through online library catalogs or Web links.

- *Reference works in specific subject areas.* These references cover a vast range of material. Examples include *The Oxford Companion to Art,* the *Encyclopedia of the Biological Sciences, Countries and Their Cultures,* and the *Concise Oxford Companion to Classical Literature.* Ask a librarian for more information.

- *Periodical articles.* Find articles in periodicals (works issued periodically, such as scholarly journals, popular magazines, and newspapers) by using a periodical index. Some indexes, such as Lexis-Nexis Academic Universe, InfoTrac, OCLC FirstSearch, and New York Times Ondisc, provide the full text of articles.[4]

5

SEARCH FOR INFORMATION WITH KEY WORDS

One crucial skill for information literacy is using key words. Key words are the main terms in your main and supporting questions. These are the words that you enter into a library database or online search box. Your choice of key words determines the quality of results that you get from Internet search engines such as google.com, and from library catalogs. For better search results:

- *Use specific key words.* Entering *firefox* or *safari* will give you more focused results than entering *web browser. Reading strategies* or *note-taking strategies* will get more specific results than *study strategies.* Do not type in your whole research question as a sentence. The search engine will look for each word and give you a lot of useless results.

- *Use unique key words.* Whenever possible, use proper names. Enter *Beatles* or *Radiohead* rather than *British rock bands.* If you're looking for nearby restaurants, enter *restaurant* and your zip code rather than the name of your city.

- *Use quotation marks if you're looking for certain words in a certain order.* "Audacity of hope" will return a list of pages with that exact phrase.

- *Search within a site.* If you're looking only for articles about college tuition from the *New York Times,* then add *new york times* or *nytimes.com* to the search box.

- *Remember to think of synonyms.* For example, "hypertension" is often called "high blood pressure."

- *When you're not sure of a key word, add a wild card character.* In most search engines, that character is the asterisk (*). If you're looking for the title of a film directed by Clint Eastwood and just can't remember the name, enter *clint eastwood directed *.*

- *Look for more search options.* Many search engines also offer advanced search features and explain how to use them. Look for the word *advanced* or *more* on the site's home page, and click on the link. If in doubt about how to use your library's search engines, ask a librarian for help.

TURN TO PEOPLE AS SOURCES OF INFORMATION

Making direct contact with people can offer a welcome relief from hours of solitary research time and give you valuable hands-on involvement. Your initial research will uncover the names of experts on your chosen topic. Consider doing an interview with one of these people—in person, over the phone, or via e-mail. To get the most from interviews:

- Schedule a specific time for the interview—and a specific place, if you're meeting the expert in person.

- Agree on the length of the interview in advance and work within that timeframe.

- Enter the interview with a short list of questions to ask.

- Allow time for additional questions that occur to you during the interview.

- If you want to record the interview, ask for permission in advance.

- When working with people who don't want to be recorded, be prepared to take handwritten notes.

- Ask experts for permission to quote their comments.

- Be courteous before, during, and after the interview; thank the person for taking time with you.

- End the interview at your agreed time.

- Follow up on interviews with a thank-you note.

EVALUATE INFORMATION

Some students assume that anything that's published in print or on the Internet is true. Unfortunately, that's not the case. Some sources of information are more reliable than others, and some published information is misleading or mistaken.

Before evaluating any source of information, make sure that you understand what it says. Use the techniques of Muscle Reading to comprehend an author's message. Then think critically about the information. Chapter 8 offers many suggestions for doing this. Some things you should be sure to look for:

- *Currency.* Notice the published date of your source material. If your topic is time-sensitive, then set some guidelines about how current you want your sources to be—for example, that they were published during the last 5 years.

- *Credibility.* Scan the source for biographical information about the author. Look for educational degrees, training, and work experience that qualify this person to publish on the topic of your research.

- *Bias.* Determine what the Web site or other source is "selling"— the product, service, or point of view it promotes. Political affiliations or funding sources might color the author's point of view. For instance, you can predict that a pamphlet on gun control policies that's printed with funding from the National Rifle Association will promote certain points of view. Round out your research with other sources on the topic.

Evaluate Internet sources with extra care. Ask the following questions:

- *Who pays for the site?* Carefully check information from an organization that sells advertising. Look for an "About This Site" link—a clue to sources of funding.

- *Who runs the site?* Look for a clear description of the person or organization responsible for the content. If the sponsoring person or organization did not create the site's content, then find out who did.

. . . .

Some students assume that anything that's published in print or on the Internet is true. Unfortunately, that's not the case.

. . . .

- *How is the site's content selected?* Look for a link that lists members of an editorial board or other qualified reviewers.

- *Does the site separate fact from opinion?* Reliable sites often follow a newspaper model, which separates reports about current events from editorials.

- *Does the site support claims with evidence?* Credible sites base their editorial stands on expert opinion and facts from scientific studies. Look for references to primary sources. If you find grandiose claims supported only by testimonials, beware. When something sounds too good to be true, it probably is.

- *Does the site link to other sites?* Think critically about these sites as well.

- *How can readers connect with the site?* Look for a way to contact the site's publisher with questions and comments. See whether you can find a physical address, e-mail address, and phone number. Sites that conceal this information might conceal other facts. Also inspect reader comments on the site to see whether a variety of opinions are expressed.

Many Web sites from government agencies and nonprofit organizations have strict and clearly stated editorial policies. These are often good places to start your research.

USE INFORMATION

Many students use information to write a paper or create a presentation. See Chapter 9 of this book for suggestions. In addition, take careful notes on your sources using the techniques explained in Chapter 6. Remember to keep a list of all your sources of information and avoid plagiarism. Be prepared to cite your sources in footnotes or endnotes, and a bibliography.

Also make time to digest all the information you gather. Ask yourself:

- Do I have answers to my main question?

- Do I have answers to my supporting questions?

- What are the main ideas from my sources?

- Do I have personal experiences that can help me answer these questions?

- If a television talk show host asked me these questions, how would I answer?

- On what points do my sources agree?

- On what points do my sources disagree?

- Do I have statistics and other facts that I can use to support my ideas?

- What new questions do I have?

The beauty of these questions is that they stimulate *your* thinking. Discover the pleasures of emerging insights and sudden inspiration. You just might get hooked on the adventure of information literacy.

MUSCLE READING FOR EBOOKS

Today you can read ebooks on many platforms—computers, mobile phones, and dedicated devices such as the Amazon Kindle and Sony Reader. Muscle your way into this new medium by using features that are not available with printed books. Though ebook features vary, see whether you can do the following.

Use navigation tools. To flip electronic pages, look for *previous* and *next* buttons or arrows on the right and left borders of each page. Many ebooks also offer a "go to page" feature that allows you to key in a specific page number.

For a bigger picture of the text, look for a table of contents that lists chapter headings and subheadings. Click on any of these headings to expand the text for that part of the book. Note that charts, illustrations, photos, tables, diagrams and other visuals might be listed separately in the table of contents.

Search. Look for a search box that allows you to enter key words and find all the places in the text where those words are mentioned.

Customize page appearance. For more readable text, adjust the font size or zoom in on a page.

Follow links to related information. Many ebook readers will supply a definition of any word in the text. All you need to do is highlight a word and click on it. Also find out if your ebook reader will connect you to Web sites related to the topic of your ebook.

Mark it up. Look for ways to electronically underline or highlight text. In addition, see whether you can annotate the book by keying in your own notes tied to specific pages. You might be able to tag each note with a key word and then sort your notes into categories based on these words.

Print. See whether you can connect your ebook device to a printer. You might find it easier to study difficult passages on paper. Note that some ebook publishers impose a limit on how much text you can print.

Sit back and listen. Some ebook readers will convert highlighted text into speech. Let your book read itself out loud.

Monitor battery life. Recharge the battery for your ebook device or laptop computer so that it has enough power to last throughout your work or school day. Seeing your screen go dark when you're in the middle of a paragraph could be a one-way ticket to confusion.

Generate notes and citations automatically. Some ebooks will summarize any text that you highlight. Though these are no substitute for your own written summaries, they can be useful starting points. Also, some ebooks will create citations—items you include in the "references" or "works cited" page of a paper.

Copy and paste. See whether you can copy and paste highlighted text to a word-processing file. This is a fast way to create summaries of a reading assignment and take notes while writing papers or creating presentations. To avoid plagiarism, put quotation marks around the text that you copy and paste. Also record the source for each copied passage.

Consult the print version. Sometimes it's hard to beat a good old-fashioned book—especially for dense tables, complex illustrations, and large, color-coded charts. These might not translate well to a small screen. Go to the library or bookstore to see whether you can find those pages in a printed copy of your ebook. ■

5

Muscle reading at work

Knowledge workers read a lot. They consume technical manuals, sales manuals, policies and procedures, memos, e-mails, Web sites, newsletters, invoices, application forms, meeting minutes, brochures, annual reports, job descriptions—and more.

The techniques of Muscle Reading can help you plow through all that material and extract what you want.

Start with a purpose.

At work, your purpose for reading is probably to produce a specific outcome—to gain a skill or gather information needed to complete a task. Fix that purpose in mind before you read in depth about a topic.

This is where step 3 of Muscle Reading—asking questions—comes in handy. See if you can express your purpose as a question.

Suppose that your purpose for reading is to learn more about marketing. Turn that purpose into a question: *What are the elements of extraordinary marketing?* Then read books and articles for specific answers.

Extract value with nonlinear reading.

Consider how you first learned to read as a child. You opened up a book, fixed your eyes on the first word, and worked straight through until the end of the sentence or page.

As you got older, you approached longer and longer documents with essentially the same strategy: Start at the beginning and plow through word by word until you reach the last period of the last paragraph.

Instead, read with the alertness of someone who's in a large group of people and searching for someone she knows. Her eyes scan the crowd at high speed until—presto!—they land on the familiar face. When reading, your brain can operate with that kind of efficiency. Rather than looking for people, however, you're scanning to land on the paragraphs that contain answers to your questions.

The key is to make several passes through the material. Make your first pass a preview—step 1 of Muscle Reading.

Then go for a second pass. Read the first sentence of each paragraph or the first and last paragraphs of each section.

If you want more detail, then make additional passes. Slow down and pick up a little more detail each time.

During each pass through a document, you can skip entire sections or take them out of order. This is the nonlinear technique.

You might even want to start at the end of a chapter or article to see if there's a summary or review section placed there. This section might be all that you need.

Create a "to-read" folder.

Much of the paper that crosses your field of attention at work will probably consist of basic background material—items that are important, but not urgent. Place these documents in a paper or digital folder, label it "To Read," and pull it out the next time you have a few minutes to spare.

Beware of blog overload.

Reading blogs can be useful. It can also become an activity that devours too many hours. To get the most value from blogs:

- *Create a schedule*. Rather than checking blogs for updates at random points throughout the workday, set specific times for visiting these sites.

- *Set limits*. If you're an avid blog reader, monitor how much time you spend on them each week. The results might surprise you.

- *Use an RSS reader to monitor blogs*. RSS readers are online tools that create summaries of frequently updated Web sites. (RSS stands for "Rich Site Summary" or "Really Simple Syndication.") Examples include NetNewsWire, My Yahoo!, and Google Reader. For each article posted on a Web site, an RSS reader displays a headline. You can add several sets of headlines, or "feeds," to your RSS reader. This allows you to scan the contents of many Web sites in one window—much as you'd skim the headlines in a newspaper.

- *Limit the number of blogs you read*. If you add a new feed to your RSS reader, see if you can delete an old one.

Read with a bias toward action.

Your reading might include passages that call for action on your part. Mark these passages with an appropriate symbol in the margin. For example, write a big letter "A" for *action* next to the relevant paragraph. Or draw a small box there and check off the box after taking the appropriate action. Another option is to enter actionable items directly in your calendar or add them to your to-do list.

The bottom line is that reading at work ultimately means one thing—getting something done. ■

masterstudentprofile

Michael Hyatt

(1955–) Chairman of Thomas Nelson Publishers—the seventh largest trade book publishing company in the U.S.—popular blogger, and professional speaker

One of the most important things you can do to grow as a leader is to read voraciously. As I have written previously, "Leaders are readers, and readers are leaders." …

In January, I started a mentoring group with eight young men. This has been a fantastic experience. …

As part of the program, we meet formally once a month for three hours. We share how things are going in our personal lives and work, recite scripture we have memorized, and pray together. However, the biggest chunk of our time is spent discussing a book that we have all read prior to the meeting.

In addition to reading the book, we have to write a one-page "Net Out" of the book. … This exercise forces us to distill the key insights from the book and then determine what we are going to do differently in our lives as a result. Every man does his Net Out a little differently, but I divide mine into four sections, with an optional fifth;

Bibliographic Heading. This includes the title of the book, the author(s), my name, and the date of my review.

Quick Summary. This is a one-paragraph summary. It's like an "elevator pitch." If you had to tell someone what the book is about in a short elevator ride, what would you say? I usually find the book's jacket copy helpful in distilling the essence of the book.

Key Insights. As I am reading the book, I highlight it as usual. I usually find something worth highlighting every few pages. Then, when I am finished, I go back through the book and record in my own words those items that particularly struck me. I usually end up with about two pages worth of insights. However … this document can be no more than one page—total. So I am forced to go back through my insights and cull the best ones. I also note the page number, so I can go back later and review the insight in more detail if I wish.

Personal Application. This is the key. Some reading (like most fiction, for example) is purely for entertainment.

However, this kind of reading is for application. I want it to change my life, even if it is only incremental. Therefore, I try to list two or three things I am going to do differently as a result of what I learned in the book. (I try to list no more than three.)

Meaningful Quotes. In almost every book, the author says things in a way that are worth remembering. I like to identify these with the letter "Q" in the margin as I am reading and then and include them on second page of the Net Out. This isn't a requirement, but I find it very helpful. I also enter these quotes into Evernote, which is my computer-based brain for remembering everything.

Again, the key is to distill this entire document into no more than a page (or, optionally, two pages with the Meaningful Quotes being on the second page or on the back of the first). The discipline of keeping it short makes the content easier to remember. As a result, I retain more of what I read. …

I am not yet doing this for every book I read, but I can see the value of doing so. It is really a small price to pay to ensure that the content "sticks" and becomes more than a vague memory.

Michael Hyatt ... is hungry for knowledge.
YOU ... can develop a hunger for ideas that help you achieve your goals.

You're One Click Away...
from learning more about Michael Hyatt online at the Master Student Profiles. You can also visit the Master Student Hall of Fame to learn more about other master students..

FIVE Cs
FOR YOUR CAREER

CHARACTER • CRITICAL THINKING • CREATIVE THINKING • COLLABORATION • COMMUNICATION

You can use research and reading skills to discover employers that interest you and make the best impression on them during your job search. Once you've got a job, use reading skills to gain skills and advance your career.

Approach reading as a way to develop character. Regular reading of challenging texts does more than fill us with stories, ideas, and information. It helps to change our outlook on the world and our behavior in fundamental ways. According to a 2007 report from the National Endowment for the Arts, literary readers:

- Help to enrich our nation's cultural life by visiting museums, going to concerts and plays, and creating original artwork more often than nonreaders.

- Are more likely to vote than nonreaders.

- Do more volunteer work than nonreaders.[5]

Also note that a lifetime habit of reading will help you develop several qualities of a master student, including focused attention, creativity, and hunger for learning.

Use information literacy to think creatively about job hunting. Get to know the reference librarians at your school library and public library. These specialists can become your allies in discovering who's hiring in your area and what kind of skills they want to see in new employees. Uncovering this kind of information usually calls for going beyond company Web sites. Librarians can help you open up new job and long-term career possibilities.

Use information literacy to think critically at work. Your supervisor might ask, "Have we priced our products above or below the going rate in our region?"

Or "What's unique about our line of services, compared to our competitors?"

Use the research skills suggested in "Developing information literacy" on page 150 to answer such questions quickly and accurately.

This is another area where reference librarians can help. Some specialize in doing research for certain types of businesses and nonprofit organizations.

Use critical thinking to read e-mails efficiently. Scan each new message, and file it right away in an appropriate place:

- If a message requires some kind of response, send it to a folder titled "Action." Review this folder daily.

- If no response is required but you might refer to the message again, then send it to a folder named "Archives."

You can search this folder any time you want to retrieve a message.

- If the message requires no response and there's little chance that you will ever refer to it, then trash it.

Think critically about when to stop reading. Free yourself of the obligation to finish every book that you start. This is especially true when reading to further your career. If a book that you've started doesn't actually create value for you, let it go and move on. There are plenty more waiting for you.

Or read only the sections of a document or book that apply specifically to your work. One immediate benefit of this approach is saving time. If the content that you really want is on page 23, you don't have to invest an hour reading pouring through the preceding 22 pages. Instead, your preview might unearth that valuable passage within a minute or two.

By the way, look for summaries at the front or back of long documents and business books Everything you want to know might be there, all in a page or two.

Expand your vocabulary to communicate effectively. One key to workplace success is expanding your vocabulary. Learn the key terms used by people in your industry or profession.

Find out which publications and Web sites are popular with your coworkers. Start reading these sources, making special note of words and concepts that are new to you.

Use your reading to create collaboration. Read a lot about topics related to work. Then talk to coworkers about what you're learning. This kind of conversation helps you remember what you read. As you respond to questions, your understanding of the material will also deepen.

In addition, see your reading as a way to create relationships that lead to effective collaboration. Find a book that will create value for members of your team, and share it with them. As business blogger Seth Godin notes:

The single best use of a business book is to help someone else. Sharing what you read, handing the book to a person who needs it ... pushing those around you to get in sync and to take action—that's the main reason it's a book, not a video or a seminar. A book is a souvenir and a container and a motivator and an easily leveraged tool. Hoarding books makes them worth less, not more.[6]

Now, make a personal commitment to developing the five Cs. Take another look at the Discovery Wheel in Chapter 2—especially the sections labeled Character, Creative and Critical Thinking, Communicating, and Collaborating. Take a snapshot of your current skills in these areas after reading and doing this chapter.

DISCOVERY

My scores on the "Five C" sections of the Discovery Wheel were:	As of today, I would give myself the following scores in these areas:	At the end of this course, I would like my scores in these areas to be:
Character _____	Character _____	Character _____
Creative & Critical Thinking _____	Creative & Critical Thinking _____	Creative & Critical Thinking _____
Communicating _____	Communicating _____	Communicating _____
Collaborating _____	Collaborating _____	Collaborating _____

Next, skim this chapter and look for a memory technique that you want to explore in depth. Choose one that would enhance your self-rating in at least one of the five Cs.

I discovered that my preferred technique is . . .

_____

_____

_____

_____

In light of the five Cs, I can use this technique to become more . . .

_____

_____

_____

_____

This technique can also enhance my character by helping me to develop master student qualities, including . . .

_____

_____

_____

_____

INTENTION
To use this technique, I intend to . . .

_____

_____

_____

_____

NEXT ACTION
The specific action I will take is . . .

_____

_____

_____

_____

Name _____

Date _____

1. Briefly explain the problem with holding on to mental pictures, as suggested by the Power Process in this chapter.

   Pictures can prevent us from seeing what is really there. Our pictures often lead to our being angry or disappointed. We set up expectations of events before they occur. Sometimes we don't even realize we have these expectations. (*Power Process: Notice your pictures and let them go*, page 134)

2. Name the acrostic that can help you remember the steps of Muscle Reading.

   POQ, RUA, RRR = **P**ry **O**ut **Q**uestions, **R**oot **U**p **A**nswers, **R**ecite, **R**eview, and **R**eview again. (*How Muscle Reading works*, page 136)

3. You must complete all the steps of Muscle Reading to get the most out of any reading assignment. True or false? Explain your answer.

   False. The nine-step process is not an all-or-nothing package. Use it appropriately and choose what steps to apply as you read. (*Muscle Reading—a leaner approach*, page 140)

4. Give three examples of what to look for when previewing a reading assignment.

   Describe at least three of the following: Look over the table of contents. Survey the entire assignment by looking at each page. Keep the preview short. Look for summary statements. Look for familiar concepts, facts, or ideas while previewing. Read all chapter headings and subheadings. Inspect drawings, diagrams, charts, tables, graphs, and photographs. Ask yourself what you will do with this material and how it can relate to your long-term goals. (*Phase 1: Before you read*, page 137)

5. Briefly explain how to use headings in a text to create an outline.

   The headings of the text can be used as the major points of an outline, and the subheadings can serve as the subcategories in the outline. (*Phase 1: Before you read*, page 137)

6. In addition to underlining and highlighting, there are other ways to mark up a text. List three possibilities.

   List any three of the following: Use asterisks or exclamation points near important sentences. Circle key terms. Write short definitions of key terms in the margin. Mark possible test questions with a "Q" in the margin. Write personal comments in the margin. Write related page number references in the margin. Write summaries of main points. Rewrite chapter titles, headings, and subheadings. Draw diagrams, pictures, or maps. Number steps in a list or series of related points. (*Phase 2: While you read*, page 138)

7. To get the most benefit from marking a book, underline at least 20 percent of the text. True or false? Explain your answer.

   False. Underlining is generally more effective when only the most important material is flagged. A small portion of underlined text, less than 10 percent, is usually sufficient for review. (*Phase 2: While you read*, page 138)

8. Compare the steps of Muscle Reading with the approach described in "Muscle Reading—a leaner approach." How do these two methods differ?

   (Answers will vary.) The leaner approach is a more structured, simplified approach than Muscle Reading, but both approaches are based on the same ideas and should be equally effective when used appropriately. Whereas Muscle Reading involves steps to take before, during, and after you read, the leaner approach is aimed at the process during reading. (*Muscle Reading—a leaner approach*, page 140)

9. Explain at least three strategies you can use when reading is tough.

   Explain at least three of the following: Read it again. Look for essential words. Hold a mini-review. Read it out loud. Talk to your instructor. Stand up. Jump to the next section or the end of the article or chapter. Find a tutor. Use another text. Try to explain it as though you were telling someone else. Ask, "What's going on here?" Stop reading. (*When reading is tough*, page 142)

10. Define the term *information literacy*.

    Information literacy is a set of skills to use whenever you want to answer questions or find information. It involves finding information from appropriate sources, evaluating the information, organizing it, and using it to achieve a purpose. The ability to do this in a world where data is literally at your fingertips is called information literacy. (*Developing information literacy*, page 150)

NOTES

Instructor Tools & Tips

"Rather than try to gauge your note-taking skill by quantity, think in this way: Am I simply doing clerk's work or am I assimilating new knowledge and putting down my own thoughts? To put down your own thoughts you must put down your own words. . . . If the notes taken show signs of having passed through a mind, it is a good test of its relevance and adequacy."

—Jacques Barzun and Henry Graff

PREVIEW

Linking Chapters 5, 6, and 7 together is very important because students sometimes tend to compartmentalize these chapters. Introducing note taking as a four-part process asks students to understand the following:

- *Why* it is important to capture the context of *what* they are taking notes on.

- This chapter will help your students identify *what* note-taking strategies are effective: observing, recording, and reviewing. Each part of the process is essential and interdependent with the others.

- After your students learn new strategies for taking notes, ask them *how* they will apply these techniques to their other courses. Practice is an important element in adopting or adapting effective note-taking techniques. Encourage your students to test the new methods over time before they evaluate the effectiveness of a particular method. In class discussions, give students time to interpret the effectiveness of their note taking. Remember to suggest that learning styles have a significant impact on note-taking skill. Visual learners can find note taking more pleasant and effective when they use personalized visual elements like colorful paper, favorite colors in highlighters and pens, or other visual elements that make the notes feel personal and unique.

- Students can also apply *what if* by connecting Chapters 5, 6, and 7 together into a study-skills section for the course.

GUEST SPEAKER

At this point in the term, students should be aware of how they are doing in their classes. It may be a good time to invite guest speakers from academic support services to talk to your students about how to get additional help they may need. Possibilities include the coordinators of the Writing Center, Tutoring Program, or Academic Success Center. Announce the guest speaker to students in advance, and ask students to prepare two or three questions before the speaker comes. For example, they might ask a Writing Center representative: "In addition to writing classes, how will this service help me in my other classes?" Students can also practice taking Cornell method notes during the guest lecturer's mini-lecture, using their own questions. The questions could be placed in the left-hand column, with the corresponding answers on the right side of the paper. Use these short segments to provide practice sessions. This helps students flex their note-taking muscles to better prepare them for longer, more rigorous segments in their college classes.

LECTURE

Eldon McMurray tells his students, "You are your own best instructor." As an in-class discussion, he asks students to tell him about their favorite recording artist or sports figure. He asks questions such as "Where does she live?" and "How old is he?" Then he switches over to asking students about their professors. He almost always gets a blank stare when he asks, "What do you know about your math instructor?" Challenge students to brainstorm ideas on how they can learn more about their instructors and how this connectedness will help them in class. Some shy students particularly like the ideas of conducting Internet research and reading about their instructors online.

Many new college students have no idea what they should do when they miss a class. They fail to contact either their instructor or their classmates to find out what handouts, information, and assignments they missed. As a follow-up to the article What to do when you miss a class (page 163), considering providing a brief lecture on this topic. It's also a good time to review classroom and campus attendance policies with your students. You might include discussion of topics that may seem obvious to you but can be perplexing to new college students—how to communicate with your college professors (benefits of e-mail, phone calls, or office visits). You might also want to explain to students how to read an office schedule to determine availability of professors or the distinction of adjunct professors, who may not have a campus office or required office hours.

master instructor
BEST PRACTICE

"*I share an additional tool for note taking with my students: Use the power of doodling. If you find that you often have drawn circles around every hole on the paper and have added doodles in every open space in your notes, perhaps you need to use your "doodle power" to your advantage. Doodlers often find that they put more effort into their artistic efforts than they do into the content of their notes. Consider using this energy to create notes in the style of a comic strip with stick figures (for speed) and balloons for dialogue. As you invest your energy in depicting the information on paper, you will become more involved in the presentation instead of allowing the doodles to distract you.*"

–Sam Sink, Wilkes Community College, North Carolina

EXERCISES/ACTIVITIES

1. **Power Process: I create it all** This in-class activity helps bring this process alive. After students have read this process and seen the "I create it all" segment from the CourseMate, ask them to recall a recent situation that went well for them at college, work, or home. Give them a few minutes to summarize the situation in their notes. Then ask them to list six ways that they created that successful situation. After they are done, ask for volunteers to share their success and how they created it. Then repeat the exercise, this time identifying a recent situation that did *not* work out well for them. For some students, this part may be much harder to do. Discuss this in class, with students volunteering to share their stories. You may need to give them an example to get the discussion started.

2. **Target class exercise** Ask your students to select three of their other courses in which they would like to put their advanced note-taking system into practice. By applying

the note-taking concepts to their other courses, they start to realize the power of the ideas presented in *From Master Student to Master Employee.* To give them a head start and to help them understand how setting the stage can contribute to effective note taking, have them prepare for taking notes in class by outlining the textbook reading that the professor's lecture will cover that day.

3. **Getting your money's worth, or "What am I paying for this ticket?"** Set up this demonstration by having a student come up at the beginning of the class and pay you $20 for a front-row seat. If there is no front-row seat available, ask a student to move so that the paying student can sit there. Do this very seriously, and the irony of the object lesson will catch everyone's attention.

   Ask students where they like to sit at a concert that costs $40 or more to attend. Then ask why tickets are so much more expensive for front-row center seats at a concert, or at the center court of a professional basketball game, or on the 50-yard line of a football game. All they have to do to get the best seat in class is be on time or come a little early. Sitting in the front requires students to be more diligent and aware, as professors have a front-row seat to observe them as well! But this offers a payback, as professors can often learn the names and relate to the eye contact and one-on-one response of students in the front row.

4. **"Be here now" in class** Ask students to designate the upper right-hand corner of their class note page as their "Be here now" corner. When they catch their mind wandering, they can jot down a note or make a tick mark at the top of the page. They can then bring their attention back to the speaker. Counting tick marks afterward allows students to quantify the number of times their minds wander, and to measure progress made in future classes. Practicing this helps them stay focused.

5. **Note-taking tools (page 161)** After students have read about the various note-taking strategies, discuss them in class. Divide the class into groups of four, and assign each group one of the new techniques to practice while you give a short lecture. Provide a safety net for this exercise by telling students that you will give them a detailed handout of the lecture at the end of class. This way, they don't have to worry about missing important information while they are trying out a new note-taking tool. After the lecture, the students discuss—with their group and then as a class—what they discovered about using the new strategy, including their initial perceptions of its strengths and weaknesses. This in-class practice encourages students to try a new note-taking tool in their other courses.

CONVERSATION/SHARING

1. **Master Student Profile: Fay Wattleton (page 181)** Ask students to discuss the characteristics that made Faye Wattleton a master student, using the list of Master Student Qualities provided in the

Introduction. Also ask them to identify *what* traits Wattleton had that they feel they do not personally possess. This is followed by further sharing on *how* students can gain these qualities.

2. **Online courses** This chapter is a good time to facilitate a conversation and sharing about online courses. Some students love them; some hate them. Ask students to share what they have liked and/or disliked about online courses so that those who haven't tried them will have more information before it's time to register for the next term. Ask students their perceptions about the following: time demands of an online class, amount of reading required, expected response time from teachers. Online students can clear up some of these misperceptions by their own examples!

HOMEWORK

Master Student Map (page 159) Students can begin practicing new note-taking techniques immediately after reading this chapter. As your students begin to transfer and apply what they learn in this course to their other courses, more *aha!* moments will begin to occur.

Why?   Why learn about new methods of note taking?

What?   What is the Cornell format? What is mind mapping?

How?   How can reviewing your notes help you be more successful in school? How is effective listening related to note taking?

What if?   What if you observe, record, and review your notes in a new way in all of your classes?

Review: The note-taking process flows (pages 170–171) For many students, 24 hours is too long to wait before reviewing and processing their notes into long-term memory. For difficult classes or upper-division theory-based courses, ask your students

to answer the questions using the strengths of each mode in the Master Student Map exercises. Students can summarize their notes during their review by answering these key questions: *Why* is this idea important? *What* are the details I need to know? *How* will I remember and prepare to be tested on this material? *What if* the test is multiple choice? *What if* the test is an essay format? *How* can I know or anticipate this format in advance of the test?

Revisit your goals One powerful way to achieve any goal is to periodically assess your progress in meeting it. Provide your students an opportunity to reflect on the materials that have been covered to date. Have students reflect on their goals set earlier in the book and make adjustments to their plan. While discussing this, suggest that your students look back at their Discovery Wheel and review their progress to date. Students will be given a formal post-course Discovery Wheel in Chapter 12.

EVALUATION

Quiz Ideas for Chapter 6

Ask students to:

- Describe the Cornell note-taking system.

- Describe strategies for taking notes when instructors talk fast.

- Explain what it takes to become an online learner.

- Explain how the Power Process: "I create it all" can help them be more successful in college.

- List four ways they can be prepared in advance of taking notes.

- Take notes using a particular style, such as Cornell notes, after watching a brief video (possibly from Video Skillbuilders on the *From Master Student to Master Employee* Web site) you show them.

Additional Digital Resources for Chapter 6

What can you ASSIGN FROM THE COURSEMATE *for From Master Student to Master Employee?*

- **Concept Maps.** These interactive concept maps not only summarize note-taking concepts from the chapter but are note-taking examples themselves. Share the following maps with students to illustrate how mapping can be put to use for taking notes:
  - Observe
  - Record
  - Review

- **Video Skillbuilders.** These interactive online tools combine video clips featuring discussions with students, instructors, and experts, with articles and activities designed to give students a fully engaging learning experience. Either view and experience these together in class, or have students view them as a homework assignment and respond to the viewing questions and reflective exercise. These modules are good matches for Chapter 6:
  - Taking Notes to Improve Your Grade
  - Textbook Note Taking: Student Methods
  - Textbook Note Taking: Traditional Methods

Note that Video Skillbuilders are available for every chapter.

- **Interactive eBook.** For students who are more likely to read onscreen than in print, assign the ebook chapter as an option where students can take notes, highlight, and search, and are directly connected to all the additional digital resources available for the chapter. Discuss electronic note-taking strategies with students who choose to read online.

CourseMate *To access CourseMate, your students need to visit* www.cengagebrain .com. *At the CengageBrain.com home page, students search for the ISBN of* From Master Student to Master Employee *(from the back cover of the book), using the search box at the top of the page. This takes them to the product page where these resources can be found.*

Did you know that THESE RESOURCES (and many more) ARE AVAILABLE on the INSTRUCTOR COMPANION SITE?

- **Looking for fresh, innovative ways to teach Chapter 6 topics?** Browse through the Best Practices library to see what other Master Instructors have been successfully doing with their students.

....

master instructor BEST PRACTICE

"*Take Note. I show students an 8-minute segment on polar bears from the PBS series Nova. It contains several statistics and Russian names. The videotape is also filled with pictures of 'cute little bears.' I ask students to take notes on the videotape. Afterwards, I give an open-notes quiz. Between the pictures of bears, the statistics, and the Russian names, many of the students find their notes less than adequate. I then introduce mind mapping and the Cornell method of taking notes. The videotape is presented a second time, and everyone takes notes again, this time using one of the new methods. Students usually see an immediate improvement. This exercise stresses three points:*

1. *Preparation and prior exposure to the material improve note taking and comprehension*
2. *Sometimes the method by which information is given has distracting elements (i.e., cute little bears)*
3. *Note-taking skills can be learned and improved.*"

–Terry Johnson, Lindsey Wilson College

....

- **Check out the PowerPoint Library for a PowerPoint specifically created for Chapter 6.** This master library of PowerPoint presentations makes it easy to find the right PowerPoint for you! If you're looking for a way to freshen up your lecture, the PowerPoint Library is a great place to start.

Please visit login.cengage.com *to log in and access the Instructor Companion Site.*

Notes

Use this **Master Student Map** to ask yourself

WHY THIS CHAPTER MATTERS . . .

- Note taking helps you remember course content and influences how well you do on tests.

WHAT IS INCLUDED . . .

HOW I CAN USE THIS CHAPTER . . .

- Experiment with several formats for note taking.
- Create a note-taking format that works well for me.
- Take effective notes in special situations—such as while reading and when instructors talk quickly.

WHAT IF . . .

- I could take notes that remain informative and useful for weeks, months, or even years to come?

© Ruslan Ivantsov/Shutterstock.com

JOURNAL ENTRY 11
Intention Statement

Get what you want from this chapter

Recall a recent incident in which you had difficulty taking notes. Perhaps you were listening to an instructor who talked fast, or you got confused and stopped taking notes altogether. Then preview this chapter to find at least three strategies that you can use right away to help you take better notes.

Strategy	Page number

POWER
process

I create it all

This article describes a powerful tool for times of trouble. In a crisis, "I create it all" can lead the way to solutions. The main point of this Power Process is to treat experiences, events, and circumstances in your life *as if* you created them.

"I create it all" is one of the most unusual and bizarre suggestions in this book. It certainly is not a belief. Use it when it works. Don't when it doesn't.

Keeping that in mind, consider how powerful this Power Process can be. It is really about the difference between two distinct positions in life: being a victim or being responsible.

A victim of circumstances is controlled by outside forces. We've all felt like victims at one time or another. Sometimes we felt helpless.

In contrast, we can take responsibility. Responsibility is "response-ability"—the ability to choose a *response* to any event. You can choose your *response* to any event, even when the event itself is beyond your control.

Many students approach grades from the position of being victims. When the student who sees the world this way gets an "F," she reacts something like this:

"Another 'F'! That teacher couldn't teach her way out of a wet paper bag. She can't teach English for anything. There's no way to take notes in that class. And that textbook—what a bore!"

The problem with this viewpoint is that in looking for excuses, the student is robbing herself of the power to get any grade other than an "F." She's giving all of her power to a bad teacher and a boring textbook.

There is another way, called *taking responsibility*. You can recognize that you choose your grades by choosing your actions. Then you are the source, rather than the result, of the grades you get. The student who got an "F" could react like this:

"Another 'F'! Oh, shoot! Well, hmmm . . . What did I do to create it?"

Now, that's power. By asking, "How did I contribute to this outcome?" you are no longer the victim. This student might continue by saying, "Well, let's see. I didn't review my notes after class. That might have done it." Or "I went out with my friends the night before the test. Well, that probably helped me fulfill some of the requirements for getting an 'F.'"

The point is this: When the "F" is the result of your friends, the book, or the teacher, you probably can't do anything about it. However, if you *chose* the "F," you can choose a different grade next time. You are in charge.

You're One Click Away...
from accessing Power Process Media online and finding out more about how to "create it all."

The Note-Taking Process FLOWS

One way to understand note taking is to realize that taking notes is just one part of the process. Effective note taking consists of three parts: observing, recording, and reviewing.

First, you **observe** an "event." This can be a statement by an instructor, a lab experiment, a slide show of an artist's works, or a chapter of required reading.

Then you **record** your observations of that event. That is, you "take notes."

Finally, you **review** what you have recorded. You memorize, reflect, apply, and rehearse what you're learning. This step lifts ideas off the page and turns them into a working part of your mind.

Each part of the note-taking process is essential, and each depends on the other. Your observations determine what you record. What you record determines what you review. And the quality of your review can determine how effective your next observations will be. If you review your notes on the Sino-Japanese War of 1894, for example, the next day's lecture on the Boxer Rebellion of 1900 will make more sense.

Legible and speedy handwriting is also useful in taking notes. Knowledge of outlining is handy too. A nifty pen, a new notebook, and a laptop computer are all great note-taking devices.

And they're all worthless—unless you participate as an energetic observer *in* class and regularly review your notes *after* class. If you take those two steps, you can turn even the most disorganized chicken scratches into a powerful tool.

This is a well-researched aspect of student success in higher education. Study after study points to the benefits of taking notes. The value is added in two ways. First, you create a set of materials that refreshes your memory and helps you prepare for tests. Second, taking notes prompts you to listen effectively during class. You translate new ideas into your own words and images. You impose a personal and meaningful structure on what you see, read, and hear. You move from passive observer to active participant.[1] It's not that you take notes so that you can learn from them later. Instead, you learn *while* taking notes.

Computer technology takes traditional note taking to a whole new level. You can capture key notes with word-processing, outlining, database, and publishing software. Your notes become living documents that you can search, bookmark, tag, and archive like other digital files.

Sometimes note taking looks like a passive affair, especially in large lecture classes. One person at the front of the room does most of the talking. Everyone else is seated and silent, taking notes. The lecturer seems to be doing all of the work.

© iStockphoto.com/cmcderm1

Don't be deceived.

Look more closely. You'll see some students taking notes in a way that radiates energy. They're awake and alert, poised on the edge of their seats. They're writing—a physical activity that expresses mental engagement. These students listen for levels of ideas and information, make choices about what to record, and compile materials to review.

In higher education, you might spend hundreds of hours taking notes. Making them more effective is a direct investment in your success.

Think of your notes as a textbook that *you* create—one that's more current and more in tune with your learning preferences than any textbook you could buy. ■

OBSERVE

The note-taking process flows

Sherlock Holmes, a fictional master detective and student of the obvious, could track down a villain by observing the fold of his scarf and the mud on his shoes. In real life, a doctor can save a life by observing a mole—one a patient has always had—that undergoes a rapid change.

An accountant can save a client thousands of dollars by observing the details of a spreadsheet. A student can save hours of study time by observing that she gets twice as much done at a particular time of day.

Keen observers see facts and relationships. They know ways to focus their attention on the details and then tap their creative energy to discover patterns. To sharpen your classroom observation skills, experiment with the following techniques, and continue to use those that you find most valuable. Many of these strategies can be adapted to the notes you take while reading.

SET THE STAGE

Complete outside assignments. Nothing is more discouraging (or boring) than sitting through a lecture about the relationship of Le Chatelier's principle to the principle of kinetics if you've never heard of Henri Louis Le Chatelier or kinetics. The more familiar you are with a subject, the more easily you can absorb important information during class lectures. Instructors usually assume that students complete assignments, and they construct their lectures accordingly.

Bring the right materials. A good pen does not make you a good observer, but the lack of a pen or notebook can be distracting enough to take the fine edge off your concentration. Make sure you have a pen, pencil, notebook, or any other materials you need. Bring your textbook to class, especially if the lectures relate closely to the text.

If you are consistently unprepared for a class, that might be a message about your intentions concerning the course. Find out if it is. The next time you're in a frantic scramble to borrow pen and paper 37 seconds before the class begins, notice the cost. Use the borrowed pen and paper to write a Discovery Statement about your lack of preparation. Consider whether you intend to be successful in the course.

Sit front and center. Students who get as close as possible to the front and center of the classroom often do better on tests for several reasons. The closer you sit to the lecturer, the harder it is to fall asleep. The closer you sit to the front, the fewer interesting or distracting classmates are situated between you and the instructor. Material on the board is easier to read from up front. Also, the instructor can see you more easily when you have a question.

Instructors are usually not trained to perform. Some can project their energy to a large audience, but some cannot. A professor who sounds boring from the back of the room might sound more interesting up close.

Sitting up front enables you to become a constructive force in the classroom. By returning the positive energy that an engaged teacher gives out, you can reinforce the teacher's enthusiasm and enhance your experience of the class.

In addition, sound waves from the human voice begin to degrade at a distance of 8 to 12 feet. If you sit more than 15 feet from the speaker, your ability to hear and take effective notes might be compromised. Get close to the source of the sound. Get close to the energy.

Sitting close to the front is a way to commit yourself to getting what you want out of school. One reason students gravitate to the back of the classroom is that they think the instructor is less likely to call on them. Sitting in back can signal a lack of commitment. When you sit up front, you are declaring your willingness to take a risk and participate.

Conduct a short preclass review. Arrive early, and then put your brain in gear by reviewing your notes from the previous class. Scan your reading assignment. Look at the sections you have underlined or highlighted. Review assigned problems and exercises. Note questions you intend to ask.

Clarify your intentions. Take a 3 × 5 card to class with you. On that card, write a short Intention Statement about what you plan to get from the class. Describe your intended level of participation or the quality of attention you will bring to the subject. Be specific. If you found your previous class notes to be inadequate, write down what you intend to do to make your notes from this class session more useful.

"BE HERE NOW" IN CLASS

Accept your wandering mind. The techniques in Chapter 3's "Process: Be here now" can be especially useful when your head soars into the clouds. Don't fight daydreaming. When you notice your mind wandering during class, look at it as an opportunity to refocus your attention. If thermodynamics is losing out to beach parties, let go of the beach.

Notice your writing. When you discover yourself slipping into a fantasyland, feel the weight of your pen in your hand. Notice how your notes look. Paying attention to the act of writing can bring you back to the here and now.

You also can use writing in a more direct way to clear your mind of distracting thoughts. Pause for a few seconds, and write those thoughts down. If you're distracted by thoughts of errands you need to run after class, list them on a 3 × 5 card and stick it in your pocket. Or simply put a symbol, such as an arrow or asterisk, in your notes to mark the places where your mind started to wander. Once your distractions are out of your mind and safely stored on paper, you can gently return your attention to taking notes.

Be with the instructor. In your mind, put yourself right up front with the instructor. Imagine that you and the instructor are the only ones in the room and that the lecture is a personal conversation between the two of you. Pay attention to the instructor's body language and facial expressions. Look the instructor in the eye.

Remember that the power of this suggestion is immediately reduced by digital distractions—Web surfing, e-mail checking, or text messaging. Taking notes is a way to stay focused. The physical act of taking notes signals your mind to stay in the same room as the instructor.

Notice your environment. When you become aware of yourself daydreaming, bring yourself back to class by paying attention to the temperature in the room, the feel of your chair, or the quality of light coming through the window. Run your hand along the surface of your desk. Listen to the chalk on the blackboard or the sound of the teacher's voice. Be in that environment. Once your attention is back in the room, you can focus on what's happening in class.

Postpone debate. When you hear something you disagree with, note your disagreement and let it go. Don't allow your internal dialogue to drown out subsequent material. If your disagreement is persistent and strong, make note of it and then move on. Internal debate can prevent you from absorbing new

What to do when you miss a class

For most courses, you'll benefit by attending every class session. This allows you to observe and actively participate. If you miss a class, then catch up as quickly as possible. Find additional ways to observe class content.

Clarify policies on missed classes.
On the first day of classes, find out about your instructors' policies on absences. See whether you will be allowed to make up assignments, quizzes, and tests. Also inquire about doing extra-credit assignments.

Contact a classmate. Early in the
semester, identify a student in each class who seems responsible and dependable. Exchange e-mail addresses and phone numbers. If you know you won't be in class, contact this student ahead of time. When you notice that your classmate is absent, pick up extra copies of handouts, make assignments lists, and offer copies of your notes.

Contact your instructor. If you miss a
class, e-mail or call your instructor, or put a note in his mailbox. Ask whether he has another section of the same course that you can attend so you won't miss the lecture information. Also ask about getting handouts you might need before the next class meeting.

Consider technology. If there is a Web
site for your class, check it for assignments and the availability of handouts you missed. Free online services such as NoteMesh allow students to share notes with one another. These services use wiki software, which allows you to create and edit Web pages using any browser. Before using such tools, however, check with instructors for their policies on note sharing.

6

information. It's okay to absorb information you don't agree with. Just absorb it with the mental tag "My instructor says . . . , and I don't agree with it."

Let go of judgments about lecture styles. Human beings are judgment machines. We evaluate everything, especially other people. If another person's eyebrows are too close together (or too far apart), if she walks a certain way or speaks with an unusual accent, we instantly make up a story about her. We do this so quickly that the process is usually not a conscious one.

Don't let your attitude about an instructor's lecture style, habits, or appearance get in the way of your education. You can decrease the power of your judgments if you pay attention to them and let them go.

You can even let go of judgments about rambling, unorganized lectures. Turn them to your advantage. Take the initiative and organize the material yourself. While taking notes, separate the key points from the examples and supporting evidence. Note the places where you got confused, and make a list of questions to ask.

Participate in class activities. Ask questions. Volunteer for demonstrations. Join in class discussions. Be willing to take a risk or look foolish, if that's what it takes for you to learn. Chances are, the question you think is dumb is also on the minds of several of your classmates.

Relate the class to your goals. If you have trouble staying awake in a particular class, write at the top of your notes how that class relates to a specific goal. Identify the reward or payoff for reaching that goal.

Think critically about what you hear. This suggestion might seem contrary to the previously mentioned technique "postpone debate." It's not. You might choose not to think critically about the instructor's ideas during the lecture. That's fine. Do it later, as you review and edit your notes. This is the time to list questions or write down your agreements and disagreements.

WATCH FOR CLUES

Be alert to repetition. When an instructor repeats a phrase or an idea, make a note of it. Repetition is a signal that the instructor thinks the information is important.

Listen for introductory, concluding, and transition words and phrases. Introductory, concluding, and transition words and phrases include phrases such as *the following three factors, in conclusion, the most important consideration, in addition to,* and *on the other hand.* These phrases and others signal relationships, definitions, new subjects, conclusions, cause and effect, and examples. They reveal the structure of the lecture. You can use these phrases to organize your notes.

Watch the board or PowerPoint presentation. If an instructor takes the time to write something down on the board or show a PowerPoint presentation, consider the material to be important.

Copy all diagrams and drawings, equations, names, places, dates, statistics, and definitions.

Watch the instructor's eyes. If an instructor glances at her notes and then makes a point, it is probably a signal that the information is especially important. Anything she reads from her notes is a potential test question.

Highlight the obvious clues. Instructors often hint strongly or tell students point-blank that certain information is likely to appear on an exam. Make stars or other special marks in your notes next to this information. Instructors are not trying to hide what's important.

Notice the instructor's interest level. If the instructor is excited about a topic, it is more likely to appear on an exam. Pay attention when she seems more animated than usual. ∎

You're One Click Away...
from finding more strategies for observing online.

JOURNAL ENTRY 12
Discovery/Intention Statement

Create more value from lectures

Think back on the last few lectures you have attended. How do you currently observe (listen to) lectures? What specific behaviors do you have as you sit and listen? Do you listen more closely in some classes than others? Briefly describe your responses in the space below.

I discovered that I . . .

_____

_____

_____

_____

Now write an Intention Statement about any changes you want to make in the way you respond to lectures.

I intend to . . .

_____

_____

_____

_____

RECORD

The note-taking process flows

Woman in white: © John Molloy/Getty Images/Frame: Shutterstock/
Digital Camera: © iStockphoto.com/tezzstock

The format and structure of your notes are more important than how fast you write or how elegant your handwriting is. The following techniques can improve the effectiveness of your notes.

GENERAL TECHNIQUES FOR NOTE TAKING

Use key words. An easy way to sort the extraneous material from the important points is to take notes using key words. Key words or phrases contain the essence of communication. They include these:

- Concepts, technical terms, names, and numbers
- Linking words, including words that describe action, relationship, and degree (for example, *most, least,* and *faster*)

Key words evoke images and associations with other words and ideas. They trigger your memory. That characteristic makes them powerful review tools. One key word can initiate the recall of a whole cluster of ideas. A few key words can form a chain from which you can reconstruct an entire lecture.

To see how key words work, take yourself to an imaginary classroom. You are now in the middle of an anatomy lecture. Picture what the room looks like, what it feels like, how it smells. You hear the instructor say:

Okay, what happens when we look directly over our heads and see a piano falling out of the sky? How do we take that signal and translate it into the action of getting out of the way? The first thing that happens is that a stimulus is generated in the neurons— receptor neurons—of the eye. Light reflected from the piano reaches our eyes. In other words, we see the piano.

The receptor neurons in the eye transmit that sensory signal— the sight of the piano—to the body's nervous system. That's all they can do—pass on information. So we've got a sensory signal coming into the nervous system. But the neurons that initiate movement in our legs are effector neurons. The information from the sensory neurons must be transmitted to effector neurons, or we will get squashed by the piano. There must be some kind of interconnection between receptor and effector neurons. What happens between the two? What is the connection?

Key words you might note in this example include *stimulus, generated, receptor neurons, transmit, sensory signals, nervous*

system, effector neurons, and *connection.* You can reduce the instructor's 163 words to these 12 key words. With a few transitional words, your notes might look like this:

> Stimulus (piano) generated
> in receptor neurons (eye)
>
> Sensory signals transmitted
> by nervous system to
> effector neurons (legs)
>
> What connects receptor to
> effector?

Note the last key word of the lecture: *connection.* This word is part of the instructor's question and leads to the next point in the lecture. Be on the lookout for questions like this. They can help you organize your notes and are often clues for test questions.

Use pictures and diagrams. Make relationships visual. Copy all diagrams from the board, and invent your own. A drawing of a piano falling on someone who is looking up, for example, might be used to demonstrate the relationship of receptor neurons to effector neurons. Label the eyes "receptor" and the feet "effector." This picture implies that the sight of the piano must be translated into a motor response. By connecting the explanation of the process with the unusual picture of the piano falling, you can link the elements of the process together.

Write notes in paragraphs. When it is difficult to follow the organization of a lecture or put information into outline form, create a series of informal paragraphs. These paragraphs should contain few complete sentences. Reserve complete sentences for precise definitions, direct quotations, and important points that the instructor emphasizes by repetition or other signals—such as the phrase "This is an important point."

Copy material from the board or a PowerPoint presentation. Record key formulas, diagrams, and problems that the teacher presents on the board or in a PowerPoint presentation. Copy dates, numbers, names, places, and other facts. You can even use your own signal or code to flag important material.

Use a three-ring binder. Three-ring binders have several advantages over other kinds of notebooks. First, pages can be removed and spread out when you review. This way, you can get the whole picture of a lecture. Second, the three-ring-binder format allows you to insert handouts right into your notes. Third, you can insert your own out-of-class notes in the correct order.

Use only one side of a piece of paper. When you use one side of a page, you can review and organize all your notes by spreading them out side by side. Most students find the benefit well worth the cost of the paper. Perhaps you're concerned about the environmental impact of consuming more paper. If so, you can use the blank side of old notes and use recycled paper.

Use 3 × 5 cards. As an alternative to using notebook paper, use 3 × 5 cards to take lecture notes. Copy each new concept onto a separate 3 × 5 card.

Keep your own thoughts separate. For the most part, avoid making editorial comments in your lecture notes. The danger is that when you return to your notes, you might mistake your own

ideas for those of the instructor. If you want to make a comment, clearly label it as your own.

Use an "I'm lost" signal. No matter how attentive and alert you are, you might get lost and confused in a lecture. If it is inappropriate to ask a question, record in your notes that you were lost. Invent your own signal—for example, a circled question mark. When you write down your code for "I'm lost," leave space for the explanation or clarification that you will get later. The space will also be a signal that you missed something. Later, you can speak to your instructor or ask to see a fellow student's notes.

Label, number, and date all notes. Develop the habit of labeling and dating your notes at the beginning of each class. Number the page too. Sometimes the sequence of material in a lecture is important. Write your name and phone number in each notebook in case you lose it.

Use standard abbreviations. Be consistent with your abbreviations. If you make up your own abbreviations or symbols, write a key explaining them in your notes. Avoid vague abbreviations. When you use an abbreviation such as *comm.* for *committee,* you run the risk of not being able to remember whether you meant *committee, commission, common,* or *commit.* One way to abbreviate is to leave out vowels. For example, *talk* becomes *tlk, said* becomes *sd, American* becomes *Amrcn.*

Leave blank space. Notes tightly crammed into every corner of the page are hard to read and difficult to use for review. Give your eyes a break by leaving plenty of space.

Later, when you review, you can use the blank spaces in your notes to clarify points, write questions, or add other material.

Take notes in different colors. You can use colors as highly visible organizers. For example, you can signal important points with red. Or use one color of ink for notes about the text and another color for lecture notes.

Use graphic signals. The following ideas can be used with any note-taking format:

- Use brackets, parentheses, circles, and squares to group information that belongs together.
- Use stars, arrows, and underlining to indicate important points. Flag the most important points with double stars, double arrows, or double underlines.
- Use arrows and connecting lines to link related groups.
- Use equal signs and greater-than and less-than signs to indicate compared quantities.

To avoid creating confusion with graphic symbols, use them carefully and consistently. Write a "dictionary" of your symbols in the front of your notebooks; an example is shown here.

$$I \quad I, (\ ), \bigcirc, \square = info$$
that belongs together

$$*, \searrow, = \ = important$$

$$**, \searrow\searrow, \equiv, !!! = extra \ important$$

$$> = greater \ than \quad < = less \ than$$
$$= \ = equal \ to$$

$$\longrightarrow \ = leads \ to, \ becomes$$
$$Ex: school \rightarrow job \rightarrow money$$

$$? = huh?, \ lost$$

$$?? = big \ trouble, \ clear \ up$$
immediately

Use recorders effectively. Some students record lectures with audio or digital recorders, but there are persuasive arguments against doing so. When you record a lecture, there is a strong temptation to daydream. After all, you can always listen to the lecture again later on. Unfortunately, if you let the recorder do all of the work, you are skipping a valuable part of the learning process.

There are other potential problems as well. Listening to recorded lectures can take a lot of time—more time than reviewing written notes. Recorders can't answer the questions you didn't ask in class. Also, recording devices malfunction. In fact, the unscientific Hypothesis of Recording Glitches states that the tendency of recorders to malfunction is directly proportional to the importance of the material. With those warnings in mind, you can use a recorder effectively if you choose. For example, you can use recordings as backups to written notes. (Check with your instructor first. Some prefer not to be recorded.) Turn the recorder on; then take notes as if it weren't there. Recordings can be especially useful if an instructor speaks fast.

THE CORNELL METHOD

A note-taking system that has worked for students around the world is the *Cornell method*.[2] Originally developed by Walter Pauk at Cornell University during the 1950s, this approach continues to be taught across the United States and in other countries as well.

The cornerstone of this method is what Pauk calls the *cue column*—a wide margin on the left-hand side of the paper. The cue column is the key to the Cornell method's many benefits. Here's how to use it.

Format your paper. On each sheet of your notepaper, draw a vertical line, top to bottom, about 2 inches from the left edge of

the paper. This line creates the cue column—the space to the left of the line. You can also find Web sites that allow you to print out pages in this format. Just do an Internet search using the key words *cornell method pdf*.

Take notes, leaving the cue column blank. As you read an assignment or listen to a lecture, take notes on the right-hand side of the paper. Fill up this column with sentences, paragraphs, outlines, charts, or drawings. Do not write in the cue column. You'll use this space later, as you do the next steps.

Condense your notes in the cue column. Think of the notes you took on the right-hand side of the paper as a set of answers. In the cue column, list potential test questions that correspond to your notes. Write one question for each major term or point.

As an alternative to questions, you can list key words from your notes. Yet another option is to pretend that your notes are a series of articles on different topics. In the cue column, write a newspaper-style headline for each "article." In any case, be brief. If you cram the cue column full of words, you defeat its purpose—to reduce the number and length of your notes.

Write a summary. Pauk recommends that you reduce your notes even more by writing a brief summary at the bottom of each page. This step offers you another way to engage actively with the material.

Cue column	Notes
What are the 3 phases of Muscle Reading?	Phase 1: Before you read Phase 2: While you read Phase 3: After you read
What are the steps in phase 1?	1. Preview 2. Outline 3. Question
What are the steps in phase 2?	4. Focus 5. Flag answers
What are the steps in phase 3?	6. Recite 7. Review 8. Review again
What is an acronym for Muscle Reading?	Pry = preview Out = outline Questions = question Focus Flag Answers Recite Review Review again

Summary
Muscle Reading includes 3 phases: before, during, and after reading. Each phase includes specific steps. Use the acronym to recall all the steps.

Use the cue column to recite. Cover the right-hand side of your notes with a blank sheet of paper. Leave only the cue column showing. Then look at each item you wrote in the cue column and talk about it. If you wrote questions, answer each question. If you wrote key words, define each word and talk about why it's important. If you wrote headlines in the cue column, explain what each one means and offer supporting details. After reciting, uncover your notes and look for any important points you missed.

MIND MAPPING

Mind mapping, a system developed by Tony Buzan,[3] can be used in conjunction with the Cornell method to take notes. In some circumstances, you might want to use mind maps exclusively.

To understand mind maps, first review the features of traditional note taking. Outlines (explained in the next section) divide major topics into minor topics, which in turn are subdivided further. They organize information in a sequential, linear way.

The traditional outline reflects only a limited range of brain function—a point that is often made in discussions about "left-brain" and "right-brain" activities. People often use the term *right brain* when referring to creative, pattern-making, visual, intuitive brain activity. They use the term *left brain* when talking about orderly, logical, step-by-step characteristics of thought. Writing teacher Gabrielle Rico uses another metaphor. She refers to the left-brain mode as our "sign mind" (concerned with words) and the right-brain mode as our "design mind" (concerned with visuals).[4] A mind map uses both kinds of brain functions. Mind maps can contain lists and sequences and show relationships. They can also provide a picture of a subject. They work on both verbal and nonverbal levels.

One benefit of mind maps is that they quickly, vividly, and accurately show the relationships between ideas. Also, mind mapping helps you think from general to specific. By choosing a main topic, you focus first on the big picture, then zero in on subordinate details. And by using only key words, you can condense a large subject into a small area on a mind map. You can review more quickly by looking at the key words on a mind map than by reading notes word for word.

Give yourself plenty of room. To create a mind map, use blank paper that measures at least 11 by 17 inches. If that's not available, turn regular notebook paper on its side so that you can take notes in a horizontal (instead of vertical) format. If you use a computer in class to take notes, consider

software that allows you to create digital mind maps that can include graphics, photos, and URL links.

Determine the main concept of the lecture, article, or chapter. As you listen to a lecture or read, figure out the main concept. Write it in the center of the paper and circle it, underline it, or highlight it with color. You can also write the concept in large letters. Record concepts related to the main concept on lines that radiate outward from the center. An alternative is to circle or box in these concepts.

Use key words only. Whenever possible, reduce each concept to a single word per line or circle or box in your mind map. Although this reduction might seem awkward at first, it prompts you to summarize and to condense ideas to their essence. That means fewer words for you to write now and fewer to review when it's time to prepare for tests. (Using shorthand symbols and abbreviations can help.) Key words are usually nouns and verbs that communicate the bulk of the speaker's ideas. Choose words that are rich in associations and that can help you recreate the lecture.

Create links. A single mind map doesn't have to include all of the ideas in a lecture, book, or article. Instead, you can link mind maps. For example, draw a mind map that sums up the five key points in a chapter, and then make a separate, more detailed mind map for each of those key points. Within each mind map, include references to the other mind maps. This technique helps explain and reinforce the relationships among many ideas. Some students pin several mind maps next to one another on a bulletin board or tape them to a wall. This allows for a dramatic—and effective—look at the big picture.

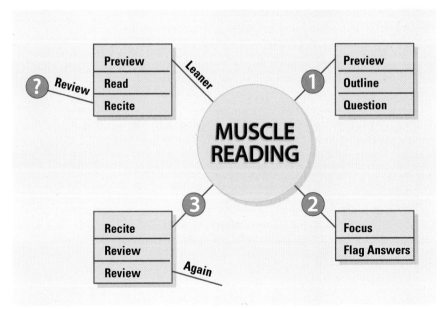

OUTLINING

A traditional outline shows the relationships among major points and supporting ideas. One benefit of taking notes in the outline format is that doing so can totally occupy your attention. You are recording ideas and also organizing them. This process can be an advantage if the material has been presented in a disorganized way. By playing with variations, you can discover the power of outlining to reveal relationships among ideas. Technically, each word, phrase, or sentence that appears in an outline is called a *heading*. Headings are arranged in different levels:

- In the first, or top, level of headings, note the major topics presented in a lecture or reading assignment.

- In the second level of headings, record the key points that relate to each topic in the first-level headings.

- In the third level of headings, record specific facts and details that support or explain each of your second-level headings. Each additional level of subordinate heading supports the ideas in the previous level of heading.

Roman numerals offer one way to illustrate the difference between levels of headings. See the following examples.

First-level heading

Second-level heading   **Third-level heading**

I. Muscle Reading includes 3 phases.
   A. Phase 1: Before you read
      1. Preview
      2. Outline
      3. Question
   B. Phase 2: While you read
      4. Focus
      5. Flag answers
   C. Phase 3: After you read
      6. Recite
      7. Review
      8. Review again

COMBINING FORMATS

Feel free to use different note-taking systems for different subjects and to combine formats. Do what works for you.

Distinguish levels with indentations only:

Muscle Reading includes 3 phases
   Phase 1: Before you read
      Preview

Distinguish levels with bullets and dashes:

MUSCLE READING INCLUDES 3 PHASES
   •Phase 1: Before you read
      – Preview

Distinguish headings by size:

MUSCLE READING INCLUDES 3 PHASES
Phase 1: Before you read
Preview

For example, combine mind maps along with the Cornell method. You can modify the Cornell format by dividing your notepaper in half. Reserve one half for mind maps and the other for linear information such as lists, graphs, and outlines, as well as equations, long explanations, and word-for-word definitions. You can incorporate a mind map into your paragraph-style notes whenever you feel one is appropriate. Minds maps are also useful for summarizing notes taken in the Cornell format.

John Sperry, a teacher at Utah Valley State College, developed a note-taking system that can include all of the formats discussed in this article:

- Fill up a three-ring binder with fresh paper. Open your notebook so that you see two blank pages—one on the left and one on the right. Plan to take notes across this entire two-page spread.

- During class or while reading, write your notes only on the left-hand page. Place a large dash next to each main topic or point. If your instructor skips a step or switches topics unexpectedly, just keep writing.

- Later, use the right-hand page to review and elaborate on the notes that you took earlier. This page is for anything you want. For example, add visuals such as mind maps. Write review questions, headlines, possible test questions, summaries, outlines, mnemonics, or analogies that link new concepts to your current knowledge.

- To keep ideas in sequence, place appropriate numbers on top of the dashes in your notes on the left-hand page. Even if concepts are presented out of order during class, they'll still be numbered correctly in your notes. ■

You're One Click Away...
from seeing more examples of notes in various formats online.

REVIEW

The note-taking process flows

Think of reviewing as an integral part of note taking rather than an added task. To make new information useful, encode it in a way that connects it to your long-term memory. The key is reviewing.

Review within 24 hours. In Chapter 5, when you read the suggestion to review what you've read within 24 hours, you were asked to sound the trumpet. If you have one, get it out and sound it again. This note-taking technique might be the most powerful one you can use. It might save you hours of review time later in the term.

Many students are surprised that they can remember the content of a lecture in the minutes and hours after class. They are even more surprised by how well they can read the sloppiest of notes at that time. Unfortunately, short-term memory deteriorates quickly. The good news is that if you review your notes soon enough, you can move that information from short-term to long-term memory. And you can do it in just a few minutes—often 10 minutes or less.

The sooner you review your notes, the better, especially if the content is difficult. In fact, you can start reviewing during class. When your instructor pauses to set up the overhead display or erase the board, scan your notes. Dot the *i*'s, cross the *t*'s, and write out unclear abbreviations. Another way to use this technique is to get to your next class as quickly as you can. Then use the 4 or 5 minutes before the lecture begins to review the notes you just took in the previous class. If you do not get to your notes immediately after class, you can still benefit by reviewing them later in the day. A review right before you go to sleep can also be valuable.

Think of the day's unreviewed notes as leaky faucets, constantly dripping and losing precious information until you shut them off with a quick review. Remember, it's possible to forget most of the material within 24 hours—unless you review.

Edit your notes. During your first review, fix words that are illegible. Write out abbreviated words that might be unclear to you later. Make sure you can read everything. If you can't read something or don't understand something you *can* read, mark it, and make a note to ask your instructor or another student about it. Check to see that your notes are labeled with the date and class and that the pages are numbered.

Fill in key words in the left-hand column. This task is important if you are to get the full benefit of using the Cornell method. Using the key word principles described earlier in this chapter, go through your notes and write key words or phrases in the left-hand column. These key words will speed up the review process later. As you read your notes, focus on extracting important concepts.

Use your key words as cues to recite. Cover your notes with a blank sheet of paper so that you can see only the key words in the left-hand margin. Take each key word in order, and recite as much as you can about the point. Then uncover your notes and look for any important points you missed.

Conduct short weekly review periods. Once a week, review all of your notes again. These review sessions don't need to take a lot of time. Even a 20-minute weekly review period is valuable. Some students find that a weekend review—say, on Sunday afternoon—helps them stay in continuous touch with the material. Scheduling regular review sessions on your calendar helps develop the habit.

As you review, step back to see the larger picture. In addition to reciting or repeating the material to yourself, ask questions about it: Does this relate to my goals? How does this compare to information I already know, in this field or another? Will I be tested on this material? What will I do with this material? How can I associate it with something that deeply interests me?

Consider typing your notes. Some students type up their handwritten notes on the computer. The argument for doing so is threefold. First, typed notes are easier to read. Second, they take up less space. Third, the process of typing them forces you to review the material.

Another alternative is to bypass handwriting altogether and take notes in class on a laptop. This solution has a potential drawback, though: Computer errors can wipe out your notes files. If you like using this method of taking notes, save your files frequently, and back up your work onto a jump drive, external hard drive, or online backup service.

Create summaries. Mind mapping is an excellent way to summarize large sections of your course notes or reading assignments. Create one map that shows all the main topics you want to remember. Then create another map about each main topic. After drawing your maps, look at your original notes, and fill in anything you missed. This system is fun and quick.

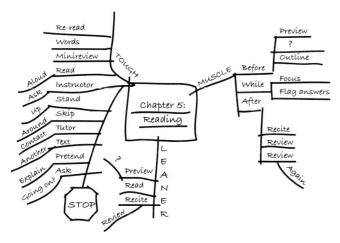

While you're reviewing, evaluate your notes. Review sessions are excellent times to look beyond the *content* of your notes and reflect on your note-taking *process*. Remember these common goals of taking notes in the first place:

- *Reduce* course content to its essentials.

- *Organize* the content.

- Demonstrate that you *understand* the content.

If your notes consistently fall short on one of these points, then review this chapter for a strategy that can help.

Hermann Ebbinghaus, a psychologist, discovered that most forgetting occurs during the first 9 hours after we learn new information—especially during the first hour. Use the strategies in this chapter to prevent forgetting and reverse this "Ebbinghaus curve." ■

Another option is to create a "cheat sheet." There's only one guideline: Fit all your review notes on a single sheet of paper. Use any note-taking format that you want—mind map, outline, Cornell method, or a combination of all of them. The beauty of this technique is that it forces you to pick out main ideas and key details. There's not enough room for anything else!

If you're feeling adventurous, create your cheat sheet on a single index card. Start with the larger sizes (5 × 7 or 4 × 6) and then work down to a 3 × 5 card.

Some instructors might let you use a summary sheet during an exam. But even if you can't use it, you'll benefit from creating one while you study for the test. Summarizing is a powerful way to review.

You're One Click Away...
from finding more strategies for reviewing online.

JOURNAL **ENTRY 13** *Discovery Statement*

Reflect on your review habits

Respond to the following statements by checking "Always," "Often," "Sometimes," "Seldom," or "Never" after each.

1. I review my notes immediately after class.

   _____ Always _____ Often _____ Sometimes _____ Seldom _____ Never

2. I conduct weekly reviews of my notes.

   _____ Always _____ Often _____ Sometimes _____ Seldom _____ Never

3. I make summary sheets of my notes.

   _____ Always _____ Often _____ Sometimes _____ Seldom _____ Never

4. I edit my notes within 24 hours.

   _____ Always _____ Often _____ Sometimes _____ Seldom _____ Never

5. Before class, I conduct a brief review of the notes I took in the previous class.

   _____ Always _____ Often _____ Sometimes _____ Seldom _____ Never

Create more VALUE *from your* NOTES

Effective notes are living documents—words and images that gain clarity as your understanding of a subject deepens. Notes that are not used continuously throughout a term can quickly become inaccurate—or even useless. Instead, you can create notes that are clear enough for you to understand and useful enough to consult for weeks, months, or years to come.

Observing, recording, and reviewing will give you a great start. In addition, experiment with the following strategies.

EDIT TO REDUCE, ORGANIZE, AND UNDERSTAND

One suggested strategy for reviewing is to evaluate your notes. This means reflecting on how well you reduced, organized, and understood the course content. The table below reviews strategies for meeting each of these goals.

As you evaluate, remember to avoid vague and absolute judgments such as *I'm a lousy note taker*. Instead, be specific and nonjudgmental. Focus on ways to improve.

RECREATE YOUR NOTES IN A NEW FORMAT

The goal of *taking* notes in the first place is to condense a lecture or discussion to its essence, leaving you with a compact set of ideas and information to study. A goal of *revising* your notes is to reflect on the subject matter and bring your insights into clear focus.

Sometimes it helps to get a different perspective on the material. You can do that by recreating your notes in a new format. If you took notes in Cornell format, convert sections to outline format. If your original notes are outlined, then convert sections to mind maps or concept maps. Use all these formats at different points in your notes for a course, or invent new formats of your own.

The benefit of playing with all these formats is that they engage your mind in different ways. Taking notes in Cornell format can help you get a handle on details—key terms and facts. Outlines force you to pay attention to the way that material is structured. And maps are visual devices that help you see connections between many topics at once. Each format yields a different cross section of the subject matter. And each format deepens your understanding.

EXPAND ON YOUR NOTES WITH A PERSONAL JOURNAL

Here is a chance for you to stretch out mentally. Use your personal journal to put class notes in a larger perspective. Reflect on the significance of your courses. Mine your own experiences for examples of the ideas you're learning about. Speculate about how you might apply what you're learning in class.

Goal	Strategies
Reduce course content to its essentials.	• Use meaningful abbreviations. • Use key words. • Focus on major topics, terms, and points; record only key details.
Clarify the organization of course content.	• Use concept maps, mind maps, and other visual devices to highlight key ideas and their relationships. • Use outlines with headings that clearly distinguish between different levels of ideas. • Create graphic cues to aid review: underline or capitalize key words and phrases; indent key passages or record them in a different color; use simple lists and numbered lists.
Reveal understanding of the course content.	• When possible, use your own words rather than the lecturer's. • Take notes in several different formats. • Use key words, but avoid condensing material so much that it becomes impossible to decode. • Record essential points in complete sentences.

A simple way to start a journal and gradually expand its content is to make lists. Experiment with many kinds of lists. For example:

- List new words and their definitions.
- List the top five ideas that you want to remember from your classes or assigned readings.
- List the five most influential people in your life and what they taught you.
- List the three most important things you want to teach your children.
- List your favorite quotations, including notable things that you and your friends say.

Also imagine that you're sitting face to face with the author of your textbook or a historical figure that you're studying. Write what you would say to this person. Argue. Debate. Note questions you want to ask this person; later, pose these questions in class. In each case, you will build your skills at creative and critical thinking. ■

Turn POWERPOINTS into POWERFUL NOTES

PowerPoint presentations are common. They can also be lethal for students who want to master course content or those who simply want to stay awake.

Some students stop taking notes during a PowerPoint presentation. This choice can be hazardous to your academic health for three major reasons:

- *PowerPoint presentations don't include everything.* Instructors and other speakers use PowerPoint to organize their presentations. Topics covered in the slides make up an outline of what your instructor considers important. Slides are created to flag the main points and signal transitions between points. However, speakers usually add examples and explanations that don't appear on the slides. In addition, slides will not include any material from class discussion, including any answers that the instructor gives in response to questions.

- *You stop learning.* Taking notes forces you to capture ideas and information in your own words. Also, the act of writing things down helps you remember the material. If you stop writing and let your attention drift, you can quickly get lost.

- *You end up with major gaps in your notes.* When it's time to review your notes, you'll find that material from PowerPoint presentations is missing. This can be a major pain at exam time.

To create value from PowerPoint presentations, take notes on them. Continue to observe, record, and review. See PowerPoint as a way to *guide* rather than to *replace* your own note taking. Even the slickest, smartest presentation is no substitute for your own thinking.

Experiment with the following suggestions. They include ideas about what to do before, during, and after a PowerPoint presentation.

BEFORE THE PRESENTATION

Sometimes instructors make PowerPoint slides available before a lecture. If you have computer access, download these files. Scan the slides, just as you would preview a reading assignment.

Consider printing out the slides and bringing them along to class. (If you own a copy of PowerPoint, then choose the "handouts" option when printing. This will save paper and ink.) You can take notes directly on the pages that you print out as in the figure below. Be sure to add the slide numbers if they are missing.

If you use a laptop computer for taking notes during class, then you might not want to bother with printing. Just open up the PowerPoint file and type your notes in the window that appears at the bottom of each slide. After class, you can print out the slides in note view. This will show the original slides plus any text that you added.

DURING THE PRESENTATION

In many cases, PowerPoint slides are presented visually by the instructor *only during class*. The slides are not provided as handouts, and they are not available online for students to print out.

This makes it even more important to take effective notes in class. Capture the main points and key details as you normally would. Use your preferred note-taking strategies.

Be selective in what you write down. Determine what kind of material is on each slide. Stay alert for new topics, main points, and important details. Taking too many notes makes it hard to keep up with a speaker and separate main points from minor details.

In any case, go *beyond* the slides. Record valuable questions and answers that come up during a discussion, even if they are not a planned part of the presentation.

AFTER THE PRESENTATION

If you printed out slides before class and took notes on those pages, then find a way to integrate them with the rest of your notes. For example, add references in your notebook to specific slides. Or create summary notes that include the major topics and points from readings, class meetings, and PowerPoint presentations.

Printouts of slides can provide review tools. Use them as cues to recite. Cover up your notes so that only the main image or words on each slide are visible. See whether you can remember what else appears on the slide, along with the key points from any notes you added.

Also consider "editing" the presentation. If you have the PowerPoint file on your computer, make another copy of it. Open up this copy, and see whether you can condense the presentation. Cut slides that don't include anything you want to remember. Also rearrange slides so that the order makes more sense to you. Remember that you can open up the original file later if you want to see exactly what your instructor presented. ■

6

How Muscle Reading Works

▸ Phase 1 – Before You Read
  ▪ **P**ry **O**ut **Q**uestions

▸ Phase 2 – While You Read
  ▪ **F**ocus and **F**lag **A**nswers

▸ Phase 3 – After You Read
  ▪ **R**ecite, **R**eview, and **R**eview Again

When your instructor talks QUICKLY

Take more time to prepare for class. Familiarity with a subject increases your ability to pick up on key points. If an instructor lectures quickly or is difficult to understand, conduct a thorough preview of the material to be covered.

Be willing to make choices. Focus your attention on key points. Instead of trying to write everything down, choose what you think is important. Occasionally, you will make a less than perfect choice or even neglect an important point. Worse things could happen. Stay with the lecture, write down key words, and revise your notes immediately after class.

Exchange photocopies of notes with classmates. Your fellow students might write down something you missed. At the same time, your notes might help them. Exchanging photocopies can fill in the gaps.

Leave large empty spaces in your notes. Leave plenty of room for filling in information you missed. Use a symbol that signals you've missed something, so you can remember to come back to it.

See the instructor after class. Take your class notes with you, and show the instructor what you missed.

Use an audio recorder. Recording a lecture gives you a chance to hear it again whenever you choose. Some audio recording software allows you to vary the speed of the recording. With this feature, you can perform magic and actually slow down the instructor's speech.

Before class, take notes on your reading assignment. You can take detailed notes on the text before class. Leave plenty of blank space. Take these notes with you to class, and simply add your lecture notes to them.

Go to the lecture again. Many classes are taught in multiple sections. That gives you the chance to hear a lecture at least twice—once in your regular class and again in another section of the class.

Learn shorthand. Some note-taking systems, known as shorthand, are specifically designed for getting ideas down fast. Books and courses are available to help you learn these systems. You can also devise your own shorthand method by inventing one- or two-letter symbols for common words and phrases.

Ask questions—even if you're totally lost. Many instructors allow a question session. This is the time to ask about the points you missed.

At times you might feel so lost that you can't even formulate a question. That's okay. One option is to report this fact to the instructor. He can often guide you to a clear question. Another option is to ask a related question. Doing so might lead you to the question you really wanted to ask.

Ask the instructor to slow down. This solution is the most obvious. If asking the instructor to slow down doesn't work, ask her to repeat what you missed. ■

✓ CRITICAL THINKING EXERCISE 17

Taking notes under pressure

With note taking, as with other skills, the more you practice, the better you become. You can use TV programs and videos to practice listening for key words, writing quickly, focusing your attention, and reviewing. Programs that feature speeches and panel discussions work well for this purpose. So do documentary films.

The next time you watch such a program, use pen and paper to jot down key words and information. If you fall behind, relax. Just leave a space in your notes and return your attention to the program. If a program includes commercial breaks, use them to review and revise your notes.

At the end of the program, spend 5 minutes reviewing all of your notes. Create a mind map based on your notes. Then sum up the main points of the program for a friend.

This exercise will help you develop an ear for key words. Because you can't ask questions or request that speakers slow down, you train yourself to stay totally in the moment.

Don't be discouraged if you miss a lot the first time around. Do this exercise several times, and observe how your mind works.

Another option is to record a program and then take notes. You can stop the recording at any point to review what you've written.

Ask a classmate to do this exercise with you. Compare your notes and look for any points that either of you missed.

Taking notes
WHILE READING

Taking notes while reading requires the same skills that apply to taking class notes: observing, recording, and reviewing. Use these skills to take notes for review and for research.

REVIEW NOTES

Review notes will look like the notes you take in class. Take review notes when you want more detailed notes than writing in the margin of your text allows. You might want to single out a particularly difficult section of a text and make separate notes. Or make summaries of overlapping lecture and text material. Because you can't underline or make notes in library books, these sources will require separate notes, too. To take more effective review notes, use the following suggestions.

Set priorities. Single out a particularly difficult section of a text and make separate notes. Or make summaries of overlapping lecture and text material.

Use a variety of formats. Translate text into Cornell notes, mind maps, or outlines. Combine these formats to create your own. Translate diagrams, charts, and other visual elements into words. Then reverse the process by translating straight text into visual elements.

However, don't let the creation of formats get in your way. Even a simple list of key points and examples can become a powerful review tool. Another option is to close your book and just start writing. Write quickly about what you intend to remember from the text, and don't worry about following any format.

Condense a passage to key quotes. Authors embed their essential ideas in key sentences. As you read, continually ask yourself, "What's the point?" Then see whether you can point to a specific sentence on the page to answer your question. Look especially at headings, subheadings, and topic sentences of paragraphs. Write these key sentences word for word in your notes, and put them within quotation marks. Copy as few sentences as you can and still retain the core meaning of the passage.

Condense by paraphrasing. Pretend that you have to summarize a chapter, article, or book on a postcard. Limit yourself to a single paragraph—or a single sentence—and use your own words. This is a great way to test your understanding of the material.

Take a cue from the table of contents. Look at the table of contents in your book. Write each major heading on a piece of paper, or key those headings into a word-processing file on your computer. Include page numbers. Next, see whether you can improve on the table of contents. Substitute your own headings for those that appear in the book. Turn single words or phrases into complete sentences, and use words that are meaningful to you.

Adapt to special cases. The style of your notes can vary according to the nature of the reading material. If you are assigned a short story or poem, for example, then read the entire work once without taking any notes. On your first reading, simply enjoy the piece. When you finish, write down your immediate impressions. Then go over the piece again. Make brief notes on characters, images, symbols, settings, plot, point of view, or other aspects of the work.

Note key concepts in math and science. When you read mathematical, scientific, or other technical materials, copy important formulas or equations. Recreate important diagrams, and draw your own visual representations of concepts. Also write down data that might appear on an exam.

RESEARCH NOTES

Take research notes when preparing to write a paper or deliver a speech. One traditional method of research is to take notes on index cards. You write *one* idea, fact, or quotation per card, along with a note about the source (where you found it). The advantage of limiting each card to one item is that you can easily arrange cards according to the sequence of ideas in your outline. If you change your outline, no problem. Just resort your cards.

Taking notes on a computer offers the same flexibility as index cards. Just include one idea, fact, or quotation per paragraph along with the source. Think of each paragraph as a separate "card." When you're ready to create the first draft of your paper or presentation, just move paragraphs around so that they fit your outline.

6

Include your sources. No matter whether you use cards or a computer, be sure to *include a source for each note that you take.*

Say, for example, that you find a useful quotation from a book. You want to include that quotation in your paper. Copy the quotation word for word onto a card, or key the quotation into a computer file. Along with the quotation, note the book's author, title, date and place of publication, and publisher. You'll need such information later when you create a formal list of your sources—a bibliography, or a list of endnotes or footnotes.

For guidelines on what information to record about each type of source, see the sidebar to this article as a place to start. Your instructors might have different preferences, so ask them for guidance as well.

Note this information about
YOUR SOURCES

Following are checklists of the information to record about various types of sources. Whenever possible, print out or make photocopies of each source. For books, include a copy of the title page and copyright page, both of which are found in the front matter. For magazines and scholarly journals, copy the table of contents.

For each *book* you consult, record the following:

- Author
- Editor (if listed)
- Translator (if listed)
- Edition number (if listed)
- Full title, including the subtitle
- Name and location of the publisher
- Copyright date
- Page numbers for passages that you quote, summarize, or paraphrase

For each *article* you consult, record the following:

- Author
- Editor (if listed)
- Translator (if listed)
- Full title, including the subtitle
- Name of the periodical
- Volume number
- Issue number
- Issue date
- Page numbers for passages that you quote, summarize, or paraphrase

For each *computer-based source* you consult (CD-ROMs and Internet documents), record the following:

- Author
- Editor (if listed)
- Translator (if listed)
- Full title of the page or article, including the subtitle
- Name of the organization that posted the site or published the CD-ROM
- Dates when the page or other document was published and revised
- Date when you accessed the source
- URL for Web pages (the uniform resource locator, or Web site address, which often starts with http://)
- Version number (for CD-ROMs)
- Volume, issue number, and date for online journals

Note: Computer-based sources may not list all the above information. For Web pages, at a minimum record the date you accessed the source and the URL.

For each *interview* you conduct, record the following:

- Name of the person you interviewed
- Professional title of the person you interviewed
- Contact information for the person you interviewed—mailing address, phone number, e-mail address
- Date of the interview

Avoid plagiarism. When people take material from a source and fail to acknowledge that source, they are committing plagiarism. Even when plagiarism is accidental, the consequences can be harsh. For essential information on this topic, see "Academic integrity: Avoid plagiarism" on page 41.

Many cases of plagiarism occur during the process of taking research notes. To prevent this problem, remember that a major goal of taking research notes is to *clearly separate your own words and images from words and images created by someone else*. To meet this goal, develop the following habits:

- If you take a direct quote from one of your sources, then enclose those words in quotation marks and note information about that source.

- If you take an image (photo, illustration, chart, or diagram) from one of your sources, then note information about that source.

- If you summarize or paraphrase *a specific passage* from one of your sources, then use your own words and note information about that source.

> The bottom line: Always present your own work—not materials that have been created or revised by someone else. If you're ever in doubt about what to do, then take the safest course: Cite a source. Give credit where credit is due.

- If your notes include any idea that is closely identified with a particular person, then note information about the source.

- When you include one of your own ideas in your notes, then simply note the source as "me."

If you're taking notes on a computer and using Internet sources, be especially careful to avoid plagiarism. When you copy text or images from a Web site, separate those notes from your own ideas. Use a different font for copied material, or enclose it in quotation marks.

You do *not* need to note a source for these:

- Facts that are considered common knowledge ("The history of the twentieth century includes two world wars").

- Facts that can be easily verified ("The United States Constitution includes a group of amendments known as the Bill of Rights").

- Your own opinion ("Hip-hop artists are the most important poets of our age").

The bottom line: Always present your own work—not materials that have been created or revised by someone else. If you're ever in doubt about what to do, then take the safest course: Cite a source. Give credit where credit is due.

Reflect on your notes. Schedule time to review all the information and ideas that your research has produced. By allowing time for rereading and reflecting on all the notes you've taken, you create the conditions for genuine understanding.

Start by summarizing major points of view on your topic. Note points of agreement and disagreement among your sources.

Also see whether you can find direct answers to the questions that you had when you started researching. These answers could become headings in your paper.

Look for connections in your material, including ideas, facts, and examples that occur in several sources. Also look for connections between your research and your life—ideas that you can verify based on personal experience. ■

6

You're One Click Away...
from finding examples of effective research and review notes online.

Get to the BONES of your BOOK with CONCEPT MAPS

Concept mapping, pioneered by Joseph Novak and D. Bob Gowin, is a tool to make major ideas in a book leap off the page.[5] In creating a concept map, you reduce an author's message to its essence—its bare bones. Concept maps can also be used to display the organization of lectures and discussions.

Concepts and links are the building blocks of knowledge. A *concept* is a name for a group of related things or ideas. *Links* are words or phrases that describe the relationship between concepts. Consider the following paragraph:

Muscle Reading consists of three phases. Phase 1 includes tasks to complete before reading. Phase 2 tasks take place during reading. Finally, Phase 3 includes tasks to complete after reading.

In this paragraph, examples of concepts are Muscle Reading, reading, phases, tasks, Phase 1, Phase 2, and Phase 3. Links include consists of, includes, before, during, and after.

To create a concept map, list concepts and then arrange them in a meaningful order from general to specific. Then fill in the links between concepts, forming meaningful statements.

Concept mapping promotes critical thinking. It alerts you to missing concepts or faulty links between concepts. In addition, concept mapping mirrors the way that your brain learns—that is, by linking new concepts to concepts that you already know.

To create a concept map, use the following steps:

1. **List the key concepts in the text.** Aim to express each concept in three words or less. Most concept words are nouns, including terms and proper names. At this point, you can list the concepts in any order.

2. **Rank the concepts so that they flow from general to specific.** On a large sheet of paper, write the main concept at the top of the page. Place the most specific concepts near the bottom. Arrange the rest of the concepts in appropriate positions throughout the middle of the page. Circle each concept.

3. **Draw lines that connect the concepts.** On these connecting lines, add words that describe the relationship between the concepts. Again, limit yourself to the fewest words needed to make an accurate link—three words or less. Linking words are often verbs, verb phrases, or prepositions.

4. **Finally, review your map.** Look for any concepts that are repeated in several places on the map. You can avoid these repetitions by adding more links between concepts. ■

You're One Click Away...
from seeing more examples of concept maps online.

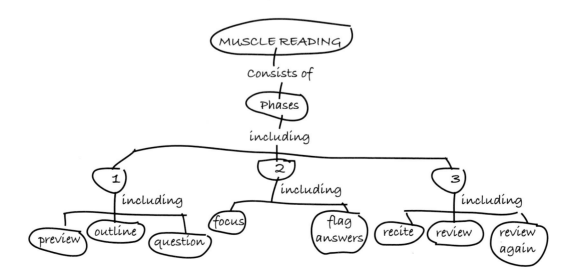

Taking *effective notes* for *online coursework*

If you are taking an online course, or a course that is heavily supported by online materials, then get ready for new challenges to note taking. You can use a variety of strategies to succeed.

Do a trial run with technology. Verify your access to course Web sites, including online tutorials, PowerPoint presentations, readings, quizzes, tests, assignments, bulletin boards, and chat rooms. Ask your instructors for Web site addresses, e-mail addresses, and passwords. Work out any bugs when you start the course and well before that first assignment is due.

If you're planning to use a computer lab on campus, find one that meets course requirements. Remember that on-campus computer labs may not allow you to install all the software needed to access Web sites for your courses or textbooks.

Develop a contingency plan. Murphy's Law of Computer Crashes states that technology tends to break down at the moment of greatest inconvenience. You might not believe this piece of folklore, but it's still wise to prepare for it:

- Find a "technology buddy" in each of your classes—someone who can contact the instructor if you lose Internet access or experience other computer problems.

- Every day, make backup copies of files created for your courses.

- Keep extra printer supplies—paper and toner or ink cartridges—on hand at all times. Don't run out of necessary supplies on the day a paper is due.

Get actively involved with the course. Your online course will include a page that lists homework assignments and test dates. That's only the beginning. Look for ways to engage with the material by submitting questions, completing assignments, and interacting with the instructor and other students.

Take notes on course material. You can print out anything that appears on a computer screen. This includes online course materials—articles, books, manuscripts, e-mail messages, chat room sessions, and more.

The potential problem is that you might skip the note-taking process altogether. ("I can just print out everything!") You would then miss the chance to internalize a new idea by restating it in your own words—a principal benefit of note taking. Result: Material passes from computer to printer without ever intersecting with your brain.

To prevent this problem, take notes in Cornell, mind map, concept map, or outline format. Write Discovery and Intention Statements to capture key insights from the materials and next actions to take. Also talk about what you're learning. Recite key points out loud, and discuss what you find online with other students.

© iStockphoto.com/RichVintage

Of course, it's fine to print out online material. If you do, treat your printouts like mini-textbooks. Apply the steps of Muscle Reading as explained in Chapter 5.

Another potential problem with online courses is the physical absence of the teacher. In a classroom, you get lots of visual and verbal clues to what kinds of questions will appear on a test. Those clues are often missing from an online course, which means that they could be missing from your notes. Ask your online instructor about what material she considers to be most important.

Set up folders and files for easy reference. Create a separate folder for each class on your computer's hard drive. Give each folder a meaningful name, such as *biology—spring2009*. Place all files related to a course in the appropriate folder. Doing this can save you from one of the main technology-related time wasters: searching for lost files.

Also name individual files with care. Avoid changing extensions that identify different types of files, such as .ppt for PowerPoint presentations or .pdf for files in the Adobe Reader portable document format. Changing extensions might lead to problems when you're looking for files later or sharing them with other users.

Take responsibility. If you register for an online course with no class meetings, you might miss the motivating presence of an instructor and classmates. Instead, manufacture your own motivation. Be clear about what you'll gain by doing well in the course. Relate course content to your major and career goals. Don't wait to be contacted by your classmates and instructor. Initiate that contact on your own.

Ask for help. If you feel confused about anything you're learning online, ask for help right away. This is especially important when you don't see the instructor face-to-face in class. Some students simply drop online courses rather than seek help. E-mail or call the instructor before you make that choice. If the instructor is on campus, you might be able to arrange for a meeting during office hours.

Manage time and tasks carefully. Courses that take place mostly or totally online can become invisible in your weekly academic schedule. This reinforces the temptation to put off dealing with these courses until late in the term.

Avoid this mistake! Consider the real possibility that an online course can take *more* time than a traditional, face-to-face lecture class. Online courses tend to embrace lots of activities—sending and receiving e-mails, joining discussion forums, commenting on blog posts, and more. New content might appear every day. One key to keeping up with the course is frequent contact and careful time management:

- Early in the term, create a detailed schedule for online courses. In your calendar, list a due date for each assignment. Break big assignments into smaller steps, and schedule a due date for each step.

- Schedule times in your calendar to complete online course work. Give these scheduled sessions the same priority as regular classroom meetings. At these times, check for online announcements relating to assignments, tests, and other course events. Check for course-related e-mails daily.

- If the class includes discussion forums, check those daily as well. Look for new posts and add your replies. The point of these tools is to create a lively conversation that starts early and continues throughout the term.

- -

Consider the real possibility that an online course can take *more* time than a traditional, face-to-face lecture class. Online courses tend to embrace lots of activities—sending and receiving e-mails, joining discussion forums, commenting on blog posts, and more.

- -

- When you receive an online assignment, e-mail any questions immediately. If you want to meet with an instructor in person, request an appointment several days in advance.

- Give online instructors plenty of time to respond. They are not always online. Many online instructors have traditional courses to teach, along with administration and research duties.

- Download or print out online course materials as soon as they're posted on the class Web site. These materials might not be available later in the term.

- If possible, submit online assignments early. Staying ahead of the game will help you avoid an all-nighter at the computer during finals week.

Find tools that help with online courses. BlackBoard and other portals for online courses offer tools to help you access the content. See whether there are any created specifically for your class.

These tools might include "apps"—software programs designed to run on smart phones, iPods, iPads, and similar devices. Most apps have specific, limited features. They're designed to just do one or two things well. Look for apps that allow you to manage to-do lists, maintain a calendar, create flash cards, take notes, make voice recordings, read ebooks, and listen to audio books.

Many apps are free. Others cost just a few dollars or come in trial versions that you can use for free.

Focus your attention. Some students are used to visiting Web sites while watching television, listening to loud music, or using instant messaging software. When applied to online learning, these habits can reduce your learning and endanger your grades. To succeed with technology, turn off the television, quit online chat sessions, and turn down the music. Whenever you go online, stay in charge of your attention.

Ask for feedback. To get the most from online learning, request feedback from your instructor via e-mail. When appropriate, also ask for conferences by phone or in person.

Sharing files offers another source of feedback. For example, Microsoft Word has a Track Changes feature that allows other people to insert comments into your documents and make suggested revisions. These edits are highlighted on the screen. Use such tools to get feedback on your writing from instructors and peers.

Note: Be sure to check with your instructors to see how they want students enrolled in their online courses to address and label their e-mails. Many teachers ask their online students to use a standard format for the subject area so they can quickly recognize e-mails from them.

Contact other students. Make personal contact with at least one other student in each of your classes—especially classes that involve lots of online course work. Create study groups to share notes, quiz each other, critique papers, and do other cooperative learning tasks. This kind of support can help you succeed as an online learner. ■

masterstudentprofile

Faye Wattleton

(1943–) President of the Planned Parenthood Federation of America from 1978 until 1992. She is currently the founder and president of the Center for the Advancement of Women.

I don't ever recall not wanting to be a nurse, or not saying I wanted to be a nurse. This was, in part, certainly my mother's influence. She wanted me to be a missionary nurse. It wasn't sufficient just to be a nurse, I had to commit to a religious cause as well. Missionary nurses work in church hospitals, in Africa and all over the world. I suspect this was suggested to me before I even understood the power of suggestion, and I always grew up saying I was going to be a nurse. I earned two degrees in nursing, but never practiced as a nurse. In the broadest sense of the word, you can say I have nursed all the time, but not in the technical sense. After undergraduate school, I taught nursing for two years. Then I went to graduate school at Columbia University and earned my master's degree. Following that I moved to Dayton, Ohio, to work in a public health department. There, I was asked to join the board of the local Planned Parenthood. Two years later, I became executive director of the local chapter. Then, seven years later, I became the national president of the organization.

I'm sure the suggestion to become a nurse was colored by the limitation on women's options in those years. Women were nurses, social workers, or teachers. I don't ever remember being explicitly told, "Oh, you can't be that because you're a girl." It just was. . . . It was never conveyed to me there were any limitations on what I could do and what my work could be, although I'm sure the idea that I be a nurse, as opposed to a doctor or something else, was due to the limitations on the role of women at that time.

Even though we lived in a working class community, there wasn't as much integration, so blacks of all economic levels lived in the black community. My father was a laborer, and my mother was a seamstress, but I went to nursing school with our doctor's son. The doctor's family lived a few blocks from us. This was before the Civil Rights movement, and before blacks moved into white or integrated neighborhoods. That experience also played a very important role in my sense of who I am ethnically, as well as what the possibilities were for me. We lived next door to professionals, as well as the housepainter who had the most beautiful house on the block because he painted and decorated it beautifully.

I try to find the best people I can in various specialties so I can learn from them. I want people who are better than me in their specialties, maybe not better than me in running the whole shebang, but better than me in the communications field or legal field. Stitching everything together to make it work as a [piece of] machinery is, for me, the challenge and the excitement.

I try very hard to listen. If there is conflict, I want to hear what the other side says. . . . As long as I feel there is mutual respect, it does not hurt me to listen to someone with whom I am really in conflict, to hear what they are saying even if I disagree. If it's a conflict I really want to resolve, I try to find ways we can come to mutual points of agreement. One thing I always believe is if you talk long enough you can almost always reach a resolution. Just the process of talking has a de-fanging influence. I have great faith in human beings finding ways to relate if they have enough contact with each other.

6

FAYE WATTLETON ... is willing to participate.

YOU ... can participate by listening with respect, even to people who disagree with you.

Excerpt from Lucinda Watson, *How They Achieved: Stories of Personal Achievement and Business Success,* © 2001, pp. 208–212, John Wiley & Sons. Reproduced with permission of John Wiley & Sons, Inc.

You're One Click Away...
from learning more about Faye Wattleton online at the Master Student Profiles. You can also visit the Master Student Hall of Fame to learn about other master students.

FIVE Cs
FOR YOUR CAREER

CHARACTER • CRITICAL THINKING • CREATIVE THINKING • COLLABORATION • COMMUNICATION

Taking notes at work allows you to apply many of the transferable skills covered in this book—including the five Cs. Remember that the ability to take clear and concise notes is one way to make yourself valuable to an employer. It might even help you get promoted.

Connect note taking to character through the qualities of a Master Student. The way that you take notes at school and work says a lot about who you are. For example, sitting front and center in class tells your instructor that you're engaged and willing to participate. Rewriting your notes into a different format demonstrates that you can organize and sort, and that you're willing to change. Making the effort to listen fully when you disagree with an instructor or coworker shows that you are willing to suspend judgment.

Taking notes calls for split-second decisions about what's important to remember. In addition, you monitor your emotional responses and stay physically active through the act of writing. Effective note taking engages your mind, emotions, and body all at once.

Think creatively by experimenting with formats. During meetings, experiment with Cornell format notes, mind mapping, outlining, concept mapping, or some combination of these. Feel free to add boldface headings, charts, tables, graphs, and other visuals that make the main ideas stand out.

Think critically about your notes. Before meetings, complete background reading on the topics to be discussed, including minutes from relevant meetings in the past. Doing this sets the stage for taking better notes in upcoming meetings. It's easier to make sense of what people say when you already know something about the meeting topics.

When taking notes during fast-paced meetings and conference calls, use suggestions from the article "When your instructor talks *quickly*" in this chapter. Focus on the main points and major details. Immediately after the call or meeting, review and edit your notes.

After meetings, review the notes you took. Edit and rewrite your notes for clarity and accuracy. If you took handwritten notes, consider entering them into a computer file.

If you're taking notes to distribute to coworkers, they will appreciate it if you get to the point and keep paragraphs short.

Use notes to promote collaboration. Take meeting notes in a way that helps your team members move projects to completion. Focus on the following topics:

Attendance. In many organizations, people expect meeting notes to include a list of attendees. For large meetings, see if you can get an advance list of the people who are expected to attend. Bring this to the meeting and check off peoples' names as they enter the room. Along with your list of attendees, include the name of your department, the date, the time, and the name of the person who led the meeting.

Agenda. Think of the agenda as a road map—a way to keep the discussion on track. Skilled planners often put an agenda in writing and distribute it in advance of a meeting. Use this agenda while you take notes.

Agreements. The purpose of most meetings is to reach an agreement about something—a policy, project, or plan. Focus on capturing the details about each agreement.

Actions. During meetings, people often commit to take some type of action in the future. Record each follow-up action and who agreed to do it.

Follow-up action is often a make-or-break point for project teams. One mark of exceptional teams is that people make agreements about what they will do—and then keep those agreements.

You can set a powerful example. Ask whether any of the points you included in your notes call for follow-up action on your part. Highlight such items in your notes. Then add them to your calendar or to-do list and follow through.

Take notes for clear communication. Your employer may have specific guidelines for taking meeting notes. Ask your supervisor about this. Note that in some cases—such as minutes taken during a board of directors meeting—notes may function as legal documents reviewed by the IRS or another independent auditor.

Now, make a personal commitment to developing the five Cs. Take another look at the Discovery Wheel in Chapter 2—especially the sections labeled Character, Creative and Critical Thinking, Communicating, and Collaborating. Take a snapshot of your current skills in these four areas after reading and doing this chapter.

DISCOVERY

My scores on the "Five C" sections of the Discovery Wheel were:	As of today, I would give myself the following scores in these areas:	At the end of this course, I would like my scores in these areas to be:
Character _____	Character _____	Character _____
Creative & Critical Thinking _____	Creative & Critical Thinking _____	Creative & Critical Thinking _____
Communicating _____	Communicating _____	Communicating _____
Collaborating _____	Collaborating _____	Collaborating _____

Next, choose your favorite note-taking technique and consider how it could enhance your skill at least one of the five Cs.

I discovered that my favorite technique for taking notes is . . .

_____

_____

_____

_____

I can use this technique to become a more effective thinker, communicator, or collaborator by . . .

_____

_____

_____

_____

INTENTION
To use this technique, I intend to . . .

_____

_____

_____

_____

NEXT ACTION
The specific action I will take is . . .

_____

_____

_____

_____

6

CHAPTER 6 QUIZ

Name _____

Date _____

1. Define the word *responsibility* as it is used in the "Power Process: I create it all."

   Responsibility is "response-ability"—the ability to choose a response to any event. You can choose your response to any event, even when the event itself is beyond your control. (*Power Process: I create it all*, page 160)

2. What are the three major parts of effective note taking as explained in this chapter? Summarize each step in one sentence.

   List each of the following and describe in a sentence (answers will vary): (1) Observe—notice spoken or written words. (2) Record—take notes. (3) Review—reread notes frequently. (*The note-taking process flows*, page 161)

3. According to the text, neat handwriting and a knowledge of outlining are the only requirements for effective notes. True or false? Explain your answer.

   False. Neat handwriting and knowing how to outline are useful, but not requirements. (*The note-taking process flows*, page 161)

4. What are some advantages of sitting in the front and center of the classroom?

   Possible advantages to sitting front and center in a lecture include the following (answers will vary): The closer you sit to the lecturer, the harder it is to fall asleep. The closer you sit to the front, the fewer interesting or distracting classmates between you and the instructor there are to watch. Material on the board is easier to read from up front. The instructor can see you more easily when you have a question. A professor who sounds boring from the back of the room might sound more interesting if you're closer. Sitting up front is a way to commit yourself to getting what you want out of your education. When you sit in front, you are declaring your willingness to take a risk and participate. (*Observe: The note-taking process flows*, page 162)

5. Describe a way to apply the "Power Process: Be here now" to the job of taking notes in class.

   (Answers will vary.) When you discover yourself slipping into fantasyland, feel the weight of your pen in your hand. Notice how your notes look. Paying attention to the act of writing can bring you back to the here and now. (*Observe: The note-taking process flows*, page 162)

6. Instructors sometimes give clues that the material they are presenting is important. List at least three of these clues.

   List at least three of the following: Be alert to repetition. Listen for introductory, concluding, and transitional words and phrases. Watch the board or PowerPoint presentation. Watch the instructor's eyes. Highlight the obvious clues. Notice the instructor's interest level. (*Observe: The note-taking process flows*, page 162)

7. Postponing judgment while taking notes means that you have to agree with everything that the instructor says. True or false? Explain your answer.

   False. The purpose of postponing debate is to prevent your internal dialogue about what is being presented from drowning out subsequent material. Thinking critically and postponing debate are not contradictory. Aim to understand the instructor's point before you criticize it. (*Observe: The note-taking process flows*, page 162)

8. Describe the two main types of key words. Then write down at least five key words from this chapter.

   (Answers will vary.) The two main types of key words are as follows: (1) Concepts, technical terms, names, and numbers (for example, *stimulus, generated, receptor neurons, transmit,* and *sensory*); (2) Linking words, including words that describe action, relationship, and degree (for example, *most, least, highest, lower,* and *faster*). (*Record: The note-taking process flows*, page 165)

9. Graphic signals include which of the following?

   (a) Brackets and parentheses

   (b) Stars and arrows

   (c) Underlining and connecting lines

   (d) Equal signs and greater-than and less-than signs

   (e) All of the above

   (e) All of the above (*Record: The note-taking process flows*, page 165)

10. Describe at least three strategies for reviewing notes.

    Describe at least three of the following: Review within 24 hours. Edit your notes. Fill in key words in the left-hand column. Use key words as recitation cues. Conduct short weekly review periods. Type up your notes. Create summaries. (*Review: The note-taking process flows*, page 170)

CHAPTER 7 TESTS

Instructor Tools & Tips

"Learn from the mistakes of others—you can never live long enough to make them all yourself." —John Luther

"Keep in mind that neither success nor failure is ever final." —Roger Babson

PREVIEW

Test taking is a high-priority issue for students. Discussing this topic together in class can help students prepare more successfully before tests while learning to manage anxiety during tests. This chapter reinforces how the strategies in *From Master Student to Master Employee* can help students reduce stress at school, at work, and at home. An article on math test strategies can help your students achieve higher test scores. Point out that Chapter 11 will help them establish better overall health habits, but learning simple breathing techniques or other stress management tools can make a big observable difference in test anxiety. Encourage your students to do a chapter reconnaissance to discover ways to predict test questions or to glean information from a test after it has been returned.

GUEST SPEAKER

Consider inviting faculty members from different departments to talk to your class about their expectations regarding tests. Ask them to prepare a few suggestions for studying materials in their discipline. Math and science are particularly problematic subjects for test anxiety. Prompt them to provide information on the importance of attending class, reading assigned textbook materials, and completing homework assignments. Have students prepare questions to ask these faculty members during a question-and-answer session.

Another suggestion for a guest speaker is to invite a counselor or staff member from the Student Health Center to talk about test anxiety and relaxation techniques.

master instructor
BEST PRACTICE

When giving a major test, I give one traditional test for individual completion. I then group students (those who need help with those that are more advanced to encourage coaching) and have the students retake the same test as a group of three or four. They are given one group answer sheet and instructed to take turns reading and answering the questions. If there is any disagreement, they discuss rationale and vote on the answer to be posted. I average the two grades together. In the next class I only address the questions that were most problematic because they have already reviewed the answers. This process encourages students to collaborate and promotes learning.

–Lorraine Fedrizzi, Niagara County Community College

LECTURE

What to do when you're stuck. Lecture on what students should do when they are stuck on a test question. Here are some strategies. A copy of this material is available on the Instructor Web site.

- **Read it again.** Eliminate the simplest sources of confusion, such as misreading the question.

- **Skip the question for now.** Do the ones you are sure of first. This advice is simple—and it works. Tell students to let their subconscious mind work on the answer while they respond to other questions. The trick is to truly let go of the puzzling question—for the moment. Questions that nag at the back of your mind can undermine your concentration and interfere with your recall while you are answering other questions.

- **Look for answers in other test questions.** A term, name, date, or other fact that escapes you might appear in another question on the test itself. Use other questions to stimulate your memory or to provide a hint or clue.

- **Treat intuition with care.** In quick-answer questions (multiple choice, true/false), go with your first instinct about which answer is correct. If you think your first answer is wrong because you misread the question, though, do change your answer.

- **Visualize the answer's "location."** Think of the answer to any test question as being recorded someplace in your notes or assigned reading. Close your eyes, take a deep breath, and see if you can visualize that place—its location on a page in the materials you studied for the test. You might also be able to recall a picture or graph, which often helps the details come flooding back into your mind. Ask the teacher for clarification if needed. The worst he can say is no!

- **Rewrite the question.** See if you can put a confusing question into your own words. Doing so might release the answer.

- **Free-write.** Just start writing anything at all. On scratch paper or in the margins of your test booklet, record any response to the test question that pops into your head. Instead of just sitting there, stumped, you're doing something—and that can reduce anxiety. Writing might also trigger a mental association that answers the question.

- **Write a close answer.** If you simply cannot think of a direct, accurate answer to the question, give it a shot anyway. Answer the question as best as you can, even if you don't think your answer is fully correct. This technique might help you get partial credit for short-answer questions, essay questions, and problems on math or science tests.

EXERCISES/ACTIVITIES

1. **Power Process: Detach (page 186)** After you have lectured on how to develop and write good essay exam answers, and have emphasized the importance of thinking, planning, and clear writing, divide students into groups of four and have them answer the following question: "Fully explain the Power Process: Detach." This provides them with an opportunity to practice developing an essay answer in a cooperative learning environment. It's also valuable because some students don't fully understand this process without class discussion. Provide students with clear guidelines for a "good answer." Write these guidelines on the board or in a handout to provide clarity. After the groups write their group essay answers, have them pass their papers to another group who then "grades" the essay. Read the highest-scoring answer, and provide your analysis as to the essay's strengths and weaknesses.

master instructor
BEST PRACTICE

"One thing that I tell my students about essay tests is to write as if they were writing to someone who knows absolutely nothing about the subject. In that way they should include all the basic information that they might not otherwise think of. I also use LIBEC, which was in a College Survival newsletter several years ago. LIBEC stands for legible, introduction, body, example, and conclusion. We talk about these steps and then my students (in groups) write answers to questions I make up from the reading in the chapter. With their group members they exchange answers and check to see if all the areas were covered. They enjoy working on an essay question with others and then evaluating what others have done."

–Barbara Fowler, Longview Community College, Missouri

2. **What to do *before* the test (pages 189–190)** This article is important to students because so many of them cram at the last minute and therefore have never practiced these strategies. Mind maps are powerful visual review tools that can be effective for students who don't know how to study effectively for tests. Have your students get into groups of four, pick a chapter from *From Master Student to Master Employee*, and create a mind map of the chapter's content on poster paper with colored markers. Tell them to sign their names at the top of the paper. This helps ensure that everyone is actively participating in the group. Hang the completed posters on the wall in the classroom, and then have the students walk around in their groups to review their classmates' work. Having had an opportunity to practice creating mind map summaries in class, they are likely to be more comfortable trying the technique on their own outside class. This activity also allows students to practice the important skill of working in groups. Refer to Interactive Concept Maps in Chapter 6 of the *From Master Student to Master Employee* Web site for an example of effective concept maps.

3. **Ways to predict test questions (page 191)** Divide students into groups, and have them practice predicting test questions for the quizzes that you give in class. Ask them to answer the questions also. Their questions and answers

should be based on what they see as the key points you have presented in lectures, activities, and homework, and the key points in the articles in the text. They are often surprised at how easy and effective this tool is! If by now you have completed Chapters 1 through 6, you can group students into six groups, asking each group to create 10 questions and answers for their assigned chapter. You can copy all chapter questions and answers to help students review these chapters for the exam.

CONVERSATION/SHARING

As the article The test isn't over *until* . . . (page 195) explains, it is vital for students to find out what questions they missed on a test and to understand why they missed them. Students can use the learning styles questions (*Why? What? How? What if?*) to review their tests. *Why* did I get this question wrong? *What* is the correct answer? *How* should I have studied this material? And they need to understand the consequences: *What if* I do not learn the correct answer for future tests? These four questions are a great foundational structure for this self-analysis. After a quiz or test, divide students into groups and have them share their analyses with each other so that they can all do better on the next evaluation.

master instructor BEST PRACTICE

" I have always tried to instruct my students to learn something from the tests that they take. This can be an area where the students can gain so much information and yet it is often overlooked. The information in the chart (page 195) is also helpful. This is a great way to say a lot in a small space. "

–Ray Emett, Salt Lake Community College

HOMEWORK

Journal Entry 14 Intention Statement (page 185) Having students complete and turn in this journal entry regarding how they feel about tests can be helpful to you in understanding the key problem areas for your students before, during, and after a test. Review students' responses to this exercise, and tailor your lectures and activities to address the needs expressed. Possible issues might include test anxiety, procrastination, and past failures. Ask students if they feel these issues influence their test experiences.

Journal Entry 15 Discovery Statement (page 118) Ask students to take a look at how they sabotage their opportunity to "create it all" by making excuses. This self-analysis helps them break the excuses habit by writing their discoveries and intentions about excuses. List common excuses on the board. Ask students, "Which ones have you used?" "Why is this excuse problematic?"

EVALUATION

Giving a quiz that includes multiple-choice, true/false, short-answer, and essay questions gives students an opportunity to practice new skills they've learned in this chapter and provides them with feedback about where they have achieved success in building new skills and where more practice is needed. For example, ask the following quiz question about Master Student Al Gore: "Briefly describe Gore's position on the crisis of climate change. Then state whether you agree with it or not, and justify your position." Using the three-part quiz forms available from your Cengage sales representative facilitates students' self-evaluation of their quiz performance and provides them with immediate feedback about their test-taking skills.

Quiz ideas for Chapter 7

Ask students to:

- Describe steps to do before taking a test.
- Describe steps to do during a test.
- Describe steps to do after taking a test.
- Describe how to deal with test anxiety

Additional Digital Resources for Chapter 7

What can you **ASSIGN FROM THE COURSEMATE** *for From Master Student to Master Employee?*

- **Master Students in Action Video.** Students will hear firsthand from other students where their test-taking challenges are and their strategies for success. The Master Students in Action videos give your students a firsthand view of how the strategies in *From Master Student to Master Employee* have helped their peers overcome obstacles. In special segments, Dave Ellis offers students his best strategies for mastering each chapter's content. Note that these videos are available for every chapter.

- **Flash cards of words to watch for in essay exams.** Students can test themselves on typical vocabulary used in essay exams so that they will know how to best formulate their response to the questions.

- **Power Process Media: Detach.** To help students understand the importance of "Detach" as described in the Power Process for Chapter 7, have them watch a video about detaching, listen to an audio version, and then answer the accompanying questions. A PowerPoint presentation that summarizes the Power Process article's main points is also included. Or have students create group multimedia PowerPoint presentations based on their understanding of how to "detach." Note that Power Process media are available for every chapter.

CourseMate *To access CourseMate, your students need to visit www.cengagebrain .com. At the CengageBrain.com home page, students search for the ISBN of* From Master Student to Master Employee *(from the back cover of the book), using the search box at the top of the page. This takes them to the product page where these resources can be found.*

Did you know that **THESE RESOURCES** *(and many more)* **ARE AVAILABLE** *on the* **INSTRUCTOR COMPANION SITE?**

- **Need some energizing lecture ideas?** Browse through the lecture ideas provided for Chapter 7, including the following:

- **IBEC Essay Test Strategy.** Help your students who lack college-level writing skills to succeed in taking essay tests by introducing them to this four-part essay test system.

- **Comparing Athletic Competitions to Tests.** Draw comparisons between what it takes to excel in athletic competition and on tests to help students understand the necessary preparations.

- **Unsure of how to assess your own students?** Look to the online Course Manual for the following articles with suggestions for how to implement testing and assessment in your course:

- Strategies for grading this course

- Assessment of skills for first-year students

- Guidelines for pre- and post-course assessment

- Suggestions for creating a pre- and post-course assessment on your campus

- Strategies for working with students who are failing your course

Tests

Use this **Master Student Map** to ask yourself

WHY THIS CHAPTER MATTERS . . .

- Adopting a few simple techniques can make a major difference in how you feel about tests—and how you perform on them.

WHAT IS INCLUDED . . .

HOW I CAN USE THIS CHAPTER. . .

- Predict test questions and use my study time more effectively.
- Harness the power of cooperative learning by studying with other people.
- Gain strategies for raising my scores on tests.
- Separate my self-image from my test scores.

WHAT IF . . .

- I could let go of anxiety about tests—or anything else?

© Ruslan Ivantsov/Shutterstock.com

JOURNAL ENTRY 14
Intention Statement

Use this chapter to transform your experience with tests

Think about how you want your experience of test taking to change. For example, you might want to walk into every test feeling well rested and thoroughly prepared. Next, preview this chapter to find at least three strategies to accomplish your goal. List those strategies below, and note the page numbers where you can find out more about each one.

Strategy	Page number
_____	_____
_____	_____
_____	_____
_____	_____
_____	_____
_____	_____
_____	_____
_____	_____
_____	_____
_____	_____
_____	_____

POWER process

DETACH

This Power Process helps you release the powerful, natural student within you. It is especially useful whenever negative emotions are getting in your way.

Attachments are addictions. When we are attached to something, we think we cannot live without it, just as a drug addict feels he cannot live without drugs. We believe our well-being depends on maintaining our attachments.

We can be attached to just about anything: beliefs, emotions, people, roles, objects. The list is endless.

One person, for example, might be so attached to his car that he takes an accident as a personal attack. Pity the poor unfortunate who backs into this person's car. He might as well have backed into the owner himself.

Another person might be attached to her job. Her identity and sense of well-being depend on it. She could become depressed if she got fired.

When we are attached and things don't go our way, we can feel angry, sad, afraid, or confused.

Suppose you are attached to getting an "A" on your physics test. You feel as though your success in life depends on getting that "A." As the clock ticks away, you work harder on the test, getting more stuck. That voice in your head gets louder: "I must get an 'A.' I MUST get an 'A.' I MUST GET AN 'A!'"

Now is a time to detach. See whether you can just *observe* what's going on, letting go of all your judgments. When you just observe, you reach a quiet state above and beyond your usual thoughts. This is a place where you can be aware of being aware. It's a tranquil spot, apart from your emotions. From here, you can see yourself objectively, as if you were watching someone else.

That place of detachment might sound far away and hard to reach. You can get there in three ways.

First, pay attention to your thoughts and physical sensations. If you are confused and feeling stuck, tell yourself, "Here I am, confused and stuck." If your palms are sweaty and your stomach is one big knot, admit it.

Second, practice relaxation. Start by simply noticing your breathing. Then breathe more slowly and more deeply. See whether you can breathe the relaxing feeling into your whole body.

Third, practice seeing current events from a broader perspective. In your mind, zoom out to a bigger picture. Ask yourself how much today's test score will matter to you in one week, one month, one year, or one decade from today. You can apply this technique to any challenge in life.

Caution: Giving up an *attachment* to being an "A" student does not mean giving up *being* an "A" student. Giving up an attachment to a job doesn't mean giving up the job. When you detach, you get to keep your values and goals. However, you know that you will be okay even if you fail to achieve a goal.

Remember that you are more than your goals. You are more than your thoughts and feelings. These things come and go. Meanwhile, the part of you that can *just observe* is always there and always safe, no matter what happens.

Behind your attachments is a master student. Release that mastery. Detach.

You're One Click Away...
from accessing Power Process Media online and finding out more about how to "detach."

DISARM TESTS

On the surface, tests don't look dangerous. Maybe that's why we sometimes treat them as if they were land mines. Suppose a stranger walked up to you on the street and asked, "Does a finite abelian P-group have a basis?" Would you break out in a cold sweat? Would your muscles tense up? Would your breathing become shallow?

Probably not. Even if you had never heard of a finite abelian P-group, you probably would remain coolly detached. However, if you find the same question on a test and you have never heard of a finite abelian P-group, your hands might get clammy.

Grades (A to F) are what we use to give power to tests. And there are lots of misconceptions about what grades are. Grades are not a measure of intelligence or creativity. They are not an indication of our ability to contribute to society. Grades are simply a measure of how well we do on tests.

Some people think that a test score measures what a student has accomplished in a course. This idea is false. A test score is a measure of what a student scored on a test. If you are anxious about a test and blank out, the grade cannot measure what you've learned. The reverse is also true: If you are good at taking tests and you are a lucky guesser, the score won't be an accurate reflection of what you know.

Grades are not a measure of self-worth. Yet we tend to give test scores the power to determine how we feel about ourselves. Common thoughts include "If I fail a test, I am a failure" or "If I do badly on a test, I am a bad person." The truth is that if you do badly on a test, you are a person who did badly on a test. That's all.

If you experience test anxiety, then you might find this line of reasoning hard to swallow. Test anxiety is a common problem among students. And it can surface in many ways, masquerading as a variety of emotions. Here are some examples:

- *Anger:* "The teacher never wanted me to pass this stupid course anyway."
- *Blame:* "If only the class were not so boring."
- *Fear:* "I'll never have enough time to study."

Believing in any of these statements leaves us powerless. We become victims of things that we don't control—the teacher, the textbook, or the wording of the test questions.

Another option is to ask: What can *I* do to experience my next test differently? How can I prepare more effectively? How can I manage stress before, during, and after the test? When you answer such questions, you take back your power.

Carrying around misconceptions about tests and grades can put undue pressure on your performance. It's like balancing on a railroad track. Many people can walk along the rail and stay balanced for long periods. Yet the task seems entirely different if the rail is placed between two buildings, 52 stories up.

It is easier to do well on exams if you don't put too much pressure on yourself. Don't give the test some magical power over your own worth as a human being. Academic tests are not a matter of life and death. Scoring low on important tests—standardized tests or medical school exams, bar exams, CPA exams—usually means only a delay.

Whether the chance of doing poorly is real or exaggerated, worrying about it can become paralyzing. The way to deal with tests is to keep them in perspective. Keep the railroad track on the ground. ■

"F" is for feedback

When some students get an "F" on an assignment, they interpret that letter as a message: "You are a failure." That interpretation is not accurate. Getting an "F" means only that you failed a test—not that you failed your life.

From now on, imagine that the letter "F" when used as a grade represents another word: *feedback*. An "F" is an indication that you didn't understand the material well enough. It's a message to do something differently before the next test or assignment. If you interpret "F" as *failure,* you don't get to change anything. But if you interpret "F" as *feedback,* you can change your thinking and behavior in ways that promote your success. You can choose a new learning strategy, or let go of an excuse about not having the time to study.

Getting prompt and meaningful feedback on your performance is a powerful strategy for learning *anything.* Tests are not the only source of feedback. Make a habit of asking for feedback from your instructors, advisors, classmates, coworkers, friends, family members, and anyone else who knows you. Just determine what you want to improve and ask, "How am I doing?"

JOURNAL ENTRY 15
Discovery Statement

Explore your feelings about tests

Complete the following sentences:

As exam time gets closer, one thing I notice that I do is . . .

_____

_____

_____

When it comes to taking tests, I have trouble . . .

_____

_____

_____

The night before a test, I usually feel . . .

_____

_____

_____

_____

The morning of a test, I usually feel . . .

_____

_____

_____

_____

During a test, I usually feel . . .

_____

_____

_____

_____

After a test, I usually feel . . .

_____

_____

_____

_____

When I learn a test score, I usually feel . . .

_____

_____

_____

_____

You're One Click Away...
from accessing and completing this Journal Entry online under Success Tools in From Master Student to Master Employee's *College Success CourseMate.*

JOURNAL ENTRY 16
Discovery/Intention Statement

Notice your excuses and let them go

Do a timed, 4-minute brainstorm of all the reasons, rationalizations, justifications, and excuses you have used to avoid studying. Be creative. Write your list of excuses in the space below. Use additional paper as needed.

Review your list. Then write a Discovery Statement about patterns that you see in your excuses.

I discovered that I . . .

Next, review your list, pick the excuse that you use the most, and circle it. In the space below, write an Intention Statement about what you will do to begin eliminating your favorite excuse. Make this Intention Statement one that you can keep, with a time line and a reward.

I intend to . . .

_____

_____

_____

_____

_____

_____

_____

_____

_____

_____

_____

_____

_____

_____

_____

_____

_____

_____

_____

_____

_____

WHAT TO DO
BEFORE THE TEST

Do daily reviews. Daily reviews include short preclass and postclass reviews of lecture notes. Also conduct brief daily reviews with textbooks: Before reading a new assignment, scan your notes and the sections you underlined or highlighted in the previous assignment. In addition, use the time you spend waiting for the bus or doing the laundry to conduct short reviews.

Concentrate daily reviews on two kinds of material. One is material you have just learned, either in class or in your reading. Second is material that involves simple memorization—equations, formulas, dates, definitions.

Begin to review on the first day of class. Most instructors outline the whole course at that time. You can even start reviewing within seconds after learning. During a lull in class, go over the notes you just took. Immediately after class, review your notes again.

Do weekly reviews. Review each subject at least once a week, allowing about 1 hour per subject. Include reviews of assigned reading and lecture notes. Look over any mind map summaries or flash cards you have created. Also practice working on sample problems.

Do major reviews. Major reviews are usually most helpful when conducted the week before finals or other critical exams. They help you integrate concepts and deepen your understanding of material presented throughout the term. These are longer review periods—2 to 5 hours at a stretch, with sufficient breaks. Remember that the effectiveness of your review begins to drop after an hour or so unless you give yourself a short rest.

After a certain point, short breaks every hour might not be enough to refresh you. That's when it's time to quit. Learn your limits by being conscious of the quality of your concentration.

During long sessions, study the most difficult subjects when you are the most alert: at the beginning of the session.

Schedule reviews. Schedule specific times in your calendar for reviews. Start reviewing key topics at least 5 days before you'll be tested on them. This allows plenty of time to find the answers to questions and close any gaps in your understanding.

Create study checklists. You can use study checklists the way a pilot uses a preflight checklist. Pilots go through a standard routine before they take off. They physically mark off each item: test flaps, check magnetos, check fuel tanks, adjust instruments, check rudder. A written list helps them to be sure they don't miss anything. Once they are in the air, it's too late. Taking an exam is like flying a plane. Once the test begins, it's too late to memorize that one equation you forgot to include in your review.

Make a checklist for each subject. List reading assignments by chapters or page numbers. List dates of lecture notes. Write down various types of problems you will need to solve. Write down other skills to master. Include major ideas, definitions, theories, formulas, and equations. For math and science tests, choose some problems and do them over again as a way to review for the test.

"'How To Do Well In School Without Studying' is over there in the fiction section."

A. BACALL

© Aaron Bacall

7

Remember that a study checklist is not a review sheet; it is a to-do list. Checklists contain the briefest possible description of each item to study.

Instead of a checklist, you may want to use a test prep plan. This written plan goes beyond a study checklist to include the following:

- The date and time of each test, along with the name of the course and instructor.
- The type of items—such as essay or multiple choice—that are likely to appear on each test.
- Specific dates and times that you intend to study for each test (which you then enter on your calendar).
- Specific strategies that you intend to use while studying for each test.

Create mind map summary sheets. There are several ways to make a mind map as you study for tests. Start by creating a map totally from memory. You might be surprised by how much you already know. After you have gone as far as you can using recall alone, go over your notes and text, and fill in the rest of the map. Another option is to go through your notes and write down key words as you pick them out. Then, without looking at your notes, create a mind map of everything you can recall about each key word. Finally, go back to your notes, and fill in material you left out.

Create flash cards. Flash cards are like portable test questions. On one side of some 3×5 cards, write questions. On the other side, write the answers. It's that simple. Always carry a pack of flash cards with you, and review them whenever you have a minute to spare. Use flash cards for formulas, definitions, theories, key words from your notes, axioms, dates, foreign language phrases, hypotheses, and sample problems. Create flash cards regularly as the term progresses. Buy an inexpensive card file to keep your flash cards arranged by subject.

Monitor your reviews. Each day that you prepare for a test, assess what you have learned and what you still want to learn. See how many items you've covered from your study checklist. Look at the tables of contents in your textbooks, and mark an X next to the sections that you've summarized. This helps you gauge the thoroughness of your reviews and alerts you to areas that still need attention.

Take a practice test. Write up your own questions based on course material—a good activity for study groups. Take your practice test several times before the actual exam. You might type this "test" so that it looks like the real thing. If possible, take your practice test in the same room where you will take the actual test.

Also meet with your instructor to go over your practice test. Ask whether your questions focus on appropriate topics and represent the kind of items you can expect to see. The instructor might decline to give you any of this information. More often, though, instructors will answer some or all of your questions about an upcoming test.

Get copies of old exams. Copies of previous exams for the class might be available from the instructor, the instructor's department, the library, or the counseling office. Old tests can help you plan a review strategy. One caution: If you rely on old tests exclusively, you might gloss over material the instructor has added since the last test. Also, check your school's policy about making past tests available to students. Some schools might not allow it. ■

You're One Click Away...
from seeing examples of mind map summary sheets and other review tools online.

How to cram (even though you "shouldn't")

Know the limitations of cramming, and be aware of its costs. Cramming won't work if you've neglected all of the reading assignments or if you've skipped most of the lectures and daydreamed through the rest. The more courses you have to cram for, the less effective cramming will be. Also, cramming is not the same as learning: You won't remember what you cram.

If you are going to cram, however, then avoid telling yourself that you *should* have studied earlier, you *should* have read the assignments, or you *should* have been more conscientious. All those *shoulds* get you nowhere. Instead, write an Intention Statement about how you will change your study habits. Give yourself permission to be the fallible human being you are. Then make the best of the situation.

Make choices Pick out a *few* of the most important elements of the course and learn them backward, forward, and upside down. For example, devote most of your attention to the topic sentences, tables, and charts in a long reading assignment.

Make a plan After you've chosen what elements you want to study, determine how much time to spend on each one.

Recite and recite again The key to cramming is repetition. Go over your material again and again.

Ways to
PREDICT TEST QUESTIONS

Predicting test questions can do more than get you a better grade. It can also keep you focused on the purpose of a course and help you design your learning strategies. Making predictions can be fun too—especially when they turn out to be accurate.

Ask about the nature of the test. Eliminate as much guesswork as possible. Ask your instructor to describe upcoming tests. Do this early in the term so you can be alert for possible test questions throughout the course. Here are some questions to ask:

- What course material will the test cover—readings, lectures, lab sessions, or a combination?
- Will the test be cumulative, or will it cover just the most recent material you've studied?
- Will the test focus on facts and details or major themes and relationships?
- Will the test call on you to solve problems or apply concepts?
- Will you have choices about which questions to answer?
- What types of questions will be on the test—true/false, multiple choice, short answer, essay?

Note: In order to study appropriately for essay tests, find out how much detail the instructor wants in your answers. Ask how much time you'll be allowed for the test and about the length of essay answers (number of pages, blue books, or word limit). Having that information before you begin studying will help you gauge your depth for learning the material.

Put yourself in your instructor's shoes. If you were teaching the course, what kinds of questions would you put on an exam? You can also brainstorm test questions with other students—a great activity for study groups.

Look for possible test questions in your notes and readings. Have a separate section in your notebook labeled "Test questions." Add several questions to this section after every lecture and assignment. You can also create your own code or graphic signal—such as a "*T!*" in a circle—to flag possible test questions in your notes. Use the same symbol to flag review questions and problems in your textbooks that could appear on a test.

Remember that textbook authors have many ways of pointing you to potential test items. Look for clues in chapter overviews and summaries, headings, lists of key words, and review questions. Some textbooks have related Web sites where you can take practice tests.

Look for clues to possible questions during class. During lectures, you can predict test questions by observing what an instructor says and how he says it. Instructors often give clues. They might repeat important points several times, write them on the board, or return to them in later classes.

Gestures can indicate critical points. For example, your instructor might pause, look at notes, or read passages word for word.

Notice whether your teacher has any strong points of view on certain issues. Questions on those issues are likely to appear on a test. Also pay attention to questions the instructor poses to students, and note questions that other students ask.

When material from reading assignments is covered extensively in class, it is likely to be on a test. For science courses and other courses involving problem solving, work on sample problems using different variables.

Save all quizzes, papers, lab sheets, and graded materials of any kind. Quiz questions have a way of reappearing, in slightly altered form, on final exams. If copies of previous exams and other graded materials are available, use them to predict test questions.

Apply your predictions. To get the most value from your predictions, use them to guide your review sessions.

Remember the obvious. Be on the lookout for these words: *This material will be on the test.* ■

What to do **during the test**

Prepare yourself for the test by arriving early. Being early often leaves time to do a relaxation exercise. While you're waiting for the test to begin and talking with classmates, avoid asking the question "How much did you study for the test?" This question might fuel anxious thoughts that you didn't study enough.

AS YOU BEGIN

Ask the teacher or test administrator if you can use scratch paper during the test. (If you use a separate sheet of paper without permission, you might appear to be cheating.) If you *do* get permission, use this paper to jot down memory aids, formulas, equations, definitions, facts, or other material you know you'll need and might forget. An alternative is to make quick notes in the margins of the test sheet.

Pay attention to verbal directions given as a test is distributed. Then scan the whole test immediately. Evaluate the importance of each section. Notice how many points each part of the test is worth; then estimate how much time you'll need for each section, using its point value as your guide. For example, don't budget 20 percent of your time for a section that is worth only 10 percent of the points.

Read the directions slowly. Then reread them. It can be agonizing to discover that you lost points on a test merely because you failed to follow the directions. When the directions are confusing, ask to have them clarified.

Now you are ready to begin the test. If necessary, allow yourself a minute or two of "panic" time. Notice any tension you feel, and apply one of the techniques explained in the article "Let Go of Test Anxiety" later in this chapter.

Answer the easiest, shortest questions first. This gives you the experience of success. It also stimulates associations and prepares you for more difficult questions. Pace yourself, and watch the time. If you can't think of an answer, move on. Follow your time plan.

If you are unable to determine the answer to a test question, keep an eye out throughout the test for context clues that may remind you of the correct answer or provide you with evidence to eliminate wrong answers.

MULTIPLE-CHOICE QUESTIONS

- **Answer each question in your head first.** Do this step before you look at the possible answers. If you come up with an answer that you're confident is right, look for that answer in the list of choices.

- **Read all possible answers before selecting one.** Sometimes two answers will be similar and only one will be correct.

- **Test each possible answer.** Remember that multiple-choice questions consist of two parts: the stem (an incomplete statement or question at the beginning) and a list of possible answers. Each answer, when combined with the stem, makes a complete statement or question-and-answer pair that is either true or false. When you combine the stem with each possible answer, you are turning each multiple-choice question into a small series of true/false questions. Choose the answer that makes a true statement.

- **Eliminate incorrect answers.** Cross off the answers that are clearly not correct. The answer you cannot eliminate is probably the best choice.

TRUE/FALSE QUESTIONS

- **Read the entire question.** Separate the statement into its grammatical parts—individual clauses and phrases—and then test each part. If any part is false, the entire statement is false.

- **Look for qualifiers.** Qualifiers include words such as *all, most, sometimes,* or *rarely.* Absolute qualifiers such as *always* or *never* generally indicate a false statement.

- **Find the devil in the details.** Double-check each number, fact, and date in a true/false statement. Look for numbers that have been transposed or facts that have been slightly altered. These are signals of a false statement.

- **Watch for negatives.** Look for words such as *not* and *cannot.* Read the sentence without these words and see whether you come up with a true/false statement. Then reinsert the negative words and see whether the statement makes more sense. Watch especially for sentences with two negative words. As in math operations, two negatives cancel each other out: *We cannot say that Chekhov never succeeded at short story writing* means the same as *Chekhov succeeded at short story writing.*

COMPUTER-GRADED TESTS

- Make sure that the answer you mark corresponds to the question you are answering.
- Check the test booklet against the answer sheet whenever you switch sections and whenever you come to the top of a column.
- Watch for stray marks on the answer sheet; they can look like answers.
- If you change an answer, be sure to erase the wrong answer thoroughly, removing all pencil marks completely.

OPEN-BOOK TEST

- Carefully organize your notes, readings, and any other materials you plan to consult when writing answers.
- Write down any formulas you will need on a separate sheet of paper.
- Bookmark the table of contents and index in each of your textbooks. Place sticky notes and stick-on tabs or paper clips on other important pages of books (pages with tables, for instance).
- Create an informal table of contents or index for the notes you took in class.
- Predict which material will be covered on the test, and highlight relevant sections in your readings and notes.

SHORT-ANSWER/FILL-IN-THE-BLANK TESTS

- Concentrate on key words and facts. Be brief.
- Overlearning material can really pay off. When you know a subject backward and forward, you can answer this type of question almost as fast as you can write.

MATCHING TESTS

- Begin by reading through each column, starting with the one with fewer items. Check the number of items in each column to see whether they're equal. If they're not, look for an item in one column that you can match with two or more items in the other column.
- Look for any items with similar wording, and make special note of the differences between these items.
- Match words that are similar grammatically. For example, match verbs with verbs and nouns with nouns.

- When matching individual words with phrases, first read a phrase. Then look for the word that logically completes the phrase.
- Cross out items in each column when you are through with them.

ESSAY QUESTIONS

Managing your time is crucial in answering essay questions. Note how many questions you have to answer, and monitor your progress during the test period. Writing shorter answers and completing all of the questions on an essay test will probably yield a better score than leaving some questions blank.

Find out what an essay question is asking—precisely. If a question asks you to *compare* the ideas of Sigmund Freud and Karl Marx, no matter how eloquently you *explain* them, you are on a one-way trip to No Credit City.

Before you write, make a quick outline. An outline can help speed up the writing of your detailed answer; you're less likely to leave out important facts; and if you don't have time to finish your answer, your outline could win you some points. To use test time efficiently, keep your outline brief. Focus on key words to use in your answer.

Introduce your answer by getting to the point. General statements such as "There are many interesting facets to this difficult question" can cause irritation to teachers grading dozens of tests.

One way to get to the point is to begin your answer with part of the question. Suppose the question is "Discuss how increasing the city police budget might or might not contribute to a decrease in street crime." Your first sentence might be this: "An increase in police expenditures will not have a significant effect on street crime for the following reasons." Your position is clear. You are on your way to an answer.

Then expand your answer with supporting ideas and facts. Start out with the most solid points. Be brief and avoid filler sentences.

Write legibly. Grading essay questions is in large part a subjective process. Sloppy, difficult-to-read handwriting might actually lower your grade.

Write on one side of the paper only. If you write on both sides of the paper, writing may show through and obscure the words on the other side. If necessary, use the blank side to add points you missed. Leave a generous left-hand margin and plenty of space between your answers, in case you want to add points that you missed later on.

Finally, if you have time, review your answers for grammar and spelling errors, clarity, and legibility. ▧

7

Words to watch for in
ESSAY QUESTIONS

The following words are commonly found in essay test questions. They give you precise directions about what to include in your answer. Get to know these words well. When you see them on a test, underline them. Also look for them in your notes. Locating such key words can help you predict test questions.

Analyze: Break into separate parts and discuss, examine, or interpret each part. Then give your opinion.

Compare: Examine two or more items. Identify similarities and differences.

Contrast: Show differences. Set in opposition.

Criticize: Make judgments about accuracy, quality, or both. Evaluate comparative worth. Criticism often involves analysis.

Define: Explain the exact meaning—usually, a meaning specific to the course or subject. Definitions are usually short.

Describe: Give a detailed account. Make a picture with words. List characteristics, qualities, and parts.

Diagram: Create a drawing, chart, or other visual element. Label and explain key parts.

Discuss: Consider and debate or argue the pros and cons of an issue. Write about any conflict. Compare and contrast.

Enumerate: List the main parts or features in a meaningful order and briefly describe each one.

Evaluate: Make judgments about accuracy, quality, or both (similar to *criticize*).

Explain: Make an idea clear. Show logically how a concept is developed. Give the reasons for an event.

Illustrate: Clarify an idea by giving examples of it. Illustration often involves comparison and contrast. Read the test directions to see whether the question calls for actually drawing a diagram as well.

Interpret: Explain the meaning of a new idea or event by showing how it relates to more familiar ideas or events. Interpretation can involve evaluation.

List: Write a series of concise statements (similar to *enumerate*).

Outline: List the main topics, points, features, or events and briefly describe each one. (This does not necessarily mean creating a traditional outline with Roman numerals, numbers, and letters.)

Prove: Support with facts, examples, and quotations from credible sources (especially those presented in class or in the text).

Relate: Show the connections between ideas or events. Provide a larger context for seeing the big picture.

State: Explain precisely and clearly.

Summarize: Give a brief, condensed account. Include main ideas and conclusions. Avoid supporting details, or include only significant details.

Trace: Show the order of events or the progress of a subject or event.

Notice how these words differ. For example, *compare* asks you to do something different from *contrast*. Likewise, *criticize* and *explain* call for different responses.

If any of these terms are still unclear to you, look them up in an unabridged dictionary.

During a test, you might be allowed to ask for an explanation of a key word. Check with instructors for policies.

 You're One Click Away...
from reviewing these key words and other helpful vocabulary terms by using online flash cards.

The test isn't over *UNTIL . . .*

Many students believe that a test is over as soon as they turn in the answer sheet. Consider another point of view: You're not done with a test until you know the answer to any question that you missed—and why you missed it.

This point of view offers major benefits. Tests in many courses are cumulative. In other words, the content included on the first test is assumed to be working knowledge for the second test, midterm, or final exam. When you discover what questions you missed and understand the reasons for lost points, you learn something—and you greatly increase your odds of achieving better scores later in the course.

To get the most value from any test, take control of what you do at two critical points: the time immediately following the test and the time when the test is returned to you.

Immediately following the test. After finishing a test, your first thought might be to nap, snack, or go out with friends to celebrate. Restrain those impulses for a short while so that you can reflect on the test. The time you invest now carries the potential to raise your grades in the future.

To begin with, sit down in a quiet place. Take a few minutes to write some Discovery Statements related to your experience of taking the test. Describe how you felt about taking the test, how effective your review strategies were, and whether you accurately predicted the questions that appeared on the test.

Follow up with an Intention Statement or two. State what, if anything, you will do differently to prepare for the next test. The more specific you are, the better.

When the test is returned. When a returned test includes a teacher's comments, view this document as a treasure trove of intellectual gold.

First, make sure that the point totals add up correctly, and double-check for any other errors in grading. Even the best teachers make an occasional mistake.

Next, look at the test items that you missed. Ask these questions:

- On what material did the teacher base test questions—readings, lectures, discussions, or other class activities?
- What types of questions appeared in the test—objective (such as matching items, true/false questions, or multiple choice), short answer, or essay?
- What types of questions did you miss?
- Can you learn anything from the instructor's comments that will help you prepare for the next test?
- What strategies did you use to prepare for this test? What would you do differently to prepare for your next test?

Also see whether you can correct any answers that lost points. To do this, carefully analyze the source of your errors, and find a solution. Consult the chart below for help. ■

Source of test error	Possible solutions
Study errors—studying material that was not included on the test, or spending too little time on material that did appear on the test	• Ask your teacher about specific topics that will be included on a test. • Practice predicting test questions. • Form a study group with class members to create mock tests.
Careless errors, such as skipping or misreading directions	• Read and follow directions more carefully—especially when tests are divided into several sections with different directions. • Set aside time during the next test to proofread your answers.
Concept errors—mistakes made when you do not understand the underlying principles needed to answer a question or solve a problem	• Look for patterns in the questions you missed. • Make sure that you complete all assigned readings, attend all lectures, and show up for laboratory sessions. • Ask your teacher for help with specific questions.
Application errors—mistakes made when you understand underlying principles but fail to apply them correctly	• Rewrite your answers correctly. • When studying, spend more time on solving sample problems. • Predict application questions that will appear on future tests, and practice answering them.
Test mechanics errors—missing more questions in certain parts of the test than others, changing correct answers to incorrect ones at the last minute, leaving items blank, miscopying answers from scratch paper to the answer sheet	• Set time limits for taking each section of a test, and stick to them. • Proofread your test answers carefully. • Look for patterns in the kind of answers you change at the last minute. • Change answers only if you can state a clear and compelling reason to do so.

7

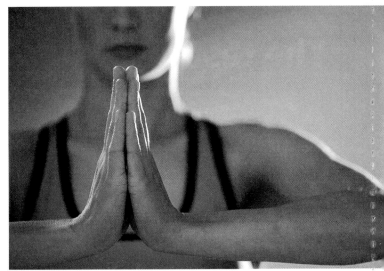
© Comstock/Masterfile

> If you freeze during tests and flub questions when you know the answers, you might be dealing with test anxiety.

Let go of
TEST ANXIETY

A little tension before a test is fine. That tingly, butterflies-in-the-stomach feeling you get from extra adrenaline can sharpen your awareness and keep you alert. You can enjoy the benefits of a little tension while you stay confident and relaxed.

Sometimes, however, tension is persistent and extreme. If it interferes with your daily life and consistently prevents you from doing your best in school, then it might be test anxiety. Anxiety has three elements: mental, physical, and emotional. The mental element includes your thoughts, including predictions of failure. The physical component includes physical sensations such as shallow breathing and muscle tension. The emotional element occurs when thoughts and physical sensations combine. The following techniques can help you deal with these elements of stress in *any* situation, from test anxiety to stage fright.

Yell "Stop!" If you notice that your mind is consumed with worries and fears—that your thoughts are spinning out of control—mentally yell "Stop!" If you're in a situation that allows it, yell it out loud. This action can allow you to redirect your thoughts. Once you've broken the cycle of worry or panic, you can use any of the following techniques.

Describe your thoughts in writing. Certain thoughts tend to increase test anxiety. One way to defuse them is to simply acknowledge them. To get the full benefit of this technique, take the time to make a list. Write down what you think and feel about an upcoming test. Capture everything that's on your mind, and don't stop to edit. One study indicates that this technique can relieve anxiety and potentially raise your test score.[1]

Dispute your thoughts. You can take the above technique one step further. Do some critical thinking. Remember that anxiety-creating thoughts about tests often boil down to this statement: *Getting a low grade on a test is a disaster.* Do the math, however: A four-year degree often involves taking about 32 courses (eight courses per year over four years for a full-time student). This means that your final grade on any one course amounts to about only 3 percent of your total grade point average. This is *not* an excuse to avoid studying. It is simply a reason to keep tests in perspective.

Praise yourself. Many of us take the first opportunity to belittle ourselves: "Way to go, dummy! You don't even know the answer to the first question on the test." We wouldn't dream of treating a friend this way, yet we do it to ourselves. An alternative is to give yourself some encouragement. Treat yourself as if you were your own best friend. Prepare carefully for each test. Then remind yourself, "I am ready. I can do a great job on this test."

Consider the worst. Rather than trying to put a stop to your worrying, consider the very worst thing that could happen. Take your fear to the limit of absurdity. Imagine the catastrophic problems that might occur if you were to fail the test. You might say to yourself, "Well, if I fail this test, I might fail the course, lose my financial aid, and get kicked out of school. Then I won't be able to get a job, so the bank will repossess my car, and I'll start drinking." Keep going until you see the absurdity of your predictions. After you stop chuckling, you can backtrack to discover a reasonable level of concern.

Breathe. You can calm physical sensations within your body by focusing your attention on your breathing. Concentrate on the air going in and out of your lungs. Experience it as it passes through your nose and mouth. If you notice that you are taking short, shallow breaths, begin to take longer and deeper breaths.

Scan your body. Simple awareness is an effective response to unpleasant physical sensations. Discover this for yourself by bringing awareness to each area of your body.

To begin, sit comfortably and close your eyes. Focus your attention on the muscles in your feet, and notice if they are relaxed. Tell the muscles in your feet that they can relax.

Move up to your ankles and repeat the procedure. Next go to your calves and thighs and buttocks, telling each group of muscles to relax.

Do the same for your lower back, diaphragm, chest, upper back, neck, shoulders, jaw, face, upper arms, lower arms, fingers, and scalp.

As you become aware of physical sensations, open up to them. If you let them arise without resistance, they will eventually pass away.

Use guided imagery. Relax completely and take a quick fantasy trip. Close your eyes, free your body of tension, and imagine yourself in a beautiful, peaceful, natural setting. Create as much of the scene as you can. Be specific. Use all of your senses.

For example, you might imagine yourself at a beach. Hear the surf rolling in and the seagulls calling to each other. Feel the sun on your face and the hot sand between your toes. Smell the sea breeze. Taste the salty mist from the surf. Notice the ships on the horizon and the rolling sand dunes. Use all of your senses to create a vivid imaginary trip.

Find a place that works for you, and practice getting there. When you become proficient, you can return to it quickly for trips that might last only a few seconds.

With practice, you can use this technique even while you are taking a test.

Exercise aerobically. This is one technique that won't work in the classroom or while you're taking a test. Yet it is an excellent way to reduce body tension. Exercise regularly during the days that you review for a test. See what effect this has on your ability to focus and relax during the test.

Do some kind of exercise that will get your heart beating at twice your normal rate and keep it beating at that rate for 15 or 20 minutes. Aerobic exercises include rapid walking, jogging, swimming, bicycling, basketball, and anything else that elevates your heart rate and keeps it elevated.

Practice defusing. To *defuse* means to step back from something and see it as separate from ourselves. When we defuse from an emotion, we no longer identify with it. We no longer say "*I am afraid*" or "*I am sad*." We say something like "There's fear again" or "I feel sadness right now." Using language such as this offers a way to step back from our internal experiences and keep them in perspective.

Before a test, you might find it especially useful to defuse from your thoughts. Borrow some techniques from Acceptance and Commitment Therapy, used by a growing number of therapists.[2] Take an anxiety-producing thought—such as *I always screw up on tests*—and do any of the following:

1. Repeat it over and over again out loud until it becomes just a meaningless series of sounds.

2. Repeat the thought while using the voice of a cartoon character such as Mickey Mouse or Homer Simpson.

3. Rephrase the thought so that you can sing it to the tune of a nursery rhyme or the song "Happy Birthday."

4. Preface the statement with "I'm having the thought that. . . . (*I'm having the thought that I always screw up on tests.*)

5. Talk back to your mind by saying, "That's an interesting thought, mind; thanks a lot for sharing." Or simply, "Thanks, mind."

> To *defuse* means to step back from something and see it as separate from ourselves. When we defuse from an emotion, we no longer identify with it.

Make contact with the present moment. If you feel anxious, see if you can focus your attention on a specific sight, sound, or other sensation that's happening in the present moment. Examine the details of a painting. Study the branches on a tree. Observe the face of your watch right down to the tiny scratches in the glass. During an exam, take a few seconds to listen to the sounds of squeaking chairs, the scratching of pencils, the muted coughs. Touch the surface of your desk and notice the texture.

Focus all of your attention on one point—anything other than the flow of thoughts through your head. This is an example of using the "Power Process: Be here now." ■

Have some **FUN!**

Contrary to popular belief, finals week does not have to be a drag. In fact, if you have used techniques in this chapter, exam week can be fun. You will have done most of your studying long before finals arrive.

When you are well prepared for tests, you can even use fun as a technique to enhance your performance. The day before a final, go for a run or play a game of basketball. Take in a movie or a concert. A relaxed brain is a more effective brain. If you have studied for a test, your mind will continue to prepare itself even while you're at the movies. Get plenty of rest too. There's no need to cram until 3:00 A.M. when you have reviewed material throughout the term.

✓ CRITICAL THINKING EXERCISE 18

Twenty things I like to do

One way to relieve tension is to mentally yell "Stop!" and substitute a pleasant daydream for the stressful thoughts and emotions you are experiencing.

To create a supply of pleasant images to recall during times of stress, conduct an 8-minute brainstorm about things you like to do. Your goal is to generate at least twenty ideas. Time yourself, and write as fast as you can in the space below.

When you have completed your list, study it. Pick out two activities that seem especially pleasant, and elaborate on them by creating a mind map in the space below. Write down all of the memories you have about that activity.

You can use these images to calm yourself in stressful situations.

Getting ready for math tests

Many students who could succeed in math shy away from the subject. Some had negative experiences in past courses. Others believe that math is only for gifted students.

At some level, however, math is open to all students. There's more to this subject than memorizing formulas and manipulating numbers. Imagination, creativity, and problem-solving skills are important too.

Consider a three-part program for math success. Begin with strategies for overcoming math anxiety. Next, boost your study skills. Finally, let your knowledge shine during tests.

OVERCOME MATH ANXIETY

Many schools offer courses in overcoming math anxiety. Ask your advisor about resources on your campus. Also experiment with the following suggestions.

Connect math to life. Think of the benefits of mastering math courses. You'll have more options for choosing a major and a career. Math skills can also put you at ease in everyday situations—calculating the tip for a waiter, balancing your checkbook, working with a spreadsheet on a computer. If you follow baseball statistics, cook, do construction work, or snap pictures with a camera, you'll use math. And speaking the language of math can help you feel at home in a world driven by technology.

Pause occasionally to get an overview of the branch of math that you're studying. What's it all about? What basic problems is it designed to solve? How do people apply this knowledge in daily life? For example, many architects, engineers, and space scientists use calculus daily.

Take a First Step. Math is cumulative. Concepts build upon each other in a certain order. If you struggled with algebra, you may have trouble with trigonometry or calculus.

To ensure that you have an adequate base of knowledge, tell the truth about your current level of knowledge and skill. Before you register for a math course, locate assigned texts for the prerequisite courses. If the material in those books seems new or

7

difficult for you, see the instructor. Ask for suggestions on ways to prepare for the course.

Notice your pictures about math. Sometimes what keeps people from succeeding at math is their mental picture of mathematicians. They see a man dressed in a baggy plaid shirt and brown wingtip shoes. He's got a calculator on his belt and six pencils jammed in his shirt pocket.

These pictures are far from realistic. Succeeding in math won't turn you into a nerd. Actually, you'll be able to enjoy school more, and your friends will still like you.

Mental pictures about math can be funny, but they can have serious effects. If math is seen as a field for white males, then women and people of color are likely to get excluded. Promoting math success for all students helps to overcome racism and sexism.

Change your conversation about math. When students fear math, they often say negative things to themselves about their abilities in this subject. Many times this self-talk includes statements such as *I'll never be fast enough at solving math problems* or *I'm good with words, so I can't be good with numbers.*

Get such statements out in the open, and apply some emergency critical thinking. You'll find two self-defeating assumptions lurking there: *Everybody else is better at math and science than I am* and *Since I don't understand a math concept right now, I'll never understand it.* Both of these statements are illogical.

Replace negative beliefs with logical, realistic statements that affirm your ability to succeed in math: *Any confusion I feel now can be resolved. I learn math without comparing myself to others.* And *I ask whatever questions are needed to aid my understanding.*

Choose your response to stress. Math anxiety is seldom just "in your head." It can also register as sweaty palms, shallow breathing, tightness in the chest, or a mild headache. Instead of trying to ignore these sensations, just notice them without judgment. Over time, simple awareness decreases their power.

In addition, use stress management techniques. "Let Go of Test Anxiety" on page 196 offers a bundle of them.

No matter what you do, remember to breathe. You can relax in any moment just by making your breath slower and deeper. Practice doing this while you study math. It will come in handy at test time.

BOOST STUDY SKILLS FOR MATH

Choose teachers with care. Whenever possible, find a math teacher whose approach to math matches your learning style. Talk with several teachers until you find one you enjoy.

Another option is to ask around. Maybe your academic advisor can recommend math teachers. Also ask classmates to name their favorite math teachers—and to explain the reasons for their choices.

In some cases, only one teacher will be offering the math course you need. The suggestions that follow can be used to learn from a teacher regardless of her teaching style.

Take math courses back to back. Approach math in the same way that you learn a foreign language. If you take a year off in between Spanish I and Spanish II, you won't gain much fluency. To master a language, you take courses back to back. It works the same way with math, which is a language in itself.

Avoid short courses. Courses that you take during summer school or another shortened term are condensed. You might find yourself doing far more reading and homework each week than you do in longer courses. If you enjoy math, the extra intensity can provide a stimulus to learn. But if math is not your favorite subject, give yourself extra time. Enroll in courses spread out over more calendar days.

Form a study group. During the first week of each math course, organize a study group. Ask each member to bring five problems to group meetings, along with solutions. Also exchange contact information so that you can stay in touch via e-mail, phone, and text messaging.

Make your text top priority. Math courses are often text driven. Budget for math textbooks and buy them as early as possible. Class activities usually closely follow the book. This fact underscores the importance of completing your reading assignments. Master one concept before going on to the next, and stay current with your reading. Be willing to read slowly and reread sections as needed.

Do homework consistently. Students who succeed in math do their homework daily—from beginning to end, and from the easy problems all the way through the hard problems. If you do homework consistently, you're not likely to be surprised on a test.

When doing homework, use a common process to solve similar problems. There's comfort in rituals, and using familiar steps can help to reduce math anxiety.

Take notes that promote success in math. Though math courses are often text-driven, you might find that the content and organization of your notes makes a big difference as well. Take notes during every class and organize them by date. Also number the pages of your notes. Create a table of contents or index for them so that you can locate key concepts quickly.

In addition, make separate notes to integrate material from class meetings and reading assignments. Paul Nolting, author of the *Math Study Skills Workbook*, suggests that you create a large table with three columns: Key Words/Rules, Examples, and Explanation.[3] Updating this table weekly is a way to review for tests, uncover questions, and monitor your understanding.

Participate in class. Success in math depends on your active involvement. Attend class regularly. Complete homework assignments *when they're due*—not just before the test. If you're confused, get help right away from an instructor, tutor, or study group. Instructors' office hours, free on-campus tutoring, and classmates are just a few of the resources available to you. Also support class participation with time for homework. Make daily contact with math.

1: Prepare

- Read each problem two or three times, slowly and out loud whenever possible.
- Consider creating a chart with three columns labeled *What I already know, What I want to find out,* and *What connects the two.* The third column is the place to record a formula that can help you solve the problem.
- Determine which arithmetic operations (addition, subtraction, multiplication, division) or formulas you will use to solve the problem.
- See if you can estimate the answer before you compute it.

2: Compute

- Reduce the number of unknowns as much as you can. Consider creating a separate equation to solve each unknown.
- When solving equations, carry out the algebra as far as you can before plugging in the actual numbers.
- Cancel and combine. For example, if the same term appears in both dividend and divisor, they will cancel each other out.
- Remember that it's OK to make several attempts at solving the problem before you find an answer.

3: Check

- Plug your answer back into the original equation or problem and see if it works out correctly.
- Ask yourself if your answer seems likely when compared with your estimate. For example, if you're asked to apply a discount to an item, that item should cost less in your solution.
- Perform opposite operations. If a problem involves multiplication, check your work by division; add, then subtract; factor, then multiply; find the square root, then the square; differentiate, then integrate.
- Keep units of measurement clear. Say that you're calculating the velocity of an object. If you're measuring distance in meters and time in seconds, the final velocity should be in meters per second.

Math tests often involve lists of problems to solve. Ask your instructor about what type of tests to expect. Then prepare for the tests using strategies from this chapter.

Ask questions fearlessly. It's a cliché, and it's true: In math, there are no dumb questions. Ask whatever questions will aid your understanding. Keep a running list of them, and bring the list to class.

Read actively. To get the most out of your math texts, read with paper and pencil in hand. Work out examples. Copy diagrams, formulas, and equations. Use chapter summaries and introductory outlines to organize your learning. From time to time, stop, close your book, and mentally reconstruct the steps in solving a problem. Before you memorize a formula, understand the basic concepts behind it.

USE TESTS TO SHOW WHAT YOU KNOW

Practice problem solving. To get ready for math tests, work *lots* of problems. Find out whether practice problems or previous tests are on file in the library, in the math department, or with your math teacher.

Isolate the types of problems that you find the most difficult. Practice them more often. Be sure to get help with these kinds of problems *before* exhaustion or frustration sets in.

To prepare for tests, practice working problems fast. Time yourself. This activity is a great one for math study groups.

Approach problem solving with a three-step process, as shown in the chart on this page. During each step, apply an appropriate strategy.

Practice test taking. In addition to solving problems, create practice tests:

- Print out a set of problems, and set a timer for the same length of time as your testing period.
- Whenever possible, work on these problems in the same room where you will take the actual test.
- Use only the kinds of supporting materials—such as scratch paper or lists of formulas—that will be allowed during the test.
- As you work problems, use deep breathing or another technique to enter a more relaxed state.

To get the most value from practice tests, use them to supplement—not replace—your daily homework.

Ask appropriate questions. If you don't understand a test item, ask for clarification. The worst that can happen is that an instructor or proctor will politely decline to answer your question.

Write legibly. Put yourself in the instructor's place. Imagine the prospect of grading stacks of illegible answer sheets. Make your answers easy to read. If you show your work, underline key sections and circle your answer.

Do your best. There are no secrets involved in getting ready for math tests. Master some stress management techniques, do your homework, get answers to your questions, and work sample problems. If you've done those things, you're ready for the test and deserve to do well. If you haven't done all those things, just do the best you can.

Remember that your personal best can vary from test to test, and even from day to day. Even if you don't answer all test questions correctly, you can demonstrate what you *do* know right now.

During the test, notice when solutions come easily. Savor the times when you feel relaxed and confident. If you ever feel math anxiety in the future, these are the times to remember.[4] ■

Notable failures

As you experiment with memory techniques, you may try a few that fail at crucial moments—such as during a test. Just remember that many people before you have failed miserably before succeeding brilliantly. Consider a few examples.

In his first professional race, cyclist **Lance Armstrong** finished last.

The first time **Jerry Seinfeld** walked onstage at a comedy club as a professional comic, he looked out at the audience and froze.

When **Lucille Ball** began studying to be an actress in 1927, she was told by the head instructor of the John Murray Anderson Drama School, "Try any other profession."

In high school, actor and comic **Robin Williams** was voted "Least Likely to Succeed."

Walt Disney was fired by a newspaper editor because "he lacked imagination and had no good ideas."

R. H. Macy failed seven times before his store in New York City caught on.

Emily Dickinson had only seven poems published in her lifetime.

Decca Records turned down a recording contract with the **Beatles** with an unprophetic evaluation: "We don't like their sound. Groups of guitars are on their way out."

In 1954, Jimmy Denny, manager of the Grand Ole Opry, fired **Elvis Presley** after one performance.

Babe Ruth is famous for his past home run record, but for decades he also held the record for strikeouts. **Mark McGwire** broke that record.

After **Carl Lewis** won the gold medal for the long jump in the 1996 Olympic Games, he was asked to what he attributed his longevity, having competed for almost 20 years. He said, "Remembering that you have both wins and losses along the way. I don't take either one too seriously."

"I've missed more than 9,000 shots in my career," **Michael Jordan** said. "I've lost almost 300 games. Twenty-six times I've been trusted to take the game winning shot . . . and missed. I've failed over and over and over again in my life. That is why I succeed."

Adapted from "But They Did Not Give Up," Division of Educational Studies, Emory University, accessed January 20, 2011, from www.des.emory.edu/mfp/OnFailingG.html.

You're One Click Away...
from finding more notable failures online.

masterstudentprofile

Al Gore

(1948–) Former vice president of the United States. Gore refocused his career on climate change, won a Nobel Peace Prize, and—in his film *An Inconvenient Truth*—invented a new type of documentary.

One hundred and nineteen years ago, a wealthy inventor read his own obituary, mistakenly published years before his death. Wrongly believing the inventor had just died, a newspaper printed a harsh judgment of his life's work, unfairly labeling him "The Merchant of Death" because of his invention—dynamite. Shaken by this condemnation, the inventor made a fateful choice to serve the cause of peace.

Seven years later, Alfred Nobel created this prize and the others that bear his name.

Seven years ago tomorrow, I read my own political obituary in a judgment that seemed to me harsh and mistaken—if not premature. But that unwelcome verdict also brought a precious if painful gift: an opportunity to search for fresh new ways to serve my purpose.

Unexpectedly, that quest has brought me here. Even though I fear my words cannot match this moment, I pray what I am feeling in my heart will be communicated clearly enough that those who hear me will say, "We must act." . . .

In the last few months, it has been harder and harder to misinterpret the signs that our world is spinning out of kilter. Major cities in North and South America, Asia, and Australia are nearly out of water due to massive droughts and melting glaciers. Desperate farmers are losing their livelihoods. Peoples in the frozen Arctic and on low-lying Pacific islands are planning evacuations of places they have long called home. Unprecedented wildfires have forced a half million people from their homes in one country and caused a national emergency that almost brought down the government in another. Climate refugees have migrated into areas already inhabited by people with different cultures, religions, and traditions, increasing the potential for conflict. Stronger storms in the Pacific and Atlantic have threatened whole cities. Millions have been displaced by massive flooding in South Asia, Mexico, and 18 countries in Africa. As temperature extremes have increased, tens of thousands have lost their lives. We are recklessly burning and clearing our forests and driving more and more species into extinction.

There is an African proverb that says, "If you want to go quickly, go alone. If you want to go far, go together." We need to go far, quickly. . . .

Fifteen years ago, I made that case at the "Earth Summit" in Rio de Janeiro. Ten years ago, I presented it in Kyoto. This week, I will urge the delegates in Bali to adopt a bold mandate for a treaty that establishes a universal global cap on emissions and uses the market in emissions trading to efficiently allocate resources to the most effective opportunities for speedy reductions.

This treaty should be ratified and brought into effect everywhere in the world by the beginning of 2010— 2 years sooner than presently contemplated. The pace of our response must be accelerated to match the accelerating pace of the crisis itself. . . .

Make no mistake, the next generation will ask us one of two questions. Either they will ask: "What were you thinking; why didn't you act?"

Or they will ask instead: "How did you find the moral courage to rise and successfully resolve a crisis that so many said was impossible to solve?"

AL GORE ... is optimistic.

YOU ... can be more optimistic by focusing on your goals.

Al Gore Nobel Lecture, Oslo, 10 December 2007. Copyright © The Nobel Foundation 2007. Reproduced by permission.

You're One Click Away...
from learning more about Al Gore online at the Master Student Profiles. You can also visit the Master Student Hall of Fame to learn about other master students.

FIVE Cs
FOR YOUR CAREER

CHARACTER • CRITICAL THINKING • CREATIVE THINKING • COLLABORATION • COMMUNICATION

Like tests, performance reviews are evaluations. Think of them as the workplace equivalent of the First Step exercise in Chapter 2. Treat these reviews as opportunities to discover your strengths—and to take your experience of the five Cs to a new level.

Connect performance reviews to character. Some employees look forward to annual performance reviews about as much as getting a root canal. To develop the qualities of a Master Student, experiment with a different attitude. When handled with skill, performance reviews are tools for re-creating your experience of work and enjoying more long-term success.

Performance reviews will probably take place in a meeting with your direct supervisor at work. Meetings follow various formats, and many organizations have their own systems for rating performance. Yet the basic idea in any case is for you to walk away with answers to three questions: What am I doing well? What could I do better? And, how can I develop the skills to do better? Answering these questions demonstrates a professional work ethic and gets to the heart of character development.

Think creatively to prepare for the review. As the date of your performance review approaches, imagine the kind of questions your supervisor will ask. For example:

- What was your biggest accomplishment since your last performance review?

- In light of your stated goals, how did you feel about your performance?

- What prevented you from performing well or meeting any of your goals?

- What can you do to overcome those obstacles?

- What can coworkers and managers do to help you overcome those obstacles?

Put your answers to such questions in writing, and revise them to clarify your thinking.

Think critically to set goals. Your organization may schedule performance reviews only once or twice per year. Another option is to see effective performance review as a continuous process.

For optimum results, begin this process on your first day at work. When you start a new job, meet with your direct supervisor to define exactly what "effective performance" means for you.

Here's where your skills at goal setting—a form of critical thinking—can be a lifesaver (see Chapter 3). Translate your definition of effective performance into goals that you can achieve. State them in specific, measurable terms. When the goal is achieved:

- What will you *have* that you don't have now?

- What will you *do* differently?

- How will you *be* different?

Whenever possible, set a specific date to meet each goal. Then put your goals in writing and share them with your supervisor. Also ask if you can submit self-reviews of your performance in preparation for the formal review.

Communicate to keep the tone positive. Sometimes performance reviews are stiff and formal. Supervisor and employees go through the motions, and both are relieved when the meeting is over.

Here is your chance to take the conversation to a deeper level.

During your performance review, refer to your list of goals and note which ones you met. Take time to celebrate your accomplishments and set new goals.

If you missed a goal, talk about how that happened. Instead of focusing on failure or placing blame, take a problem-solving approach. If you made a mistake, talk about what you learned from the experience and what you intend to do differently in the future. Revise the goal and create a new plan for achieving it.

Remember that communication is the creating of shared understanding. Take the assumptions and guesswork out of performance reviews by getting everyone's expectations out on the table, and in writing.

Turn performance reviews into opportunities to collaborate. Effective performance reviews include time for you to *give* feedback as well as receive it. Discuss what you like about your job and what you would like to change. Meeting your goals might call for changes in your job description or extra resources—new equipment, training, coaching, or more. Ask for these.

Instead of complaining about working conditions during your review, make suggestions. "My office is way too noisy for me to be productive" is a complaint. "Let's set up a quiet room in our building where people can go to do work that requires long periods of concentration" is a suggestion. Suggestions are easier to hear than complaints and naturally lend themselves to follow-up action. That action is often taken by a team of people who collaborate to make a change in the workplace.

Now make a personal commitment to develop the five Cs. Take another look at the Discovery Wheel in Chapter 2—especially the sections labeled Character, Creative and Critical Thinking, Communicating, and Collaborating. Take a snapshot of your current skills in these areas after reading and doing this chapter.

DISCOVERY

My scores on the "Five C" sections of the Discovery Wheel were:	As of today, I would give myself the following scores in these areas:	At the end of this course, I would like my scores in these areas to be:
Character _____	Character _____	Character _____
Creative & Critical Thinking _____	Creative & Critical Thinking _____	Creative & Critical Thinking _____
Communicating _____	Communicating _____	Communicating _____
Collaborating _____	Collaborating _____	Collaborating _____

Next, choose your favorite test-taking technique and consider how it could enhance your skill in at least one of the five Cs.

I discovered that my favorite technique for taking tests is . . .

_____

_____

_____

_____

This technique will help me further develop at least one of the five Cs because . . .

_____

_____

_____

_____

INTENTION
To use this technique, I intend to . . .

_____

_____

_____

_____

NEXT ACTION
The specific action I will take is . . .

_____

_____

_____

_____

7

Name _____

Date _____

1. Describe how using the "Power Process: Detach" differs from giving up.

    Detaching (giving up an attachment to a goal) doesn't mean you give up on the goal. When you detach, you get to keep your values and goals. However, you know you will be okay even if you fail to achieve the goal.   (*Power Process: Detach*, page 186)

2. According to the text, test scores measure your accomplishments in a course. True or false? Explain your answer.

    False. Test scores are a measure of how well we do on tests.   (*Disarm tests*, page 187)

3. Briefly explain the difference between a *daily review* and a *major review*.

    Daily reviews include short preclass and postclass reviews of lecture notes and brief text reviews. Major reviews are usually done about a week before an exam and are much longer study periods, such as 2 to 5 hours per session.   (*What to do* before *the test*, page 189)

4. Define the term *study checklist*, and give three examples of what to include on such checklists.

    Study checklists are lists of everything one needs to review for a given test. They are similar to a to-do list or a study plan. List at least three of the following examples of what to include (answers will vary): reading assignments listed by page or chapter number; dates of lecture notes; types of problems to be solved; other skills to master; a brief description of each item to study.   (*What to do* before *the test*, page 189)

5. According to the text, you are not finished with a test until you know the answer to any question you missed—and why you missed it. True or false? Explain your answer.

    True. When you discover what questions you missed and understand the reasons for lost points, you learn something—and you greatly increase your odds of achieving better scores later in the course. (*The test isn't over* until..., page 195)

6. When answering multiple-choice questions, the recommended strategy is to read all of the possible answers before answering the question in your head. True or false? Explain your answer.

    False. You should answer the question in your head before looking at the possible answers. If you are confident you are correct in the answer you come up with, you should then look for that answer in the list of choices. (*What to do during the test*, page 192)

7. The presence of absolute qualifiers, such as *always* or *never*, generally indicates a false statement. True or false? Explain your answer.

    True. Because very few things are 100 percent, and you need to think of only one exception to make a statement false, this is generally a trick question. Such qualifiers generally indicate a false statement. (*What to do during the test*, page 192)

8. Describe three techniques for dealing with test anxiety.

    Describe at least three of the following: Breathe; describe sensations; scan your body; use guided imagery; exercise aerobically; find alternatives to chemicals; accept your emotions; practice detachment; and make contact with the present moment.   (*Let go of test anxiety*, page 196)

9. The text offers a three-step process for solving math problems. Name these steps, and list a strategy related to each one.

    (Answers will vary.) *First, prepare:* Read each problem. Create a three-column chart—What I know, what I want to find out, and what connects the two. Determine which arithmetic operations or formulas you will use. Estimate the answer before computing it. *Second, compute*: Reduce the number of unknowns. Carry out algebraic equations before using actual numbers. Cancel and combine. Remember that it's okay to make several attempts. *Third, check*: Plug your answer in to see if it works out correctly. Compare your answer to your estimate. Perform opposite operations. Keep units of measurement clear. (*Getting ready for math tests*, page 199)

10. Suggestions for taking essay tests include the following:

    (a) Find out what an essay question is asking—precisely.

    (b) Make a quick outline before you write.

    (c) Introduce your answer by getting to the point.

    (d) Write legibly.

    (e) All of the above

    (e) All of the above (*What to do during the test*, page 192)

CHAPTER 8

CREATIVE & CRITICAL THINKING

Instructor Tools & Tips

"I always wanted to be somebody, but I should've been more specific."
—Lily Tomlin

"Creativity was in each one of us as a small child. In children it is universal. Among adults it is almost nonexistent. The great question is: What has happened to this enormous and universal human capacity?"
—Tillie Olsen

PREVIEW

Critical thinking is an essential skill for success in the classroom and in the workplace. Although critical thinking has already been introduced through the Master Student Map, Learning Styles Applications, chapter exercises, Journal Entries, and Practicing Critical Thinking exercises, Chapter 8 takes a more in-depth look at how students can practice the strategies presented in Chapters 1 through 7, using higher levels of thinking. At this point, your students will have taken their first tests in their other courses and will have become familiar with the learning strategies presented in the earlier chapters of *From Master Student to Master Employee*. Now you can help them take the next step toward thinking critically in higher education. The skills they learn in this chapter can be applied immediately to one decision that most of your students must make—choosing a major.

A primary objective of the student success course is to nurture the fundamental skill of critical thinking. From the beginning of this text, your students have been using the Master Student Map as a means of thinking critically.

When they ask *why* they need this chapter, have them complete a chapter reconnaissance of *what* new materials are in this chapter. Together you can discuss *how* these new ideas will help them become better students. Remind your students that, with these techniques, they can open the door of possibility (*What if?*) to solve problems more creatively and make decisions with confidence. Remind students to find the value in their own lives. The key is to

plug into these questions: *What* does this material mean to me personally? *How* can I use this information to improve my life?

GUEST SPEAKER

Critical thinking is a priority for many workplace scenarios. A police officer, attorney, or law school professor would be a great guest speaker for this chapter. These guests can provide students with a dramatic reality check that will help you reinforce the importance of critical thinking in the real world. Ask your guests to prepare to talk for approximately 10 minutes on the importance of critical thinking in their jobs.

Another guest speaker idea is to invite a colleague from the department that offers critical and/or creative thinking courses, or logic courses, to talk about classes that students can take to expand on the concepts they learn in this chapter.

LECTURE

Use the following excerpt from Vincent Ryan Ruggiero's *Instructor's Resource Manual to Accompany Becoming a Critical Thinker*, Fifth Edition, copyright 2006 (reprinted by permission) to help you prepare lectures for this chapter:

As a result of the historic neglect of thinking, many people harbor misconceptions about thinking instruction. The following misconceptions are the most damaging:

That thinking can't be taught. A related misconception is that thinking can be taught only to "gifted" people. The basis of both misconceptions is the pessimistic view that intelligence is fixed and therefore cannot be increased. Formal research and the experience of innumerable thinking-skills instructors disprove this notion.

That thinking is taught automatically in certain courses. Some people reason that English courses teach thinking automatically because they deal with the expression of ideas and because expression is intimately connected to thought. Others make similar claims for science because it deals with scientific method, history because it deals with the record of human thought and action, or psychology because it deals with behavior. Research has long made clear that no course content, by itself, can teach thinking; in other words, thinking skills are developed only when students receive direct instruction in them and have frequent opportunities for guided practice.

That thinking skills are necessarily subject-specific. According to this view, economists use one set of thinking skills, biologists another, and anthropologists yet another; no generic thinking skills exist. Yet close examination of what thinkers do in everyday situations reveals great similarity in their patterns of thought. Moreover, the patterns of error are also remarkably similar. That is why the list of logical fallacies has remained essentially the same since the time of the ancient Greeks. Though different academic disciplines may employ certain patterns of thinking more often and in slightly different ways than others, the fundamental fact is that the human mind created the academic disciplines and is neither defined nor limited by them.

That students learn to think by being exhorted or inspired. Exhortation and inspiration can surely motivate students to learn, but these approaches have little if any teaching force, particularly where skills are involved. No one ever learned to master driving a car or playing the piccolo or dribbling a basketball by hearing a lecture. Similarly, intellectual skills are learned by doing and by receiving guidance and encouragement from knowledgeable people.

EXERCISES/ACTIVITIES

1. Have students practice problem solving and noticing assumptions by completing an in-class case study. Have them do this in groups of four. Individually, they read the short case study in class. Then they discuss it in their group. Facilitate a full-class discussion so that students can hear what other groups came up with. For examples and more information about using case studies in your classroom, go to the Instructor Web site.

master instructor
BEST PRACTICE

"*As a warm-up exercise or icebreaker for this chapter, I put my students into groups and give each group an ordinary household object (such as a napkin, candle, coaster, cup). Then I have the groups brainstorm ways to use the objects in a different fashion than the most obviously intended purpose. This helps students embrace different ways of thinking and stretches their minds to see things in new ways.*"

–Michelle Martin, TeamUp Consultant

2. Divide students into groups, and have them work through the following problem using the four-step process in the article Four ways to solve problems (pages 228–229). Consider this scenario: A worker has difficulty affording the rising gas prices, making it difficult to get to work and back each day on her salary. Students should define the problem, avoiding preconceived notions. For example, if the problem is that Jane has to drive too far to work, perhaps considering the value of maintaining a good job, the problem may include changing housing, rather than jobs. Students should work through steps 1–3, creating a plan for solving the problem. Students may consider the following issues to solve this problem: changing jobs, finding alternate modes of travel, and changing housing. This process will emphasize the fact that there can be several valid options to solve the same problem. Have each group make a 90-second summary report to the class about their position on the issue and their justification for that position.

3. Ask students to reread Thinking: Moving from 'aha!' to follow through (page 209). Describe the following scenario: Adrian is an employee who listens attentively and observes trends in the workplace. He is punctual, dependable, and always "on task." He has a thorough understanding of the dynamics and issues in his job. Adrian is aware of the suggestion box in the employee break room, asking for suggestions to problems in the office, but he chooses not to submit suggestions, preferring to stay "below the radar." Ask students, "Is it possible or advisable for Adrian to *understand* office problems (Bloom's Level 2) without *analyzing* (Level 4), *evaluating* (Level 5), or *creating* solutions (Level 6)?" Now ask how this lack of higher level Bloom's response can affect Adrian's security and advancement in the workplace. How does an employer view the "follow-through" phase?

CONVERSATION/SHARING

Begin with a discussion about the media's influence on our lives, using the think-pair-share discussion pattern. Model this process for students first. Discuss products that we buy because of media influence and marketing. Ask the students to think critically about the topic and then have them free-write for a minute about their thoughts on the matter and about the learning style questions. They need to feel that they can jot down their own ideas without worrying about what you might expect or want them to say. Then have students work in pairs to share their ideas. Cycle through the learning style questions, and then discuss the topic as a class. More detailed information about this exercise is available on the Instructor Web site.

Power Process: Finding a bigger problem (page 208) Some students feel trapped by their personal situation or by learning problems, to the point that their ability to succeed in school is seriously impaired. This article can help students recognize that there are other ways to view their problems. Students can look for a way to get involved in activities that take them outside their own circumstances. Find an example of a child or young person who found a way to make a difference in his or her community, emphasizing that everyone is capable of making a difference. Ask students to find out about one group or organization in your community where they could make a positive contribution. Ask students to share their discoveries.

Five Cs for Your Career (pages 232–233) Chapters 1, 8, 9, and 10 address essential transferable skills sought out by employers, Discuss the topics addressed in these chapters in context of the 5 Cs to give students a greater understanding of the role they play in their continued success. You may find self-scores for Creative and Critical Thinking, Communicating, and Collaborating improve as they learn more about these skill sets. Ask student to share their Discovery/ Intention Statements as you move through these chapters.

HOMEWORK

Examining different points of view This can be assigned in class or as homework. Have students read a newspaper article about a current, controversial issue and then answer the first two learning style questions (*Why?* and *What?*) based on the information in the article. Then have them form groups of four to discuss their ideas. Eventually, someone will say that there is not enough information in the article to explore all of the various views on the topic. This provides an opportunity to ask students to continue this project outside the classroom, using campus resources (such as the library and the Internet) to fully answer the second and third (*What?* and *How?*) learning style questions. They should also work on the fourth question *(What if?)* at home. At the next class meeting, have the students discuss their findings and draw conclusions.

Selecting classes Too often, the hectic process of registering for classes results in a schedule based on convenience rather than critical decision making. Ask students to follow the systematic procedure described in the article Gaining skill at decision making (page 227) to decide which classes to take next semester—before the schedule of classes has been published. Emphasize that the section "Use time as an ally" has a flip side. Sometimes acting quickly to make a decision, such as selecting classes, can allow you to select the most desirable teachers and class times—using time as an ally.

EVALUATION

With the skills students have learned about essay test answers in Chapter 7, they are prepared to answer an essay question that requires critical thinking. Ask them to justify

master instructor
BEST PRACTICE

"*Choosing your major is a major topic in my course. My background is in career counseling, and statistics back up the assumption that students make better grades and are less likely to drop out if they have selected a major and have a good handle on a future career. In my class (and at our school), students are required to complete an exploration paper. In my class, we set academic and career goals (even if it's to select a major and career) [and] generate career ideas using a variety of methods (including interest/skills/ personality inventories). Students select one career and major to research, complete an informational interview, and finally write a paper reviewing what they have done/researched and any conclusions they have drawn.*"

–Terry Carles, Valencia Community College

their answers to open-ended questions about common mistakes in logic, learning through inquiry, or thinking critically about information on the Internet.

Quiz Ideas for Chapter 8

Ask students to:

- Describe comcmon mistakes in logic and give examples.
- Describe the difference between creative and critical thinking.
- Describe ways to overcome stereotypes.

Additional Digital Resources for Chapter 8

What can you **ASSIGN FROM THE COURSEMATE** for *From Master Student to Master Employee?*

• **Video Skillbuilders.** These interactive online tools combine video clips featuring discussions with students, instructors, and experts, with articles and activities designed to give students a fully engaging learning experience. Either view and experience these together in class, or have students view them as a homework assignment and respond to the viewing questions and reflective exercise. These modules are good matches for Chapter 8:

- Critical Thinking: What Is Critical Thinking?
- Critical Thinking in Action: Career Planning
- Exploring Majors

Note that Video Skillbuilders are available for every chapter.

• **Power Process Media.** To help students understand the importance of "finding a bigger problem" as described in the Power Process for Chapter 8, have them watch a video on this subject, listen to an audio version, and then answer the accompanying questions. A PowerPoint presentation that summarizes the Power Process article's main points is also included. Or have students create group multimedia PowerPoint presentations based on their understanding of how to "find a bigger problem." Note that Power Process media are available for every chapter.

• **Chapter Reflections.** This diverse set of questions can get students actively using their critical thinking skills, whether by a Learning Style Application, discussion questions, or experimenting with strategies.

CourseMate *To access CourseMate, your students need to visit www.cengagebrain .com. At the CengageBrain.com home page, students search for the ISBN of* From Master Student to Master Employee *(from the back cover of the book), using the search box at the top of the page. This takes them to the product page where these resources can be found.*

Did you know that **THESE RESOURCES** (and many more) **ARE AVAILABLE** on the **INSTRUCTOR COMPANION SITE?**

• **Looking for fresh, innovative ways to teach Chapter 8 topics?** Browse through the Best Practices library to see what other Master Instructors have been successfully doing with their students.

• **Questions about how to incorporate critical thinking into your course?** Look to the online *Course Manual* for the following articles with suggestions for how to make critical thinking skills an integral part of your course:

- Strategies for encouraging more class participation from your students
- Improving learning and problem-solving Skills
- Using journaling in your course

master instructor BEST PRACTICE

" Who Says So? *Entering first-year students often lack any formal training in the skills of critical thinking. This demonstration aims to provide a model lesson for getting a class to think about five common categories or statements usually lumped together as accepted "truths." Ask students to list on a slip of paper any six statements they take to be true. Then solicit 20 or so random samples of "truths," writing these on the board. These audience-generated statements are the raw material from which you can uncover a pattern by asking this simple question: Who is your authority for the truth of this statement? The following patterns are typically uncovered:*

- *I say so: My personal experience is the authority for the truthfulness of the statement.*
- *"They" say so: Cultural consensus or common sense is the authority.*
- *Science says so: Some aspect of the scientific method is the authority.*
- *"We" say so: Some prior established rule is the authority (e.g., one dime is worth two nickels).*
- *God says so: A sacred text or tradition is the authority.*

If by chance any category is not represented in this random sample, supply some examples of your own in order to complete the whole pattern. Conclude the lesson by pointing out that we use very different criteria for testing and judging the truth of a statement in each one of the uncovered categories. Thus, it is never wrong for students (or anybody else) to begin their critical thinking process about any statement by asking the basic question: Who says so? **"**

–Carol Lindquist, Borough of Manhattan Community College

Please visit login.cengage.com *to log in and access the Instructor Companion Site.*

Creative & Critical Thinking

Use this **Master Student Map** to ask yourself

WHY THIS CHAPTER MATTERS . . .

- The ability to think creatively and critically helps you succeed in any course and opens up new career possibilities.

WHAT IS INCLUDED . . .

HOW I CAN USE THIS CHAPTER. . .

- Solve problems creatively.
- Make decisions with more confidence.
- Protect myself from stereotypes, misleading claims, and manipulative advertising.
- Boost my skills in speaking, listening, reading, and writing.

WHAT IF . . .

- I could meet any challenge with a fresh perspective that creates new possibilities for my life?

© Ruslan Ivantsov/Shutterstock.com

JOURNAL ENTRY 17
Intention Statement

Choose to create value from this chapter

Remember a time in your life when you felt unable to choose among several different solutions to a problem or struggled with making a decision. Then scan this chapter to find useful suggestions for creative thinking, critical thinking, decision making, and problem solving. Below, note at least three techniques that you definitely intend to use.

Strategy	Page number

Find a bigger problem

It is impossible to live a life that's free of problems. Besides, problems serve a purpose. They provide opportunities to participate in life. Problems stimulate us and pull us forward.

Seen from this perspective, our goal becomes not to eliminate problems, but to find problems that are worthy of us. Worthy problems are those that challenge us to think, consider our values, and define our goals. Solving the biggest problems offers the greatest potential benefits for others and ourselves. Engaging with big problems changes us for the better. Bigger problems give more meaning to our lives.

Problems expand to fill whatever space is available. Suppose that your only problem for today is to write a thank-you letter to a job interview. You could spend the entire day thinking about what you're going to say, writing the letter, finding a stamp, going to the post office—and then thinking about all of the things you forgot to say.

Now suppose that you get a phone call with an urgent message: A close friend has been admitted to the hospital and wants you to come right away. It's amazing how quickly and easily that letter can get finished when there's a bigger problem on your plate.

True, the smaller problems that enter our lives still need to be solved. The goal is simply to solve them in less time and with less energy.

Bigger problems are easy to find—world hunger, child abuse, environmental pollution, terrorism, human rights violations, drug abuse, street crime, energy shortages, poverty, and wars. These problems await your attention and involvement.

Tackling a bigger problem does not have to be depressing. In fact, it can be energizing—a reason for getting up in the morning. A huge project can channel your passion and purpose.

When we take on a bigger problem, we play full out. We do justice to our potentials. We start to love what we do and do what we love. We're awake, alert, and engaged. Playing full out means living our lives as if our lives depended on it.

Perhaps a little voice in your mind is saying, "That's crazy. I can't do anything about global problems." In the spirit of critical thinking, put that idea to the test. Get involved in solving a bigger problem. Then notice the difference that you *can* make. And just as important, notice how your other problems dwindle—or even vanish.

You're One Click Away...
from accessing Power Process Media online and finding out more about how to "find bigger problems."

Jan Martin Will/Shutterstock.com

THINKING: Moving from "aha!" to follow-through

This chapter offers you a chance to practice two types of thinking: creative thinking and critical thinking. Both are essential to your success in school and in the workplace.

One path to having good ideas is to have *lots* of ideas. Open up alternatives. Consider many options. Define problems in different ways. Keep asking new questions and looking for fresh answers. These are elements of creative thinking.

Next, pick and choose from among the ideas you create. Combine them. Refine them. Look for ways to take a new concept and turn it into a persuasive paper, a stunning presentation, a useful service, or a product that's ready to sell and ship. This is where critical thinking comes into play.

Creative thinking is the process of generating ideas to look at issues in new and different ways. Critical thinking is when we narrow down our choice by picking and choosing from among these ideas to come up with new and exciting ways to think and do things.

Use creative thinking to cultivate "aha!" Central to creative thinking is something called the "aha!" experience. Nineteenth-century poet Emily Dickinson described *aha!* this way: "If I feel physically as if the top of my head were taken off, I know that is poetry." Aha! is the burst of creative energy heralded by the arrival of a new, original idea. It is the sudden emergence of an unfamiliar pattern, a previously undetected relationship, or an unusual combination of familiar elements. It is an exhilarating experience.

Aha! does not always result in a timeless poem or a Nobel Prize. It can be inspired by anything from playing a new riff on a guitar to figuring out why your car's fuel pump doesn't work. A nurse might notice a patient's symptom that everyone else missed. That's an aha! An accountant might discover a tax break for a client. That's an aha! A teacher might devise a way to reach a difficult student. Aha!

Use critical thinking to follow through. The flip side of aha! is following through. Thinking is both fun and work. It is both effortless and uncomfortable. It's the result of luck and persistence. It involves spontaneity and step-by-step procedures, planning and action, convergent and creative thinking.

Employers want people who can find aha! and do something with it to develop new products and services. This calls for the abilities to spot assumptions, weigh evidence, separate fact from opinion, organize thoughts, and avoid errors in logic. All these skills involve demanding work. Just as often, they can be energizing and fun.

Use critical thinking to make wise choices. Society depends on persuasion. Advertisers want us to spend money on their products. Political candidates want us to "buy" their stands on the issues. Teachers want us to agree that their classes are vital to our success. Parents want us to accept their values. Authors want us to read their books. Broadcasters want us to spend our time in front of the radio or television, consuming their programs and not those of the competition. The business of persuasion has an impact on all of us.

A typical American sees thousands of television commercials each year—and TV is just one medium of communication. Add to that the writers and speakers who enter our lives through radio shows, magazines, books, billboards, brochures, Internet sites, and fund-raising appeals—all with a product, service, cause, or opinion for us to embrace.

This flood of appeals leaves us with hundreds of choices about what to buy, where to go, and who to be. It's easy to lose our heads in the crosscurrent of competing ideas—unless we develop skills in critical thinking. When we think critically, we can make choices with open eyes.

8

> This flood of appeals leaves us with hundreds of choices about what to buy, where to go, and who to be. It's easy to lose our heads in the crosscurrent of competing ideas—unless we develop skills in critical thinking.

It has been said that human beings are rational creatures. Yet no one is born an effective thinker. Critical thinking is a learned skill. This is one reason that you study so many subjects in higher education—math, science, history, psychology, literature, and more. A broad base of courses helps you develop as a thinker. You see how people with different viewpoints arrive at conclusions, make decisions, and solve problems. This gives you a foundation for dealing with complex challenges in your career, your relationships, and your community.

Use critical thinking to avoid deception. One of the reasons that critical thinking is so challenging—and so rewarding—is that we have a remarkable capacity to fool ourselves. Some of our ill-formed thoughts and half-truths have a source that hits a little close to home. That source is ourselves.

For example, consider someone who stakes her identity on the fact that she is a valued employee. During a recession, she gets laid off. On her last day at work, she learns that her refusal to take part in on-the-job training sessions was the major reason that the company let her go. This brute fact contradicts her belief in her value. Her response: "I didn't need that training. I already knew that stuff anyway. Nobody at that company could teach me anything."

A skilled critical thinker would go beyond such self-justifying statements and ask questions instead: "What training sessions did I miss? Could I have learned something from them? Were there any signs that I was about to be laid off, and did I overlook them? What can I do to prevent this from happening again?"

Master students are willing to admit the truth when they discover that their thinking is fuzzy, lazy, based on a false assumption, or dishonest. These students value facts. When a solid fact contradicts a cherished belief, they are willing to change the belief.

More uses of creative and critical thinking. Clear thinking promotes your success inside and outside the classroom. Any time that you are faced with a choice about what to believe or what to do, your thinking skills come in to play. Consider the following applications.

- *Thinking informs reading, writing, speaking, and listening.* These elements are the basis of communication—a process that occupies most of our waking hours.

- *Thinking promotes social change.* The institutions in any society—courts, governments, schools, businesses, nonprofit groups—are the products of cultural customs and trends. All social movements—from the American Revolution to the Civil Rights movement—come about through the work of engaged individuals who actively participated in their communities and questioned what was going on around them. As creative and critical thinkers, we strive to understand and influence the institutions in our society.

- *Thinking uncovers bias and prejudice.* Working through our preconceived notions is a first step toward communicating with people of other races, ethnic backgrounds, and cultures.

- *Thinking reveals long-term consequences.* Crises occur when our thinking fails to keep pace with reality. An example is the world's ecological crisis, which arose when people polluted the earth, air, and water without considering the long-term consequences. Imagine how different our world would be if our leaders had thought like the first female chief of the Cherokees. Asked about the best advice her elders had given her, she replied, "Look forward. Turn what has been done into a better path. If you are a leader, think about the impact of your decision on seven generations into the future."

Master the cycle of creative and critical thinking. The key is to make conscious choices about what kind of thinking to do in any given moment. Generally speaking, creative thinking is more appropriate in the early stages of planning and problem solving. Feel free to dwell in this domain for a while. If you narrow down your options too soon, you run the risk of missing an exciting solution or of neglecting a novel viewpoint.

Remember that creative thinking and critical thinking take place in a continuous cycle. After you've used critical thinking to narrow down your options, you can return to creative thinking at any time to generate new ones.

Use the suggestions in this chapter to claim the thinking powers that are your birthright. The creative thinker and the critical thinker are qualities of the master student who lives inside you. ■

> Master students are willing to admit the truth when they discover that their thinking is fuzzy, lazy, based on a false assumption, or dishonest. These students value facts. When a solid fact contradicts a cherished belief, they are willing to change the belief.

WAYS TO CREATE IDEAS

Anyone can think creatively. Use the following techniques to generate ideas about anything—whether you're studying math problems, remodeling a house, or writing a best seller.

Conduct a brainstorm. Brainstorming is a technique for creating plans, finding solutions, and discovering new ideas. When you are stuck on a problem, brainstorming can break the logjam. For example, if you run out of money 2 days before payday every week, you can brainstorm ways to make your money last longer. You can brainstorm ways to pay for your education. You can brainstorm ways to find a job.

The overall purpose of brainstorming is to generate as many solutions as possible. Sometimes the craziest, most outlandish ideas, while unworkable in themselves, can lead to new ways to solve problems. Use the following steps to try out the brainstorming process:

- *Focus on a single problem or issue.* State your focus as a question. Open-ended questions that start with the words *what, how, who, where,* and *when* often make effective focusing questions. For example, What is my ideal career? What is my ideal major? How can I raise the quality of relationships? What is the single most important change I can make in my life right now?

- *Relax.* Creativity is enhanced by a state of relaxed alertness. If you are tense or anxious, use relaxation techniques such as those described in "Let Go of Text Anxiety" in Chapter 7.

- *Set a quota or goal for the number of solutions you want to generate.* Goals give your subconscious mind something to aim for.

- *Set a time limit.* Use a clock to time it to the minute. Digital sports watches with built-in stopwatches work well. Experiment with various lengths of time. Both short and long brainstorms can be powerful.

- *Allow all answers.* Brainstorming is based on attitudes of permissiveness and patience. Accept every idea. At this stage, there are no wrong answers. If it pops into your head, put it

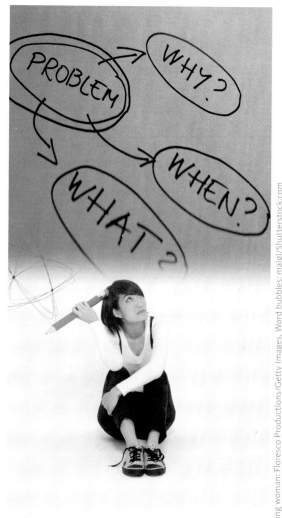

Sitting woman: Floresco Productions/Getty Images, Word bubbles: maigi/Shutterstock.com

down on paper. Quantity, not quality, is the goal. Avoid making judgments and evaluations during the brainstorming session. If you get stuck, think of an outlandish idea, and write it down. One crazy idea can unleash a flood of other, more workable solutions.

- *Brainstorm with others.* Group brainstorming is a powerful technique. Group brainstorms take on lives of their own. Assign one member of the group to write down solutions. Feed off the ideas of others, and remember to avoid evaluating or judging anyone's ideas during the brainstorm.

After your brainstorming session, evaluate the results. Toss out any truly nutty ideas, but not before you give them a chance.

Focus and let go. Focusing and letting go are alternating parts of the same process. Intense focus taps the resources of your conscious mind. Letting go gives your subconscious mind time to work. When you focus for intense periods and then let go for a while, the conscious and subconscious parts of your brain work in harmony.

Focusing attention means being in the here and now. To focus your attention on a project, notice when you pay attention and when your mind starts to wander. And involve all of your senses. For example, if you are having difficulty writing a paper at a computer, practice focusing by listening to the sounds as you type. Notice the feel of the keys as you strike them. When you know the sights, sounds, and sensations you associate with being truly in focus, you'll be able to repeat the experience and return to your paper more easily.

Be willing to recognize conflict, tension, and discomfort in yourself. Notice them and fully accept them rather than fight against them. Look for the specific thoughts and body sensations that make up the discomfort. Allow them to come fully into your awareness, and then let them pass.

You might not be focused all of the time. Periods of inspiration might last only seconds. Be gentle with yourself when you notice that your concentration has lapsed. In fact, that might be a time to

8

let go. *Letting go* means not forcing yourself to be creative. Practice focusing for short periods at first, and then give yourself a break. Play a board game. Go outside and look for shapes in the clouds. Switch to a new location. Take a nap when you are tired. Thomas Edison, the inventor, took frequent naps. Then the lightbulb clicked on.

Cultivate creative serendipity. The word *serendipity* was coined by the English author Horace Walpole from the title of an ancient Persian fairy tale, "The Three Princes of Serendip." The princes had a knack for making lucky discoveries. Serendipity is that knack, and it involves more than luck. It is the ability to see something valuable that you weren't looking for.

History is full of people who make serendipitous discoveries. Country doctor Edward Jenner noticed "by accident" that milkmaids seldom got smallpox. The result was his discovery that mild cases of cowpox immunized them. Penicillin was also discovered "by accident." Scottish scientist Alexander Fleming was growing bacteria in a laboratory petri dish. A spore of *Penicillium notatum,* a kind of mold, blew in the window and landed in the dish, killing the bacteria. Fleming isolated the active ingredient. A few years later, during World War II, it saved thousands of lives. Had Fleming not been alert to the possibility, the discovery might never have been made.

Keep your eyes open. You might find a solution to an accounting problem in a Saturday morning cartoon. You might discover a topic for your term paper at the corner convenience store. Multiply your contacts with the world. Resolve to meet new people. Join a study or discussion group. Read. Go to plays, concerts, art shows, lectures, and movies. Watch television programs you normally wouldn't watch.

Also expect discoveries. One secret for success is being prepared to recognize "luck" when you see it.

Keep idea files. We all have ideas. People who treat their ideas with care are often labeled "creative." They not only recognize ideas but also record them and follow up on them.

One way to keep track of ideas is to write them down on 3 × 5 cards. Invent your own categories, and number the cards so you can cross-reference them. For example, if you have an idea about making a new kind of bookshelf, you might file a card under "Remodeling." A second card might also be filed under "Marketable Ideas." On the first card, you can write down your ideas, and on the second, you can write, "See card #321—Remodeling."

Include in your files powerful quotations, random insights, notes on your reading, and useful ideas that you encounter in class. Collect jokes too.

Keep a journal. Journals don't have to be exclusively about your own thoughts and feelings. You can record observations about the world around you, conversations with friends, important or offbeat ideas—anything.

To fuel your creativity, read voraciously, including newspapers, magazines, blogs, and other Web sites. Explore beyond mainstream journalism. Hundreds of low-circulation specialty magazines and online news journals cover almost any subject you can imagine. Keep letter-size file folders of important documents. Bookmark Web sites in your browser. Use an online service such as Evernote, Delicious, or Pinboard to save articles that you want to read and refer to later. Create idea files on your computer.

Safeguard your ideas, even if you're pressed for time. Jotting down four or five words is enough to capture the essence of an idea. You can write down one quotation in a minute or two. And if you carry 3 × 5 cards in a pocket or purse, you can record ideas while standing in line or sitting in a waiting room.

Review your files regularly. Some amusing thought that came to you in November might be the perfect solution to a problem in March.

Collect and play with data. Look from all sides at the data you collect. Switch your attention from one aspect to another. Examine each fact, and avoid getting stuck on one particular part of a problem. Turn a problem upside down by picking a solution first and then working backward. Ask other people to look at the data. Solicit opinions.

Living with the problem invites a solution. Write down data, possible solutions, or a formulation of the problem on 3 × 5 cards, and carry them with you. Look at them before you go to bed at night. Review them when you are waiting for the bus. Make them part of your life, and think about them frequently.

Look for the obvious solutions or the obvious "truths" about the problem—then toss them out. Ask yourself, "Well, I know *x* is true, but if *x* were *not* true, what would happen?" Or ask the reverse: "If that *were* true, what would follow next?"

Put unrelated facts next to each other and invent a relationship between them, even if it seems absurd at first. In *The Act of Creation,* novelist Arthur Koestler says that finding a context in which to combine opposites is the essence of creativity.[1]

Make imaginary pictures with the data. Condense it. Categorize it. Put it in chronological order. Put it in alphabetical order. Put it in random order. Order it from most to least complex. Reverse all of those orders. Look for opposites.

It has been said that there are no new ideas—only new ways to combine old ideas. Creativity is the ability to discover those new combinations.

Create while you sleep. A part of our mind works as we sleep. You've experienced this fact directly if you've ever fallen asleep with a problem on your mind and awakened the next morning with a solution. For some of us, the solution appears in a dream or just before we fall asleep or wake up.

You can experiment with this process. Ask yourself a question as you fall asleep. Keep pencil and paper or a recorder near your bed. The moment you wake up, begin writing or speaking, and see whether an answer to your question emerges.

Many of us have awakened from a dream with a great idea, only to fall asleep again and lose it forever. To capture your ideas, keep a notebook by your bed at all times. Put the notebook where you can find it easily.

There is a story about how Benjamin Franklin used this suggestion. Late in the evenings, as he was becoming drowsy, he would sit in his rocking chair with a rock in his right hand and a metal bucket on the floor beneath the rock. The moment he fell asleep, the rock would fall from his grip into the bottom of the bucket, making a loud noise that awakened him. Having placed a pen and paper nearby, he immediately wrote down what he was thinking. Experience taught him that his thoughts at these moments were often insightful and creative.

Promote creative thinking in groups. Sometimes creative thinking dies in committee. People are afraid to disagree with a forceful leader and instead keep their mouths shut. Or a longstanding group ignores new members with new ideas. The result can be "group think," where no one questions the prevailing opinion. To stimulate creative thinking in groups, try these strategies:

- *Put your opinion on hold.* If you're leading a meeting, ask other people to speak up first. Then look for the potential value in *any* idea. Avoid nonverbal language that signals a negative reaction, such as frowning or rolling your eyes.

- *Rotate group leadership.* Ask group members to take turns. This strategy can work well in groups where people have a wide range of opinions.

- *Divide larger groups into several teams.* People might be more willing to share their ideas in a smaller group.

- *Assign a devil's advocate.* Give one person free permission to poke holes in any proposal.

- *Invite a guest expert.* A fresh perspective from someone outside the group can spark an aha!

- *Set up a suggestion box.* Let people submit ideas anonymously, in writing.

Refine ideas and follow through. Many of us ignore the part of the creative process that involves refining ideas and following through. How many great moneymaking schemes have we had that we never pursued? How many good ideas have we had for short stories that we never wrote? How many times have we said to ourselves, "You know, what they ought to do is attach two handles to one of those things, paint it orange, and sell it to police departments. They'd make a fortune." And we never realize that we are "they."

Genius resides in the follow-through—the application of perspiration to inspiration. One powerful tool you can use to follow through is the Discovery and Intention Journal Entry system. First write down your idea in a Discovery Statement, and then write what you intend to do about it in an Intention Statement. You also can explore the writing techniques discussed in Chapter 9: Communicating as a guide for refining your ideas.

Another way to refine an idea is to simplify it. And if that doesn't work, mess it up. Make it more complex.

Finally, keep a separate file in your ideas folder for your own inspirations. Return to it regularly to see whether there is anything you can use. Today's defunct term paper idea could be next year's "A" in speech class.

Trust the process. Learn to trust the creative process—even when no answers are in sight. We are often reluctant to look at problems if no immediate solution is at hand. Trust that a solution will show up. Frustration and a feeling of being stuck are often signals that a solution is imminent.

Sometimes solutions break through in a giant AHA! More often they come in a series of little aha!s. Be aware of what your aha!s look, feel, and sound like. This understanding sets the stage for even more flights of creative thinking. ■

You're One Click Away...
from finding more strategies online for creative thinking.

CREATE on your feet

A popular trend in executive offices is the stand-up desk—a raised working surface at which you stand rather than sit.

Standing has advantages over sitting for long periods. You can stay more alert and creative when you're on your feet. One theory is that our problem-solving ability improves when we stand, due to increased heart rate and blood flow to the brain.

Standing can ease lower-back pain too. Sitting for too long aggravates the spine and its supporting muscles.

Photo courtesy of David Ellis

Standing while working is a technique with tradition. If you search the Web for stand-up desks, you'll find models based on desks used by Thomas Jefferson, Winston Churchill, and writer Virginia Woolf. Consider setting your desk up on blocks or putting a box on top of your desk so that you can stand while writing, preparing speeches, or studying. Discover how long you can stand comfortably while working, and whether this approach works for you.

Creative thinking
at WORK

What does creative thinking have to do with working? Everything.

Every product you've ever bought started out as an idea in someone's head. Before it was manufactured, assembled, or sold, it was created. The same is true of any service that you can purchase—from pet sitting to digital publishing.

Creative thinking at work can change lives and create fortunes. Daniel Ek created Spotify because he wanted to create a legal music service that's more convenient than piracy. Marco Arment created an Internet-based tool called Instapaper because he wanted to "clip" articles that he found online and save them to read later. And William Kamkwamba used scrap materials to create a windmill that still powers his family's home in Malawi.[2]

Creative thinking at work is not accidental. Instead, it's carefully cultivated and sustained through dozens of simple daily choices. Get started with the following strategies.

Set aside a physical space for creative thinking. Step into any office and notice whether it's designed for creative thinking. If people hide behind desks and close their office doors, there's probably not much room for free-wheeling conversation and collaboration. If you see open workspaces and large, bright meeting rooms, then you're probably in an organization that values innovation.

Most people don't get the luxury—or the permission—to tear down cubicles and completely redesign their work spaces. Fortunately, you don't have to do that. Other options are to:

- Open shades and windows to allow more light and fresh air into an office.
- Scrounge up some high stools—which encourage alertness and an upright posture—for people to sit on during meetings.
- Ask your coworkers to stand up during meetings, which encourages people to get to the point and adjourn earlier.
- Use floor lamps to flood a room with warm light.
- Play music while people are filing into a room and waiting for a meeting to start.
- Set up meeting space so that people sit in a circle, which promotes informal conversation.

Set aside solitary time for creative thinking. A calendar that's filled with work and social activities doesn't always allow time for thinking that's free of interruptions. If you want to think creatively, then schedule time for it.

See if you can set aside one hour per week for this purpose. To free your mind from its usual patterns, get away from your work environment during a break or lunch time. Power down your phone and other digital devices for a little while, and grab a pen and some paper instead. Then walk to a library, coffee shop, or safe public space where you can be alone.

Next, sit in silence for a little while and practice the "Power Process: Be here now." Shift into a more receptive state of mind by simply noticing what you hear, see, and feel.

After a few moments, turn your attention to a single question, and let it roll around in your mind for a while. For example:

- What is my biggest current challenge at work?
- What would allow me to do my job with more fun and favorable outcomes?
- What is working well in my job, and how can I get to experience more of it?
- What frustrations do my coworkers, customers, or clients experience on a daily basis, and what would make life easier for them?

Jot down any answers that occur to you, and save them for your next creative thinking session.

Set aside group time for creative thinking. Use the questions from the Master Student Map at the beginning of each chapter in this book to fuel creative thinking with coworkers. You can adapt those questions to any project that your team is assigned to complete. For example:

- *Why are we doing this project?* Will it increase revenues, decrease costs, or improve services to our customers or clients? If this project aligns with none of those goals, then why bother?
- *What will we do to meet our goal?* What's the very next action that must occur in order for this project to move forward? Who will take that action? When?
- *How will we know whether our project succeeds?* What visible or measurable outcomes would occur? What would people say or do differently? What new products or services would result?
- *What if we did nothing?* Would the problem we're trying to solve go away on its own? Would it be better handled by another group of people with different skills? Could we free up time and energy for another project that's more urgent or important?

Questions such as these might make people uncomfortable. That's okay. Hang out with them until they take you to the next level of creative thinking at work. ■

Becoming a CRITICAL THINKER

Thinking is a path to intellectual adventure. Although there are dozens of possible approaches to thinking well, the process boils down to asking and answering questions.

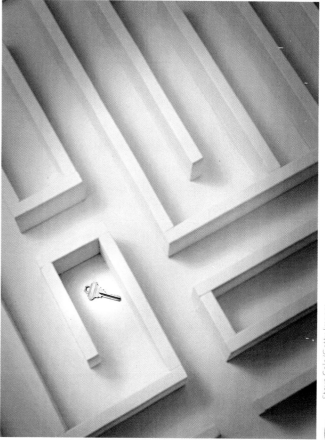

Steve Cole/Getty Images

One quality of a master student is the ability to ask questions that lead to deeper learning. Your mind is an obedient servant. It will deliver answers at the same level as your questions. Becoming a critical thinker means being flexible and asking a wide range of questions.

GETTING READY FOR CRITICAL THINKING

A psychologist named Benjamin Bloom named six levels of thinking. (He called them *educational objectives*, or goals for learning).[3] Each level of thinking calls for asking and answering different kinds of questions.

LEVEL 1: Remembering. At this level of thinking, the key question is *Can I recall the key terms, facts, or events?* To prompt level 1 thinking, an instructor might ask you to do the following:

- List the nine steps of Muscle Reading.
- State the primary features of a mind map.
- Name the master student profiled in Chapter 6 of this book.

To study for a test with level 1 questions, you could create flash cards to review ideas from your readings and class notes. You could also read a book with a set of questions in mind and underline the answers to those questions in the text. Or, you could memorize a list of definitions so that you can recite them exactly. These are just a few examples.

Although remembering is important, this is a relatively low level of learning. No critical or creative thinking is involved. You simply recognize or recall something that you've observed in the past.

LEVEL 2: Understanding. At this level, the main question is *Can I explain this idea in my own words?* Often this means giving examples of an idea based on your own experience.

Suppose that your instructor asks you to do the following:

- Explain the main point of the "Power Process: I create it all."
- Summarize the steps involved in creating a concept map.
- Compare mind mapping with concept mapping, stating how they're alike and how they differ.

Other key words in level 2 questions are *discuss, estimate,* and *restate.* All of these are cues to go one step beyond remembering and to show that you truly *comprehend* an idea.

LEVEL 3: Applying. Learning at level 3 means asking: *Can I use this idea to produce a desired result?* That result might include completing a task, meeting a goal, making a decision, or solving a problem.

Some examples of level 3 thinking are listed here:

- Write an affirmation about succeeding in school, based on the guidelines in this text.
- Write an effective goal statement.
- Choose a mnemonic to remember the names of the Great Lakes.

Some key words in level 3 questions include *apply, solve, construct, plan, predict,* and *produce.*

LEVEL 4: Analyzing. Questions at this level boil down to this: *Can I divide this idea into parts or steps?* For example, you could do the following:

- Divide the steps of Muscle Reading into three major phases.
- Take a list of key events in the Vietnam War and arrange them in chronological order.
- Organize the 20 memory techniques from Chapter 4 into different categories.

Other key words in level 4 questions are *classify, separate, distinguish,* and *outline.*

LEVEL 5: Evaluating. Learning at level 5 means asking, *Can I rate the truth, usefulness, or quality of this idea—and give reasons for my rating?* This is the level of thinking you would use to do the following:

- Judge the effectiveness of an Intention Statement.
- Recommend a method for taking lecture notes when an instructor talks fast.
- Rank the Power Processes in order of importance to you—from most useful to least useful.

Level 5 involves genuine critical thinking. At this level you agree with an idea, disagree with it, or suspend judgment until you get more information. In addition, you give reasons for your opinion and offer supporting evidence.

Some key words in level 5 questions are *critique, defend,* and *comment.*

LEVEL 6: Creating. To think at this level, ask, *Can I invent something new based on this idea?* For instance, you might do the following:

- Invent your own format for taking lecture notes.
- Prepare a list of topics that you would cover if you were teaching a student success course.

- Imagine that you now have enough money to retire and then write goals you would like to accomplish with your extra time.
- Create a Power Point presentation based on ideas found in this chapter. Put the material in your own words, and use visual elements to enhance the points.

Creative thinking often involves analyzing an idea into parts and then combining those parts in a new way. Another source of creativity is taking several ideas and finding an unexpected connection among them. In either case, you are thinking at a very high level. You are going beyond agreement and disagreement to offer something unique—an original contribution of your own.

Questions for creative thinking often start with words such as *adapt, change, collaborate, compose, construct, create, design,* and *develop.* You might also notice phrases such as *What changes would you make . . . ? How could you improve . . . ? Can you think of another way to . . . ? What would happen if . . . ?*

GAINING SKILL AS A CRITICAL THINKER

Critical and creative thinking are exciting. The potential rewards are many, and the stakes are high. Your major decisions in life—from choosing a major to choosing a spouse—depend on your skills at critical and creative thinking.

All levels of thinking are useful. Notice that the lower levels of thinking (1 to 3) give you fewer options than the highest

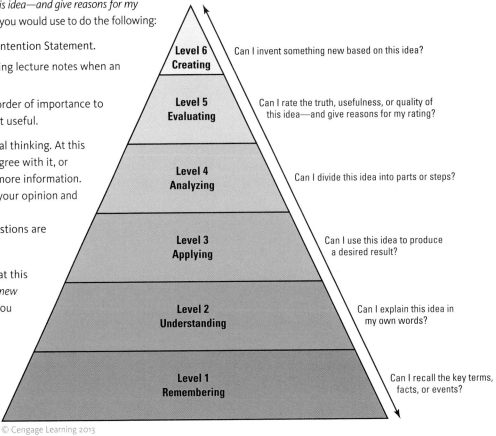

Level 6 Creating — Can I invent something new based on this idea?

Level 5 Evaluating — Can I rate the truth, usefulness, or quality of this idea—and give reasons for my rating?

Level 4 Analyzing — Can I divide this idea into parts or steps?

Level 3 Applying — Can I use this idea to produce a desired result?

Level 2 Understanding — Can I explain this idea in my own words?

Level 1 Remembering — Can I recall the key terms, facts, or events?

© Cengage Learning 2013

levels (4 to 6). Lower levels of thinking are sometimes about finding the "right" answer to a question. At levels 4, 5, and 6, you might discover several valid answers or create several workable solutions.

Also notice that the levels build on each other. Before you agree or disagree with an idea, make sure that you *remember* it accurately and truly *understand* it. Your understanding will go deeper if you can *apply* and *analyze* the idea as well. Master students stay aware of their current level of thinking. They can also move to other levels with a clear intention.

Remember that the highest levels of thinking call for the highest investments of time and energy. Also, moving from a lower level of thinking to a higher level often requires courage, along with an ability to tolerate discomfort. Give yourself permission to experiment, practice, and learn from mistakes.

The suggestions here will help you to deepen your skills at critical thinking. To learn more about creative thinking, see "Thinking: Moving from "aha!" to follow through" on page 209 and "Ways to create ideas" on page 211.

Find various points of view on any issue. Imagine George Bush, Cesar Chavez, and Barack Obama assembled in one room to debate the most desirable way to reshape our government. Picture Madonna, Oprah Winfrey, and Mark Zuckerberg leading a workshop on how to plan your career. When seeking out alternative points of view, let scenes like these unfold in your mind.

Dozens of viewpoints exist on every important issue—reducing crime, ending world hunger, preventing war, educating our children, and countless other concerns. In fact, few problems have any single, permanent solution. Each generation produces its own answers to critical questions, based on current conditions. Our search for answers is a conversation that spans centuries. On each question, many voices are waiting to be heard.

You can take advantage of this diversity by seeking out alternative views with an open mind. When talking to another person, be willing to walk away with a new point of view—even if it's the one you brought to the table, supported with new evidence.

Examining different points of view is an exercise in analysis, which you can do with the suggestions that follow.

Define terms. Imagine two people arguing about whether an employer should limit health care benefits to members of a family. To one person, the word *family* means a mother, father, and children; to the other person, the word *family* applies to any individuals who live together in a long-term, supportive relationship. Chances are the debate will go nowhere until these two people realize that they're defining the same word in different ways.

Conflicts of opinion can often be resolved—or at least clarified—when we define our key terms up front. This is especially true with abstract, emotion-laden terms such as *freedom, peace,*

progress, or *justice.* Blood has been shed over the meaning of those words. Define terms with care.

Look for assertions. Speakers and writers present their key terms in a larger context called an *assertion.* An assertion is a complete sentence that directly answers a key question. For example, consider this sentence from the article "Master student qualities" in the Introduction to this book: "Mastery means attaining a level of skill that goes beyond technique." This sentence is an assertion that answers an important question: How do we recognize mastery?

Look for at least three viewpoints. When asking questions, let go of the temptation to settle for just a single answer. Once you have come up with an answer, say to yourself, "Yes, that is one answer. Now what's another?" Using this approach can sustain honest inquiry, fuel creativity, and lead to conceptual breakthroughs. Be prepared: The world is complicated, and critical thinking is a complex business. Some of your answers might contradict others. Resist the temptation to have all of your ideas in a neat, orderly bundle.

Practice tolerance. One path to critical thinking is tolerance for a wide range of opinions. Taking a position on important issues is natural. When we stop having an opinion on things, we've probably stopped breathing.

Problems occur when we become so attached to our current viewpoints that we refuse to consider alternatives. Likewise, it can be disastrous when we blindly follow everything any person or group believes without questioning its validity. Many ideas that are widely accepted in Western cultures—for example, civil

> Each generation produces its own answers to critical questions, based on current conditions. Our search for answers is a conversation that spans centuries. On each question, many voices are waiting to be heard.

8

liberties for people of color and the right of women to vote—were once considered dangerous. Viewpoints that seem outlandish today might become widely accepted a century, a decade, or even a year from now. Remembering this idea can help us practice tolerance for differing beliefs and, in doing so, make room for new ideas that might alter our lives.

Look for logic and evidence. Uncritical thinkers shield themselves from new information and ideas. As an alternative, you can follow the example of scientists, who constantly search for evidence that contradicts their theories. The following suggestions can help you do so.

The aim of using logic is to make statements that are clear, consistent, and coherent. As you examine a speaker's or writer's assertions, you might find errors in logic—assertions that contradict each other or assumptions that are unfounded.

Also assess the evidence used to support points of view. Evidence comes in several forms, including facts, expert testimony, and examples. To think critically about evidence, ask questions such as these:

- Are all or most of the relevant facts presented?
- Are the facts consistent with one another?
- Are facts presented accurately—or in a misleading way?
- Are opinions mistakenly being presented as facts?
- Are enough examples included to make a solid case for the viewpoint?
- Do the examples truly support the viewpoint?
- Are the examples typical? That is, could the author or speaker support the assertion with other examples that are similar?
- Is the expert credible—truly knowledgeable about the topic?
- Does this evidence affirm or contradict something that I already know?

Consider the source. Look again at that article on the problems of manufacturing cars powered by natural gas. It might have been written by an executive from an oil company. Check out the expert who disputes the connection between smoking and lung cancer. That "expert" might be the president of a tobacco company.

This is not to say that we should dismiss the ideas of people who have a vested interest in stating their opinions. Rather, we should take their self-interest into account as we consider their ideas.

Understand before criticizing. Polished debaters are good at summing up their opponents' viewpoints—often better than the people who support those viewpoints themselves. Likewise, critical thinkers take the time to understand a statement of opinion before agreeing or disagreeing with it.

Effective understanding calls for listening without judgment. Enter another person's world by expressing her viewpoint in your own words. If you're conversing with that person, keep revising your summary until she agrees that you've stated her position accurately. If you're reading an article, write a short summary of it. Then scan the article again, checking to see whether your synopsis is on target.

Watch for hot spots. Many people have mental "hot spots"—topics that provoke strong opinions and feelings. Examples are abortion, homosexuality, gun control, and the death penalty.

To become more skilled at examining various points of view, notice your own particular hot spots. Make a clear intention to accept your feelings about these topics and to continue using critical thinking techniques in relation to them.

One way to cool down our hot spots is to remember that we can change or even give up our current opinions without giving up ourselves. That's a key message behind the "Power Processes: Ideas are tools" and "Detach." These articles remind us that human beings are much more than the sum of their current opinions.

Be willing to be uncertain. Some of the most profound thinkers have practiced the art of thinking by using a magic sentence: "I'm not sure yet."

Those are words that many people do not like to hear. Our society rewards quick answers and quotable sound bites. We're under considerable pressure to utter the truth in 10 seconds or less.

In such a society, it is courageous and unusual to take the time to pause, to look, to examine, to be thoughtful, to consider many points of view—and to be unsure. When a society adopts half-truths in a blind rush for certainty, a willingness to embrace uncertainty can move us forward.

Write about it. Thoughts can move at blinding speed. Writing slows down that process. Gaps in logic that slip by us in thought or speech are often exposed when we commit the same ideas to paper. Writing down our thoughts allows us to compare, contrast, and combine points of view more clearly—and therefore to think more thoroughly.

Notice your changing perspectives. Researcher William Perry found that students in higher education move through stages of intellectual development.[4] In earlier stages, students tend to think there is only one correct viewpoint on each issue, and they look to their instructors to reveal that truth. Later, students acknowledge a variety of opinions on issues and construct their own viewpoints.

Remember that the process of becoming a critical thinker will take you through a variety of stages. Give yourself time, and celebrate your growing mastery. ■

WAYS TO FOOL YOURSELF: *common mistakes* IN LOGIC

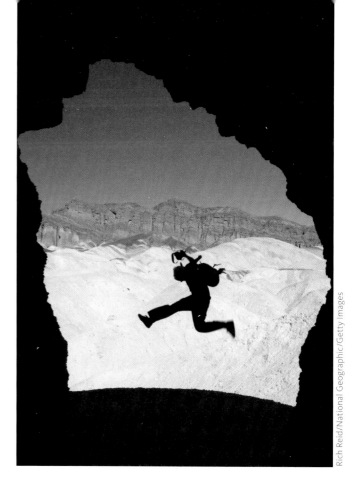

Rich Reid/National Geographic/Getty Images

Logic is a branch of philosophy that seeks to distinguish between effective and ineffective reasoning. Students of logic look for valid steps in an *argument,* or a series of statements. The opening statements of the argument are the premises, and the final statement is the conclusion.

Effective reasoning is not just an idle pastime for unemployed philosophers. Learning to think logically offers many benefits: When you think logically, you take your reading, writing, speaking, and listening skills to a higher level. You avoid costly mistakes in decision making. You can join discussions and debates with more confidence, cast your election votes with a clear head, and become a better-informed citizen. People have even improved their mental health by learning to dispute illogical beliefs.[5]

Over the last 2,500 years, specialists have listed some classic land mines in the field of logic—common mistakes in thinking that are called *fallacies.* The study of fallacies could fill a yearlong course. Following are 15 examples to get you started. Knowing about them before you string together a bunch of assertions can help you avoid getting fooled.

1 Jumping to conclusions. Jumping to conclusions is the only exercise that some lazy thinkers get. This fallacy involves drawing conclusions without sufficient evidence. Take the bank officer who hears about a student's failing to pay back an education loan. After that, the officer turns down all loan applications from students. This person has formed a rigid opinion on the basis of hearsay. Jumping to conclusions—also called *hasty generalization*—is at work here.

Following are more examples of this fallacy:

- *When I went to Mexico for spring break, I felt sick the whole time. Mexican food makes people sick.*

- *Google's mission is to "organize the world's information." Their employees must be on a real power trip.*

- *During a recession, more people go to the movies. People just want to sit in the dark and forget about their money problems.*

Each item in the above list includes two statements, and the second statement does not necessarily follow from the first. More evidence is needed to make any possible connection.

2 Attacking the person. The mistake of attacking the person is common at election time. An example is the candidate who claims that her opponent has failed to attend church regularly during the campaign. People who indulge in personal attacks are attempting an intellectual sleight of hand to divert our attention away from the truly relevant issues.

3 Appealing to authority. A professional athlete endorses a brand of breakfast cereal. A famous musician features a soft drink company's product in a rock video. The promotional brochure for an advertising agency lists all of the large companies that have used its services.

In each case, the people involved are trying to win your confidence—and your dollars—by citing authorities. The underlying assumption is usually this: *Famous people and organizations buy our product. Therefore, you should buy it too.* Or: *You should accept this idea merely because someone who's well-known says it's true.*

8

Appealing to authority is usually a substitute for producing real evidence. It invites sloppy thinking. When our only evidence for a viewpoint is an appeal to authority, it's time to think more thoroughly.

4 **Pointing to a false cause.** The fact that one event follows another does not necessarily mean that the two events have a cause-and-effect relationship. All we can actually say is that the events might be correlated. For example, as children's vocabularies improve, they can get more cavities. This does not mean that cavities are the result of an improved vocabulary. Instead, the increase in cavities is due to other factors, such as physical maturation and changes in diet or personal care.

Suppose that you see this newspaper headline: "Student tries to commit suicide after failing to pass bar exam." Seeing this headline, you might conclude that the student's failure to pass the exam lead to a depression that caused his suicide attempt. However, this is simply an assumption that can be stated in the following way: *When two events occur closely together in time, the first event is the cause of the second event.* Perhaps the student's depression was in fact caused by another traumatic event not mentioned in the headline, such as breaking up with a longtime girlfriend.

5 **Thinking in all-or-nothing terms.** Consider these statements: *Doctors are greedy. You can't trust politicians. Students these days are in school just to get high-paying jobs; they lack idealism. Homeless people don't want to work.*

These opinions imply the word *all*. They gloss over individual differences, claiming that all members of a group are exactly alike. They also ignore key facts—for instance, that some doctors volunteer their time at free medical clinics and that many homeless people are children who are too young to work.

All-or-nothing thinking is one of the most common errors in logic. To avoid this fallacy, watch out for words such as *all, everyone, no one, none, always,* and *never.* Statements that include these words often make sweeping claims that require a lot of evidence. See whether words such as *usually, some, many, few,* and *sometimes* lead to more accurate statements. Sometimes the words are implied. For example, the implication in the claim "Doctors are greedy" is that *all* doctors are greedy.

6 **Basing arguments on emotion.** The politician who ends every campaign speech with flag waving and slides of his mother eating apple pie is staking his future on appeals to emotion. So is the candidate who paints a grim scenario of the disaster and ruination that will transpire unless she is elected. Get past the fluff and histrionics to see whether you can uncover any worthwhile ideas.

7 **Using a faulty analogy.** An *analogy* states a similarity between two things or events. Some arguments rest on analogies that hide significant differences. On June 25, 1987, the Associated Press reported an example: U.S. representative Tom DeLay opposed a bill to ban chlordane, a pesticide that causes cancer in laboratory animals. Supporting this bill, he argued, would be like banning cars because they kill people. DeLay's analogy was faulty. Banning automobiles would have a far greater impact on society than banning a single pesticide, especially if safer pesticides are available.

8 **Creating a straw man.** The name of this fallacy comes from the scarecrows traditionally placed in gardens to ward off birds. A scarecrow works because it looks like a man. Likewise, a person can attack ideas that *sound like* his opponent's ideas but are actually absurd. For example, some legislators attacked the Equal Rights Amendment by describing it as a measure to abolish separate bathrooms for men and women. In fact, supporters of this amendment proposed no such thing.

9 **Begging the question.** Speakers and writers beg the question when their colorful language glosses over an idea that is unclear or unproven. Consider this statement: *Support the American tradition of individual liberty and oppose mandatory seat belt laws!* Anyone who makes such a statement "begs" (fails to answer) a key question: Are laws that require drivers to use seat belts actually a violation of individual liberty?

10 **Confusing fact and opinion.** Facts are statements verified by direct observation or compelling evidence that creates widespread agreement. In recent years, some politicians argued for tax cuts on the grounds that the American economy needed to create more jobs. However, it's not a fact that tax cuts automatically create more jobs. This statement is almost impossible to verify by direct observation, and there's actually evidence against it.

11 **Creating a red herring.** When hunters want to throw a dog off a trail, they can drag a smoked red herring (or some other food with a strong odor) over the ground in the opposite direction. This distracts the dog, who is fooled into following a false trail. Likewise, people can send our thinking on false trails by raising irrelevant issues. Case in point: In 2006, some people who opposed a presidential campaign by U.S. Senator Barack Obama emphasized his middle name: Hussein. This was an irrelevant attempt to link the senator to Saddam Hussein, the dictator and former ruler of Iraq.

12 **Appealing to tradition.** Arguments based on an appeal to tradition take a classic form: *Our current beliefs and behaviors have a long history; therefore, they are correct.* This argument has been used to justify the divine right of kings, feudalism, witch burnings, slavery, child labor, and a host of other traditions that are now rejected in most parts of the world. Appeals to tradition ignore the fact that unsound ideas can survive for centuries before human beings realize that they are being fooled.

13 **Appealing to "the people."** Consider this statement: *Millions of people use Wikipedia as their main source of factual information. Wikipedia must be the best reference work in the world.* This is a perfect example of the *ad populum* fallacy. (In Latin, that phrase means "to the people.") The essential error is assuming that popularity, quality, and accuracy are the same.

Appealing to "the people" taps into our universal desire to be liked and to associate with a group of people who agree with us.

No wonder this fallacy is also called "jumping on the bandwagon." Following are more examples:

- *Internet Explorer is the most widely used Web browser. It must be the best one.*
- *Dan Brown's books, including* The Da Vinci Code, *did not sell as well as the Harry Potter books by J. K. Rowling. I guess we know who's the better writer.*
- *Same-sex marriages must be immoral. Most Americans think so.*

You can refute such statements by offering a single example: Many Americans once believed that slavery was moral and that people of color should not be allowed to vote. That did not make either belief right.

14 Distracting from the real issue. The fallacy of distracting from the real issue occurs when a speaker or writer makes an irrelevant statement and then draws a conclusion based on that statement. For example: *The most recent recession was caused by people who borrowed too much money and bankers who loaned too much money. Therefore, you should never borrow money to go to school.* This argument ignores the fact that a primary source of the recession was loans to finance housing—not loans to finance education. Two separate topics are mentioned, and statements about one do not necessarily apply to the other.

15 Sliding a slippery slope. The fallacy of sliding a slippery slope implies that if one undesired event occurs, then other, far more serious events will follow: *If we restrict our right to own guns, then all of our rights will soon be taken away. If people keep downloading music for free, pretty soon they'll demand to get everything online for free. I notice that more independent bookstores are closing; it's just a matter of time before people stop reading.*

When people slide a slippery slope, they assume that different types of events have a single cause. They also assume that a particular cause will operate indefinitely. In reality, the world is far more complex. Grand predictions about the future often prove to be wrong.

Finding fallacies before they become a fatal flaw (bonus suggestions). Human beings have a long history of fooling themselves. This article presents just a partial list of logical fallacies. You can prevent them and many more by following a few suggestions:

- When outlining a paper or speech, create a two-column chart. In one column, make a list of your main points. In the other column, summarize the evidence for each point. If you have no evidence for a point, a logical fallacy may be lurking in the wings.

- Go back to some of your recent writing—assigned papers, essay tests, journal entries, and anything else you can find. Look for examples of logical fallacies. Note any patterns, such as repetition of one particular fallacy. Write an Intention Statement about avoiding this fallacy.

- Be careful when making claims about people who disagree with you. One attitude of a critical thinker is treating everyone with fairness and respect. ∎

You're One Click Away...
from practicing hunting for fallacies online.

Master Employees
IN ACTION

You're One Click Away...
from a video about Master Students in Action.

"*I am lucky to work for a company that actively encourages creativity. Although we are expected to fulfill all the responsibilities of our position, there is also time set aside during which we can pursue more free-thinking activities. I stay motivated by remembering that there is an outlet for my creativity and always come back to the more mundane tasks with a renewed energy.*"

—Kate Chiu,
Associate Director of Communications

THINKING CRITICALLY about information on the *INTERNET*

Sources of information on the Internet range from the reputable (such as the Library of Congress) to the flamboyant (such as the *National Enquirer*). People are free to post *anything* on the Internet, including outdated facts as well as intentional misinformation.

Newspaper, magazine, and book publishers often employ fact checkers, editors, and lawyers to screen out errors and scrutinize questionable material before publication. Authors of Web pages and other Internet sources might not have these resources or choose to use them.

Taking a few simple precautions when you surf the Internet can keep you from crashing onto the rocky shore of misinformation.

Distinguish between *ideas* and *information*. To think more powerfully about what you find on the Internet, remember the difference between information and ideas. For example, consider the following sentence: *Nelson Mandela became president of South Africa in 1994.* That statement provides information about South Africa. In contrast, the following sentence states an idea: *Nelson Mandela's presidency means that apartheid has no future in South Africa.*

Information refers to facts that can be verified by independent observers. *Ideas* are interpretations or opinions based on facts. These include statements of opinion and value judgments. Several people with the same information might adopt different ideas based on that information.

People who speak of the Internet as the "information superhighway" often forget to make the distinction between information and ideas. Don't assume that an idea is more current,

reasonable, or accurate just because you find it on the Internet. Apply your critical thinking skills to all published material—print and online.

Look for overall quality. Examine the features of a Web site in general. Notice the effectiveness of the text and visuals as a whole. Also note how well the site is organized and whether you can navigate the site's features with ease. Look for the date that crucial information was posted, and determine how often the site is updated.

Next, get an overview of the site's content. Examine several of the site's pages, and look for consistency of facts, quality of information, and competency with grammar and spelling. Are the links within the site easy to navigate?

Also evaluate the site's links to related Web pages. Look for links to pages of reputable organizations. Click on a few of those links. If they lead you to dead ends, it might indicate that the site you're evaluating is not updated often—a clue that it's not a reliable source for late-breaking information.

Look at the source. Find a clear description of the person or organization responsible for the Web site. Many sites include this information in an "About" link.

The domain in the uniform resource locator (URL) for a Web site gives you clues about sources of information and possible bias. For example, distinguish among information from a for-profit commercial enterprise (URL ending in .com); a nonprofit organization (.org); a government agency (.gov); and a school, college, or university (.edu).

If the site asks you to subscribe or become a member, then find out what it does with the personal information that you provide. Look for a way to contact the site's publisher with questions and comments.

Look for documentation. When you encounter an assertion on a Web page or some other Internet resource, note the types and quality of the evidence offered. Look for credible examples, quotations from authorities in the field, documented statistics, or summaries of scientific studies.

Remember that wikis (peer-edited sites) such as Wikipedia do not employ editors to screen out errors or scrutinize questionable material before publication. Do not rely on these sites when researching a paper or presentation. Also, be cautious about citing blogs, which often are not reviewed for accuracy. Such sources may, however, provide you with key words and concepts that help lead you to scholarly research on your topic.

Set an example. In the midst of the Internet's chaotic growth, you can light a path of rationality. Whether you're sending a short e-mail message or building a massive Web site, bring your own critical thinking skills into play. Every word and image that you send down the wires to the Web can display the hallmarks of critical thinking—sound logic, credible evidence, and respect for your audience. ■

> People who speak of the Internet as the "information superhighway" often forget to make the distinction between information and ideas. Don't assume that an idea is more current, reasonable, or accurate just because you find it on the Internet.

OVERCOME STEREOTYPES
with critical thinking

Consider assertions such as these: "College students like to drink heavily," "People who speak English as a second language are hard to understand," and "Americans who criticize the president are unpatriotic."

These assertions are examples of stereotyping—generalizing about a group of people based on the behavior of isolated group members. The word *stereotype* originally referred to a method used by printers to produce duplicate pages of text. This usage still rings true. When we stereotype, we gloss over individual differences and assume that every member of a group is a "duplicate." These assumptions are learned, and they can be changed.

Stereotypes infiltrate every dimension of human individuality. People are stereotyped on the basis of their race, ethnic group, religion, political affiliation, geographic location, birthplace, accent, job, economic status, age, gender, sexual orientation, IQ, height, hair color, or hobbies.

Stereotypes have many possible sources: fear of the unknown, uncritical thinking, and negative encounters between individual members of different groups. Whatever their cause, stereotypes abound.

In themselves, generalizations are neither good nor bad. In fact, they are essential. Mentally sorting people, events, and objects into groups allows us to make sense of the world. But when we consciously or unconsciously make generalizations that rigidly divide the people of the world into "us" versus "them," we create stereotypes and put on the blinders of prejudice.

You can take several steps to free yourself from stereotypes.

Look for errors in thinking. Some of the most common errors in thinking are the following:

- *Selective perception.* Stereotypes can literally change the way we see the world. If we assume that homeless people are lazy, for instance, we tend to notice only the examples that support our opinion. Stories about homeless people who are too young or too ill to work will probably escape our attention.

- *Self-fulfilling prophecy.* When we interact with people based on stereotypes, we set them up in ways that confirm our thinking. For example, when people of color were denied access to higher education based on stereotypes about their intelligence, they were deprived of opportunities to demonstrate their intellectual gifts.

- *Self-justification.* Stereotypes can allow people to assume the role of victim and to avoid taking responsibility for their own lives. An unemployed white male might believe that affirmative action programs are making it impossible for him to get a job—even as he overlooks his own lack of experience or qualifications.

Create categories in a more flexible way. Stereotyping has been described as a case of "hardening of the categories." Avoid

> The word *stereotype* originally referred to a method used by printers to produce duplicate pages of text. This usage still rings true. When we stereotype, we gloss over individual differences and assume that every member of a group is a "duplicate."

this problem by making your categories broader. Instead of seeing people based on their skin color, you could look at them on the basis of their heredity. (People of all races share most of the same genes.) Or you could make your categories narrower. Instead of talking about "religious extremists," look for subgroups among the people who adopt a certain religion. Distinguish between groups that advocate violence and those that shun it.

Test your generalizations about people through action. You can test your generalizations by actually meeting people of other cultures. It's easy to believe almost anything about certain groups of people as long as we never deal directly with individuals. Inaccurate pictures tend to die when people from different cultures study together, work together, and live together. Consider joining a school or community organization that will put you in contact with people of other cultures. Your rewards will include a more global perspective and an ability to thrive in a multicultural world.

Be willing to see your own stereotypes. The "Power Process: Notice your pictures and let them go" can help you see your own stereotypes. One belief about yourself that you can shed is *I have no pictures about people from other cultures.* Even people with the best of intentions can harbor subtle biases. Admitting this possibility allows you to look inward even more deeply for stereotypes.

Every time we notice an inaccurate picture buried in our mind and let it go, we take a personal step toward embracing diversity. ■

 You're One Click Away...
from finding more examples online of stereotypes and critical responses to them.

8

✓ CRITICAL THINKING EXERCISE 19

Take your thinking to another level

Recall an idea or suggestion from the chapter that you'd like to explore in more detail. Summarize it, and include the page number where it appears:

You've just done some thinking at **Level 1: Remembering**—Now, take your thinking about this idea or suggestion to **one** of the higher levels:

Level 2: Understanding—Explain this idea in your own words and give examples from your own experience.

Level 3: Applying—Use the idea to produce a desired result.

Level 4: Analyzing—Divide this idea into parts or steps.

Level 5: Evaluating—Rate the truth, usefulness or quality of the idea—and give reasons for your rating.

Level 6: Creating—Invent something new based on the idea.

Demonstrate your higher-level thinking by writing a brief paragraph in the space below. If you want to show your thinking in another way, then check with your instructor. In either case, clearly state your intended level of thinking (For example, "To *apply* this idea, I would . . . .")

Asking questions—
learning through inquiry

Thinking is born of questions. Questions wake us up. Questions alert us to hidden assumptions. Questions promote curiosity and create new distinctions. Questions open up options that otherwise go unexplored. Besides, teachers love questions.

There's a saying: "Tell me, and I forget; show me, and I remember; involve me, and I understand." Asking questions is a way to stay involved. One of the main reasons you are in school is to ask questions—a process called *inquiry-based learning*. This process takes you beyond memorizing facts and passing tests. Asking questions turns you into a lifelong learner.

One of the main reasons you are in school is to ask questions. This kind of learning goes beyond memorizing facts and passing tests. Educated people do more than answer questions. They also *ask* questions. They continually search for better questions, including questions that have never been asked before.

Questions have practical power. Asking for directions can shave hours off a trip. Asking a librarian for help can save hours of research time. Asking how to address an instructor, whether by first name or formal title, can change your relationship with that person. Asking your academic advisor a question can alter your entire education. Asking people about their career plans can alter *your* career plans.

Asking questions is also a way to improve relationships with friends and coworkers. When you ask a question, you offer a huge gift to people—an opportunity for them to speak their brilliance and for you to listen to their answers.

George Bernard Shaw, the playwright, knew the power of questions. "Some men see things as they are, and say, Why?" he wrote. "I dream of things that never were, and say, Why not?"

Students often say, "I don't know what to ask." If you have ever been at a loss for questions, here are some ways to discover them. Apply these strategies to any subject you study in school or to any area of your life that you choose to examine.

Ask questions that create possibilities. In Japan, there is a method called *Naikan* that is sometimes used in treating alcoholism. This program is based on asking three questions: "What have I received from others? What have I given to others? And what troubles and difficulties have I caused others?"[8] Taking the time to answer these questions in detail, and with rigorous honesty, can turn someone's life around.

Asking questions is also a way to help people release rigid, unrealistic beliefs: "Everyone should be kind to me." "If I make a mistake, it's terrible." "Children should always do what I say." In her book *Loving What Is*, Byron Katie recommends that you ask four questions about such beliefs: Is it true? Can you absolutely know that it's true? How do you react when you believe that thought? And, who would you be *without* that thought?[9]

At any moment you can ask a question that opens up a new possibility for someone. Suppose a friend walks up to you and says, "People just never listen to me."

You listen carefully. Then you say, "Let me make sure I understand. Who, specifically, doesn't listen to you? And how do you know they're not listening?"

Another friend comes up to you and says, "I just lost my job to someone who has less experience. That should never happen."

"Wow, that's hard," you say. "I'm sorry you lost your job. Who can help you find another job?"

Then a relative seeks your advice. "My mother-in-law makes me mad," she says.

"You're having a hard time with this person," you say. "What does she say and do when you feel mad at her? And are there times when you *don't* get mad at her?"

These kinds of questions—asked with compassion and a sense of timing—can help people move from complaining about problems to solving them.

8

Ask questions for critical thinking. In their classic *How to Read a Book*, Mortimer Adler and Charles Van Doren list four different questions to sum up the whole task of thinking critically about any body of ideas:[10]

What is this piece of writing about as a whole? To answer this question, state the main topic in one sentence. Then list the related subtopics.

What is being said in detail, and how? List the main terms, assertions, and arguments. Also state what problems the writer or speaker is trying to solve.

Is it true? Examine the logic and evidence behind the ideas. Look for missing information, faulty information, and errors in reasoning. Also determine which problems were solved and which remain unsolved.

What of it? After answering the first three questions, prepare to change your thinking or behavior as a result of encountering new ideas.

Discover your own questions. Students sometimes say, "I don't know what questions to ask." Consider the following ways to create questions about any subject you want to study, or about any area of your life that you want to change.

Let your pen start moving. Sometimes you can access a deeper level of knowledge by taking out your pen, putting it on a piece of paper, and writing down questions—even before you know what to write. Don't think. Just watch the pen move across the paper. Notice what appears. The results might be surprising.

Ask about what's missing. Another way to invent useful questions is to notice what's missing from your life and then ask how to supply it. For example, if you want to take better notes, you can write, "What's missing is skill in note taking. How can I gain more skill in taking notes?" If you always feel rushed, you can write, "What's missing is time. How do I create enough time in my day to actually do the things that I say I want to do?"

Pretend to be someone else. Another way to invent questions is first to think of someone you greatly respect. Then pretend you're that person. Ask the questions you think she would ask.

Begin a general question; then brainstorm endings. By starting with a general question and then brainstorming a long list of endings, you can invent a question that you've never asked before. For example:

- What can I do when . . . an instructor calls on me in class and I have no idea what to say? When a teacher doesn't show up for class on time? When I feel overwhelmed with assignments?

- How can I . . . take the kind of courses that I want? Expand my career options? Become much more effective as a student, starting today?

- When do I . . . decide on a major? Transfer to another school? Meet with an instructor to discuss an upcoming term paper?

- What else do I want to know about . . . my academic plan? My career plan? My options for job hunting? My friends? My relatives? My spouse?

- Who can I ask about . . . my career options? My major? My love life? My values and purpose in life?

Ask questions to promote social change. If your friends are laughing at racist jokes, you have a right to ask why. If you're legally registered to vote and denied access to a voting booth, you have a right to ask for an explanation. Asking questions can advance justice.

Ask what else you want to know. Many times you can quickly generate questions by simply asking yourself, "What else do I want to know?" Ask this question immediately after you read a paragraph in a book or listen to someone speak.

Start from the assumption that you are brilliant. Then ask questions to unlock your brilliance. ■

15 questions to try on for size

1. What is the most important problem in my life to solve right now?
2. What am I willing to do to solve this problem?
3. How can I benefit from solving this problem?
4. Who can I ask for help?
5. What are the facts in this situation?
6. What are my options in this situation?
7. What can I learn from this situation?
8. What do I want?
9. What am I willing to do to get what I want?
10. What will be the consequences of my decision in one week? One month? One year?
11. What is the most important thing for me to accomplish today?
12. What's the best possible use of my time right now?
13. What am I grateful for?
14. Who loves me?
15. Whom do I love?

Gaining skill at DECISION MAKING

© Mike Baldwin / Cornered

© Mike Baldwin

We make decisions all the time, whether we realize it or not. Even avoiding decisions is a form of decision making. The student who puts off studying for a test until the last minute might really be saying, "I've decided this course is not important" or "I've decided not to give this course much time." In order to escape such a fate, decide right now to experiment with the following suggestions.

Recognize decisions. Decisions are more than wishes or desires. There's a world of difference between "I wish I could be a better student" and "I will take more powerful notes, read with greater retention, and review my class notes daily." Decisions are specific and lead to focused action. When we decide, we narrow down. We give up actions that are inconsistent with our decision. Deciding to eat fruit for dessert instead of ice cream rules out the next trip to the ice cream store.

Establish priorities. Some decisions are trivial. No matter what the outcome, your life is not affected much. Other decisions can shape your circumstances for years. Devote more time and energy to the decisions with big outcomes.

Base your decisions on a life plan. The benefit of having long-term goals for our lives is that they provide a basis for many of our daily decisions. Being certain about what we want to accomplish this year and this month makes today's choices more clear.

Balance learning styles in decision making. To make decisions more effectively, use all four modes of learning explained in Chapter 2: First Steps. The key is to balance reflection with action, and thinking with experience. First, take the time to think creatively, and generate many options. Then think critically about the possible consequences of each option before choosing one. Remember, however, that thinking is no substitute for experience. Act on your chosen option, and notice what happens. If you're not getting the results that you want, then quickly return to creative thinking to invent new options.

Choose an overall strategy. Every time you make a decision, you choose a strategy—even when you're not aware of it. Effective decision makers can articulate and choose from among several strategies. For example:

- *Find all of the available options, and choose one deliberately.* Save this strategy for times when you have a relatively small number of options, each of which leads to noticeably different results.

- *Find all of the available options, and choose one randomly.* This strategy can be risky. Save it for times when your options are basically similar and fairness is the main issue.

- *Limit the options, and then choose.* When deciding which search engine to use on the World Wide Web, visit many sites and then narrow the list down to two or three that you choose.

Use time as an ally. Sometimes we face dilemmas—situations in which any course of action leads to undesirable consequences. In such cases, consider putting a decision on hold. Wait it out. Do nothing until the circumstances change, making one alternative clearly preferable to another.

Use intuition. Some decisions seem to make themselves. A solution pops into our mind, and we gain newfound clarity. Using intuition is not the same as forgetting about the decision or refusing to make it. Intuitive decisions usually arrive after we've gathered the relevant facts and faced a problem for some time.

Evaluate your decision. Hindsight is a source of insight. After you act on a decision, observe the consequences over time. Reflect on how well your decision worked and what you might have done differently.

Think choices. This final suggestion involves some creative thinking. Consider that the word *decide* derives from the same roots as *suicide* and *homicide*. In the spirit of those words, a decision forever "kills" all other options. That's kind of heavy. Instead, use the word *choice,* and see whether it frees up your thinking. When you *choose,* you express a preference for one option over others. However, those options remain live possibilities for the future. Choose for today, knowing that as you gain more wisdom and experience, you can choose again. ■

 You're One Click Away...
from finding more strategies online for making decisions.

8

Four ways to
solve problems

Many people use the terms *decision making* and *problem solving* interchangeably, as if the two processes are the same. Of course, there are many overlaps. Both processes hinge on your ability to think critically and creatively. Yet when actually trying your hand at these processes, you'll discover that problem solving exists at an even higher level of complexity than decision making.

To understand this point, start by considering the nature of decision making. When faced with a decision, you're asked to make a judgment call. Often the decision boils down to a single question that can be answered yes or no, or a choice between two major options: Is the defendant guilty or not guilty? Do we hire this person or keep looking for another? Do I cast my vote for this candidate or someone else?

Problem solving, on the other hand, calls for making a *series* of decisions and answering questions that are more open ended: How can I raise enough money to fund my education? How can I manage my time so that I finish projects by the due date? How can I resolve conflicts with my partner?

Think of problem solving as a process with four P's: Define the *problem*, generate *possibilities*, create a *plan*, and *perform* your plan.

Define the **problem**

Generate **possibilities**

Create a **plan**

Perform your plan

What is the problem?

What if there are several possible solutions?

How would this possible solution work?

Why is one solution more workable than another?

1 Define the problem. To define a problem effectively, understand what a problem is—a mismatch between what you want and what you have. Problem solving is all about reducing the gap between these two factors.

Tell the truth about what's present in your life right now, without shame or blame. For example: "I often get sleepy while reading my physics assignments, and after closing the book I cannot remember what I just read."

Next, describe in detail what you want. Go for specifics: "I want to remain alert as I read about physics. I also want to accurately summarize each chapter I read."

Remember that when we define a problem in limiting ways, our solutions merely generate new problems. As Albert Einstein said,

"The world we have made is a result of the level of thinking we have done thus far. We cannot solve problems at the same level at which we created them."[6]

This idea has many applications for success in school. An example is the student who struggles with note taking. The problem, she thinks, is that her notes are too sketchy. The logical solution, she decides, is to take more notes, and her new goal is to write down almost everything her instructors say. No matter how fast and furiously she writes, she cannot capture all of the instructors' comments.

Consider what happens when this student defines the problem in a new way. After more thought, she decides that her dilemma is not the *quantity* of her notes but their *quality*. She adopts a new format for taking notes, dividing her notepaper into two columns. In the right-hand column, she writes down only the main points of each lecture. And in the left-hand column, she notes two or three supporting details for each point.

Over time, this student makes the joyous discovery that there are usually just three or four core ideas to remember from each lecture. She originally thought the solution was to take more notes. What really worked was taking notes in a new way.

For added clarity, see if you can state the problem as a single question. This focuses your thinking and makes it easier to isolate and analyze the underlying issues.

You might find it tempting to gloss over this first step in problem solving, especially if your learning style favors moving into action quickly. However, consider the advantages of delaying action until you've taken time to define a problem precisely. The definition phase paves the way for the remaining three. Once you define a problem, you're well on the way to no longer having a problem. A clear definition of the problem can immediately suggest appropriate ways to solve it.

Also remember that problems often come in pairs. First is the immediate problem that you want to solve. Next is the underlying issue—a breakdown in a system, policy, or procedure that *created* the immediate problem. To solve the underlying issue, ask: How can we prevent this problem from happening again?

2 Generate possibilities. Now put on your creative thinking hat. Open up. Brainstorm as many possible solutions to the problem as you can. At this stage, quantity counts. As you generate possibilities, gather relevant facts. For example, when you're faced with a dilemma about what courses to take next term, get information on class times, locations, and instructors. If you haven't decided which summer job offer to accept, gather information on salary, benefits, and working conditions.

Certain comments can put the brakes on new ideas and squelch creativity in record time. For example, when considering a new policy or procedure, people can speak from a mindset of inertia: "We've never done it that way before." They can also speak from a sense of resignation: "We'll never get this idea past the boss." Or they can use the weight of tradition to smother new ideas: "We've been using this procedure for years, and it's too late to change now." When you notice such voices and consciously choose to put them on hold, you start to unleash your imagination.

Alex Osborn, who first described brainstorming, compared the process of creating ideas to using the gas pedal on a car floorboard and evaluating ideas to using the brake pedal. If you drive with a foot on the brake pedal and the other foot on the gas pedal at the same time, you can damage your car. Likewise, trying to evaluate ideas at the same time that you create them compromises your ability to make innovative decisions.

3 Create a plan. After rereading your problem definition and list of possible solutions, choose the solution that seems most workable. Think about specific actions that will reduce the gap between what you have and what you want. Visualize the steps you will take to make this solution a reality, and arrange them in chronological order. To make your plan even more powerful, put it in writing.

If you're working in a group, ask participants to visualize what the solution will look like and how it will operate when it's fully implemented in the future. With that image in mind, ask participants to list the steps they'll take to make the solution a reality and arrange those steps in chronological order.

4 Perform your plan. This step gets you off your chair and out into the world. Now you actually *do* what you've planned. Ultimately, your skill in solving problems lies in how well you

> Visualize the steps you will take to make this solution a reality, and arrange them in chronological order. To make your plan even more powerful, put it writing.

perform your plan. Through the quality of your actions, you become the architect of your own success.

Be sure to evaluate the results of your actions. The messy complexity of life and the fact that people and circumstances are constantly changing means that solutions seldom "stay put." In fact, any solution has the potential to create new problems. If that happens, cycle through the four steps of problem solving again.

Bonus tip: Be grateful for problems. In the work world, problems create jobs. Problems create a reason for an employer, customer, or client to pay you. For example, medical assistants solve problems that prevent a physician's office or medical clinic from running smoothly. Paralegals solve problems with the accuracy and usefulness of legal research and records. People who develop "apps" solve problems for people who want their mobile devices to be as useful as their desktop computer.

Seen from this perspective, you can greet problems with gratitude, as explained in the "Power Process: Love your problems (and experience your barriers)." In fact, you can advance your career and boost your income by seeking out bigger problems at your job and gaining the skills to deal with them. There are plenty of jobs for people who know how to solve problems. ■

8

You're One Click Away...
from finding more strategies online for problem solving.

✔ CRITICAL THINKING EXERCISE 20

Move from problems to solutions

Many students find it easy to complain about school and to dwell on problems. This exercise gives you an opportunity to change that habit and respond creatively to any problem you're currently experiencing—whether it be with memorizing or some other aspect of school or life.

The key is to dwell more on solutions than on problems. Do that by inventing as many solutions as possible for any given problem. See whether you can turn a problem into a *project* (a plan of action) or a *promise* to change some aspect of your life. Shifting the emphasis of your conversation from problems to solutions can raise your sense of possibility and unleash the master learner within you.

In the space below, describe at least three problems that could interfere with your success as a student. The problems can be related to transportation issues, lack of access to technology, teachers, relationships with coworkers, personal relationships, finances, or anything else that might get in the way of your success.

My problem is that . . .

_____

_____

_____

_____

_____

_____

My problem is that . . .

_____

_____

_____

_____

_____

_____

My problem is that . . .

_____

_____

_____

_____

Next, brainstorm at least five possible solutions to each of those problems. Ten solutions would be even better. (You can continue brainstorming on a separate piece of paper or on a computer.) You might find it hard to come up with that many ideas. That's okay. Stick with it. Stay in the inquiry, give yourself time, and ask other people for ideas.

I can solve my problem by . . .

_____

_____

_____

_____

_____

I can solve my problem by . . .

_____

_____

_____

_____

I can solve my problem by . . .

_____

_____

_____

_____

masterstudentprofile

Irshad Manji

(1969–) Controversial journalist, broadcaster, and author of *The Trouble with Islam*, who uses her "Muslim voice of reform, to concerned citizens worldwide" in an effort to explore faith and community, and the diversity of ideas.

It's to be expected that an author with a book on the verge of publication will lose her cool over a last-minute detail or two. Some might get nervous that their facts won't hold up and run a paranoid, final check. Others might worry about what to wear to their book party. When Irshad Manji's book was about to hit the stands, her concern was a bit different. She feared for her life.

Certain her incendiary book *The Trouble with Islam* would set off outrage in the Muslim community, she called the police, told them she was working on a book that was highly critical of Islam, and asked if they could advise her on safety precautions.

They came to visit her Toronto apartment building several times and suggested she install a state-of-the-art security system, bulletproof windows, and hire a counterterrorism expert to act as her personal bodyguard.

In her short, plucky book she comes down hard on modern-day Islam, charging that the religion's mainstream has come to be synonymous with literalism. Since the 13th century, she said, the faith hasn't encouraged—or tolerated—independent thinking (or as it's known in the faith, *ijtihad*).

The book, which is written like a letter, is both thoughtful and confrontational. In person, Ms. Manji embodied the same conflicting spirit. She was affable and wore a broad smile. Her upbeat, nervous energy rose to the task of filling in every potentially awkward pause. (One of her favorite factoids: "Prophet Mohammed was quite a feminist.")

Her journey scrutinizing Islam started when she was an 8-year-old and taking weekly religious classes at a *madrasa* (religious school) in suburban Vancouver. Her anti-Semitic teacher Mr. Khaki never took her questions seriously; he merely told her to accept everything because it was in the Koran. She wanted to know why she had to study it in Arabic, which she didn't understand, and was told the answers were "in the Koran."

Her questioning ended up getting her kicked out of school at 14, and she embarked on a 20-year-long private study of the religion. While she finds the treatment poured on women and foreigners in Islamic nations indefensible, she said that she continues to be a believer because the religion provides her with her values. "And I'm so glad I did because it was then I came to realize that there was this really progressive side of my religion and it was this tradition of critical thinking called *ijtihad*. This is what allows me to stay within the faith."

She calls herself a "Muslim refusenik" because she remains committed to the religion and yet she doesn't accept what's expected of Muslim women. As terrorist acts and suicide bombings refuse to subside, she said it's high time for serious reform within the Islamic faith.

She said many young Muslim supporters are still afraid to come out about their support of her. "Even before 9/11 it was the young Muslims who were emerging out of these audiences and gathering at the side of the stage. They'd walk over and say, 'Irshad, we need voices such as yours to help us open up this religion of ours because if it doesn't open up, we're leaving the mosques.'"

She wants Muslims to start thinking critically about their religion and to start asking more questions. "Most Muslims have never been introduced to the possibility, let alone the virtue, of asking questions about our holy book," she said. "We have never been taught the virtue of interpreting the Koran in different ways."

8

IRSHAD MANJI ... is courageous.

YOU ... can practice courage by questioning assumptions and creating bold, new ideas.

You're One Click Away...
from learning more about Irshad Manji online at the Master Student Profiles. You can also visit the Master Student Hall of Fame to learn about other master students.

FIVE Cs
FOR YOUR CAREER

CHARACTER • CRITICAL THINKING • CREATIVE THINKING • COLLABORATION • COMMUNICATION

Build character by making ethical decisions at work. Some workplace behaviors are clearly unethical. Examples are submitting false expense reports, operating machinery while intoxicated, stealing from a cash drawer, diverting corporate funds for personal uses, taking home office supplies, or using work time to download explicit sexual images from the Internet. Other behaviors fall into a "gray area" that calls for careful thinking about whether ethics are being violated.

You don't have to be a philosopher in order to make sound ethical decisions at work. Start with a working definition of *ethics* as using moral standards to guide your behavior. Next, turn your own moral standards into a checklist of pointed questions. For example, is this action legal? Is this action consistent with my organization's mission, goals, and policies? Will I be able to defend this action tomorrow, next month, and next year? Am I willing to make this decision public—to share it wholeheartedly with my boss, my family, and my friends? Has everyone who will be affected by this decision had the chance to voice their concerns?

Think creatively by looking for an unmet need. Sometimes needs are met as a result of serendipity—a happy and creative coincidence of ideas. Spence Silver, a research scientist at 3M, invented a new chemical by accident while looking for ways to improve tape adhesives. This chemical did not stick strongly when coated onto tape backings. Even so, Silver believed it had potential uses.

His invention languished for years until Art Fry, who worked in new product development at 3M, attended a seminar by Silver. Fry had long been frustrated with the scrap paper bookmarks he used to mark his place in his church hymnal during choir practice. One day it suddenly occurred to Fry that Silver's adhesive could be used to make a perfect bookmark—one that could be fastened temporarily to a page and then easily but securely refastened on another page. That "aha!" yielded the Post-it® in 1980, with billions sold since then.

Think critically to use your mind like an expert. In their book *The New Division of Labor: How Computers Are Creating the Next Job Market*, Frank Levy and Richard J. Murname argue that prospering in a global economy calls for expert thinking. This means "solving new problems for which there are no routine solutions."[7]

The chef who creates a new meal without increasing restaurant costs shows expert thinking. So does a car mechanic who solves a problem not covered in the owner's manual.

Jobs that do not involve expert thinking are more likely to be outsourced or automated. For example, travel agents and underwriters (people who determine eligibility for an insurance policy or loan) traditionally made decisions according to step-by-step formulas. Those kinds of decisions are now made by computers.

An expert has deep knowledge about a field along with an ability to identify new relationships between ideas. Develop expert thinking by taking advanced courses in your major or field and seizing opportunities to work on project teams.

Think collaboratively with the Decreasing Options Technique. The Decreasing Options Technique (DOT) offers an efficient way to sort and rank a large pool of ideas created by groups of people in meetings. With DOT, you can sort and prioritize dozens of ideas, reducing them to a manageable number for discussion. This technique is especially useful for large groups that are asked to arrive at a decision in a short time. DOT also allows for contribution from all participants—not just those who are most vocal. Here's how it works:

- *Conduct a brainstorm, summarizing each idea in a single, word, phrase, or sentence on a large sheet of paper.* Write letters that are big enough to be seen across the meeting room. Place only one idea on each sheet of paper.

- *Post the sheets where everyone can see them.* To save time, ask participants to submit ideas before the meeting takes place. That way you can summarize and post ideas ahead of time.

- *Ask participants whether they can eliminate some ideas as obviously unworkable.* Also group similar ideas together and eliminate duplications.

- *"Dot" ideas.* Give each participant a handful of sticker dots. Then ask participants to go around the room and place a dot next to the ideas that they consider most important. A variation on this process is to give each participant a limited number of dots. You can also assign different levels of priority to each color of sticker.

- *Stand back and review the ideas.* The group's favored ideas will stand out clearly as the sheets with the most dots. Now you can bring these high-priority ideas to the discussion table.

Communicate some ideas to individuals before groups. If you come up with an idea that has the potential to create big changes in your workplace, consider *not* sharing it first during a regular staff meeting. Instead, "pitch" the idea to key decision makers on an individual basis. Plan to do this over several weeks of months.

This strategy has several advantages. For one, these people can help you think critically about the idea. And if they like it, you can ask them for support when you decide to share it more publicly. At that time, you'll already have some "buy-in" for your big idea.

Now make a personal commitment to develop the five Cs. Take another look at the Discovery Wheel in Chapter 2—especially the sections labeled Character, Creative and Critical Thinking, Communicating, and Collaborating. Take a snapshot of your current skills in these areas after reading and doing this chapter.

DISCOVERY

My scores on the "Five C" sections of the Discovery Wheel were:	As of today, I would give myself the following scores in these areas:	At the end of this course, I would like my scores in these areas to be:
Character _____	Character _____	Character _____
Creative & Critical Thinking _____	Creative & Critical Thinking _____	Creative & Critical Thinking _____
Communicating _____	Communicating _____	Communicating _____
Collaborating _____	Collaborating _____	Collaborating _____

Next, skim this chapter and look for a creative or critical thinking technique that you want to explore in depth. Choose one that would enhance your self-rating in at least one of the five Cs.

I discovered that my preferred technique is . . .

_____

_____

_____

_____

In light of the five Cs, I can use this technique to become more . . .

_____

_____

_____

_____

INTENTION
To use this technique, I intend to . . .

_____

_____

_____

_____

NEXT ACTION
The specific action I will take is . . .

_____

_____

_____

_____

8

CHAPTER 8 QUIZ

Name _____

Date _____

1. List the six levels of thinking described by Benjamin Bloom.

   (1) Remembering, (2) understanding, (3) applying, (4) analyzing, (5) evaluating, and (6) creating (*Becoming a critical thinker,* page 215)

2. List the key question associated with each level of thinking of Bloom's taxonomy.

   (1) *Remembering:* Can I recall the key terms, facts, or events? (2) *Understanding:* Can I explain this idea in my own words? (3) *Applying:* Can I use this idea to produce a desired result? (4) *Analyzing:* Can I divide this idea into parts or steps? (5) *Evaluating:* Can I rate the truth, usefulness, or quality of this idea—and give reasons for my rating? (6) *Creating:* Can I invent something new based on this idea? (*Becoming a critical thinker,* page 215)

3. Briefly explain the difference between *creative thinking* and *critical thinking.*

   Creative thinking is the process of generating lots of ideas to look at issues in new and different ways; critical thinking is when we narrow down our choices by picking and choosing from among these ideas to come up with new and exciting ways to think and do things. (*Thinking: Moving from "aha!" to follow-through,* page 209)

4. Discuss what is meant in this chapter by *aha!*

   Aha! is the burst of creative energy that comes with the arrival of a new or original idea. (*Thinking: Moving from "aha!" to follow-through,* page 209)

5. Briefly describe three strategies for creative thinking.

   (Answers will vary.) List and describe three of the following: Conduct a brainstorm, focus and let go, cultivate creative serendipity, keep idea files, collect and play with data, create while you sleep, refine ideas and follow through, and trust the process. (*Ways to create ideas,* page 211)

6. List three types of logical fallacies, and give an example of each type.

   Jumping to conclusions—assuming that you failed the course and therefore dropping the class because you got a poor grade on one test. *Attacking the person*—diverting attention from political issues by making a personal attack on the opposing candidate or the candidate's family. *Appealing to authority*—thinking that a breakfast cereal is healthy for you because a professional athlete has endorsed it. *Pointing to a false cause*—saying, for example, "As children's vocabularies improve, they can get more cavities." *Thinking in all-or-nothing terms*—believing that all students these days are in school only to get high-paying jobs. *Basing arguments on emotions*—deciding that a politician who kisses babies and eats apple pie must be a nice person. *Faulty analogy*—saying, for example, "The people at the vitamin store are all very healthy, so if I take the vitamins they sell, I'll be healthy, too." *Creating a straw man*—saying that the quality of everyone's health care will go down if the United States adopts national health care. *Begging the question*—asserting that banning smoking in public places violates personal freedom. *Confusing fact and opinion*—thinking, for example, "We must have tax cuts in order to create more jobs." *Creating a red herring*—emphasizing that Barack Obama's middle name is the same as Saddam Hussein's last name. *Appealing to tradition*—for example, saying, "We have to do it this way because historically we've always done it this way." *Appealing to "the people"*—thinking that completing assignments in such a way as to please your instructor is the best way for you to learn. *Distracting from the real issue*—addressing a point that's only slightly related to the issue at hand because that's the only point you're knowledgeable enough to discuss. *Sliding a slippery slope*—concluding that because you failed one test, you are incapable of completing a college degree. (*Ways to fool yourself: Common mistakes in logic,* page 219)

7. Name the logical fallacy involved in this statement: "Everyone who's ever visited this school agrees that it's the best in the state."

   (Answers will vary.) All-or-nothing thinking (surely not everyone agrees). (*Ways to fool yourself: Common mistakes in logic,* page 219).

8. What cultivates an *aha!* moment, and what leads to following through from that moment?

   Creative thinking is necessary to cultivate an aha! moment, while critical thinking is used to follow through. (*Thinking: Moving from "aha!" to follow-through,* page 209)

9. List the three strategies for making a decision that were mentioned in the text.

   (1) Find all of the available options, and choose one deliberately. (2) Find all the available options, and choose one randomly. (3) Limit the options, and then choose. (*Gaining skill at decision making,* page 227)

10. List three examples of questions you can ask to promote inquiry-based learning.

    (Answers will vary.) Three of many options listed: What is the most important problem in my life to solve right now? Whom can I ask for help? What's the best us of my time right now? (*Asking questions—learning through inquiry,* page 225)

CHAPTER 9 COMMUNICATING

Instructor Tools & Tips

"Listening means trying to see the problem the way the speaker sees it—which means not sympathy, which is feeling for him, but empathy, which is feeling with him." —S. I. Hayakawa

"You have two ears and one mouth. Remember to use them in more or less that proportion." —Paula Bern

PREVIEW

Communicating effectively is discussed indirectly in many chapters of *From Master Student to Master Employee.* By taking a closer look at effective communication in this chapter, you can help your students in the related skills of speaking, listening, and writing now that they have the necessary foundations to work toward mastery. This chapter provides an opportunity to explore new strategies for effective public speaking (including overcoming fear of public speaking) and to avoid plagiarism. Communication abilities are essential workplace skills that can be practiced and mastered in the college setting. Use this *Annotated Instructor's Edition* and other resources available to you to highlight and discuss key concepts in class and to devise assignments that allow students to practice communication skills outside the classroom. And consider this: Developing relationships through effective communication is essential for first-year student success and retention at your college. You can emphasize that these skills are equally important in students' personal lives and in the workplace, making communication a valuable life skill.

GUEST SPEAKER

A librarian or a colleague from the Speech/Communications department makes a timely guest speaker as a lead-in to the articles on plagiarism and public speaking. Share the related articles with the guest speaker ahead of time so that the speaker's presentation can be focused to complement the text. Let students know who is coming so that they can prepare questions to ask your guest speaker. Ask the guest speaker to discuss the importance of public speaking and communication beyond the classroom.

LECTURE

Appropriate lecture topics for this chapter include active listening and concentration, effective writing, plagiarism, public speaking, and the Power Process: Employ your word. Consider inviting a guest lecturer for one or more of these topics or using the PowerUP! DVD to lecture for you on the Power Process. For additional ideas, visit the Instructor Web site.

EXERCISES/ACTIVITIES

1. **Five ways to say "I" (page 243)** Students who have not taken an interpersonal communications course often do not know how to create "I" statements. Dividing students into groups and having them practice writing and speaking "I" statements can help them understand how to do so and enable them to gauge their effectiveness in communicating.

2. **Dealing with compliments** This is one of Dave Ellis's favorite class activities. Ask students to pair up with a classmate they have gotten to know during the semester. One will be the speaker; the other, the listener. The speaker says, "What I like about you is . . ." and finishes the sentence with a quality he likes in that person. He continues to repeat this sentence for 45 seconds, each time stating a different quality. If your students get stuck and cannot think of a quality, encourage them to say, "What I like about you is *everything*" over and over again until they can think of another specific compliment. This keeps the barrage of compliments going. The listener receives the compliments and acknowledges them nonverbally. After 45 seconds, the students switch roles and repeat the exercise. Then have a class discussion about how it felt to *give* and to *receive* compliments. Ask students if it is more difficult to give or receive compliments.

3. **Making presentations (pages 255–258)** In this activity, students prepare and present a 5-minute process speech about their future career plans. This provides them with an opportunity to stand up and speak before the entire class. To lay the groundwork, review the criteria for an effective speech. This practice in a familiar and comfortable environment helps reduce speech anxiety for students who will likely make future presentations in other courses. For suggestions on grading student speeches, review information on the Instructor Web site.

master instructor
BEST PRACTICE

"I assign a PowerPoint project to my College Success students. I lead the class in researching their chosen career through an online career assessment tool and through career research tools. Once students prepare their PowerPoint presentation, each presents a 5-minute speech, using the PowerPoint as a visual aid. This assignment can be customized to incorporate current class topics and research tools, including the Video Skillbuilders available on the Web site."

–Annette McCreedy, Nashville State Community Collegee

4. **Making presentations (pages 255–258)** Participating in class is another excellent way for students to practice speaking in public. Many students experience communication apprehension when they are called on in class or when they must speak before a group. Ask your students to write a Discovery Statement about their memory of this type of situation. Have them describe their physical sensations, the effectiveness of their presentation, feedback from the audience, and so forth. Ask your students to write an Intention Statement concerning how they intend to participate in class in order to experience talking to a group of people. Ask them to be specific about which class they intend to speak in, how they will set up the opportunity to speak (e.g., having questions ready, sitting in front, asking to give a presentation, and so forth), and how they intend to record their observations of the experience. Tie class participation into the course grade, reminding students that willingness to participate is a valuable skill in the workplace as well as the classroom.

CONVERSATION/SHARING

This chapter is certainly one that your students will be energized to discuss. It will be especially easy for them to create schema using their prior knowledge of the subject before learning new information. Spend time focusing on the *What if?* in this chapter. Ask students *What if* they use the ideas presented in this chapter to help them succeed in the workplace. Ask your students to consider the importance of communication for the major they have chosen) or to their future career choice (looking ahead to Chapter 12).

HOMEWORK

Power Process: Employ your word (page 236) To help illustrate the effectiveness of this Power Process, have students individually think about and then write two promises, one to themselves and one to a significant person in their lives. This helps demonstrate how to use the ideas in the article. Ask students to answer the following concerning their promises: "Which level is this promise?" "What are the possible consequences if I do not keep these promises?" Remind students that the promises they are making are, culturally, the highest level of commitment we make to each other.

Three phases of effective writing (pages 249–253) Are you looking for an assignment that can help your students practice their writing *and* provide them with an opportunity to win a $1,000 scholarship? This is a perfect place to announce the Cengage Learning Scholarship Essay Contest. Host a contest in your classes, select the best essay (that answers the scholarship essay question, posted on the *From Master Student to Master Employee* Web site), and submit this winning essay to the national contest. Remind your students that they have the formula for writing a successful essay in their hands! Previous winning essays are available at the Student Web site for reflection.

Three phases of effective writing (pages 249–253) Convincing your students that writing is as important in the workplace as it is in the classroom is an essential point to drive home. Stress that learning to write well pays many dividends and that writing effectively can help students express themselves. Writing will help them to organize information and adapt their ideas to different audiences. Finally, point out that good writing is a marketable skill. To verify this, have your students look at help-wanted ads in the newspaper or online and determine how many job descriptions call for good writing skills. Have your students look for other transferable skills that they can master in the classroom and utilize in the workplace. Students can write Discovery and Intention Statements after reviewing the help-wanted ads. Ask your students to highlight skills other than writing that will be applicable to their intended career choice.

Master Student Profile: Cesar Chavez (page 259) Remind students that the Master Student Profiles can be a source of inspiration. You can also use the Master Student Profiles to discuss the topics covered in the article. Ask your students why they think that Cesar Chavez was selected for the communication chapter. You can assign additional reading or research (another opportunity for students to practice their research and writing) related to this article. Have your students begin with the biographical information and links that are provided on the *From Master Student to Master Employee* Web site.

EVALUATION

 Quiz Ideas for Chapter 9

Ask students to:

- Describe five ways to communicate with a difficult boss.

- Describe three strategies for effective nonverbal listening and three strategies for verbal listening.

- Describe five strategies for effective writing for the workplace.

- Present an example of a problem between a student and the Admissions/Records Office, and ask students to share how they would effectively complain in order to get the situation resolved.

- Write Discovery and Intention Statements regarding the Power Process: Employ your word.

Additional Digital Resources for Chapter 9

What can you **ASSIGN FROM THE COURSEMATE** *for From Master Student to Master Employee?*

• **Video Skillbuilders.** These interactive online tools combine video clips featuring discussions with students, instructors, and experts, with articles and activities designed to give students a fully engaging learning experience. Either view and experience these together in class, or have students view them as a homework assignment and respond to the viewing questions and reflective exercise. These modules are good matches for Chapter:

- Persuasive Communication: Effective Strategies
- Persuasive Communication: Communicating in a Group

Note that Video Skillbuilders are available for every chapter.

• **Master Student Profile: Cesar Chavez.** Students can read more about Cesar. Note that every chapter includes more information about the featured Master Student Profile.

• **Plagiarism Prevention Zone.** For strategies on how to avoid plagiarism when writing, direct students to the Plagiarism Prevention Zone, where they can access various tutorials and opportunities to practice writing ethically.

CourseMate *To access CourseMate, your students need to visit www.cengagebrain .com. At the CengageBrain.com home page, students search for the ISBN of* From Master Student to Master Employee *(from the back cover of the book), using the search box at the top of the page. This takes them to the product page where these resources can be found.*

Did you know that **THESE RESOURCES** *(and many more)* **ARE AVAILABLE** *on the* **INSTRUCTOR COMPANION SITE**?

• **Having trouble connecting with your students?** Many strategies for addressing students are included in the online Course Manual including how to handle students who resist the class, don't feel they need it, or are plain insulted at having to take the course. Work on improving your communication skills to reach these students.

• **Looking for test banks?** Customizable, text-specific content quizzes are a great way to test student's knowledge and understanding of the text and are available for every chapter. Because they are provided in ExamView, BlackBoard, and WebCT as well as Word, you will have no problem accessing the multiple-choice, true/false, completion, and short-answer questions.

Please visit login.cengage.com *to log in and access the Instructor Companion Site.*

Communicating

Use this **Master Student Map** to ask yourself

WHY THIS CHAPTER MATTERS ...

- Communication skills are as important to your success as technical skills.

WHAT IS INCLUDED ...

HOW I CAN USE THIS CHAPTER...

- Make and keep agreements as a tool for creating my future.
- Listen in a way that contributes to other people.
- Speak and write in ways that win acceptance for my ideas.

WHAT IF ...

- I could consistently create the kind of relationships that I've always wanted?

© Ruslan Ivantsov/Shutterstock.com

JOURNAL ENTRY 18
Intention Statement

Commit to create value from this chapter

Think of a time when you found it difficult to write a paper or prepare a presentation. Then scan this chapter for ideas that can help you in a similar situation. List at least three ideas below, along with the page numbers where you intend to read more about them.

Strategy	Page number
_____	_____
_____	_____
_____	_____
_____	_____
_____	_____
_____	_____
_____	_____
_____	_____
_____	_____
_____	_____
_____	_____
_____	_____
_____	_____
_____	_____
_____	_____
_____	_____

POWER process

Employ your word

When you give your word, you are creating—literally. The person you are is, for the most part, a result of the agreements you make. Others know who you are by your words and your commitments. And you can learn who you are by observing which commitments you choose to keep and which ones you choose to avoid.

Relationships are built on agreements. When we break a promise to be faithful to a spouse, to help a friend move to a new apartment, or to pay a bill on time, relationships are strained.

The words we use to make agreements can be placed into six different levels. We can think of each level as one rung on a ladder—the ladder of powerful speaking. As we move up the ladder, our speaking becomes more effective.

The first and lowest rung on the ladder is *obligation*. Words used at this level include *I should, he ought to, someone had better, they need to, I must,* and *I had to.* Speaking this way implies that something other than ourselves is in control of our lives. When we live at the level of obligation, we speak as if we are victims.

The second rung is *possibility*. At this level, we examine new options. We play with new ideas, possible solutions, and alternative courses of action. As we do, we learn that we can make choices that dramatically affect the quality of our lives. We are not the victims of circumstance. Phrases that signal this level include *I might, I could, I'll consider, I hope to,* and *maybe.*

From possibility, we can move up to the third level—*preference.* Here we begin the process of choice. The words *I prefer* signal that we're moving toward one set of possibilities over another, perhaps setting the stage for eventual action.

Above preference is a fourth rung called *passion.* Again, certain words signal this level: *I want to, I'm really excited to do that,* and *I can't wait.*

Action comes with the fifth rung—*planning.* When people use phrases such as *I intend to, my goal is to, I plan to,* and *I'll try like mad to,* they're at the level of planning. The Intention Statements you write in this book are examples of planning.

The sixth and highest rung on the ladder is *promising.* This is where the power of your word really comes into play. At this level, it's common to use phrases such as these: *I will, I promise to, I am committed,* and *you can count on it.* Promising is where we bridge from possibility and planning to action. Promising brings with it all of the rewards of employing your word.

You're One Click Away...
from accessing Power Process Media online and finding out more about how to "employ your word."

© iStockphoto.com/claylib

Communicating creates our world

Certain things are real for us because we can see them, touch them, hear them, smell them, or taste them. Books, pencils, tables, chairs, and food all are real in this sense. They enter our world in a straightforward, uncomplicated way.

Many other aspects of our lives, however, do not have this kind of observable reality. None of us can point to a *purpose,* for example. Nor would a purpose step up and introduce itself or buy us lunch. The same is true about other abstract concepts, such as *quality, intelligence, trust, human rights,* or *student success.*

Concepts such as these shape our experience of life. Yet they don't really exist until we talk about them. These concepts come alive for us only to the degree that we have conversations about them. Communicating brings our world into being.

According to communication theorist Lee Thayer, there are two basic life processes. One is acquiring and processing energy. The other is acquiring and processing information, also known as *communication.*[1] From this point of view, communicating is just as fundamental to life as eating.

Through communication, we take raw impressions and organize them into patterns. With our senses, we perceive sights, sounds, and other sensations. However, none of our sense organs is capable of perceiving *meaning.* We create meaning by finding patterns in our sensations and sharing them through conversation.

Communication can be defined as the process of creating shared meaning. When two people agree about the meaning of an event, they've communicated. However, communication is a constant challenge. Each of us creates meaning in a way that is unique.

When people speak or listen, they don't exchange meaning. They exchange symbols—words, images, gestures. And symbols are open to interpretation. This means that communication is always flawed to some extent. We can never be sure that the message we send is the message that others receive. This creates a constant challenge in our relationships.

Much of this chapter is about two low-tech methods for creating shared meaning—speaking and listening, face-to-face.

Often we can make an immediate difference in the quality of a relationship by starting with the way we listen. "You have two ears and one mouth," author Paula Bern reminds us. "Remember to use them in more or less that proportion."

Then, when it's your turn to speak, consider the benefits of open and honest communication. Sometimes it's tempting to hold back—to say only a fraction of what you're thinking or feeling. This can be one more way to keep a conflict alive. An alternative is to "empty your bucket." There are times when you can benefit everyone by letting your words and feelings flow spontaneously. Don't worry about speaking perfectly. Just reveal what's on your mind. Get all of your cards on the table. This too calls for balance. Sometimes people say *too* much. And they take a lot of time to lay the groundwork for their main point, making their listeners wait in suspense. This technique works well for actors on a stage who want to add drama to a scene. It doesn't work so well off-stage, especially when people are in conflict. When people feel forced to listen, they can become impatient and irritable. To prevent this problem, get to your point right away. Then elaborate. Provide supporting details while respecting everyone's time.

Another powerful way to boost your communication skills is to remember that disagreement can be positive. Breakdowns in communication are going to happen. Most of them can be resolved. Managing conflict in effective ways can actually bring people closer together.

With practice we can overcome many of the challenges inherent in human communication. That's what this chapter is about. As you enhance your skills at listening, speaking, and writing, you can create a new world. ■

9

In our daily contact with other people and the mass media, we are exposed to hundreds of messages. Yet the obstacles to receiving those messages accurately are numerous.

Communication— keeping the channels open

For one thing, only a small percentage of communication is verbal. We also send messages with our bodies and with the tone of our voices. Throw in a few other factors, such as a hot room or background noise, and it's a wonder we can communicate at all.

Written communication adds a whole other set of variables. When you speak, you supplement the meaning of your words with the power of body language and voice inflection. When you write, those nonverbal elements are absent. Instead, you depend on your skills at word choice, sentence construction, and punctuation to get your message across. The choices that you make in these areas can aid—or hinder—communication.

In addition, technology has transformed the ways that we communicate at school and at work. Voice mail, e-mail, and instant messaging offer even less context than longer forms of writing.

The brevity of such messages—and the haste in which they are composed—further reduces the odds of creating shared meaning.

In communication theory, the term *noise* refers to any factor that distorts meaning. When noise is present, the channels of communication start to close. Noise can be external (a lawn mower outside a classroom) or internal (the emotions of the sender or receiver, such as speech anxiety). To a large extent, skillful communication means reducing noise and keeping channels open.

© Moodboard/Corbis; static: © Paul Edmondson/Corbis; ear: © Masterfile Royalty Free

One powerful technique for doing these crucial things is to separate the roles of sending and receiving. Communication channels get blocked when we try to send and receive messages at the same time. Instead, be aware of when you are the receiver and when you are the sender. If you are receiving (listening or reading), just receive; avoid switching into the sending (speaking or writing) mode. When you are sending, stick with it until you are finished.

Communication works best when each of us has plenty of time to receive what others send *and* the opportunity to send a complete message when it's our turn. Communication is a two-way street. When someone else talks, just listen. Then switch roles so that you can be the sender for a while. Keep this up until you do a reasonably complete job of creating shared meaning. ■

CRITICAL THINKING EXERCISE 21

Practice sending or receiving

The purpose of this exercise is to help you slow down the pace of communication and clearly separate the roles of sending and receiving. Begin by applying the following steps to conversations on neutral topics. With some practice, you'll be ready to use this technique in situations that could escalate into an argument.

First, find a partner, and choose a topic for a conversation. Also set a time limit for doing this exercise. Then complete the following steps:

1. Get two 3 × 5 cards. Label one of them *sender*. Label the other *receiver*. Choose one card, and give the other one to your partner.

2. If you chose the *sender* card, then start speaking. If you chose the *receiver* card, then listen to your partner without saying a word.

3. When the sender is done speaking, exchange cards and switch roles. The person who listened in Step 2 now gets to speak. However, *do not exchange cards until the sender in Step 2 declares that she has expressed everything she wants to say.*

4. Keep switching cards and roles until your time is up.

After completing these steps, reflect on the experience. What has this exercise taught you about your current skills as a speaker and listener?

Choosing to LISTEN

Effective listening is not easy. It calls for concentration and energy. But it's worth the trouble. People love a good listener. The best salespeople, managers, coworkers, teachers, parents, and friends are the best listeners.

Through skilled listening, you can gain insight into other people and yourself. You can also promote your success in school through more powerful notes, more productive study groups, and better relationships with students and instructors.

To listen well, begin from a clear intention. *Choose* to listen well. Once you've made this choice, you can use the following techniques to be even more effective at listening. Notice that these techniques start with suggestions for nonverbal listening, which involves remaining silent while another person talks. The second set of suggestions is about verbal listening, where you occasionally speak up in ways that help you fully receive a speaker's message.

NONVERBAL LISTENING

Be quiet. Silence is more than staying quiet while someone is speaking. Allowing several seconds to pass before you begin to talk gives the speaker time to catch her breath and gather her thoughts. She might want to continue. Someone who talks nonstop might fear she will lose the floor if she pauses.

If the message being sent is complete, this short break gives you time to form your response and helps you avoid the biggest barrier to listening—listening with your answer running. If you make up a response before the person is finished, you might miss the end of the message, which is often the main point.

In some circumstances, pausing for several seconds might be inappropriate. Ignore this suggestion completely, like in an emergency where immediate action is usually necessary.

Maintain eye contact. Look at the other person while he speaks. Maintaining eye contact demonstrates your attentiveness and helps keep your mind from wandering. Your eyes also let you observe the speaker's body language and behavior. If you avoid eye contact, you can fail to see *and* fail to listen.

This idea is not an absolute. Maintaining eye contact is valued more in some cultures than others. Also, some people learn primarily by hearing; they can listen more effectively by turning off the visual input once in a while.

Display openness. You can display openness through your facial expression and body position. Uncross your arms and legs. Sit up straight. Face the other person, and remove any physical barriers between you, such as a pile of books.

Send acknowledgments. Let the speaker know periodically that you are still there. Words and nonverbal gestures of acknowledgment convey to the speaker that you are interested

> Observe a person in a conversation who is not talking. Is he listening? Maybe. Maybe not. Is he focusing on the speaker? Preparing his response? Daydreaming?

and that you are receiving her message. These words and gestures include "Mmhmm," "Okay," "Yes," and head nods.

These acknowledgments do not imply your agreement. When people tell you what they don't like about you, your head nod doesn't mean that you agree. It just indicates that you are listening.

Release distractions. Even when your intention is to listen, you might find your mind wandering. Thoughts about what *you* want to say or something you want to do later might claim your attention. There's a simple solution: Notice your wandering mind without judgment. Then bring your attention back to the act of listening.

You can also set up your immediate environment to release distractions. Turn off or silence your cell phone. Stash your laptop and other digital devices. Send the message that your sole intention in the moment is to listen.

Another option is to ask for a quick break so that you can make a written note about what's on your mind. Tell the speaker that you're writing so that you can clear your mind and return to full listening.

Suspend judgments. Listening and agreeing are two different activities. As listeners, our goal is to fully receive another person's message. This does not mean that we're obligated to agree with the message. Once you're confident that you accurately understand a speaker's point of view, you are free to agree or disagree with it. The key to effective listening is understanding *before* evaluating.

Be willing to look for value in any idea. Recall the "Power Process: Ideas are tools." It reminds us to look for potential value

9

in anything we see, hear, or read. What often prevents us from doing this is a subtle fear of letting "ridiculous" or "dangerous" ideas out in the open. During a genuine conversation, however, it's more likely that truly inaccurate or unworkable ideas will be exposed for what they are—and die a natural death.

When presented with a new idea, some of us take pride in being critical thinkers. We look for problems. We probe for weaknesses. We continue to doubt the idea until there's clear proof. Our main question seems to be "What's wrong with this idea?"

This approach can be useful when it is vital to expose flaws in ideas or reasoning. On the other hand, when we constantly look for what's wrong with new ideas, we might not recognize their value. A different and potentially more powerful approach is to ask yourself: *What if this idea is true?* This opens up all sorts of new possibilities and variations. Rather than looking for what's wrong, we can look for what's potentially valuable. Faced with a new idea, we can stay in the inquiry, look deeper, and go further.

Keep listening for new answers. Much of your education will be about finding answers to questions. Every subject you study—from algebra to history to philosophy—poses a unique set of questions. Some of the most interesting questions are those that admit many answers: How can we create a just society? How can we transmit our values to the next generation? What are the purposes of higher education? How can we prevent an environmental crisis?

Other questions are more personal: What career shall I choose? Shall I get married? Where shall I live and how shall I spend my leisure time? What shall I have, do, and be during my time on earth?

Perhaps you already have answers to these questions. Answers are wonderful, especially when they relate to our most persistent and deeply felt questions. Answers can also get in the way. Once we're convinced that we have the "right" answer, it's easy to stop looking for more answers. We then stop learning. Our range of possible actions becomes limited.

Instead of latching on to one answer, we can open up for more. Instead of being content with the ideas that we usually hear, we can keep listening for new ones. Even when we're convinced that we've finally handled a problem, we can ask people to brainstorm until we find five more solutions. The light bulb, the airplane, the computer chip, the notion of the unconscious—these and many other tools became possible when their inventors practiced the art of continually looking for additional answers.

When we keep listening for answers, we uncover fresh possibilities for thinking, feeling, and behaving. Like children learning to walk, we experience the joy of discovery.

VERBAL LISTENING

Choose when to speak. When we listen to another person, we often interrupt with our own stories, opinions, suggestions, and comments. Consider the following dialogue:

©iStockphoto.com/stevecoleimages

"Oh, I'm so excited! I just found out that I've been nominated to be in *Who's Who in American Musicians*."

"Yeah, that's neat. My Uncle Elmer got into *Who's Who in American Veterinarians*. He sure has an interesting job. One time I went along when he was treating a cow, and you'll never believe what happened. . . ."

To avoid this kind of one-sided conversation, delay your verbal responses. This does not mean that you remain totally silent while listening. It means that you wait for an *appropriate* moment to respond.

Watch your nonverbal responses too. A look of "Good grief!" from you can deter the other person from finishing his message.

Feed back meaning. Sometimes you can help a speaker clarify her message by paraphrasing it. This does not mean parroting what she says. Instead, briefly summarize. Psychotherapist Carl Rogers referred to this technique as *reflection*.[2]

Feed back what you see as the essence of the person's message: "Let me see whether I understood what you said. . . ." or "What I'm hearing you say is . . ." Often, the other person will say, "No, that's not what I meant. What I said was . . ."

There will be no doubt when you get it right. The sender will say, "Yeah, that's it," and either continue with another message or stop sending when he knows you understand.

When you feed back meaning, be concise. This is not a time to stop the other person by talking on and on about what you think you heard.

Notice verbal *and* nonverbal messages. You might point out that the speaker's body language seems to convey the exact opposite of what her words do. For example: "I noticed you said you are excited, but you look bored."

Keep in mind that the same nonverbal behavior can have various meanings across cultures. Someone who looks bored might simply be listening in a different way.

Listen for requests and intentions. An effective way to listen to complaints is to look for the request hidden in them. "This class is a waste of my time" can be heard as "Please tell me what I'll gain if I participate actively in class." "The instructor talks too fast" might be asking "What strategies can I use to take notes when the instructor covers material rapidly?"

We can even transform complaints into intentions. Take this complaint: "The parking lot by the dorms is so dark at night that I'm afraid to go to my car." This complaint can result in having a light installed in the parking lot.

Viewing complaints as requests gives us more choices. Rather than responding with defensiveness ("What does he know anyway?"), resignation ("It's always been this way and always will be"), or indifference ("It's not my job"), we can decide whether to grant the request (do what will alleviate the other's difficulty) or help the person translate his own complaint into an action plan.

Allow emotion. In the presence of full listening, some people will share things that they feel deeply about. They might shed a few tears, cry, shake, or sob. If you feel uncomfortable when this happens, see whether you can accept the discomfort for a little while longer. Emotional release can bring relief and trigger unexpected insights.

> # When we keep listening for answers, we uncover fresh possibilities for thinking, feeling, and behaving. Like children learning to walk, we experience the joy of discovery.

Ask for more. Full listening with unconditional acceptance is a rare gift. Many people have never experienced it. They are used to being greeted with resistance, so they habitually stop short of saying what they truly think and feel. Help them shed this habit by routinely asking, "Is there anything more you want to say about that?" This question sends the speaker a message that you truly value what she has to say.

Be careful with questions and advice. Questions are directive. They can take conversations in a new direction, which may not be where the speaker wants to go. Ask questions only to clarify the speaker's message. Later, when it's your turn to speak, you can introduce any topic that you want.

Also be cautious about giving advice. Unsolicited advice can be taken as condescending or even insulting. Skilled listeners recognize that people are different, and they do not assume that they know what's best for someone else.

Take care of yourself. People seek good listeners, and there are times when you don't want to listen. You might be distracted with your own concerns. Be honest. Don't pretend to listen. You can say, "What you're telling me is important, but I'm pressed for time right now. Can we set aside another time to talk about this?" It's okay not to listen.

Stay open to the adventure of listening. Receiving what another person has to say is an act of courage. Listening fully—truly opening yourself to the way another person sees the world—means taking risks. Your opinions may be challenged. You may be less certain or less comfortable than you were before.

Along with the risks come rewards. Listening in an unguarded way can take your relationships to a new depth and level of honesty. This kind of listening can open up new possibilities for thinking, feeling, and behaving. And when you practice full listening, other people are more likely to receive when it's your turn to send. ∎

You're One Click Away...
from finding more strategies online for full listening.

9

Choosing to SPEAK

You have been talking with people for most of your life, and you usually manage to get your messages across. There are times, though, when you don't. Often, these times are emotionally charged.

We all have this problem. Sometimes we feel wonderful or rotten or sad or scared, and we want to express it. Emotions, though, can get in the way of the message. And although you can send almost any message through tears, laughter, fist pounding, or hugging, sometimes words are better. Begin with a sincere intention to reach common ground with your listener. Then experiment with the suggestions that follow.

Replace "you" messages with "I" messages. It can be difficult to disagree with someone without his becoming angry or your becoming upset. When conflict occurs, we often make statements about the other person, or "you" messages:

"You are rude."
"You make me mad."
"You must be crazy."
"You don't love me anymore."

This kind of communication results in defensiveness. The responses might be similar to these:

"I am not rude."
"I don't care."
"No, *you* are crazy."
"No, *you* don't love *me!*"

"You" messages are hard to listen to. They label, judge, blame, and assume things that may or may not be true. They demand rebuttal. Even praise can sometimes be an ineffective "you" message. "You" messages don't work.

Psychologist Thomas Gordon suggests that when communication is emotionally charged, consider limiting your statements to descriptions about yourself.[3] Replace "you" messages with "I" messages:

"You are rude" might become "I feel upset."
"You make me mad" could be "I feel angry."
"You must be crazy" can be "I don't understand."
"You don't love me anymore" could become "I'm afraid we're drifting apart."

Suppose a friend asks you to pick him up at the airport. You drive 20 miles and wait for the plane. No friend. You decide your friend missed her plane, so you wait 3 hours for the next flight. No

friend. Perplexed and worried, you drive home. The next day, you see your friend downtown.

"What happened?" you ask.
"Oh, I caught an earlier flight."
"You are a rude person," you reply.

Look for and talk about the facts—the observable behavior. Everyone will agree that your friend asked you to pick her up, that she did take an earlier flight, and that you did not receive a call from her. But the idea that she is rude is not a fact—it's a judgment.

She might go on to say, "I called your home, and no one answered. My mom had a stroke and was rushed to Valley View. I caught the earliest flight I could get." Your judgment no longer fits.

When you saw your friend, you might have said, "I waited and waited at the airport. I was worried about you. I didn't get a call. I feel angry and hurt. I don't want to waste my time. Next time, you can call me when your flight arrives, and I'll be happy to pick you up."

"I" messages don't judge, blame, criticize, or insult. They don't invite the other person to counterattack with more of the same. "I" messages are also more accurate. They report our own thoughts and feelings.

At first, "I" messages might feel uncomfortable or seem forced. That's okay. Use the "Five ways to say 'I'" explained on page 243.

Remember that questions are not always questions. You've heard these "questions" before. A parent asks, "Don't you want to look nice?" Translation: "I wish you'd cut your hair, lose the blue jeans, and put on a tie." Or how about this question from a spouse: "Honey, wouldn't you love to go to an exciting hockey game tonight?" Translation: "I've already bought tickets."

We use questions that aren't questions to sneak our opinions and requests into conversations. "Doesn't it upset you?" means "It upsets me," and "Shouldn't we hang the picture over here?" means "I want to hang the picture over here."

Communication improves when we say, "I'm upset" and "Let's hang the picture over here."

Choose your nonverbal messages. How you say something can be more important than what you say. Your tone of voice and gestures add up to a silent message that you send. This message can support, modify, or contradict your words. Your posture, the way you dress, how often you shower, and even the poster hanging on your wall can negate your words before you say them.

Most nonverbal behavior is unconscious. We can learn to be aware of it and choose our nonverbal messages. The key is to be clear about our intention and purpose. When we know what we want to say and are committed to getting it across, our inflections, gestures, and words work together and send a unified message.

Notice barriers to sending messages. Sometimes fear stops us from sending messages. We are afraid of other people's reactions, sometimes justifiably. Being truthful doesn't mean being insensitive to the impact that our messages have on others. Tact is a virtue; letting fear prevent communication is not.

Assumptions can also be used as excuses for not sending messages. "He already knows this," we tell ourselves.

Predictions of failure can be barriers to sending too. "He won't listen," we assure ourselves. That statement might be inaccurate. Perhaps the other person senses that we're angry and listens in a guarded way. Or perhaps he is listening and sending nonverbal messages we don't understand.

Or we might predict, "He'll never do anything about it, even if I tell him." Again, making assumptions can defeat your message before you send it.

It's easy to make excuses for not communicating. If you have fear or some other concern about sending a message, be aware of it. Don't expect the concern to go away. Realize that you can communicate even with your concerns. You can choose to make them part of the message: "I am going to tell you how I feel, but I'm afraid that you will think it's stupid."

Talking to someone when you don't want to could be a matter of educational survival. Sometimes a short talk with an advisor, a teacher, a friend, or a family member can solve a problem that otherwise could jeopardize your education.

Speak candidly. When we brood on negative thoughts and refuse to speak them out loud, we lose perspective. And when we keep joys to ourselves, we diminish our satisfaction. A solution is to share regularly what we think and feel. Psychotherapist Sidney Jourard referred to such openness and honesty as *transparency* and wrote eloquently about how it can heal and deepen relationships.[4]

Sometimes candid speaking can save a life. For example, if you think a friend is addicted to drugs, telling her so in a supportive, nonjudgmental way is a sign of friendship.

Imagine a community in which people freely and lovingly speak their minds—without fear or defensiveness. That can be your community.

This suggestion comes with a couple of caveats. First, there is a big difference between speaking candidly about your problems and griping about them. Gripers usually don't seek solutions. They just want everyone to know how unhappy they are. Instead, talk about problems as a way to start searching for solutions.

Second, avoid bragging. Other people are turned off by constant references to how much money you have, how great your partner is, how numerous your social successes are, or how much status your family enjoys. There is a difference between sharing excitement and being obnoxious.

Offer "feedforward." Giving people feedback about their past performance can be a powerful way to help them learn. Equally useful is "feedforward," which means exploring new options for the future.

Marshall Goldsmith, a management consultant, suggests a way to do this. First, talk about a specific, high-impact behavior that you'd

FIVE WAYS to say "I"

An "I" message can include any or all of the following five elements. Be careful when including the last two elements, though, because they can contain hidden judgments or threats.

Observations. Describe the facts—the indisputable, observable realities. Talk about what you—or anyone else—can see, hear, smell, taste, or touch. Avoid judgments, interpretations, or opinions. Instead of saying, "You're a slob," say, "Last night's lasagna pan was still on the stove this morning."

Feelings. Describe your own feelings. It is easier to listen to "I feel frustrated" than to "You never help me." Stating how you feel about another's actions can be valuable feedback for that person.

Wants. You are far more likely to get what you want if you say what you want. If someone doesn't know what you want, she doesn't have a chance to help you get it. Ask clearly. Avoid demanding or using the word *need*. Most people like to feel helpful, not obligated. Instead of saying, "Do the dishes when it's your turn, or else!" say, "I want to divide the housework fairly."

Thoughts. Communicate your thoughts, but use caution. Beginning your statement with the word "I" doesn't automatically make it an "I" message. "I think you are a slob" is a "you" judgment in disguise. Instead, say, "I'd have more time to study if I didn't have to clean up so often."

Intentions. The last part of an "I" message is a statement about what you intend to do. Have a plan that doesn't depend on the other person. For example, instead of "From now on, we're going to split the dishwashing evenly," you could say, "I intend to do my share of the housework and leave the rest."

9

like to change—for example, "I want to be a better listener." Then gather with a small group of trusted friends and ask for suggestions about ways to accomplish your goal. To make this process work, avoid any conversation about what's happened in the past. Focus instead on next actions you intend to take. Also listen to what others suggest without criticizing their ideas.[5]

Speak up! Look for opportunities to practice speaking strategies. Join class discussions, and keep a running list of questions and comments to share. Start conversations about topics that excite you. Ask for information and clarification. Ask for feedback on your skills.

Also speak up when you want support. Consider creating a team of people who help one another succeed. Such a team can develop naturally from a study group that works well. Ask members whether they would be willing to accept and receive support in achieving a wide range of academic and personal goals. Meet regularly to do goal-setting exercises from this book and brainstorm success strategies.

After you have a clear statement of your goals and a plan for achieving them, let family members and friends know. When appropriate, let them know how they can help. You may be surprised at how often people respond to a genuine request for support. ■

You're One Click Away...
from finding more strategies online for speaking your mind.

CRITICAL THINKING EXERCISE 22

Write an "I" message

Pick something about school that irritates you. Then pretend that you are talking to a person who is associated with this irritation. Write down what you would say to this person as a "you" message.

_____

_____

_____

_____

_____

_____

_____

Now write the same complaint as an "I" message. Include at least the first three elements suggested in "Five Ways to Say 'I.'"

_____

_____

_____

_____

_____

_____

_____

_____

Discover communication styles

The concept of *communication styles* can be useful when you want to discover sources of conflict with another person—or when you're in a conversation with someone from a different culture.

Consider the many ways in which people express themselves verbally. These characteristics can reflect an individual's preferred communication style:

- *Extroversion*—talking to others as a way to explore possibilities for taking action.
- *Introversion*—thinking through possibilities alone before talking to others.
- *Dialogue*—engaging in a discussion to hear many points of view before coming to a conclusion or decision.
- *Debate*—arguing for a particular point of view from the outset of a discussion.
- *Openness*—being ready to express personal thoughts and feelings early in a relationship.
- *Reserve*—holding back on self-expression until a deeper friendship develops.
- A *faster pace* of conversation—allowing people to speak quickly and forcefully while filling any gaps in conversation.
- A *slower pace* of conversation—allowing people to speak slowly and quietly while taking time to formulate their thoughts.

These are just a few examples of differences in communication styles. You might be able to think of others.

The point is that people with different communication styles can make negative assumptions about each other. For example, those who prefer fast-paced conversations might assume that people who talk slowly are indecisive. And people who prefer slower-paced conversations might assume that people who talk quickly are pushy and uninterested in anyone else's opinion.

Take this opportunity to think about your preferred communication styles and assumptions. Do they enhance or block your relationships with other people? Think back over the conversations you've had during the past week. Then complete the following sentences, using additional paper as needed.

1. I discovered that I prefer conversations that allow me to. . .

_____

_____

_____

2. I discovered that I usually feel uncomfortable in conversations when other people. . .

_____

_____

_____

3. When people do the things listed in Item 2, I tend to make certain assumptions, such as. . .

_____

_____

_____

4. As an alternative to making the assumptions listed in Item 3, I intend to. . .

_____

_____

_____

9

COMMUNICATING
with your boss

Much of the literature about personal success is about strategies for promoting yourself. Consider another point of view: Success at work means promoting your boss. If you actively help your boss to complete projects on time and within budget, the rewards can come back to you in the form of pay raises and promotions.

If the mere *thought* of talking to your boss fills you with fear, take a deep breath. This is a skill you can master. The keys include preparation, practice, and taking time to see the world from your boss's point of view.

Minimize surprise with regular communication. When you're struggling with a task or know about a project that's poised for breakdown, tell your boss immediately. Save surprises for the occasional spontaneous birthday party.

There are two reasons for this suggestion. First, your boss would probably like to hear about problems directly from you—rather than learn about them from someone else. Second, the sooner she knows about problems, the sooner she can help you take steps to solve them.

Also take the time to tell your boss about things that are going well. If you're going to finish a project early or deliver it under budget, then share the good news. Your boss would like to hear about such things from the people that report directly to him.

Beyond sharing problems and successes, be prepared to give your boss a routine status report on all your active projects. Some bosses require a written report. In addition, be able to give a quick verbal summary whenever your boss asks for it.

In summary, this strategy boils down to four words: Talk often. Be honest.

Observe the chain of command. All organizations—especially big ones—have a chain of command. There's a chief executive, owner, president, director, or someone else who makes the final decisions. Just beneath this person is a board of directors or some other group of top-level managers. In turn, these managers supervise others who have direct responsibility for getting projects done.

You've probably heard about people who "go over their boss's head." It happens when employees bypass their immediate supervisor and initiate a discussion with someone who falls higher on the chain of command. Doing this is usually a sure-fire way to alienate your boss.

Of course, no rule is absolute. At times—such as during a sustained conflict with your boss—you might decide to communicate with a person who has more authority. Before you do this, make sure that:

- You've done everything possible to resolve the conflict or otherwise complete the communication with your boss.
- You've told your boss about your decision.
- You've thoroughly considered the consequences—and are willing to live with them.

Before you approach your boss ... Bosses are busy people. To communicate with them effectively, respect their time. Be prepared. Before you ask your boss for a meeting:

- List the topics that you want to cover.
- Clarify the points you want to make about each topic.
- Gather all the facts you need to make your points, and verify their accuracy.
- Anticipate the questions your boss might ask and prepare some answers.
- Think of potential solutions to any problem that you mention.
- If you have an idea to propose, see if you can pair it with a clear and compelling benefit.

When dealing with a complex issue, put the above points in writing. You might also want to rehearse your part of the conversation, or role-play it with someone you know outside of work.

For a successful meeting, avoid communicating with your boss when either of you feels angry or upset. You're more likely to think clearly and communicate persuasively when emotions are in check.

While speaking to your boss ... Any of the ideas in this chapter can help you develop a positive relationship with your boss. In particular, consider the following.

Get to the point. When you have a routine update, keep it short. If you have a bigger issue to discuss, summarize it in a sentence or two, and ask for a meeting to discuss it in more detail.

Offer details. Saying, "I'm stuck" will probably leave your boss wanting more. You're more likely to get a meaningful response if you add specifics, followed by a request. For example: "Two of our vendors raised their prices. Could I please have an extra day to revise my budget?"

Remember that your boss is under pressure to make quick decisions about how to respond to any new development. These decisions are easier when you provide the key facts and figures.

Use words that promote collaboration and defuse resistance. When communicating with your boss, "I" statements can work magic. "I'd like your support in solving a problem" is easier for your boss to hear than "You never give me any support."

To further reduce resistance to your ideas, avoid absolute words such as *always, every,* and *never*—for instance, "My team can never agree on anything." Such terms imply that your point of view on an issue is the final truth. This practically invites disagreement.

As an alternative, choose words such as *often, sometimes,* and *perhaps*: "My team *often* has problems reaching consensus; how can I coach them to be more effective?"

You can use a similar strategy when your boss says something that you disagree with. Instead of saying, "I totally disagree," consider starting your response with words such as:

- *I can see that. Another option is . . .*
- *Have you thought about . . .*
- *It might be more effective if we . . .*

Statements such as this show that you're open-minded, that there's room for discussion, and that you're willing to learn.

Listen actively. In a fast-paced work environment, conversations can take place at breakneck speed. It's okay to admit that you missed something your boss said. Ask her to repeat or clarify it. Your request shows that you're tuned in to the conversation and that you value what your boss has to say.

Monitor your body language. When your boss speaks, make direct eye contact. Notice points of tension in your body and consciously relax them. If your arms are folded tightly, let them hang loose at your sides. If you're holding your breath, then inhale deeply and let it go with a long exhale. A skilled boss will pick up on your nonverbal signals and notice when you're staying fully present to the conversation.

Stay open to feedback. Experiment with the attitude that *any* response from your boss is valuable. If your boss agrees with you, that's useful feedback. If your boss disagrees with you, that's equally useful feedback. The most important thing is to stay in a conversation and keep the lines of communication open.

Remember that your boss might have information that you don't have—or that she might be dealing with office politics that are hidden from you. When your boss disagrees with you or denies your request, don't take it personally.

Communicate with a difficult boss. People get promoted to supervisory roles for many reasons. And it's not always because they have good "people skills." At some point in your career, you are likely to work for a boss that you and your coworkers actively dislike.

This situation can be draining and dispiriting. In extreme cases, you might wonder whether your boss is deliberately *trying* to make you miserable.

That's seldom the case. More likely, your boss's behavior results from many factors that have nothing to do with you.

Instead of complaining about your boss's actions, focus on managing responses. Although you can't control your boss's behavior, you can control your own:

Get support outside of work. Discuss your feelings about your boss with someone other than a coworker. Venting your anger and sadness can take some of the sting out of those emotions.

Cultivate supportive relationships in your life. These serve as reminders that you are a person worth loving, no matter what boss you have.

Avoid complaining about your boss to colleagues. Complaining will only create a more negative work environment. It won't change your boss, and it might damage your reputation.

Support your boss publicly. When your boss's name comes up in conversations with coworkers, find something positive to say. If news of your public support gets back to your boss, you could gain credibility and lower his defenses at the same time.

Spend more time with your boss. Our natural reaction to people we dislike is to avoid them. Consider the possible benefits of doing exactly the opposite. Volunteering to work on extra projects with your boss might give you insight into the pressures and personal problems she's struggling with.

In addition, collaborating with your boss to meet a shared goal increases the chances of having positive experiences with her. Over time, these experiences might change your relationship for the better. ◾

9

✔ CRITICAL THINKING EXERCISES 23

VIPs (Very Important Persons)

STEP 1 Under the column below titled "Name," write the names of at least seven people who have positively influenced your life. They might be relatives, friends, teachers, or perhaps persons you have never met. (Complete each step before moving on.)

STEP 2 In the next column, rate your gratitude for this person's influence (from 1 to 5, with 1 being a little grateful and 5 being extremely grateful).

STEP 3 In the third column, rate how fully you have communicated your appreciation to this person (again, 1 to 5, with 1 being not communicated and 5 being fully communicated).

STEP 4 In the final column, put a "U" to indicate the persons with whom you have unfinished business (such as an important communication that you have not yet sent).

	Name	Grateful (1–5)	Communicated (1–5)	U
1.				
2.				
3.				
4.				
5.				
6.				
7.				

STEP 5 Now select two persons with "U's" beside their names, and write each of them a letter. Express the love, tenderness, and joy you feel toward them. Tell them exactly how they have helped change your life and how glad you are that they did.

STEP 6 You also have an impact on others. Write below the names of people whose lives you have influenced. Consider sharing with these people why you enjoy being a part of their lives.

_____

_____

_____

_____

_____

_____

_____

_____

_____

_____

_____

_____

_____

THREE phases of

EFFECTIVE WRITING

9

Effective writing is essential to your success. Papers, presentations, essay tests, e-mail, social networking sites—and even the occasional text message—call for your ability to communicate ideas with force and clarity.

This chapter outlines a three-phase process for writing anything:

1. Getting ready to write
2. Writing a first draft
3. Revising your draft

PHASE 1: Getting ready to write

Schedule and list writing tasks. You can divide the ultimate goal—a finished paper—into smaller steps that you can tackle right away. Estimate how long it will take to complete each step. Start with the date your paper is due and work backward to the present. Say that the due date is December 1, and you have about 3 months to write the paper. To give yourself a cushion, schedule November 20 as your targeted completion date. Plan what you want to get done by November 1, and then list what you want to get done by October 1.

Choose a topic. It's easy to put off writing if you have a hard time choosing a topic. However, it is almost impossible to make a wrong choice of topic at this stage. You can choose a different topic later if you find the one you've chosen isn't working out.

Using your instructor's guidelines for the paper or speech, write down the list of possible topics that you created earlier. Then choose one. If you can't decide, use scissors to cut your list into single items, put them in a box, and pull one out. To avoid getting stuck on this step, set a precise time line: "I will choose a topic by 4:00 p.m. on Wednesday."

There's no need to brainstorm topics in isolation. You can harness the energy and the natural creative power of a group to assist you in creating topics for your paper. For ideas about ways to brainstorm, see Chapter 8: Creative & Critical Thinking.

Narrow your topic. The most common pitfall is selecting a topic that's too broad. "Harriet Tubman" is not a useful topic for your American history paper because it's too broad. Covering that topic would take hundreds of pages. Instead, consider "Harriet Tubman's activities as a Union spy during the Civil War." Your topic statement can function as a working title.

Write a thesis statement. Clarify what you want to say by summarizing it in one concise sentence. This sentence, called a *thesis statement*, refines your working title. It also helps in making a preliminary outline.

You might write a thesis statement such as "Harriet Tubman's activities with the Underground Railroad led to a relationship with the Union army during the Civil War." A thesis statement that's clear and to the point can make your paper easier to write. Remember, you can always rewrite your thesis statement as you learn more about your topic.

A thesis statement is different from a topic. Like newspaper headlines, a thesis statement makes an assertion or describes an action. It is expressed in a complete sentence, including a verb. "Diversity" is a topic. "Cultural diversity is valuable" is a thesis statement.

Consider your purpose. Effective writing flows from a purpose. Discuss the purpose of your assignment with your instructor. Also think about how you'd like your reader or listener to respond after considering your ideas. Do you want your audience to think differently, to feel differently, or to take a certain action?

How you answer these questions greatly affects your writing strategy. If you want someone to think differently, make your writing clear and logical. Support your assertions with evidence. If you want someone to feel differently, consider crafting a story. Write about a character your audience can empathize with, and tell how that character resolves a problem that the audience can relate to. And if your purpose is to move the reader into action, explain exactly what steps to take, and offer solid benefits for doing so.

To clarify your purpose, state it in one sentence. For example, "I will define the term *success* in such a clear and convincing way that I win a scholarship from the publisher of this textbook."

Do initial research. At the initial stage, the objective of your research is not to uncover specific facts about your topic. That comes later. First, you want to gain an overview of the subject. Discover the structure of your topic—its major divisions and branches.

Say that you want to persuade the reader to vote for a certain candidate. You must first learn enough about this person to summarize his background and state his stands on key issues.

Outline. An outline is a kind of map. When you follow a map, you avoid getting lost. Likewise, an outline keeps you from wandering off the topic.

To start an outline, gather a stack of 3 × 5 cards. Brainstorm ideas you want to include in your paper. Write one phrase or sentence per card. Then experiment with the cards. Group them into separate stacks, each stack representing one major category. After that, arrange the stacks in order. Finally, arrange the cards within each stack in a logical order. Rearrange them until you discover an organization that you like. If you write on a computer, consider using the outlining feature of your word-processing software.

Do in-depth research. You can find information about research skills in Chapter 5: Reading and Chapter 6: Notes. The following are further suggestions.

Use 3 × 5 cards. If they haven't found their way into your life by now, joy awaits you. These cards work wonders when you conduct research. Just write down one idea per card. This makes it easy to organize—and reorganize—your ideas.

Organizing research cards as you create them saves time. Use rubber bands to keep source cards—cards that include the bibliographical information for a source—separate from information cards—cards that include nuggets of information from a source—and to maintain general categories.

You can also save time in two other ways. First, copy all of the information correctly. Always include the source code and page number on information cards. Second, be neat and organized. Write legibly, using the same format for all of your cards.

In addition to source cards and information cards, generate idea cards. If you have a thought while you are researching, write it down on a card. Label these cards clearly as containing your own ideas.

An alternative to 3 × 5 cards is a computer outlining or database program. Some word-processing packages also include features that can be used for outlining and note taking.

☐ Avoid ~~at all costs and at all times~~ ~~the really, really~~ terrible mistake of using ~~way too many~~ unnecessary words, ~~a mistake that some student writers often make when they sit down to write papers for the various courses in which they participate at the fine institutions of higher learning which they are fortunate to attend.~~

occasionally to glance at your notes and outline. The idea is to avoid stopping to edit your work. You can save that for the next step.

Speak it. To get ideas flowing, start talking. Admit your confusion or lack of clear ideas. Then just speak. By putting your thoughts into words, you'll start thinking more clearly. Novelist E. M. Forster said, "'Speak before you think' is creation's motto."[6]

Use free writing. Free writing, a technique championed by writing teacher Peter Elbow, sends a depth probe into your creative mind.[7] There's only one rule in free writing: Write without stopping. Set a time limit—say, 10 minutes—and keep your pencil in motion or your fingers dancing across the keyboard the whole time. Give yourself permission to keep writing. Ignore the urge to stop and rewrite, even if you think what you've written isn't very good. There's no need to worry about spelling, punctuation, or grammar. It's okay if you stray from the initial subject. Just keep writing, and let the ideas flow. Experiment with free writing as soon as your instructor assigns a paper.

PHASE 2: WRITING A FIRST DRAFT

Gather your notes and outline. If you've planned your writing project and completed your research, you've already done much of the hard work. Now you can relax into writing your first draft. To create your draft, gather your notes and arrange them to follow your outline. Then write about the ideas in your notes. Write in paragraphs, with one idea per paragraph. If you have organized your notes logically, related facts will appear close to one another.

Ease into it. Some people find that it works well to forget the word *writing*. Instead, they ease into the task with activities that help generate ideas. You can free associate, cluster, meditate, daydream, doodle, draw diagrams, visualize the event you want to describe, talk into a voice recorder—anything that gets you started.

Remember that the first draft is not for keeps. You can worry about quality later, when you revise. Your goal at this point is simply to generate lots of material.

Many writers prefer to get their first draft down quickly. Their advice is just to keep writing. Of course, you may pause

Make writing a habit. The word *inspiration* is not in the working vocabulary for many professional writers. Instead of waiting for inspiration to strike, they simply make a habit of writing at a certain time each day. You can use the same strategy. Schedule a block of time to write your first draft. The very act of writing can breed inspiration.

Respect your deep mind. Part of the process of writing takes place outside our awareness. There's nothing mysterious about this process. Many people report that ideas come to them while they're doing something totally unrelated to writing. Often this happens after they've been grappling with a question and have reached a point where they feel stuck. It's like the composer who said, "There I was, sitting and eating a sandwich, and all of a sudden this darn tune pops into my head." You can trust your deep mind. It's writing while you eat, sleep, and brush your teeth.

9

Get physical. Writing, like jogging or playing tennis, is a physical activity. You can move your body in ways that are in tune with the flow of your ideas. While working on the first draft, take breaks. Go for a walk. Speak or sing your ideas out loud. From time to time, practice relaxation techniques and breathe deeply.

PHASE 3: REVISING YOUR DRAFT

Plan to revise a paper two or three times. Make a clean copy of each revision, and then let the last revised draft sit for at least 3 or 4 days.

Schedule time for rewrites before you begin, and schedule at least 1 day between revisions so that you can let the material sit. On Tuesday night, you might think your writing sings the song of beautiful language. On Wednesday, you will see that those same words, such as the phrase "sings the song of beautiful language," belong in the trash basket.

Keep in mind the saying "Write in haste; revise at leisure." When you edit and revise, slow down and take a microscope to your work. One guideline is to allow 50 percent of writing time for planning, researching, and writing the first draft. Then give the remaining 50 percent to revising.

While you're in the revising phase, consider making an appointment to see your instructor during office hours. Bring along a current draft of your paper. Be willing to share your thesis and outline. Ask for revision tips. If your school has a writing assistance center, see someone there as well.

One effective way to revise your paper is to read it out loud. The eyes tend to fill in the blanks in our own writing. The combination of voice and ears forces us to pay attention to the details.

Another technique is to ask other people to review your paper. If you do this in class, it's called peer editing. This is never a substitute for your own review, but other people can often see mistakes you miss. Remember, when other people criticize or review your work, they're not attacking you. They're just commenting on your paper. With a little practice, you can actually learn to welcome feedback.

When it's your turn to edit someone else's writing, remember two guidelines: First, be positive. Find something that you like about the paper and talk about that. Second, offer a specific suggestion. Begin this statement with words such as: "I think your paper would be even stronger if…."

After getting feedback on your draft, revise it while keeping the following suggestions in mind.

Cut. Look for excess baggage. Avoid at all costs and at all times the really, really terrible mistake of using way too many unnecessary words, a mistake that some student writers often make when they sit down to write papers for the various courses in which they participate at the fine institutions of

> Approach your rough draft as if it were a chunk of granite from which you will chisel the final product. In the end, much of your first draft will be lying on the floor. What is left will be the clean, clear, polished product. Sometimes the revisions are painful.

higher learning that they are fortunate enough to attend. (Example: The previous sentence could be edited to "Avoid unnecessary words.")

Approach your rough draft as if it were a chunk of granite from which you will chisel the final product. In the end, much of your first draft will be lying on the floor. What is left will be the clean, clear, polished product. Sometimes the revisions are painful. Sooner or later, every writer invents a phrase that is truly clever but makes no contribution to the purpose of the paper. Grit your teeth and let it go.

Note: For maximum efficiency, make the larger cuts first—sections, chapters, pages. Then go for the smaller cuts—paragraphs, sentences, phrases, words. Stay within the word limit that your instructor assigns.

Paste. In deleting both larger and smaller passages in your first draft, you've probably removed some of the original transitions and connecting ideas. The next task is to rearrange what's left of your paper or speech so that it flows logically. Look for consistency within paragraphs and for transitions from paragraph to paragraph and section to section.

If all or part of your draft doesn't hang together, reorder your ideas. Imagine yourself with scissors and glue, cutting the paper into scraps—one scrap for each point. Then paste these points down in a new, more logical order.

Fix. Now it's time to look at individual words and phrases. Define any terms that the reader might not know, putting them in plain English whenever you can. Scan your paper for any passages that are written in the language of texting or instant messaging. Rewrite those into full sentences.

In general, rely on vivid nouns and verbs. Using too many adjectives and adverbs weakens your message and adds unnecessary bulk to your writing. Write about the details, and be specific. Also, use the active rather than the passive voice.

> Instead of writing in the passive voice:
> > *A project was initiated.*
> You can use the active voice:
> > *The research team began a project.*

> Instead of writing verbosely:
> > *After making a timely arrival and perspicaciously observing the unfolding events, I emerged totally and gloriously victorious.*
> You can write to the point, as Julius Caesar did:
> > *I came, I saw, I conquered.*
> Instead of writing vaguely:
> > *The speaker made effective use of the television medium, asking in no uncertain terms that we change our belief systems.*
> You can write specifically:
> > *The reformed criminal stared straight into the television camera and shouted, "Take a good look at what you're doing! Will it get you what you really want?"*

Prepare. In a sense, any paper is a sales effort. If you hand in a paper that is wearing wrinkled jeans, its hair tangled and unwashed, and its shoes untied, your instructor is less likely to buy it. To avoid this situation, format your paper following accepted standards for margin widths, endnotes, title pages, and other details.

Ask your instructor for specific instructions on how to cite the sources used in writing your paper. You can find useful guidelines in the *MLA Handbook for Writers of Research Papers,* a book from the Modern Language Association. Also visit the MLA Web site at www.mla.org/style.

If you cut and paste material from a Web page directly into your paper, be sure to place that material in quotation marks and cite the source. And before referencing an e-mail message, verify the sender's identity. Remember that anyone sending e-mail can pretend to be someone else.

Use quality paper for your final version. For an even more professional appearance, bind your paper with a plastic or paper cover.

> In a sense, any paper is a sales effort. If you hand in a paper that is wearing wrinkled jeans, its hair tangled and unwashed, and its shoes untied, your instructor is less likely to buy it.

Proof. As you ease down the homestretch, read your revised paper one more time. This time, go for the big picture and look for the following:

- A clear thesis statement
- Sentences that introduce your topic, guide the reader through the major sections of your paper, and summarize your conclusions
- Details— such as quotations, examples, and statistics—that support your conclusions
- Lean sentences that have been purged of needless words
- Plenty of action verbs and concrete, specific nouns

Finally, look over your paper with an eye for spelling and grammar mistakes. If you're writing with software that checks for such errors, take advantage of this feature. Also keep in mind that even the best software will miss some mistakes. Computers still cannot replace a skilled human proofreader.

When you're through proofreading, take a minute to savor the result. You've just witnessed something of a miracle— the mind attaining clarity and resolution. That's the *aha!* in writing. ■

 You're One Click Away...
from finding more paths online to effective writing.

9

Writing
for the WORKPLACE

Writing is essential to career success. Companies crank out documents daily: contracts, budgets, project plans, grant proposals, reports, marketing campaigns, advertisements, e-mails, job descriptions, and more. Employers value people who write well.

The skills that you develop in writing for teachers will also help you write clearly for coworkers. Remember, however, that readers at work are often pressed for time and impatient. Do them a courtesy by using the following strategies.

Get to the point, pronto! Don't worry about warming up to your point with a long introduction. Put your main idea in the first paragraph—if possible, the first sentence. If your document will go over two pages, then add a summary at the top. Keep this to one paragraph and place the key "take away" idea there.

Answer key questions. Put yourself in your reader's place. She may be reading your document after a long day of meetings and still have 10 items on her to-do list. When she sees your report, she's likely to ask: *What's the problem you're addressing? What's your solution? And why should I care?* Organize your document so that it directly answers such questions in a logical order.

Make it clear how you want readers to respond. You might want them to schedule a meeting, approve your budget, give a green light to your project plan, or give you a raise. Whatever your purpose, make sure that your request is polite and clear.

Let the text breathe. Allow white space between paragraphs. For long documents, include each of your main points in a large, newspaper-style headline (also called a *heading*). For ideas that come in a series, use numbered or bulleted lists.

Write for online audiences. Today's information technology allows you to manipulate text and images in ways that were unheard of just a few years ago. Even so, you are subject to limitations imposed by the computer screen. Those limitations relate especially to the workhorse of online communication—good old-fashioned alphanumeric characters, also known as plain text.

The computer screen is a poor medium for presenting lengthy text. To communicate effectively online, get to the point quickly and keep the word count down. The following techniques will help you do that:

- When creating an e-mail message or web page, write about half the words you would use on a printed page.

- Whenever possible, keep your text to one screen or less.

- Use short words, short sentences, and short paragraphs.

- Set short line lengths—no more than 65 characters.

- Write in the second person, addressing the reader as *you*.

- Use active verbs and write in the present tense.

- Avoid "fluff"—clichés, filler, and empty claims; stick to essential ideas and verifiable facts.

- Define technical terms that readers may not know.

- Include long documents as attachments that readers can print out.

Research indicates that when people sit at their computers, they don't read word for word. Instead, they scan. And, many of them will not scroll downward past the first screen of text. Assist readers who scan by giving your writing a visible structure:

- Break up your text with headings printed in boldface.

- Keep headings short.

- To clarify the structure of your document, use minor headings as well as major headings.

- Write headings that are informative enough to make sense when displayed out of context—such as a list of "hits" from a search engine.

- Break up paragraphs with bulleted lists, numbered lists, and graphics.

- Keep lists short.

- Highlight important key words or phrases, but don't overdo it.

Write e-mails that get results. Be conscious of the amount of e-mail that busy people receive. Send e-mail messages only to the people who need them, and only when necessary.

Write an informative subject line. Rather than offering a generic description of your message, include a capsule summary—a complete sentence with the main point of your message.

Before hitting the *send* button, review what you've written. Every message you send says something about your attention to detail. Keep the tone professional—more formal than the text messages you send to friends.

Use the "reply-all" feature only when everyone who received a message truly needs to know your response. People will appreciate your help in keeping their incoming messages to a minimum. ■

> Some people tune out during a speech. Just think of all the times you've listened to instructors, lecturers, and politicians. Remember all the wonderful daydreams you had during their speeches.

James Steidl/Shutterstock.com

Making PRESENTATIONS

Your audiences are like you. The way you plan and present your speech can determine the number of audience members who will stay with you until the end. Polishing your speaking and presentation skills can also help you think on your feet and communicate clearly. You can use these skills in any course and in any career you choose.

Remember the power of presentations. Presentations can move people to change their opinions, change their vote, or change their lives. Democracy rests on the free exchange of ideas, accomplished largely by the power of the spoken word. Your speaking can change the world.

As you read this article, remember that the word *presentation* includes the traditional topic of public speaking and elements used to supplement the spoken word. Those supplements include handout materials, group discussions and exercises, and visual elements that are created and displayed with a computer and other technology.

Creating a presentation is much like writing a paper. Divide the project into three phases:

1. Preparing your presentation
2. Delivering your presentation
3. Reflecting on your presentation

PHASE 1: PREPARING YOUR PRESENTATION

Start from your passions. If your instructor allows you to choose the topic of presentation, then choose one that you find interesting. Imagine that the first words in your presentation will be: "I'm here to talk to you because I feel passionately about . . ."

How would you complete the sentence? Turn your answer into your main topic.

Consider a "process speech." In this type of presentation, your purpose is to explain a way to do or make something. Examples are changing a tire, planting asparagus, or preparing a healthy meal in 15 minutes. Choose a short, step-by-step process with a concrete outcome. This makes it easier to organize, practice, and deliver your first presentation.

In the introduction to your process speech, get the audience's attention and establish rapport. State the topic and purpose of your speech. Relate the topic to something that audience members care about. During the body of your speech, explain each step in the process, following a logical order. To conclude, quickly summarize the process and remind your audience of its usefulness.

Analyze your audience. Developing a speech is similar to writing a paper. Begin by writing out your topic, purpose, and thesis statement as described in "Phase 1: Getting ready to write" on page 250. Then carefully analyze your audience by using the strategies in the chart on page 256.

Remember that audiences want to know that your presentation relates to their needs and desires. To convince people that you have something worthwhile to say, think of your main topic or point. Then see whether you can complete this sentence: *I'm telling you this because . . .*

Organize your presentation. List three to five questions that your audience members are likely to ask about your topic. Put those questions in logical order. Organize your presentation so that it directly answers those questions.

9

If your topic is new to listeners . . .	• Explain why your topic matters to them. • Relate the topic to something that listeners already know and care about. • Define any terms that listeners might not know.
If listeners already know about your topic . . .	• Acknowledge this fact at the beginning of your speech. • Find a narrow aspect of the topic that may be new to listeners. • Offer a new perspective on the topic, or connect it to an unfamiliar topic.
If listeners disagree with your thesis . . .	• Tactfully admit your differences of opinion. • Reinforce points on which you and your audience agree. • Build credibility by explaining your qualifications to speak on your topic. • Quote expert figures that agree with your thesis—people whom your audience is likely to admire. • Explain that their current viewpoint has costs for them, and that a slight adjustment in their thinking will bring significant benefits.
If listeners may be uninterested in your topic . . .	• Explain how listening to your speech can help them gain something that matters deeply to them. • Explain ways to apply your ideas in daily life.

Also consider the length of your presentation. As a general guideline, plan on delivering about a hundred words per minute. Remember that you could lose points if your presentation goes over the assigned time limit.

Aim for a lean presentation—enough words to make your point but not so many as to make your audience restless. Leave your listeners wanting more. When you speak, be brief and then be seated.

Speeches are usually organized in three main parts: the introduction, the main body, and the conclusion.

Write the introduction. Rambling speeches with no clear point or organization put audiences to sleep. Solve this problem with your introduction. The following introduction, for example, reveals the thesis and exactly what's coming. It reveals that the speech will have three distinct parts, each in logical order:

Dog fighting is a cruel sport. I intend to describe exactly what happens to the animals, tell you who is doing this, and show you how you can stop this inhumane practice.

Whenever possible, talk about things that hold your interest. Include your personal experiences and start with a bang. Consider this introduction to a speech on the subject of world hunger:

I'm very honored to be here with you today. I intend to talk about malnutrition and starvation. First, I want to outline the extent of these problems, then I will discuss some basic assumptions concerning world hunger, and finally I will propose some solutions.

You can almost hear the snores from the audience. Following is a rewrite:

More people have died from hunger in the past 5 years than have been killed in all of the wars, revolutions, and murders in the past

150 years. Yet there is enough food to go around. I'm honored to be here with you today to discuss solutions to this problem.

Some members of an audience will begin to drift during any speech, but most people pay attention for at least the first few seconds. Highlight your main points in the beginning sentences of your speech.

A related option is to simply announce the questions you intend to answer. You can number these questions and write them on a flip chart. Or create an overview slide with the list of questions.

People might tell you to start your introduction with a joke. Humor is tricky. You run the risk of falling flat or offending somebody. Save jokes until you have plenty of experience with public speaking and know your audiences well.

Also avoid long, flowery introductions in which you tell people how much you like them, how thrilled you are to address them, and how humble you feel standing in front of them. If you lay it on too thick, your audience won't believe a word of it.

Draft your introduction, and then come back to it after you've written the rest of your speech. In the process of creating the main body and conclusion, your thoughts about the purpose and main points of your speech might change. You might even want to write the introduction last.

Write the main body. The main body of your speech is the content, which accounts for 70 to 90 percent of most speeches. In the main body, you develop your ideas in much the same way that you develop a written paper. If you raised questions in your introduction, be sure to directly answer them.

Transitions are especially important. Give your audience a signal when you change points. Do so by using meaningful pauses and verbal emphasis as well as transitional phrases: "On the other hand, until the public realizes what is happening to children in these countries . . ." or "The second reason hunger persists is . . ."

In long speeches, recap from time to time. Also preview what's to come. Hold your audience's attention by using facts, descriptions, expert opinions, and statistics.

Write the conclusion. At the end of the speech, summarize your points and draw your conclusion. You started with a bang; now finish with drama. The first and last parts of a speech are the most important. Make it clear to your audience when you've reached the end. Avoid endings such as "This is the end of my speech." A simple standby is "So in conclusion, I want to reiterate three points: First, . . ." When you are finished, stop talking.

Create speaking notes. Some professional speakers recommend writing out your speech in full, and then putting key words or main points on a few 3 × 5 cards. Number the cards so that if you drop them, you can quickly put them in order again. As you finish the information on each card, move it to the back of the pile. Write information clearly and in letters large enough to be seen from a distance.

The disadvantage of the 3 × 5 card system is that it involves card shuffling. Some speakers prefer to use standard outlined notes. Another option is mind mapping. Even an hour-long speech can be mapped on one sheet of paper. You can also use memory techniques to memorize the outline of your speech. (For more options, see the sidebar to this article.)

Create supporting visuals. Presentations often include visuals such as PowerPoint slides and posters. With PowerPoint, you can also add video clips from your computer or cell phone. These visuals can reinforce your main points and help your audience understand how your presentation is organized.

Use visuals to *complement* rather than *replace* your speaking. If you use too many visuals—or visuals that are too complex—your audience might focus on them and forget about you.

To use PowerPoint and similar software to full advantage:

- Ask your instructor whether it's acceptable to use technology in your presentation.

- Ask yourself whether slides will actually benefit your presentation. If you use PowerPoint simply because you *can*, you run the risk of letting the technology overshadow your message.

- Use fewer slides rather than more. For a 15-minute presentation, 10 slides are enough.

- Use slides to *show* rather than *tell*. Save them for illustrations, photos, charts, and concepts that are hard to express in words. Don't expect your audience to read a lot of text.

- Limit the amount of text on each visual. Stick to key words presented in short sentences or phrases.

- Use a consistent set of plain fonts that are large enough for all audience members to see. Avoid using more than two fonts, and avoid UPPERCASE letters.

- Stick with a simple consistent color scheme. Use dark text on a light background. Keep backgrounds consistent, and avoid colors that compete with each other.

Create handouts and activities. Especially when your presentation will last more than an hour, give your audience some paper to hold. Consider sharing your speaking notes with your audience. Even a simple list of the topics you plan to cover can help your audience stay oriented.

On your handouts, leave enough space for people to take notes on your presentation. Also, distribute handouts *before* you speak rather than interrupt your presentation to distribute them.

For lengthy presentations, plan to let your audience get into the action. Leave time for questions and comments. Break large audiences into small groups for discussions and role-playing exercises.

If you make people sit still for more than a half-hour, you risk losing them to fatigue or boredom. Let them stretch, stand, talk, and move. This will wake everyone up—and engage people with learning styles that favor concrete experience and active experimentation.

Overcome fear of public speaking. You may not be able to eliminate fear of public speaking entirely, but you can take three steps to reduce and manage it.

© Nick Bland

First, prepare thoroughly. Research your topic thoroughly. Knowing your topic inside and out can create a baseline of confidence. To make a strong start, memorize the first four sentences that you plan to deliver, and practice them many times. Delivering them flawlessly when you're in front of an audience can build your confidence for the rest of your speech.

Second, accept your physical sensations. You've probably experienced physical sensations that are commonly associated with stage fright: dry mouth, a pounding heart, sweaty hands, muscle jitters, shortness of breath, and a shaky voice. One immediate way to deal with such sensations is to simply notice them. Tell yourself, "Yes, my hands are clammy. Yes, my stomach is upset. Also, my face feels numb." Trying to deny or ignore such facts can increase your fear. When you fully accept sensations, however, they start to lose power.

Third, focus on content, not delivery. Michael Motley, a professor at the University of California–Davis, distinguishes between two orientations to speaking. People with a *performance orientation* believe that the speaker must captivate the audience by using formal techniques that differ from normal conversation. In contrast, speakers with a *communication orientation* see public speaking simply as an extension of one-to-one conversation. The goal is not to perform but to communicate your ideas to an audience in the same ways that you would explain them to a friend.[8]

Adopting a communication orientation can reduce your fear of public speaking. Instead of thinking about yourself, focus on your message. Your audience is more interested in *what* you have to say than *how* you say it. Forget about giving a "speech." Just give people valuable ideas and information that they can use.

Practice your presentation. The key to successful public speaking is practice. Do this with your "speaker's voice." Your voice sounds different when you talk loudly, and this fact can be unnerving. Get used to it early on.

Practice in the room in which you will deliver your speech. Keep an eye on the time to make sure that you stay within the limit.

Hear what your voice sounds like over a sound system. If you can't practice your speech in the actual room, at least visit the site ahead of time. Also make sure that the materials you will need for your speech, including any audio-visual equipment, will be available when you want them.

Whenever possible, make a recording. Many schools have video recording equipment available for student use. Use it while you practice. Then view the finished recording to evaluate your presentation.

Listen for repeated words and phrases. Examples include *you know, kind of,* and *really,* plus any little *uh*'s, *umm*'s, and *ah*'s. To get rid of them, tell yourself that you intend to notice every time they pop up in your daily speech. When you hear them, remind yourself that you don't use those words anymore.

Keep practicing. Avoid speaking word for word, as if you were reading a script. When you know your material well, you can deliver it in a natural way. Practice your presentation until you could deliver it in your sleep. Then run through it a few more times.

PHASE 2: DELIVERING YOUR PRESENTATION

Before you begin, get the audience's attention. If people are still filing into the room or adjusting their seats, they're not ready to listen. When all eyes are on you, then begin.

Dress for the occasion. The clothing you choose to wear on the day of your speech delivers a message that's as loud as your words. Consider how your audience will be dressed, and then choose a wardrobe based on the impression you want to make.

Project your voice. When you speak, talk loudly enough to be heard. Avoid leaning over your notes or the podium.

Maintain eye contact. When you look at people, they become less frightening. Also, remember that it is easier for the audience to listen to someone when that person is looking at them. Find a few friendly faces around the room, and imagine that you are talking to each of these people individually.

Notice your nonverbal communication. Be aware of what your body is telling your audience. Contrived or staged gestures will look dishonest. Be natural. If you don't know what to do with your hands, notice that. Then don't do anything with them.

Notice the time. You can increase the impact of your words by keeping track of the time during your speech. It's better to end early than to run late.

Pause when appropriate. Beginners sometimes feel that they have to fill every moment with the sound of their voice. Release that expectation. Give your listeners a chance to make notes and absorb what you say.

Have fun. Chances are that if you lighten up and enjoy your presentation, so will your listeners.

PHASE 3: REFLECTING ON YOUR PRESENTATION

Many students are tempted to sigh with relief when their presentation is done and put the event behind them. Resist this temptation. If you want to get better at making presentations, then take time to reflect on each performance. Did you finish on time? Did you cover all of the points you intended to cover? Was the audience attentive? Did you handle any nervousness effectively?

Write Journal Entries about what you discovered and intend to do differently for your next presentation. Remember to be as kind to yourself as you would be to someone else after a presentation. In addition to noting areas for improvement, note what you did well. Congratulate yourself on getting up in front of an audience and completing your presentation.

Also welcome feedback from others. Most of us find it difficult to hear criticism about our speaking. Be aware of resisting such criticism, and then let go of your resistance. Listening to feedback will increase your skill. ∎

Checklist: Formats for speaking notes

Option 1: A bare-bones outline.
When your presentation is short and the setting is informal, prepare with a brief outline:

- Write out your opening in a complete sentence.
- Summarize each of your major points in a key word or short phrase.
- Write out your closing in a complete sentence.

Option 2: A detailed outline.
For longer and more formal settings, consider making a detailed outline:

- Write out your introduction and conclusion word for word.
- List each major point in a complete sentence.
- If you include quotations, statistics, or technical details, also write these out completely and include their sources.
- Number each page of notes.

Option 3: A full manuscript.
This option is for speeches in formal settings, such as presentations of research results at an academic conference. To promote your comfort on the podium and make your presentation more natural, make your manuscript easy to read:

- Print out the text triple-spaced in a large font that's easy to read.
- Print key words and phrases in bold so that you remember to emphasize them.
- Use an ellipse (...) to indicate any spots where you plan to pause.
- Number each page of notes.

master**student**profile

Cesar Chavez

(1927–1993) Leader of the United Farm Workers (UFW) who organized strikes, boycotts, and fasts to improve conditions for migrant workers.

A few men and women have engraved their names in the annals of change through nonviolence, but none have experienced the grinding childhood poverty that Chavez did after the Depression-struck family farm on the Gila River was foreclosed in 1937. Chavez was 10. His parents and the five children took to the picking fields as migrant workers.

Chavez's faith sustained him, but it is likely that it was both knowing and witnessing poverty and the sheer drudgery and helplessness of the migrant life that drove him.

He never lost the outreach that he had learned from his mother, who, despite the family's poverty, told her children to invite any hungry people in the area home to share what rice, beans, and tortillas the family had.

He left school to work. He attended 65 elementary schools but never graduated from high school . . . .

It was in the fields, in the 1950s, that Chavez met his wife, Helen. The couple and their eight children gave much to "La Huelga," the strike call that became the UFW trademark, from their eventual permanent home near Bakersfield. Chavez did not own the home . . . but paid rent out of his $900 a month as a union official.

Yet, in the fields in the 1930s, something happened that changed Chavez's life. He was 12 when a Congress of Industrial Organizations union began organizing dried-fruit industry workers, including his father and uncle. The young boy learned about strikes, pickets, and organizing.

For two years during World War II, Chavez served in the U.S. Navy; then it was back to the fields and organizing. There were other movements gaining strength in the United States during those years, including community organizing.

From 1952 to 1962, Chavez was active outside the fields, in voter registration drives and in challenging police and immigration abuse of Mexicans and Mexican-Americans.

At first, in the 1960s, only one movement had a noticeable symbol: the peace movement. By the time the decade ended, the United Farm Workers, originally established as the National Farm Workers Association, gave history a second flag: the black Aztec eagle on the red background.

In eight years, a migrant worker son of migrants helped change a nation's perception through nonviolent resistance. It took courage, imagination, and the ability to withstand physical and other abuse.

The facts are well-known now. During the 1968 grape boycott, farmers and growers fought him, but Chavez stood firm. Shoppers hesitated, then pushed their carts past grape counters without buying. The growers were forced to negotiate.

The UFW as a Mexican-American civil rights movement in time might outweigh the achievements of the UFW as a labor movement, for Chavez also represented something equally powerful to urban Mexican-Americans and immigrants—a nonviolent leader who had achieved great change from the most humble beginnings.

Word of Chavez's death spread to the union halls decorated with the Virgin of Guadalupe and UFW flag, to the fields, to the small towns and larger cities. And stories about the short, compact man with the ready smile, the iron determination, the genuine humility and the deep faith were being told amid the tears.

© Bettmann/CORBIS

CESAR CHAVEZ ... was courageous.

YOU ... can practice courage by listening deeply with an open mind and speaking candidly—with compassion.

9

Arthur Jones, "Millions Reaped What Cesar Chavez Sowed," *National Catholic Reporter*, May 7, 1993, vol. 29, no. 27, pp. 5–8. Copyright © 1993 by *National Catholic Reporter*. Reproduced by permission.

You're One Click Away...
from learning more about Cesar Chavez online at the Master Student Profiles. You can also visit the Master Student Hall of Fame to learn about other master students.

FIVE Cs
FOR YOUR CAREER

CHARACTER • CRITICAL THINKING • CREATIVE THINKING • COLLABORATION • COMMUNICATION

In the workplace, all of us are in the business of persuasion. When you write a cover letter and résumé, your aim is to persuade someone to invite you for a job interview. The purpose of a job interview is to do some further persuasion. And once you get hired, you'll have many goals that depend on persuasion—anything from convincing your supervisor to approve a raise to convincing a customer to client to spend money.

Aristotle, the ancient Greek philosopher wrote a text on *rhetoric* (the art of persuasion) that is still widely quoted. He recommends that any persuasive speech include three main elements, presented in the following order.

First, establish credibility through your character. *Ethos* is a Greek word for character. Aristotle believed that audiences want to know whether a speaker is credible and honest. So, your first goal is to establish that you know what you're talking about and that you can be trusted. Do this by telling a humorous story about yourself Also mention your association with people whom your audience already trusts. Ironically, you can sometimes gain credibility by being modest about your qualifications—a quality that audiences may perceive as honesty.

Think creatively to engage emotions. Aristotle also spoke about *pathos*, the Greek word for passion or emotion. Human beings have instinctive desires for security, appreciation, recognition, pleasure, and love. Whenever possible, tie your presentation to one of these basic drives. Show that adopting your ideas or acting on your recommendation will help audience members get something that they want.

Be sure to emphasize a benefit that people feel strongly about. In the workplace, that often means increasing revenues, decreasing costs, improving customer service, and streamlining procedures.

Think critically to provide reasons. *Logos*, the Greek word for logic, comes last in Aristotle's system. Aristotle believed that rational arguments in favor of your point of view have little force unless your audience first trusts you and feels emotionally engaged. Logic and evidence are important, but for maximum impact, present them after you've already established *ethos* and *pathos*.

Seize opportunities to develop complex communication skills. The ability to persuade people based on character, emotional appeal, and logical reasons is also called *complex communication*.

In their book *The New Division of Labor: How Computers Are Creating the Next Job Market*, Frank Levy and Richard J. Murname emphasize the value of complex communication. They define it as acquiring information, explaining it, and persuading coworkers that your explanation implies a definite course of action.[9] Complex communication is required for any job that involves direct teaching, selling, or negotiation.

Complex communication cannot be automated (done by a computer) or outsourced (delegated to someone outside your organization, often for lower wages). This means that people who master complex communication enjoy greater job security. Start developing this cluster of skills now through courses that require you to write papers and make presentations that aim at persuasion.

Start effective collaborations by selling your ideas to coworkers. When you join a workplace-based team, supplement Aristotle's ideas with an additional strategy for persuasion: Focus on outcomes rather than process. This is crucial when you're proposing a change in policies or procedures—especially one that calls for new behaviors from your team members, boss, or other coworkers.

When people resist change, one way that they shoot down a new idea is to quibble about how it will be implemented. In response, say that you want to save that discussion for later—*after* talking about the benefits of your idea. Once people latch on to the value of your goal, they'll be more open-minded about the means to achieve it.

Now, make a personal commitment to developing the five Cs. Take another look at the Discovery Wheel in Chapter 2—especially the sections labeled Character, Creative and Critical Thinking, Communicating, and Collaborating. Take a snapshot of your current skills in these areas after reading and doing this chapter.

DISCOVERY

My scores on the "Five C" sections of the Discovery Wheel were:	As of today, I would give myself the following scores in these areas:	At the end of this course, I would like my scores in these areas to be:
Character _____	Character _____	Character _____
Creative & Critical Thinking _____	Creative & Critical Thinking _____	Creative & Critical Thinking _____
Communicating _____	Communicating _____	Communicating _____
Collaborating _____	Collaborating _____	Collaborating _____

Next, skim this chapter and look for a communication strategy that you want to explore in depth. Choose one that would enhance your self-rating in at least one of the five Cs.

I discovered that my preferred technique is . . .

_____

_____

_____

_____

In light of the five Cs, I can use this technique to become more . . .

_____

_____

_____

_____

INTENTION
To use this technique, I intend to . . .

_____

_____

_____

_____

NEXT ACTION
The specific action I will take is . . .

_____

_____

_____

_____

CHAPTER 9 QUIZ

Name _____

Date _____

1. Name the six rungs on the ladder of powerful speaking from the "Power Process: Employ your word."
   (1) obligation, (2) possibility, (3) preference, (4) passion, (5) planning, and (6) promising   (*Power Process: Employ your word*, page 236)

2. Write one example of a statement on the lowest rung of the ladder of powerful speaking—and another example of a statement on the highest rung.
   (Answers will vary.) Example for lowest rung: "I should feed and walk the dog soon"; example for highest rung: "You can count on the fact that I will graduate in 2 years."   (*Power Process: Employ your word*, page 236)

3. One strategy for effective communication is to separate the roles of sending and receiving. Briefly explain how to do this.
   (Answers will vary.) Communication channels get blocked when we try to send and receive messages at the same time. Instead, be aware of when you are the receiver and when you are the sender. If you are receiving (listening or reading), just receive; avoid switching into the sending (speaking or writing) mode. When you are sending, stick with it until you are finished. When someone else talks, just listen. Then switch roles so that you can be the sender for a while. Keep this up until you do a reasonably complete job of creating shared meaning.   (*Communication: Keeping the channels open*, page 238)

4. This chapter suggests techniques for nonverbal and verbal listening. Briefly explain the difference between these two approaches to listening, and give one example of each approach.
   During nonverbal listening, the listener does not speak and stays focused on what the sender is saying. Examples of nonverbal listening are (list one of the following): maintaining eye contact, displaying openness, sending acknowledgments, releasing distractions, and suspending judgments. During verbal listening, the listener responds to what the sender is saying to indicate that the listener understands what is being communicated. Examples of verbal listening are (list one of the following): feeding back meaning, noticing verbal and nonverbal messages, listening for requests and intentions, allowing emotion, asking for more, being careful with questions and advice, taking care of yourself, and staying open to the adventure of listening.   (*Choosing to listen*, page 239)

5. You can listen skillfully to a speaker even when you disagree with that person's viewpoint. True or false? Explain your answer.
   True. Listening and agreeing are two different activities. As listeners, our goal is to fully receive another person's message. This does not mean that we're obligated to agree with the message. Once you're confident that you accurately understand a speaker's point of view, you are free to agree or disagree with it. The key to effective listening is understanding before evaluating.   (*Choosing to listen*, page 239)

6. Reword the following complaint as a request: "You always interrupt when I talk!"
   Possible rewordings include "Before you begin to talk, please let me finish" and "I'd like to finish making my point; please allow me to do that."   (*Choosing to listen*, page 239)

7. List the five parts of an "I" message (the five ways to say "I").
   (1) observations, (2) feelings, (3) wants, (4) thoughts, and (5) intentions   (*Five ways to say "I,"* page 243)

8. List three strategies for effective writing in the workplace.
   Any three of the following: Get to the point; answer key questions; make it clear how you want readers to respond; let the text breathe; write for online audiences; write e-mail that gets results.   (*Writing for the workplace*, page 254)

9. Give examples of phrases that you can use to promote collaboration and defuse resistance when communicating with your boss.
   Phrases include the following: "I can see that." "Another option is … " "Have you thought about … " "It might be more effective if we … "   (*Communicating with your boss*, page 246)

10. According to the text, you can completely eliminate your fear of public speaking. True or false? Explain your answer.
    False. You may not be able to eliminate the fear of public speaking entirely, but you can take steps to reduce and manage it by preparing thoroughly, accepting physical sensations, and focusing on content, not delivery.   (*Making presentations*, page 255)

CHAPTER 10 COLLABORATING

Instructor Tools & Tips

"Candor is a compliment; it implies equality. It's how true friends talk."
—Peggy Noonan

"We don't see things as they are, we see things as we are." —Anaïs Nin

"We must all hang together, or assuredly we will all hang separately."
—Benjamin Franklin

PREVIEW

From Master Student to Master Employee values people skills as a key element to success at school, at work, in our neighborhoods, and in our global community. This chapter focuses specifically on the theme of collaboration and cooperative learning. Collaboration is one of the five Cs, essential skills for academic and career success. Successful teams generate superior results despite difficulties. Team members feel accountable for the productivity of their team and work together to clear any difficulties standing in the way. The exercises and activities here and in the additional ancillaries encourage students to work together to achieve common goals and to build networks of peer support. Students can learn to overcome stereotyping, respect differences, embrace diversity, respond effectively to conflict and grow as a team member or leader.

GUEST SPEAKER

Consider inviting a local employer to come to your class to discuss desired qualities of a team worker and the importance of having people skills. Alternatively, a representative from your human resources department may be able to provide a similar presentation to your students. Another option would be a prominent college employee who is involved in the union or faculty senate and could present on making the most of meetings and managing conflict.

LECTURE

The articles Leadership in a diverse world, Building relationships across cultures, and the Power Process: Choose your conversations and your community, all can provide the basis for a lecture unit on Chapter 10. See additional lecture ideas on the Instructor Web site.

EXERCISES/ACTIVITIES

1. **Cooperative learning: Studying in groups (pages 265–266)** This article addresses the topic of working together in group study sessions. Use the Master Student Map to begin the discussion of tests and cooperative learning. Divide your class into four groups, assigning each group one of the learning styles. Next, ask students to write down as many answers to their question (*Why? What? How? What if?*) in relation to test taking as they can in 1 minute (with their books closed). After a minute, have each group pick their best answer and report about it to the class. Then have the students open their textbooks and compare their lists to the Master Student Map.

Why?	Why does this chapter appear in *From Master Student to Master Employee?*
What?	What is included in this chapter?
How?	How can you use this chapter? How can test taking apply to the workplace?
What if?	What if you use the techniques in this chapter to be better prepared for tests?

2. **Building relationships across cultures (pages 278–281)** Joanne Zitik, a diversity consultant for Center Focus, creates diversity exercises for workshops and courses for employees, managers, and executives in organizations. Some of her guidelines for the exercises also apply to the classroom, including these:

   - Use adult learning approaches and techniques. Refer to the Adult Learner Toolbox online.

   - Carefully consider the timing of when you introduce an exercise. For example, be sure to build trust among the students before tackling an exercise that encourages them to delve deeply into and/or reveal things about themselves.

- Make sure that students know that it is all right to "pass" and not participate in an exercise.
- Do not repeat derogatory words and phrases; try to move students away from stereotypes and derogatory language.
- Ask the students to observe confidentiality so that what is said during the exercise is not repeated outside the course.
- Make sure that the exercise is facilitated by a person who has had ample diversity and inclusion training.

master instructor
BEST PRACTICE

❝I like to show my class a video titled Wealth, Innovation and Diversity, that is narrated by futurist Joel Barker (published by Star Thrower Productions). Beginning with the Irish potato famine, the video illustrates the vital importance of diversity, casting it in a whole new light. It is diversity that makes human beings strong enough to survive. When we violate the principle of diversity, we pay a price in human suffering every time. When we celebrate diversity, we prosper as a people and as a nation.❞

–Lorraine Fedrizzi, Niagara County Community College

3. **Diversity circle** Some diversity trainers use the diversity circle exercise to help workers appreciate diversity and overcome misperceptions. The exercise can be easily adapted for classroom use. Form a group of about 10 students. Arrange your chairs into a circle, and put one additional chair in the center of the circle. A "diverse" group member volunteers to sit in the center chair and become the first "awareness subject." Because all people are diverse in some way (whether by age, gender, ability, background), everyone is eligible to occupy the center chair.

The person in the center tells the others how she has felt about being diverse or different and how people have reacted to her diversity. For example, an Inuit described how fellow workers were hesitant to ask him out for a beer because they worried about whether he could handle alcohol.

An equally effective alternative to the procedure just described is to ask each class member to come to the front of the class and describe a significant way in which he or she is different. After each class member has spoken, have the students discuss their observations and interpretations. Ask the students, "What lessons did you learn about interpersonal relations from this exercise that will help you be a more effective leader?"[1]

[1] Andrew J. Dubrin, *Leadership*, 4th ed. Copyright © 2004 by Houghton Mifflin Company. Reprinted by permission.

CONVERSATION/SHARING

What?	What does collaboration mean to you?
How?	How has collaboration played a role in your home, school, and work life?
Why?	Why does collaboration matter to you?
What if?	What if you applied the concepts of collaboration to other parts of your life?

4. **Managing conflict (pages 274–276)** Ask students to generate issues that create conflict among roommates. Then ask them to find suggestions from the chapter to deal with these issues. Ask students to consider how much time they will spend with their work mates and relate these issues/suggestions to situations that arise in a working environment.

5. **Power Process: Choose your conversations and your community (page 264)** Raise your students' "conversation consciousness" by asking them to reflect on the conversations described in the Power Process. Point out the various options available for the scenario, creating either a positive or a negative experience. Ask students to reflect on their own conversations. These conversations might occur during class meetings, course lectures, or social events; in the workplace; or even while reading or watching television. Students can describe a publication they read regularly (in print or online), pointing out the conversations they have when they read and the insights they gain from this material. Invite your students to write Discovery and Intention Statements highlighting the amount of time they currently spend talking about the past, present, and future, and stating how they intend to change their conversations. A central thesis of *From Master Student to Master Employee* is that education works when it is value driven. We can choose to engage in value-driven conversations—those that move us toward our goals and affirm our intentions. Values were discussed further in Chapter 1. Refer to the Power Process: Define your values; align your actions on page 28.

6. **Leadership in a diverse world (pages 284–286)** The topic of leadership provides another opportunity for in-class discussion.

master instructor
BEST PRACTICE

❝I encourage students to collaborate with each other inside and outside of the classroom and use each other as resources, stressing that collaboration is two-sided and provides mutual benefits for participants. Collaboration on homework is a good thing as long as group members actively participate. At the beginning of class, I sometimes group students and have them collaborate over the homework before it is turned in. Any class members who did not do the homework are grouped together.❞

–Lorraine Fedrizzi, Niagara County Community College

Ask your students who are leaders (on campus, in the workplace, at their church, at home, in their circle of friends) to share what it's like to be a leader. Then, divide the students into small groups and have them discuss the following questions: What are the advantages and disadvantages of being a leader? What are the challenges and perks? Does holding a leadership position help your self-esteem?

HOMEWORK

Ask students to identify a prominent person in the media whom they consider a great leader and write a brief paper on the qualities they admire in this individual.

Ask students to go to a club meeting on campus and write a paper evaluating the effectiveness of the leadership of the meeting and what they might do differently to improve the meeting.

Five Cs for Your Career (pages 288–289) Chapters 1, 8, 9, and 10 address essential skills for career success. Now that all of these chapters have been covered, ask students to write a brief paper on why an employer would hire them over other candidates based on the five Cs. What do they now know about themselves that an employer will value? How do they plan to get this information across to the employer during the hiring process?

EVALUATION

Quiz Ideas for Chapter 10

Ask students to:

- List strategies to conduct a successful study group.

- List several reasons teams fall apart and strategies to deal with these potential breakdowns.

- Describe ways to manage conflict and give examples.

- Write an essay about the value of diversity.

- Write about how to build relationships across cultures.

- Explain how choosing your conversations and community could promote student success.

Additional Digital Resources for Chapter 10

What can you **ASSIGN FROM THE COURSEMATE** *for From Master Student to Master Employee?*

• **Master Students in Action Video.** Students will hear firsthand from other students about their experiences and challenges with diversity. The Master Students in Action videos give your students a firsthand view of how the strategies in *From Master Student to Master Employee* have helped their peers overcome obstacles. In special segments, Dave Ellis offers students his best strategies for mastering each chapter's content. Note that these videos are available for every chapter.

• **Cultural Differences.** These additional articles are available for every chapter and make important connections between diversity and chapter topics for students. You can choose whether to incorporate a discussion about diversity as you cover each chapter topic, or consider having students choose one to read and create a presentation on for the class.

• **Toolboxes.** To account for the diversity of students in your classes, when appropriate for your student population, consider assigning additional reading from the following toolboxes—specialized collections of articles geared for these students:

• Adult Learner Toolbox
• Community College Toolbox
• Student Athlete Toolbox

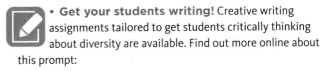

To access CourseMate, your students need to visit www.cengagebrain .com. At the CengageBrain.com home page, students search for the ISBN of From Master Student to Master Employee *(from the back cover of the book), using the search box at the top of the page. This takes them to the product page where these resources can be found.*

Did you know that **THESE RESOURCES** *(and many more)* **ARE AVAILABLE** *on the* **INSTRUCTOR COMPANION SITE?**

• **Questions about how to handle the diversity of your own students?** Look to the online Course Manual for various articles detailing strategies for teaching in all kinds of specialized classroom settings, including the following:

• Racially and ethnically diverse students
• International and ESL Students
• Returning adults
• Students with disabilities
• Lesbian, gay, bisexual, and transgender students

• **Get your students writing!** Creative writing assignments tailored to get students critically thinking about diversity are available. Find out more online about this prompt:

• **Teach Critical Thinking with Movies.** Ask students to view the movie *Babe*, which depicts the experience of a young animal navigating cultural discrimination and conflict. Or have students watch *Castaway*—the lead character is forced to reevaluate his notions of time, companionship, food, shelter, and water on which he relied before he was washed onto a desert island. Ask students to list how he coped with each of these needs on the island to model the steps of critical problem solving.

Please visit login.cengage.com to log in and access the Instructor Companion Site.

Collaborating

Use this **Master Student Map** to ask yourself

WHY THIS CHAPTER MATTERS ...

- In a competitive job market, your ability to collaborate with coworkers and build long-term relationships can make you stand out.

WHAT IS INCLUDED ...

HOW I CAN USE THIS CHAPTER...

- Learn to work effectively in study groups and teams.
- Gain skills to resolve conflict between people.
- Take projects from initial planning to successful completion.

WHAT IF ...

- I could learn from and work with anyone—even people who differ from me in significant ways?

© Ruslan Ivantsov/Shutterstock.com

JOURNAL ENTRY 20
Intention Statement

Commit to create value from this chapter

Think of a time when you were asked to complete a project with a group of people and felt frustrated with the results. Then scan this chapter for ideas that can help you in a similar situation. List at least three ideas below, along with the page numbers where you intend to read more about them.

Strategy	Page number

POWER process

Choose your conversations and your community

Conversations can exist in many forms. One form involves people talking out loud to each other. At other times, the conversation takes place inside our own heads, and we call it *thinking*. We are even having a conversation when we read a magazine or a book, watch television or a movie, or write a letter or a report. These observations have three implications that wind their way through every aspect of our lives.

One implication is that conversations exercise incredible power over what we think, feel, and do. They shape our attitudes, our decisions, our opinions, our emotions, and our actions. If you want clues as to what a person will be like tomorrow, listen to what she's talking about today.

Second, given that conversations are so powerful, it's amazing that few people act on this fact. Most of us swim in a constant sea of conversations, almost none of which we carefully and thoughtfully choose.

The real power of this process lies in a third discovery: We can choose our conversations. Certain conversations create real value for us. They give us fuel for reaching our goals. Other conversations distract us from what we want. They might even create lasting unhappiness and frustration.

Suppose that you meet with an instructor to ask about some guidelines for writing a term paper. She launches into a tirade about your writing skills and lack of preparation for higher education. This presents you with several options. One possibility is to talk about what a jerk the instructor is and give up on the idea of learning to write well. Another option is to refocus the conversation on what you can do to improve your writing skills, such as working with a writing tutor or taking a basic composition class. These two sets of conversations will have vastly different consequences for your success in school.

Another important fact about conversations is that the people you associate with influence them dramatically. If you want to change your attitudes about anything—prejudice, politics, religion, humor—choose your conversations by choosing your community. Spend time with people who speak about and live consistently with the attitudes you value. Use conversations to change habits. Use conversations to explore new ways of seeing the world and to create new options in your life.

When we choose our conversations, we discover a tool of unsurpassed power. This tool has the capacity to remake our thoughts—and thus our lives. It's as simple as choosing the next article you read or the next topic you discuss with a friend.

Start choosing your conversations today, and watch what happens.

 You're One Click Away...
from accessing Power Process Media online and finding out more about how to "choose your conversations."

cobalt88/Shutterstock.com

Yuri Arcurs/Shutterstock.com

COOPERATIVE LEARNING: Studying in groups

Study groups can lift your mood on days when you just don't feel like working. If you skip a solo study session, no one else will know. If you declare your intention to study with others who are depending on you, your intention gains strength.

Study groups are especially important if going to school has thrown you into a new culture. Joining a study group with people you already know can help ease the transition. To multiply the benefits of working with study groups, seek out people of other backgrounds, cultures, races, and ethnic groups. You can get a whole new perspective on the world, along with some valued new friends.

Joining a study group also helps you to develop a number of skills for working on teams in the workplace. Effective teams consist of people who know how to resolve conflict, give each other constructive feedback, collaborate to reach a common goal, and build consensus based on creative and critical thinking. None of us is born with these skills. You can start learning them now and use them to advance your career in the future.

FORM A STUDY GROUP

Choose a focus for your group. Many students assume that the purpose of a study group is to help its members prepare for a test. That's one valid purpose—and there are others.

Through his research on cooperative learning, psychologist Joe Cuseo has identified several kinds of study groups.[1] For instance, members of *test review* groups compare answers and help one another discover sources of errors. *Note-taking* groups focus on comparing and editing notes, often meeting directly after the day's class. Members of *research* groups meet to help one another find, evaluate, and take notes on background materials for papers and presentations. *Reading* groups can be useful for courses in which test questions are based largely on textbooks. Meet with classmates to compare the passages you underlined or highlighted and the notes you made in the margins of your books.

Look for dedicated students. Find people you are comfortable with and who share your academic goals. Look for students who pay attention, participate in class, and actively take notes. Invite them to join your group.

Of course, you can recruit members in other ways. One way is to make an announcement during class. Another option is to post signs asking interested students to contact you. Or pass around a sign-up sheet before class. These methods can reach many people, but they do take more time to achieve results. And you have less control over who applies to join the group.

Limit groups to four people. Research on cooperative learning indicates that four people are an ideal group size.[2] Larger groups can be unwieldy.

Studying with friends is fine, but if your common interests are pizza and jokes, you might find it hard to focus.

Hold a planning session. Ask two or three people to get together for a snack and talk about group goals, meeting times, and other logistics. You don't have to make an immediate commitment.

As you brainstorm about places to meet, aim for a quiet meeting room with plenty of room to spread out materials. Your campus library probably has study rooms. Campus tutoring services might also have space and other resources for study groups.

Do a trial run. Test the group first by planning a one-time session. If that session works, plan another. After a few successful sessions, you can schedule regular meetings.

CONDUCT YOUR GROUP

Ask your instructor for guidelines on study group activity. Many instructors welcome and encourage study groups. However, they have different ideas about what kinds of collaboration are acceptable. Some activities—such as sharing test items or writing papers from a shared outline—are considered cheating and can have serious consequences. Let your instructor know that you're forming a group, and ask for clear guidelines.

Set an agenda for each meeting. At the beginning of each meeting, reach agreement on what you intend to do. Set a time limit for each agenda item, and determine a quitting time. End each meeting with assignments for all members to complete before the next meeting.

Assign roles. To make the most of your time, ask one member to lead each group meeting. The leader's role is to keep the

10

discussion focused on the agenda and ask for contributions from all members. Assign another person to act as recorder. This person will take notes on the meeting, recording possible test questions, answers, and main points from group discussions. Rotate both of these roles so that every group member takes a turn.

Cycle through learning styles. As you assign roles, think about the learning styles present in your group. Some people excel at raising questions and creating lots of ideas. Others prefer to gather information and think critically. Some like to answer questions and make decisions, while others excel at taking action. Each of these distinct modes of learning are explained in Chapter 2 on pages 57, LSI-6, and 59–62. To create an effective group, match people with their preferred activities. Also change roles periodically. This gives group members a chance to explore new learning styles.

Teach each other. Teaching is a great way to learn something. Turn the material you're studying into a list of topics and assign a specific topic to each person, who will then teach it to the group. When you're done presenting your topic, ask for questions or comments. Prompt each other to explain ideas more clearly, find gaps in understanding, consider other points of view, and apply concepts to settings outside the classroom.

Test one another. During your meeting, take a practice test created from questions contributed by group members. When you're finished, compare answers. Or turn testing into a game by pretending you're on a television game show. Use sample test questions to quiz one another.

Compare notes. Make sure that all the group's members heard the same thing in class and that you all recorded the important information. Ask others to help explain material in your notes that is confusing to you.

Create wall-size mind maps or concept maps to summarize a textbook or series of lectures. Work on large sheets of butcher paper, or tape together pieces of construction paper. When creating a mind map, assign one branch to each member of the study group. Use a different colored pen or marker for each branch of the mind map. (For more information on concept maps and mind maps, see Chapter 6: Notes.)

Monitor effectiveness. On your meeting agenda, include an occasional discussion about your group's effectiveness. Are you meeting consistently? Is the group helping members succeed in class?

Use this time to address any issues that are affecting the group as a whole. If certain members are routinely unprepared for study sessions, brainstorm ways to get them involved. If one person tends to dominate meetings, reel her in by reminding her that everyone's voice needs to be heard.

To resolve conflict among group members, keep the conversation constructive. Focus on solutions. Move from vague complaints ("You're never prepared") to specific requests ("Will you commit to bringing ten sample test questions next time?"). Asking a "problem" member to lead the next meeting might make an immediate difference.

Use technology to collaborate. Web-based applications allow you to create virtual study groups and collaborate online. For example, create and revise documents with sites such as Google Docs (www.docs.google.com) and Zoho Writer (www.writer.zoho.com).

Create and share PowerPoint and keynote presentations with tools such as SlideShare (www.slideshare.net).

Use Basecamp (www.basecamphq.com), Joint Contact (www.jointcontact.com), or 5pm (www.5pmweb.com) to manage projects. You can share files, create a group calendar, assign tasks, chat online, post messages, and track progress toward milestones (key due dates).

Create group mind maps with MindMeister (www.mindmeister.com) and Mindomo (www.mindomo.com).

For more options, do an Internet search with the key words *collaborate online*.

If your course has an online component, look for collaboration tools there. For example, Blackboard has some handy features for this purpose—chat, e-mail, and discussion groups. ■

Master Employees IN ACTION

"While the courses were important, the personal/ social aspects of my college career were perhaps more important. Through those aspects I learned about time management, project management, and people management skills."

—Andy Fisher,
Executive Marketing Manager

© iStockphoto.com /Neustockimages

 You're One Click Away...
from a video about Master Students in Action.

4 simple "PEOPLE SKILLS"

New technology will make it easier for companies to automate and outsource the tasks that were once done by employees. However, the jobs that *don't* go to robots or overseas workers tend to have a characteristic in common: They involve face-to-face contact with coworkers, customers, and clients. This means that having people skills can give you a measure of job security.

Some people downplay the importance of these skills. "They're just common sense," these folks say. That might be true. At the same time, think about all the crabby bosses and irritating coworkers that you've met. Even if people skills are common sense, they're not always commonly practiced. Use the following suggestions as reminders.

1 Smile. The power of a smile is obvious and often forgotten. When combined with eye contact and a relaxed, receptive posture, it sends an unmistakable message to the people you meet: *I'm glad that you're here, and I care about what you have to say.*

At the same time, remember that people can usually spot a fake smile from a mile away. If you fear that your nonverbal language is sending a negative message, then seek a solution. Perhaps there is a conflict between you and a coworker that calls for some attention. Use the communication strategies in Chapter 9 to find a resolution. Also see "Managing conflict" in this chapter.

2 Shake hands. The next time you shake hands with someone, notice how it feels. This simple gesture can send a message that the people involved are open for more conversation—or anxious to get away from each other.

You already know how to give firm, friendly handshakes. The key is to offer them consistently in the workplace, even with people you don't know well or even like all that much. The simple human connection that comes through touch can lower people's defenses just enough for a constructive dialogue to begin.

3 Make small talk. Meeting new clients, customers, and coworkers means making small talk. Conversation about sports, movies, TV shows, and the weather might seem trivial at first. In the workplace, it almost never is. When done in a skillful way, small talk puts people at ease and invites them to a larger conversation that unfolds over time.

To succeed with small talk, look for common ground. Even if you're a newly hired employee in your twenties who's face to face with a recent retiree in her seventies, you can find a shared interest. Look for it.

As a place to start, remember that people often enjoy talking about themselves. If you're meeting someone for the first time, but you both work for the same organization, that's a place to start. Ask the other person about how his or her career path led them to this point. Then listen closely to the answers. Just relax, ask more questions, and let people talk.

If other people ask about you, follow their lead. Respond openly while taking care not to dominate the conversation.

Your skill at small talk will improve over time, so look for chances to practice it. If your employer, clients, or customers invite you to a social event, make it a point to attend. To develop deeper relationships, go beyond the regularly scheduled events. Also invite individuals to lunch or dinner. Informal contact with coworkers that maintains a professional tone can lead you to see them in a whole new way.

4 Express appreciation. There's a powerful way to boost morale at work that's both simple and free—tell people that you appreciate them. Coworkers want to know that their efforts are being noticed. Even if you can't offer them a raise or a promotion, you can offer recognition.

Many of us remember to thank people during the dramatic moments in their lives—at the end of successful project, for example, or at the climax of a long career. It's just as important to celebrate the small victories—the meeting that was masterfully conducted, the e-mail that was gracefully written, the sale that was successfully closed.

When such things happen, express appreciation. Also describe the specific behavior that you appreciate, and do it in the presence of your coworkers. People will remember when you do. ■

10

Getting to "done"—
the practical art of
project management

At some point in your career, you'll be asked to manage a project. This request will summon your skills at collaboration, communication, and conflict resolution. If you want to shine, then start preparing for that moment of leadership now.

Adopt a project mindset. Stripped to its essence, a project is any outcome that you want to create in any area of your life. More specifically, it's an outcome that calls for completing multiple actions over a specific period of time.

Get a head start by adapting the four questions from the Master Student Map that begins each chapter of this book:

- *Why* do this project? In the work world, projects serve many purposes. Those usually fall into three main categories—to increase revenues, save costs, or improve services. In addition, the people on a team usually want to uphold certain standards while getting a project done. These can include integrity, flexibility, fairness, and other shared values.

- *What* is the desired outcome? Skilled project managers keep their eyes on the prize. They know exactly what the desired outcome looks like. They can point to clear signs that their team is succeeding and that a project is actually getting done.

- *How* will we produce that outcome? In a word, it takes action. Projects are finished only when team members promise to complete specific tasks and then keep their word.

- *What if* we can expand on the outcome? When projects get done, everyone involved benefits. Lessons are gained. New possibilities emerge. Master project managers lift their eyes to the future. Based on what they learn, they ask: What's next? What new projects shall we take on? What's worth doing, and how can we do it better?

Divide and conquer. The skeleton of any project plan consists of four main elements—milestones, actions, reference materials, and "someday" items.

Milestones are due dates for major parts of the project. If your team is developing a new software package, for example, project milestones include the dates of the alpha, beta, and final product releases.

To manage these commitments, pull out your calendar. Enter the start date for the project and the final due date. Then assign a due date for each project milestone. This calls for a balance of creative and critical thinking. Choose dates that are realistic *and* challenging. Also build in some extra time for unexpected events.

Actions are lists of the tasks that you'll complete in order to meet the milestones and final due date. These are items that you enter on a to-do list. As a project manager, you might keep a master to-do list for the project, assign items to specific people, and follow up to make sure that all items get done.

Writing action items is an art in itself. On your to-do list, start each one with an active verb such as *call, e-mail, print,* or *deliver*. Choose a word that points to a visible behavior.

Reference materials include background information that you might want to review as you complete action items. Examples are product catalogs, notes from meetings, and articles from Web sites, magazines, and newspapers. Whenever possible, collect these materials in digital form so that you can easily search for specific items with keywords.

Someday items are ideas for other projects and actions that you might want to do in the future.

To keep track of the four project elements, consider using calendars and documents that can be shared. Online applications such as Basecamp and the Action Method are designed specifically for project teams. Evernote, Springpad, Microsoft OneNote, and similar applications work for storing reference items.

Another option, especially for simpler projects, is to use the all-purpose project planner on the next pages. Make as many photocopies of this form as you want.

Engage the key players. Remind the members of your project team about upcoming milestones. Ask about their progress in completing action items. Answer questions and offer support. Schedule short team meetings to answer questions that call for everyone's input.

In addition, hold the vision for your team. Keep talking about the outcome you're working to create and the benefits it will bring. The art of getting to "done" often means keeping the horizon in sight. ■

The All-Purpose Project Planner

Project name:

_____

Project outcome:

_____

_____

_____

_____

Project start date:

_____

Project end date:

_____

Team members	E-mail:	Phone number:
_____	_____	_____
_____	_____	_____
_____	_____	_____
_____	_____	_____
_____	_____	_____

Location of reference materials: "Someday" items for possible follow-up:

_____   _____

_____   _____

_____   _____

_____   _____

_____   _____

_____   _____

10

Describe the milestones for this project, along with their related actions and who is responsible for each action. When an action is completed, check off the box in the "Done" column.

Milestone: _____ **Due Date:** _____

Action	Assigned to	Done
		☐
		☐
		☐
		☐
		☐
		☐
		☐
		☐
		☐
		☐

Milestone: _____ **Due Date:** _____

Action	Assigned to	Done
		☐
		☐
		☐
		☐
		☐
		☐
		☐
		☐
		☐
		☐

Milestone: _____ **Due Date:** _____

Action	Assigned to	Done
		☐
		☐
		☐
		☐
		☐
		☐
		☐
		☐
		☐
		☐

Collaborate
in effective teams

Most work in organizations get done by teams. Collaboration and cooperative learning are key. Yet not all teams are created equal. Some produce long-term, positive change. Other teams produce bland reports that make a direct trip to the recycling bin.

Team members get discouraged when they suggest new ideas that immediately get rejected. After proposing changes to a company's policies and procedures, for example, team members might face resistance: *This suggestion will never work. . . . That's just not the way we do things around here. . . . We can't break with tradition.* These responses are examples of "groupthink," which happens when people automatically rule out new options simply because they're . . . well, new.

When this happens, creative thinking dies in committee. Team members stop asking questions. People feel afraid to disagree with a forceful leader and instead keep their mouths shut. The team's effectiveness takes a nosedive.

Use the following suggestions to prevent the problems that take teams down.

Choose team members who are willing to learn. Set the stage for success by selecting team members based on the cycle of learning as described in Chapter 2. Remember David Kolb's idea that people learn from experience through four kinds of activity that occur in a repeating cycle. Teams learn in the same way. This means choosing members who will:

- Get fully involved with the team and commit to its purpose (concrete experience).
- Talk about the team's experiences and stay open to new ideas (reflective observation).
- Think critically about which agreements and actions will achieve the team's purpose (abstract conceptualization).
- Make decisions and take action (active experimentation).

Not everyone you know will have all these skills, so invite team members with a variety of learning styles. Look beyond your circle of friends and people who tend to think and act alike. Your team is more likely to succeed with a variety of people who can choose tasks based on their strengths and preferences.

Determine an optimal size for your team. Collective learning is easier when the team is an optimal size. Think carefully about how many people to include. There is no magic number that will guarantee a successful team. Keep it small enough to manage and large enough to achieve the team's goals.

Draw lessons from past experiences with teams. During your team's first meeting, set aside time to reflect on everyone's past experience with teams. Share your best and worst experiences. Based on this discussion, create your own list of what makes a successful team. Then make some basic agreements about ways to prevent the problems you've experienced with teams in the past.

Create a project plan. After sharing your collective lessons about teamwork, get the big picture of your project:

- Clarify the purpose of your team—the specific outcome you will produce along with the benefits that outcome will create.

© Rafal Olechowski/Shutterstock

- Next, set dates for producing that outcome and each of the milestones along the way.
- Follow up with a list of actions that your team will take to meet the milestones and who will be responsible for completing each action.

Be sure to put all your agreements on these points in writing and share them with every team member. For more details, see "Getting to 'done'—the practical art of project management" and "The all-purpose project planner" earlier in this chapter.

Encourage new ideas. In an empowered team, all ideas are welcome, problems are freely admitted, and any item is open for discussion. In other words, people who want a team to succeed will treat ideas as tools. Instead of automatically looking for what's wrong with a proposal, they search for potential applications. Even a proposal that seems outlandish at first might become workable with a few modifications.

During meetings, allow members to fully express any idea before thinking critically about it. To make this happen more often:

- *Put your opinions on hold.* If you're leading a meeting, pose a question and ask other people to contribute answers. Then look for the potential value in *any* idea. Avoid nonverbal language that signals a negative reaction, such as frowning or rolling your eyes.

- *Divide large teams into working groups.* People might be more willing to ask questions and volunteer answers in a smaller group.
- *Assign a "devil's advocate."* Give one person free permission to ask tough questions and poke holes in any proposal.
- *Invite a guest expert.* A fresh perspective from someone outside the group can stimulate fresh questions and spark insights.
- *Set up a suggestion box.* Let team members submit questions and ideas anonymously, in writing.

Even out the workload. One potential trap for teams is that one person ends up doing most of the work. This person might feel resentful and complain.

If you find yourself in this situation, transform your complaint into a request. Instead of scolding team members for being lazy, request help. Ask team members to take over tasks that you've been doing. Delegate specific jobs.

Practice integrity. Collaborations work to the degree that people make agreements and keep them. When team members promise to take an action and fail to deliver, the team's process immediately breaks down.

If you want your team to be effective, then use the "Power Process: Employ your word." See your shared project as a laboratory for practicing integrity and truth telling. If you don't know the answer to a question, then admit it and ask for help. If you need more time or resources to complete a task, then ask for them. And if you know that you'll be unable to deliver on a promise, then negotiate with your team to agree on one that you can actually keep.

When a team member lapses in practicing integrity, avoid shaming and blaming that person. Instead, take a problem-solving approach. Talk about what happened and how to prevent it in the future. Then recommit as a whole team to creating your desired outcome.

Share the leadership role. Teams often begin by choosing a leader with a vision, charisma, and expertise. As your team matures, however, consider letting other members take turns in a leadership role. This strategy can work especially well in groups where people have a wide range of opinions. Sharing the leadership role is one way to encourage a diversity of viewpoints and help people expand their learning styles.

Sustain team focus with two key questions. Pause for a moment to consider the challenge of leading project teams. These usually consist of people with different skills, different preferences, different perspectives on the world—and a host of other job duties as well. Your task is to keep these people enthused and engaged right up to the moment that you cross the last item off your collective to-do list. If this sounds complicated, that's because it is.

When a team tries to tackle too many problems or achieve too many goals, the members can easily get distracted. They can forget the team's purpose and lose their enthusiasm for the whole project. Often you can restore your team's focus and energy level

by asking: "What is the single most important goal that our team can meet?" and "What is the single most important thing we can do *now* to meet that goal?"

Keep stakeholders informed. Stakeholders include anyone outside your team who has an interest in the outcome of your project, including your immediate supervisors and their managers. Give these people brief and regular updates about progress toward your team's milestones and final outcome.

Celebrate and recap. When your project is finished, take time to celebrate with your team members. Talk about what you learned and how to apply those lessons in the future.

Also celebrate your growing skills in the five Cs—character, creative thinking, critical thinking, communication, and collaboration. Working in teams helps you to develop all these qualities of a Master Student. ■

You're One Click Away...
from finding more strategies online
for constructive collaboration.

JOURNAL ENTRY 21
Discovery/Intention Statement

Reflect on your experience with collaboration

Take a few minutes to reflect on your previous experiences with study groups and workplace teams. You know which of them worked well, and which did not. Complete the following sentences:

I discovered that teams tend to break down when . . .

_____

_____

_____

_____

To prevent such problems with my next team, I intend to . . .

_____

_____

_____

_____

Make the most of meetings

Four of the most dreaded words in many offices are: "Let's schedule a meeting." Some managers even call meetings about having fewer meetings.

Perhaps you've worked a job that was plagued by time-wasting meetings. These tend to be:

- Open-ended—scheduled without a time limit.
- Unstructured—conducted without a clear agenda or format.
- Standing—set up for a regular time each week, even when there's no pressing issue to discuss.
- Inconclusive—ended without agreements about desired outcomes or next actions.

When you plan to avoid such problems, meetings can actually become useful.

BEFORE THE MEETING

The value that you create from a meeting often depends on how well you prepare. Before you attend a meeting, ask for an agenda and think about what you have to add. If you're not sure, then check with the meeting organizer about what she wants you to contribute.

Remember to add the meeting date and time to your calendar. If there are any tasks that you want to complete before the meeting takes place, then do them immediately or add them to your to-do list.

Also think about what could happen during the meeting. Anticipate questions that might be asked and think about how to respond. If you need to dig up some background information or prepare materials to hand out at the meeting, plan to complete these tasks well in advance.

DURING THE MEETING

To stay engaged throughout a meeting—and remember what was discussed—take notes. You can use any of the note-taking formats explained in Chapter 6. Just be sure to flag key items in your notes with appropriate symbols. For example, place a

- star (*) or exclamation mark (!) next to key points in your notes
- question mark (?) next to items that are unclear.
- big letter "A" next to items that call for further action.

One major reason for ineffective meetings is lack of follow-up action by the people who present. The solution is to practice integrity. Make a commitment to complete your assigned tasks and then keep your promises.

AFTER THE MEETING

Treat your meeting notes like class notes. Review them within 24 hours, and edit them for clarity. If you can complete an action item within a few minutes, do it immediately. Otherwise, add the item to your to-do list or calendar. Also create a paper-based or digital folder for each active project. File meeting notes by date in the appropriate folder.

WHEN IT'S YOUR TURN TO LEAD A MEETING

When you're asked to lead a meeting, see it as an opportunity to practice your collaboration, communication, and thinking skills.

Think carefully about benefits and costs. Before you schedule a meeting, ask whether it's truly necessary. Weigh the possible benefits against the costs of asking people to interrupt other work. Save meetings for the times when a problem requires input from several people at once.

Eliminate recurring meetings. Convince your coworkers to hold meetings only when there is a specific question to answer or problem to solve. This rules out most meetings that are automatically scheduled for a certain day and time each week. If you want to update coworkers on the status of a project, use e-mail or project management software instead.

Schedule carefully. Give people plenty of notice that you want to meet. Many people like to get some focused work done during the opening and closing hours of their workday. If you book a room for 8 A.M. on Monday or 4 P.M. on Friday, don't expect a crowd.

Plan a focused agenda and attendee list. Before each meeting, send out a written agenda. Keep it to three items, tops. To focus everyone's thinking, state each item as a question to answer. Instead of listing "project schedule," for example, write: "When is a realistic date for finishing this project?"

Set clear starting and stopping times. Experiment with scheduling less time for meetings. If people know that a meeting will only last 20 minutes, they're more likely to show up on time.

End each meeting with a to-do list. Save the last five minutes of each meeting for agreeing on the very next actions to complete. Also make sure that each action is assigned to a specific person. You'll know that meetings are working when the energy level in the room stays high and when people leave the meeting with clear commitments to produce an outcome. ∎

10

MANAGING CONFLICT

Conflict management is one of the most practical skills you'll ever learn. Here are strategies that can help.

The first five strategies discussed are about dealing with the *content* of a conflict—defining the problem, exploring viewpoints, and discovering solutions. The remaining strategies are about finding a *process* for resolving any conflict, no matter what the content.

To bring these strategies to life, think of ways to use them in managing a conflict that you face right now.

FOCUS ON CONTENT

Back up to common ground. Conflict heightens the differences between people. When this happens, it's easy to forget how much we still agree with each other.

As a first step in managing conflict, back up to common ground. List all of the points on which you are *not* in conflict: "I know that we disagree about how much to spend on a new car, but we do agree that the old one needs to be replaced." Often, such comments put the problem in perspective and pave the way for a solution.

State the problem. Using "I" messages, as explained earlier in this chapter, state the problem. Tell people what you observe, feel, think, want, and intend to do. Allow the other people in a particular conflict to do the same.

Each person might have a different perception of the problem. That's fine. Let the conflict come into clear focus. It's hard to fix something unless people agree on what's broken.

Remember that the way you state the problem largely determines the solution. Defining the problem in a new way can open up a world of possibilities. For example, "I need a new roommate" is a problem statement that dictates one solution. "We could use some agreements about who cleans the apartment" opens up more options, such as resolving a conflict about who will wash the dishes tonight.

State all points of view. If you want to defuse tension or defensiveness, set aside your opinions for a moment. Take the time to understand the other points of view. Sum up those viewpoints in words that the other parties can accept. When people feel that they've been heard, they're often more willing to listen.

Ask for complete communication. In times of conflict, we often say one thing and mean another. So before responding to what the other person says, use active listening. Check to see whether you have correctly received that person's message by saying, "What I'm hearing you say is. . . . Did I get it correctly?"

Focus on solutions. After stating the problem, dream up as many solutions as you can. Be outrageous. Don't hold back. Quantity—not quality—is the key. If you get stuck, restate the problem and continue brainstorming.

Next, evaluate the solutions you brainstormed. Discard the unacceptable ones. Talk about which solutions will work and how difficult they will be to implement. You might hit upon a totally new solution. Choose one solution that is most acceptable to everyone involved, and implement it. Agree on who is going to do what by when. Then keep your agreements.

Finally, evaluate the effectiveness of your solution. If it works, pat yourselves on the back. If not, make changes or implement a new solution.

Focus on the future. Instead of rehashing the past, talk about new possibilities. Think about what you can do to prevent problems in the future. State how you intend to change, and ask others for their contributions to the solution.

FOCUS ON PROCESS

Commit to the relationship. The thorniest conflicts usually arise between people who genuinely care for each other. Begin by affirming your commitment to the other person: "I care about you, and I want this relationship to last. So I'm willing to do whatever it takes to resolve this problem." Also ask the other person for a similar commitment.

Allow strong feelings. Permitting conflict can also mean permitting emotion. Being upset is all right. Feeling angry is often appropriate. Crying is okay. Allowing other people to see the strength of our feelings can help resolve the conflict. This suggestion can be especially useful during times when differences are so extreme that reaching common ground seems impossible.

Expressing the full range of your feelings can transform the conflict. Often what's on the far side of anger is love. When we express and release resentment, we might discover genuine compassion in its place.

Notice your need to be "right." Some people approach conflict as a situation where only one person wins. That person has the "right" point of view. Everyone else loses.

When this happens, step back. See whether you can approach the situation in a neutral way. Define the conflict as a problem to be solved, not as a contest to be won. Explore the possibility that you might be mistaken. There might be more than one acceptable solution. The other person might simply have a different learning style than yours. Let go of being "right," and aim for being effective at resolving conflict instead.

Sometimes this means apologizing. Conflict sometimes arises from our own errors. Others might move quickly to end the conflict when we acknowledge this fact and ask for forgiveness.

Slow down the communication. In times of great conflict, people often talk all at once. Words fly like speeding bullets, and no one listens. Chances for resolving the conflict take a nosedive.

When everyone is talking at once, choose either to listen or to talk—not both at the same time. Just send your message. Or just receive the other person's message. Usually, this technique slows down the pace and allows everyone to become more levelheaded.

To slow down the communication even more, take a break. Depending on the level of conflict, this might mean anything from a few minutes to a few days.

A related suggestion is to do something nonthreatening together. Share an activity with the others involved that's not a source of conflict.

Communicate in writing. What can be difficult to say to another person face-to-face might be effectively communicated in writing. When people in conflict write letters or e-mails to each other, they automatically apply many of the suggestions in this article. Writing is a way to slow down the communication and ensure that only one person at a time is sending a message.

There is a drawback to this tactic, though: It's possible for people to misunderstand what you say in a letter or e-mail. To avoid further problems, make clear what you are *not* saying: "I am saying that I want to be alone for a few days. I am *not* saying that I want you to stay away forever." Saying what you are *not* saying is often useful in face-to-face communication as well.

Before you send your letter or e-mail, put yourself in the shoes of the person who will receive it. Imagine how your comments could be misinterpreted. Then rewrite your note, correcting any wording that might be open to misinterpretation.

Resolve conflicts with
ROOMMATES

People who live together share a delicate bond. Relationships with even best friends or closest relatives can quickly deteriorate over disagreements about who pays the bills or washes the dishes.

You can prevent conflicts with roommates by negotiating agreements now. For example, adopt a policy about borrowing. Loaning your roommate a book or a tennis racket might seem like a small thing. Yet these small loans can become a sore point in a relationship. Some people have difficulty saying no and resent lending things. If so, keep borrowing to a minimum.

Meet with your roommates to discuss the following:

- What you will do about sharing belongings such as computers, audio and video equipment, food, or clothing
- How you will create a study environment at home
- How you will split household costs and make sure that bills get paid on time
- How you will resolve conflicts when someone thinks that a roommate is not keeping your agreements

Expand this list to include other issues that matter to you. For maximum clarity, put your agreements in writing.

10

There's another way to get the problem off your chest, especially when strong, negative feelings are involved: Write the nastiest, meanest e-mail response you can imagine, leaving off the address of the recipient so you don't accidentally send it. Let all of your frustration, anger, and venom flow onto the page. Be as mean and blaming as possible. When you have cooled off, see whether there is anything else you want to add.

Then destroy the letter or delete the e-mail. Your writing has served its purpose. Chances are that you've calmed down and are ready to engage in skillful conflict management.

Get an objective viewpoint. With the agreement of everyone involved, set up a video camera, and record a conversation about the conflict. In the midst of a raging argument, when emotions run high, it's almost impossible to see ourselves objectively. Let the camera be your unbiased observer. Another way to get an objective viewpoint is to use a mediator—an objective, unbiased third party. Even an untrained mediator—as long as it's someone who is not a party to the conflict—can do much to decrease tension. Mediators can help everyone get their point of view across. The mediator's role is not to give advice, but to keep the discussion on track and moving toward a solution.

Allow for cultural differences. People respond to conflict in different ways, depending on their cultural background. Some stand close, speak loudly, and make direct eye contact. Other people avert their eyes, mute their voices, and increase physical distance.

When it seems to you that other people are sidestepping or escalating a conflict, consider whether your reaction is based on cultural bias.

Agree to disagree. Sometimes we say all we have to say on an issue. We do all of the problem solving we can do. We get all points of view across. And the conflict still remains, staring us right in the face.

What's left is to recognize that honest disagreement is a fact of life. We can peacefully coexist with other people—and respect them—even though we don't agree on fundamental issues. Conflict can be accepted even when it is not resolved.

See the conflict within you. Sometimes the turmoil we see in the outside world has its source in our own inner world. A cofounder of Alcoholics Anonymous put it this way: "It is a spiritual axiom that every time we are disturbed, no matter what the cause, there is something awry with us."

When we're angry or upset, we can take a minute to look inside. Perhaps we are ready to take offense—waiting to pounce on something the other person said. Perhaps, without realizing it, we did something to create the conflict. Or maybe the other person is simply saying what we don't want to admit is true.

When these things happen, we can shine a light on our own thinking. A simple spot-check might help the conflict disappear—right before our eyes. ■

You're One Click Away...
from discovering more ways online to manage conflict.

JOURNAL ENTRY 22
Discovery/Intention Statement

Recreate a relationship

Think about one of your relationships for a few minutes. It can involve a parent, sibling, spouse, child, friend, hairdresser, or anyone else. In the space below, write down some things that are not working in the relationship. What bugs you? What do you find irritating or unsatisfying?

I discovered that . . .

_____

_____

_____

_____

_____

_____

_____

_____

Now think for a moment about what you want from this relationship. More attention? Less nagging? More openness, trust, financial security, or freedom? Choose a suggestion from this chapter, and describe how you could use it to make the relationship work.

I intend to . . .

_____

_____

_____

_____

_____

_____

_____

_____

_____

Developing
EMOTIONAL INTELLIGENCE

In his book *Working with Emotional Intelligence*, Daniel Goleman defines emotional intelligence as a cluster of traits:

- *Self-awareness*—recognizing your full range of emotions and knowing your strengths and limitations.
- *Self-regulation*—responding skillfully to strong emotions, practicing honesty and integrity, and staying open to new ideas.
- *Motivation*—persisting to achieve goals and meet standards of excellence.
- *Empathy*—sensing other people's emotions and taking an active interest in their concerns.
- *Skill in relationships*—listening fully, speaking persuasively, resolving conflict, and leading people through times of change.

Goleman concludes that "IQ washes out when it comes to predicting who among a talented pool of candidates *within* an intellectually demanding profession will become the strongest leader." At that point, emotional intelligence starts to become more important.[3]

If you're emotionally intelligent, you're probably described as someone with good "people skills." You're aware of your feelings. You act in thoughtful ways, show concern for others, resolve conflict, and make responsible decisions.

Your emotional intelligence skills will serve you in school and in the workplace, especially when you collaborate on project teams. You can deepen your skills with the following strategies.

RECOGNIZE THREE ELEMENTS OF EMOTION

Even the strongest emotion consists of just three elements: physical sensations, thoughts, and action. Usually they happen so fast that you can barely distinguish them. Separating them out is a first step toward emotional intelligence.

Imagine that you suddenly perceive a threat—such as a supervisor who's screaming at you. Immediately your heart starts beating in double-time and your stomach muscles clench (physical sensations). Then thoughts race through your head: *This is a disaster. She hates me. And everyone's watching.* Finally, you take action, which could mean staring at her, yelling back, or running away.

NAME YOUR EMOTIONS

Naming your emotions is a first step to going beyond the "fight or flight" reaction to any emotion. Naming gives you power. The second that you attach a word to an emotion, you start to gain perspective. People with emotional intelligence have a rich vocabulary to describe a wide range of emotions. For example, do an Internet search with the key words *feeling list*. Read through the lists you find for examples of ways that you can name your feelings in the future.

ACCEPT YOUR EMOTIONS

Another step toward emotional intelligence is accepting your emotions—*all* of them. This can be challenging if you've been taught that some emotions are "good," whereas others are "bad." Experiment with another viewpoint: You do not choose your emotional reactions. However, you can choose what you *do* in response to any emotion.

EXPRESS YOUR EMOTIONS

One possible response to any emotion is expressing it. The key is to speak without blaming others for the way you feel. The basic tool for doing so is using "I" messages, as described on page 243.

RESPOND RATHER THAN REACT

The heart of emotional intelligence is moving from mindless reaction to mindful action. See whether you can introduce an intentional gap between sensations and thoughts on the one hand and your next action on the other hand. To do this more often:

- *Run a "mood meter."* Check in with your moods several times each day. On a 3 × 5 card, note the time of day and your emotional state at that point. Rate your mood on a scale of 1 (relaxed and positive) to 10 (very angry, very sad, or very afraid).
- *Write Discovery Statements.* In your journal, write about situations in daily life that trigger strong emotions. Describe these events—and your usual responses to them—in detail.
- *Write Intention Statements.* After seeing patterns in your emotions, you can consciously choose to behave in new ways. Instead of yelling back at the angry supervisor, for example, make it your intention to simply remain silent and breathe deeply until he finishes. Then say, "I'll wait to respond until we've both had a chance to cool down."

MAKE DECISIONS WITH EMOTIONAL INTELLIGENCE

When considering a possible choice, ask yourself, "How am I likely to feel if I do this?" You can use "gut feelings" to tell when an action might violate your values or hurt someone.

Think of emotions as energy. Anger, sadness, and fear send currents of sensation through your whole body. Ask yourself how you can channel that energy into constructive action. ■

You're One Click Away...
from learning more ways online to develop emotional intelligence.

10

Building relationships
across cultures

Communicating with people of other cultures is a learned skill—a habit. According to Stephen R. Covey, author of *The Seven Habits of Highly Effective People*, a habit is the point at which desire, knowledge, and skill meet:[4]

- Desire is about *wanting* to do something.
- Knowledge is *understanding* what to do.
- And skill is the *ability* to do it.

© Peter Dazeley/Getty Images

© Fuse/Jupiter Images

Master students merge these qualities in the way that they relate to people of different cultures.

Knowing techniques for communicating across cultures is valuable. And what gives them power is a sincere desire and commitment to create understanding. If you truly value cultural diversity, then you can discover ways to build bridges between people. Use the following suggestions and invent more of your own.

Start with self-discovery. One step to developing diversity skills is to learn about yourself and understand the lenses through which you see the world. One way to do this is to intentionally switch lenses—that is, to consciously perceive familiar events in a new way.

For example, think of a situation in your life that involved an emotionally charged conflict among several people. Now mentally put yourself inside the skin of another person in that conflict. Ask yourself, "How would I view this situation if I were that person?"

You can also learn by asking, "What if I were a person of the opposite gender? Or if I were member of a different racial or ethnic group? Or if I were older or younger?" Do this exercise consistently, and you'll discover that we live in a world of multiple realities. There are many different ways to interpret any event—and just as many ways to respond, given our individual differences.

Also reflect on how people can have experiences of privilege *and* prejudice. For example, someone might tell you that he's more likely to be promoted at work because he's white and male—*and* that he's been called "white trash" because he lives in a trailer park.

See whether you can recall incidents such as these from your own life. Think of times when you were favored because of your gender, race, or age—and times when you were excluded or ridiculed based on one of those same characteristics. In doing this, you'll discover ways to identify with a wider range of people.

Learn about other cultures. People from different cultures read differently, write differently, think differently, eat differently, and learn differently than you. If you know this from the beginning, you can be more effective with your classmates, coworkers, and neighbors.

One key to understanding styles is to look for several possible interpretations of any behavior. For example:[5]

- Consider the hand signal that signifies *okay* to many Americans—thumb and index finger forming a circle. In France, that signal denotes the number zero. In Japan, it is a symbol for money. And in Brazil, it is considered an obscene gesture.

- When Americans see a speaker who puts her hands in her pockets, they seldom attribute any meaning to this behavior. But in many countries—such as Germany, Indonesia, and Austria—this gesture is considered rude.

- During a conversation, you might prefer having a little distance between yourself and another person. But in Iran, people may often get so close to you that you can feel their breath.

These examples could be extended to cover many areas—posture, eye contact, physical contact, facial expressions, and more. And the various ways of interpreting these behaviors are neither right nor wrong. They simply represent differing styles in making meaning out of what we see.

You might find yourself fascinated by the styles that make up a particular culture. Consider learning as much about that culture as possible. Immerse yourself in it. Read novels, see plays, go to concerts, listen to music, look at art, take courses, learn the language.

Look for differences between individualist and collectivist cultures. Individualist cultures flourish in the United States, Canada, and Western Europe. If your family has deep roots in one of these areas, you were probably raised to value personal fulfillment and personal success. You received recognition or rewards when you stood out from your peers by earning the highest grades in your class, scoring the most points during a basketball season, or demonstrating another form of individual achievement.

In contrast, collectivist cultures value cooperation over competition. Group progress is more important than individual success. Credit for an achievement is widely shared. If you were raised in such a culture, you probably place a high value on your family and were taught to respect your elders. Collectivist cultures dominate Asia, Africa, and Latin America.

In short, individualist cultures often emphasize "I." Collectivist cultures tend to emphasize "we." Forgetting about the differences between them can strain a friendship or wreck an international business deal.

If you were raised in an individualist culture:

- *Remember that someone from a collectivist culture may place a high value on "saving face."* This idea involves more than simply avoiding embarrassment. This person may *not* want to be singled out from other members of a group, even for a positive achievement. If you have a direct request for this person or want to share something that could be taken as a personal criticism, save it for a private conversation.

- *Respect titles and last names.* Although Americans often like to use first names immediately after meeting someone, in some cultures this practice is acceptable only among family members. Especially in work settings, use last names and job titles during your first meetings. Allow time for informal relationships to develop.

- *Put messages in context.* For members of collectivist cultures, words convey only part of an intended message. Notice gestures and other nonverbal communication as well.

If you were raised in a collectivist culture, you can creatively "reverse" the above list. Keep in mind that direct questions from an American student or coworker are meant not to offend, but only to clarify, an idea. Don't be surprised if you are called by a nickname, if no one asks about your family, or if you are rewarded for a personal achievement. In social situations, remember that indirect cues might not get another person's attention. Practice asking clearly and directly for what you want.

Reach out. If carrying out any of these suggestions feels awkward, just apply the "Power Process: Be here now." Then use the suggestions in this article. By intentionally expanding your comfort zone over time, you can break down social barriers and gain a new level of ease at being with people.

A more formal option is to arrange an intergroup dialogue—a "*facilitated*, face-to-face meeting between students from two or more social identity groups that have a history of conflict or potential conflict." Examples are Christians and Muslims, blacks and whites, and people with disabilities and those without disabilities. The goal is sustained and meaningful conversation about controversial issues.[6] Groups typically gather for 2-hour meetings over 6 to 12 weeks.

The format for intergroup dialogues was developed at the University of Michigan and is now being used at campuses across the country. Ask your academic advisor whether such a program is available at your school.

Look for common ground. Students in higher education often find that they worry about many of the same things—including tuition bills, the quality of dormitory food, and the shortage of on-campus parking spaces. More important, our fundamental goals as human beings—such as health, physical safety, and economic security—cross culture lines.

10

> The key is to honor the differences among people while remembering what we have in common. Diversity is not just about our differences—it's also about our similarities.

The key is to honor the differences among people while remembering what we have in common. Diversity is not just about our differences—it's also about our similarities. On a biological level, less than 1 percent of the human genome accounts for visible characteristics such as skin color. In terms of our genetic blueprint, we are more than 99 percent the same.[7]

Speak and listen with cultural sensitivity. After first speaking with someone from another culture, don't assume that you've been understood or that you fully understand the other person. The same action can have different meanings at different times, even for members of the same culture. Check it out. Verify what you think you have heard. Listen to see whether what you spoke is what the other person received.

If you're speaking with someone who doesn't understand English well, keep the following ideas in mind:

- Speak slowly, distinctly, and patiently.
- To clarify your statement, don't repeat individual words over and over again. Restate your entire message with simple, direct language and short sentences.
- Avoid slang and figures of speech.
- Use gestures to accompany your words.
- English courses for nonnative speakers often emphasize written English, so write down what you're saying. Print your message in capital letters.
- Stay calm, and avoid sending nonverbal messages that you're frustrated.

If you're unsure about how well you're communicating, ask questions: "I don't know how to make this idea clear to you. How might I communicate better?" "When you look away from me during our conversation, I feel uneasy. Is there something else we need to talk about?" "When you don't ask questions, I wonder whether I am being clear. Do you want any more explanation?" Questions such as these can get cultural differences out in the open in a constructive way.

Look for individuals, not group representatives. Sometimes the way we speak glosses over differences among individuals and reinforces stereotypes. For example, a student worried about her grade in math expresses concern over "all those Asian students who are skewing the class curve." Or a white music major assumes that her black classmate knows a lot about jazz or hip-hop music. We can avoid such errors by seeing people as individuals—not spokespersons for an entire group.

Find a translator, mediator, or model. People who move with ease in two or more cultures can help us greatly. Diane de Anda, a professor at the University of California, Los Angeles, speaks of three kinds of people who can communicate across cultures. She calls them *translators, mediators,* and *models.*[8]

A *translator* is someone who is truly bicultural—a person who relates naturally to both people in a mainstream culture and people from a contrasting culture. This person can share her own experiences in overcoming discrimination, learning another language or dialect, and coping with stress.

Mediators are people who belong to the dominant or mainstream culture. Unlike translators, they might not be bicultural. However, mediators value diversity and are committed to cultural understanding. Often they are teachers, counselors, tutors, mentors, or social workers.

Models are members of a culture who are positive examples. Models include students from any racial or cultural group who participate in class and demonstrate effective study habits. Models can also include entertainers, athletes, and community leaders.

Your school might have people who serve these functions, even if they're not labeled translators, mediators, or models. Some schools have mentor or "bridge" programs that pair new students with teachers of the same race or culture. Ask your student counseling service about such programs.

Develop support systems. Many students find that their social adjustment affects their academic performance. Students with strong support systems—such as families, friends, churches, self-help groups, and mentors—are using a powerful strategy for success in school. As an exercise, list the support systems that you rely on right now. Also list new support systems you could develop.

Support systems can help you bridge culture gaps. With a strong base of support in your own group, you can feel more confident in meeting people outside that group.

Be willing to accept feedback. Members of another culture might let you know that some of your words or actions had a meaning other than what you intended. For example, perhaps a comment that seems harmless to you is offensive to them. And they may tell you directly about it.

Avoid responding to such feedback with comments such as "Don't get me wrong," "You're taking this way too seriously," or "You're too sensitive." Instead, listen without resistance. Open yourself to what others have to say. Remember to distinguish between the *intention* of your behavior and its actual *impact* on other people. Then take the feedback you receive and ask yourself how you can use it to communicate more effectively in the future.

You can also interpret such feedback positively—a sign that others believe you can change and that they see the possibility of a better relationship with you.

If you are new at responding to diversity, expect to make some mistakes along the way. As long as you approach people in a spirit of tolerance, your words and actions can always be changed.

Speak up against discrimination. You might find yourself in the presence of someone who tells a racist joke, makes a homophobic comment, or utters an ethnic slur. When this happens, you have a right to state what you observe, share what you think, and communicate how you feel. Depending on the circumstance, you might say:

- "That's a stereotype, and we don't have to fall for it."
- "Other people are going to take offense at that. Let's tell jokes that don't put people down."
- "I realize that you don't mean to offend anybody, but I feel hurt and angry by what you just said."
- "I know that an African American person told you that story, but I still think it's racist and creates an atmosphere that I don't want to be in."

This kind of speaking may be the most difficult communicating you ever do. However, if you *don't* do it, you give the impression that you agree with biased speech.

In response to your candid comments, many people will apologize and express their willingness to change. Even if they don't, you can still know that you practiced integrity by aligning your words with your values.

Change the institution. None of us lives in isolation. We all live in systems, and these systems do not always tolerate diversity. As a student, you might see people of color ignored in class. You might see people of a certain ethnic group passed over in job hiring or underrepresented in school organizations. And you might see gay and lesbian students ridiculed or even threatened with violence. One way to stop these actions is to point them out.

You can speak more effectively about what you believe by making some key distinctions. Remember the following:

- *Stereotypes* are errors in thinking—inaccurate ideas about members of another culture.
- *Prejudice* refers to positive or negative feelings about others, which are often based on stereotypes.
- *Discrimination* takes places when stereotypes or prejudice gets expressed in policies and laws that undermine equal opportunities for all cultures.

Federal civil rights laws, as well as the written policies of most schools, ban racial and ethnic discrimination. If your school receives federal aid, it must set up procedures that protect students against such discrimination.

Throughout recent history, students have fueled social change. Student action helped to shift Americans' attitudes toward segregated universities, the Vietnam War, the military draft, and the invasion of Iraq. When it comes to ending discrimination, you are in an environment where you can make a difference. Run for student government. Write for school publications. Speak at rallies. Express your viewpoint. This is training for citizenship in a multicultural world. ■

You're One Click Away...
from gaining more strategies online for building relationships across cultures.

Master Employees
IN ACTION

You're One Click Away...
from a video about Master Students in Action.

"*When I first became a manager, I dreaded conducting the annual performance reviews for my group. I expected my employees—many of whom had been with the company far longer than I had—to resent me evaluating their performances. But for the most part, I was happily surprised. Most people genuinely wanted ideas about how they could improve their performance. After all, if we can't accept constructive criticism, none of us would be able to hold onto our jobs for long.*"

—*Jeff Rogers,*
Research Manager

10

© iStockphoto.com/Danny Kusters

✓ CRITICAL THINKING EXERCISE 24

Becoming a culture learner

To learn about other cultures in depth, actively move through the cycle of learning described by psychologist David Kolb (and explained more fully when you completed your Learning Styles Inventory beginning on page LSI-1). This exercise, which has three parts, illustrates one way to apply the cycle of learning. Use additional paper as needed to complete each part.

Part 1: Feeling

Think of a specific way to interact with people from a culture different from your own. For example, attend a meeting for a campus group that you normally would not attend. Or sit in a campus cafeteria with a new group of people. In the space below, describe what you will do to create your experience of a different culture.

_____

_____

_____

_____

Part 2: Watching

Describe the experience you had while doing Part 1 of this exercise. Be sure to separate your observations—what you saw, heard, or did—from your interpretations. In addition, see whether you can think of other ways to interpret each of your observations. Use the table below for this part of the exercise. An example is included to get you started.

Part 3: Thinking

Next, see whether you can refine your initial interpretations and develop them into some informed conclusions about your experience in Part 1. Do some research about other cultures, looking specifically for information that can help you understand the experience. (Your instructor and a librarian can suggest ways to find such information.) Whenever possible, speak directly to people of various cultures. Share your observations from Part 1, and ask for *their* interpretations. Reflect on the information you gather. Does it reinforce any of the interpretations you listed in Part 2? Does it call for a change in your thinking? Summarize your conclusions in the space below.

_____

_____

_____

_____

_____

Observation	Your Initial Interpretation	Other Possible Interpretations
For 30 minutes starting at noon on Tuesday, I sat alone in the northeast section of the cafeteria in our student union. During this time, all of the conversations I overheard were conducted in Spanish.	I sat alone because the Spanish-speaking students did not want to talk to me. They are unfriendly.	The Spanish-speaking students are actually friendly. They were just not sure how to start a conversation with me. Perhaps they thought I wanted to eat alone or study. Also, I could have taken the initiative to start a conversation.

ASKING FOR HELP

The world responds to people who ask. If you're not consistently getting what you want in life, then consider the power of asking for help.

"Ask, and you shall receive" is a gem of wisdom from many spiritual traditions. Yet acting on this simple idea can be challenging.

Some people see asking for help as a sign of weakness. Actually, it's a sign of strength. Focus on the potential rewards. When you're willing to receive and others are willing to give, resources become available. Circumstances fall into place. Dreams that once seemed too big become goals that you can actually achieve. You benefit, and so do other people.

Remember that asking for help pays someone a compliment. It means that you value what people have to offer. Many will be happy to respond. The key is asking with skill.

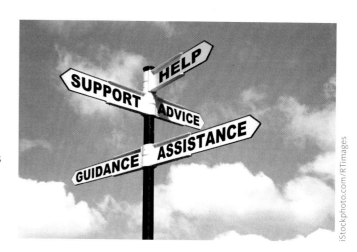

iStockphoto.com/RTimages

ASK WITH CLARITY

Before asking for help, think about your request. Take time to prepare, and consider putting it in writing before you ask in person.

The way you ask has a great influence on the answers you get. For example, "I need help with money" is a big statement. People might not know how to respond. Be more specific: "Do you know any sources of financial aid that I might have missed?" Or: "My expenses exceed my income by $200 each month. I don't want to work more hours while I'm in school. How can I fill the gap?"

ASK WITH SINCERITY

People can tell when a request comes straight from your heart. Although clarity is important, remember that you're asking for help—not making a speech. Keep it simple and direct. Just tell the truth about your current situation, what you want, and the gap between the two. It's okay to be less than perfect.

ASK WIDELY

Consider the variety of people who can offer help. They include parents, friends, classmates, coworkers, mentors, and sponsors. People such as counselors, advisors, and librarians are *paid* to help you.

Also be willing to ask for help with tough issues in any area of life—sex, health, money, career decisions, and more. If you consistently ask for help only in one area, you limit your potential.

To get the most value from this suggestion, direct your request to an appropriate person. For example, you wouldn't ask your instructors for advice about sex. However, you can share any concern with a professional counselor.

ASK WITH AN OPEN MIND

When you ask for help, see whether you can truly open up. If an idea seems strange or unworkable, put your objections on hold for the moment. If you feel threatened or defensive, just notice the feeling. Then return to listening. Discomfort can be a sign that you're about to make a valuable discovery. If people only confirm what you already think and feel, you miss the chance to learn.

ASK WITH RESPONSIBILITY

If you want people to offer help, then avoid statements such as "You know that suggestion you gave me last time? Wow, that really bombed!"

When you act on an idea and it doesn't work, the reason may have nothing to do with the other person. Perhaps you misunderstood or forgot a key point. Ask again for clarity. In any case, the choice about what to do—and the responsibility for the consequences—is still yours.

ASK WITH AN OPENING FOR MORE IDEAS

Approaching people with a specific, limited request can work wonders. So can asking in a way that takes the conversation to a new place. You can do this with creative questions: "Do you have any other ideas for me?" "Would it help if I approached this problem from a different angle?" "Could I be asking a better question?"

ASK AGAIN

People who make a living by selling things know the power of a repeated request. Some people habitually respond to a first request with "no." They might not get to "yes" until the second or third request.

Some cultures place a value on competition, success, and "making it on your own." In this environment, asking for help is not always valued. Sometimes people say no because they're surprised or not sure how to respond. Give them more time and another chance to come around. ∎

10

Jeff Hunter/Getty Images

LEADERSHIP in a DIVERSE world

Many people mistakenly think that the only people who are leaders are those with formal titles such as *supervisor* or *manager*. In fact, though, some leaders have no such titles. Some have never supervised others. Like Mahatma Gandhi, some people change the face of the world without ever reaching a formal leadership position.

No one is born knowing how to lead. We acquire the skills over time. Begin now, while you are in higher education. Campuses offer continual opportunities to gain leadership skills. Volunteer for clubs, organizations, and student government. Look for opportunities to tutor or to become a peer advisor or mentor. No matter what you do, take on big projects—those that are worthy of your time and talents.

The U. S. Census Bureau predicts that the groups once classified as minorities—Hispanics, African Americans, East Asians, and South Asians—will become the majority by the year 2042. For Americans under age 18, this shift will take place in 2023.[9] Translation: Your next boss or coworker could be a person whose life experiences and views of the world differ radically from yours.

We live in a world where Barack Obama, a man with ancestors from Kenya and Kansas, became president of the United States; where Bobby Jindal, the son of immigrants from India, became governor of Louisiana; and where Oprah Winfrey, an African American woman, can propel a book to the top of the best seller list simply by recommending it on her television show. These people set examples of diversity in leadership that many others will follow.

Although many of us will never become so well-known, we all have the capacity to make significant changes in the world around us. Through our actions and words, we constantly influence what happens in our classrooms, offices, communities, and families. We are all leaders, even if sometimes we are unconscious of that fact.

To become a more effective leader, understand the many ways you naturally influence others. This kind of self-awareness—and the ability to harness that influence for positive goals—are qualities of master students. Also prepare to apply your leadership skills in a multicultural world.

> To become a more effective leader, understand the many ways you naturally influence others. This kind of self-awareness—and the ability to harness that influence for positive goals—are qualities of master students.

The following strategies can help you have a positive impact on your relationships with your friends and family members. Also use them when you join study groups and project teams in the workplace.

Own your leadership. Let go of the reluctance that many of us feel toward assuming leadership. It's impossible to escape leadership. Every time you speak, you lead others in some small or large way. Every time you take action, you lead others through your example. Every time you ask someone to do something, you are in essence leading that person. Leadership becomes more effective when it is consciously applied.

Be willing to be uncomfortable. Leadership is a courageous act. Leaders often are not appreciated or even liked. They can feel isolated—cut off from their colleagues. This isolation can sometimes lead to self-doubt and even fear. Before you take on a leadership role, be aware that you might experience such feelings. Also remember that none of these feelings has to stop you from leading.

Allow huge mistakes. The more important and influential you are, the more likely it is that your mistakes will have huge consequences. The chief financial officer for a large company can make a mistake that costs thousands or even millions of dollars. A physician's error could cost a life. As commander-in-chief of the armed forces, the president of a country can make a decision that costs thousands of lives. At the same time, these people are in a position to make huge changes for the better—to save thousands of dollars or lives through their power, skill, and influence.

People in leadership positions can become paralyzed and ineffective if they fear making a mistake. It's necessary for them to act even when information is incomplete or when they know a catastrophic mistake is a possible outcome.

Take on big projects. Leaders make promises. And effective leaders make big promises. These words—*I will do it* and *You can count on me*—distinguish a leader.

Look around your world to see what needs to be done, and then take it on. Consider taking on the biggest project you can think of—ending world hunger, eliminating nuclear weapons, wiping out poverty, promoting universal literacy. Think about how you'd spend your life if you knew that you could make a difference regarding these overwhelming problems. Then take the actions you considered. See what a difference they can make for you and for others.

Tackle projects that stretch you to your limits—projects that are worthy of your time and talents.

Provide feedback. An effective leader is a mirror to others. Share what you see. Talk with others about what they are doing effectively—and what they are doing ineffectively.

Keep in mind that people might not enjoy your feedback. Some would probably rather not hear it at all. Two things can help. One is to let people know up front that if they sign on to work with you, they can expect feedback. Also give your feedback with skill. Use "I" messages as explained in Chapter 9: Communicating. Back up any criticisms with specific observations and facts. And when people complete a task with exceptional skill, point that out too.

Paint a vision. Help others see the big picture—the ultimate purpose of a project. Speak a lot about the end result and the potential value of what you're doing.

There's a biblical saying: "Without vision, the people perish." Long-term goals usually involve many intermediate steps. Unless we're reminded of the purpose for those day-to-day actions, our work can feel like a grind. Leadership is the art of helping others lift their eyes to the horizon—keeping them in touch with the ultimate value and purpose of a project. Keeping the vision alive helps spirits soar.

Model your values. "Be the change you want to see" is a useful motto for leaders. Perhaps you want to see integrity, focused attention, and productivity in the people around you. Begin by modeling these qualities yourself. It's easy to excite others about a goal when you are enthusiastic about it yourself. Having fun while being productive is contagious. If you bring these qualities to a project, others might follow suit.

Make requests—lots of them. An effective leader is a request machine. Making requests—both large and small—is an act of respect. When we ask a lot from others, we demonstrate our respect for them and our confidence in their abilities.

10

At first, some people might get angry when we make requests of them. Over time, however, many will see that requests are compliments and opportunities to expand their skills. Ask a lot from others, and they might appreciate you because of it.

Follow up. What we don't inspect, people don't respect. When other people agree to do a job for you, follow up to see how it is going. You can do so in a way that communicates your respect and interest—not your fear that the project might flounder. When you display a genuine interest in other people and their work, they are more likely to view you as a partner in achieving a shared goal.

Focus on problems, not people. Sometimes projects do not go as planned. Big mistakes occur. If this happens, focus on the project and the mistakes—not the personal faults of your colleagues. People do not make mistakes on purpose. If they did, we would call them "on-purposes," not mistakes. Most people will join you in solving a problem if your focus is on the problem, not on what they did wrong.

Acknowledge others. Express genuine appreciation for the energy and creativity that others have put into their work. Take the time to be interested in what others have done and to care about the results they have accomplished. Thank and acknowledge them with your eyes, your words, and the tone of your voice.

Share credit. As a leader, constantly give away the praise and acknowledgment that you receive. When you're congratulated for your performance, pass the praise on to others. Share the credit with the group.

When you're a leader, the results you achieve depend on the efforts of many others. Acknowledging that fact often is more than telling the truth—it's essential if you want to continue to count on the support of others in the future.

Delegate. Ask a coworker or classmate to take on a job that you'd like to see done. Ask the same of your family or friends. Delegate tasks to the mayor of your town, the governor of your state, and the leaders of your country.

Take on projects that are important to you. Then find people who can lead the effort. You can do this even when you have no formal role as a leader.

We often see delegation as a tool that's available only to those above us in the chain of command. Actually, delegating up or across an organization can be just as effective. Consider delegating a project to your boss. That is, ask him to take on a job that you'd like to see accomplished. It might be a job that you cannot do, given your position in the company.

Balance styles. Think for a moment about your own learning style. To lead effectively, assess your strengths, and look for people who can complement them. If you excel at gathering

information and setting goals, for example, then recruit people who like to make decisions and take action. Also enlist people who think creatively and generate different points of view.

Look for different styles in the people who work with you. Remember that learning results from a balance between feeling, watching, thinking, and doing. (For more information, see Chapter 2: First Steps.) The people you lead will combine these characteristics in infinite variety. Welcome that variety, and accommodate it.

You can defuse and prevent many conflicts simply by acknowledging differences in style. Doing so opens up more options than blaming the differences on "politics" or "personality problems."

Listen. As a leader, be aware of what other people are thinking, feeling, and wanting. Listen fully to their concerns and joys. Before you criticize their views or make personal judgments, take the time to understand what's going on inside them. This is not merely a personal favor to the people you work with. The more you know about your coworkers or classmates, the more effectively you can lead them.

Communicate assertively—not aggressively or passively. *Aggressive* communication is ineffective. People who act aggressively are domineering. They often get what they want by putting down other people or using strong-arm methods. When aggressive people win, other people lose.

Assertive communication is asking directly and confidently for what you want *and* showing respect for others at the same time. This is one sign of an effective leader. Assertive people are committed to win–win solutions.

Some of us don't act assertively out of fear that we will appear aggressive. This is *passive* communication—neither assertive nor aggressive—that gets us nowhere. By remaining quiet and submissive, we allow others to infringe on our rights. When others run our lives, we fail to have the lives we want.

For more on how to speak assertively, see the suggestions for speaking with "I" messages in Chapter 9.

Practice. Leadership is an acquired skill. No one is born knowing how to make requests, give feedback, create budgets, do long-range planning, or delegate tasks. We learn these things over time, with practice, by seeing what works and what doesn't.

As a process of constant learning, leadership calls for all of the skills of master students. Look for areas in which you can make a difference, and experiment with these strategies. Right now there's something worth doing that calls for your leadership. Take action, and others will join you. ■

You're One Click Away...
from gaining more perspectives online on leadership.

masterstudentprofile

Nilofer Merchant

(1968–) Corporate director, consultant, and author, has led successful start-up businesses and launched products that account for $18 billion in revenues

Learners are those that recognize that they will find out what they don't know and they'll keep modifying their ideas, perspectives, and approaches to adapt to the change around them. Zealots are the opposite. The word *Zealot* comes from the Greek root to be "jealous of the truth"—to guard it as your own. Not surprising, Zealots hold an absolute conviction that they are right. Right, as in: us/them, black/white, same/different, and a good/evil world. ...

An odd fact? The Learner and the Zealot will be wrong about the same [a]mount [sic] of the time. Sad, but true. But the Zealot, once forced to deal with the wrongness will go with a "sure mistakes were made but not by me" alibi. Zealots are simply unable to say "I don't know," and will often make the wrongness about the world around them, the situation at hand, blame someone else, and forever explain away the error. The Zealots deny the failure as *theirs*, at almost any cost. They, therefore, miss the inherent opportunity in it, which is to learn and discover what they actually need to know.

Here's where Learners have an opportunity: learners are open to seeing things anew, and when they do this, they benefit from the unique upside of being open to what could be, which is a creative space. After all, isn't *being open* the very essence of innovation, of curiosity, of exploration, of the many creative acts like that of art, of our own individuality, of the rub that fuels entrepreneurs, or even what allows each of us to grow as people? When we can see a wrong or a gap, and our own hand in it, we can see the world anew, make another choice, and chart a new course.

But many people, myself included at times, avoid the role of Learner. We human-ites don't want to be or appear "stupid." We don't want to face the hard and sometimes humbling task of then figuring out a different story that makes more sense. Instead, we human-ites love to *know*, we love the feeling of *mastery*, and the *confidence* our knowledge (our MBA, our job status) gives us.

I had this very human-ite experience myself a few weeks ago... as I was "interviewing" for a role, and got asked the question of what I was most proud of. I had a moment of pause where I thought about what kind of answer to give:

If I wanted to lean towards my bravado and knowingness, or to be a bit more of my fuller self which includes doubt and unknowingness. I went with the fuller picture, figuring the guy could take it. I answered that my humility to always question and be okay being in a state of not knowing was the thing I was most proud of....

But, after the call ended, I wanted to change my answer. I played back the response, and it sounded so mealy-mouth, so weak, so un-polished and I started to question who would say yes to wanting a humble person? I had the strongest urgent to call the guy back, and point out that my peer CEO group voted for me as the MVP for several years in a row. That had a little more awesomeness, it was a little more *Hoo-Yah*, and was a little less ... humble. I resisted making the call, or writing the email to change my answer. But, *ooooh*, how I wanted to. I still feel that angst in my chest. ...

Learning takes active inquiry and the use of questions. Learning takes humility and living in a state of not knowing, yet. Learning takes a certain courage that we can outpace others, if we admit to not knowing so we can learn what we need to learn. Above all, taking the learning, open stance is an act of faith—a belie[f] [sic] that you don't need to fake it, you can be genuine *and* you will still arrive where you need to be.

Photo courtesy of Nilofer Merchant

Learning Being or Zealot? Which are you? ...

Nilofer Merchant ... is willing to be uncomfortable.

YOU ... can master discomfort by remembering that there's always more to learn—and that you have to skills to learn it.

10

You're One Click Away...
from learning more about Nilofer Merchant online at the Master Student Profiles. You can also visit the Master Student Hall of Fame to learn more about other master students.

FIVE Cs
FOR YOUR CAREER

CHARACTER • CRITICAL THINKING • CREATIVE THINKING • COLLABORATION • COMMUNICATION

Discover links between collaboration and character. Remember that as you experiment with the strategies presented in this chapter, you will develop many qualities of a master student. Examples are responsibility, the ability to organize and sort, and the willingness to change, take risks, and participate. Master students are master collaborators.

Think creatively to plan projects. Chapter 3 offers suggestions for creating a to-do list. There's another type of list that you can maintain to excel at work—a *project* list.

Review the key areas of responsibility—such as marketing, hiring, product design, or customer service—that make up your job. Then use creative thinking techniques to brainstorm a list of the most important outcomes that you want to produce in each area during the coming year. Remember that each of these outcomes is a potential project that you can plan by using suggestions from this chapter.

Think critically to manage projects. After you've created a list of potential projects, use your critical thinking skills to narrow that list to outcomes that you will actually commit to produce. Remember that project lists are typically much shorter than to-do lists. In fact, your project list for the upcoming three months might fit on a 3 × 5 card.

To stay on top of your workload and manage time effectively, review and update your projects list weekly. At any moment during the workday, you can scan this list in a few seconds and ask yourself: *Will the task I'm doing right now take me closer to these outcomes? If not, what else could I do next?* Asking these questions several times each week is one shortcut to thinking and acting like a skilled knowledge worker.

Use basic communication skills to set the stage for collaboration. One of the most fundamental and practical communication skills that you can develop is the ability to initiate and sustain a conversation with someone you've just met. In the workplace, you will regularly meet new coworkers, customers, and clients. The ability to put people at ease through "small talk" will make you valuable to employers. Review "Four simple people skills" in this chapter for relevant strategies.

Collaboration depends on high-level communication skills, including the ability to listen closely, suspend judgment, and sympathize with another person's experiences. Every conversation, no matter how informal, is a chance to develop those skills.

By the way, there's one simple and powerful suggestion for making small talk that's easy to forget. Notice any repetitive "filler" words that crop up in your speech such as *like, you know, um*, and *ah*. Those are words that people just um, like, *totally* overused, you know? Remind yourself that you don't use them anymore.

See study groups as ways to develop collaboration skills now. Teamwork is often required in the workplace. Almost every job is accomplished by the combined efforts of many people. For example, manufacturing a single car calls for the contribution of designers, welders, painters, electricians, marketing executives, computer programmers, and many others.

Joining study groups now, while you are in school, can help you expand your learning styles and develop the skills of a successful team player. Many of those skills center on outcome-based and action-oriented thinking. During your study group's first meeting, set clear goals to achieve. Define the focus of your group (test review, note taking, research, reading). End each meeting with a clear list of actions to complete before the next meeting, along with a record of who will take each action. Doing this consistently will give you a head start for your next team-based project at work.

Now, make a personal commitment to developing the five Cs. Take another look at the Discovery Wheel in Chapter 2—especially the sections labeled Character, Creative and Critical Thinking, Communicating, and Collaborating. Take a snapshot of your current skills in these areas after reading and doing this chapter.

DISCOVERY

My scores on the "Five C" sections of the Discovery Wheel were:	As of today, I would give myself the following scores in these areas:	At the end of this course, I would like my scores in these areas to be:
Character _____	Character _____	Character _____
Creative & Critical Thinking _____	Creative & Critical Thinking _____	Creative & Critical Thinking _____
Communicating _____	Communicating _____	Communicating _____
Collaborating _____	Collaborating _____	Collaborating _____

Next, skim this chapter and look for a collaboration strategy that you want to explore in depth. Choose one that would enhance your self-rating in at least one of the five Cs.

I discovered that my preferred technique is . . .

_____

_____

_____

_____

This technique can help me become more effective at one or more of the five Cs because . . .

_____

_____

_____

_____

INTENTION
To use this technique, I intend to . . .

_____

_____

_____

_____

NEXT ACTION
The specific action I will take is . . .

_____

_____

_____

_____

10

Name _____

Date _____

1. List three strategies for conducting an effective study group.
   Any three of the following: Ask your instructor for guidelines. Set an agenda for each meeting. Assign roles. Cycle through learning styles. Teach each other. Test one another. Compare notes. Create wall-size mind maps or concept maps to summarize a textbook or series of lectures. Monitor effectiveness. Use technology to collaborate. (*Cooperative learning: Studying in groups*, page 265)

2. List the four ways people skills are practiced.
   (1) Smile. (2) Shake hands. (3) Make small talk. (4) Express appreciation. (*Four simple "people skills,"* page 267)

3. Name the four main elements of a project plan.
   (1) Milestones, (2) actions, (3) reference materials, and (4) "someday" items (*Getting to "done"—the practical art of project management*, page 268)

4. Effective teams include people who
   (a) get fully involved with the team and commit to its purpose.
   (b) talk about the team's experiences and stay open to new ideas.
   (c) think critically about which agreements and actions will achieve the team's purpose.
   (d) make decisions and take action.
   (e) all of the above.
   (e) all of the above. (*Collaborate in effective teams*, page 271)

5. List four characteristics of time-wasting meetings.
   (1) Open-ended, (2) unstructured, (3) standing, and (4) inconclusive (*Make the most of meetings*, page 273)

6. Briefly describe two strategies for dealing with the *content* of a conflict between people.
   Describe any two: Back up to common ground. State the problem. State all points of view. Ask for complete communication. Focus on solutions. Focus on the future. (*Managing conflict*, page 274)

7. Briefly describe two strategies for dealing with the *process* of resolving any conflict.
   Describe any two of the following: Commit to the relationship. Allow strong feelings. Notice your need to be "right." Slow down the communication. Communicate in writing. (*Managing conflict*, page 274)

8. Define the term *emotional intelligence*.
   Emotional intelligence goes way beyond IQ; it includes an awareness of your feelings, acting in thoughtful ways, showing concern for others, resolving conflict, and making responsible decisions. (*Developing emotional intelligence*, page 277)

9. According to the text, emotions consist of three elements. What are they?
   Physical sensations, thoughts, and action (*Developing emotional intelligence*, page 277)

10. In her Master Student Profile, Nilofer Merchant distinguishes between Learners and Zealots. Briefly explain how they differ.
    Learners are willing to learn new information and modify their ideas, perspectives, and approaches to adapt to the change around them; they are open to seeing things anew or differently. Zealots hold an absolute conviction and are not open to new information; when things go wrong Zealots do not take personal responsibility. (*Master student profile Nilofer Merchant*, page 287)

HEALTH

Instructor
Tools & Tips

ANNOTATED INSTRUCTOR'S EDITION

"To be somebody, you must last."
—Ruth Gordon

"Emotion, which is suffering, ceases to be suffering as soon as we have a clear picture of it." —Baruch Spinoza

PREVIEW

Staying healthy while pursuing higher education is an important skill all students need to master. Juggling work, college courses, and family responsibilities can be quite stressful. It is essential that first-year students start their education on the right foot with strategies for maintaining their "machine." This chapter provides resources for beginning conversations about such topics as eating well, exercising, personal safety, self-esteem, and alcohol abuse and addiction. Don't hesitate to seek an opinion—from your campus health center or a community outreach program—when you need an expert's voice to support the text.

Some of you may feel uncertain *how* to begin discussing serious health issues in your classroom. You will likely find helpful advice in your personal health plan. Don't feel you must have all the answers. Share your own personal health journey with your students if you feel comfortable doing so. It often helps students to hear that we, as teachers and mentors, face challenges as well. The secret is being open to growing and improving our behaviors and beliefs. Healthy living is often an informed, proactive process. One way to begin this process is to have students revisit the answers they filled in on their Discovery Wheel. Using the Discovery and Intention Journal Entry system, a discussion about stress can begin with *what* factors are causing your students to feel stress, and this can lead to asking *why* these issues might be considered stressful. As a class, you can brainstorm possible *what if* scenarios to reduce students' stress. Then have your students write Intention Statements about steps they can take the next time they are experiencing high levels of stress.

GUEST SPEAKER

Invite a guest speaker from the student wellness or health center for this portion of the class. If your school offers health and wellness classes, consider inviting a

faculty member from this department. You could even contact your county health department as a resource. Often, students will pay more attention to a visiting professional. Ask your presenter to discuss the importance of health and the relationship of health to learning. Be sure to allow time for a question-and-answer period.

Another idea is to ask if a local chapter of Alcoholics Anonymous or Narcotics Anonymous can provide a guest speaker or, better yet, a panel of speakers. Although these programs emphasize anonymity, some participants, as part of their program of recovery, choose to share their story as a way of educating others. These individuals can have a powerful impact on your students.

Or use the Video Skillbuilders that were designed to go along with this chapter.

Keeping your mind and body and shape Students often overlook the role their health plays in their success in college. Many college students are living on their own for the first time and may not know how to cook and prepare healthy meals. Many students don't have time to prepare meals and fall into the fast-food habit. In this video, students talk about being overwhelmed by school and work, and not efficiently managing their days in order to provide time for meal preparation and eating, exercise, and a good night's sleep.

Healthy Living: Making the right choices Difficulties encountered by college students don't always originate during freshman year. Problems may begin during high school. They may occur at home. But college is a different environment, and students may be distracted. Whether it's about living arrangements, time management, or new friends, students have many choices to make. Drinking, sexually transmitted diseases, and psychological problems may create unsafe and unhealthy conditions. The students on the video relate examples of the results of extreme behavior.

An excellent health resource is choosemyplate.gov. Invite students to explore the tips, resources, and interactive tools in this informative site. Discuss the role of peer pressure and other challenges found in the college environment, often a less structured environment where choices and freedom abound. These choices can lead to unhealthy choices and habits. Encourage your older students to share their experiences in these areas.

LECTURE

master instructor **BEST PRACTICE**

"I've been involved in AIDS education since the 1980s. The best weapon we have to fight HIV/AIDS is education, so we spend about 30 to 45 minutes on this topic in my College Success classes. The college years are the time for many students to experiment with sexual behaviors. Many know that they need to practice abstinence to be totally safe or, if sexually active, to practice safer sex. However, many students do not know what behaviors are considered risky or what skills are involved in practicing safer sex. So I teach not only the fact that condoms may prevent the transmission of HIV but also specific skills in condom usage. My primary objectives are for students to learn effective communication skills in negotiating the use of a condom with their partners as well as learning the skills needed to stay safe during sexual activities. I use explicit language; I incorporate humor and frank discussion as well as a demonstration on how to use a condom. This is one topic where you will find the entire class will "Be here now.""

–Deborah Warfield, *Seminole Community College*

EXERCISES/ACTIVITIES

Master Student Profile: Randy Pausch (page 315) After students read the inspirational story about Randy Pausch, ask them to think about how their childhood dreams can be connected to their career goals. Remind students that they can view "The Last Lecture" by Randy Pausch online in its entirety.

CONVERSATION/SHARING

Power Process: Surrender (page 292) Use the following example to open a discussion about this Power Process with your students:

Sally and Jane leave work on Friday at the same time. Both are caught in rush-hour traffic. Sally frets, honks her horn, and changes lanes as frequently as possible, with the hope of

master instructor **BEST PRACTICE**

"When change is requested of students, they often unconsciously say, "I can't. …" I ask my students to take a closer look at times when they say these statements and begin to replace the "I can't" with "I won't."

Have your students make a list of those "I can't" statements. From this list, have them select one and restate the sentence with won't instead of can't. Then, ask students to describe any distinction between these two statements. Generally students will say that the "I won't" statement implies some choice in the matter, and the experience changes from being one of victimization to taking some responsibility.

The last step is to have students replace the "I won't" with "I don't know how." Again I ask students to describe any distinction between this statement and the "I won't" statement. Students often experience a weight off their shoulders or realize they were operating under a false expectation such as "I should know this." Students at this point can write a Discovery and Intention Statement about their experience.

Chapter 11 provides students with an opportunity to practice taking more responsibility for their thoughts (intrapersonal communications) and to use the steps in critical thinking.

I have students list some of their negative thinking. They often say things like "I'll never get as much sleep as suggested" or "I'll never reduce my anxiety before test taking."

I ask student to rewrite their sentences to look like this: "I thought I would never get enough sleep" or "I thought I would never reduce my anxiety before test taking."

I have students rewrite these statements over and over again, emphasizing the word thought. At some point, students will smile and say, "Oh I get it—I just 'thought' I would never get enough sleep," or "I see it now—I 'thought' I would never reduce my anxiety before test taking."

We often turn our thoughts into reality or a belief without going through the steps in critical thinking. This is related to a self-fulfilling prophecy, or self-efficacy, described in the article 'Developing a strong self-image' in Chapter 11 and the Power Process: I create it all in Chapter 6."

–Fred Kester, *Yavapai College*

saving time. She curses the light when it changes to red, gets aggravated at cars that don't start moving fast enough when the light changes to green, frantically listens to the traffic reports on the radio, agonizes about all the things she's missing at home, worries because she is getting very low on gas, and arrives home at 6:09 P.M. with a headache. Jane surrenders. Rather than fighting and resisting the traffic, she accepts it and flows with it. She listens to her favorite radio station, plans her activities for the weekend, thinks of a better way for taking purchase orders at work, sees a new Chinese restaurant she wants to try, notices the trees and plants telling her that spring is here, repeats her affirmations about self-improvement, anticipates the warm greeting she will receive from her family, and arrives home at 6:09 P.M. with a smile.

More examples like this one are available on the Instructor Web site.

HOMEWORK

Choose to rest College students frequently complain that they have trouble getting a good night's sleep. For a homework assignment, have them research solutions to sleep disorders online and bring an interesting article to class. Have them share these articles in small groups and then discuss the body's need for rest and how sleep deprivation can affect their schoolwork.

Alcohol, tobacco, and drugs: The Truth (page 309) Some college students are trying to enhance their focus, memory, and brain performance by taking controlled medications that are prescribed for other purposes. These drugs include Ritalin, Adderall, and Provigil. Assign students to research the intended medical purposes of these drugs as well as the precautions and side effects associated with them.

EVALUATION

Quiz Ideas for Chapter 11

Ask students to:
- Describe strategies to find more time to exercise.
- Write Discovery and Intention Statements about ways to develop self-esteem.

- Describe tools for dealing with emotional pain.
- Identify several strategies that can be used to quit smoking.
- List three new strategies for improving their diet.

master instructor BEST PRACTICE

"Stress Management Plan. *I have students do this project to help them understand how to cope with stress.*

1. *Research several possible stress-management strategies.*
   - *Explore stress-management strategies.*
   - *Try to explore an area that you would be interested in incorporating into your life. This may include physical exercise, journaling, music therapy, or humor therapy.*
   - *Choose one strategy that you would consider using on a regular basis and complete number 2 below.*

2. *Write a two- to three-page essay or create a PowerPoint presentation in which you:*
   - *Describe the stress-management strategy. Give some background. For example, if you choose yoga, give some history of yoga and how people have used this as effective stress reduction.*
   - *Then relate that strategy to your personal life, and discuss how you plan to incorporate the stress-management plan into your lifestyle.*
   - *Include photos or clip art in work.***"**

—Annette McCreedy, Nashville State Community College

Additional Digital Resources for Chapter 11

What can you **ASSIGN FROM THE COURSEMATE** *for From Master Student to Master Employee?*

• **Video Skillbuilders.** These interactive online tools combine video clips featuring discussions with students, instructors, and experts, with articles and activities designed to give students a fully engaging learning experience. Either view and experience these together in class, or have students view them as a homework assignment and re-spond to the viewing questions and reflective exercise. This module is a good match for Chapter 11:

- Healthy Living: Making the Right Choices
- Keeping Your Mind and Body in Shape

Note that Video Skillbuilders are available for every chapter.

• **Power Process Media: Surrender.** To help students understand the importance of "surrender" as described in the Power Process for Chapter 11, have them watch a video about surrendering, listen to an audio version, and then answer the accom-panying questions. A PowerPoint presentation that summarizes the Power Process article's main points is also included. Or have students create group multimedia PowerPoint presentations based on their understanding of how to "surrender." Note that Power Process media are available for every chapter.

• **The Wellness Wheel.** Like the Discovery Wheel, the Wellness Wheel offers students the opportunity to assess their strengths and weaknesses associated with self-image, emotions, energy, relationships, chemicals, self-care, and prevention. Students simply rate their responses to the questions and the wheel does the rest!

CourseMate *To access CourseMate, your students need to visit www.cengagebrain.com. At the CengageBrain.com home page, students search for the ISBN of From Master Student to Master Employee (from the back cover of the book), using the search box at the top of the page. This takes them to the product page where these resources can be found.*

Did you know that **THESE RESOURCES** *(and many more)* **ARE AVAILABLE** *on the* **INSTRUCTOR COMPANION SITE?**

• **Need some energizing lecture ideas?** Browse through the lecture ideas provided for Chapter 11, including the following:

- **Addiction.** Facts and statistics about a variety of wellness issues can help students make choices.
- **Burnout.** Discuss with your students the warning signs of burnout and prevention techniques.

• **Looking for fresh, innovative ways to teach Chapter 11 topics?** Browse through the Best Practices library to see what other Master Instructors have been successfully doing with their students.

Please visit login.cengage.com to log in and access the Instructor Companion Site.

Health

Use this **Master Student Map** to ask yourself

WHY THIS CHAPTER MATTERS . . .

- Succeeding in higher education calls for a baseline of physical and emotional well-being.

WHAT IS INCLUDED . . .

HOW I CAN USE THIS CHAPTER. . .

- Maintain my physical and mental energy.
- Enhance my self-esteem.
- Make decisions about alcohol and other drugs in a way that supports my success.

WHAT IF . . .

- I could meet the demands of daily life with energy and optimism to spare?

© Ruslan Ivantsov/Shutterstock.com

JOURNAL ENTRY 23
Discovery Statement

Take a First Step about your health

This chapter allows you to look closely at your health. Aim to change your behavior in specific ways that make a dramatic, positive difference in your life. Start with a one-sentence First Step:

What concerns me more than anything else about my health right now is . . .

_____
_____
_____
_____
_____
_____
_____
_____
_____
_____
_____
_____
_____
_____
_____

Note: You can expand on your response—and keep it private—by writing it on a separate piece of paper.

POWER process

Surrender

Life can be magnificent and satisfying. It can also be devastating. Sometimes there is too much pain or confusion. Problems can be too big and too numerous. Life can bring us to our knees in a pitiful, helpless, and hopeless state. A broken relationship, a sudden diagnosis of cancer, a dependence on drugs, or a stress-filled job can leave us feeling overwhelmed—powerless.

In these troubling situations, the first thing we can do is to admit that we don't have the resources to handle the problem. No matter how hard we try and no matter what skills we bring to bear, some problems remain out of our control. When this is the case, we can tell the truth: "It's too big and too mean. I can't handle it." In that moment, we take a step toward greater health.

Desperately struggling to control a problem can easily result in the problem controlling us. Surrender is letting go of being the master in order to avoid becoming the slave.

Many traditions make note of this idea. Western religions speak of surrendering to God. Hindus say surrender to the Self. Members of Alcoholics Anonymous talk about turning their lives over to a Higher Power. Agnostics might suggest surrendering to their intellect, their intuition, or their conscience.

In any case, surrender means being receptive. Once we admit that we're at the end of our rope, we open ourselves up to help. We learn that we don't have to go it alone. We find out that other people have faced similar problems and survived. We give up our old habits of thinking and behaving as if we have to be in control of everything. We stop acting as general manager of the universe. We surrender. And that creates a space for something new in our lives.

Surrender is not "giving up." It is not a suggestion to quit and do nothing about your problems. Giving up is fatalistic and accomplishes nothing. You have many skills and resources. Use them. You can apply all of your energy to handling a situation and still surrender at the same time. You can surrender to weight gain even as you step up your exercise program. You can surrender to a toothache even as you go to the dentist. You can surrender to the past while adopting new habits for a healthy future.

Surrender includes doing whatever you can in a positive, trusting spirit. Let go, keep going, and know when a source of help lies beyond you.

You're One Click Away...
from accessing Power Process Media online and finding out more about how to "surrender."

Hannamariah/Shutterstock.com

Wake up TO HEALTH

Some people see health as just a matter of common sense. These people might see little value in reading a health chapter. After all, they already know how to take care of themselves.

Yet *knowing* and *doing* are two different things. Health information does not always translate into healthy habits.

We expect to experience health challenges as we age. Even youth, though, is no guarantee of good health. Over the last 3 decades, obesity among young adults has tripled. Twenty-nine percent of young men smoke. And 70 percent of deaths among adults ages 18 to 29 result from unintentional injuries, accidents, homicide, and suicide.[1]

As a student, your success in school is directly tied to your health. Lack of sleep and exercise have been associated with lower grade point averages among undergraduate students. So have alcohol use, tobacco use, gambling, and chronic health conditions.[2] And any health habit that undermines your success in school can also undermine your success in later life.

On the other hand, we can adopt habits that sustain our well-being. One study found that people lengthened their lives an average of 14 years by adopting just four habits: staying tobacco-free, eating more fruits and vegetables, exercising regularly, and drinking alcohol in moderation if at all.[3]

Health also hinges on a habit of exercising some tissue that lies between your ears—the organ called your brain. One path to greater health starts not with new food or a new form of exercise, but with new ideas.

Consider the power of beliefs. Some of them create barriers to higher levels of health: "Your health is programmed by your heredity." "Some people are just low on energy." "Healthy food doesn't taste very good." "Over the long run, people just don't change their habits." Be willing to test these ideas and change them when it serves you.

People often misunderstand what the word *health* means. Remember that this word is similar in origin to *whole, hale, hardy,* and even *holy*. Implied in these words are qualities that most of

us associate with healthy people: alertness, vitality, vigor. Healthy people meet the demands of daily life with energy to spare. Illness or stress might slow them down for a while, but then they bounce back. They know how to relax, create loving relationships, and find satisfaction in their work.

To open up your inquiry into health—and to open up new possibilities for your life—consider three ideas.

First, health is a continuum. On one end of that continuum is a death that comes too early. On the other end is a long life filled with satisfying work and fulfilling relationships. Many of us exist between those extremes at a point we might call average. Most of the time we're not sick. And most of the time we're not truly thriving either.

Second, health changes. Health is not a fixed state. In fact, health fluctuates from year to year, day to day, and moment to moment. Those changes can occur largely by chance. Or they can occur more often by choice, as we take conscious control of our thinking and behavior.

Third, even when faced with health challenges, we have choices. We can choose attitudes and habits that promote a higher quality of life. For example, people with diabetes can often manage the disease by exercising more and changing their diet.

Health is one of those rich, multilayered concepts that we can never define completely. In the end, your definition of *health* comes from your own experience. The proof lies not on these pages but in your life—in the level of health that you create, starting now.

You have choices. You can remain unaware of habits that have major consequences for your health. Or you can become aware of current habits (discovery), choose new habits (intention), and take appropriate action.

Health is a choice you make every moment, with each thought and behavior. Wake up to this possibility by experimenting with the suggestions in this chapter.

Olena Pivnenko/Shutterstock.com

11

✔ CRITICAL THINKING EXERCISE 25

Take a First Step about your health

This exercise expands on the Journal Entry that opened this chapter. The purpose is to explore your current level of health in more detail. To do this, complete the following sentences. If a sentence does not apply to you, then skip it. As with the Discovery Wheel, the usefulness of this writing will be determined by your honesty and courage.

Note: If you'd like to keep your responses to this exercise confidential, then write on separate paper.

My eating habits lead me to be . . .

_____

_____

What I would most like to change about my diet is . . .

_____

_____

The way I usually exercise is . . .

_____

_____

The last time I did 20 minutes or more of aerobic exercise was . . .

_____

_____

It would be easier for me to work out regularly if I . . .

_____

_____

The most important benefit for me in exercising more is . . .

_____

_____

In the last 10 days, the number of alcoholic drinks I have had is . . .

_____

_____

When it comes to my use of drugs other than alcohol, what concerns me is . . .

_____

_____

Someone who knows me fairly well would say I am emotionally . . .

_____

_____

The best thing I could do for myself and my relationships would be to . . .

_____

_____

The number of hours I sleep each night is . . .

_____

_____

I have trouble sleeping when . . .

_____

_____

Next, review what you've just written, and focus on the area of your health that concerns you the most right now. Preview this chapter and choose one strategy for making a positive change in this area. In the space below, describe exactly what you will do to use this strategy.

_____

_____

_____

_____

_____

Choose Your FUEL

Food is your primary fuel for body and mind. And even though you've been eating all your life, entering higher education is bound to change the way that you fuel yourself.

There have been hundreds of books written about nutrition. One says don't drink milk. Another says the calcium provided by milk is an essential nutrient we need daily. Although such debate seems confusing, take comfort. There is actually wide agreement about how to fuel yourself for health.

Today, federal nutrition guidelines are summarized visually as a *dinner plate*. The idea is to eat more of the foods shown in the bigger sections of the dinner plate. To see an example and build your personal food pyramid, go online to www.choosemyplate.gov.

The various food guidelines available agree on several core principles:[4]

- Emphasize fruits, vegetables, whole grains, and fat-free or low-fat milk and milk products.

- Include lean meats, poultry, fish, beans, eggs, and nuts.

- Choose foods that are low in saturated fats, trans fats, cholesterol, salt (sodium), and added sugars.

Michael Pollan, a writer for the *New York Times Magazine,* spent several years sorting out the scientific literature on nutrition.[5] He boiled the key guidelines down to seven words in three sentences:

- *Eat food.* In other words, choose whole, fresh foods over processed products with a lot of ingredients.

- *Not too much.* If you want to manage your weight, then control how much you eat. Notice portion sizes. Pass on snacks, seconds, and desserts—or indulge just occasionally.

- *Mostly plants.* Fruits, vegetables, and grains are loaded with chemicals that help to prevent disease. Plant-based foods, on the whole, are also lower in calories than foods from animals (meat and dairy products).

Finally, forget diets. *How* you eat can matter more than *what* you eat. If you want to eat less, then eat slowly. Savor each bite. Stop when you're satisfied instead of when you feel full. Use meal times as a chance to relax, reduce stress, and connect with people. ■

You're One Click Away...
from discovering more strategies online for fueling your body.

© iStockphoto.com/jgroup

Prevent and treat eating disorders

Eating disorders affect many students. These disorders involve serious disturbances in eating behavior. Examples are overeating or extreme reduction of food intake, as well as irrational concern about body shape or weight. Women are much more likely to develop these disorders than are men, though cases are on the rise among males.

Bulimia involves cycles of excessive eating and forced purges. A person with this disorder might gorge on a pizza, doughnuts, and ice cream and then force herself to vomit. Or she might compensate for overeating with excessive use of laxatives, enemas, or diuretics.

Anorexia nervosa is a potentially fatal illness marked by self-starvation. People with anorexia may practice extended fasting or eat only one kind of food for weeks at a time.

These disorders are not due to a failure of willpower. They are real illnesses in which harmful patterns of eating take on a life of their own.

Eating disorders can lead to many complications, including life-threatening heart conditions and kidney failure. Many people with eating disorders also struggle with depression, substance abuse, and anxiety. They need immediate treatment to stabilize their health. This is usually followed by continuing medical care, counseling, and medication to promote a full recovery.

If you're worried you might have an eating disorder, visit a doctor, campus health service, or local public health clinic. If you see signs of an eating disorder in someone else, express your concern with "I" messages, as explained in Chapter 9: Communicating.

For more information, contact the National Eating Disorders Association at 1-800-931-2237 or online at www.nationaleatingdisorders.org.

11

joyfull/Shutterstock.com

Choose to EXERCISE

Our bodies need to be exercised. The world ran on muscle power back in the era when we had to hunt down a woolly mammoth every few weeks and drag it back to the cave. Now we can grab a burger at a drive-up window. Today we need to make a special effort to exercise.

Exercise promotes weight control and reduces the symptoms of depression. It also helps to prevent heart attack, diabetes, and several forms of cancer.[6] Exercise also refreshes your body and your mind. If you're stuck on a math problem or blocked on writing a paper, take an exercise break. Chances are that you'll come back with a fresh perspective and some new ideas.

If you get moving, you'll create lean muscles, a strong heart, and an alert brain. If the word *exercise* turns you off, think *physical activity* instead. Here are some things you can do:

Stay active throughout the day. Park a little farther from work or school. Do your heart a favor by walking some extra blocks. Take the stairs instead of riding elevators. For an extra workout, climb two stairs at a time.

An hour of daily activity is ideal, but do whatever you can. Some activity is better than none.

No matter what you do, ease into it. For example, start by walking briskly for at least 15 minutes every day. Increase that time gradually, and add a little jogging.

Adapt to your campus environment. Look for exercise facilities on campus. Search for classes in aerobics, swimming, volleyball, basketball, golf, tennis, and other sports. Intramural sports are another option. School can be a great place to get in shape.

Do what you enjoy. Stay active with aerobic activities that you enjoy. You might like martial arts, kickboxing, yoga, ballroom dance classes, stage combat classes, or mountain climbing. Check your school catalog for such courses.

Vary your routine. Find several activities that you like to do, and rotate them throughout the year. Your main form of activity during winter might be ballroom dancing, riding an exercise bike, or skiing. In summer, you could switch to outdoor sports.

Whenever possible, choose weight-bearing activities such as walking, running, or stair climbing.

Get active early. Work out first thing in the morning. Then it's done for the day. Make it part of your daily routine, just like brushing your teeth.

Exercise with other people. Making exercise a social affair can add a fun factor and raise your level of commitment.

Join a gym without fear. Many health clubs welcome people who are just starting to get in shape.

Look for gradual results. If your goal is to lose weight, be patient. Because 1 pound equals 3,500 calories, you might feel tempted to reduce weight loss to a simple formula: *Let's see … if I burn away just 100 calories each day through exercise, I should lose 1 pound every 35 days.*

Actually, the relationship between exercise and weight loss is complex. Many factors—including individual differences in metabolism and the type of exercise you do—affect the amount of weight you actually lose.[7]

When you step on the bathroom scale, look for small changes over time rather than sudden, dramatic losses. Gradual weight loss is more healthy, anyway—and easier to sustain over the long term.

Weight loss is just one potential benefit of exercise. Choosing to exercise can lift your mood, increase your stamina, strengthen your bones, stabilize your joints, and help prevent heart disease. It can also reduce your risk of high blood pressure, diabetes, and several forms of cancer. If you do resistance training—such as weight machines or elastic-band workouts—you'll strengthen your muscles as well. For a complete fitness program, add stretching exercises to enjoy increased flexibility.[8]

Before beginning any vigorous exercise program, consult a health care professional. This is critical if you are overweight, over age 60, in poor condition, or a heavy smoker, or if you have a history of health problems. ■

You're One Click Away...
from discovering more ways online to follow through on your exercise goals.

iStockphoto.com/AlbanyPictures

CHOOSE EMOTIONAL HEALTH

The number of students in higher education who have emotional health problems is steadily increasing.[9] According to the American College Health Association, 31 percent of college students report that they have felt so depressed that it was difficult to function. Almost half of students say that they've felt overwhelming anxiety, and 60 percent report that they've felt very lonely.[10]

Emotional health includes many factors: your skill at managing stress, your ability to build loving relationships, your capacity to meet the demands of school and work, and your beliefs about your ability to succeed. People with mental illness have thoughts, emotions, or behaviors that consistently interfere with these areas of life.

You can take simple and immediate steps to prevent emotional health problems or cope with them if they do occur. Remember that strategies for managing test-related stress can help you manage *any* form of stress. (See "Let go of test anxiety" on page 196.) Here are some other suggestions to promote your emotional health.

Take care of your body. Your thoughts and emotions can get scrambled if you go too long feeling hungry or tired. Follow the suggestions in this chapter for eating, exercise, and sleep.

Solve problems. Although you can't "fix" a bad feeling in the same way that you can fix a machine, you can choose to change a situation associated with that feeling. There might be a problem that needs a solution. You can use feeling bad as your motivation to solve that problem.

Sometimes an intense feeling of sadness, anger, or fear is related to a specific situation in your life. Describe the problem. Then brainstorm solutions and choose one to implement. Reducing your course load, cutting back on hours at work, getting more financial aid, delegating a task, or taking some other concrete action might solve the problem and help you feel better.

Stay active. A related strategy is to do something—*anything* that's constructive, even if it's not a solution to a specific problem.

11

For example, mop the kitchen floor. Clean out your dresser drawers. Iron your shirts. This sounds silly, but it works.

The basic principle is that you can separate emotions from actions. It is appropriate to feel miserable when you do. It's normal to cry and express your feelings. It is also possible to go to class, study, work, eat, and feel miserable at the same time. Unless you have a diagnosable problem with anxiety or depression, you can continue your normal activities until the misery passes.

Japanese psychiatrist Morita Masatake, a contemporary of Sigmund Freud, based his whole approach to treatment on this insight: We can face our emotional pain directly and still take constructive action. One of Masatake's favorite suggestions for people who felt depressed was that they tend a garden.[11]

Focus on one task at a time. It's easy to feel stressed if you dwell on how much you have to accomplish this year, this term, this month, or even this week. One solution is to plan using the suggestions in Chapter 3: Time & Money.

Remember that an effective plan for the day does two things. First, it clarifies what you're choosing *not* to do today. (Tasks that you plan to do in the future are listed on your calendar or to-do list.) Second, an effective plan reduces your day to a series of concrete tasks—such as making phone calls, going to classes, running errands, or reading chapters—that you can do one at a time.

If you feel overwhelmed, just find the highest-priority task on your to-do list. Do it with total attention until it's done. Then go back to your list for the next high-priority task. Do *it* with total attention. Savor the feeling of mastery and control that comes with crossing each task off your list.

Don't believe everything you think. According to Albert Ellis and other cognitive psychologists, stress results not from events in our lives, but from the way we *think* about those events.[12] If we believe that people should always behave in exactly the way we expect them to, for instance, we set ourselves up for misery. The same happens if we believe that events should always turn out exactly as we want.

There are two main ways to deal with such thoughts. First, don't believe them. Dispute such thoughts and replace them with more realistic ones: *I can control my own behavior, but not the behavior of others.* And: *Some events are beyond my control.* Changing our beliefs can reduce our stress significantly.

Second, you can just release stress-producing thoughts without disputing them. Meditation is a way to do this. While meditating, you simply notice your thoughts as they arise and pass. Instead of reacting to them, you observe them. Eventually, your stream of thinking slows down. You might enter a state of deep relaxation that also yields life-changing insights.

Many religious organizations offer meditation classes. You can also find meditation instruction through health maintenance organizations, YMCAs or YWCAs, and community education programs.

Remember that emotional pain is not a sickness. Emotional pain has gotten a bad name. This reputation is undeserved. There

Choose to rest

A lack of rest can decrease your immunity to illness and impair your performance in school. You still might be tempted to cut back drastically on your sleep once in a while for an all-night study session. Instead, read Chapter 3: Time & Money for some time management ideas. Depriving yourself of sleep is a choice you can avoid.

If you have trouble falling asleep, experiment with the following suggestions:

- Exercise daily. For many people, regular exercise promotes sounder sleep. However, finish exercising several hours before you want to go to sleep.

- Avoid naps during the daytime.

- Monitor your caffeine intake, especially in the afternoon and evening.

- Avoid using alcohol to feel sleepy. Drinking alcohol late in the evening can disrupt your sleep during the night.

- Develop a sleep ritual—a regular sequence of calming activities that end your day. You might take a warm bath and do some light reading. Turn off the TV and computer at least 1 hour before you go to bed.

- Keep your sleeping room cool.

- Keep a regular schedule for going to sleep and waking up.

- Sleep in the same place each night. When you're there, your body gets the message: "It's time to go to sleep."

- Practice relaxation techniques while lying in bed. A simple one is to count your breaths and release distracting thoughts as they arise.

- Make tomorrow's to-do list before you go to sleep so you won't lie there worrying that tomorrow you'll forget about something you need to do.

- Get up and study or do something else until you're tired.

- See a doctor if sleeplessness persists.

is nothing wrong with feeling bad. It's okay to feel miserable, depressed, sad, upset, angry, dejected, gloomy, or unhappy.

It might not be pleasant to feel bad, but it can be good for you. Often, bad is an appropriate way to feel. When you leave a place you love, sadness is natural. When you lose a friend or lover, misery might be in order. When someone treats you badly, it is probably appropriate to feel angry. When a loved one dies, it is necessary to grieve. The grief might appear in the form of depression, sadness, or anger.

There is nothing wrong with extreme emotional pain. If depression, sadness, or anger persists, then get help. Otherwise, allow yourself to experience these emotions. They're often appropriate.

Sometimes we allow ourselves to feel bad only if we have a good reason. For example: "Well, I feel very sad, but that is because I just found out my best friend is moving to Europe." It's all right to know the reason why you are sad. It's also fine not to know. You can feel bad for no apparent reason. The reason doesn't matter. Because you cannot directly control any feeling, simply accept it.

There's no way to predict how long emotional pain will last. The main point is that it does not last forever. There's no need to let a broken heart stop your life. Although you can find abundant advice on the subject, just remember a simple and powerful idea: This too shall pass.

Sometimes other people—friends or family members, for example—have a hard time letting you feel bad. They might be worried that they did something wrong and want to make it better. They want you to quit feeling bad. Tell them you will—eventually. Assure them that you will feel good again, but that for right now you just want to feel bad.

Share what you're thinking and feeling. Revealing your inner world with a family member or friend is a powerful way to gain perspective. The simple act of describing a problem can sometimes reveal a solution or give you a fresh perspective.

Get help. Remember a basic guideline about *when* to seek help: whenever problems with your thinking, moods, or behavior consistently interfere with your ability to sleep, eat, go to class, work, or create positive relationships.

You can get help at the student health center on campus. This is not just a service for treating colds, allergies, and flu symptoms. Counselors expect to help students deal with adjustment to campus, changes in mood, academic problems, and drug abuse and dependence.

Students with anxiety disorders, clinical depression, bipolar disorder, and other diagnoses might get referred to a professional outside the student health center. The referral process can take time, so seek help right away. Your tuition helps to pay for these services. It's smart to use them now.

You can find resources to promote emotional health even if your campus doesn't offer counseling services. Start with a personal physician—one person who can coordinate all of your health care. (For suggestions, go to your school's health center.) A personal physician can refer you to another health professional if it seems appropriate.

These two suggestions can also work after you graduate. Promoting emotional health is a skill to use for the rest of your life. ■

You're One Click Away...
from finding more pathways to robust emotional health online.

Master Employees
IN ACTION

You're One Click Away...
from a video about Master Students in Action.

" *In college I always enjoyed running. It helped me stay healthy and clear my head. It is even more important to me now since it helps me deal with the pressures of my job while also countering the fact that the majority of my time at work is spent sitting at a desk.* "

—*Jane Casson, Copywriter*

11

Developing a strong
SELF-IMAGE

Your *self-image* is the way you see yourself. It includes beliefs and feelings about your potential to succeed.

Self-image can erode in ways that are imperceptible to us. Over time, we can gradually buy into a reduced sense of our own possibilities in life. These views make it less likely that

we'll take risks, create a vision for the future, and set and achieve goals.

Self-image is related to what psychologists call *self-efficacy*. This field of research is closely associated with psychologist Albert Bandura of Stanford University.[13] *Efficacy* refers to the ability to produce a desired effect. *Self-efficacy* refers to your belief in your ability to determine the outcomes of events—especially outcomes that are strongly influenced by your own behavior.

A strong self-image allows you to tackle problems with confidence, set long-term goals, and see difficult tasks as creative challenges rather than potential disasters. With a strong self-image, you believe that your action counts. You see yourself as someone who can make a positive difference in the world.

No one has to live with a poor self-image. Your self-image is flexible. It changes over time, and you can influence it with the following strategies.

> **The challenge of higher education often puts our self-image at risk. The rigors of class work, financial pressures, and new social settings can test our ability to adapt and change.**

SET UP SITUATIONS IN WHICH YOU CAN WIN

Start by planning scenarios in which you can succeed. Bandura calls these "mastery situations." For example, set yourself up for success by breaking a big project down into small, doable tasks.

Then tackle and complete the first task. This accomplishment can help you move on to the next task with higher self-efficacy. Success breeds more success.

SET GOALS WITH CARE

If you want to boost your self-image, be picky about your goals. According to the research, goals that you find easy to meet will not make much of a difference in the way you see yourself. Instead, set goals that call on you to overcome obstacles, make persistent effort, and even fail occasionally.

At the same time, it is important to avoid situations in which you are *often* likely to fail. Setting goals that you have little chance of meeting can undermine your self-image. Ideal goals are both challenging *and* achievable.

ADOPT A MODEL

In self-efficacy research, the word *model* has a special definition. This term refers to someone who is similar to you in key ways and who succeeds in the kinds of situations in which you want to succeed. To find a model, gather with people who share your interests. Look for people with whom you have a lot in common— and who have mastered the skills that you want to acquire. Besides demonstrating strategies and techniques for you to use, these people hold out a real possibility of success for you.

CHANGE THE CONVERSATION ABOUT YOURSELF

Monitor what you say and think about yourself. Remember that your self-talk might be so habitual that you don't even notice it. Whether or not you are fully aware of these thoughts, they can make or break your sense of self-image.

Pay close attention. Notice when you speak or think negatively about yourself. Telling the truth about your weaknesses is one thing. Consistently underrating yourself is another. In the conversation about yourself, go for balance. Tell the truth about the times you set a goal and missed it. Also take the time to write and speak about the goals you meet and what works well in your life.

People with a strong self-image attribute their failures to skills that they currently lack—and that they can acquire in the future. This approach chooses not to look on failures as permanent, personal defects. Rather than saying, "I just don't have what it takes to become a skilled test taker," say, "I can adopt techniques to help me remember key facts even when I feel stressed."

INTERPRET STRESS IN A NEW WAY

Achieving your goals might place you right in the middle of situations in which you feel stress. You might find yourself meeting new people, leading a meeting, speaking in public, or doing something else that you've never done before. That can feel scary.

Remember that stress comes in two forms—thoughts and physical sensations. Thoughts can include mental pictures of yourself making mistakes or being publicly humiliated. They also can be statements such as "This is the worst possible thing that could happen to me." Sensations can include shortness of breath, dry mouth, knots in the stomach, tingling feelings, headaches, and other forms of discomfort.

The way you interpret stress as you become aware of it can make a big difference in your self-image. During moments when you want to do well, you might rely on a stream of personal impressions to judge your performance. In those moments, see whether you can focus your attention. Rather than attaching negative interpretations to your experience of stress, simply notice your thoughts and sensations. Release them instead of dwelling on them or trying to resist them. As you observe yourself over time, you might find that the physical sensations associated with your sense of stress and your sense of excitement are largely the same. Instead of viewing these sensations as signs of impending doom when they are caused by stress, see them as a boost of energy and enthusiasm that you can channel into performing well.

COMPARE YOURSELF TO YOURSELF

Our own failures are often more dramatic to us than the failures of others. Our own successes are often more invisible to us. When we're unsure of ourselves, we can look in any direction and see people who seem more competent and more confident than we do. When we start the comparison game, we open the door to self-doubt.

There is a way to play the comparison game and win: Instead of comparing yourself with others, compare yourself to yourself. Measure success in terms of self-improvement rather than in terms of triumphs over others. Take time to note any progress you've made toward your goals over time. Write Discovery Statements about that progress. Celebrate your success in any area of life, no matter how small that success might seem.

SURROUND YOURSELF WITH SUPPORT

Seek out people who share your values and support your goals. This might mean going beyond your family. If you are the first student in your family to attend college, for example, your family might support you and still not understand your experiences. Find additional support by joining a study group, getting to know instructors, meeting with your advisor, and getting involved in a campus organization.

When you find supportive people, be willing to receive their encouragement. Instead of deflecting compliments ("It was nothing"), fully receive the positive things that others say about you ("Thank you"). Also, take public credit for your successes. "Well, I was just lucky" can change to "I worked hard to achieve that goal." ■

You're One Click Away...
from learning more ways to change your self-image online.

11

SUICIDE is no solution

While preparing for and entering higher education, people typically face major changes. The stress they feel can lead to depression and anxiety. Both are risk factors for suicide—the second leading cause of death on college campuses.[14] To prevent suicide, start by recognizing danger signals:

- **Talking about suicide.** People who attempt suicide often talk about it first. They might say, "I just don't want to live anymore." Or "I want you to know that no matter what happens, I've always loved you." Or "Tomorrow night at 7:30, I'm going to end it all with a gun."

- **Planning for it.** People planning suicide will sometimes put their affairs in order. They might close bank accounts, give away or sell precious possessions, or make or update a will. They might even develop specific plans on how to kill themselves.

- **Having a history of previous attempts.** The American Foundation for Suicide Prevention estimates that up to 50 percent of the people who kill themselves have attempted suicide at least once before.[15]

- **Dwelling on problems.** Expressing extreme helplessness or hopelessness about solving problems can indicate that someone might be considering suicide.

- **Feeling depressed.** Although not everyone who is depressed attempts suicide, almost everyone who attempts suicide feels depressed.

TAKE PROMPT ACTION

Most often, suicide can be prevented. If you suspect that someone you know is considering suicide, do whatever it takes to ensure the person's safety. Let this person know that you will persist until you are certain that she's safe. Any of the following actions can help:

- **Take it seriously.** Taking suicidal comments seriously is especially important when you hear them from young adults. Suicide threats are more common in this age group and might be dismissed as normal. Err on the side of being too careful rather than negligent.

- **Listen fully.** Encourage the person at risk to express thoughts and feelings appropriately. If he claims that he doesn't want to talk, be inviting, be assertive, and be persistent. Be totally committed to listening.

- **Speak powerfully.** Let the person at risk know that you care. Trying to talk someone out of suicide or minimizing problems is generally useless. Acknowledge that problems are serious and that they can be solved. Point out that suicide is a permanent solution to a temporary problem—and that help is available.

- **Get professional help.** Suggest that the person see a mental health professional. If she resists help, offer to schedule the appointment for her and to take her to it. If this fails, get others involved, including the depressed person's family or school personnel.

> Trying to talk someone out of suicide or minimizing problems is generally useless. Acknowledge that problems are serious and that they can be solved. Point out that suicide is a permanent solution to a temporary problem.

- **Remove access to firearms.** Most suicides are attempted with guns. Get rid of any guns that might be around. Also remove all drugs and razors.

- **Ask the person to sign a "no-suicide contract."** Get a promise, in writing, that the person will not hurt himself before speaking to you. A written promise can provide the "excuse" he needs not to take action.

- **Handle the event as an emergency.** If a situation becomes a crisis, do not leave the person alone. Call a crisis hotline, 911, or a social service agency. If necessary, take the person to the nearest hospital emergency room, clinic, or police station.

- **Follow up.** Someone in danger of attempting suicide might resist further help even if your first intervention succeeds. Ask the person whether she's keeping counseling appointments and taking prescribed medication. Help this person apply strategies for solving problems. Stay in touch.

TAKE CARE OF YOURSELF

If you ever begin to think about committing suicide, remember that you can apply any of the above suggestions to yourself. For example, look for warning signs and take them seriously. Seek out someone you trust. Tell this person how you feel. If necessary, make an appointment to see a counselor, and ask someone to accompany you. When you're at risk, you deserve the same compassion that you'd willingly extend to another person.

Find out more from the American Foundation for Suicide Prevention at 1-800-273-8255 or www.afsp.org. Another excellent resource is the It Gets Better Project at www.itgetsbetter.org. ■

Choose to STAY SAFE

TAKE GENERAL PRECAUTIONS

Three simple actions can significantly increase your personal safety. One is to always lock doors when you're away from home. If you live in a dorm, follow the policies for keeping the front doors secure. Don't let an unauthorized person walk in behind you. If you commute to school or have a car on campus, keep your car doors locked.

The second action is to avoid walking alone, especially at night. Many schools offer shuttle buses to central campus locations. Use them. As a backup, carry enough spare cash for a taxi ride.

Third, be prepared for a crisis. Ask your instructors about what to do in classroom emergencies. Look for emergency phones along the campus routes that you normally walk. You can always use your cell phone to call 911 for help.

Also, be willing to make that call when you see other people in unsafe situations. For example, you might be at a party with a friend who drinks too much and collapses. In this situation, some

© iStockphoto.com/Allkindza

underage students might hesitate to call for help. They fear getting charged with illegal alcohol possession. Don't make this mistake. Every minute that you delay calling 911 puts your friend at further risk.

PREVENT SEXUAL ASSAULT

You need to know how to prevent sexual assault while you're on campus. This problem could be more common at your school than you think. People often hesitate to report rape for many reasons, such as fear, embarrassment, and concerns that others won't believe them.

Both women and men can take steps to prevent rape from occurring in the first place:

- Get together with a group of people for a tour of the campus. Make a special note of danger spots, such as unlighted paths and unguarded buildings. Keep in mind that rape can occur during daylight and in well-lit places.

- Ask whether your school has escort services for people taking evening classes. These might include personal escorts, car escorts, or both. If you do take an evening class, ask whether there are security officers on duty before and after the class.

- Take a course or seminar on self-defense and rape prevention. To find these courses, check with your student counseling service, community education center, or local library.

If you are raped, get medical care right away. Go to the nearest rape crisis center, hospital, student health service, or police station. Also arrange for follow-up counseling. It's your decision whether to report the crime. Filing a report does not mean that you have to press charges. And if you do choose to press charges later, having a report on file can help your case. ■

Observe thyself

You are an expert on your body. You are more likely to notice changes before anyone else does. Pay attention to these changes. They are often your first clue about the need for medical treatment or intervention. Watch for signs such as the following:

- Weight loss of more than 10 pounds in 10 weeks with no apparent cause
- A sore, scab, or ulcer that does not heal in 3 weeks
- A skin blemish or mole that bleeds, itches, or changes size, shape, or color
- Persistent or severe headaches
- Sudden vomiting that is not preceded by nausea
- Fainting spells
- Double vision

- Blood that is coughed up or vomited
- Black and tarry bowel movements
- Rectal bleeding
- Pink, red, or unusually cloudy urine
- Discomfort or difficulty when urinating or during sexual intercourse
- Lumps or thickening in a breast
- Vaginal bleeding between menstrual periods or after menopause

If you are experiencing any of these symptoms, get help from your doctor or campus health service—*before* a minor illness or injury leads to more-serious problems.

11

Choose sexual health:
PREVENT INFECTION

People with a sexually transmitted infection (STI) might feel no symptoms for years and not even discover that they are infected. Know how to protect yourself.

STIs can result from vaginal sex, oral sex, anal sex, or any other way that people contact semen, vaginal secretions, and blood. Without treatment, some of these infections can lead to blindness, infertility, cancer, heart disease, or even death.[16]

There are at least 25 kinds of STIs. Common examples are chlamydia, gonorrhea, and syphilis. Sexual contact can also spread the human papillomavirus (HPV, the most common cause of cervical cancer) and the human immunodeficiency virus (HIV, the virus that causes AIDS).

Most STIs can be cured if treated early. (Herpes and AIDS are important exceptions.) Prevention is better. Some guidelines for prevention follow.

Abstain from sex. Abstain from sex, or have sex exclusively with one person who is free of infection and has no other sex partners. These are the only ways to be absolutely safe from STIs.

Talk to your partner. Before you have sex with someone, talk about the risk of STIs. If you are infected, tell your partner.

Use condoms. Male condoms are thin membranes stretched over the penis prior to intercourse. Condoms prevent semen from entering the vagina. For the most protection, use latex condoms— not ones made of lambskin or polyurethane. Use a condom every time you have sex, and for any type of sex.

Condoms are not guaranteed to work all of the time. They can break, leak, or slip off. In addition, condoms cannot protect you from STIs that are spread by contact with herpes sores or warts.

Talk to your doctor before using condoms, lubricants, spermicides, and other products that contain nonoxynol-9. This chemical can irritate a woman's vagina and cervix and can actually increase the risk of STIs.

Stay sober. People are more likely to have unsafe sex when drunk or high.

Do not share needles. Sharing needles or other paraphernalia with other drug users can spread STIs.

Take action soon after you have sex. Urinate soon after you have sex. Wash your genitals with soap and water.

Get vaccinated. Vaccines are available to prevent hepatitis B and HPV infection. See your doctor.

Get screened for STIs. The only way to find out whether you're infected is to be tested by a health care professional. If you have sex with more than one person, get screened for STIs at least once each year. Do this even if you have no symptoms. Remember that many schools offer free STI screening.

The more people you have sex with, the greater your risk of STIs. You are at risk even if you have sex only once with one person who is infected.

The U.S. Centers for Disease Control and Prevention recommends chlamydia screening for all sexually active women under age 26. Women age 25 and older should be screened if they have a new sex partner or multiple sex partners.[17]

Recognize the symptoms of STIs. Symptoms include swollen glands with fever and aching; itching around the vagina; vaginal discharge; pain during sex or when urinating; sore throat following oral sex; anal pain after anal sex; sores, blisters, scabs, or warts on the genitals, anus, tongue, or throat; rashes on the palms of your hands or soles of your feet; dark urine; loose and light-colored stools; and unexplained fatigue, weight loss, and night sweats.

Get treated right away. If you think you have an STI, go to your doctor, campus health service, or local public health clinic. Early treatment might prevent serious health problems. To avoid infecting other people, abstain from sex until you are treated and cured. ■

You're One Click Away...
from learning more about preventing sexually transmitted infections online.

Choose sexual health:
PREVENT UNWANTED PREGNANCY

You and your partner can avoid unwanted pregnancy. There are many options. But choosing among them can be a challenge. Think about whether you want to have children someday, the number of sexual partners you have, your comfort with using a birth control method, possible side effects, and your overall health.

Even birth control methods that are usually effective can fail when used incorrectly. To prevent pregnancy, make sure you understand your chosen method. Then use it *every* time you have sex. Start with the ideas listed below. Also talk to your doctor.

Abstinence. Abstinence is choosing *not* to have sex—vaginal, oral, or anal. You might feel pressured to change your mind about this choice. However, many people exist happily without having sex. Abstinence, when practiced without exception, is the only sure way to prevent pregnancy and sexually transmitted infections (STIs).

Natural family planning. Natural family planning is based on abstaining from sex when a woman is most fertile (likely to become pregnant). It is sometimes called the "rhythm method." For women with a regular menstrual cycle, this fertile time is about 9 days each month. It includes the days right before and after ovulation. There are no side effects with natural family planning. However, it is difficult to know for sure when a woman is ovulating. Before you consider natural family planning, talk to a qualified instructor.

Barrier methods. Several methods of birth control create barriers that prevent sperm from reaching a woman's egg. One is the sponge. This is a soft disk made of polyurethane that contains nonoxynol-9—a spermicide (chemical that kills sperm). To use a sponge, a woman runs it under water and then places it inside her vagina to cover the cervix (the opening to the womb). If you choose to use the sponge, ask your doctor for instructions on when to remove it after you have intercourse. Keep in mind that nonoxynol-9 can irritate tissue in the vagina and anus with frequent use, making it easier for STIs to enter the body. Some

women are sensitive to nonoxynol-9, so the sponge is not an option for them.

Other barrier methods include the diaphragm, cervical cap (FemCap), and cervical shield (Lea's Shield). These are cups made out of silicone or latex. The woman fills them with a spermicide and then places them inside her vagina to cover the cervix before having sex. The diaphragm and cervical cap come in various sizes, meaning that a woman has to see her doctor to get fitted for one. The cervical shield comes in only one size. Again, ask a doctor about when to remove these devices.

Male condoms, another type of barrier, are wrapped over an erect penis before sex. For better protection, use them with a spermicide. Also, use a new condom every time you have sex. The male latex condom is the only form of birth control known to protect against STIs.

If you use male condoms, keep some precautions in mind. Do not use them with oil-based lubricants such as petroleum jelly, lotions, baby oil, or massage oils. All of these can cause condoms to break. Instead, use lubricated condoms or add a water-based lubricant, such as K-Y Jelly. Remember that "natural" condoms—condoms made from lambskin—do not prevent STIs. Also, storing condoms in a warm place—such as a car or wallet—can weaken them and lead to breakage.

Female condoms are made of polyurethane. They are lubricated and placed inside the woman's vagina. Carefully follow the instructions about when to insert the female condom. Use a new condom each time you have sex. Do not use a female condom and a male condom at the same time.

Spermicides come in several forms: tablets, suppositories, cream, film, gel, and foam. They work best with a barrier method, such as a condom, cervical cap, or diaphragm. Note that some spermicides include nonoxynol-9, which can irritate tissue in the vagina and anus and make it easier for STIs to enter the body. Also, vaginal yeast infections can make spermicides less effective.

Hormonal methods. There are several hormonal methods for preventing pregnancy. These methods work by preventing ovulation, fertilization, or implantation of a fertilized egg.

11

An oral contraceptive—the *Pill*—is a synthetic hormone that "tells" a woman's body not to produce eggs. Many kinds are available. Talk to your doctor to make an informed choice. You might be advised to avoid the Pill if you are older than 35 and smoke, if you've had blood clots, or if you've had cancer. Antibiotics can interfere with the Pill, so ask your doctor about other methods of birth control when you're taking this medication.

Women can choose from several methods that release hormones to stop ovulation. These include a skin patch (Ortho Evra), an injection (Depo-Provera), and a vaginal ring (NuvaRing). Again, ask your doctor about possible side effects and for specific instructions on how to use these methods.

Implants. Some devices for preventing pregnancy are placed inside a woman's body and left there for several years. These devices release a hormone that prevents sperm from reaching an egg. They can also prevent a fertilized egg from implanting in the lining of the uterus. The rod (Implanon) goes under the skin of the upper arm. Intrauterine devices (IUDs) go inside a woman's uterus. They include the copper IUD (ParaGard) and the hormonal IUD (Mirena).

Talk to your doctor about how implants are inserted, how long they stay inside you, and which option would be most effective for you.

Emergency contraceptives. When women have vaginal sex without using birth control, or when they use birth control that fails, they can take "morning-after" pills. These pills are taken in two doses, 12 hours apart. The pills release hormones that stop ovulation or stop sperm from fertilizing an egg. This method works best when the pills are taken within 72 hours after sex.

Permanent methods. Some birth control methods are only for people who do not want to have children, or want to stop having children. One method is surgical sterilization. For women this means cutting, tying, or sealing the fallopian tubes (where eggs travel to get implanted in the uterus). Men get a vasectomy, which prevents sperm from going to the penis. Remember that sperm can stay in a man's body for about 3 months after surgery. Use another form of birth control during this time.

Women can also be sterilized without surgery. The doctor inserts an implant (Essure) that causes scar tissue to form in the fallopian tubes. Until the scarring appears—usually in about 3 months—another form of birth control is needed.

Where to get birth control. You can buy condoms, sponges, and spermicides over the counter at a store. Other birth control devices—including morning-after pills for women under age 18—require a prescription.

> Be sure you know how to use your chosen method of birth control. A doctor might assume that you already have this knowledge. If you don't, ask questions freely. Remember that some methods require practice and special techniques.

Note: **Withdrawal does not work.** Withdrawal happens when a man takes his penis out of the woman's vagina before he has an orgasm. Don't rely on this method for birth control. It requires extraordinary self-control. In addition, men can release some sperm before they have an orgasm. This can lead to pregnancy. If the man has an STI, the withdrawal method can pass the infection on to the woman as well.

Evaluate birth control methods. Be sure you know how to use your chosen method of birth control. A doctor might assume that you already have this knowledge. If you don't, ask questions freely. Remember that some methods require practice and special techniques. For example, male condoms have an inside and outside surface, and they work best when there's a little space left at the tip for fluid.

The following chart summarizes the effectiveness of various birth control methods and possible side effects. However, effectiveness rates can only be estimated. The estimates depend on many factors—for example, the health of the people using them, their number of sex partners, and how often they have sex. *Remember that a method can work only if used consistently and correctly.* ■

Method	Failure Rate (number of pregnancies expected per 100 women)	Some Side Effects and Risks
Sterilization surgery for women	Less than 1	• Pain • Bleeding • Complications from surgery • Ectopic (tubal) pregnancy
Sterilization implant for women (Essure)	Less than 1	• Pain • Ectopic (tubal) pregnancy
Sterilization surgery for men	Less than 1	• Pain • Bleeding • Complications from surgery
Implantable rod (Implanon)	Less than 1 Might not work as well for women who are overweight or obese.	• Acne • Weight gain • Ovarian cysts • Mood changes • Depression • Hair loss • Headache • Upset stomach • Dizziness • Sore breasts • Changes in period • Lowered interest in sex
Intrauterine device (ParaGard, Mirena)	Less than 1	• Cramps • Bleeding between periods • Pelvic inflammatory disease • Infertility • Tear or hole in the uterus
Shot/Injection (Depo-Provera)	Less than 1	• Bleeding between periods • Weight gain • Sore breasts • Headaches • Bone loss with long-term use
Oral Contraceptives (combination pill, or "the Pill")	5 Being overweight may increase the chance of getting pregnant while using the Pill.	• Dizziness • Upset stomach • Changes in your period • Changes in mood • Weight gain • High blood pressure • Blood clots • Heart attack • Stroke • New vision problems
Oral contraceptives (continuous/extended use, or "no-period Pill")	5 Being overweight may increase the chance of getting pregnant while using the Pill.	• Same as combination pill • Spotting or bleeding between periods • Hard to know if pregnant
Oral contraceptives (progestin-only pill, or "mini-Pill")	5 Being overweight may increase the chance of getting pregnant while using the Pill.	• Spotting or bleeding between periods • Weight gain • Sore breasts

11

Method	Failure Rate (number of pregnancies expected per 100 women)	Some Side Effects and Risks
Skin patch (Ortho Evra)	5 May not work as well in women weighing more than 198 pounds.	• Similar to side effects for the combination pill • Greater exposure to estrogen than with other methods
Vaginal ring (NuvaRing)	5	• Similar to side effects for the combination pill • Swelling of the vagina • Irritation • Vaginal discharge
Male condom	11–16	• Allergic reactions
Diaphragm with spermicide	15	• Irritation • Allergic reactions • Urinary tract infection • Toxic shock if left in too long
Sponge with spermicide (Today Sponge)	16–32	• Irritation • Allergic reactions • Hard time taking it out • Toxic shock if left in too long
Cervical cap with spermicide	17–23	• Irritation • Allergic reactions • Abnormal Pap smear • Toxic shock if left in too long
Female condom	20	• Irritation • Allergic reactions
Natural family planning (rhythm method)	25	• None
Spermicide alone	30 It works best if used along with a barrier method, such as a condom.	• Irritation • Allergic reactions • Urinary tract infection
Emergency contraception ("morning-after pill," "Plan B")	15 It must be used within 72 hours of having unprotected sex. Should not be used as regular birth control; only in emergencies.	• Upset stomach • Vomiting • Stomach pain • Fatigue • Headache

Source: womenshealth.gov, "Birth Control Methods: Frequently Asked Questions," March 6, 2009, accessed January 9, 2011, from www.4women.gov/faq/birth-control-methods.cfm#b.

Alcohol, tobacco, and drugs:
The Truth

The truth is that getting high can be fun. In our culture, and especially in our media, getting high has become synonymous with having a good time. Even if you don't smoke, drink, or use other drugs, you are certain to come in contact with people who do.

For centuries, human beings have devised ways to change their feelings and thoughts by altering their body chemistry. The Chinese were using marijuana 5,000 years ago. Herodotus, the ancient Greek historian, wrote about a group of people in eastern Europe who threw marijuana on hot stones and inhaled the vapors. More recently, during the American Civil War, customers could buy opium and morphine at neighborhood stores.[18]

Today we are still a drug-using society. Of course, some of those uses are therapeutic and lawful, including taking drugs as prescribed by a doctor or psychiatrist. The problem comes when we turn to drugs as *the* solution to any problem. Are you uncomfortable? Often the first response is "Take something."

We live in times when reaching for instant comfort via chemicals is not only condoned but encouraged. If you're bored, tense, or anxious, you can drink a can of beer, down a glass of wine, or light up a cigarette. If you want to enhance your memory, take a "smart drug," which includes prescription stimulants and caffeine. And these are only the legal options. If you're willing to take risks, you can pick from a large selection of illegal drugs on the street. And if that seems too risky, you can abuse prescription drugs.

There is a big payoff in using alcohol, tobacco, caffeine, cocaine, heroin, or other drugs—or people wouldn't do it. The payoff can be direct, such as relaxation, self-confidence, comfort, excitement, or the ability to pull an all-nighter. At times, the payoff is avoiding rejection or defying authority.

In addition to the payoffs, there are costs. For some people, the cost is much greater than the payoff. Even if drug use doesn't make you broke, it can make you crazy. This is not necessarily the kind of crazy where you dress up like Napoleon. Rather, it is the kind where you care about little else except finding more drugs—friends, school, work, and family be damned.

Substance abuse is only part of the picture. People can also relate to food, gambling, money, sex, and even work in compulsive ways.

Some people will stop abusing a substance or activity when the consequences get serious enough. Other people don't stop. They continue their self-defeating behaviors, no matter the consequences for themselves, their friends, or their families. At that point, the problem goes beyond abuse. It's addiction.

With addiction, the costs can include overdose, infection, and lowered immunity to disease. These can be fatal. Long-term heavy drinking, for example, damages every organ system in the human body. And about 440,000 Americans die annually from the effects of cigarette smoking, including secondhand smoke.[19]

Lectures about the reasons for avoiding alcohol and drug abuse and addiction can be pointless. We don't take care of our bodies because someone says we should. We might take care of ourselves when we see that the costs of using a substance outweigh the benefits.

Acknowledging that alcohol, tobacco, and other drugs can be fun infuriates a lot of people. Remember that this acknowledgment is *not* the same as condoning drug use. The point is this: People are more likely to abstain when they're convinced that using these substances leads to more pain than pleasure over the long run. You choose. It's your body. ■

11

Addiction: How do I know?

People who have problems with drugs and alcohol can hide this fact from themselves and from others. It is also hard to admit that a friend or loved one might have a problem. The purpose of this exercise is to give you an objective way to look at your relationship with drugs or alcohol. There are signals that indicate when drug or alcohol use has become abusive or even addictive. This exercise can also help you determine if a friend might be addicted.

Answer the following questions quickly and honestly with yes, no, or n/a (not applicable). If you are concerned about someone else, rephrase each question using that person's name.

_____ Are you uncomfortable discussing drug abuse or addiction?

_____ Are you worried about your own drug or alcohol use?

_____ Are any of your friends worried about your drug or alcohol use?

_____ Have you ever hidden from a friend, spouse, employer, or coworker the fact that you were drinking? (Pretended you were sober? Covered up alcohol breath?)

_____ Do you sometimes use alcohol or drugs to escape lows rather than to produce highs?

_____ Have you ever gotten angry when confronted about your use?

_____ Do you brag about how much you consume? ("I drank her under the table.")

_____ Do you think about or do drugs when you are alone?

_____ Do you store up alcohol, drugs, cigarettes, or caffeine (in coffee or soft drinks) to be sure you won't run out?

_____ Does having a party almost always include alcohol or drugs?

_____ Do you try to control your drinking so that it won't be a problem? ("I drink only on weekends now." "I never drink before 5:00 p.m." "I drink only beer.")

_____ Do you often explain to other people why you are drinking? ("It's my birthday." "It's my friend's birthday." "It's Veterans Day." "It sure is a hot day.")

_____ Have you changed friends to accommodate your drinking or drug use? ("She's okay, but she isn't excited about getting high.")

_____ Has your behavior changed in the last several months? (Grades down? Lack of interest in a hobby? Change of values or of what you think is moral?)

_____ Do you drink or use drugs to relieve tension? ("What a day! I need a drink.")

_____ Do you have medical problems (stomach trouble, malnutrition, liver problems, anemia) that could be related to drinking or drugs?

_____ Have you ever decided to quit drugs or alcohol and then changed your mind?

_____ Have you had any fights, accidents, or similar incidents related to drinking or drugs in the last year?

_____ Has your drinking or drug use ever caused a problem at home?

_____ Do you envy people who go overboard with alcohol or drugs?

_____ Have you ever told yourself you can quit at any time?

_____ Have you ever been in trouble with the police after or while you were drinking?

_____ Have you ever missed school or work because you had a hangover?

_____ Have you ever had a blackout (a period you can't remember) during or after drinking?

_____ Do you wish that people would mind their own business when it comes to your use of alcohol or drugs?

_____ Is the cost of alcohol or other drugs taxing your budget or resulting in financial stress?

_____ Do you need increasing amounts of the drug to produce the desired effect?

_____ When you stop taking the drug, do you experience withdrawal?

_____ Do you spend a great deal of time obtaining and using alcohol or other drugs?

_____ Have you used alcohol or another drug when it was physically dangerous to do so (such as when driving a car or working with machines)?

_____ Have you been arrested or had other legal problems resulting from the use of a substance?

Now count the number of questions to which you answered yes. If you answered yes more than once, then talk with a professional. This does not necessarily mean that you are addicted. It does point out that alcohol or other drugs are adversely affecting your life. Talk to someone with training in recovery from chemical dependency. Do not rely on the opinion of anyone who lacks such training.

If you filled out this questionnaire about another person and you answered yes two or more times, then your friend might need help. You probably can't provide that help alone. Seek out a counselor or a support group such as Al-Anon. Call the local Alcoholics Anonymous chapter to find out about an Al-Anon meeting near you.

Some facts . . .

The National Institute on Alcohol Abuse and Alcoholism reports the following annual consequences of excessive and underage drinking by college students.[20] For more information, go online to www.collegedrinkingprevention.gov.

Death	1,825 college students between the ages of 18 and 24 die from alcohol-related unintentional injuries, including motor vehicle crashes.
Injury	599,000 students between the ages of 18 and 24 are unintentionally injured under the influence of alcohol.
Assault	696,000 students between the ages of 18 and 24 are assaulted by another student who has been drinking.
Sexual Abuse	97,000 students between the ages of 18 and 24 are victims of alcohol-related sexual assault or date rape.
Unsafe Sex	400,000 students between the ages of 18 and 24 had unprotected sex. More than 100,000 students between the ages of 18 and 24 report having been too intoxicated to know if they consented to having sex.
Academic Problems	About 25 percent of college students report academic consequences of their drinking, including missing class, falling behind, doing poorly on exams or papers, and receiving lower grades overall.
Health Problems/Suicide Attempts	More than 150,000 students develop an alcohol-related health problem, and between 1.2 and 1.5 percent of students indicate that they tried to commit suicide within the past year due to drinking or drug use.
Drunk Driving	3,360,000 students between the ages of 18 and 24 drive under the influence of alcohol.
Vandalism	About 11 percent of college student drinkers report that they have damaged property while under the influence of alcohol.
Property Damage	More than 25 percent of administrators from schools with relatively low drinking levels and over 50 percent from schools with high drinking levels say their campuses have a "moderate" or "major" problem with alcohol-related property damage.
Police Involvement	About 5 percent of 4-year college students are involved with the police or campus security as a result of their drinking, and 110,000 students between the ages of 18 and 24 are arrested for an alcohol-related violation such as public drunkenness or driving under the influence.
Alcohol Abuse and Dependence	31 percent of college students met criteria for a diagnosis of alcohol abuse and 6 percent for a diagnosis of alcohol dependence in the past 12 months, according to questionnaire-based self-reports about their drinking.

11

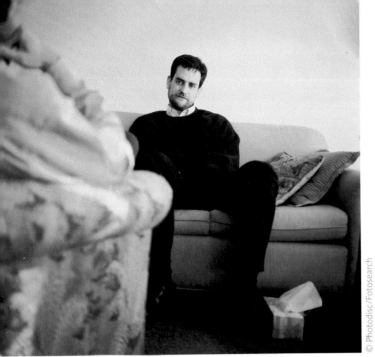
© Photodisc/Fotosearch

FROM
DEPENDENCE
TO
RECOVERY

The technical term for drug addiction is *drug dependence*. This disease is defined by the following:

- *Loss of control*—continued substance use or activity in spite of adverse consequences.

- *Pattern of relapse*—vowing to quit or limit the activity or substance use and continually failing to do so.

- *Tolerance*—the need to take increasing amounts of a substance to produce the desired effect.

- *Withdrawal*—signs and symptoms of physical and mental discomfort or illness when the substance is taken away.[21]

This list can help you determine whether dependence is a barrier for you right now. The items above can apply to anything from cocaine use to compulsive gambling.

If you have a problem with dependence in any form, get help. Consider the following suggestions.

Use responsibly. Show people that you can have a good time without alcohol or other drugs. If you do choose to drink, consume alcohol with food. Pace yourself. Take time between drinks.

Avoid promotions that encourage excess drinking. "Ladies Drink Free" nights are especially dangerous. Women are affected more quickly by alcohol, making them targets for rape. Also stay out of games that encourage people to guzzle. And avoid people who make fun of you for choosing not to drink.

Pay attention. Whenever you use alcohol or another drug, do so with awareness. Then pay attention to the consequences. Act with deliberate decision rather than out of habit or under pressure from others.

Look at the costs. There is always a tradeoff to dependence. Drinking six beers might result in a temporary high, and you will probably remember that feeling. You might feel terrible the morning after consuming six beers, but some people find it easier to forget *that* pain. Stay aware of how dependence makes you feel.

Before going out to a restaurant or bar, set a limit for the number of drinks you will consume. If you consistently break this promise to yourself and experience negative consequences afterward, then you have a problem.

Admit the problem. People with active dependencies are a varied group—rich and poor, young and old, successful and unsuccessful. Often these people do have one thing in common: They are masters of denial. They deny that they are unhappy. They deny that they have hurt anyone. They are convinced that they can quit any time they want. They sometimes become so adept at hiding the problem from themselves that they die.

Take responsibility for recovery. Nobody plans to become an addict. If you have pneumonia, you seek treatment and recover without guilt or shame. Approach drug dependence in the same way. You can take responsibility for your recovery without blame, shame, or guilt.

Get help. People cannot treat dependence on their own. Behaviors tied to dependence are often symptoms of an illness that needs treatment.

Two broad options exist for getting help. One is the growing self-help movement. The other is formal treatment. People recovering from addiction often combine the two.

Many self-help groups are modeled after Alcoholics Anonymous (AA). AA is made up of recovering alcoholics and addicts. These people understand the problems of abuse firsthand,

and they follow a systematic, 12-step approach to living without it. AA is one of the oldest and most successful self-help programs in the world. Chapters of AA welcome people from all walks of life, and you don't have to be an alcoholic to attend most meetings. Programs based on AA principles exist for many other forms of dependence as well.

Some people feel uncomfortable with the AA approach. They can use other options, including private therapy and group therapy. Also investigate organizations such as Women for Sobriety, the Secular Organizations for Sobriety, and Rational Recovery. Use whatever works for you.

Treatment programs are available in almost every community. They might be residential (you live there for weeks or months at a time) or outpatient (you visit several hours a day). Find out where these treatment centers are located by calling a doctor, a mental health professional, or a local hospital. If you don't have insurance, it is usually possible to arrange some other payment program. Cost is no reason to avoid treatment.

Get help for a friend or family member. You might know someone whose behavior meets the criteria for dependence. If so, you have every right to express your concern to that person. Wait until the person is clearheaded. Then mention specific incidents. For example: "Last night you drank five beers when we were at my apartment, and then you wanted to drive home. When I offered to call a cab for you instead, you refused." Also be prepared to offer a source of help, such as the phone number of a local treatment center. ■

You're One Click Away...
from learning more online about recovery from dependence.

Succeed in quitting
SMOKING

There is no magic formula for becoming tobacco-free. However, you can take steps to succeed sooner rather than later. The American Cancer Society suggests the following.[22]

Make a firm choice to quit. All plans for quitting depend on this step. If you're not ready to quit yet, then admit it. Take another look at how smoking affects your health, finances, and relationships.

Set a date. Choose a "quit day" within the next month. That's close enough for a sense of urgency—and time to prepare. Consider a date with special meaning, such as a birthday or anniversary. Let friends and family members know about the big day.

Get personal support. Involve other people. Sign up for a quit smoking class. Attend Nicotine Anonymous or a similar group.

Consider medication. Medication can double your chances of quitting successfully.[23] Options include bupropion hydrochloride (Zyban) and varenicline (Chantix), as well as the nicotine patch, gum, nasal spray, inhaler, and lozenge.

Prepare the environment. Right before your quit day, get rid of all cigarettes and ashtrays at home and at work. Stock up on oral substitutes such as sugarless gum, candy, and low-fat snacks.

Deal with cravings for cigarettes. Distract yourself with exercise or another physical activity. Breathe deeply. Tell yourself that you can wait just a little while longer until the craving passes. Even the strongest urges to smoke will pass. Avoid alcohol use, which can increase cravings.

Learn from relapses. If you break down and light up a cigarette, don't judge yourself. Quitting often requires several attempts. Think back over your past plans for quitting and how to improve on them. Every relapse contains a lesson about how to succeed next time.

11

WARNING: ADVERTISING *can be dangerous to* YOUR HEALTH

The average American is exposed to hundreds of advertising messages per day. Unless you are stranded on a desert island, you are affected by advertising.

Advertising serves a useful function. It helps us make choices about how we spend our money. We can choose among thousands of companies that provide goods and services. Advertising makes us aware of the options.

Advertising also plays on our emotions. And some ads are dangerously manipulative.

Consider how advertising can affect your health. Advertising alcohol, tobacco, pain relievers, and other health-related products is a big business. Much of the revenue earned by newspapers, magazines, radio, television, and Web sites comes from ads for these products. This means that advertisers are a major source of information about health and illness.

Advertising influences our food choices. The least nutritious foods often bring in the most advertising money. So, advertisers portray the primary staples of our diet as sugary breakfast cereals, candy bars, and soft drinks.

Ads for alcohol glorify drinking. Advertisers imply that daily drinking is the norm. Pleasant experiences are enhanced by drinking. Holidays naturally include alcohol. Parties are a flop without it. Relationships are more romantic over cocktails. Everybody drinks.

Advertising also targets our emotional health. The message behind many ads is: *Buying our product will make you okay*. This message is used to sell clothes, makeup, and hair products to make us look okay; drugs, alcohol, and food to make us feel okay; perfumes, toothpaste, and deodorants to make us smell okay.

According to many ads, buying the right product is essential to having the right relationships in our lives.

A related problem concerns images of women. Ads give us the impression that women love to spend hours discussing floor wax, deodorants, tampons, and laundry detergent—and that they think constantly about losing weight and looking sexy. In some ads, women handle everything from kitchen to bedroom to boardroom—true superwomen.

Images such as these are demeaning to women and damaging to men. Women lose when they allow their self-image to be influenced by ads. Men lose when they expect real-life women to look and act like the women on television.

Advertising creates illusions. The next time you're in a crowd, notice how few people look like those in ads.

Advertising often excludes people of color. If our perceptions were based solely on advertising, we would be hard-pressed to know that our society is racially and ethnically diverse. See how many examples of cultural stereotypes you can find in the ads you encounter this week.

Use advertising as a continual opportunity to develop the qualities of a critical thinker. Every time you're exposed to an ad, ask: What's the main message, and what's the evidence for it?

Stay aware of how a multibillion-dollar industry affects your health. ■

JOURNAL ENTRY 24
Discovery/Intention Statement

Advertisements and your health

Think of a time when—after seeing an advertisement or a commercial—you craved a certain food or drink, or you really wanted to buy something. Describe a specific ad and exactly how it affected you.

I discovered that I . . .

_____

_____

_____

Now describe anything you'd like to do differently in the future when you notice that advertising affects you in the way you just described.

I intend to . . .

_____

_____

_____

masterstudentprofile

Randy Pausch

(1960–2008) Pausch was a professor at Carnegie Mellon University, who, shortly after being diagnosed with pancreatic cancer, gave a "last lecture"—a reflection on his personal and professional journey—that became a hit on YouTube (this lecture was later adapted into a book of the same title). He devoted the remaining 9 months of his life to creating a legacy.

It's a thrill to fulfill your own childhood dreams, but as you get older, you may find that enabling the dreams of others is even more fun.

When I was teaching at the University of Virginia in 1993, a twenty-two-year-old artist-turned-computer-graphics-wiz named Tommy Burnett wanted a job on my research team. After we talked about his life and goals, he suddenly said, "Oh, and I have always had this childhood dream."

Anyone who uses "childhood" and "dream" in the same sentence usually gets my attention.

"And what is your dream, Tommy?" I asked.

"I want to work on the next *Star Wars* film," he said.

Remember, this was in 1993. The last *Star Wars* movie had been made in 1983, and there were no concrete plans to make any more. I explained this. "That's a tough dream to have because it'll be hard to see it through," I told him. "Word is that they're finished making *Star Wars* films."

"No," he said, "they're going to make more, and when they do, I'm going to work on them. That's my plan."

Tommy was six years old when the first *Star Wars* film came out in 1977. "Other kids wanted to be Hans Solo," he told me. "Not me. I wanted to be the guy who made the special effects—the space ships, the planets, the robots."

He told me that, as a boy, he read the most technical *Star Wars* articles he could find. He had all the books that explained how the models were built, and how the special effects were achieved. . . . I figured Tommy's big dream would never happen, but it might serve him well somehow. I could use a dreamer like that. I knew from my NFL desires that even if he didn't achieve his, they could serve him well, so I asked him to join our research team. . . .

When I moved to Carnegie Mellon, every member of my team from the University of Virginia came with me—everyone except Tommy. He couldn't make the move. Why? Because he had been hired by producer/director George Lucas' company, Industrial Light & Magic. And it's worth noting that they didn't hire him for his dream; they hired him for his skills. In his time with our research group, he had become an outstanding programmer in the Python language, which as luck would have it, was the language of choice in their shop. Luck is indeed where preparation meets opportunity.

It's not hard to guess where this story is going. Three new *Star Wars* films would be made—in 1999, 2002, and 2005—and Tommy ended up working on all of them.

On *Star Wars Episode II: Attack of the Clones,* Tommy was a lead technical director. There was an incredible fifteen-minute battle scene on a rocky red planet, pitting clones against droids, and Tommy was the guy who planned it all out. He and his team used photos of the Utah desert to create a virtual landscape for the battle. Talk about cool jobs. Tommy had one that let him spend each day on another planet.

RANDY PAUSCH . . . was energetic.
YOU . . . can build energy with effective habits for eating, sleeping, and managing stress.

You're One Click Away...
from learning more about Randy Pausch online at the Master Student Profiles. You can also visit the Master Student Hall of Fame to learn about other master students.

©iStockphoto.com/Mustang_79

FIVE Cs
FOR YOUR CAREER

CHARACTER • CRITICAL THINKING • CREATIVE THINKING • COLLABORATION • COMMUNICATION

You don't need another lecture about the health risks of drug dependence, unprotected sex, sleep deprivation, and a high-calorie diet. You already know about that stuff. What people might forget, however, is that poor health can hurt their chances for getting a job, keeping a job, earning more money, and enjoying their career over the long term.

Discover the link between health and character. One quality of a master student is a strong work ethic. This implies showing up for work, staying alert, and tackling tasks with energy. Employers reward people with these characteristics, and the strategies in this chapter can help you demonstrate them.

Think creatively to protect your emotional health. When the economy contracts, competition for jobs increases. People who are persistent and flexible in their strategies will gain an edge.

Remember a simple and commonly overlooked strategy for thinking creatively about job hunting: If one approach fails to work for you, then use another one. Do this even if you assumed it's an approach you'd never use.

Keep in mind that reading help-wanted ads and sending out résumés are just two common approaches to job hunting. Others are networking, going to state and federal employment agencies, working temporary jobs, volunteering, taking a part-time job while looking for a full-time position, joining a job club, starting a business, and directly approaching companies that interest you—whether or not they have an advertised job opening.

Skilled job hunters stay optimistic by staying flexible. If you've sent out 100 résumés that failed to generate any job interviews, then sending out another 100 might not be the best use of your time and energy. Brainstorm and use some new strategies instead.

Think critically to protect your emotional health. Job hunting during a recession can raise anyone's anxiety level. If you face this challenge, then use the stress management strategies from this chapter to your advantage.

For example, think critically about common stress-inducing beliefs. Despite what people say, for example, it is never true that "there are no jobs out there." Jobs are always opening up as people retire, find new jobs in their career field, or change careers entirely. In

January 2009—during a recession—4,300,000 people in the United States found new jobs. In addition, 3,000,000 jobs went unfilled.[24]

Communicate in ways that protect your health. Review your responses to the Journal Entries and Critical Thinking Exercises in this chapter. Do any of them raise issues that you'd like to share with someone that you trust? The act of communicating what you're thinking and feeling can restore your emotional balance, refresh your thinking, and relieve the physical signs of distress.

To get the greatest health benefits, communicate with people who will listen deeply and resist the urge to offer unsolicited advice. If they do offer advice, then remind them that that the best way for them to help is to simply receive what you have to say in a nonjudgmental way.

If you use any of the techniques in this chapter for a few weeks and don't find that they make a difference, then turn to a professional. Sometimes expert help with a specific situation—such as a lack of money—can relieve a significant source of stress and change the rest of your life for the better. Turn to the appropriate campus resource, such as the financial aid office.

The power of communication applies especially when you're dealing with an issue that affects your emotional health. If you become withdrawn, have thoughts about death or suicide, feel depressed for more than a few days, or have prolonged feelings of hopelessness, then see your doctor or a counselor at your student health center.

No matter what the source of distress, help is available if you openly and honestly communicate your need for it.

Collaborate with your employer to protect your health. If you receive health benefits through your job, then take full advantage of them. Your benefits might include screenings for a variety of conditions, paid time off for medical appointments, and discounts for health club memberships. Set up a meeting with someone at work who can explain all the options available to you.

Protecting your health is a win–win situation for you and your employer. You benefit from gaining more physical energy and psychological flexibility. Your employer benefits from reduced health care costs.

Now, make a personal commitment to developing the five Cs. Review the Discovery Wheel in Chapter 2—especially the sections labeled Character, Creative and Critical Thinking, Communicating, and Collaborating. Then take a snapshot of your current skills in these areas after reading and doing this chapter.

DISCOVERY

My scores on the "Five C" sections of the Discovery Wheel were:	As of today, I would give myself the following scores in these areas:	At the end of this course, I would like my scores in these areas to be:
Character _____	Character _____	Character _____
Creative & Critical Thinking _____	Creative & Critical Thinking _____	Creative & Critical Thinking _____
Communicating _____	Communicating _____	Communicating _____
Collaborating _____	Collaborating _____	Collaborating _____

Next, skim this chapter and look for a health-related strategy that you want to explore in depth. Choose one that would enhance your self-rating in at least one of the five Cs.

I discovered that my preferred technique is . . .

_____
_____
_____
_____

This technique can help me become more effective at one or more of the five Cs because . . .

_____
_____
_____
_____

INTENTION
To use this technique, I intend to . . .

_____
_____
_____
_____

NEXT ACTION
The specific action I will take is . . .

_____
_____
_____
_____

CHAPTER 11 QUIZ

Name _____

Date _____

1. How does the "Power Process: Surrender" differ from giving up?

   Surrender is not "giving up." Surrender includes doing whatever you can in a positive, trusting spirit. Let go, keep going, and know when a source of help lies beyond you. (*Power Process: Surrender*, page 292)

2. List Michael Pollan's guidelines for nutrition.

   "Eat food. Not too much. Mostly plants." (*Choose your fuel*, page 295)

3. List two ways you can build more physical activity into your day, outside of a scheduled time for exercise.

   Choose two of the following (answers will vary): Stay active throughout the day; adapt to your campus environment; do what you enjoy; vary your routine; get active early; exercise with other people; join a gym without fear; and look for gradual results. (*Choose to exercise*, page 296)

4. The text suggests two ways to "not believe everything you think." Briefly summarize those suggestions.

   First, don't believe these thoughts; replace them with more realistic thoughts. Second, just release stress-producing thoughts through meditation or other means. (*Choose emotional health*, page 297)

5. According to the text, emotional pain is a sickness that always calls for professional help. True or false? Explain your answer.

   False. Emotional pain is not a sickness. Although not pleasant, emotional pain is healthy and does not have to be a permanent state. (*Choose emotional health*, page 297)

6. Briefly define the term *self-efficacy*, and describe a strategy for developing it.

   Self-efficacy refers to your belief in your ability to determine the outcomes of events. With a strong self-image, you believe that your action counts. Strategies for developing strong self-efficacy include (describe any one of the following): Set up situations in which you can win; set goals with care; adopt a model; change the conversation about yourself; interpret stress in a new way; compare yourself to yourself; and surround yourself with support. (*Developing a strong self-image*, page 300)

7. Name three behaviors that signal a danger of suicide.

   Answers include any three of the following. Danger signals of suicide include: talking about suicide, planning for it, having a history of previous attempts, dwelling on problems, and feeling depressed. (*Suicide is no solution*, page 302)

8. Key signs of dependence include the following:

   (a) Loss of control

   (b) A pattern of relapse

   (c) Tolerance

   (d) Withdrawal

   (e) All of the above

   (e) All of the above (*From dependence to recovery*, page 312)

9. One of the suggestions for dealing with addiction is "Pay attention." This implies that it's okay to use drugs, as long as you do so with full awareness. True or false? Explain your answer.

   False. The suggestion to "Pay attention" refers to being aware of the consequences of behavior under the influence of drugs. Respond to that awareness with deliberate decision rather than out of habit or under pressure from others. (*From dependence to recovery*, page 312)

10. The only option for long-term recovery from dependence is treatment based on the steps of Alcoholics Anonymous. True or false? Explain your answer.

    False. Many recovery groups are based on the AA system, but there are many other systems, such as private therapy. People should explore different systems and pursue the one that works best for them. (*From dependence to recovery*, page 312)

CAREER MANAGEMENT

Instructor Tools & Tips

"Live as if you were to die tomorrow. Learn as if you were to live forever."
—Gandhi

"Learning is not a task or a problem—it is a way to be in the world. Man learns as he pursues goals and projects that have meaning for him." —Sidney Jourard

PREVIEW

Chapter 12 is about helping students succeed as they begin to make transitions from master student to master employee. Perhaps the most important aspect of this chapter is that it offers students an opportunity to solidify the relationship between college success and success in the workplace. The lead article (The master employee, page 321) helps students continue to make the connection between school and the workplace. Research shows that characteristics predictive of success in higher education are the same characteristics that promote success in the workplace. Use these culminating ideas to promote success in gaining employment and applying skills from this course to the workplace.

GUEST SPEAKER

A local employer who looks to your institution to find workers is an appropriate choice for a guest speaker for this chapter. Another possibility is to invite a career counselor or your Human Resources Director who can help students prepare to apply for jobs, interview, and enter the workplace.

Now is also the time to ask your current students to consider coming back next term to be your guest speakers on the first day of class. Your new students will be very interested in meeting your former students. They can be an inspiration to new students who are not fully committed to continuing in your class. You might want to consider filming current students as you ask them to share their experiences and personal growth. These testimonials will make a powerful impact on incoming students next semester.

LECTURE

Appropriate lecture topics for this chapter include the following: what students can do next term to keep the tools learned in this course fresh in their minds, the connection between the skills learned in this course and the skills employers are looking for, networking strategies, putting together an effective résumé, interviewing successfully for a job, and skills for starting a new job.

Fine tune your résumé with an effective cover letter (page 329)
The cover letter is an excellent place for students to highlight their strengths—especially those strengths that are related to things employers care about. Recent data from the National Association of Colleges and Employers (NACE, 2006) suggest that employers are looking for new employees who have the following characteristics: strong work ethic, motivation/initiative, organizational commitment, interpersonal skills, adaptability, self-confidence, integrity/dependability, job-related skills, communication skills, and good manners/politeness.

Engage your students in a discussion of how they have demonstrated these characteristics as students, part-time workers, or campus leaders, and then brainstorm how they might incorporate examples of these characteristics in their cover letter.

EXERCISES/ACTIVITIES

1. The Discovery Wheel—coming full circle (pages 347–350) Begin this in-class assignment by having your students complete the Discovery Wheel in this final chapter. Ask them to compare the scores they have just given themselves with the scores from the Discovery Wheel they completed in Chapter 2. Then have students subtract their first Discovery Wheel scores from their second Discovery Wheel scores. This difference can be very insightful. It represents the change in the students' self-confidence. Many students see dramatic improvements. This comparison is a powerful tool—the Discovery Wheel reveals the truth about students to themselves.

Some students also like to divide the first Discovery Wheel scores by the second Discovery Wheel scores and note the percentage change. They describe the result as a percentage increase in their academic awareness.

Note: Occasionally, you will have a student whose scores go down. This is an important example of the power of telling the truth and how the truth can change. Sometimes, students' scores are lower now that they are more aware of the meanings and significance of topics and questions. The results of the Discovery Wheel in the beginning of the term may have been slightly skewed by lack of understanding and/or reflection.

2. **Use job interviews to "hire" an employer (pages 330–332)** Set up a day of mock interviews with your students. Have students prepare to answer key interviewing questions. Instruct each student to write one interviewing question on a 3 × 5 card. Collect these cards and use them at your mock interviews to ask students key questions. Encourage your students to dress as they would for an interview. Invite juniors and seniors to be the interviewees, or pair students up with their peers in class.

Encourage students, whenever possible, to describe themselves using language that would be familiar to employers. Students can draw from skills categories such as the characteristics desired in new employees suggested by the NACE (provided in the previous section). You should also encourage your students to prepare concrete examples that they can use to bolster their assertions. Here is a sample interview response: "I have a strong sense of direction and am quite persistent in my efforts. For example, I knew in my freshman year that I wanted to assume a student leadership role in my undergraduate department. I took the following steps in an effort to work toward that goal. . . ."

Alternatively, a free video, *The Interviewing Process: Strategies for Making the Right Impression*, is available for you to use in your course. This video, which includes tips from career counselor Susan Loffredo, provides strategies for a successful job search and walks students through the interviewing process from start to finish. Simulated interviewing scenarios conducted by actual professionals and managers allow your students to have a bird's eye view of what a real interview looks like. To enhance this video, accompanying activities and discussion questions to help students better understand the strategies for successful interviewing are available on the Instructor Web site.

Your students might also benefit from reviewing other exercises throughout the book (e.g., learning styles, multiple intelligences, career interests) as they develop cover letters, résumés, and responses to interview questions.

3. **Power Process: Be it (page 320)** As this class nears its completion, it's exciting for students to reflect on their educational and career goals one last time before exiting the course. Once they learn to use the tools and strategies presented in *From Master Student to Master Employee*, many students raise their level of expectation to include additional educational and career achievements. They now know how easy it can be for them to pursue goals they would never have considered before. In class, ask them to brainstorm individually a list of their hopes, dreams,

and goals. Have them answer the following questions on a sheet of paper: What do you want to be? What do you want to do? What do you want to have? For example, a student might write:

I want to be a poet.

I want to go to Stanford University.

I want to have a career that enables me to travel throughout the world.

Then ask the students to sit in a large circle. Ask them to change the *want*'s to *be*'s. In the example above, the changes might look like this:

I am a poet.

I am a Stanford University student.

I am in a career that enables me to travel throughout the world.

Ask them to look at their revised statements and read them silently to themselves. Seeing this change on paper will make students feel as if the future is happening in the present! Ask the students to read their affirmation statements out loud to out loud to a partner in class.

CONVERSATION/SHARING

The culminating chapter of *From Master Student to Master Employee* focuses on the transfer of knowledge that is best displayed by Mode 4 learners who ask, "*What if?*" Your students will have practiced using the metacognitive map for a whole semester. Now you can challenge them to think of questions related to Chapter 12 and Mode 4. *What if* they apply the skills they learned in this course to all of their future courses? *What if* they apply these skills in the workplace? *What if* they select one major and then want to change majors because they have changed career goals? This is a great time to connect the discussion to transferable skills (refer to the Introduction, page 23). As a class, list some of these transferable skills on the board. Ask specifically: "*How* are these skills related to the workplace?" Ask students to share examples in their own lives.

Encourage your students to look ahead to the following semester and make a commitment to review the chapters of this textbook, one per week, to keep the concepts and strategies fresh in their mind. As part of the final week's assignment, have students reread the textbook's Introduction: Making Transitions, which will make even more sense to them now that they have read the entire book. This assignment demonstrates the benefits of a later, second reading of the text. Ask students to engage in a group conversation about what they discovered on rereading the Introduction.

HOMEWORK

Critical Thinking Exercise 30: Create your career plan—now (page 346) This exercise will help students focus and commit to considering a specific career, and to identifying in writing the steps to get there. You can refer your students to the Web site Occupational Outlook Handbook (http://www.bls.gov/ooh/) by the Bureau of Labor

Statistics. This valuable government resource provides specifics on training and education needs, earnings, expected job prospects, and other details for hundreds of different types of jobs.

Build an irresistible résumé (pages 327–329) The materials provided in *From Master Student to Master Employee* related to résumé building should be considered preliminary guidelines. These are tools to help students get started and perhaps gain employment while they are in school. If your students are not yet ready to create their own résumés, consider having them create a résumé that answers a specific help-wanted ad that they pull from the newspaper or a Web site with job listings. This mock résumé can be used as a goal setting tool. What skills do you want to be able to write on your résumé? How can you successfully practice these skills in higher education or at an internship?

The CL Assessment and Portfolio Builder tool can be used in guiding students to create effective résumés. Have your students complete the assessment and fill in their Accomplishments Report. This report can be used to populate their résumé and will help students focus on their accomplishments. The report will also show students where they need to continue to build skills through community services, campus activities or internships.

Build an irresistible résumé (pages 327–329) Have your students follow up their work on their résumés by writing a cover letter that addresses their accomplishments and skills, aligning them to a position they are applying for (building on the previous exercise). This exercise provides another opportunity for students to practice their writing skills. Use the examples in the text as models. Have your students do peer editing in the classroom. More information on peer editing techniques is available on the Instructor Web site.

Creating portfolios

Your first-year student success course is a perfect place for students to begin collecting their work in a way that reflects their academic development and accomplishments. Encourage students to personalize their portfolios and help them reflect on their growth over time. A portfolio is a work in progress. Each student's portfolio will be unique and different from all others at the conclusion of the course. Consider having a sharing day and end-of-semester celebration so that students can review and reflect on one another's portfolios.

Create a personal profile. Personal profiles help to catalog your students' background, education, employment, activities, hobbies, and college skills. The profile can be used as a resource for learning more about your students. A sample personal profile form is available for downloading and distributing to your students from the Instructor Web site. Consider customizing the profile to your liking and to your campus. Consider allowing students to omit sensitive items if they prefer not to answer them (especially if you are requiring that they submit the profile for a grade).

Review goal-setting exercises. *From Master Student to Master Employee* provides students with many opportunities for setting

goals. Beginning with Critical Thinking Exercise 11: Get real with your goals (page 83), students can begin to plan long-term goals, mid-term goals and short-term goals. Periodically, they are encouraged to revisit these goals and make updates. Filing this material in a portfolio enables them to easily measure their growth and note their changes throughout their semester and college experience. The CL Assessment and Portfolio Builder provides students with another opportunity for self-reflection and future planning. The CL Assessment and Portfolio Builder is an online tool that you can use in your classroom to reinforce goal setting, accomplishments, attitudes, and values to your students. Have your students assess the skills that they come to college with, and work with your students to plan for accomplishments throughout their college experience and their future in the workplace.

Prepare for the future. As students assess their majors and career interests, they can use their portfolios to keep track of their education plans, lists of courses they need to complete in order to graduate, and other program requirements. Suggest that students also consider what types of materials may be relevant to share with prospective employers. For example, if a student writes for a publication on your campus, he can add his published articles to his portfolio and share them during an interview. If a student participates in campus organizations or service-learning projects, she can add photographs and materials documenting her activities to her portfolio.[1]

Even if students do not have previous work experience, encourage them to focus on student accomplishments, extracurricular activities, offices held, and skills which can transfer to the workplace. Remind students to refer to their multiple intelligences from Chapter 2 for personal strengths that can be an advantage on the job.

EVALUATION

Quiz Ideas for Chapter 12

Here are some ideas for final exam questions for your course:

1. Which Master Student Profile in the text inspired you the most, and why?

2. What were the three most valuable textbook articles that you read in this course? How did they change the way you are as a student?

3. If you were to write a top 10 list of reasons why students entering college should take this course their first semester, what would be your top 5 reasons?

4. Name the five most important skills you learned in this course, and explain how you will ensure that you use, and do not lose, these skills as you continue your college experience after this course ends.

---

[1] Some ideas for this homework assignment were collected from the work of Eve Evans Walden, *Portfolio to Accompany Becoming a Master Student,* 9th ed. Copyright © 2001 by Houghton Mifflin Company. Reprinted by permission.

Additional Digital Resources for Chapter 12

What can you **ASSIGN FROM THE COURSEMATE** for *From Master Student to Master Employee?*

- **Video Skillbuilders.** These interactive online tools combine video clips featuring discussions with students, instructors, and experts, with articles and activities designed to give students a fully engaging learning experience. Either view and experience these together in class, or have students view them as a homework assignment and respond to the viewing questions and reflective exercise. This module is a good match for Chapter 12:

  - Career Planning: In College
  - Career Planning: After College

Note that Video Skillbuilders are available for every chapter.

- **Career Resource Center.** The Career Resource Center offers tips, exercises, articles, and ideas to help students succeed on their journey from college to career.

  - *The Bridge from College to Career* lets students practice new skills acquired in college that can be applied as they enter the job market.

  - *Finding the Perfect Job* helps students fine-tune their résumé writing and interviewing skills.

  - *Skills for Your Future* provides strategies for problem solving and decision making to help students learn to work with others and communicate on the job.

- **The SCANS Wheel.** Like the Discovery Wheel, the SCANS Wheel offers students the opportunity to assess their strengths and weaknesses associated with transferable skills, like basic skills, thinking, personal, resources, interpersonal, information, and systems. Students simply rate their responses to the questions, and the wheel does the rest!

CourseMate *To access CourseMate, your students need to visit www.cengagebrain .com. At the CengageBrain.com home page, students search for the ISBN of* From Master Student to Master Employee *(from the back cover of the book), using the search box at the top of the page. This takes them to the product page where these resources can be found.*

Did you know that **THESE RESOURCES** *(and many more)* **ARE AVAILABLE** *on the* **INSTRUCTOR COMPANION SITE?**

- **What are your next steps?** Look to the online Course Manual to discover ways to evaluate the success of your course and how you can play a role in student retention with these articles:

  - Creating evaluations of your course
  - Start now: Evaluate today's class
  - The role of faculty in retaining students on campus

- **Looking for fresh, innovative ways to teach Chapter 12 topics?** Browse through the Best Practices library to see what other Master Instructors have been successfully doing with their students.

master instructor BEST PRACTICE

Master Student Hall of Fame PowerPoint. *Students select a previous Master Student from the Cengage online Master Student Hall of Fame, research that Master Student, create a PowerPoint, and present it at one of our last classes of the semester. I scaffold student success on the PowerPoint project by teaching them to create a planning schedule for larger projects, to prevent procrastination. I have those who are experienced PowerPoint creators raise their hands so that the students who will need extra help can go to a fellow classmate or sit by them while we're working on it. I bring in an IT instructor as a guest speaker to teach them advanced skills like adding video or speech, or to answer questions that they need help with. We do Internet research for tips on a quality PowerPoint, and the students present at least one tip each to the class. As students present, we give positive and constructive feedback for their future PowerPoint assignments in other classes. It is a very motivating and inspirational time because of the people they are telling us about who overcame obstacles to achieve success and because for many it is their very first PowerPoint, and they're thrilled to achieve it.*

–Dana Dildine, Eastern New Mexico University

Please visit login.cengage.com *to log in and access the Instructor Companion Site.*

Career Management

Use this **Master Student Map** to ask yourself

WHY THIS CHAPTER MATTERS . . .

- You can gain strategies to succeed as a job hunter, worker, career planner, and lifelong learner.

WHAT IS INCLUDED . . .

HOW I CAN USE THIS CHAPTER. . .

- Learn effective strategies for job hunting.
- Use work as a path to lifelong learning.
- Create a long-term vision for my career.

WHAT IF . . .

- I could work in ways that align with my core values, connect with my passions, and contribute to others?

© Ruslan Ivantsov/Shutterstock.com

JOURNAL ENTRY 25
Discovery/Intention Statement

Reflect on your experience of working

Reflect on all the jobs you've held in your life. What aspect of working would you most like to change? Answers might include job hunting with less frustration, resolving conflicts with coworkers, building a better relationship with your boss, or coping with office politics. Describe the change that would make the biggest positive difference in your job satisfaction over the long run.

I discovered that I . . .

_____

_____

_____

_____

Now preview this chapter for ideas that could help you make the positive change you just described. List three to five suggestions in the following space, along with the page numbers where you intend to read more about them.

Strategy	Page number
_____	_____
_____	_____
_____	_____

⏻ POWER process Be it

Use this Power Process to enhance all of the techniques in this book.

Consider that most of our choices in life fall into three categories. We can do the following:

- Increase our material wealth (what we have).
- Improve our skills (what we do).
- Develop our "being" (who we are).

Many people devote their entire lifetime to the first two categories. They act as if they are "human havings" instead of human beings. For them, the quality of life hinges on what they have. They devote most of their waking hours to getting more—more clothes, more cars, more relationships, more degrees, more trophies. "Human havings" define themselves by looking at the circumstances in their lives—what they have.

Some people escape this materialist trap by adding another dimension to their identities. In addition to living as "human havings," they also live as "human doings." They thrive on working hard and doing everything well. They define themselves by how efficiently they do their jobs, how effectively they raise their children, and how actively they participate in clubs and organizations. Their thoughts are constantly about methods, techniques, and skills.

In addition to focusing on what we have and what we do, we can also focus on our being. That last word describes how we *see* ourselves.

All of the techniques in this book can be worthless if you operate with the idea that you are an ineffective student. You might do almost everything this book suggests and still never achieve the success in school that you desire.

Instead, picture yourself as a master student right now. Through higher education, you are simply gaining knowledge and skills that reflect and reinforce this view of yourself. Change the way you see yourself. Then watch your actions and results shift as if by magic.

Remember that "Be it" is not positive thinking or mental cheerleading. This Power Process works well when you take a First Step—when you tell the truth about your current abilities. The very act of accepting who you are and what you can do right now unleashes a powerful force for personal change.

If you can first visualize where you want to be, if you can go there in your imagination, if you can *be* it today, then you set yourself up to succeed.

If you want it, be it.

You're One Click Away...
*from from accessing Power Proce
Media online and finding out mo
about how to "be it."*

The master employee

The title of this book—*From Master Student to Master Employee*—implies that these two types of mastery have something in common.

To some people, this idea sounds half-baked. They separate life into two distinct domains: work and school. One is the "real" world. The other is the place where you attend classes to get ready for the real world.

Consider another point of view—the idea that success in higher education promotes success on the job.

There's some pretty hard-nosed evidence for this idea. One piece of evidence is the fact that higher levels of education are correlated with higher levels of income.[1] Another is that mastery in school and in work seems to rest on a common set of transferable skills.

Consider the Secretary's Commission on Achieving Necessary Skills (SCANS) issued by the U.S. Department of Labor.[2] According to this classic document, one crucial skill for the workplace is a personal quality called *responsibility*. This skill is demonstrated by any employee who:

Exerts a high level of effort and perseverance toward goal attainment. Works hard to become excellent at doing tasks by setting high standards, paying attention to details, working well, and displaying a high level of concentration even when assigned an unpleasant task.

Displays high standards of attendance, punctuality, enthusiasm, vitality, and optimism in approaching and completing tasks.

A better definition of mastery would be hard to find. If you've ever exerted a high level of effort to complete an assignment, paid attention to the details of a lecture, or displayed a high level of concentration while reading a tough textbook, then you've already demonstrated some key aspects of character and mastery.

Remember that when you graduate from school, you don't leave your capacity for mastery locked inside a classroom. Excellence in one setting paves the way for excellence in other settings.

For example, a student who knows how to show up for class on time is ready to show up for work on time. The student who knows how to focus attention during a lecture is ready to focus attention during a training session at work. And a student who's worked cooperatively in a study group brings a lot of skills to the table when joining a workplace team. You can multiply this list by developing any of the skills explored in this book.

Just like a master student, a master employee embraces change, takes risks, and looks for chances to exercise leadership. A master employee completes tasks efficiently, communicates openly and respectfully, and commits to lifelong learning.

You can learn to do all this, and more. *Master student* and *master employee* are names for qualities that already exist in you, waiting to be expressed as you embrace new ideas and experiment with new behaviors.

If you used this book fully—if you actively participated in reading the contents, writing the Journal Entries, doing the Critical Thinking Exercises, and putting the suggestions to work—then you have had quite a journey in developing the qualities of a master employee.

Recall some high points of that journey. The first half of this book is about nuts and bolts of education—gaining knowledge. It presents the concept of character and ideas for making the transition to higher education. It suggests that you take a First Step by telling the truth about your skills and setting goals to expand them. Also included are guidelines for planning time, managing money, training your memory, improving reading skills, taking useful notes, and succeeding at tests.

All of this activity prepares you for another aim of education—creating and applying knowledge. This means thinking creatively and critically, communicating more effectively, building collaboration skills, and living with vibrant health. All are steps on the path of becoming a master employee.

Soon you are about to make another transition—not to another chapter of this book, but to the next chapter of your life. So what's next for you? Use this chapter to explore that question. Learn more about job hunting and thriving in the work force. In addition, get a big picture of your unique contribution to the world. Begin creating the life of your dreams with a vision that can power your career for decades to come. ■

12

© Marcel Mooij/Shutterstock

Tap the *hidden* **job market**

One of the most useful job skills you can ever develop is the ability to discover job openings *before* they are advertised. (Most never are.) The more you can tap the hidden job market, the less you need to fear getting fired, laid off, or stuck in a job that no longer serves you.

Conventional job hunting is passive. It relies on sending out résumés and waiting for responses. Instead, get active. Remember that even during a recession, the state of the economy at large does not determine your individual prospects for finding a job. All of the following tools are at your disposal.

Think like an employer. Imagine yourself working as the hiring manager for a small business or head of human resources for a larger company. Your organization has a job opening, and your task is to fill it as soon as possible. You have the following options:

1. Hiring someone you know—a current or former employee or intern—with appropriate qualifications.

2. Hiring someone who is *recommended* by a current or former employee or intern.

3. Asking other members of your professional network to recommend a person for the job.

4. Hiring someone else who has already contacted you and demonstrated that he or she has the appropriate qualifications.

5. Contracting with an employment agency to screen potential applicants.

6. Running blind ads in newspapers or posting openings online—and preparing for the dreaded onslaught of résumés.

If you're like most people in charge of hiring new employees, you'll choose from options 1 to 4 whenever possible, and in roughly that order. That makes sense: You'd prefer to hire someone you know well, or have met. This is probably safer than risking your luck on a total stranger.

Now consider the traditional approach to *finding* a job, which usually relies on tasks that follow in a different order:

1. Responding blindly to help-wanted ads or online job boards with a résumé and cover letter.

2. Contacting employment agencies.

3. Making direct contact with people who have the power to hire you, even when their organization does not have an advertised job opening.

4. Asking people in your professional network if they know of job openings that match your qualifications.

5. Asking people who work in your chosen field to recommend you for job openings.

6. Asking a current or former employer about job openings and opportunities to get promoted.

Carefully compare these two numbered lists. The traditional job-hunting method proceeds in *exactly the opposite direction* that employers use. Employers prefer to hire someone that they know. However, many job seekers ignore this. It's no wonder that people find the process of hiring and getting hired to be so frustrating.

To prevent this disconnection, think like an employer. Get to know people. Do research to discover organizations that interest you. Find out who does the hiring at those organizations, and contact those people directly.

This is not to say that help-wanted ads, job boards, and employment agencies are a waste of time. They might work. The suggestion here is simply not to rely on them exclusively. To succeed at job hunting, use a variety of methods. If one method doesn't get results, then choose another one.

When people say "There are no jobs," maybe what they really mean is, "My current job hunting method is not working." There's a world of difference between those statements. The first one kills options. The second one *creates* options.

Discover your network. Networking is one of the most powerful ways to tap the hidden job market. Mastering this skill can do more for your career over the long-term than endlessly revising your résumé or trying to craft the perfect cover letter.

Some people hear the word *networking* and wince. They think of it as sleazy or a waste of time. In reality, information interviews can be effective and fun. When you ask questions that allow people to reflect on their work, you can help *them* to create a more compelling and detailed vision for their future. This is a form

of contribution. And when you can give something back to the people you meet—such as useful information or an introduction to someone else—you add even more value to the relationship.

You might not believe that you have a network. If so, then just notice that thought and gently let it go. *Everyone* has a network. The key is to discover it and develop it.

Networking is a useful strategy even if you're currently employed. If you get laid off or choose to change your career in the future, then your network will be in place when you want it.

Begin by listing contacts—any person who can help you find a job. Contacts can include roommates, classmates, teachers, friends, relatives, and their friends. Also list former employers and current employers.

In addition, go to your school's alumni office and see if you can get contact information for past graduates—especially people who are working in your career field. This is a rich source of contacts that many students ignore.

Start your contact list now. Record each person's name, phone number, and e-mail address on a separate 3 × 5 card or Rolodex card. Another option is to keep your list on a computer, using word processing, database, contact management software, or an app on your smart phone.

Contact people in your network. Next, send a short e-mail to a person on your list—someone who's doing the kind of work that you'd love to do. Invite that person to coffee or lunch. If that's not feasible, then ask for a time to make a phone call. Explain that you'd like to have a 20-minute conversation to learn more about what these people do. In other words, you're asking for an *information interview* rather than a job interview. Whenever possible, make this contact after getting an introduction from someone that both of you know.

Before you meet with your contacts in person or over the phone, create a short list of questions to ask. Plan to ask them how they chose their career and found their job. Ask about what they enjoy, what they find challenging, and what trends are shaping their work. Find out what kind of work they'd like to be doing in a year, five years, and even ten years from today. In particular, ask about how people find jobs in their field, and if there is anyone else you could meet with for more information.

During the actual interview, listen closely to what people say. Take notes and highlight any follow-up actions that you'd like to take. Keep the focus of the conversation on the other person rather than you.

Keep in mind that people are busy. Stick to your agreed time limit for the conversation—unless it's clear that both of you want to continue. When you're done, say thank you. If you met in person for coffee or a meal, then offer to pay the bill.

After the interview, send a thank-you note. Refer to a specific topic or point from your conversation. If the person made a suggestion and you acted on it, then be sure to mention this.

Go beyond your network. Through your job research and information interviews, you'll learn about many people in your

12

career field. Some of them might be people who fall outside your current network. You can reach out to them anyway.

Tap the power of the Internet. Get the name of the person that you'd like to meet and key it into your favorite search engine. You might be able to find contact information through a Web site such as pipl (**pipl.com**), PeekYou (**peekyou.com**), or wink (**wink.com**) as well.

Scan the search results to find out whether this person has a Web site, blog, or both. Also look for their presence on social networks such as Facebook, Twitter, and LinkedIn. With this information you do many things to connect. For example:

- Comment on a blog post that the person wrote.
- Join Twitter and post an update about this person or "retweet" one of their updates.
- Create your own Web site, add a blog, and write a post about this person.
- Send a short e-mail—or handwritten note—that expresses your appreciation for their work.

In any case, do not ask anything of people at this stage. Your goal is simply to show up on their personal "radar." Over time, they might initiate a contact with you. Then you can feel free to respond and suggest an information interview.

Be specific about the job you want—and why you can do it. After doing some information interviews, you'll learn more about the language used by people in your career field. Listen closely for common job titles. When you find one that matches the kind of work that you want to do, make a habit of using that title.

Don't worry about limiting your options by focusing on just one specific job title or career option for now. If your current choice doesn't work out, you can choose another one later.

When you meet the person who can hire you for the job you want, then be prepared to answer a common question: *Why should I hire you?* Answers such as *Because I can make a contribution to this company* or *Because I'm well qualified* are too general. Don't worry about being the best-qualified person for the position. Just give specific reasons why you'd be a good "hire."

This means doing research. Find out what problems the company wants to solve. Discover what kind of services and products they want to offer. Then prepare some compelling evidence that you make a contribution in these areas. This evidence can take various forms, depending on the job that you want. It might be a list of measurable outcomes that you achieved on a previous job. It might also be something tangible that you've just created, such as a Web site or a detailed, written proposal that describes a project you can do for a company.

Offer a limited amount of work for free. If you really want to get a potential employer's attention, then offer to work for free. This is not a joke. When done with care, working for free offers a low-risk way for you and an employer to get to know each other. If it works out, you could get hired full-time and start earning a salary. If it doesn't work out, the employer loses nothing. You

Smart things to do if you're unemployed

Take care of business. Make appointments to see your doctor and dentist while you still have health insurance coverage from your old job. File for unemployment benefits.

Teach yourself a new skill. Though Web-based tutorials and community education classes, there are plenty of free and low-cost sources of information and training.

Plan and complete a project that interests you. For example, build a Web site. Start a blog. Write an e-book on a topic you know well. Approach small businesses and offer to do a project in return for a testimonial or recommendation.

Do something off-beat that recharges your batteries. Travel. Go on a meditation retreat. Visit friends. Clean out your house, apartment, or garage. Develop a hobby. Learn to cook. Spend more time with friends and family members. Catch up on sleep. Exercise. Find a wealthy boyfriend or girlfriend (just kidding … kind of).

Make job hunting your job. This means working as hard at your job hunt as you would at any full-time job. Spend at least 40 hours per week building and tapping into your network. Plan specific activities for each day and do them on a regular schedule. If possible, meet with people when your mood and energy level peaks for the day.

Consider alternative work styles. Ask the people in your network if they have experiences with temporary work, contract work, and self-employment.

Rethink your job search strategies. Change your strategies and monitor the results. If you're relying on classified ads to find job openings, for example, then do more networking. If you've been posting your résumé online and waiting for responses, then consider making more phone calls.

Even in the best job market, there will be competition for jobs. Use tough times to experiment with new strategies and get more skilled at job hunting. One key to staying positive during tough times is always to have another option at hand.

get to walk away from the company on friendly terms and learn something from the experience as well.

There are four caveats to this suggestion. First, be sure to do your homework. Go online to find companies and entrepreneurs that really interest you. Supplement this with library research. Also ask people you know for suggestions.

Second, make sure that you have something to offer these companies and individuals. Find out what kinds of products and services they want to develop. Then look for a match between their wants and your skills.

Third, set a limit on the amount of time that you're willing to work for free. Put this limit in writing and ask the potential employer to agree to it. You might send an e-mail that goes something like this: "I have some specific ideas for the home page of your company's Web site that could increase the number of customer responses and raise its ranking on Google and other search engines. Over the next two weeks, I will develop some prototypes for a new home page. If you like my ideas, then I'd like to meet with you about getting hired on a contract or full-time basis to implement them."

Finally, develop another source of income to pay the bills. Work part-time at another job. Another option is to find a full-time job with a flexible schedule that allows you to "moonlight"

for potential employers. Doing this might mean reducing your expenses and learning to live on a bare-bones budget for a short time. See Chapter 3: Time & Money for suggestions.

Cope with emotional ups and downs. Job hunting and rejection go hand in hand. If you've been turned down for several job offers but are still getting interviews, then your job hunting methods are basically working well. Remember that you can perform well in an interview and still get turned down for a job, especially when there are several equally qualified applicants.

Coping with rejections can pose many challenges. Your self-confidence can crack when people don't return your calls or when job applications disappear into the void with no response.

Whatever your feelings, take a First Step about them. There's power in telling the truth to yourself and to a good listener. (See Chapter 11: Health for more ideas about managing stress.)

You can go into more depth by writing Discovery Statements about your changing moods. Follow up with Intention Statements about the next strategies that you will use for your job search. One cornerstone of emotional health is that you can *do* something constructive even when you *feel* sad or mad. Moving into action can change your mood and bring you even closer to the job you've been waiting for. ■

Get the scoop on
potential employers

One of the best compliments you can get during an information interview or job interview is, "You really know a lot about our organization." This is one benefit of researching potential employers. Another is getting the information you need to write convincing cover letters and résumés that are targeted to that specific company and job.

List questions to answer. For example: How old is the company? What are its core services, products, and projects? Where is it located? How many people does it employ? What are its competitors? Has the company grown in recent years? What are current trends affecting companies like this one? What issues will they face over the next five years?

Go to your school's career center. Many businesses and nonprofit organizations distribute recruiting materials to campus career centers. See what's available at your

school. Find out which companies do campus visits or sponsor local job fairs.

Go online. Start with a general guide such as Career Guide to Industries, published by the U.S. Bureau of Labor Statistics, (http://www.bls.gov/oco/cg/). Here you'll find information about working conditions, earnings, and the job market in your state. A similar source is CareerOneStop (careerinfonet.org). Use the Employer Locator feature of that site to research specific organizations in your area.

You can find useful information through many other reputable Web sites. Examples are CNNfn (money.cnn. com), Bloomberg (bloomberg.com), the Wall Street Journal (wsj.com), the New York Times (nytimes.com), and Top Money News (usatoday.com/money/mfront. htm). Glassdoor (glassdoor.com) and LinkedIn (linkedin. com) offer reviews of companies and information about their salary ranges.

12

✓ CRITICAL THINKING EXERCISE 27

Activate your network

Review the article "Tap the hidden job market." Then imagine that you're starting a full-time job search as of today. The following questions will help you move into action. Answer the questions in the space provided, using additional paper as needed. If you are unsure about what to write, then list the questions you have and what you will do to find the answers.

What specific job will you apply for? If you choose self-employment, what product or service will you offer?

_____

_____

_____

_____

_____

_____

_____

Who currently belongs to your network? List as many names as you can.

_____

_____

_____

_____

_____

_____

Do you know people who are currently doing the kind of work that you want to do? List their names.

_____

_____

_____

_____

_____

_____

_____

Among the people you just listed, who are the first three people that you will contact?

_____

_____

_____

_____

_____

_____

_____

Visualize yourself going on information interviews with these people. What questions will you ask?

_____

_____

_____

_____

_____

_____

_____

_____

BUILD AN IRRESISTIBLE résumé

A résumé is much more than a list of your qualifications. This document says a lot about who you are, what you love to do, and how you contribute to the world by using your skills. You can gain a lot from thinking about those things now, even if you don't plan to apply for a job in the near future. Start *building* your résumé now, even if you don't plan to *use* one for a while.

BUILD YOUR RÉSUMÉ FROM A SKILLS PERSPECTIVE

According to one perspective, there's no need to think about a résumé until your last term in school. At that time you go to a career planning workshop or two, check the job listings, and start sending out applications. And if you don't land a job—well, you can always go back to school.

Instead, take a skills perspective. Ask one question about every experience you have in higher education: *How will this help me develop a valuable skill?* Remembering this question will help you choose courses, instructors, and extracurricular activities with a new level of clarity. Then, when it's your time to send out a résumé, you'll be ready to demonstrate your mastery.

An education is much more than a grade point average and list of course credits. The whole point is to become a different person. Graduating means being able to *do* things that you could not do when you started school.

Today you can start developing the ability to think critically, speak persuasively, and write clearly. You can learn to work in teams, solve complex problems, innovate, and act with integrity. These are skills that allow you to prosper in the workplace and find your place in a global economy. From this perspective, a résumé is something that you build during your whole time in higher education.

START BUILDING SKILLS FOR YOUR IDEAL RÉSUMÉ

To get the most from your education, think about the résumé you want to have when you graduate. With that vision of the person you want to be, choose the skills that you want to gain.

If you've actively participated with this course and this book, then you've got a head start. Review "Master student qualities" on page 3. Reread your responses to the Journal Entries and exercises throughout this book. Also review the articles in this chapter about values, transferable skills, declaring a major, and choosing your career.

With those insights fresh in mind, start planning. Write goals to develop specific skills. Then list the actions you will take to develop those skills. Add reminders of these actions to your to-do list and calendar so that you can actually achieve your goals.

Many of your plans will involve taking courses. In addition, look for ways to gain and use skills outside the classroom. Sign up for internships and service learning projects related to your major. Find part-time jobs related to your career plan. Seize every opportunity to take theories and test them in the work world. These experiences will help you develop an expertise, build a job network, and make a seamless transition to your next career.

REMEMBER THE REASON FOR A RÉSUMÉ

When you *do* write a résumé to apply for a job, approach it as a piece of persuasive writing—not a dry recitation of facts or a laundry list of previous jobs. The key purpose of your resume is to get you to the next step in the hiring process.

There is no formula for a great résumé. Employers have many different preferences for what they want to see. Just remember that an effective résumé states how you can benefit a potential employer. Second, it offers evidence that you can deliver those benefits. Make sure that every word in your résumé serves those goals.

To write an effective résumé, consider your audience. Picture a person who has a several hundred résumés to plow through, and almost no time for that task. She may spend only 20 seconds scanning each résumé before making a decision about whom to call for interviews. Remember to be concise. Employers will not read long resumes with attachments and pages of details.

Your goal is to get past this first cut. Neatness, organization, and correct grammar and punctuation are essential. Meet these goals, and then make an even stronger impression with the following strategies.

USE THIS RÉSUMÉ CHECKLIST

The following suggestions will guide you through one common résumé format:

- *Let people know how to contact you.* Start your résumé with contact information. This includes your name, mailing address, e-mail address, and phone number. If you have a Web site, add that as well. Make sure that your e-mail address, voice mail greeting, and Web site convey a professional image.

- *State your objective.* This is a description of the job that you want. Keep this to one sentence, and tailor it to the specific position for which you're applying. Craft your objective to get attention. Ask yourself: From an employer's perspective, what kind of person would make an ideal candidate for this job? Then write your objective to directly answer this question with two or three specific qualities that you can demonstrate.

12

- *Focus the objective on what you can do for the employer.* Here is the first place to state the benefits you can deliver. Avoid self-centered phrases like "a job in the software industry where I can develop my sales skills." Instead, state your objective as "a sales position for a software company that wants to continually generate new customers and exceed its revenue goals."

- *Highlight your experience.* Follow your objective with the body of your resume. One common heading is *experience*. Write this section carefully. Here is where you give a few relevant details about your past jobs, listed in order starting with your most recent position. This is the heart of a *chronological* résumé. An alternative to the chronological format is the *functional* résumé. It highlights your skills, strengths, and personal achievements rather than past jobs. This format might be useful for people with limited experience or gaps in their work history.

- *Highlight your education.* A second common heading for the body of a résumé is "education." List any degree that you attained beyond high school, along with honors, awards, and significant activities. If you are currently enrolled in classes, note that as well. Include your planned degree and date of graduation.

- *Include references.* Many résumés end with a line such as "references are available on request." Before you add this statement, make sure that you can deliver a list of people who have already agreed to write a reference for you. Ask for their permission and current contact information.

- *Write so that the facts leap off the page.* Whenever possible, use phrases that start with an action verb: "*supervised* three people," "*generated* leads for sales calls," "*wrote* speeches and *edited* annual reports," "*designed* a process that reduced production expenses by 20 percent." Active verbs refer directly to your skills. Make them relevant to the job you're seeking, and tie them to specific accomplishments whenever possible. Be prepared to discuss these accomplishments during a job interview.

- *Cut the fluff.* Leave out information that could possibly eliminate you from the hiring process and send your résumé hurtling into the circular file. Avoid boilerplate language—stock wording or vague phrases such as "proven success in a high-stress environment," "highly motivated self-starter," or "a demonstrated capacity for strategic thinking."

- *Get feedback.* Ask friends and family members if your résumé is persuasive and easy to understand. Also get feedback from someone at your school's career-planning center. Revise your résumé based on their comments. Then revise some more. Create sparkling prose that will intrigue a potential employer enough to call you for an interview.

- *Take charge of your online résumé.* While you're writing a résumé, take a break to check your online presence. Type your name into an Internet search engine such as Google and see what results you get. These search results make up your online résumé.

Employers will check social networking sites such as Facebook, MySpace, and Twitter to learn about you. Review your posts, photos, videos, and files on all social networks you have joined, deleting content as well as unsubscribing from any inactive social network accounts. Be mindful as you post future content. Add updates about your academic achievements, extracurricular activities, and internships.

You can also use social networking to actively support your job search. For example, start a Twitter stream about topics related to your major and career plan. Link your followers to useful articles, and start following people who are working your chosen field.

ROUND OUT YOUR RÉSUMÉ WITH A PORTFOLIO

Photographers, contractors, and designers regularly show portfolios filled with samples of their work. Today, employers and educators increasingly see the portfolio as a tool that's useful for everyone. Some schools require students to create them, and some employers want to see a portfolio before they hire.

Portfolios consist of artifacts. An *artifact* is any object that's important to you and that reveals something about yourself. Examples include awards, recommendation letters, job descriptions for positions you've held, writing samples, presentations, articles about projects you've done, lists of grants or scholarships you've received, programs from performances you've given, and transcripts of your grades. Your portfolio can also include photographs, audio or video recordings, Web sites, or representations of anything else you've created.

To save hours when creating your portfolio, start documenting your artifacts. Record the "five W's" about each one: *who* was involved with it, *what* you did with it, *when* it was created, *where*

it was created, and *why* the artifact is important to you. Update this information as you collect new artifacts. Whenever possible, manage this information with a computer, using word-processing or database software.

When you're ready to create a portfolio for a specific audience, write your purpose—for example, to demonstrate your learning or to document your work experience as you prepare for a job interview.

Also think about your audience—the people who will see your portfolio. Predict what questions they will ask and make sure they're answered in your portfolio. Screen artifacts with your purpose and audience in mind. If a beautiful artifact fails to meet your purpose or fit your audience, leave it out for now.

Consider presenting your portfolio online in the form of a personal Web site with an online portfolio of your work or keeping a blog and writing a post every 2 weeks or so. Focus your posts on topics related to your career plan. Search for blogs by people with similar interests and add constructive comments to their posts.

SEE YOUR RÉSUMÉ AS A WORK IN PROGRESS

To create an effective résumé, plan to revise it regularly. Save a copy on a flash drive or computer hard drive in a file you can update. See which version of your résumé leads to the most interviews.

Look at a lot of sample résumés, especially from people in your career field. There is no ideal format for a résumé. Just focus on doing what works.

Also combine your résumé with other strategies. If you just send out résumés and neglect to make personal contacts, you will be disappointed with the results. Instead, research companies and do information interviews. Contact potential employers directly—even if they don't have a job opening at the moment. Find people in organizations who have the power to hire you. Then use every job contact you have to introduce yourself to those people and schedule an interview. To get the most from your résumé, use it to support a variety of job-hunting strategies. ■

FINE TUNE YOUR
cover letter

Remember the primary question in an employer's mind: What do you have to offer us? Using a three-part structure can help you answer this question.

1. Gain attention

In your first sentence, address the person who can hire you and grab that person's attention. Make a statement that appeals directly to her self-interest. Write something that moves a potential employer to say, "We can't afford to pass this person up. Call him right away to set up an appointment."

To come up with ideas for your opening, complete the following sentence: "The main benefits that I can bring to your organization are . . . ." Another option: "My work experience ties directly to several points mentioned in your job description. First, ..."

Perhaps someone the employer knows told you about this job opening. Mention this person in your opening paragraph, especially if she has a positive reputation in the organization.

2. Build interest

Add a fact or two to back up your opening sentence. If you're applying for a specific job opening, state this.

If you're not, then offer an idea that will intrigue the employer enough to respond anyway. Another option is to give a summary of your key qualifications for a specific job. Briefly refer to your experience and highlight a few key achievements.

3. Take care of business

Refer the reader to your résumé. Mention that you'll call at a specific point to follow up. Then make good on your promise.

And don't forget . . .

- Whenever possible, address your letter to a specific person. Make sure to use this person's correct title and mailing address. If you cannot find a specific name, then address your letter to "Dear Hiring Manager for [name of the position]."

- Use a simple typeface that is easy to read.

- Tailor each letter you write to the specific company and position you are applying for. Sending a "stock letter" implies that you don't really care about the job.

- Thank your reader for her time and consideration.

12

Use job interviews to "hire" an employer

Helder Almeida/Shutterstock.com

Job interviews are times for an employer to size up applicants and screen most of them out. The reverse is also true: Interviews offer *you* a chance to size up potential employers. Careful preparation and follow-up can help you get the information—and the job—that you want.

PUT INTERVIEWS IN CONTEXT

Mention the phrase *job hunting*, and many people think about poring through the help-wanted sections in newspapers and Web sites, sending out hundreds of résumés, and going to employment agencies. The desired result is an interview that leads to a job offer.

There's a big problem with these typical job-hunting strategies: They don't work well.[3] Many employers turn to help-wanted listings, résumés, and employment agencies only as a last resort. When they have positions to fill, they prefer instead to hire people they already know. Employers also listen closely when friends, family members, and coworkers recommend someone *they* know.

Richard Bolles, author of *What Color Is Your Parachute? A Practical Manual for Job-Hunters and Career-Changers,* recommends the following steps in job hunting:

- Discover which skills you want to use in your career.
- Discover which jobs draw on the skills you want to use.
- Interview people who are doing the kind of jobs you'd want to do.

- Research companies you'd like to work for, and find out what kinds of problems they face on a daily basis.
- Identify a person at each one of these companies who has the power to hire you.
- Arrange an interview with that person, even if the company has no job openings at the moment.
- Stay in contact with the people who interviewed you, knowing that a job opening can occur at any time—even during a recession.[4]

Notice that getting an interview comes toward the bottom of the above list—*after* you take the time to discover a lot about yourself and the work world. Those are keys to unlocking the hidden job market.

START BUILDING YOUR NETWORK—NOW

Networking is often described as the most effective way to get a job. Start by sharing your career plans with friends, relatives, neighbors, coworkers, students, instructors, and advisors. Basically, your network includes *anyone* who can hire you or refer you to an employer.

It's never too early to start building your network. Look for student and professional organizations that relate to your career plan. Go to conferences, conventions, and job fairs. Talk often about your skills and the work you want to do. Even a casual conversation in the grocery store or dentist's office can lead to job

> # When you want a job, tell everyone—especially people who have the power to hire you. This sets the stage for getting interviews.

openings. Keep a list of the people you meet and brief notes about what you discussed.

Also begin networking online. Do this by creating profiles on Web sites such as Twitter, Facebook, and LinkedIn. Develop your online presence with your career goals in mind. Take part in online discussion groups. Read career-related blogs and post comments. Connect with members of your network. Also consider building a personal Web site that can function as an online résumé and portfolio.

Anything about you that appears online can affect your job search. So, post only information that you want to be made public. At least once each year, do an Internet search on your name and review the results. Remove content that could hurt your job prospects.

The bottom line: When you want a job, tell everyone—especially people who have the power to hire you. This sets the stage for getting interviews.

BEFORE YOU GO TO THE INTERVIEW

To get the most from your interviews, learn everything you can about each organization that interests you. Start by searching the Internet. Then head to your campus and public libraries. Tell a reference librarian that you're researching specific companies in preparation for a job interview, and ask for good sources of information.

Before you interview for a job at any organization, learn about:

- The organization's products and services
- Major developments in the organization during the past year
- Directions that the organization plans to go during the upcoming year
- Names of the organization's major divisions
- Names of people who could hire you
- The types of jobs they offer

Next, prepare for common questions. Many interviewers have the following questions on their mind, even if they don't ask them directly:

- How did you find out about us?
- Will we be comfortable working with you?

- How can you help us?
- Will you learn this job quickly?
- What makes you different from other people applying for this job?

Write out brief answers to those questions. Mention personal characteristics such as those listed in "Master student qualities" on page 3. Also describe your skills and specific examples of how you used them to create positive results.

Next, summarize the main points you want to make on a single sheet of paper. Then practice delivering them verbally to the point where you barely refer to the sheet. Your goal is to sound prepared without delivering canned answers.

For extra practice, prepare for the following questions:

What do you want to tell me about yourself? For interviewers, this question serves several purposes. First, it encourages you to open up. The interviewer wants to get a sense of who you are as a person—beyond your cover letter and résumé. The question also tests your ability to think on your feet. A skilled interviewer will pay as much attention to *how* you answer the question as to *what* you say. Focus on the top two to three things that you want the interviewer to recall about you. Talk about aspects of your education and experience that most qualify you for the job. Do *not* give the story of your life.

What are your weaknesses? Interviewers want to know that you have enough self-awareness to spot your limitations. By planning in advance, you will be prepared to share a weakness that points to one of your strengths. For example, you might be slow to complete some tasks because you show a high level of attention to detail. At the same time, declare your intention to improve.

Why should I hire you? The full version is *Why should I hire you instead of any of the other people who are applying for this job?* Take a cue from the field of advertising, and develop your "unique selling proposition." This is the main thing that sets you apart from other job applicants. Focus on a key benefit that you can deliver—one that's unusual or distinctive. Begin your answer with a reference to the interviewer's organization. For example, mention a current development such as new product, service, or initiative. Then talk specifically about how you can enhance that new development.

If you plan to bring examples of work from your portfolio, contact the employer ahead of time to find out how many people will be at the interview so you can bring the correct number of copies.

Also plan to dress appropriately for your interview. Don't choose clothing, shoes, jewelry, or cologne that will clash with an employer's expectations. If you have tattoos, be careful about revealing them.

Round out your preparation by reviewing the "Power Process: Be it." To convince an employer that you can do a job, first convince yourself. Be authentic. Start from a conviction that you already *are* an excellent candidate, and that the job connects with your values. Your passion and personality counts as much as any prepared answer.

12

DURING THE INTERVIEW

Plan to arrive early for your interview. While you're waiting, observe the workplace. Notice what people are saying and doing. See whether you can "read" the company culture by making informal observations.

Just before the interview begins, remind yourself that you have one goal—to get the *next* interview. The top candidates for a job often talk to several people in a company.

When you meet the interviewer, do three things right away: smile, make eye contact, and give a firm handshake. Nonverbal communication creates a lasting impression.

After making small talk, the interviewer will start asking questions. Draw on the answers you've prepared. At the same time, respond to the *exact* questions that you're asked. Speak naturally and avoid the impression that you're making a speech or avoiding a question.

Stay aware of how much you talk. Avoid answers that are too brief or too long. Respond to each question for a minute or two. If you have more to say, end your answer by saying, "Those are the basics. I can add more if you want."

A skilled interviewer will allow time for *you* to ask questions about the company. Use this time to your full advantage. Some good questions to ask:

- When does the job begin?
- What is a typical day like?
- What would I work on if I were to get the job?
- What training is offered for this job?
- Are there opportunities to advance?
- Who will supervise me in this job?
- Could I take a tour of the workplace?

Save questions about benefits, salary, and vacation days for the second interview. When you get to that point, you know that the employer is interested in you. You might have leverage to negotiate.

Be sure to find out the next step in the hiring process and when it will take place. Also ask interviewers for their business cards and how they want you to follow up. Some people are fine with a phone call, fax, e-mail, or other form of online communication. Others prefer a good, old-fashioned letter.

If you're truly interested in the job and feel comfortable with the interviewer, ask one more question: "Do you have any concerns about hiring me?" Listen carefully to the reply. Then respond to each concern in a polite way.

AFTER THE INTERVIEW

Congratulate yourself for getting as far in the hiring process as an interview. Write a Discovery Statement that describes your strengths, along with what you learned about your potential employer. Also write an Intention Statement about ways to be more effective during your next interview.

Now comes follow-up. This step can give you the edge that leads to a job offer.

Pull out the business cards from the people who interviewed you. Write them thank-you notes, following each person's preference for paper-based or online contact. Do this within 2 business days after the interview. If you talked to several people at the same company, then write a different note to each one.

Besides thanking each person for an interview, mention something that you discussed. Include a reminder of why you're a "fit" for the job. Proofread each note carefully.

Also alert your references that they might get a contact from the interviewers.

Within 5 business days, find a reason to contact the interviewer again. For example, e-mail a link to an interesting article and explain how it might be useful. If you have a Web site with a blog, let them know about a recent post. Reinforce the value you will bring to their team.

If you have permission to make contact by phone, also do so within 10 business days of the interview.

If you get turned down for the job after your interview, don't take it personally. Every interview is a source of feedback about what works—and what doesn't work—in contacting employers. Use that feedback to interview more effectively next time.

Also remember that each person you talked to is now a member of your network. This is true even if you do not get a job offer. Follow up by asking interviewers to keep you in mind for future job openings. Using this approach, you gain from every interview, no matter what the outcome. ■

> Stay aware of how much you talk. Avoid answers that are too brief or too long. Respond to each question for a minute or two. If you have more to say, end your answer by saying, "Those are the basics. I can add more if you want."

You're One Click Away...
from discovering more job-hunting strategies online.

Craft the story of you

Job interviewers are like most of us—they enjoy a good story. That's what they really want when they say things like *Tell me a little about yourself.* Instead of responding with a verbal version of your résumé, craft a compelling story that the interviewer will immediately want to share with colleagues.

You can take a cue from storytelling experts— Hollywood screenwriters. Many films are based on a three-act structure:

- Act I is about a *complication* (problem) faced by the main character.
- Act II is about the *challenges* that character faces in dealing with the complication.
- Act III is about *closure*—how the character resolved the complication by changing herself, changing the circumstances of her life, or both.

For this exercise, take a significant event from your work experience and write a story about it. Keep it short—three paragraphs, with one paragraph for each "act" of your story. Remember that your overall goal is to narrate true events in a memorable way.

Start with an interesting complication. For instance, you might write about the time that:

- You were assigned to train a coworker that no one wanted to work with.
- You faced a sudden funding shortfall for your nonprofit organization and had only one month to raise the money you needed.
- You worked on a project team with people who wouldn't talk to each other.

Then describe about the challenges that followed and how you solved them. Here's an example:

I was the manager on duty at a coffee shop. We usually got extremely busy during the morning rush hour—from 8 A.M. to 9 A.M.—when many of our customers stopped by on their way to work. On one morning, the line stretched almost out the door. (Complication)

A customer stepped up to the counter and ordered a large espresso drink that was complicated to make—a skim, extra-hot, half-decaffeinated latté with extra whipped cream. My coworker, who was making the drinks, forgot the "extra-hot" part. The customer took her latté, shouted that it was "frigid" and called us incompetent. Then she stormed over to a table, sat down, and sulked. (Challenge)

I gave her a few minutes to cool down. Then I went over and apologized that we'd made a mistake with her drink, and offered to make another one for free. I'd seen her come in the store before, so I also asked what it would take for her to become a regular customer. It turned out that she had restaurant experience, and she answered my question with some great ideas for making our service more efficient. The next time she came in, she saw that we'd acted on several of her suggestions. After that, she stopped by the shop every day. (Closure)

Now write your story in the space below. Then practice telling it in a way that sounds natural and unscripted.

_____

_____

_____

_____

_____

_____

_____

_____

_____

_____

_____

_____

_____

_____

_____

_____

_____

_____

_____

12

Succeeding as a new employee

Your first year at a new job represents a distinct stage in your life, especially if it's your first job after getting a degree. You're no longer a student. Nor are you a seasoned professional in your new position. You've left one world behind, and your new world is still an unknown.

The way that you manage this year might affect your career for years to come. Make the most of this key transition period with the following strategies.

Prepare for culture clash. People in the worlds of higher education and work play by different rules. For example:

- Students might get used to structured courses with lots of direction from teachers; in the workplace, they might get little direction from supervisors.
- Students might be used to a flexible schedule—and get saddled with a tight "eight to five" schedule at work.
- Students might thrive on mastering ideas and facts—and be forced to master office politics at work.
- Students can get used to focusing on their individual development—and discover that work is all about becoming a team player.
- Students might get used to moving in groups of people who know about their academic accomplishments—and find themselves among strangers on the first day at a new job.

One powerful way to prepare for this clash of cultures is to simply know that it's coming. In addition, review the Introduction to this book for suggestions about mastering the transition to higher education. The strategies presented there—such as admitting your feelings, giving yourself time, and taking constructive action—can help you as you make *any* transition, including the transition to a new job.

Focus on attitudes first. As a new employee, your first concern might be succeeding at job *tasks*. The top questions on your mind might be "Am I really prepared to *do* this job?" and "Can I actually complete the projects that my boss gives me?"

Meanwhile, your boss's top concern might be *attitudes*. She's probably asking herself, "Is this new person open to coaching?" and "Will he fit in with our team?" If your boss could talk candidly about her desires for "new hires," she might say, "Send me someone with a positive attitude, a work ethic, and plenty of energy. We'll teach him everything else he needs to know."

Remember that your boss scoped out your qualifications *before* you got hired. Because she hired you, she's probably confident that you can handle job tasks now or learn to do them within a reasonable period. To really shine as a new employee, remember the "soft" skills—those that relate to personality and people.

People in 12-step programs, such as Alcoholics Anonymous, talk about the usefulness of HOW attitudes—Honesty, Openness, and Willingness. This is also a useful acronym for succeeding as a new employee:

- Be honest when you don't understand directions, and be willing to ask questions.
- Be open to feedback about your performance, and be willing to change your behavior on the basis of the feedback.
- Be willing to complete the mundane tasks that are part of almost every job, and understand what it means to "pay your dues."

Another thing to keep in mind: Technical skills help people get hired. However, the lack of transferable skills—such as communicating tactfully and collaborating skillfully—can get them fired.

Use a knowledge of learning styles to decode the culture. Every organization, large or small, develops its own culture. One way to succeed in the workplace is to "decode" company cultures—the basic assumptions and shared values that shape human behavior in the workplace every day. You can use this knowledge to prevent misunderstanding, resolve conflict, and forge lasting relationships.

Being culturally savvy starts with discovering "the way we do things around here"—the beliefs and behaviors that are widely shared by your coworkers. In terms of the learning styles discussed in Chapter 2: First Steps, this calls for *reflective observation*. In other words, keep your eyes open. See what actions are rewarded and which are criticized. Observe what people do and say to gain credibility in your organization.

You may disagree with what you see and find yourself making negative judgments about your coworkers. Remember that you cannot fully observe behaviors and judge them at the same time. Play the role of a social scientist and collect facts impartially.

Next, create theories about how people succeed in your organization. In terms of the learning cycle, this is the stage of *abstract conceptualization*. In particular, notice the unwritten "rules" that govern your workplace. Your coworkers may behave on the basis of beliefs such as these:

- Never make the boss look bad.
- Some commitments are not meant to be kept.

- If you want to get promoted, then be visible.
- Everyone is expected to work some overtime.
- Before you try to change the rules around here, prove that you know what you're doing.
- Before we assign you to a big project, build a solid track record of small successes.

Once you understand the norms and standards of your company, you can consciously choose whether to accept them. This calls for two other stages in the cycle of learning—*actively experimenting* with new behaviors and gaining *concrete experiences*. In any case, decoding any culture begins with a First Step—telling the truth about how it works right now.

Master office politics. The unspoken rules for getting recognized and rewarded are usually what people mean when they talk about office politics. One way to deal with office politics is to pretend they don't exist. The downfall of this strategy is that such rules are a fact of life.

Another option is to be politically savvy *and* still hold fast to your values. You can move through the ranks of power and meet ethical career goals at the same time. Here are some specific strategies:

Grow "industry-smart." Read trade journals and newsletters related to your field. Keep up with current developments. Speak the language shared by the decision makers in your organization.

Promote your boss. During your first year with an organization, the single most important person in your work life is probably your boss. This is the person who most closely monitors your performance. This is also the person who can become your biggest advocate. Find out what this person needs and wants. Learn about her goals and then assist her to meet them.

Be visible. To gain credibility in your organization, get involved in a high-profile project that you believe in. Then perform well. Go beyond the minimum standards. Meet the project goals—and deliver even more.

Get close to the power centers. People who advance to top positions are often those who know the language of sales, marketing, and information technology. These departments are power centers. They directly affect the bottom line.

Knowing this means that you can enhance your company's profitability—no matter what position you hold. Look for ways to save money and time. Suggest workable ways to streamline procedures or reduce costs. Focus on solutions to problems, no matter how small, and you'll play the ultimate political game—making a contribution. ■

Surviving your first day

Dress the part. Many students cultivate an eclectic wardrobe that won't pass the test for a new job. Even employers with "casual days" prefer to meet new employees in standard business attire. Think back to what people in the office were wearing when you showed up for your job interview. To make a positive impression, put special effort into looking your best on your first day.

Notice your "nonverbals." Remember to shake hands firmly and say hello in a friendly voice. Make eye contact and smile. Also check out your other nonverbal messages. In meetings, for example, check to see whether your posture says, *I'm here now and paying attention to what you say.*

Take notes. During your first day you'll cover lots of details. First, there's the obvious stuff—where to sit, where to park, where to eat, where to make photocopies, where to take breaks, where to go to the bathroom. Then there's the higher level stuff, such as phone numbers, user IDs, and passwords for Internet access. Be prepared with paper and pen to write this information down.

Pack a briefcase. Companies just love to push paper at new employees—brochures, forms, maps, manuals, and more. When you receive such material, look at it for a few seconds. This communicates in a small and significant way that you pay attention to details. Then place the papers in a professional-looking folder or briefcase.

Go easy on yourself. Notice whether there's a self-critical voice in your head that's saying something like "You're not fooling anyone—you really have no idea what you're doing here." No one else hears that voice, just like no one expects you to perform to perfection on your first day.

Do not say these words: "Wow, that's not how we did things at my last job." This invites an inevitable response: "Well, then why did you leave that job?" Expect procedures to differ from job to job, and look for chances to suggest improvements in the future.

12

© Markus/Shutterstock

LEARNING ON *the job*

The workplace is a laboratory for learning from experience. In this laboratory, we get to immerse ourselves in action and accomplish tasks. We get to reflect on our daily experiences and draw lessons from them. Resolving conflict, solving problems, and learning from mistakes are all part of the process. Learning and working are inseparable.

Also remember that employers value a "quick study"—someone who can get up to speed at a new job in minimum time. In addition, some of the information you acquired in school might become quickly outdated. Learning how to learn—a key transferable skill—is an asset if you want to prosper in the job market and advance in your career.

Let go of old ideas about learning. Educational literature is full of distinctions such as "theory versus application" and "beginner versus advanced." These distinctions can be useful. If you want

to learn on the job, you can often benefit by letting them go. In workplace-based learning, for example:

- There is no "finish" line such as a graduation ceremony. Rather, you learn continuously, taking periodic progress checks to assess your current skills.

- Outside of formal training programs, there are no course divisions. A new job might call on you to integrate knowledge of several subjects at once.

- There is no syllabus for learning a subject, with assignments carefully laid out in a planned sequence. You might learn concepts in an "illogical" order as dictated by the day-to-day demands of a job.

If this sounds like a prescription for chaos, consider that it reflects the ways you've always learned outside the classroom. Teaching yourself anything from a new golf swing to a new song on the guitar has a lot in common with the way you teach yourself on the job.

Seize informal opportunities to learn. At work, your learning may take place in unplanned, informal ways. Look for opportunities to

- Do self-directed reading on topics related to new job tasks.
- Observe people who demonstrate a skill that you would like to develop.
- Ask questions on the spot.
- Attend trade shows for new products or services offered by your company's competitors.
- Join professional organizations in your field that offer workshops and seminars.
- Make yourself into the company expert on a new product or procedure by digging into brochures, Web sites, professional journals, technical manuals, and other sources of information that your coworkers may have overlooked.

Learn as an intern. Another way to learn while you earn is an internship. As an intern, you work in a job that relates directly to your career interests. Internships blend classroom learning with on-the-job experience. You get to put your work content *and* transferable skills into action.

Internships often give you academic credit. Some involve paid positions, whereas others are volunteer opportunities. Interns usually prepare for their assignments by completing courses in a specific field. Note that internships may be called by other names, such as *co-op experience, practicum, externship*, and *field experience*.

> Use your goal-setting skills to set due dates for acquiring new skills or producing new outcomes in your worklife.

To find an internship, make an appointment with someone at the career center or counseling center at your school. There you can connect with employers in your area who are looking for interns. You will likely submit a résumé and cover letter explaining your career interests. This is valuable in itself as experience in applying for jobs.

You can also locate organizations that interest you and contact them directly about internships. Even companies that do not have formal internship programs may accept applications.

Start looking for internships early. During a fall semester, for example, start searching for internships for the spring or summer. Talk to friends, parents, family, neighbors, and instructors to discover whether they know about internships for you. In addition, ask a reference librarian to help you find internship guides. Some look like college catalogs, listing popular positions with key contacts and due dates for applications.

To get the most from your internships, act professionally every moment that you're on the job:

Get direction. Find an internship supervisor and meet with that person regularly. Ask this person to explain your tasks and offer feedback on how you're doing.

Set a goal. Think about what you'd most like to gain from your internship. For example, your main goal might be to gain information about a career that you can't get from any other source, clarify your choice of a major, or meet people who can recommend you for a job in the future.

Ask questions. You are not expected to be an expert. If you are in doubt about how to complete any task, ask for help.

Meet people. Some internships allow you to work in several areas of a company. If yours does not, then attend company events where you can meet a variety of people.

Take the initiative. If you see a way to save time or money for the organization, then suggest it to your supervisor. If your idea works, be sure to share the credit with her.

Look for value in any experience. Interns are sometimes asked to make photocopies, run errands, and do other "grunt" work. Complete these tasks with a constructive attitude. Use them to demonstrate that you have integrity and a strong work ethic. These are key transferable skills.

Reflect on your internship. Internships offer a great way to test a career choice, even if you find out that you don't like a particular job. You can benefit from ruling out a career choice early on—especially if it involves a major with a lot of required courses.

Write Discovery Statements about what you learn from your internship. List details about what you accomplished. Also write Intention Statements about what you want from your next work experience. You'll find these journal entries useful whenever you hunt for a job and plan your career.

Stay in touch. Remember that any internship might lead you to a full-time, professional job following graduation. Keep in contact with the people you meet. Even if they are working at another company when you graduate, they can help you find job openings.

Work with a mentor. Another strategy for learning at work is to find a mentor—a partner in your professional and personal development. Often people will be flattered to take on such a role in your life.

Prepare to be mentored. Before you ask someone to mentor you, reflect on your goals for this relationship. Begin with *what* you want to gain rather than *whom* to ask for mentoring. List the specific skills that you want to develop with a mentor's involvement. Over time, you might work with several mentors, each with different expertise, to develop a variety of skills.

For maximum clarity, put your ideas in writing. Write Discovery Statements to list your current skills, recent examples of how you've used them, and insights from your mentor.

Also write Intention Statements. Use your goal-setting skills to set due dates for acquiring new skills or producing new outcomes in your work life. Also state when you want to begin and end the mentoring sessions. Keep in mind that many mentoring relationships are short term, taking place over weeks or months rather than years.

Approach potential mentors. Make a list of several people who have demonstrated competence in the skills you want to gain, along with the energy and desire to take on a mentee—that is, you. If you can find people at your workplace with a positive reputation and influence in your organization, that's an added plus.

Next, contact each person on your list and mention that you're seeking a mentor. Summarize your goals and timetable. Also suggest ways that you can create value for a mentor, such as helping that person complete a project or achieve one of *his* development goals. The more you give to the mentor relationship, the more you'll get out of it.

If a potential mentor is too busy to work with you right now, ask if she can refer you to someone else. After meeting with several people, choose one person to work with.

Schedule regular meetings with your mentor. During these meetings, put all your listening skills to work. Resist the temptation to debate, argue, or justify your behavior. Simply receive what your mentor has to say. Ask questions to clarify anything you don't understand.

Accept your mentor's feedback. Remember that a mentor is not a boss, parent, or taskmaster. Instead, you're looking for coaching. A coach helps you clarify your goals and then offers nonjudgmental observations of your behavior along with suggestions for improvement. However, the responsibility for your day-to-day performance and long-term development lies with you.

When you asked for mentoring, you signed on for objective feedback and suggestions—including ideas you may have resisted in the past. A commitment to change implies the willingness to think, speak, and act in new ways. Stay open to suggestions.

Beyond listening, move into action. When your mentor offers an insight, look for an immediate way to apply it. Experiment with a new behavior every day.

Whenever possible, create a way to measure your progress. For example, you could note the number of times you practice a new habit. Or you could summarize ratings from your performance reviews at work. Include these measurements in your Discovery

©iStockphoto.com/AlexRaths

Statements, and share them with your mentor. Follow up with Intention Statements that describe exactly what new behaviors you want to implement. Focus on small, simple changes that you can make immediately.

Seek closure—and continue. When you come to the end of a mentoring relationship, offer your thanks and celebrate your accomplishments. Solidify your learning by listing the top five insights or skills you gained.

In addition, choose your next step. List upcoming opportunities to practice your newly acquired skills. Also consider the benefits of working with a mentor again in the future. This is a development tool that you can use for the rest of your life.

Coach yourself. Do a daily debriefing on your way home from work. Take a few minutes to ask yourself powerful questions—the kind that a good mentor would ask. For example:

- What did I accomplish today?
- What did I find challenging today?
- Based on what I learned today, what will I do differently tomorrow?
- With whom did I interact today?
- Do I want to follow up with any of those people tomorrow?
- What questions do I have for those people?
- How can I express my appreciation for a coworker tomorrow?

By asking and answering quality questions, you set yourself up for a lifetime of learning at work. ▪

Create a personal development plan

Writing a personal development plan means thinking creatively and critically about the changes you'd like to make in your work life. You already have a powerful tool for this purpose—the Discovery and Intention Journal Entry System. Get started by completing the following sentences:

I could fix a persistent problem at work by getting better at . . .

_____

_____

_____

_____

_____

_____

_____

In performance reviews and other evaluations, I have been told more than once that I could get better at . . .

_____

_____

_____

_____

_____

_____

_____

In the future, my organization will need people who excel at . . .

_____

_____

_____

_____

_____

I could get a better job by improving my skill at . . .

_____

_____

_____

_____

_____

_____

_____

_____

_____

The one skill that's most important for me to develop right now is . . .

_____

_____

_____

_____

_____

_____

_____

_____

The next action that I intend to take in developing this skill is . . .

_____

_____

_____

_____

_____

12

Creating VALUE from *any* **job**

Job disappointment has countless symptoms, including statements such as "My boss is a jerk," "I'm so bored," and "This is too hard." Sometimes those thoughts lead to a conclusion: "I quit." In many cases of job dissatisfaction, however, there are solutions that do less damage to your immediate income—and your long-term job prospects.

Manage your expectations. Instead of changing jobs, consider changing the way you think. Managing your expectations is especially useful if you've just graduated from school and find yourself working in an entry-level position in your field. Students who are used to stimulating class discussions and teachers with a passion for their subject might be shocked by the realities of the workplace: people who hide behind a cubicle and avoid human contact, managers with technical skills but no people skills, coworkers who get promoted on the basis of political favors rather than demonstrated skills.

If you were planning to run a company within six months after joining it, then perhaps your expectations were unrealistic. Sometimes the problem boils down to "shoulds" such as these:

- My first job after graduating *should* draw on all the skills I developed in school.
- Everyone I meet on a job *should* be interesting, competent, and kind.
- Every task that I perform at work *should* be enjoyable.
- My work environment *should* be problem-free.

See if you can replace the *should* in such statements with *can* or *could*. For example: "Even though I'm not using all my skills, I *can* use this job to learn about corporate culture and coping with office politics." Or "I *could* use this job to develop at least one skill that I can transfer to my next job."

Practice problem solving. Sometimes you can benefit by adjusting more than your attitude. Apply your transferable skills at problem solving. Write Discovery Statements about the following:

- How you felt when you started the job
- When you started feeling unhappy with the job
- Any specific events that triggered your dissatisfaction

This writing can help you pinpoint the sources of job dissatisfaction. Possibilities include conflict with coworkers, a mismatch between your skills and the job requirements, or a mismatch between your personal values and the values promoted in the workplace.

No matter what the problem, you can brainstorm solutions. Ask friends and family members for help. If you're bored with work, for example, then propose a project that will create value for your boss and offer to lead it. If your supervisor seems unhappy with your performance, ask for coaching to do better.

Also reread this book for possible solutions. If you feel stressed, review the stress-management techniques in Chapter 7: Tests and Chapter 11: Health. Choose at least one technique to use on a daily basis. When you're in conflict with a coworker, apply strategies for resolving conflict presented in Chapter 9: Communicating. If you want more challenging assignments, then ask for them.

Moving into action to solve the problem leads to a key discovery: You have a lot of influence on the quality of your work life, no matter what boss you have.

Focus on process. Practice shifting your focus from the content of your job to the processes you use—from *what* you do to *how* you do it. Even if a task seems boring or beneath you, see if you can do it impeccably and with total attention. As you do, project a professional image in everything from the way you dress to the way you speak.

One strategy for handling a "dead-end" job is to do it so well that you get noticed—and promoted to a new job. ■

JOURNAL ENTRY 27
Discovery/Intention Statement
Create value from any job

You can use this Journal Entry any time that you feel unhappy at work. Complete the following sentences, using additional paper as needed.

The transferable skills I am learning on this job include . . .

_____

_____

The work-content skills that I am learning on this job include . . .

_____

_____

The aspects of this job that I *do* control include . . .

_____

_____

_____

I intend to make this job more satisfying by . . .

_____

_____

_____

Discover *yourself:*
Explore *career assessments*

Career assessments are also called *interest assessments, vocational aptitude tests,* or *skill inventories.* They can be useful resources for discovering your work-related preferences and planning your career. Although assessments cannot offer the final word on what kind of work is best for you, they can yield ideas that might not occur to you—and suggest useful ways to follow up.

Your school's career planning or counseling center will probably offer some assessments. To get the most out of them, keep the following ideas in mind.

Add the human touch. Meet with an experienced career counselor at your school. A counselor can help you select appropriate assessments and understand the results. (This is true even when an assessment is listed as "self-directed.") A counselor can also suggest next steps for creating your career plan and connect you with other services.

Remember that assessments are not tests. Some assessments include the word *test* in their title. Even so, there are no right or wrong answers to the questions they include.

Ask about cost. Many assessments are available online for free. Others require payment up to $100 or more. The fee-based assessments might include a session with a personal career counselor via the phone, e-mail, or Web-based conferencing.

Check with the career center at your school to find out which free assessments they offer. Pay for an assessment only when you're convinced that the benefits will justify the cost.

Remember that assessments differ in quality. Some assessments are backed by decades of research. Others were created last week. Do not expect *any* single assessment—free or fee based—to give a comprehensive picture of your personality and career interests.

Take several assessments and compare the results. Some assessments will help you identify major aspects of your personality and give only general guidelines for choosing a career. Other assessments will crank out a list of specific job titles for you to consider. Take both kinds of assessments to see what they have to offer.

Keep the results on file. If you take an assessment online, print out the results. Keep them in a folder along with other career planning documents.

Consider taking an assessment more than once—for example, once during this semester and again next year. Doing so will allow you to compare the new results with the earlier results and see if they differ. This can lead to useful insights about your changing career interests.

Combine assessments with other forms of self-discovery. Assessments are just one way to gather ideas for your career plan. Use activities such as the Journal Entries and Critical Thinking Exercises in this book to round out any assessment results.

Remember that what you do with the results is always a personal choice. No assessment can dictate your career direction or substitute for your gut instincts. If the result of an assessment seems wildly off base to you, then it probably is. Take what seems most valuable from each assessment and leave the rest.

Look for assessments online. You can start by doing an Internet search with the keywords *career assessment* or *self-assessment.* Inspect the results of your search carefully. Some of the more reputable assessments you might find are listed here:

- *Campbell™ Interest and Skill Survey*, a well-known assessment that includes several hundred multiple-choice items. This assessment links to specific information about 60 possible careers.
- *Keirsey™ Temperament Sorter*, based on the Myers-Briggs Type Indicator®, a prominent personality assessment. Use the Keirsey results as a basis for taking more career-focused assessments.
- *Career Liftoff Interest Inventory (CLII)*, a 240-item assessment linked to a set of codes for classifying job interests.
- *Career Maze*, an online assessment that aims to provide an 82-item list of your personal characteristics and ways to connect them with specific jobs.

Have fun. Approach assessments with a spirit of adventure and play. You're just gathering data, not putting yourself on trial. The purpose of taking any assessment and planning your career is to discover new paths to fulfillment—and to create the career of your dreams. ■

12

✓ CRITICAL THINKING EXERCISE 29

Use informal ways to discover yourself

During career planning, take time to explore your interests in an informal and playful way. The results can be revealing and useful.

Answer the following questions by writing the first ideas that come to mind. Use additional paper as needed or create a computer file for your writing. Have fun and stay open to new insights.

Imagine that you're at a party, and you're having a fascinating conversation with someone you just met. What does this person do for a living? What is your conversation about?

_____

_____

_____

What do you enjoy doing most with your unscheduled time? List any hobby or other activity that you do not currently define as "work."

_____

_____

_____

_____

Think about the kinds of books, newspaper and magazine articles, and television shows that are most likely to capture your attention. What subjects or situations do they involve?

_____

_____

_____

_____

Do you visit certain Web sites on a regular basis? What are those sites? Why do you find them interesting?

_____

_____

_____

_____

What kinds of problems do you most enjoy solving—those that involve ideas, people, or products? Give an example.

_____

_____

_____

_____

_____

Finally, reread your answers to the previous questions. List three to five interests that are critical to your choice of career.

_____

_____

_____

_____

Create your CAREER plan

There's an old saying: "If you enjoy what you do, you'll never work another day in your life." If you clearly define your career goals and your strategy for reaching them, you can plan your education effectively and create a seamless transition from one job to the next for the rest of your life.

Terry Vine/Getty Images

Career planning involves continuous exploration. There are dozens of effective paths to take. Begin now with the following ideas.

YOUR CAREER IS A CHOICE, NOT A DISCOVERY

Many people approach career planning as if they were panning for gold. They keep sifting through the dirt, clearing the dust, and throwing out the rocks. They are hoping to strike it rich and discover the perfect career.

Other people believe that they'll wake up one morning, see the heavens part, and suddenly know what they're supposed to do. Many of them are still waiting for that magical day to dawn.

You can approach career planning in a different way. Instead of seeing a career as something you discover, you can see it as something you choose. You don't find the right career. You create it.

There's a big difference between these two approaches. Thinking that there's only one "correct" choice for your career can lead to a lot of anxiety: "Did I choose the right one?" "What if I made a mistake?"

Viewing your career as your creation helps you relax. Instead of anguishing over finding the right career, you can stay open to possibilities. You can choose one career today, knowing that you can choose again later.

Suppose that you've narrowed your list of possible careers to five, and you still can't decide. Then just choose one. Any one. Many people will have five careers in a lifetime anyway. You might be able to pursue all five of your careers, and you can do any one of them first. The important thing is to choose.

One caution is in order. Choosing your career is not something to do in an information vacuum. Rather, choose after you've done a lot of research. That includes research into yourself—your skills and interests—and a thorough knowledge of what careers are available.

After you've gathered all of the data, there's only one person who can choose your career: you. This choice does not have to be a weighty one. In fact, it can be like going into your favorite restaurant and choosing from a menu that includes only your favorite dishes. At that point, it's difficult to make a mistake. Whatever your choice, you know you'll enjoy it.

YOU HAVE A WORLD OF CHOICES

Our society offers a limitless array of careers. You no longer have to confine yourself to a handful of traditional categories, such as

12

business, education, government, or manufacturing. People are constantly creating new products and services to meet emerging demands. The number of job titles is expanding so rapidly that we can barely keep track of them.

In addition, people are constantly creating new goods and services to meet emerging needs. For instance, there are people who work as *ritual consultants,* helping people plan weddings, anniversaries, graduations, and other ceremonies. *Space planners* help individuals and organizations arrange furniture and equipment efficiently. *Auto brokers* visit dealers, shop around, and buy a car for you. *Professional organizers* will walk into your home or office and advise you on managing time and paperwork. *Pet psychologists* will help you raise a happy and healthy animal. And *life coaches* will assist you in setting and achieving goals relating to your career or anything else.

The global marketplace creates even more options for you. Through Internet connections and communication satellites that bounce phone calls across the planet, you can exchange messages with almost anyone, anywhere. Your customers or clients could be located in Colorado or China, Pennsylvania or Panama. Your skills in thinking globally and communicating with a diverse world could help you create a new product or service for a new market—and perhaps a career that does not even exist today.

PLAN BY NAMING NAMES

One key to making your career plan real and to ensuring that you can act on it is naming. Go back over your plan to see whether you can include specific names whenever they're called for:

- *Name your job.* List the skills you enjoy using, and find out which jobs use them (the *Occupational Outlook Handbook* is a good resource for this activity). What are those jobs called? List them. Note that the same job might have different names.

- *Name your company—the agency or organization you want to work for.* If you want to be self-employed or start your own business, name the product or service you'd sell. Also list some possible names for your business. If you plan to work for others, name the organizations or agencies that are high on your list.

- *Name your contacts.* Take the list of organizations you just compiled. Find out which people in these organizations are responsible for hiring. List those people, and contact them directly. If you choose self-employment, list the names of possible customers or clients. All of these people are job contacts.

- *Name your location.* Ask whether your career choices are consistent with your preferences about where to live and work. For example, someone who wants to make a living as a studio musician might consider living in a large city such as New York or Toronto. This contrasts with the freelance graphic artist who conducts his business mainly by phone, fax, and e-mail. He might be able to live anywhere and still pursue his career.

DESCRIBE YOUR IDEAL LIFESTYLE

In addition to choosing the content of your career, you have many options for integrating work into the context of your

life. You can work full-time. You can work part-time. You can commute to a cubicle in a major corporation. Or you can work at home and take the 30-second commute from your bedroom to your desk.

Close your eyes. Visualize an ideal day in your life after graduation. Vividly imagine the following:

- Your work setting
- Your coworkers
- Your calendar and to-do list for that day
- Other sights and sounds in your work environment

This visualization emphasizes the importance of finding a match between your career and your lifestyle preferences—the amount of flexibility in your schedule, the number of people you see each day, the variety in your tasks, and the ways that you balance work with other activities.

CONSIDER SELF-EMPLOYMENT

Instead of joining a thriving business, you could create one of your own. If the idea of self-employment seems far-fetched, consider that as a student, you already *are* self-employed. You are setting your own goals, structuring your time, making your own financial decisions, and monitoring your performance. These are all transferable skills that you could use to become your own boss. Remember that many successful businesses—including Facebook and Yahoo!—were started by college students.

TEST YOUR CHOICE—AND BE WILLING TO CHANGE

Career-planning materials and counselors can help you test your choice and change it if you decide to do so. Read books about careers. Search for career-planning Web sites. Ask career counselors about skills assessments that can help you discover more about your skills and identify jobs that call for those skills. Take career-planning courses and workshops sponsored by your school. Visit the career-planning office on campus.

Once you have a career choice, translate it into workplace experience. For example:

- Contact people who are actually doing the job you're researching, and ask them a lot of questions about what it's like (an *information interview*).
- Choose an internship or volunteer position in a field that interests you.
- Get a part-time or summer job in your career field.

If you find that you enjoy such experiences, you've probably made a wise career choice. And the people you meet are possible sources of recommendations, referrals, and employment in the future. If you did *not* enjoy your experiences, celebrate what you learned about yourself. Now you're free to refine your initial career choice or go in a new direction.

Career planning is not a once-and-for-all proposition. Rather, career plans are made to be changed and refined as you gain new information about yourself and the world. You might not walk straight into your dream job right after graduation. And you can approach *any* position in a way that takes you one step closer to your career goal. Do your best at every job, and stay flexible.

Career planning never ends, and the process is the same, whether you're choosing your first career or your fifth.[5] ■

You're One Click Away...
from finding more strategies online for career planning.

Another option: *Don't plan your career*

When they hear the term *career plan*, some people envision a long document that lists goals with due dates and action steps. This is one type of career plan, and it can be useful for people with careers in stable industries. However, there are few of those left anymore.

In the spirit of the "Power Process: Ideas are tools," consider another approach: Don't plan your career—at least in the conventional way. In an economy that's constantly shedding jobs and adding new ones, you can gain stability with an alternative approach to managing your career.

Choose your direction rather than your destination

Instead of listing specific jobs that you'd like to have in the future, go back to your values. Determine what matters to you most about working. For example:

- Do you want to work primarily with people? Ideas? Specific products or materials?
- Do you want to manage people—or answer only to yourself and a handful of clients?
- What's the one thing that you do best—and enjoy doing—that creates value for people?

Put your answers to such questions in writing, and revise them at least once each year. This will give your career a clear and stable career direction no matter what happens to the economy.

Take one new step in that direction

Determine the very next action you will take to move in your chosen direction. Create an intention that you can act on immediately. If you want to become self-employed, for instance, then contact one person who started a successful business, and ask for an information interview.

Reflect on what you learned—and choose your next step

Write Discovery Statements about the results of acting on your intention. What did you learn? In light of those lessons, what is the *next* step you'll take to move in your desired career direction?

The key is to take frequent action and reflect on the results. This process of determining your values and aligning your actions can teach you much about the work world—and open up opportunities that you might have never planned.

12

✔ CRITICAL THINKING EXERCISE 30

Create your career plan—now

Write your career plan. Now. Start the process of career planning, even if you're not sure where to begin. Your response to this exercise can be just a rough draft of your plan, which you can revise and rewrite many times. The point is to get your ideas in writing.

The final format of your plan is up to you. You might include many details, such as the next job title you'd like to have, the courses required for your major, and other training that you want to complete. You might list companies to research and people that could hire you. You might also include target dates to complete each of these tasks.

Another option is to represent your plan visually through flowcharts, time lines, mind maps, or drawings. You can generate these by hand or use computer software.

For now, experiment with career planning by completing the following sentences. Use the space provided, and continue on additional paper as needed. When answering the first question, write down what first comes to your mind. The goal is to begin the process of discovery. You can always change direction after some investigation.

1. The career I choose for now is . . .

_____

_____

_____

_____

_____

_____

_____

_____

_____

_____

2. The major steps that will guide me to this career are . . .

_____

_____

_____

_____

_____

_____

_____

_____

_____

_____

_____

_____

_____

_____

3. The immediate steps I will take to pursue this career are . . .

_____

_____

_____

_____

_____

_____

_____

_____

_____

_____

DISCOVERY WHEEL—COMING FULL CIRCLE

This book doesn't work. It is worthless. Only you can work. Only you can make a difference and use this book to become a more effective student.

The purpose of this book is to give you the opportunity to change your behavior. The fact that something seems like a good idea doesn't necessarily mean that you will put it into practice. This exercise gives you a chance to see what behaviors you have changed on your journey toward becoming a master student and master employee.

Answer each question quickly and honestly. Record your results on the Discovery Wheel on the next few pages. Then compare it with the one you completed in Chapter 2.

The scores on this Discovery Wheel indicate your current strengths and weaknesses on your path toward becoming a master student.

As you complete this self-evaluation, keep in mind that your commitment to change allows you to become a master student. *Your scores might be lower here than on your earlier Discovery Wheel.* That's okay. Lower scores might result from increased self-awareness and honesty, as well as other valuable assets.

Note: The online version of this exercise does not include number ratings, so the results will be formatted differently from those described here. If you did your previous Discovery Wheel online, do it online again. This will help you compare your two sets of responses more accurately.

5 points = This statement is always or almost always true of me.

4 points = This statement is often true of me.

3 points = This statement is true of me about half the time.

2 points = This statement is seldom true of me.

1 point = This statement is never or almost never true of me.

You're One Click Away...
from having your Discovery Wheel scores calculated automatically for you online.

1. _____ I live by a set of values that translates into daily actions.
2. _____ I am willing to accept challenges even when I'm not sure how to meet them.
3. _____ I take responsibility for the quality of my education—and my life.
4. _____ I am gaining skills to support my success in school and in the workplace.
5. _____ I monitor my attitudes and change them when appropriate.
6. _____ I monitor my habits and change them when appropriate.
7. _____ I take effective action even when I don't feel "motivated."
8. _____ I demonstrate a professional work ethic.

_____ **Total score (1) Character**

1. _____ I enjoy learning.
2. _____ I understand and apply the concept of multiple intelligences.
3. _____ I connect my courses to my purpose for being in school.
4. _____ I make a habit of assessing my personal strengths and areas for improvement.
5. _____ I am satisfied with how I am progressing toward achieving my goals.
6. _____ I use my knowledge of learning styles to support my success in school.
7. _____ I am willing to consider any idea that can help me succeed in school—even if I initially disagree with that idea.
8. _____ I regularly remind myself of the benefits I intend to get from my education.

_____ **Total score (2) Self-discovery**

12

1. _____ I set long-term goals and periodically review them.

2. _____ I set short-term goals to support my long-term goals.

3. _____ I write a plan for each day and each week.

4. _____ I assign priorities to what I choose to do each day.

5. _____ I can access a variety of resources to finance my education.

6. _____ I take on debts carefully and repay them on time.

7. _____ I have long-range financial goals and a plan to meet them.

8. _____ I pay off the balance on credit card accounts each month.

_____ **Total score (3) Time & Money**

1. _____ I am confident of my ability to remember.

2. _____ I can remember people's names.

3. _____ At the end of a lecture, I can summarize what was presented.

4. _____ I apply techniques that enhance my memory skills.

5. _____ I can recall information when I'm under pressure.

6. _____ I remember important information clearly and easily.

7. _____ I can jog my memory when I have difficulty recalling.

8. _____ I can relate new information to what I've already learned.

_____ **Total score (4) Memory**

1. _____ I preview and review reading assignments.

2. _____ When reading, I ask myself questions about the material.

3. _____ I underline or highlight important passages when reading.

4. _____ When I read textbooks, I am alert and awake.

5. _____ I relate what I read to my life.

6. _____ I select a reading strategy to fit the type of material I'm reading.

7. _____ I take effective notes when I read.

8. _____ When I don't understand what I'm reading, I note my questions and find answers.

_____ **Total score (5) Reading**

1. _____ When I am in class, I focus my attention.

2. _____ I take notes in class.

3. _____ I am aware of various methods for taking notes and choose those that work best for me.

4. _____ I distinguish important material and note key phrases in a lecture.

5. _____ I copy down material that the instructor writes on the board or overhead display.

6. _____ I can put important concepts into my own words.

7. _____ My notes are valuable for review.

8. _____ I review class notes within 24 hours.

_____ **Total score (6) Notes**

1. _____ I use techniques to manage stress related to exams.

2. _____ I manage my time during exams and am able to complete them.

3. _____ I am able to predict test questions.

4. _____ I adapt my test-taking strategy to the kind of test I'm taking.

5. _____ I understand what essay questions ask and can answer them completely and accurately.

6. _____ I start reviewing for tests at the beginning of the term.

7. _____ I continue reviewing for tests throughout the term.

8. _____ My sense of personal worth is independent of my test scores.

_____ **Total score (7) Tests**

1. _____ I have flashes of insight and think of solutions to problems at unusual times.

2. _____ I use brainstorming to generate solutions to a variety of problems.

3. _____ When I get stuck on a creative project, I use specific methods to get unstuck.

4. _____ I apply the results of my thinking to make effective decisions and solve problems.

5. _____ I am willing to consider different points of view and alternative solutions.

6. _____ I can detect common errors in logic.

7. _____ I construct viewpoints by drawing on information and ideas from many sources.

8. _____ As I share my viewpoints with others, I am open to their feedback.

_____ **Total score (8) Creative & Critical Thinking**

1. _____ I am honest with others about who I am, what I feel, and what I want.
2. _____ Other people tell me that I am a good listener.
3. _____ I can communicate anger, sadness, and fear without blaming others.
4. _____ I can make friends and create valuable relationships in a new setting.
5. _____ I am open to being with people I don't especially like in order to learn from them.
6. _____ I can effectively plan and research a large writing assignment.
7. _____ I create first drafts without criticizing my writing, then edit later for clarity, accuracy, and coherence.
8. _____ I know ways to prepare and deliver effective presentations.

_____ **Total score (9) Communicating**

1. _____ I build rewarding relationships with people from diverse backgrounds.
2. _____ I work cooperatively with others to meet shared goals.
3. _____ I add value to study groups and to teams in the workplace.
4. _____ I can plan a project with multiple steps and deliver quality results on time.
5. _____ I am willing to assume a leadership role when that's appropriate.
6. _____ I can resolve conflict with family members, friends, and coworkers.
7. _____ I ask for help when a problem is too big for me to handle alone.
8. _____ I respond effectively to my emotions and stay aware of how other people feel.

_____ **Total score (10) Collaborating**

1. _____ I have enough energy to study and work—and still enjoy other areas of my life.
2. _____ If the situation calls for it, I have enough reserve energy to put in a long day.
3. _____ The way I eat supports my long-term health.
4. _____ The way I eat is independent of my feelings of self-worth.
5. _____ I exercise regularly to maintain a healthful weight.
6. _____ My emotional health supports my ability to learn.
7. _____ I notice changes in my physical condition and respond effectively.
8. _____ I am in control of any alcohol or other drugs I put into my body.

_____ **Total score (11) Health**

1. _____ I see learning as a lifelong process.
2. _____ I relate school to what I plan to do for the rest of my life.
3. _____ I have a written career plan and update it regularly.
4. _____ I am building positive relationships with people who support my career plan.
5. _____ I use effective strategies to find a job.
6. _____ I find ways to create value from any job.
7. _____ I use mentoring, internships, on-the-job training, and other strategies to learn at work.
8. _____ I stay up to date on new developments in my career field.

_____ **Total score (12) Career**

12

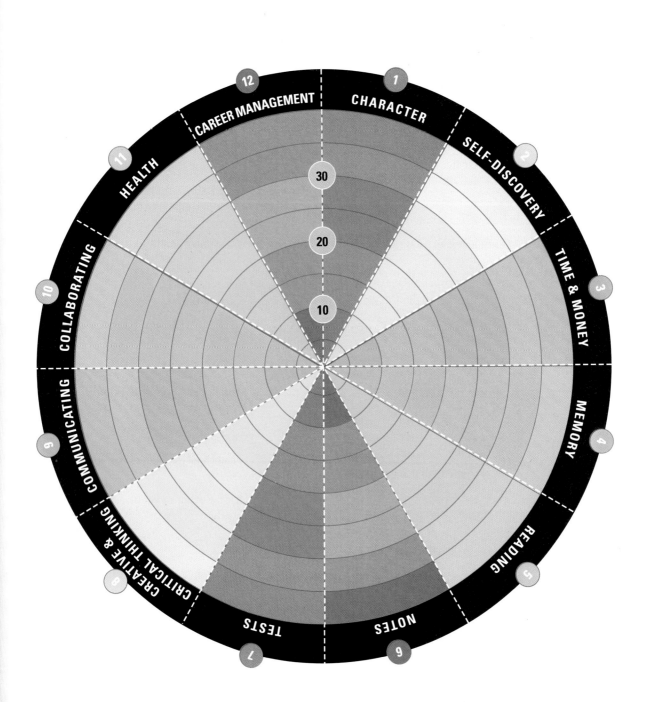

FILLING IN YOUR DISCOVERY WHEEL

Using the total score from each category, shade in each section of the Discovery Wheel. ■

masterstudentprofile

Ruth Handler

(1916–2002) Co-founder of Mattel, who invented the Barbie doll in 1959. After being diagnosed with breast cancer and undergoing a mastectomy, she designed a prosthetic breast that was later patented as Nearly Me.

When Ruth Handler first proposed the idea of a grown-up doll to the toy designers at Mattel—the company she and her husband ran—the designers thought she was crazy. Little girls want to pretend to be mommies, she was told.

No, said Handler. Little girls want to pretend to be bigger girls. And she knew this because she spent a lot of time observing one little girl in particular—her daughter, Barbara, nicknamed "Barbie."

All her life, Ruth has considered the word "no" just another challenge.

When Ruth graduated from East Denver High School and announced her intention to attend college, her family didn't give her a lot of encouragement. Marrying her high-school sweetheart—a broke-but-talented artist named Elliot Handler—was more traditional than going to college. But she ended up at the University of Denver. And she married Elliot anyway. When she took two semesters of business education at the University of California at Los Angeles, she was the only married woman in her class. And she became the first woman to complete the program.

Ruth fell in love with Southern California and was hired as a stenographer at Paramount Studios in Hollywood. The year was 1937. Ruth worked at Paramount until 1941, when she became pregnant with Barbara, and stayed home until after the birth of her son, Ken, in 1944. Staying home made Ruth restless; she wanted to help [her husband] Elliot run his giftware and costume jewelry business. "You make something; I'll sell it," she told him.

In 1944, while the United States was embroiled in World War II, Elliot designed a new style of picture frame made out of the then-revolutionary new plastics. His partner, Harold "Matt" Matson, built samples and Ruth took the frames to a chain of photography studios and got a large order. The three celebrated, calling their new business "Mattel" after MATT and ELliot.

Soon after, plastic was needed for the war effort and became unavailable for civilian use. Fortunately, Elliot came up with the idea of making frames out of scrap wood. Ruth took the samples back to the photography studio and got an even bigger order. Mattel could continue operating. The leftover wood from the picture frames led to a thriving business making doll house furniture.

Worldwide, Mattel sold millions of Ruth Handler's Barbie dolls, boosting the company's sales to $18 million. Within ten years, customers had bought $500 million worth of Barbie products.

Over the years, Ruth moved up from cofounder of the company to executive vice president to president to cochairman of the board of directors. These titles were practically unheard of for women in the 1960s.

Handler remembers one episode that occurred despite her executive status. A brokerage house was holding a meeting with the investment community at a private club, and Handler was to be the keynote speaker. When she arrived at the club, the program planners ushered her into the club through the alley and kitchen. Later, she discovered that she was sneaked into the building because the club didn't allow women.

© Bettmann/Corbis

Ruth Handler ... was a generalist.
YOU ... can think like a generalist by staying alert for problems that demand solutions—even when this means going outside of your current specialty.

Profile Ruth Handler from Ethlie Ann Vare and Greg Placek, *Women Inventors and Their Discoveries.* Copyright © 1993, The Oliver Press, pp. 125, 128, 130–131. Reproduced by permission.

You're One Click Away...
from learning more about Ruth Handler online at the Master Student Profiles. You can also visit the Master Student Hall of Fame to learn about other master students.

FIVE Cs
FOR YOUR CAREER

CHARACTER • CRITICAL THINKING • CREATIVE THINKING • COLLABORATION • COMMUNICATION

See character as a career asset. At the end of every workday, character boils down to two ideas that are weaved throughout this book: Define your values and align your actions. Another word for acting in alignment with your values is *integrity*, and it is a personal quality that your employers, clients, or customers will come to value.

When people know that they can count on you to make commitments and follow through, they'll be more willing to work with you over the long term. Integrity is more than an abstract word. It's also a practical strategy for surviving layoffs and increasing job security.

Think creatively about mistakes. Recall a mistake you made at work and then write about it. In a Discovery Statement, describe what you did to create a result you didn't want ("I discovered that I tend to underestimate the number of hours projects take"). Then write an Intention Statement describing something you can do differently in the future ("I intend to keep track of my actual hours on each project so that I can give more accurate estimates"). Doing these two things will help you mine valuable lessons and graduate from the school of hard knocks—with honors.

Thinking critically about your successes. You can also use journal entries to think critically about things that go well in your work life. Throughout your career, keep track of the positive outcomes you produce at work, including financial successes. Summarize these results in a sentence or two and add them to your résumé as well. Whenever you deliver a project on time and on budget, write Discovery Statements about how you created that result. Follow up with Intention Statements about ways to be even more effective on your next project.

Stay in communication about trends that will affect your career. Keep up to date with breaking changes in the job market as you decide what's next in your career. This is easier to do than ever before, thanks to the way that technology allows people to connect.

The Internet. Use your skills in searching the Internet to find Web sites devoted to your field. Start by keying your job title into a search engine such as Google or Yahoo! Also follow thought leaders and major players in your industry on social networks such as Twitter, Facebook, and LinkedIn.

Periodicals. Read the business sections of the *New York Times* and the *Wall Street Journal*, for example. Most newspapers also have online editions, as do magazines such as *Wired* and *Business Week*.

Professional associations. People in similar jobs like to band together and give each other a heads up on emerging trends— one reason for professional associations. These range from the American Medical Association to the Society of Actuaries. There's bound to be one for people in your field. Ask colleagues and search the Internet. *Note:* Many associations maintain Web sites and publish newsletters or trade magazines.

Conferences and conventions. Many professional associations sponsor annual meetings. Here's where you can meet people face to face and use your networking skills. Print and online publications are powerful sources of news, but sometimes nothing beats plain old schmoozing. Ask people at work what professional organizations they have joined.

Use the Power Processes to become a rock-star collaborator. They're full of ideas for producing results *and* building relationships.

Take the "Power Process: I create it all," for example. Before blaming a snafu on a coworker, look for any ways that you might have contributed to the problem. Even if you did *not* contribute to the problem, look for ways that you can contribute to the solution. Write Intention Statements to clarify what you will think, say, and do in the future to create a more positive work environment. In the workplace, problem solvers are valued.

By the way, one of the ideas behind "I create it all" is to create a gap between stimulus and response. See if you can fill this gap with a conscious *choice* rather than an unconscious *reaction*. For example, if a coworker reprimands you, that's a stimulus. You can wait anywhere from a few seconds to few days before choosing your response. Slow down and carefully plan what to say or do next. Make your point in a way that serves everybody and tones down the conflict.

Now, make a personal commitment to developing the five Cs. Review the Discovery Wheel in Chapter 2—especially the sections labeled Character, Creative and Critical Thinking, Communicating, and Collaborating. Then take a snapshot of your current skills in these areas after reading and doing this chapter.

DISCOVERY

My scores on the "Five C" sections of the Discovery Wheel were:	As of today, I would give myself the following scores in these areas:
Character _____	Character _____
Creative & Critical Thinking _____	Creative & Critical Thinking _____
Communicating _____	Communicating _____
Collaborating _____	Collaborating _____

Next, skim this chapter and look for five strategies that you want to explore in more depth even after this course ends. Choose strategies that will enhance your self-rating in all or most of the five Cs.

The techniques that I want to explore are . . .

_____
_____
_____
_____

These techniques can help me become more effective at the five Cs because . . .

_____
_____
_____
_____
_____

INTENTION
To use this technique, I intend to . . .

_____
_____
_____
_____

NEXT ACTION
The specific actions I will take to follow through on my intentions are . . .

_____
_____
_____
_____

Name _____

Date _____ _____

1. List the three categories of choices explained in the "Power Process: Be it."
   (1) what we have; (2) what we do; and (3) who we are. *(Power Process: Be it, page 320)*

2. What is the key purpose of a résumé?
   The key purpose is to get you to the next step in the hiring process. *(Build an irresistible résumé, page 327)*

3. Career assessments are free and give fairly exact directions for the kind of jobs that you should do. True or false? Explain your answer.
   False. No assessment can dictate your precise career direction. Career assessments are another resource for discovering what kind of work is best for you, your work-related preferences and planning your career. Some do charge a fee. *(Discover yourself: Explore career assessments, page 341)*

4. According to the text, you'll be more effective at learning on the job if you are willing to:
   (a) Learn continuously, taking periodic progress checks to assess your current skills
   (b) Integrate knowledge of several subjects at once
   (c) Learn concepts in an "illogical" order as dictated by the day-to-day demands of a job
   (d) All of the above
   (d) All of the above. *(Learning on the job, page 336)*

5. Briefly describe the process of creating a career plan through the process of "naming names."
   Naming names means being very specific: Name your specific job, name the company you want to work for, name your contacts in securing that job, and name where you want to live and work. *(Create your career plan, page 343)*

6. Give three examples of ways to test your career choice.
   Three ways to test a career choice are to interview people who are actually doing the job, obtain an internship or volunteer position in that field, and get a part-time or summer job in that field. For example, a person considering a career as a veterinarian might interview and ask questions of a working veterinarian, seek out a volunteer or internship position at a local animal care shelter, and get a part-time job at a veterinarian's office for the summer. (Answers will vary.) *(Create your career plan, page 343)*

7. In addition to sending a thank-you note, what is another strategy that you can use to follow up on a job interview?
   E-mail a link to an interesting article and explain how it might be useful. If you have a Web site with a blog, let the interviewer know about a recent post. Reinforce the value you will bring to the company's team. Make a follow-up phone call, if you have permission. *(Use job interviews to "hire" an employer, page 330)*

8. List three questions that job interviewers often have in mind, even if they don't directly ask the questions.
   Any three of the following: "How did you find out about us?" "Will we be comfortable working with you?" "How can you help us?" "Will you learn this job quickly?" "What makes you different from other people applying for this job?" *(Use job interviews to "hire" an employer, page 330)*

9. List three questions that you can ask yourself at the end of the workday to effectively coach yourself.
   Any three of the following: "What did I accomplish today?" "What did I find challenging today?" "Based on what I learned today, what will I do differently tomorrow?" "With whom did I interact today?" "Do I want to follow up with any of those people tomorrow?" "What questions do I have for those people?" "How can I express my appreciation for a coworker tomorrow?" *(Learning on the job, page 336)*

10. If your scores are lower on the Discovery Wheel the second time you complete it, this means your skills have not improved. True or false? Explain your answer.
    False. Lower scores the second time you complete the Discovery Wheel might result from increased self-awareness and honesty, among other valuable assets. *(Critical Thinking Exercise 31: The Discovery Wheel—Coming full circle, page 347)*

Master Student Index Cards

From Master Student to Master Employee

From Master Student to Master Employee

From Master Student to Master Employee

From Master Student to Master Employee

Master Student Index Cards (continued)

From Master Student to Master Employee

From Master Student to Master Employee

From Master Student to Master Employee

From Master Student to Master Employee

Endnotes

INTRODUCTION

1. Excerpts from *Creating Your Future*. Copyright © 1998 by David B. Ellis. Reprinted by permission. All rights reserved.
2. U.S. Department of Labor, Bureau of Labor Statistics, "Education Pays . . . ," May 27, 2010, accessed December 30, 2010, from www.bls.gov/emp/ep_chart_001.htm.
3. Randy Moore, "The Importance of Admissions Scores and Attendance to First-Year Performance," *Journal of the First-Year Experience & Students in Transition, 2006* 18, no. 1, (2006): 105–125.
4. Albert Bandura, *Social Foundations of Thought and Action* (Englewood Cliffs, NJ: Prentice-Hall, 1986).
5. U.S. Census Bureau, "Facts for Feature: Back to School 2007–2008," accessed February 2, 2009, from http://www.prnewswire.com/news-releases/us-census-bureau-facts-for-feature-back-to-school-2007-2008-58050122.html.
6. Encyclopaedia Britannica Online Reference Center, "Ford, Henry," accessed April 15, 2011, from http://www.library.eb.com/eb/ article-22461.
7. FordCarz, "Henry Ford Quotations," 2003, accessed April 15, 2009, from http://www.fordcarz.com/henry-ford-quotations-about-cars.html.

CHAPTER 1

1. James O. Prochaska, John C. Norcross, and Carlo C. DiClemente, *Changing for Good* (New York: Avon, 1994).
2. Richard Malott, "Self Management Checklist," Counselling Services, University of Victoria, 2003, accessed October 13, 2006, from http://www.coun.uvic.ca/learning/motivation/self-management.html.
3. Brad Isaac, "Jerry Seinfeld's Productivity Secret," *Lifehacker,* July 24, 2007, accessed January 8, 2011, from http://lifehacker.com/281626/jerry-seinfelds-productivity-secret.
4. B. F. Skinner, *Science and Human Behavior* (Boston: Free Press, 1965).
5. Michael Hyatt, "What Should You Look For in the People You Hire?" November 29, 2011, accessed April 16, 2012, from http://michaelhyatt.com/what-should-you-look-for-in-the-people-you-hire.html.
6. Jonathan D. Glater, "Colleges Chase as Cheats Shift to Higher Tech," *New York Times*, May 18, 2006, accessed March 9, 2011, from www.nytimes.com/2006/05/18/education/18cheating.html.
7. Center for Human Resources, *National Evaluation of Learn and Serve America,* July 1999, accessed February 5, 2011, from www.cpn.org/topics/youth/k12/pdfs/Learn_and_Serve1999.pdf.

CHAPTER 2

1. David A. Kolb, *Experiential Learning: Experience as the Source of Learning and Development* (Englewood Cliffs, NJ: Prentice-Hall, 1984).

2. Douglas A. Bernstein, Louis A. Penner, Alison Clarke-Stewart, and Edward J. Roy, *Psychology* (Boston: Houghton Mifflin, 2006), 368–369.
3. Howard Gardner, *Frames of Mind: The Theory of Multiple Intelligences* (New York: Basic Books, 1993).

CHAPTER 3

1. Alan Lakein, *How to Get Control of Your Time and Your Life* (New York: New American Library, 1973; reissue 1996).
2. Linda Sapadin, with Jack Maguire, *It's About Time! The Six Styles of Procrastination and How to Overcome Them* (New York: Penguin, 1997).
3. Mei-Ching Lien, Eric Ruthruff, and James C. Johnston, "Attentional Limitations in Doing Two Tasks at Once: The Search for Exceptions," *Current Directions in Psychological Science* 15, no. 2 (2005): 89–93.
4. Clive Thompson, "Meet the Lifehackers," *New York Times*, October 16, 2005, accessed January 24, 2011, from www.nytimes.com/2005/10/16/magazine/16guru.html.
5. John Medina, *Brain Rules: 12 Principles for Surviving and Thriving at Work, Home, and School* (Seattle, WA: Pear Press, 2009), 87.
6. Suze Orman, *Suze Orman's 2009 Action Plan: Keeping Your Money Safe & Sound* (New York: Spiegel & Grau, 2009).
7. "Education Pays 2010," College Board, 2010, accessed February 7, 2011, from http://trends.collegeboard.org/education_pays.

CHAPTER 4

1. Donald Hebb, quoted in D. J. Siegel, "Memory: An Overview," *Journal of the American Academy of Child and Adolescent Psychiatry* 40, no. 9 (2001): 997–1011.
2. D. J. Siegel, "Memory: An Overview," *Journal of the American Academy of Child and Adolescent Psychiatry* 40, no. 9 (2001): 997–1011.
3. Daniel L. Schacter, *The Seven Sins of Memory: How the Mind Forgets and Remembers* (Boston: Houghton Mifflin, 2001), 13–15.
4. Siegel, "Memory: An Overview."
5. Schacter, *The Seven Sins of Memory,* 35–36.
6. Alzheimer's Association, "Brain Health," 2010, accessed January 20, 2011, from www.alz.org/brainhealth/overview.asp.

CHAPTER 5

1. National Endowment for the Arts, "To Read or Not to Read: A Question of National Consequence," November 7, 2007, accessed January 18, 2011, from http://www.nea.gov/research/ToRead_ExecSum.pdf.
2. Jeffrey D. Karpicke and Janell R. Blunt, "Retrieval Practice Produces More Learning than Elaborative Studying with Concept Mapping," *Science* 20 (January 2011), accessed January 21, 2011, from www.sciencemag.org/content/early/2011/01/19/science.1199327.abstract.

3. O. Pineño and R. R. Miller, "Primacy and Recency Effects in Extinction and Latent Inhibition: A Selective Review with Implications for Models of Learning," *Behavioural Processes* 69 (2005): 223–235.
4. From Raimes/Jerskey. *Universal Keys for Writers*, 2e. pg. 709–712. Copyright (c) 2008 Heinle/Arts & Sciences, a part of Cengage Learning, Inc. Reproduced by permission. www.cengage.com/permissions.
5. National Endowment for the Arts, "To Read or Not to Read: A Question of National Consequence," November 7, 2007. Accessed May 9, 2012, from http://www.nea.gov/research/ToRead_ExecSum.pdf.
6. Seth Godin, "How to Read a Business Book," May 21, 2008, accessed April 26, 2012 from http://sethgodin.typepad.com/seths_blog/2008/05/how-to-read-a-b.html.

CHAPTER 6

1. Gayle A. Brazeau, "Handouts in the Classroom: Is Note Taking a Lost Skill?" *American Journal of Pharmaceutical Education* 70, no. 2 (April 15, 2006): 38.
2. Walter Pauk and Ross J. Q. Owens, *How to Study in College*, 10th ed. (Boston: Cengage Learning, 2011).
3. Tony Buzan, *Use Both Sides of Your Brain* (New York: Dutton, 1991).
4. Gabrielle Rico, *Writing the Natural Way* (New York: Penguin, 2000).
5. Joseph Novak and D. Bob Gowin, *Learning How to Learn* (New York: Cambridge University Press, 1984).

CHAPTER 7

1. Gerardo Ramirez and Sian L. Beilock, "Writing About Testing Worries Boosts Exam Performance in the Classroom," *Science* 331 (January 14, 2011): 211–213.
2. Steven Hayes and Spencer Smith, *Get Out of Your Mind and Into Your Life: The New Acceptance and Commitment Therapy* (Oakland, CA: New Harbinger, 2005), 69–86.
3. Paul D. Nolting, *Math Study Skills Workbook* (Boston: Cengage Learning, 2012), 57.
4. This article incorporates detailed suggestions from reviewer Frank Baker.

CHAPTER 8

1. Arthur Koestler, *The Act of Creation* (New York: Dell, 1964).
2. Todd Anderson, "8 Insights From Upstart Inventors Under 30," *The 99 Percent*, accessed May 4, 2012, from http://the99percent.com/articles/7165/8-Insights-From-Upstart-Inventors-Under-30.
3. L. W. Anderson and D. R. Krathwohl, *A Taxonomy For Learning, Teaching, and Assessing: A Revision Of Bloom's Taxonomy of Educational Objectives* (New York: Addison Wesley Longman, 2001).
4. William G. Perry, Jr., *Forms of Intellectual and Ethical Development in the College Years: A Scheme* (New York: Holt, Rinehart, and Winston, 1970).
5. Martin E. P. Seligman, *Authentic Happiness: Using the New Positive Psychology to Realize Your Potential for Lasting Fulfillment* (New York: Simon and Schuster, 2002).
6. Quoted in Alice Calaprice, ed., *The Expanded Quotable Einstein* (Princeton, NJ: Princeton University Press, 2000).
7. Frank Levy and Richard J. Murnane, *The New Division of Labor: How Computers Are Creating the Next Job Market* (Princeton, NJ: Princeton University Press, 2004).

CHAPTER 9

1. Lee Thayer, "Communication—Sine Qua Non of the Behavioral Sciences," *Vistas in Science*, ed. David L. Arm (Albuquerque: University of New Mexico, 1968).
2. Carl Rogers, *On Becoming a Person* (Boston: Houghton Mifflin, 1961).
3. Thomas Gordon, *Parent Effectiveness Training: The Tested New Way to Raise Responsible Children* (New York: New American Library, 1975).
4. Sidney Jourard, *The Transparent Self* (New York: Van Nostrand, 1971).
5. Marshall Goldsmith, "Try Feedforward Instead of Feedback," accessed January 26, 2011, from http://www.marshallgoldsmithlibrary.com/cim/articles_display.php?aid=110w.
6. Quoted in Richard Saul Wurman, Loring Leifer, and David Sume, *Information Anxiety #2* (Indianapolis: QUE, 2001), 116.
7. Peter Elbow, *Writing with Power: Techniques for Mastering the Writing Process* (New York: Oxford University Press, 1981).
8. M. T. Motley, *Overcoming Your Fear of Public Speaking: A Proven Method* (New York: Houghton Mifflin, 1998).
9. Frank Levy and Richard J. Murnane, *The New Division of Labor: How Computers Are Creating the Next Job Market* (Princeton, NJ: Princeton University Press, 2004), 76–95.

CHAPTER 10

1. Joe Cuseo, "Academic-Support Strategies for Promoting Student Retention and Achievement during the First Year of College," University of Ulster Office of Student Transition and Retention, accessed September 4, 2003, from http://www.ulst.ac.uk/star/data/cuseoretention.htm-peestud.
2. Ibid.
3. Daniel Goleman, *Emotional Intelligence: Why It Can Matter More Than IQ* (New York: Bantam, 1995), xiv–xv.
4. Stephen R. Covey, *The Seven Habits of Highly Effective People: Restoring the Character Ethic* (New York: Simon & Schuster, 1989).
5. Vincent A. Miller, *Guidebook for International Trainers in Business and Industry* (New York: Van Nostrand Reinhold, 1979), 46–55.
6. Ximena Zúñiga, "Fostering Intergroup Dialogue on Campus: Essential Ingredients," *Diversity Digest*, accessed February 6, 2011, from www.diversityweb.org/Digest/W98/fostering.html.
7. Maia Szalavitz, "Race and the Genome," Howard University Human Genome Center, March 2, 2001, accessed February 6, 2011, from www.genomecenter.howard.edu/article.htm.
8. Diane de Anda, *Bicultural Socialization: Factors Affecting the Minority Experience* (Washington, D.C.: National Association of Social Workers, 1984).
9. U.S. Census Bureau, "An Older and More Diverse Nation by Midcentury," August 14, 2008, accessed March 14, 2011, from http://www.census.gov/newsroom/releases/archives/population/cb08-123.html.

CHAPTER 11

1. Centers for Disease Control and Prevention, "Health Habits of Adults Aged 18–29 Highlighted in Report on Nation's Health," February 18, 2009, accessed March 15, 2011, from http://www.cdc.gov/media/pressrel/2009/r090218.htm.
2. University of Minnesota, "Health and Academic Performance: Minnesota Undergraduate Students," accessed April 10, 2009, from http://www.bhs.umn.edu/surveys/survey-results/Systemwide_Report_07.pdf, 2007.

3. Kay-Tee Khaw, Nicholas Wareham, Sheila Bingham, Ailsa Welch, Robert Luben, and Nicholas Day, "Combined Impact of Health Behaviours and Mortality in Men and Women: The EPIC-Norfolk Prospective Population Study," *PLoS Medicine* 5, no. 1 (2008), accessed March 15, 2011, from www.plosmedicine .org/article/info:doi/10.1371/journal.pmed.0050012.

4. U.S. Department of Agriculture, "Dietary Guidelines for Americans, 2010," January 31, 2011, accessed March 15, 2011, from http ://www.cnpp.usda.gov/Publications/DietaryGuidelines/2010 /PolicyDoc/PolicyDoc.pdf.

5. Michael Pollan, "Unhappy Meals," *New York Times,* January 28, 2007, accessed March 15, 2011, from http://www.nytimes .com/2007/01/28/magazine/28nutritionism.t.html.

6. Harvard Medical School, *HEALTHbeat: 20 No-Sweat Ways to Get More Exercise* (Boston: Harvard Health Publications, October 14, 2008).

7. Jane Brody, "Exercise = Weight Loss, Except When It Doesn't," *New York Times,* September 12, 2006, accessed March 15, 2011, from www.nytimes.com/2006/09/12/health/nutrition/12brody .html.

8. Harvard Medical School, *HEALTHbeat Extra: The Secret to Better Health—Exercise* (Boston: Harvard Health Publications, January 27, 2009).

9. Mary Duenwald, "The Dorms May Be Great, but How's the Counseling?" *New York Times,* October 26, 2004, accessed March 15, 2011, from http://www.nytimes.com/2004/10/26 /health/psychology/26cons.html.

10. American College Health Association, American College Health Association–National College Health Assessment II: Reference Group, Executive Summary Fall 2008 (2009). Accessed March 15, 2011, from http://www.acha-ncha.org/docs/ACHA-NCHA _Reference_Group_ExecutiveSummary_Fall2008.pdf.

11. Morita Masatake's ideas are discussed in David Reynolds, *A Handbook for Constructive Living* (New York: Morrow, 1995), 98.

12. Albert Ellis, *Overcoming Destructive Beliefs, Feelings, and Behaviors: New Directions for Rational Emotive Behavior Therapy* (Amherst, NY: Prometheus, 2001).

13. Albert Bandura, "Self-Efficacy," in V. S. Ramachaudran, ed., *Encyclopedia of Human Behavior,* vol. 4 (New York: Academic Press, 1994), 71–81.

14. M. Schaffer, E.L. Jeglic, and B. Stanley, "The Relationship between Suicidal Behavior, Ideation, and Binge Drinking among College Students," *Archives of Suicide Research* 12 (2008): 124–132.

15. American Foundation for Suicide Prevention, "Risk Factors for Suicide" (2010), accessed March 15, 2011, from http://www.afsp.org /index.cfm?page_id=05147440-E24E-E376-BDF4BF8BA6444E76.

16. Minnesota Department of Health, "Sexually Transmitted Disease Facts" (2009), accessed March 15, 2011, from www .health.state.mn.us/divs/idepc/dtopics/stds/stdfactssummary .html#complications.

17. Centers for Disease Control and Prevention, "Trends in Reportable Sexually Transmitted Diseases in the United States, 2007" (2009), accessed March 15, 2011, from www.cdc.gov/nchhstp /newsroom/docs/STDTrendsFactSheet.pdf.

18. Andrew Weil and Winifred Rosen, *From Chocolate to Morphine: Everything You Need to Know About Mind-Altering Drugs* (Boston: Houghton Mifflin, 1993), 45.

19. U.S. Centers for Disease Control and Prevention, "Tobacco-Related Mortality," March 9, 2011, accessed March 16, 2011, from http://www.cdc.gov/tobacco/data_statistics/fact_sheets /health_effects/tobacco_related_mortality.

20. National Institutes of Health, National Institute on Alcohol Abuse and Alcoholism, "A Snapshot of Annual High-Risk College Drinking Consequences," July 1, 2010, accessed January 9, 2011, from www.collegedrinkingprevention.gov /StatsSummaries/snapshot.aspx.

21. American Psychological Association, *Diagnostic and Statistical Manual of Psychoactive Substance Abuse Disorders* (Washington, D.C.: American Psychological Association, 1994).

22. American Cancer Society, "Guide to Quitting Smoking" (2008), accessed March 15, 2011, from http://www.cancer.org/Healthy /StayAwayfromTobacco/GuidetoQuittingSmoking/index.

23. American Cancer Society, "Guide to Quitting Smoking."

24. Richard Bolles, *The Job-Hunters' Survival Guide: How to Find Hope and Rewarding Work, Even When "There Are No Jobs"* (Berkeley, CA: Ten Speed Press, 2009), 8, 92.

CHAPTER 12

1. U.S. Department of Labor, Bureau of Labor Statistics, "Education Pays . . . ," March 23, 2012, http://www.bls.gov/emp/emptab7 .htm (accessed May 30, 2012).

2. U.S. Department of Labor, "Secretary's Commission on Achieving Necessary Skills (SCANS)," March 9, 2006, http://wdr.doleta.gov/SCANS/ (accessed May 30, 2012).

3. Richard N. Bolles, *What Color Is Your Parachute? A Practical Manual for Job-Hunters and Career-Changers* (Berkeley, CA: 2005), 28–30.

4. Richard N. Bolles, *What Color Is Your Parachute?* 40–42.

5. Adapted from Dave Ellis, Stan Lankowitz, Ed Stupka, and Doug Toft, *Career Planning,* 3rd ed. Copyright © 2003 by Houghton Mifflin Company. Reprinted by permission.

Additional Reading

BOOKS

Allen, David. *Getting Things Done: The Art of Stress-Free Productivity.* New York: Penguin, 2001.

Belsky, Scott. *Making Ideas Happen: Overcoming the Obstacles between Vision and Reality.* New York: Portfolio, 2010.

Bolles, Richard N. *What Color Is Your Parachute? A Practical Manual for Job-Hunters and Career-Changers.* Berkeley, CA: Ten Speed, updated annually.

Bronson, Po. *What Should I Do with My Life? The True Story of People Who Answered the Ultimate Question.* New York: Random House, 2003.

Colvin, George. *Talent is Overrated: What Really Separates World-Class Performers from Everybody Else.* New York: Portfolio, 2008.

Coplin, Bill. *10 Things Employers Want You to Learn in College: The Know-How You Need to Succeed.* Berkeley, CA: Ten Speed, 2004.

Covey, Stephen R. *The Seven Habits of Highly Effective People: Powerful Lessons in Personal Change.* New York: Simon & Schuster, 1989.

Cushman, Kathleen. *First in the Family: Advice About College From from First-Generation Students.* Providence, RI: Next Generation Press, 2006.

Davis, Deborah. *The Adult Learner's Companion,* 2nd ed. Boston: Cengage, 2012.

Downing, Skip. *On Course: Strategies for Creating Success in College and in Life,* 6th ed. Boston: Cengage, 2011.

Ellis, Dave. *Becoming a Master Student,* 14th ed. Boston: Cengage, 2013.

Friedman, Thomas. *The World Is Flat 3.0: A Brief History of the Twenty-First Century.* New York: Picador, 2007.

Godin, Seth. *Linchpin: Are You Indispensable?* New York: Portfolio, 2010.

Godin, Seth. *Purple Cow: Transform Your Business by Being Remarkable.* New York: Portfolio, 2009.

Greene, Susan D., and Melanie C. L. Martel. *The Ultimate Job Hunter's Guidebook.* Boston: Cengage, 2012.

Levy, Frank, and Richard J. Murnane. *The New Division of Labor: How Computers Are Creating the Next Job Market.* Princeton, NJ: Princeton University Press, 2004.

Light, Richard J. *Making the Most of College: Students Speak Their Minds.* Cambridge, MA: Harvard University Press, 2001.

Newport, Cal. *How to Win at College.* New York: Random House, 2005.

Nolting, Paul D. *Math Study Skills Workbook,* Fourth Edition. Boston: Cengage, 2012.

Orman, Suze. *2009 Action Plan: Keeping Your Money Safe & Sound.* New York: Spiegel & Grau, 2009.

Peddy, Shirley, Ph.D. *The Art of Mentoring: Lead, Follow and Get Out of the Way.* Houston, TX: Bullion Books, 2001.

Robinson, Adam. *What Smart Students Know: Maximum Grades, Optimum Learning, Minimum Time.* New York: Crown, 1993.

Sethi, Ramit. *I Will Teach You to Be Rich.* New York: Workman, 2009

Toft, Doug, ed. *Master Student Guide to Academic Success.* Boston: Cengage, 2005.

Trapani, Gina. *Lifehacker: 88 Tech Tricks to Turbocharge Your Day.* Indianapolis, IN: Wiley, 2007.

U.S. Department of Education. *Funding Education Beyond High School: The Guide to Federal Student Aid.* Published yearly, http://studentaid.ed.gov/students/publications/student_guide/index.html.

Watkins, Ryan, and Michael Corry. *E-learning Companion: A Student's Guide to Online Success,* 3rd ed. Boston: Cengage, 2011.

Wurman, Richard Saul. *Information Anxiety 2.* Indianapolis: QUE, 2001.

WEB SITES

Art of Non-Conformity Blog
http://chrisguillebeau.com/3x5/
Strategies for personal development, life planning, and becoming an entrepreneur

Brain Pickings
www.brainpickings.org
Links to articles about art, philosophy, science, and technology—an Internet-powered engine for cross-disciplinary and creative thinking

Brazen Careerist
http://www.brazencareerist.com/
Articles, online courses, and other resources for students in higher education and young professionals

GTD Times
www.gtdtimes.com
A community of people interested in Getting Things Done®, centered on the work of David Allen, author of Getting Things Done: The Art of Stress-Free Productivity

I Will Teach You to Be Rich
www.iwillteachyoutoberich.com
Guidance from author and speaker Ramit Sethi on job hunting on taking charge of your money, geared to people starting their career

JobHuntersBible.com
www.jobhuntersbible.com
A rich set of online resources from Richard Bolles, author of the bestseller What Color Is Your Parachute? A Practical Manual for Job-Hunters and Career-Changers *and* The Job-Hunters' Survival Guide: How to Find Hope and Rewarding Work, Even When "There Are No Jobs"

Lifehacker
http://lifehacker.com
Tips and tricks for success at school, work, and home, geared to people interested in technology

Study Hacks
http://calnewport.com/blog
Unconventional ideas for succeeding in school and planning your life from Cal Newport, author of How to Win at College

The 99%
http://The99percent.com
Strategies for taking projects from planning to completion

Index

Master Instructor Notes

Master Instructor Notes

Master Instructor Notes

Master Instructor Notes

Master Instructor Notes

Master Instructor Notes